A HISTORY

OF THE

COLDSTREAM GUARDS.

The Naval & Military Press Ltd

Published by

The Naval & Military Press Ltd
Unit 10 Ridgewood Industrial Park,
Uckfield, East Sussex,
TN22 5QE England

Tel: +44 (0) 1825 749494
Fax: +44 (0) 1825 765701

www.naval-military-press.com
www.nmarchive.com

In reprinting in facsimile from the original, any imperfections are inevitably reproduced and the quality may fall short of modern type and cartographic standards.

Field Marshal H.R.H. Adolphus Frederick, Duke of Cambridge, K.G., G.C.B., G.C.H.
Colonel Coldstream Guards 1805-1850.
FROM A PRINT IN THE POSSESSION OF THE REGIMENT.

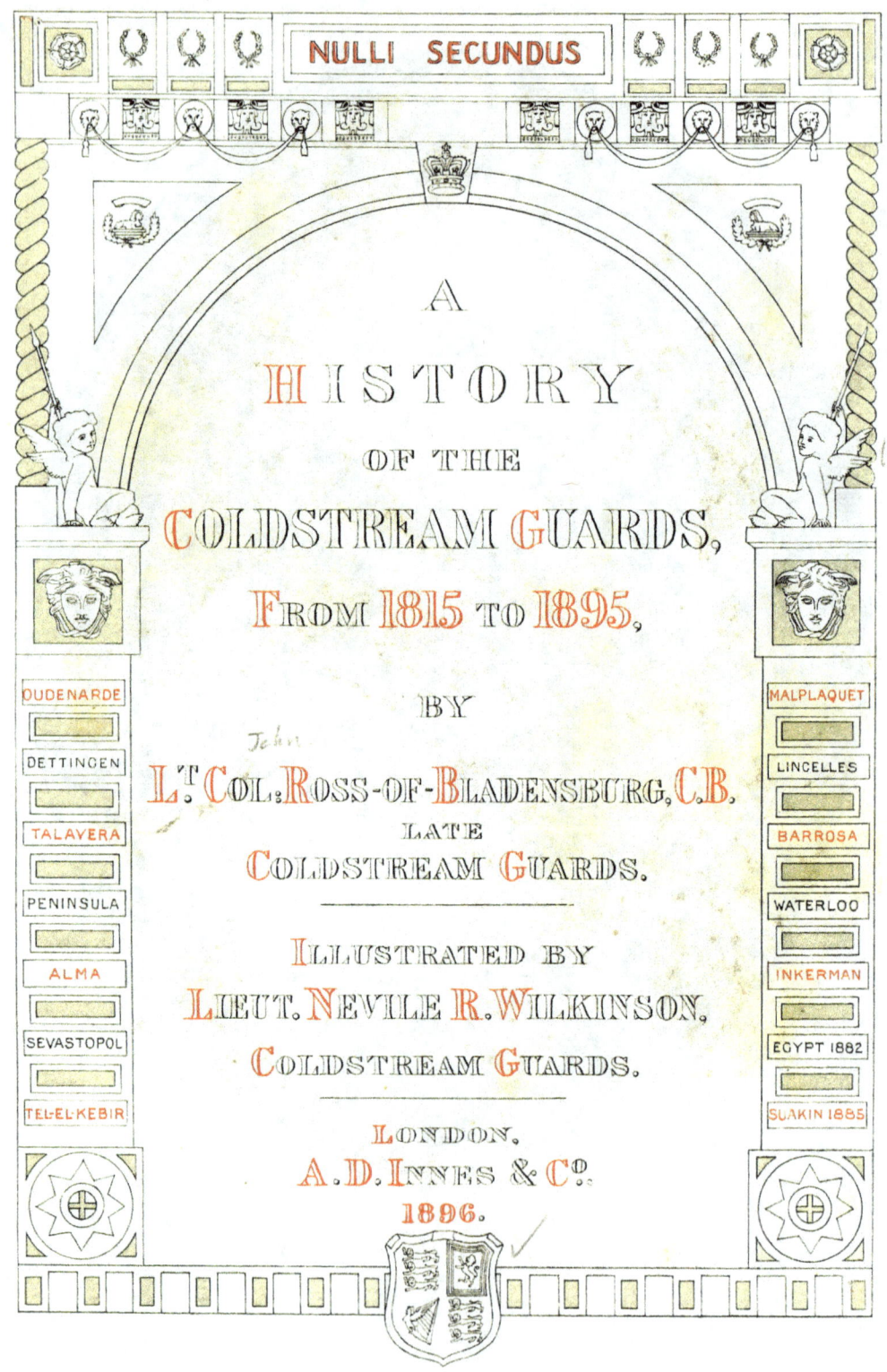

A HISTORY OF THE COLDSTREAM GUARDS, FROM 1815 TO 1895,

BY

LT. COL. ROSS-OF-BLADENSBURG, C.B.
LATE COLDSTREAM GUARDS.

Illustrated by
LIEUT. NEVILE R. WILKINSON,
COLDSTREAM GUARDS.

LONDON,
A. D. INNES & CO.
1896.

THIS HISTORY

OF

HER MAJESTY'S COLDSTREAM REGIMENT OF FOOT GUARDS,

FROM THE YEAR 1815 TO 1885,

IS, BY MOST GRACIOUS PERMISSION,

HUMBLY DEDICATED TO

HER MAJESTY THE QUEEN-EMPRESS.

PREFACE.

THE following pages are a continuation of Colonel MacKinnon's *Origin and Services of the Coldstream Guards*, from the victory of Waterloo down to the year 1885. They have been compiled with great care and much labour, and the reader will, I trust, feel justified in adding, with accuracy and marked ability.

The first few chapters deal with events that took place in France, after Waterloo, including the military occupation of the North-Eastern frontier by the Allies, up to the year 1818.

The period onwards to the Crimean War, although containing but few accounts of interest concerning the career of the Regiment, is valuable as continuing, to a considerable extent, the history of events in Europe so far as that is consistent with the subject of the present volume.

There is reference, nevertheless, to the part taken by the Regiment in the suppression of the Canadian rebellion.

From the date, however, of 1854, the subject assumes a different character, and is of absorbing interest to every Officer and man associated with the Coldstream Guards.

The events connected with that campaign have been carefully selected from thoroughly authentic sources; they are recorded in no spirit of vainglory or self-sufficiency, but as a true and faithful tale of the share which the Regiment took in that eventful war,— illustrating, as it does, acts of gallantry, a noble and uncomplaining endurance of difficulties and hardships, and a strict performance of duty under very trying circumstances.

The accuracy of the record of the more recent Egyptian campaigns is of special value, from the fact of the author of this work having himself taken an active part in one of them.

The perusal of these records will be accompanied by the conviction which exists in the minds of all of us, that those who replace their gallant predecessors will, when their turn comes, deserve equally well of their country.

FRED^K. STEPHENSON, *General*,
Colonel, Coldstream Guards.

1896.

AUTHOR'S NOTE.

I BEG to return sincere thanks to the many members of the Coldstream Guards, past and present, who have helped me to compile the volume I now venture to issue to the public; and to assure them that, but for their assistance, it would have been far less worthy of their acceptance than even it is at the present time. It is not possible for me, in the short space at my disposal, to mention all by name to whom I am indebted in this respect. But I should fail in my duty did I not, at least, express my gratitude to General Sir Frederick Stephenson, G.C.B., and to General Hon. Sir Percy Feilding, K.C.B., for the interest they have shown in my work, and for the trouble they have taken to enable me to carry it out.

Major Vesey Dawson was indefatigable in compiling all that concerns the Nulli Secundus Club. Captain Shute prepared an Appendix on the Coldstream Hospital. Mr. Sutton spared no pains in supplying information which the Regimental Orderly Room affords; and Mr. Studd arranged materials that required considerable labour. Major Goulburn, Grenadier Guards, moreover, lent me the interesting Crimean Diary of the late Colonel Tower; and Colonel Malleson kindly looked through the proofs, and made many valuable suggestions.

I also offer my acknowledgments to Messrs. Blackwood and Sons, and to Messrs. Seeley and Co., for their courteous permission to use the maps in Mr. Kinglake's *Invasion of the Crimea* and in Sir E. Hamley's *War in the Crimea*.

Lastly, I must express the pleasure it gives me that my work is illustrated by so able and accomplished an artist as Mr. Wilkinson.

It only now remains for me to explain that as Colonel MacKinnon's *Origin and Services of the Coldstream Guards* does not contain illustrations of uniforms worn by the Regiment during the many generations of its existence, we preferred to give representations, not of the familiar figures of this century, but of those that are less known. Thus, though the following pages only describe events from the year 1815 to 1885, the plates generally refer to a more remote period of the history of the Regiment.

JOHN ROSS-OF-BLADENSBURG,
Lt.-Colonel.

October, 1896.

CONTENTS.

CHAPTER I.

THE CAPITULATION OF PARIS.

PAGE

Flight of Napoleon from the field of Waterloo—Reaction in Paris—Napoleon's abdication—Surrender to Captain Maitland—Provisional Government set up in France—Advance of the Allies from Waterloo—Operations of Marshal Grouchy—Allies hope to cut the enemy off from Paris—Blücher's energy to secure that object—Unsuccessful efforts of the Provisional Government to obtain a suspension of hostilities—The Allies before Paris—The Prussians move round to the south of the city—Co-operation of Wellington—Capitulation of the capital, July 3rd—Advance of Austrians and Russians—" Waterloo men "—The " Wellington pension "—Rank of Lieutenant granted to Ensigns of the Brigade of Guards—The soldier's small account-book introduced into the British army 1

CHAPTER II.

MILITARY OCCUPATION OF FRANCE.

Termination of the war—Difficulties of the situation—The Allies occupy Paris—Dissolution of the Provisional Government—Entry of Louis XVIII. into the capital—New French Government formed—Blücher and the *Pont de Jena*—Arrival of the Allied Sovereigns—Reviews in France—Paris in the hands of the Allies—Treatment of the French by the Prussians; by the British—The wreck of the French Imperial forces disbanded—Life in Paris—The Louvre stripped of its treasures of art—Prosecution of Imperialist leaders—Labedoyère, Ney, Lavalette—Peace of Paris, November 20th 24

CHAPTER III.

OCCUPATION OF FRENCH FORTRESSES.

Organization of the Allied army of occupation, under the supreme command of the Duke of Wellington—Return of the remainder to their respective countries—Instructions of the Allied Courts to Wellington—Convention relating to the

CONTENTS.

occupation, attached to the Treaty of Paris—Positions assigned to each contingent on the north-eastern frontier of France—March from Paris to Cambrai—Military precautions—Camps of instruction and field exercises—Reduction of the army of occupation—Difficulties with the French—Congress of Aix-la-Chapelle—Evacuation of France—The Guards Brigade leave Cambrai, after nearly three years' stay there, and embark at Calais—Valedictory Orders—The Coldstream sent to Chatham—Conclusion of military service in French territory 48

CHAPTER IV.

FIRST PART OF THE LONG EUROPEAN PEACE.

Distress in England after the war—Reductions in the Army and Navy—Stations of the Brigade—French Eagles captured, deposited in the Chapel Royal, Whitehall—Reforms in interior economy—Death of George III., and Accession of George IV.—Cato Street Conspiracy—Trial of Queen Caroline—Coronation of George IV.—Guards in Dublin—Distress in 1826—Death of the Duke of York—Changes in uniform—Death of George IV.; succeeded by William IV.—Political agitation at home, revolution abroad; the Reform Act—Coronation of William IV.—First appearance of cholera—Death of the King, and Accession of Her Majesty Queen Victoria—Changes and reforms introduced during the reign of William IV. 72

CHAPTER V.

SECOND PART OF THE LONG EUROPEAN PEACE.

Beginning of the reign of Queen Victoria—Troops during Parliamentary elections—Coronation of the Queen—Fire at the Tower of London, 1841—Rebellion in Canada—Two Guards Battalions sent there, 1838, of which one the 2nd Battalion Coldstream Guards—Return home, 1842—Visit of the Russian Tsar Nicholas I. to England—European revolution—Bi-centenary celebration of the formation of the Coldstream Guards, 1850—Death of the Colonel of the Regiment, H.R.H. the Duke of Cambridge; succeeded by General the Earl of Strafford—Exhibition in London—Death of the Duke of Wellington—Changes and reforms up to 1854—Camp at Chobham 103

CHAPTER VI.

BEGINNING OF THE WAR IN THE EAST.

Position of Russia in Europe—State of the Continent in 1853—British alliance with France—The Tsar's quarrel with Turkey—Commencement of hostilities on the Danube—The affair of Sinope—How it drew England and France into the war—Three Battalions of the Brigade of Guards ordered on foreign service—Concentration of the Allies in the Mediterranean—Guards Brigade at Malta—Thence to Scutari—Want of transport—The Allies moved to Varna—Good feeling between the British and French troops—Course of the war on the Danube—Siege of Silistria—Retreat of the Russians into Bessarabia—Intervention of Austria—The Allies in Bulgaria—Sickness among the troops—Return to Varna—Preparations for the invasion of the Crimea—The organization and strength of the Allies 130

CHAPTER VII.

THE INVASION OF THE CRIMEA.

Small results gained by the Allies—Sudden determination to attack Sevastopol—Russian position in the Trans-Caucasian provinces—Conditions under which the Crimea was invaded—The allied Armada sails from Varna to Eupatoria—Landing effected at "Old Fort"—The move to Sevastopol; the order of march—The enemy on the Alma river, opposes the advance of the Allies—Description of the field of battle; strength and position of the enemy—Commencement of the battle of the Alma—Advance of the Light and the Second Divisions—Deployment of the First Division—Advance of the Guards and Highland Brigades—Defeat of the Russians—No pursuit—Losses—Bravery and steadiness of the British troops—The Allies lose valuable time after the battle—Arriving at last before their objective, Sevastopol, they refuse to attack it—General description of Sevastopol 156

CHAPTER VIII.

BEFORE SEVASTOPOL.

Predicament in which the Allies found themselves—Flank march round Sevastopol—Occupation of Balaklava by the British and of Kamiesh Bay by the French—The Allies refuse to assault Sevastopol; they prefer to bombard it—Depression of the Russians, who fear a prompt assault—Description of the defences round the south side of Sevastopol; successful efforts of the enemy to strengthen them—Description of the upland of the Chersonese, occupied by the Allies; their position and labours—First bombardment and its results—No attack; a regular siege inevitable—Draft of Officers and men to the Coldstream arrive in the Crimea—Establishment of the Regiment—Russian reinforcements begin to arrive—Battle of Balaklava; Cavalry charges—*Sortie* of the Russians against the British right flank; its failure 180

CHAPTER IX.

THE BATTLE OF INKERMAN.

Large Russian reinforcements reach the Crimea—Position and strength of the enemy; of the Allies—Description of the field of Inkerman—Commencement of the battle, 5th of November—The progress of the first part of the fight—The Guards Brigade advance to the scene of action—The struggle round the Sandbag battery—Arrival of the Fourth Division under General Cathcart—The manœuvre of the latter, and its failure—The arrival of the French—Successes of the British artillery—Repulse of the Russian attack; the retreat of the enemy; there is no pursuit—Operations of the garrison of Sevastopol and of the Russian force in the Tchernaya Valley during the day—Great losses incurred on both sides—Reaction among the soldiery after the battle 204

CHAPTER X.

THE WINTER OF 1854-55 IN THE CRIMEA.

Prostration of both sides after the battle of Inkerman—Sevastopol not to be taken in 1854—Tardy arrangements to enable the army to remain in the Crimea during the winter—Violent hurricane of the 14th of November; stores scattered and destroyed—The winter begins in earnest—How the Government at home attended to the wants of the army at the seat of war—Absence of a road between the base at Balaklava and the front—Miserable plight to which the army was reduced—Indignation in England, and the measures taken to relieve the troops—Admirable manner in which the misfortunes were borne by the British soldiers—Operations on both sides during the winter—The Turks occupy Eupatoria; successful action fought there—The Guards Brigade sent to Balaklava 231

CHAPTER XI.

THE FALL OF SEVASTOPOL.

Stay of the Brigade at Balaklava—Improvement in the condition of the men—Return of the Guards to the front, June 16th—Changed aspect of affairs before Sevastopol—Review of events during the time spent at Balaklava—Second bombardment—Interference by Napoleon III. in the course of the war; operations paralysed — General Canrobert resigns, and is succeeded by General Pélissier—Energy displayed by the latter—Third bombardment—Fourth bombardment; assault of Sevastopol—Its failure—Death of Lord Raglan; succeeded by General Simpson—Siege operations continued—Battle of the Tchernaya—Fifth bombardment—Sixth bombardment; second assault—The Malakoff is captured—Fall of the south side of Sevastopol—The Russians evacuate the town, and retreat to the north side—State in which the Allies found Sevastopol 249

CHAPTER XII.

THE END OF THE RUSSIAN WAR.

Home events during the war—Sympathy of Her Majesty with her Crimean soldiers—Badges of distinction added to the Colours—Inactivity of the Allies after the fall of Sevastopol—Expeditions against the Russian coast—Sir W. Codrington succeeds Sir J. Simpson as Commander of the Forces—The winter of 1855-56—Negotiations for a peace, which is concluded, March 30th—Events after the cessation of hostilities—A British cemetery in the Crimea—Embarkation and return home—The Crimean Guards Brigade at Aldershot; visit of Her Majesty the Queen—Move to London, and cordial reception there—Distribution of the Victoria Cross—Summary of events connected with the war—Losses—Appointment of H.R.H. the Duke of Cambridge as Commander-in-Chief, and of Major-General Lord Rokeby to command the Brigade of Guards 267

CHAPTER XIII.

A PERIOD OF WAR, 1856-1871.

Reductions after the war—Comparison between the situations in Europe, in 1815 and in 1856—Fresh troubles and complications imminent—Many wars and disturbances—Scientific instruction introduced into the army—Practical training of the troops carried out—The material comfort of the soldier attended to—Military activity in England in 1859—The Earl of Strafford succeeded by General Lord Clyde—Death of H.R.H. the Prince Consort—Misunderstanding with the United States of America—Chelsea barracks completed—Marriage of H.R.H. the Prince of Wales—Death of Lord Clyde; succeeded by General Sir W. Gomm—The Brigade of Guards Recruit Establishment—Public duties in London—Fenian troubles in Ireland; the 1st and 2nd Battalions succeed each other there; the Clerkenwell outrage—Reforms in the armament of the British infantry 292

CHAPTER XIV.

ARMY REFORM, 1871-85.

Effect produced in England by the military successes of Prussia—Short service and the reserve system introduced—Abolition of army purchase—Abolition of the double rank in the Foot Guards—Substitution of the rank of Sub-Lieutenant for that of Ensign or Cornet—Manœuvres and summer drills—Changes in the drill-book—Illness and recovery of H.R.H. the Prince of Wales—Death of Surgeon-Major Wyatt, and of Field-Marshal Sir W. Gomm—General Sir W. Codrington appointed Colonel of the Coldstream Guards—Death of Captains Hon. R. Campbell and R. Barton—Company training—Pirbright Camp established—Medical service in the Brigade—Change in the establishment of the Regiment—Death of Sir W. Codrington, and appointment of General Sir Thomas Steele as Colonel—Troubles in Ireland—Alarm in London—The Royal Military Chapel 319

CHAPTER XV.

THE WAR IN EGYPT, 1882.

Origin of the war—Emancipation of Egypt from Turkish rule; introduction of European control—Deposition of Ismail Pasha—Tewfik becomes Khedive—Military revolts—Disorganization of the country—Joint action of the English and French; its failure—Naval demonstration—Bombardment of the forts of Alexandria—The French withdraw and leave Great Britain to act alone—British troops sent to Egypt—The Suez Canal seized—Base of operations established at Ismailia—Action of Tel el-Makhuta—Clearing the communications—Actions at Kassassin, August 28th and September 7th—Character of the Egyptian army—Night march on Tel el-Kebir—The enemy is overwhelmed, September 13th—Pursuit; losses—End of the war—Return of the Coldstream to England 350

CHAPTER XVI.

FIRST PART OF THE WAR IN THE SUDAN, 1884-85—EXPEDITION UP THE NILE.

General description of the possessions of the Khedive in 1882—Rebellion in the Sudan; rapid rise of the Mahdi—Policy of the British Government—General Gordon sent to Khartum; he is cut off and besieged there—General Lord Wolseley goes to Egypt—Formation of a Camel Corps, of which the Guards compose a Regiment—Problem how to effect the rescue of Gordon—The Nile route selected—Advance to Korti—News from General Gordon—Two columns advance from Korti: one across the Bayuda Desert, the other up the river—Battles of Abu Klea and Abu Kru—The Nile reached near Metemmeh—Sir C. Wilson's effort to proceed to Khartum—Death of General Gordon—Change of plan entailed by this event—Battle of Kirbekan—Retrograde movement of both columns—Troops placed in summer quarters 372

CHAPTER XVII.

SECOND PART OF THE WAR IN THE SUDAN, 1884-85—SUAKIN CAMPAIGN.

Reasons for the expedition to Suakin—Departure of the Coldstream—Orders to Lieut.-General Sir G. Graham—Position of the enemy—Advance against Hashin—Engagement at Tofrek—Attack on a convoy, escorted by the Coldstream and Royal Marines—Advance to Tamai—Construction of the railway—Attack on T'Hakul—Abrupt end of the campaign—The Coldstream proceed to Alexandria, and thence to Cyprus—Evacuation of the Sudan; how the Mahdi took advantage of it; how the Dongolese were treated—Position taken up south of Wady Halfa—Defeat of the Arabs at Ginnis—Return of the Guards Camel regiment—Return of the Coldstream from Cyprus—Honourable distinctions added to the Colours—Officers of the Regiment in December, 1885 ... 393

APPENDIX I.

1. Despatch of M.-Gen. Sir John Byng to H.R.H. the Duke of York, on the Battle of Waterloo, Nivelles, June 19, 1815 ... 413
2. General Orders, Nivelles, June 20, 1815 ... 414
3. Proclamation of the Duke of Wellington to the French People, Malplaquet, June 22, 1815 ... 415

APPENDIX II.

1. General Order, Paris, October 28, 1815 ... 416
2. Orders for Billeting the British Troops in France, October 29, 1815 ... 416
3. Alarm Posts of British Divisions in France, October 30, 1815 ... 418

APPENDIX III.

Orders for a British Contingent to occupy French Fortresses, November 9, 1815 ... 418

APPENDIX IV.

Distribution of the British Contingent in France, April 10, 1816 ... 421

APPENDIX V.

Short Account of the Band of the Coldstream Guards ... 424

APPENDIX VI.

1. Farewell Order to the Allied Army of Occupation in France, November 10, 1818 ... 426
2. Farewell Order to the British Contingent, Cambrai, November 10, 1818 ... 427
3. General Order, Paris, December 1, 1818 ... 427

APPENDIX VII.

Coldstream Guards Hospital ... 428

CONTENTS.

PAGE

APPENDIX VIII.

The Nulli Secundus Club; and List of Members from its Formation, 1783, to 1896 ... 429

APPENDIX IX.

General Order, Constantinople, April 30, 1854 ... 436

APPENDIX X.

Death of Field-Marshal Lord Raglan, G.C.B. ... 437

APPENDIX XI.

Ages and previous Occupations of the Non-commissioned Officers and Men of the 1st Battalion Coldstream Guards, and Drafts sent to the East, engaged in the War with Russia ... 439

APPENDIX XII.

1. Return of the Numbers Killed in the Crimea ... 440
2. Return of the Numbers Wounded in the Crimea, Dead, Invalided, etc. ... 440
3. Deaths in the 1st Battalion Coldstream Guards by Months during the War with Russia ... 441

APPENDIX XIII.

The Victoria Cross ... 442

APPENDIX XIV.

1. The British Forces employed in the Egyptian Campaign, 1882 ... 444
2. Extracts from General Orders issued after the Battle of Tel el-Kebir ... 446
3. Extract of Report on Army Signalling in Egypt, 1882 ... 447

APPENDIX XV.

Stations occupied by the Coldstream Guards, 1833-1885* ... 448

APPENDIX XVI.

1. Coldstream Roll † ... 458
2. Commanding Officers of the Coldstream Guards, from 1650 to 1896 ... 478
3. Regimental Staff Officers † ... 482
4. Warrant Officers ... 485

---

* Continued from Appendix 273 of Mackinnon's *Origin and Services of the Coldstream Guards*.

† Continued from Appendix 285 of Mackinnon's *Origin, etc.*

LIST OF ILLUSTRATIONS.

		PAGE
FIELD-MARSHAL H.R.H. ADOLPHUS FREDERICK DUKE OF CAMBRIDGE, K.G.	*Frontispiece*	
PIKEMAN, 1669; DRUM MAJOR, 1670; GRENADIER COMPANY, 1670	*To face*	18
SERGEANT, 1658; DRUMMER, 1658	,,	36
MUSQUETEER, 1650	,,	66
MUSKETEER, 1669	,,	86
OFFICER *temp.* JAMES II.	,,	102
MUSKETS AND RIFLES FROM 1830 TO 1890	,,	126
PRIVATE, 1742	,,	230
COLOURS, 1669, 1684, 1685	,,	248
COLOURS OF THE COLONEL, LIEUT-COLONEL, AND MAJORS, 1750, AND THE QUEEN'S COLOUR, 1893	,,	266
DRUMMER, 1745	,,	286
SERGEANT, 1775; OFFICER, 1795	,,	300
OFFICER, 1839; OFFICER, 1849	,,	318
OFFICER, 1849; PRIVATE'S UNDRESS CAP, 1850	,,	342
SERGEANT DRUMMER, 1895	,,	392

MAPS.

		PAGE
1. Sketch Map to illustrate the British Occupation of France from 1815 to 1810	To face	54
2. Black Sea and surrounding Country	,,	149
3. Country between Eupatoria and Sevastopol	,,	165
4. Battle of the Alma	,,	174
5. Sketch Map of Country near Sevastopol	,,	182
6. Sevastopol	,,	194
7. Battle of Inkerman	,,	216
8. The Neighbourhood of Tel el-Kebir from the Suez Canal to Zagazig and the Country round Suakin	,,	360
9. Sketch Maps to illustrate Egyptian and Sudan Expeditions, 1882–1885	,,	379

CORRIGENDA.

Page 86, line 31, *for* "May 25th" *read* "May 27th."
 ,, 90, ,, 13, *for* "May 15, 1829" *read* "May 16, 1829."
 ,, 118, ,, 12, *for* "November 13th" *read* "November 9th."

INTRODUCTION.

THE central figure in Europe, during the first fifteen years of this century, was the Emperor Napoleon, the great military leader, who, having restored order in France—violently disturbed by the terror, anarchy, and confusion of the Revolution that broke out in 1789,—succeeded in ruling that country, and in imposing his arbitrary will upon its people. A master of the science of war, and gifted with the genius that makes a man supreme in the field of battle, he organized the military qualities of his subjects, who, under his guidance, invaded their neighbours, destroyed their institutions, and overran Europe from one end to the other. One opponent only remained unsubdued, and that was England; and so strong was her resistance to this modern Attila, that she succeeded not only in breaking his power, but in adding also to her own importance and influence in the world.

Napoleon, though a General of the first order,—whose campaigns will always commend themselves to the student of the art of war,—was less remarkable for his knowledge of that other science which makes a man a statesman. He lived by the sword, and he perished by the sword. He destroyed the prosperity of the people he subdued, but he could not cement a friendship with them. His object was war and only war, and he reaped its reward—military fame; but he did not use the absolute power he wielded, for the advantage of France, nor was he able to establish his name among the greatest and most enlightened rulers of mankind.

After a period of victory, he exhausted the resources of his country, and then there was formed against him a coalition of European Princes, who gradually closed their forces around him with ever tightening grasp, and pursued him to the heart of his Empire. At last, he was defeated and undone, and acknowledged his impotence to carry on any longer the mighty struggle in which he had been engaged (1814). Europe then restored the Bourbons as Kings of France, and determined that Napoleon should be expelled therefrom, and interned in the island of Elba,—an Emperor of a very narrow dominion, and a Monarch only in name. But scarcely had he been there a year, when he broke loose. Landing in France, he made the King (Louis XVIII.) fly from Paris; and, amid the acclamations of the people, he once more re-established himself upon the throne (March, 1815).

The Allied Sovereigns now combined to drive this disturber of the peace from France, and took immediate steps to invade that country again. In June, two of the Powers had their forces in Belgium,—the British and their immediate allies (the Dutch, Hanoverians, etc.), under the Duke of Wellington; and the Prussians, under Marshal Blücher. The rest were still east of the Rhine. Perceiving that his antagonists were not yet able to move forward together against him, the French Emperor resolved to strike the first blow, by advancing northwards and by attacking Wellington and Blücher. Accordingly, he left Paris on the 12th of June, and on the 16th he fought the battles of Ligny, where he defeated the Prussians and drove them off the field, and of Quatre-Bras, from which place the British, though they held their ground, eventually fell back slowly towards Waterloo. Giving orders to Marshal Grouchy, who was placed at the head of a considerable force, to pursue Blücher, and to prevent him from forming a junction with Wellington, Napoleon advanced, and attacked the British at Waterloo (June 18th). Here the most decisive battle of the present age took place. Stubbornly did the British troops maintain their position; while Blücher, rallying his forces, and leaving behind only a small corps to contain Grouchy, marched with the remainder to the field of Waterloo. The French were now enveloped, and completely and irretrievably defeated.

There was a Guards Division at the battle of Waterloo, commanded by Lieutenant-General Sir George Cooke, formed of two Brigades. The 1st Guards Brigade (Major-General P. Maitland) was composed of the 2nd and 3rd First (now Grenadier) Guards; and the 2nd Guards Brigade (Major-General Sir John Byng) of the 2nd Coldstream and the 2nd Third (now Scots) Guards. Sir George Cooke being severely wounded during the course of the day, the command of the Guards Division devolved upon Sir John Byng.

THE HISTORY

OF

THE COLDSTREAM GUARDS.

1815–1885.

CHAPTER I.

THE CAPITULATION OF PARIS.

Flight of Napoleon from the field of Waterloo—Reaction in Paris—Napoleon's abdication—Surrender to Captain Maitland—Provisional Government set up in France—Advance of the Allies from Waterloo—Operations of Marshal Grouchy—Allies hope to cut the enemy off from Paris—Blücher's energy to secure that object—Unsuccessful efforts of the Provisional Government to obtain a suspension of hostilities—The Allies before Paris—The Prussians move round to the south of the city—Co-operation of Wellington—Capitulation of the capital, July 3rd—Advance of Austrians and Russians—"Waterloo men"—The "Wellington pension"—Rank of Lieutenant granted to Ensigns of the Brigade of Guards—The soldier's small account-book introduced into the British army.

THE battle of Waterloo broke the power of Napoleon for ever. So confident of victory had that great soldier been, that he did not even make any preparations for retreat, and hence, when he was defeated, a terrible rout ensued. The wreck of the French army, blocking the only road which was available, hurried from the scene of disaster in a confused mass of fugitives. The Prussians, who were comparatively fresh, took up the pursuit, and relentlessly they pressed it home, driving the enemy back, increasing his panic, and completing his misfortunes. Through the whole night of the 18th-19th of June, a fierce and active pursuit was maintained;

while the British troops, exhausted by the labours and anxieties of the day, bivouacked as they stood, on the bloody but glorious field of victory.

Napoleon, stupefied by the unexpected result of the battle, forced his way through the surging mass of his now disorganized troops to Quatre-Bras, and as he went along, he had ever increasing evidence of the catastrophe that had overwhelmed him. He sent a message to Grouchy, announced his defeat, but gave the Marshal no orders. He then rode to Charleroi, and, almost unattended, pushed on to Philippeville, where he made his first effort to repair his broken fortunes. He ordered Marshal Soult to rally the *débris* of his forces at Laon; he despatched a letter to General Rapp, who was in command on the German frontier, and to General Lamarque, engaged in La Vendée, with orders to march to Paris; and he was sanguine enough to declare that he could reorganize a sufficient force to cover the capital, and to give time for the concentration of a much larger army, wherewith to renew the war and to save France from the invasion that threatened her.[*] But he was far from being reassured. He could scarcely deny even to himself that the end of his career had at last come in earnest, and that the stupendous ascendency which he exercised over his countrymen had disappeared now and for ever. Once before had he been obliged to acknowledge himself vanquished, and the glamour of invincibility no longer surrounded his person. He had engaged in a desperate undertaking. The whole of Europe was arming against him, and was determined to put him down. His first bold venture to try and beat the Allies in detail had signally failed. The armies of Great Britain and of Prussia had hopelessly crushed the flower of his forces. He had henceforward to reckon with Austria and Russia, and with a formidable coalition flushed with victory. His countrymen never forgave a military leader who had suffered a disaster in the field. He knew that his prestige was weakened, that the influence which his name inspired was shaken, that his resources were at an end, and that his enemies were gathering about him from every quarter.

Tormented by these gloomy thoughts, he pursued his journey, and reached Philippeville; and there he snatched a few hours repose. But the fear of the Prussians haunted his followers, and

[*] George Hooper, *Waterloo: the Downfall of the First Napoleon*, pp. 239, 263 (London, 1862).

he was hurried on, still in a state of indecision.* The momentous question had now to be faced, and immediately decided. What was Napoleon to do? Should he remain in the field in command of his troops, rally the shattered remnants of the grand army, and cover Paris, or should he fly to the capital, assert his authority there, and trust to the magic of his name to retain his supremacy over France? His own desire was to stay among his men, and to abide the result at the head of an army, devoted to his person and to his interests. Had he done so, his fate would have been less humiliating than it eventually proved to be. But his failing health, and the shock he had experienced, paralysed the active energies of the man, and, dreading a revolution in the seat of government, he agreed, against his better judgment, to start at once for Paris. He reached his destination early on the 21st, exhausted and shaken both in body and mind.

Paris was struck dumb by this event. On the 18th, the guns of the Invalides thundered a salute in honour of the battle of Ligny, and on the two following days the details of the French victory over the Prussians were published in glowing colours; but towards the evening of the 20th, the news of trouble began to leak out, and on the morrow the Emperor arrived at the Elysée palace attended only by a few of his personal Staff. "Dans le premier moment on refusa à croire; ce fut ensuite une anxiété cruelle; puis une morne stupeur." † And now at length the fatal news was fully realized, and spread like wildfire through the excited people, and all knew for certain that the army of Napoleon had been annihilated, that his military genius had played him false, and that the catastrophe was at once complete and irretrievable.

Then the weakness of the Emperor's power began to show itself, and the instability of the foundation upon which he had constructed his Imperial system became apparent. France, who drained her resources freely to serve her passion for glory, now spurned the defeated hero who had made her glorious. His rule, though it pandered to her vanity, did not rest upon the true affections of the people; and his want of success at the critical moment was an unpardonable offence, to be atoned only by

---

* Alphonse de Lamartine, *The History of the Restoration of the Monarchy in France*, ii. 443 (London, 1852).

† Hooper, p. 265.

abdication. Enemies created everywhere by his arbitrary will, by his reckless policy, and by the jealousy his brilliant genius inspired, now saw their opportunity to revenge themselves, and they arose to crush him. Alone in Paris, without an army, he was almost a prisoner in the hands of his foes, where he could not hope to recover from the disaster which had overwhelmed him, or employ his talents for the military protection of the country. The Chambers took the control of public affairs; and Napoleon, prostrated by recent events, and unable to resolve upon any definite course of action, acquiesced sullenly in allowing the reins of government to be snatched from his hands. He was forced to await the decision of a special Council of State that was summoned to settle the future of the Emperor and the policy to be pursued by the nation. Lafayette, who was named member of the Council, and was its leading spirit, insisted that the defence of the country should not be the only question discussed, but that negotiations for the restoration of peace should be also proceeded with; and he succeeded in carrying a resolution, to the effect that, as the Allies had signified their determination not to treat with Napoleon, the two Chambers should themselves nominate negotiators, who were, under their authority alone, to come to terms with the conquerors.* It was a revolution; and it was nearly complete on the morning of the 22nd. In the divided councils of the Emperor, Lafayette gained a great advantage, and giving voice to the one thought that filled all minds in that moment of anguish, he resolved that Napoleon's deposition should forthwith, and at all hazards, be carried into immediate execution.

A struggle—a one-sided struggle—took place between the Emperor and the Chambers. The former could only rely upon his previous military prestige and upon the halo of influence that still might be supposed to surround his name; but he did nothing to rouse himself out of the lethargy that oppressed his moral faculties. The latter, representing the reactionary and Republican parties, were tired of Napoleon and of his greatness. They regarded him as the sole obstacle to peace, and as a fallen leader who must be swept away in the interests of the country. So fickle were the French to the man they received as their ruler in defiance of Europe four months before, and who had been their unquestioned

* Hooper, 275; Lamartine, ii. 480.

master for nearly fifteen years, and so intent were they to be rid of him, that they only granted him—and that with difficulty—but one short hour to make up his mind to vacate his throne; in default, he was to be discrowned by force. Napoleon was indignant, but he did not resist. "I have not returned from Elba," he said, "to deluge Paris with blood;"[*] and, fearing to provoke a civil war, he accepted the inevitable, and abdicated in favour of his son within thirty-six hours of his arrival in the capital.

And yet his overweening pride was still thirsting for power, and this act of renunciation was neither tendered nor accepted in good faith. Napoleon II., as he was called, was a child, and was in Austria, and the Emperor still clung to the delusive hope that he might be re-installed in the power he had lost, though he could only wield it in the name of his son. On the other hand, the Chambers, fearing to drive their antagonist to extremes, and dreading above all things a revival of his wonted energy, agreed to an equivocal recognition of Napoleon II. In this way they also satisfied the cravings of the army for Imperialism; but the assent was a mere fictitious one, which was intended to have no meaning and which had no result. The Empire was indeed doomed, its founder dishonoured, and his dynasty destroyed. It was a wretched end to a glorious career, not even redeemed by that fortitude and personal dignity which mark the fall of the truly great. This final downfall is without parallel in history, and the weakness of human nature and the vanity of man's personal ambition stand out prominently, as the main features of the drama. The last scene was approaching, and may be described in a few words.

The moment Napoleon abdicated, he ceased to be a factor in the great events that followed. He was even an obstacle in the way of those who had usurped his place, and was treated with a contumely he had little deserved at the hands of flatterers, who, having basked in his smiles, had now constituted themselves the arbiters of his lot. Driven almost with indignity to the suburban retreat of La Malmaison, where his personality could not affect the Parisians, he still dreamt of power, but did nothing to grasp it. At last he was obliged to fly to the coast before the Allies, who were approaching the capital. Despairing of making good his escape, and feeling keenly the humiliation of his position, should capture await him in the land where for so long he had

[*] Lamartine, ii. 478.

been the idol, he yielded himself a prisoner to Captain Maitland, who commanded H.M.S. *Bellerophon*—stationed near Rochfort to intercept the Imperial fugitive,—as to the representative of "the most powerful, the most constant, and the most generous" of his enemies (July 15th). This is the last of Napoleon, and henceforward he lived and died a captive in the island of St. Helena, hated by his gaolers, forgotten by his country, and forsaken by his kindred.

> " But where is he, the modern, mightier far,
>   Who, born no king, made monarchs draw his car;
>   The new Sesostris, whose unharness'd kings,
>   Freed from the bit, believe themselves with wings,
>   And spurn the dust o'er which they crawl'd of late,
>   Chain'd to the chariot of the chieftain's state?
>   Yes! where is he, the champion and the child
>   Of all that's great or little, wise or wild?
>   Whose game was empires, and whose stake was thrones?
>   Whose table earth—whose dice were human bones?
>   Behold the grand result in yon lone isle,
>   And as thy nature urges, weep or smile." *

The overthrow of her great military hero brought no satisfaction or relief to France. She needed a chief to direct, and a policy to shape her actions; but at the most critical moment, when the Allies were thundering at her gates, she deliberately deprived herself of the one, and had not thought of the other. Napoleon was rejected; but who was to take his place, and who was to safeguard her interests? The noisy demagogues had effectively stirred up a revolution, and had deposed the only soldier who could have stood between her and the victorious enemy. Their momentary success was complete; but they left nothing except chaos behind them, and their work was folly because it was destructive. It is true, they did conceive some hope that they could rear up a Republic or a Constitutional Monarchy upon the ruins of the Imperial system, and none for a moment believed that the unconditional restoration of the Royal Family was imminent. The "obstacle to peace" was removed; but the peace that France desired was denied her, and she was not to be allowed to have a voice in shaping her own destinies. The Allies were masters of the situation; and they were as intent upon taking

* Byron, *Age of Bronze*, iii.

ample securities against the people who had for so long scourged Europe, as against the man who had led them on to plunder Christendom. The man was gone, but the people remained; and in their eagerness to repudiate him, they forgot that they too had some account to render to the conquerors.*

A Provisional Government was set up in Paris on the evening of the 22nd of June, composed of five persons, among whom was Fouché, Duc d'Otranto, late Minister of Police under Napoleon, and one of his bitterest enemies. He had the address to be named President, and in the anarchy produced by the panic which the crisis created, he alone preserved his faculties unimpaired. Seizing the supreme control of the State during the moment of interregnum, he became dictator, and the sole and irresponsible advocate of his country's cause. A Republican by conviction, a regicide, and holding to the extravagant tenets which were enunciated in 1789, he was far more keenly alive to his own immediate interests than to his avowed principles; and perceiving clearly that his credit and reward could best be secured by obliging France to accept—even against her will—a Bourbon *régime*, he devoted his great talents and his incomparable powers of intrigue to bring about the unconditional restoration of King Louis. His treachery was deeply resented by the nation, but what could they do? Napoleon had been abandoned, and there was no one to replace him,—none to form a patriotic administration, none to give effect to the national aspirations of the people, none to cope with the difficulties that had arisen, none to secure those terms which a proud and vigorous race had a right to expect, even when overwhelmed by adversity. In the universal prostration which succeeded the battle of Waterloo, Fouché, "one of the most hateful among the hateful tribunes of the Terror," † reigned in France, an autocrat, hated by all, feared by all, and obeyed by all.‡

While these events were taking place in Paris, the victorious Allies were advancing towards that city, there to reap the fruits of their success, to restore the peace of Europe, and to impose their will upon the now distracted country that lay at their mercy. After the battle there was a meeting between the Duke of

---

* Hooper, *Waterloo*, pp. 280, 285.
† M. Guizot, *History of France*, 1789-1848, edited by Madame de Witt, *née* Guizot, viii. 231 (London, 1881).
‡ Hooper, p. 286, etc.

Wellington and Marshal Blücher, at which operations for the immediate future were decided. The former engaged to advance the following day, and returned for the night to his head-quarters at Waterloo; the latter agreed to pursue the enemy without delay, and to endeavour to cut off Grouchy. He then went to Genappe, and, on the 20th, his advanced troops were in French territory. Early on the 19th, the army commanded by Wellington left their bivouacs, the 2nd Battalion Coldstream Guards starting from the farm of Hougomont, which they had held—in conjunction with the 2nd Battalion of the Third Guards, and with the light companies of the First Guards (2nd and 3rd Battalions)—with such credit to themselves. They reached Nivelles that evening, where Major-General Sir John Byng wrote his despatch on the battle, and on the stubborn contest that centred round Hougomont.*

On the 20th, the Guards Division reached Binche, and on that day the Duke of Wellington issued a General Order, which not only conveyed his thanks to the army under his command, for their conduct in the decisive action on the 18th, but which also warned the troops of the absolute necessity of treating the inhabitants of France as a friendly people.† This admonition of the rules which prevail in war time among civilized nations, was not indeed needed by the seasoned troops of British origin, who had been trained in the humane usages invariably adopted by England, to respect the liberties and the property of the people over whose lands war has to be waged. It was rather addressed to the Anglo-allies (Dutch, Belgians, and Germans), to enforce the maxim that hostilities are not conducted against the population, and that ill treatment of peasants only exasperates the enemy, and does nothing to secure his final subjugation. It is to be remarked that this policy was not followed by the Prussians, with the result that the latter never gained the good will of the French, while the British, on the contrary, were looked upon by that proud and sensitive people with respect, and almost without distrust.

On the morning of the 22nd of June, Wellington was at Malplaquet, the scene of one of Marlborough's greatest triumphs over the same enemy. Before leaving, he issued a proclamation in French to the people whose territories were then entered by the

* Appendix No. I. 1. † Appendix I. 2.

British troops, to the effect that the invaders had come to deliver them from the iron yoke that oppressed them; and that the population would be well treated by the army, provided they did not join the cause of the "Usurper" (Napoleon), who had been "pronounced to be the enemy of the human race, with whom neither peace nor truce could be made." * Neither in this effort to conciliate the population did Prince Blücher follow the example of his colleague; on the contrary he displayed resentment against the natives of a country whose military genius had, in the past, humbled in the dust the pride of his own nation. It was perhaps natural that he should assume this attitude when the provocation which the Prussians received is taken into account, but it was not calculated to reassure the French in their despair, nor to reconcile them to the restoration of the Royal Family.

In order to give a general view of the whole military situation, it will now be necessary to refer briefly to the incidents of the war that took place close to Waterloo, on the day of the battle, where Marshal Grouchy was struggling with Blücher's rear-guard. On the 18th he was at Wavre, with 32,000 men, of whom 5000 were cavalry; and there he was held in check during the whole day by Thieleman's Prussian Corps, only 15,000 strong. It was not until evening that he turned the right of the Prussians, when at length he opened a road for his troops, whereon to advance to the main body of the French army, known to be somewhere near Waterloo. As it was then too late to continue the action, Grouchy hoped next day to complete the victory he had achieved, ere he pushed forward to join his chief. On the morning of the 19th he received no tidings from the Emperor, and he believed that all was well; but Thieleman, though he was not informed of the full details of the disaster to which the French had been subjected, heard that a great battle had been fought, and that they were defeated; so he, too, determined to attack Grouchy in the morning. A battle consequently took place on the 19th, in which the Prussians, though they contested the ground inch by inch, were forced to fall back towards Louvain by the superiority of the masses they engaged. At the very moment of victory, Grouchy received the message which Napoleon had sent him from Quatre-Bras, announcing the total destruction of the French army, and thus revealing to him the full extent of the danger in which he was

* Appendix I. 3.

placed. Perceiving at once the necessity that his corps should be saved from the general wreck, he determined to retreat through Namur upon Givet, and began to move without delay. General Pirch I., having been detached from the main Prussian army on the evening of the 18th to intercept him, joined Thieleman, who also advanced as soon as he perceived that he was no longer being pursued by the corps which had defeated him. Both Prussian Generals endeavoured to arrest the enemy, but they failed to do so; and Grouchy, who marched with great rapidity and resolution, ably seconded by the valour of his subordinate Generals, reached Givet on the 21st, and entered French territory in safety. He was then ordered to join Marshal Soult, who was attempting to rally the broken fragments of the main army at Laon. This occurred on the fatal 22nd, the same day that Napoleon, coerced by the political leaders in Paris, closed his public career, and signed his abdication of the French throne in favour of his son.

Grouchy's corps was the only one that, having taken part in the campaign in Belgium, remained intact. The main French army had been panic-stricken at Waterloo, and a large mass of those who survived the battle fled straight to Paris, or deserted their standards, and were nowhere to be found; many flung away their arms, and dispersed to their homes. The disruption of the great army was complete, and the defeat signal and decided beyond all former precedent. The co-operation of the greater bulk of Napoleon's forces in subsequent military events was impossible, and little resistance was to be apprehended from these men. But there was a remnant of true soldiers still available, who, seeking their Colours, concentrated some 20,000 strong near Philippeville. On the 22nd they were at Laon, and about that time the French could dispose of some 50,000 men for the defence of the northern frontier. The situation was a desperate one, and would have been fatal even to Napoleon himself in the full vigour of his military genius; but the position was all the more impossible, since the Saxons, the Austrians, and the Russians were by this time upon the eastern frontier of France, and were ready to advance in a concentrated and concentric march upon the capital.

On the 22nd of June, Wellington reached Le Cateau Cambresis. He had three divisions at Bavay, and four echeloned along the road to Le Cateau—the Guards Division being at Gommignie. Besides this, other troops were employed against Le Quesnoi and Valenciennes, which were occupied by men of the Garde Nationale. Blücher was at Catillon-sur-Sambre with his troops in the vicinity, including Thieleman, who had returned from the pursuit of Grouchy, but excluding Pirch I., who was ordered to remain in rear for the purpose of reducing the fortresses which defended the French frontier. The Prussians were also at that time blockading Landrecies and Maubeuge—also garrisoned by local levies, from whom little resistance was to be expected. The Anglo-Prussian Allies halted on the 23rd, for the purpose of collecting their stragglers, and of bringing up ammunition; and thereby a much-needed rest was afforded to men who, for more than eight days, had been constantly and actively occupied in the arduous labours of the war. During the halt the two Generals, Wellington and Blücher, met to decide how a united advance could best be made upon Paris. As a result of this conference, it was agreed that the Allies should not pursue the enemy directly, but, covered by the Oise, push along the right bank of that river, upon Compiègne and Creil, so as to turn his left, and if possible, cut him off from Paris,—the movement to be masked by the Prussian cavalry, whose presence, it was hoped, would induce the French to retard their retreat.* Wellington, moreover, anxious that the moral effect of the battle of Waterloo should be fully reaped, and that Napoleon should have no time to recover from the disaster, hastened the arrival of King Louis into French territory, offering to secure Cambrai as his residence until Paris should be captured. Hearing, also, that that fortress was imperfectly guarded, he sent Sir Charles Colville forward with a detachment to seize it (June 23rd). The attack was successful, in so far that the town was taken with little loss; but the citadel held out until the 25th, when the Governor capitulated to the King. His Majesty by this time reached the British head-quarters, and he temporarily established his Court in Cambrai.

On the 24th the combined armies continued their advance. The British pushed on two brigades towards Cambrai, but otherwise only altered their position slightly, as they were waiting for their pontoon train. The Prussians, however, moved forward, taking Guise and St. Quentin. During the day, intelligence was received of Napoleon's abdication, but the news was at first

* Capt. Siborne, *History of the War in France and Belgium* in 1815, ii. 370 (2nd edit., London, 1844). See Map No. 1, p. 54.

discredited. Later, it became confirmed; but both Commanders determined that terms of peace could only be signed at Paris, and they rejected all overtures made to them by the Provisional Government to arrest their march upon the capital. On the 25th of June, the British head-quarters were at Joncourt, the Coldstream Guards being at Le Cateau.

Blücher, on the other hand, hearing that the French had not been deceived by the cavalry demonstration made in the direction of Laon, now came to the conclusion that they were hastening towards Paris; he therefore determined to secure the passages over the Oise, and he pushed on to these points with the utmost rapidity. A squadron entered Compiègne in the evening of the 26th, and early the following day a Prussian brigade supported it, just in time to prevent this place from falling into the hands of the enemy; for Grouchy, who had superseded Soult, ordered D'Erlon to occupy the bridge with the remnants of his Corps, about 4000 strong. D'Erlon, finding the Prussians in position, cannonaded it, and very soon afterwards retired, unpursued by the Prussians, who were too much exhausted to advance; so that it was mid-day before the advantage gained could be pressed home. These operations were connected with the movements of other Prussian columns, one of which also succeeded in capturing the bridge of Creil just before the French arrived there. Brushing the enemy away, the invaders continued to march to Senlis, where D'Erlon was met and driven off the straight line of his retreat. The bridge of St. Maxence was found partially destroyed, and the river had to be crossed in boats, but that of Verberie was taken. By the evening of the 27th, Blücher's advanced troops were on the left of Grouchy, intercepting the road to Paris, and with every hope of being able to prevent him from reaching the capital before the Prussians.* At dawn of the 28th, a small force under Pirch II. came into collision with the enemy near Villers-Cotterets, and, being greatly outnumbered at that point, they were in some danger of being overpowered. The French, however, were in no condition to fight; they had lost heart, and many were deserting their Colours. Being disorganized by their reverses, and by the fear that Blücher's energy inspired, they now allowed Pirch to get away unhurt. The latter had succeeded by his manœuvre to delay them, so that during the day they were repeatedly attacked with considerable loss, and most

* Siborne, ii. p. 403.

of them were forced to turn to their left to cross the river Marne, and so reach Paris by a circuitous route. By the evening of the 28th, the Prussians had not only captured sixteen guns and four thousand prisoners, forced the French from their true line of retreat, and increased the terror and confusion which prevailed among them, but they also succeeded in following some few detachments of the enemy, who had been enabled to fly straight to Paris. In this manner their advanced posts were within five miles of the capital, near Le Bourget and Stains, where they carried panic and dismay into the heart of the city.* Blücher established his head-quarters at Senlis.

During this vigorous pursuit, the Anglo-allies were also advancing southwards. On the 26th, Sir John Byng assaulted the fortress of Peronne with the 1st Guards Brigade, who carried the outworks by storm with little loss, soon after which the town capitulated. The British head-quarters were at Vermand and the army in the vicinity, advanced cavalry patrols having penetrated as far as Roye. The Coldstream Guards halted at Coulaincourt. Next day the army crossed the river Somme at Willecourt; the Duke was at Nesle, and Roye was occupied. On the 28th, the British right was near St. Just, and Montdidier was occupied; the left was in rear of La Tulle, where the roads meet that run from Compiègne and Roye; the reserve reached the latter place, and the Guards Division was at Conchy, where the rest of the First Army-Corps was posted.

The rapid approach of the invaders upon Paris made it plain to the Provisional Government that they had no power to arrest the progress of the Allies for a single moment; and although the north side of the city was secured by a line of fortified works, sufficiently strong to resist a *coup de main*, yet the wreck of Napoleon's army had not reached the capital, and time was imperatively required to bring them there and to organize some defence. An armistice was once more sought on the 27th, and again on the 28th, in the despairing hope that the Government might be allowed some breathing-time in which to consider their position, and make some show of resistance, in order to save France the humiliation which was clearly in store for her. But the allied Commanders were inexorable, and, refusing all such negotiations, they pursued their operations with the same activity

* Siborne, ii. 415.

as in the past. Wellington indeed frankly told the Commissioners who approached him on behalf of the Provisional Government, that he—

"must see some steps taken to re-establish a government in France which should afford the Allies some chance of peace" before he could sanction a suspension of hostilities; that he personally "conceived the best security for Europe was the restoration of the King, and that the establishment of any other government than the King's in France must inevitably lead to new and endless wars;" and he concluded by these words: "That, in my opinion, Europe had no hope of peace if any person excepting the King were called to the throne of France; that any person so called must be considered an usurper, whatever his rank and quality; that he must act as an usurper, and must endeavour to turn the attention of the country from the defects of his title towards war and foreign conquests; that the Powers of Europe must, in such a case, guard themselves against this evil; and that I could only assure them" (the Commissioners) "that, unless otherwise ordered by my Government, I would exert any influence I might possess over the Allied Sovereigns to induce them to insist upon securities for the preservation of peace, besides the treaty itself, if such an arrangement as they had stated were adopted"—viz., any arrangement whereby a prince, other than the King, were called to the throne of France. *

On the 29th, Blücher pressed on towards Paris, and reconnoitred the defences thrown round the northern side of the city. The remnants of the great army which had been shattered at Waterloo also entered the capital on that day, and the French mustered some 80,000 to 90,000 men there—troops from the provincial depôts and from the country having been called for the defence of the seat of government, and as many discharged veterans as could be collected having been assembled in a special corps some 17,000 strong. Besides this, there was plenty of artillery available, and about 30,000 of the Garde Nationale; but on the latter no great reliance could be placed. Marshal Davoût, Prince d'Eckmühl, was appointed Commander-in-chief. The British forces were still in rear, and occupied positions between Gournay and St. Maxence, the Guards Division being near St. Martin Longeau. At dawn, on the 30th of June, the advanced French post at Aubervilliers was attacked by the 4th Prussian Corps under Bülow, and the enemy was driven back, and pursued as far as the canal in rear of that village; but it became evident that to dislodge him from that line, a more serious effort would be necessary.

* Siborne, ii. 427, etc.

The Duke of Wellington having proceeded to Blücher's headquarters during the night of the 29th-30th, a conference was held as to the future operations to be pursued. It was then agreed to move the Prussians to their right, to take advantage of the capture of the bridge of St. Germains which had already been effected, and to extend the investment of the capital round the west and south of the city, threatening to cut it off from those provinces that furnished it with supplies. The British army at the same time was to move into the posts which their allies had taken up north of the city, and to mask the defences which the enemy had erected there. During the night of the 29th-30th and the following day, these operations were carried out, the 4th Prussian Corps covering the movement until the British arrived. In the evening, the latter were about Louvres, twelve miles away from Paris; the Guards Division being at La Chapelle. The two Prussian Corps, under Thieleman and Ziethen, were close to St. Germain; while two regiments of Hussars, under Lieut.-Colonel von Sohr, having been thrown forward, bivouacked at Marley, on the road to Versailles. During the day, Bülow's Corps had been engaged, as we have seen. On the 1st of July he began to move off, and in the afternoon he was relieved by the advanced British forces, who took his place; the Guards Division were at Le Bourget and the forest of Bondy, five miles from the capital.

On this day the enemy gained an advantage over the Prussians —the only one of the campaign, except the delusive victory at Ligny,—for the cavalry brigade under von Sohr, ordered to reconnoitre round the southern suburbs, proceeding too far away from its supports, was attacked, and, though the men defended themselves bravely, they were cut to pieces. This transient success, however, produced no effect upon the main result, and was but a passing incident in the drama now soon to close. Next day, the 2nd, Blücher continued his march round Paris; and his troops, under Ziethen, came into collision with the enemy near Sèvres, who was driven back to Issy, and, later in the evening, into the town. Thieleman pushed forward advanced troops to Chatillon; and the reserve, under Bülow, was near Versailles. The British remained in the positions on the north front of the capital, sending detachments across the Seine, which occupied the villages of Asnières, Courbevoie, and Suresnes, to keep up communications with the Prussians. On the 3rd, Vandamme made an attempt to drive Ziethen's troops out of Issy, and a battle took place, which, lasting about four hours, ended disastrously for the French, who were repulsed, and forced to take refuge within the barriers of the city. This effort was the end of the operations, and no more fighting took place, for the Provisional Government, holding that the defence of Paris was not practicable against the victorious Allies, now agreed to treat for a capitulation.

A great change had by this time come over public feeling in Paris, and this was mainly the work of Fouché. France, left without a chief in the moment of her abasement, fell into the hands of Napoleon's ex-Minister of Police. Once installed in power, he issued a proclamation to the people he was deliberately deluding (June 24th). It held out extravagant hopes that, under his guidance, France would at last be contented with an honourable peace. It was a dishonest proclamation, for it made impossible promises; and yet, in the national degradation which marked the crisis, the people had perforce to obey the man, who, while in secret correspondence with the Allies for the restoration of the King, told them—

"After twenty-five years of political tempests, the moment has arrived when everything wise and sublime that has been conceived respecting social institutions may be perfected in yours. Let reason and genius speak, and from whatever side their voices may proceed, they shall be heard. . . . Who is the man, that, born on the soil of France, whatever may be his party or political opinions, will not range himself under the national standard, to defend the independence of his country! Armies may be in part destroyed, but the experience of all ages and of all nations proves that a brave people, combating for justice and liberty, cannot be vanquished. The Emperor, in abdicating, has offered himself a sacrifice. The members of the Government devote themselves to the due execution of the authority with which they have been invested by your representatives." *

Nor was it long before Fouché gained sufficient influence over Davoût to make it clear to him that the Empire had come to an end, and that the only solution possible out of the *impasse* in which France had become involved, was submission to the will of the conquerors and the restoration of the Bourbons. Once gained over, the Marshal did not hesitate to obey, and efforts to ensure the defence of the capital were undertaken with deliberate

* Siborne, ii. 378.

half-hearted vigour.* The Parisians were rapidly becoming indifferent to their fate; they cared not who was to rule them, provided they were allowed to live in peace. The era of glory had afforded them some satisfaction, but it had its drawbacks, and late events had brought these to a crisis; therefore they were glad to welcome the strongest, and to have done with conquests. The Chambers, also, had exhausted all their energies in destroying the man whose military genius might have served the country at this terrible juncture. They succeeded admirably in their design; and now they devoted themselves to academical studies, and busied themselves in discussing a new constitution, quite oblivious of the fact that their labours must be fruitless. All sections of the nation were easily dealt with by Fouché; and even the army, devoted to their late incomparable leader, soon submitted to his will.

Besides the efforts already made to obtain a suspension of hostilities from the allied Commanders, Marshal Davoût approached them on the 30th of June, but again unsuccessfully. On the same day, he also joined in a protest addressed to the Chambers against the return of the Bourbons—a protest intended, perhaps, rather to satisfy the susceptibilities of the army than for any other purpose. The Chambers, in their reply, alluded to their proposed constitution; and stated that, while they were prepared to accept whatever dynasty the Allies might insist on fixing upon the throne, they were convinced that the accession of the new Monarch could only become an accomplished fact, when he had agreed to the conditions they meant to impose upon his prerogative. They "will never," they said, "acknowledge as legitimate Chief of the State him who, on ascending the throne, shall refuse to acknowledge the rights of the nation, and to consecrate them by a solemn compact." †

But neither the Chambers nor the army were to determine the fate of the country; for Fouché, alone among Frenchmen, was possessed of power, and he only had any voice in shaping its policy in this crisis. Wellington, anxious above all things that Paris should submit without further bloodshed, consented, on the 2nd of July, to a suspension of hostilities, on the basis of the evacuation of the capital by the army. But he was not altogether master of the situation, for Marshal Blücher, to whom he was so greatly indebted for his victory over the enemy, had different ideas, and wished to humble the French in a manner that would have been

* Hooper, *Waterloo*, p. 286. † Siborne, ii. 450.

impolitic as well as hostile to the best interests of a stable peace. It required, therefore, all the Duke's tact to make him understand, that the best way to end the war, was to accept a capitulation, and to give up all ideas of incurring the responsibility of taking so large a city as Paris by force of arms. Blücher, fortunately, had some respect for the good sense of his colleague, and agreed to these views, and, on the 3rd, he consented to treat. Thereupon hostilities ceased abruptly, while Vandamme was being driven back, in the manner that has been already described, near Issy.*

Commissioners met on the 3rd, at the Palace of Saint-Cloud, and speedily agreed to a Military Convention, which stipulated the following conditions :—

(1) The army to evacuate Paris within three days, and to take up a position in rear of the Loire, the movement to be complete within eight days ; (2) St. Denis, St. Ouen, Clichy, and Neuilly to be given up to the Allies on the 4th, Montmartre on the 5th, and, on the 6th, all barriers, giving access into the city, to be placed in the power of the Allies ; (3) Order to be maintained in Paris by the Garde Nationale, and by the municipal *Gens d'armerie;* (4) The actual authorities to be respected "so long as they shall exist;" (5) Private and public property, except that which relates to war, to be respected, and all individuals to enjoy their rights and liberties, "without being disturbed or called to account, either as to the situations which they hold, or may have held, or as to their conduct or political opinions ;" (6) The capital to be furnished with supplies.†

These stipulations, ratified by the British and Prussian Commanders, were carried out by the French with scrupulous fidelity. In spite of the violence of the troops, whose enthusiasm for the Imperial system had scarcely abated, the army, 70,000 men and 200 guns, marched towards the Loire on the 4th, under Marshal Davoût.‡ The Chambers continued their sittings, still intent upon their proposed constitution. On the 7th, the Allies determined to enter Paris, heralding the re-instatement of Louis XVIII., the Bourbon king.

* Hooper, 296.
† Siborne, ii. 470, where the text of the Convention is given in full.
‡ Davoût told Marshal Macdonald that the effective of the army going beyond the Loire amounted to 150,000 men, 30,000 horses, and 750 guns (*Souvenirs du Maréchal Macdonald*, p. 393).

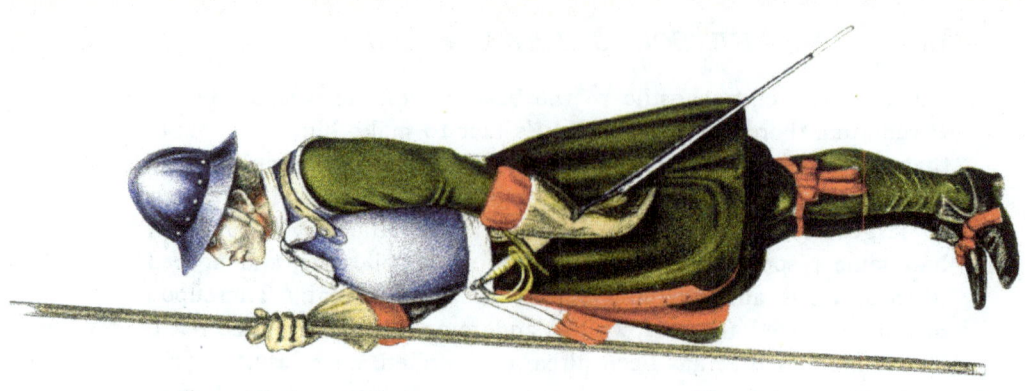
PIKEMAN 1669.

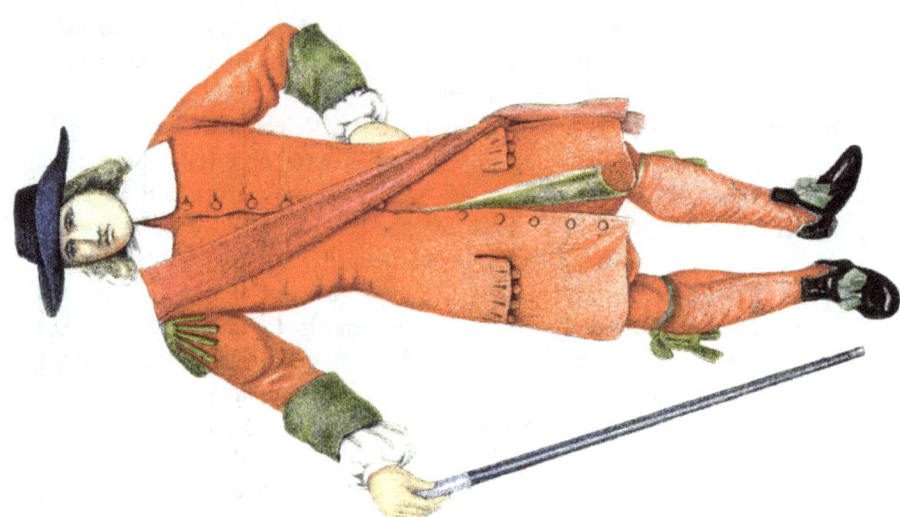
DRUM MAJOR 1670.

GRENADIER COMPANY 1670.

During this time the Germans, Austrians, and Russians were advancing to the capital, and, although the war was practically concluded by the Military Convention just signed, yet it languished for a few months longer in some of the provinces. The North-German Corps (26,000 men), formed of contingents brought together by the petty Princes, was occupied in the beginning of July, in reducing some of the French fortresses on the north-east frontier. The Austrian army, under Prince Schwartzenburg, including Saxons and South Germans, and amounting to more than 250,000 men, had its advanced troops between the Seine and the Marne, near La Ferté-sous-Jouarre, on the 10th of July. The Russians, under Marshal Barclay de Tolly (nearly 170,000 men), were at Paris and in its vicinity by the middle of July. A combined Austro-Sardinian army (60,000) was in the south-east of France, and completed, during that month, the subjugation of the districts in that quarter.*

Besides the various expressions of thanks to the gallant army that destroyed the power of Napoleon at Waterloo, to which allusion has already been made, letters were published in General Orders, July 2nd, from the Commander-in-Chief, H.R.H. the Duke of York, and from the Secretary of State for the Colonies and for War, Earl Bathurst, conveying the admiration felt at the conduct of the troops.† On the 5th, the resolutions of thanks passed by the House of Lords and by the House of Commons were published in General Orders;‡ and, on the 17th, those of the Common Council of the City of London (dated July 7th) were communicated to the troops in the same manner.

Towards the end of July it was determined, in recognition of the "conspicuous valour" displayed by the army "in the late glorious victory," to grant: (1) increase to the pensions allowed to Officers for wounds, according as they might be promoted in the service; (2) to all Subalterns in the Infantry of the Line and in the Cavalry, and to all Ensigns of the Guards, at Waterloo, two years' service, so as to qualify them for extra pay after five, instead of seven, years' service; (3) to every Non-commissioned officer, private, etc., present at the battle, the distinction of being called a

---

* Siborne, ii. 481, etc.

† *The Despatches of Field-Marshal the Duke of Wellington during his Various Campaigns, etc.*, compiled by Colonel Gurwood, viii. 186 (London, 1847).

‡ *Ibid.*, viii. 198.

"Waterloo man," and to every "Waterloo man" two years' service in reckoning his service for increase of pay or for pension, when discharged,—but this indulgence was not otherwise to affect the conditions of his original enlistment. These arrangements were notified on the 5th of August.*

The Reverend John Norcross, Framlingham Rectory, Suffolk, having promised to settle an annuity of ten pounds—to be called the "Wellington Pension"—upon one of his "brave countrymen who fought in the late tremendous but glorious conflict," to be selected by the Duke, the latter chose Lance-Sergeant Graham, Coldstream Guards, for that honour. The record shows that Sergeant Graham "assisted Lieut.-Colonel Macdonell in closing the gate" (at Hougomont) "which had been left open for the communication, and which the enemy was in the act of forcing; he shot the leading man. His brother, a corporal in the same company, was lying wounded in a barn on fire; Sergeant Graham removed him a short distance secure from the fire, and returned again to his duty. Three years and two months in the Regiment." Another man, also recommended to the Duke, was Private John Lister, Third Guards, whose conduct was noted for particular bravery during the whole day.†

On the 29th of July, H.R.H. the Prince Regent granted to all Ensigns of the three Regiments of Foot Guards then serving, and afterwards to be appointed, the rank of Lieutenant, as a mark of Royal approbation of the distinguished gallantry of the Brigade of Guards in the important battle which had just taken place. Thereby was completed the system of the "double rank" which had existed in the Household Infantry for many years. Captains of the First and Coldstream Guards had been given the rank of Lieutenant-Colonel in 1687, and four years later, in 1691, Captains of the Scots Guards received the same privilege; while all Lieutenants of the three Regiments of Foot Guards were upon that occasion given commissions of Captains in the army.‡

During the halt which was made at Le Cateau on the 23rd

---

* *Supplementary Despatches, etc., of Field-Marshal Arthur Duke of Wellington*, compiled by his son, xi. 98 (London, 1864).

† *Ibid.*, xi. 35, 121. *Wellington Despatches* (Gurwood), viii. 249.

‡ Colonel MacKinnon, *Origin and Services of the Coldstream Guards*, i. 190, 211, and ii. 368 (London, 1833). The Prince Regent also conferred upon the First Guards the title of Grenadier Guards, "in commemoration of their having defeated the Grenadiers of the French Imperial Guard upon this memorable occasion" (*ibid.*, ii. 368).

of June, a return was ordered, giving the number of killed, wounded, and missing, casualties of the fighting that took place between the 16th and 18th inclusive.*

Some changes took place in the army during the six months that followed the battle of Waterloo.

The Prince of Orange, having to return to Holland, on the 22nd of June, Major-General Sir John Byng assumed temporarily the command of the First Army-Corps until the 12th of July, when he reverted to his position of Commander of the Division of Guards until the 23rd; he was then replaced by Major-General Sir Kenneth Howard (late Coldstream Guards), and he re-assumed the command of the 2nd Guards Brigade, the 1st being still under Major-General Maitland. Owing to the absence of the Prince of Orange, the command of the First Army-Corps devolved upon Sir Kenneth Howard on the 22nd of August, when Sir J. Byng again reverted to the Guards Division, and remained at their head till further orders; thereupon Colonel Hepburn (Third Guards) became Brigadier of the 2nd Guards Brigade. On the 2nd of October, Sir J. Byng having obtained leave of absence to proceed to England, Major-General Maitland took command of the Division until his return.

* A return, dated Adjutant-General's Office, April 13, 1816, was transmitted to the Duke of Wellington from the Horse-Guards on July 16th of that year, showing the number of sergeants, trumpeters, drummers, farriers, and rank and file of the British army, who were killed, wounded, or missing in the actions fought in Flanders on the 15th, 16th, and 18th of June, 1815. The following concerns the Division of Guards:—

	Killed.	Died of Wounds.	Wounded.						Missing.	
			Suffered Amputation.	Discharged.	Transferred to Vet. or Garr. Battns.	Rejoined Regiment.	Remain in Hospital.	Total.	Rejoined Regiment.	Not since heard of; supposed dead.
Grenadier Guards, 2nd Battn.	61	29	6	44	—	197	26	302	10	38
,, ,, 3rd ,,	71	30	14	48	—	361	33	486	3	32
Coldstream ,, 2nd ,,	47	26	6	—	—	208	1	241	4	—
Third ,, ,, ,,	39	47	12	21	—	96	19	195	17	2
Total Guards Division	218	132	38	113	—	862	79	1224	34	72
Total British Army	1715	856	236	506	167	5068	854	7687	482	353

Supplementary Despatches, etc., xiv. 632, 633.)

On the 20th of June, Captain Walton, Coldstream Guards, was temporarily appointed Brigade-Major of the 2nd Guards Brigade, vice Stothert, Third Guards, who was severely wounded, and who subsequently died. On the 6th of November, Captain Prince was appointed Adjutant of the 2nd Battalion Coldstream Guards vice Major C. Bentinck, who, upon the death of Captain Lascelles, was posted to the 1st Battalion as Senior Adjutant.*

The following Officers, belonging to the 1st Battalion, were ordered, on the 22nd of June, to hold themselves in readiness for foreign service, viz. Colonel Sir. H. Bouverie, Captains Shirley and Girardot, and Ensigns Clifton and Salwey; next day Captain Sandilands received a similar order. With the exception of Sir H. Bouverie and Ensign Clifton, these Officers were posted to the 2nd Battalion on the 27th till further orders, and at the head of a detachment of two hundred men, they reached Paris on the 19th of July. Previous to this date, on the 1st, a redistribution of Subaltern Officers of the Battalion in France had been made, by which: Captain Anstruther was posted to the Grenadier company, Captain Sowerby and Ensign Short to the 1st, Ensign Hon. J. Forbes to the 2nd, Captain Cowell and Ensign Hon. W. Forbes to the 3rd, Ensign Gordon to the 4th, Ensign Douglas to the 5th, Captain Lord Hotham to the 6th, Ensign Buckley to the 7th, Ensign Hervey to the 8th, Captain Bowles and Ensigns Gooch and Buller to the Light-infantry companies.

It was about this time that the present soldier's small account-book was introduced into the British army. By a letter from Lord Palmerston, the Secretary-at-War, to the Duke of Wellington, dated War Office, August 31, 1815, "in order to remedy the inconvenience and delay experienced in the adjustment of the claims of the soldiers," it was determined that "a book should be kept by every Non-commissioned officer, trumpeter, drummer, fifer, and private man of His Majesty's regular forces, calculated to show the actual state of his accounts."† This book was introduced by Horse Guards letter on the 6th of October following, and regulations were made to ensure that the accounts should be correctly

* The Junior Adjutant was invariably posted to the 2nd Battalion at that time, and on becoming Senior Adjutant he was transferred to the 1st Battalion. This custom prevailed until about 1840. Major C. Bentinck, while Junior Adjutant, served at the battle of Waterloo as Deputy Assistant-Adjutant-General, his place in the Battalion having been taken by Captain Walton.

† *Supplementary Despatches*, etc., xi. 151.

made up to the 24th of each month, and to oblige the men to keep their small books in their own possession, and in good order.

The Coldstream Guards contained the following Officers, in November, 1815:—

Colonel.—Field-Marshal H.R.H. Adolphus, Duke of Cambridge, K.G.
Lieut.-Colonel.—Colonel Hon. H. Brand, C.B.
Majors.—*First Major*—Colonel Sir R. D. Jackson, K.C.B.
    Second „ —Colonel A. Woodford, C.B.
Captains.—Colonel Sir H. Bouverie, K.C.B.; Lieut.-Colonels James Macdonell, C.B.; J. Hamilton; and L. Adams (*Mounted*).
    Lieut.-Colonels H. Loftus; W. H. Raikes; F. Sutton; F. Milman; T. Gore; T. Barrow; D. MacKinnon; Hon. J. Walpole; H. Dawkins; Colonels Hon. A. Abercromby, C.B.; Sir C. Campbell, K.C.B.; Lieut.-Colonel Hon. E. Acheson, C.B.; Colonel Sir R. Arbuthnot, K.C.B.; Lieut.-Colonels Sir W. Gomm, K.C.B.; Hon. H. Pakenham, C.B.; and H. Wyndham.
Lieutenants.—Lieut.-Colonel T. Steele; Major G. Bowles; Captains T. Sowerby; P. Sandilands; Lieut.-Colonel J. Fremantle, C.B.; Captains J. Prince (Adjutant); J. V. Harvey; W. Walton (Brigade-Major in France); A. Wedderburn; C. White; T. Bligh; C. Shawe; Major C. Bentinck (Adjutant); Captains J. Talbot; W. Baynes; W. Stothert; J. S. Cowell; W. Grimstead; Lord Hotham; W. Anstruther; Hon. J. Rous; C. Shirley; J. Drummond; Hon. R. Moore; C. Girardot; T. Chaplin; E. Clifton; H. Salwey; G. G. Morgan.
Ensigns.—Lieutenants T. Duncombe; Hon. J. Forbes; T. Powys; H. Gooch; A. Cuyler; M. Beaufoy; W. Kortright; H. Armytage; Hon. W. Rous; H. Bentinck; F. Shawe; H. St. J. Mildmay; F. Buller; H. Griffiths; J. Buller; J. Montagu; J. Hervey; H. Vane; F. Douglas; R. Bowen; F. FitzClarence; A. Gordon; Hon. W. Forbes; C. Short; H. Serjeantson; R. Beamish; Lord Wallscourt; Jasper Hall; J. Jenkinson; W. Cornwall; H. Murray; and E. Duke.
Quartermasters.—T. Dwelly; and B. Selway.
Surgeon-Major.—J. Simpson. *Battalion Surgeons.*—J. Rose; and W. Whymper. *Assistant Surgeons.*—T. Maynard; G. Smith; S. Worrell; and W. Hunter.
Solicitor.—J. Wilkinson, Esq.

CHAPTER II.

MILITARY OCCUPATION OF FRANCE

Termination of the war—Difficulties of the situation—The Allies occupy Paris—Dissolution of the Provisional Government—Entry of Louis XVIII. into the capital—New French Government formed—Blücher and the *Pont de Jena*—Arrival of the Allied Sovereigns—Reviews in France—Paris in the hands of the Allies—Treatment of the French by the Prussians; by the British—The wreck of the French Imperial forces disbanded—Life in Paris—The Louvre stripped of its treasures of art—Prosecution of Imperialist leaders—Labedoyère, Ney, Lavalette—Peace of Paris, November 20th.

THE long period of the wars of the French Revolution, which devastated the continent of Europe for more than twenty years, had now definitely come to an end, and another era was about to dawn upon the civilized world. France, who had provoked the struggle and prolonged the strife to satisfy the craving of a restless ambition, was at last crushed; and the military chief, whose genius had called into activity the warlike character of her inhabitants, was captured. The common enemy was no longer to be feared; but the balance of power in Europe had been rudely shaken, and new ideas had taken deep root in France into the political and social life of the people. A government had to be established in Paris, of a nature calculated to repress disorder, to calm the natural turbulence of the nation, and to give the Allies pledges for future good behaviour. In short, the French were to be invited to re-enter into the European comity of nations, and to conform to the re-settlement which was rendered necessary after the general disturbance that had taken place. But, in effecting this, the interests of the enemy could not be taken into account. Once before, France had been subdued, and, in 1814, the Allies had expelled Napoleon, and sought to restore a general peace without unduly oppressing the people who had been the aggressors. The attempt failed, for the Emperor returned to Paris, and thereby he re-kindled the torch of war, and revived the baneful policy which threatened his neighbours with destruction. France had participated in Napoleon's act, and had received him once more as her ruler; and, being defeated, she had little to expect from the forbearance of the victors. She was thus treated as a conquered country, and was subjected to some of the indignities which her soldiery had, in their turn, inflicted for so long a time upon her present masters.

And yet the task of a French reconstruction was by no means an easy one. The vitality of the nation, homogeneous and patriotic, at once forbade the Allies from any attempt to dismember it, even if their mutual jealousies had allowed them to adopt such a proposal. The only feasible plan was to give the people a ruler who could and would control the explosive forces which existed among them, and put an end to the dangers that menaced Europe by reason of the warlike and unscrupulous character they had displayed in the past. But the Allies, in carrying out this policy, forgot that it was of the first consequence to the future wellbeing of the Monarchy, to place Louis in an independent position, and, instead of restoring him to his kingdom by force of hostile bayonets only, to attain to the same end, by fostering the movement towards Royalism, which France began to develop after the battle of Waterloo. The downfall of Napoleon and the rejection of his dynasty had left three solutions, and only three, for the future government of the country. A Republic might have been formed; a popular King might be set up in the person of an Orleanist prince, who would accept the tricolor flag; and, lastly, the legitimate rule of Louis could be established. The first two solutions were contrary to the spirit of the age, they gave no security for future tranquillity, and the Allies set their faces firmly against either of them. There remained the third, which was the avowed object of the conquerors, and it was obvious that it could best be reached by causing the people to recall their King of their own accord. This had been the proposition of Marshal Davoût and of others; and, while their views were possibly more in advance than could have been agreed to without modification, yet, had the matter been left in English hands, there is little doubt that the King's restoration would have been effected, with the least shock possible to French susceptibilities, and the new order based on a firmer foundation than was given to it. But the British Government had others to consult, and the Allies, smarting under the injuries to which they had been subjected for more than twenty years, were not inclined to be too conciliatory.

Nor was this the only difficulty; for the French themselves, hopelessly divided into two hostile camps, were unable to come to any satisfactory agreement. On the one hand, there were the followers of the King, reactionary in feeling, who remembered with bitterness the cruelties they had experienced during revolutionary times, and who, now that they were supported by victorious armies, demanded the revival pure and simple of the *ancien régime*. On the other hand, there was Imperial and Revolutionary France—the nation itself,—who, having irrevocably adopted new canons of social and political existence, endeavoured to make terms with the party in power for the protection of the people. There was little sympathy between the two; but the latter had no leader, and had placed themselves unreservedly in the unworthy hands of Fouché, who, having gauged the situation, deserted those he was bound to support, and sought his own personal aggrandisement by joining the party that attached itself to the King.

The keen anxiety of Louis XVIII. to save France from the humiliations that were to be imposed upon her was undoubted; so also was his earnest desire to reign in accordance with the liberal spirit which the times required. He hoped to reconcile all sections of the population, and to prove himself their deliverer, not only from internal disorder, but also from foreign oppression. But though his good will and generosity were unquestioned, his prejudices remained, and were not to be eradicated even by misfortune, and his followers and intimate counsellors were not endowed with a similar noble spirit of forgetfulness for past ill-treatment. France, therefore, by the will of the Allies and with the full consent of the Royalist faction, was again to be unconditionally placed in the King's hands, his prerogative was to be unfettered, and his power was to be absolute. Nor were his first proclamations, issued to his subjects and dated the 25th and 28th of June, calculated to give much satisfaction to a people who dreaded his rule. The King's party, in short, had not the wisdom to perceive that a stable Restoration must be accompanied by a complete amnesty in favour of those, at least, who had no further power to resist—and resistance to the old French Monarchy had entirely ceased in the country. Hence, although

Louis repudiated all intentions of restoring feudal rights, or of dispossessing those who had illegally acquired lands during the Revolution, yet he did not hesitate to threaten with punishment the men by whose assistance he imagined Napoleon had been able to install himself once again as Emperor.*

"Up to the moment of the capitulation of Paris," says a contemporary writer, "the Chambers continued their deliberations, and on the day when the humiliation of the country seemed complete, the national representatives issued a declaration of the rights of Frenchmen, resembling in its spirit and in its principal features the Bill of Rights claimed by the Parliament of England from William III., and it is surely a tribute of no ordinary value offered to the Constitution of England, that, at the very time when her army was at the gates of the French capital, our national institutions were the objects of the perpetual eulogy, and the subjects of the imitation, of the statesmen of the hostile nation. The constancy of the Chambers was put to a severe trial. The King had arrived at Compiègne, and nearly a million of foreign troops were hastening from every quarter to re-instate him on the throne, and yet not one member in either House thought proper to propose his restoration. . . . The national representatives also addressed the people with a firmness of tone, and in a spirit of independence, that will entitle them to the admiration of future ages :—'A Monarch,' say they, in language similar to that held by the Convention Parliament of England, 'cannot offer any guarantee, if he does not swear to observe the Constitution framed by the national representation, and accepted by the people ; it hence follows, that any government which shall have no other title than the acclamation and the will of a party, or which shall be imposed by force, and every government which shall not guarantee the rights and liberties of a people claiming the privileges of freemen, will have only an ephemeral existence, and will neither secure the tranquillity of France nor of Europe.'" †

---

* The vengeance against Napoleon's adherents was thus announced in the Royal proclamation of the 28th of June, which was countersigned by Prince Talleyrand, at one time a revolutionist, and afterwards Foreign Minister of the Emperor: "I wish to exclude from my presence none but those whose celebrity is a matter of grief to France and of horror to Europe. In the plot which they hatched, I perceive many of my subjects misled and some guilty. I promise—I who never promised in vain (all Europe knows)—to pardon to misled Frenchmen, all that has passed since the day when I quitted Lille, amidst so many tears, up to the day when I re-entered Cambrai, amidst so many acclamations. But the blood of my people has flowed, in consequence of a treason of which the annals of the world present no example. That treason has summoned foreigners into the heart of France. Every day reveals to me a fresh disaster. I owe it then to the dignity of my Crown, to the interest of my people, to the repose of Europe, to except from pardon the instigators and authors of this horrible plot. They shall be designated to the vengeance of the laws by the two Chambers, which I propose forthwith to assemble" (*Annual Register*, 1815 ; *State Papers*, p. 393).

† Edward Baines, *History of the Wars of the French Revolution, from the Breaking-out*

How little the arrangements made in 1815 secured the permanent tranquillity of France, is shown by the history of that country during the last eighty years; but to these events it is not our intention to revert, for our object is only to give as faithful a picture as possible of what did occur at this crisis, to describe the part which was taken in these events by the Regiment whose annals we are engaged in recording, and to explain the condition of affairs which presented itself to both Officers and men during this moment of victory and of anxiety.

The barriers of Paris were placed in the hands of the Allies in the afternoon of the 6th—in accordance with the terms of the Military Convention—amid persistent cries from the populace of: "No Bourbons!" "The Representative Government for ever!" intermingled with some in favour of the fallen Emperor. On the 7th, the Prussians under Blücher marched into the town in force, and took possession of the Luxembourg and of other places. The Duke of Wellington, with the tact which distinguished his conduct during this moment of triumph, contented himself with taking part in this demonstration by despatching one brigade only into the city, "with orders to camp in the Champs Elysées, and near to the Place Louis Quinze, where the Duke of Wellington will have his head-quarters to-day."* The main body of the British army were encamped in the Bois de Boulogne, to which place the Guards Division were also brought, without any display

As soon as Paris was occupied by foreign troops, the Provisional Government dissolved itself, on the plea that the country had been deceived by the conquerors! The message of dissolution communicated to the Chambers, written by Fouché himself, asserted that up to the 6th it had been believed that "the Allied Sovereigns were not unanimous upon the choice of a prince who was to reign in France;" that it was only then declared that "all the Sovereigns had engaged to place Louis XVIII. upon the throne." The message went on to say that, as foreign troops had just occupied the Tuileries, where the Government was sitting, "we can only breathe wishes for our country; and, our deliberations being no longer free, we think it our duty to separate." Upon receiving this news, the Chamber of Peers immediately followed the example

of the War in 1792, *to the Restoration of a General Peace in* 1815, ii. 488 (London, 1818).

* *Supplementary Despatches, etc.,* xi. 2.

given, and also dissolved. The Deputies, however, determined to show a bolder front; and proclaiming that they were at their posts by the will of the people, and that bayonets only could disperse them, they continued their deliberations upon the proposed Constitution, which they determined to offer to the King for his acceptance, as if there was still a government in the country, and as if nothing had happened to disturb their equanimity. But the following day (July 8th), the farce came to an end, and they were excluded from their place of meeting by the bayonet; the gates were locked, a body of the Garde Nationale warned them off and made them retire, and thus they too were obliged to dissolve.*

Paris was now ready to receive Louis, and his public entry took place on the 8th. The tricolor flag was everywhere replaced by the white standard of the Bourbons, and the people, who had vociferously welcomed Napoleon on his return from Elba, not four months before, now came in immense crowds to greet the King, and acclaimed his restoration with enthusiastic joy. The scene was gay, and the sight that presented itself to the inhabitants such as they loved to behold; but, beneath the surface of these outward appearances, the minds of those who had any power of reflection were filled with depression and sadness. "Even the Royalists were downcast: their patriotic feelings were deeply wounded by the defeat of France; they augured ill of the restoration of the King in the rear of the English bayonets." †

Next day, the new Government was formed, and announced to the public, at the head of which was Prince Talleyrand, who also became Minister for Foreign Affairs. It included, besides, men belonging to different parties, for Louis was anxious to get the confidence of all; and lastly, it contained the name of Fouché, who, having succeeded in shaping the anarchy, which followed the

---

* Baines, *Wars of the French Revolution*, ii. 490.

† Archibald Alison, *History of Europe from the Commencement of the French Revolution in 1789 to the Restoration of the Bourbons in 1815*, x. 964 (2nd edit., 1844). "No one who has not witnessed it, or who has not been convinced of it by the accounts of others, could form an idea of the rapidity with which the public cry can be changed in France. At nine in the morning of the day on which the King last returned to Paris, a man was torn to pieces in the Place Vendôme for wearing the white cockade; at one, a Marshal of France (Moncey or Mortier), riding into Paris with the white cockade, was pursued by the populace, and with difficulty saved himself; and, at three, the King entered the capital, accompanied by shouts of acclamation far greater than those which greeted him the year before. All those who in an adverse sense were clamorous in the morning, had changed or disappeared" (Mr. Arbuthnot to Lord Liverpool, October 30, 1815: *Supplementary Despatches, etc.*, xi. 220).

fatal 18th of June, to the benefit of the Royal cause, received, much against the King's inclination, the portfolio of Minister of Police!

"Louis XVIII. was thus once more seated upon the throne of his fathers, but he reigned only in the Tuileries. To the foreign troops by which he was surrounded he was solely indebted for his elevation. The national will had not been consulted; and the same potent agency which placed him on the throne could alone maintain him in his present position. Indebted to the enemies of his country for his elevation, surrounded by a discordant ministry, compelled to impose heavy burdens upon his people as the price of his restoration, and forced to subscribe to conditions humiliating to the glory of France, the opening of his second reign was inauspicious in the extreme; but it was not utterly hopeless. Whatever might have been the errors of his former government, or however unpromising his present circumstances, he enjoyed personally the respect of the French nation. The people were wearied with revolutions. Their military passion, which, before the return of Napoleon, constituted the great danger of the French Monarchy, was subdued; and the nation wished for peace and a moderate share of freedom, both of which the King possessed the power and the inclination to confer." *

The difficulties of the situation were not lightened by the extraordinary conduct of Marshal Blücher at this juncture. That brave Commander could never forget the sufferings which the Imperial armies had caused in Prussia, nor the indignities imposed upon his country by the intolerance and the arrogance of Napoleon, when at the zenith of his power, in Berlin. He regarded the French nation as responsible for the outrages which had been inflicted, and, now that he was able to have his revenge, he determined to take it. He refused to hold any communications with the King, or with the new authorities who had been re-introduced into office by the co-operation of his own Government; and he desired Baron Müffling, appointed Military Governor of Paris, to levy a contribution of 100,000,000 francs on the town, as well as clothing sufficient for 110,000 men.† But not content, he went still further, and insisted that one of the bridges over the Seine, known as the bridge of Jena, should be destroyed, because it bore the name of the battle which had been so disastrous to Prussia. Wellington, informed of this mad project, endeavoured to intervene;

* Baines, *Wars of the French Revolution*, ii. 491.
† *Supplementary Despatches*, etc., xi. 3.

but so blinded was his impetuous and hot-headed colleague, that he declined to listen to any remonstrance, and began forthwith to undermine the arches. The Duke thereupon placed a guard of British soldiers on the threatened bridge, with orders to drive away by force any one who should attempt to damage it; and he intimated his determination to prevent this senseless destruction by arms if necessary.* Blücher now at last was brought to reason, and gave way; and thus an act of vandalism was prevented which was not only a distinct infraction of the Convention of July 3rd, stipulating that all property was to be respected, but would also have cast a deep and lasting stain on the honour and good name of the Allies.

Shortly after this (July 11th), the Emperors of Austria and Russia and the King of Prussia arrived in Paris, when Guards of Honour were found by the Brigade of Guards.†

About the same time, Lord Castlereagh and the other statesmen of the allied Powers reached the capital, to negotiate the terms of peace to which France was to be obliged to subscribe. The conclusions agreed to, and the incidents which took place during the occupation of Paris, will be noticed presently, but, meanwhile, we must make a short allusion to certain military displays made by the Allies during this period. On the 24th of July a celebrated review of the Anglo-allied army, which had just been reinforced by several regiments who had come to France from America— where peace had been concluded—took place near Paris, before the Emperor of Russia and the other Allied Sovereigns. There were as many as 60,000 British soldiers present, the whole of the troops being under the command of the Duke of Wellington.‡ The demonstration was more of a pageant than anything else, and as correct a representation as possible was given of the battle of Salamanca. It is perhaps worth remarking that, in the General

---

* It appears that a Battalion of the Grenadier Guards were employed upon this duty (*The Reminiscences and Recollections of Captain Gronow*, i. 129, and ii. 39; London, 1892).

† His Majesty, Alexander I. of Russia, expressly requested that he should be escorted and guarded by British troops (*Supplementary Despatches, etc.*, xi. 25).

‡ So critical was the situation in France considered to be, that the British Government sent large reinforcements to Wellington during the summer of 1815, with the intention of making him stronger at Paris than he had been at Waterloo. After that battle more than 20,000 English troops were sent to the Continent (Lord Liverpool to Lord Castlereagh, Aug. 11, 1815; see *Correspondence, etc., of Viscount Castlereagh*, third series, ii. 477: London, 1853).

Orders issued, dated July 22nd, these words occur, "The Field Marshal begs that Officers may be dressed uniformly, and, if possible, according to the King's orders;"* while the following was also published in Battalion Orders of the 2nd Battalion Coldstream Guards: "Officers are to appear in plain grey overalls, jackets hooked and buttoned regimentally, sashes to be tied on the left side." On the 10th of September, a great review, which seems to have created a considerable impression at the time, also took place of all the Russian troops that were in France, near Chalons, where 160,000 men (including 28,000 cavalry) and 540 guns were brought together.†

These displays, having as much for object an easy demonstration to the inhabitants that they were completely in the power of Europe, as an exhibition made for the purpose of satisfying the national vanity of the different armies concerned, were perhaps not necessary to prove to the French that their new Government rested only upon alien arms for support. Everywhere, except south of the Loire,—where the last remnants of Napoleon's army had collected under Marshal Davoût,—was the country in the military occupation of foreigners; and in Paris especially, there were no regular troops to be seen, other than those of Great Britain, of Prussia, and of their allies. They guarded the King and the Royal palaces; they stood at the barriers of the town, and they performed all the military duties of the capital. They were to be seen at all the public buildings, at the various and numerous hôtels where the Allied Sovereigns and their Counsellors and principal Officers lodged, and even at the places of entertainment where the people flocked during the balmy weather of a French summer. Nor were these duties of a ceremonial

---

* *Supplementary Despatches, etc.*, xi. 51.

† Alison, *History of Europe, from* 1789 *to* 1815, x. 973. Captain Gronow mentions a curious incident that occurred at one of the reviews held by the Russian Emperor of his own troops. The British Foot Guards found a Guard for Alexander I., at which a dinner was provided, similar to that at St. James's. On one occasion the Captain of the Emperor's Guard was informed that there were four Russian General Officers in his custody. The latter were asked to dinner, and as their health was drunk, they were invited to reveal the nature of their offence, which called for such a punishment to men of their military rank. In reply, they said that the Emperor had not been satisfied with the manner in which they had marched past that day; whereupon one of the British Officers present, filling his glass, drank "Confusion to all tyrants—Vive Napoleon!" "The poor Russians appeared thunderstruck, and observed that if they drank the toast proposed, it would cost them their heads." It seems, this story came to the ears of Alexander, and the Duke had to explain it, for he sent for the Officers of the Guard, and begged them to repress their jokes for the future (Gronow, *Reminiscences, etc.*, ii. 19).

character; for guard-houses were placed in nearly all the principal thoroughfares, the bridges were held by troops, there were chains of sentries everywhere, patrols were constantly on the move and on the alert, and guns were kept loaded and ready for any serious emergency.

Paris was placed under the command of Baron Müffling; his orders, dated July 23rd, for the preservation of order, were thus conceived:—

"The Garde Nationale will perform police duties, and the garrison, composed of the Allied troops, occupying the great centres of the town, will remain in reserve. In case the latter have to act, for the Garde Nationale may refuse to quell disturbances, guns will be fired, when the regular forces will assemble at their alarm posts. The British brigade will form up in the Avenue de Neuilly, one battalion in Place Beauveau, and another at the junction of the Boulevard de la Madeleine and Rue St. Honoré. The Austrian brigade will have two battalions and a battery in Place Vendôme, a battalion guarding the Emperor, and a fourth battalion in Rue du Montblanc, near the Boulevards des Capucins and des Italiens; the cavalry to be in the Boulevard de la Madeleine. The brigade of Prussian Guards will occupy the Esplanade des Invalides with two battalions; they will have a third battalion at the Quay d'Orsay, a fourth on the Pont Royal, a fifth on the Pont Neuf, a sixth in the Luxembourg, and a seventh, together with the cavalry and the artillery, in the Champs de Mars. The Prussian Grenadier brigade will occupy the Place de la Bastille, the Pont du Jardin des Plantes, and the Place du Panthéon, with a battalion each; and the Quai de la Tournelle and l'Ile du Palais with two battalions each; the cavalry and artillery to be posted in the Place Walhubert. Guards in the town and at the barriers to remain at their posts. The Governor's head-quarters are in Place Vendôme; the Commandants of the north and south of the city, in Place Louis XV. and on Pont Neuf, respectively. Patrols to keep up communication between the different stations." *

An English traveller who, having visited France in 1814, returned in 1815, thus describes some of his experiences:—

"The state of things had entirely altered, and plain indications were given on the road to Paris, and at its entrance, that the visitor in 1815 would find it placed in circumstances very different from those which it held in the preceding year. The time for the real humiliation and severe punishment of the nation had now arrived; there was no longer a disposition to save it from drinking out the bitter contents of the cup of defeat; in short, Paris, as representing France, was now in the condition

* *Supplementary Despatches, etc.*, xi. 53.

of one that is beaten and bound, previously to being mulcted in a heavy forfeiture. . . . I found Paris in a state of very discomposed feeling and opinion. Every Frenchman seemed acutely alive to the calamity that had fallen upon France, and all diversities of political sentiment met in one point of union, namely that of indignation against those who acted as the conquerors of the country. A Royalist would say, 'Ah, it is very impolitic in the Allies to think of taking any territory or money from France, for good Frenchmen, united under the Bourbons, will become more formidable than the nation ever was under Bonaparte, and woe to Europe, in the course of a year or two, for what she now inflicts on us.' A military man would gurgle a *sacré* out of his throat, and anticipate the day of revenge, under some new leader, when France would show that she had not been beaten, although she had been betrayed. . . . Going round, late in the evening, by one of the more unfrequented walks, running through the woods of Saint-Cloud, I came suddenly upon a strong column of British infantry, posted in silence and order among the trees, on the hill immediately above the amusements, that jingled upon the ear from below. The regiment was in complete order for action, the Officers were all at their posts; and as I passed them by in the deep shadow, I heard not a word or even a breath, though I was close to five or six hundred men. The Allied Sovereigns were seldom seen except at reviews, for they did not now, as at a former time, go about to public places to scrape acquaintance with the Parisians and keep them in good spirits. The aspect of the alliance, as it was now settled on the inhabitants of Paris, was clouded and severe; and a very considerable degree of reserve was maintained by the representatives of the various Powers. Even the Court of the Tuileries was not frequently visited by them; there were few or no courtly entertainments and ceremonies. However friendly the Allied Sovereigns might feel towards Louis personally, their determination to make France know that the consequences of war are sometimes serious, occasioned a sense of restraint, and an appearance of coolness, as between them and the Royal Family of the Bourbons." *

The military occupation of France, painful as it was to the inordinate pride of the people—especially after their armies had run riot in every capital of the Continent,—was rendered still more unbearable by the excesses which the Prussians indulged in. Following the example set by their gallant, but irrational, Commander, both Officers and men exercised their authority in a harsh and often in a brutal manner. Forgetful of what they owed to Louis XVIII., whose restoration absolved the French from past offences, and mindful only of the grievous tyranny which they had

---

* John Scott, *Paris revisited in* 1815, pp. 264, etc. (2nd edit.: London, 1816).

experienced, they made the unfortunate inhabitants feel the full measure of their revenge, by their arrogance and exactions.

"Blücher's troops were billeted in every house; he obliged the inhabitants to feed and clothe them; and he issued an order (which I well recollect seeing), commanding the authorities to supply each soldier with a bedstead containing a bolster, a woollen mattress, two new blankets, and a pair of linen sheets. The rations per day, for each man, were two pounds of butcher's meat, a bottle of wine, a quarter of a pound of butter, ditto rice, a glass of brandy, and some tobacco.* . . . Blücher's Generals occupied all the best hôtels in the Faubourg St. Germain; General Thieleman that of Marshal Ney, where he forcibly took possession of the plate, carriages, and horses. Other Prussian Generals acted in a similar manner. The Russian and Austrian armies with the two Emperors entered Paris soon after our arrival. The Emperors imitated Blücher in some respects; they refused to quarter their soldiers in the large and wholesome barracks which were in readiness to receive them; they preferred billeting them with the peaceable merchants and tradespeople, whom they plundered and bullied in the most outrageous manner." †

It is pleasant to record that the Duke of Wellington adopted an entirely different system in his relations with the inhabitants; everything was paid for regularly, property was respected, and the people were unmolested. In short, the British army set an example of humanity, generosity, and forbearance, which not only did honour to their country and to their noble profession, but which also (notwithstanding national antipathies), gained them the respect and almost the affection of the French themselves.‡

In this connection, a quaint conversation between the English traveller (already quoted) and some Highlanders he came across in Peronne, may be noticed here. The latter, bivouacked, not billeted,—they said they seldom troubled the inhabitants for billets,—had only one thing to regret, viz. that they did not get the liberty " that ither sogers get—the Prussians and them," for " there's nae use in our

---

* It is said that the Prussians cost the French not less than three francs per day for each man (*Paris revisited in* 1815, p. 361).

† Gronow, *Reminiscences*, i. 206.

‡ " The Prussians, who were in bivouac near us " (in the Bois de Boulogne, early in July), " amused themselves by doing as much damage as they could, without any aim or object; they cut down the finest trees and set the wood on fire at several points. There were about 3000 of the Guards there, encamped in the wood, and I should think about 10,000 Prussians. Our camp was not remarkable for its courtesy towards them; in fact, our intercourse was confined to the most ordinary demands of duty, as allies, in an enemy's country " (Gronow, *Reminiscences*, i. 81).

being mealy-mou'd, if the ithers are to tak' what they like, the d—d Prussians ken better what they're about," and although, " ilka body praises us, but very few gie us ony thing." In reply to the question, whether the Duke of Wellington took severe measures to enforce his principles regarding the lives and property of the inhabitants at the seat of war, they said: " Na, sir, no here, for the men ken him gailies now ; but in Spain we aften had ugly jobs. He hung fifteen men in ae day there, after he had been ordering about it God knows how long. And d—n me if he didna ance gar the Provost-Marshal flog mare than a dizen of the wimen ; for the wimen thought themselves safe, and so they were war' than the men. They got sax and therty lashes a piece on the bare doup, and it was lang afore it was forgotten on 'em. Ane o' 'em was Meg Donaldson, the best woman in our regiment, for whatever she might tak' she didna keep it a' to hersel'." *

The demeanour of the British troops was friendly to the French, and few brawls took place between them ; this contrasted with what occurred to the Prussians, who had frequent and fierce encounters with the populace. The English soldiers were usually to be seen on the Boulevard du Temple, which at that time was an open space (but has since then been built over), and there they used to amuse themselves by watching jugglers, mountebanks, rope-dancers and other shows. A certain number of men of the armies of occupation were admitted free into the theatres ; and we are told that a party of Guardsmen, headed by a sergeant, saw a piece admirably put on the stage, entitled *Les Anglaises pour rire*, in which Englishwomen were grotesquely caricatured. Not understanding the language, nor the acting, and being indignant at the insults they supposed were levelled against their countrywomen, the honest fellows stormed the stage, and drove off, not only the actors, but the police who attempted to arrest them. "It must be remembered that the only revenge which the Parisians were able to take upon their conquerors, was to ridicule them ; and the English generally took it in good humour, and laughed at the extravagant drollery of the burlesque." Notwithstanding these minor disputes, good feeling existed ; and although numerous Prussians were assassinated in Paris and in the country, there was only one soldier of British nationality found dead in the streets of the capital, and, in his case, there were no signs of violence upon him.†

---

* *Paris revisited in* 1815, p. 253.   † Gronow, *Reminiscences*, i. 92.

DRUMMER. 1658.

SERGEANT. 1658.

That Wellington should be appealed to, to lighten the burden placed on the miserable people who groaned under the invader's despotism, is natural enough; and there are petitions recorded on the part of the inhabitants of Le Cateau and Roye, asking that British troops might continue to garrison those towns, so that they might be placed under their protection.* But it was not always that he could do anything for them. We find, for instance, M. de Breteuil, who, according to himself, was "one of the most faithful subjects of Louis XVIII." and who had "given the King proofs of devotion," complaining bitterly that not only was his house and property, situated at three leagues distant from St. Quentin, pillaged, but that the town itself was mulcted in a sum of 1,200,000 francs, of which he had to pay 20,000 (£800), because he had a single house there, "which brings in nothing, and is, on the contrary, full of soldiers." To this complaint, Wellington could only reply, "I have no troops in St. Quentin, and never had any in that town. I think you ought to address yourself to Marshal Prince Blücher." †

Nor was the King unmindful of what he owed to the British army for their discipline; for, having invited the principal Officers to the Tuileries, and having formed them in a circle about him, he told them, in broken English, in the presence of the Emperor of Austria, "I congratulate you, gentlemen, upon the result of your valour and conduct; but I am most grateful to you for your generosity and humanity towards my poor misguided people; the father and the family will for ever hold it remembrance." ‡

In order to give employment to the men under his command, and to help the French peasants, at a time when labour was very scarce, the Duke of Wellington allowed British soldiers to reap the harvest. The owners of the harvest were to make their own bargains with the men direct, but application for labourers were to be made

---

* *Supplementary Despatches*, etc., xi. 85, 101.   † *Ibid.*, xi. 19.

‡ Letter of Lieut.-Colonel Sir W. Gomm, who was present upon that occasion, to his Aunt, July 16, 1815, *Letters and Journals of Field-Marshal Sir W. Gomm, G.C.B.*, p. 376 (London, 1881). See also Alison's *History of Europe*, 1789-1815, x. 968. The Duc de Richelieu (Foreign Minister) wrote on this subject to the Duke of Wellington, January 19, 1816, "Sa Majesté m'a spécialement recommandé de saisir cette occasion pour faire connaître à Votre Excellence combien elle a été satisfaite de la conduite des troupes Anglaises dans la capitale, et du soin qui a été mis par les chefs à alléger les charges indispensablement attachées à la présence de ces troupes. Sa Majesté sait à cet égard tout ce qu'elle vous doit, My Lord; et elle a voulu que je vous donnasse de nouveau l'assurance qu'elle ne perdrait jamais le souvenir des témoignages de déférence et d'affection qu'elle a reçus de vous" (*Supplementary Despatches*, etc., xi. 282).

by the mayors of districts, and not by private individuals. Commanding Officers also were to know exactly where each soldier was employed; and the men were to return to their regiments every night, if possible, or at all events twice a week.*

Towards the end of October, the Division of Guards, hitherto in the Bois de Boulogne, marched into Paris, and occupied on the 30th, the Casernes Rue Verte, Montblanc, and Rue Temple, the Palais Louis XV., and the Abbatoire de Roule. The 2nd Battalion Coldstream Guards were thus lodged in barracks in the capital; and the general alarm post for the Division was the Palais Louis XV.† At the same time, a general change of quarters took place among the whole of the British troops, and camps were abandoned for houses. Wellington issued on the 28th of October, strict orders for the protection of the inhabitants, to apply whenever men were to be billeted, or when they were marching through the country.‡

We left the wreck of Napoleon's beaten army south of the Loire, where they were under the command of Marshal Davoût. There was nothing more for them now to hope, and their Commander soon persuaded them to conform to the circumstances of the hour, and, throwing aside their Eagles, to hoist the white flag of the Bourbons, and to adopt the white cockade. This they did, and shortly after, by Royal decree, dated the 23rd of July, they were disbanded. At the same time, a new army was forthwith to be formed, to consist of eighty Legions of infantry (103 officers and 1,687 men each), one to be raised in every Department, and to bear its name; forty-seven regiments of cavalry, and twelve regiments of artillery, —or a military force of some 200,000 regular troops. Disbanded

---

* *Supplementary Despatches, etc.*, xi. 73.

† *Orders for the Piquet*: "In the event of any disturbance in the neighbourhood, the Piquet will fall in in front of the barrack gate, and detach a sergeant's party to the right and left, if necessary, to observe what is going on. The Lieutenant on this duty will send an immediate Report to the Officer Commanding the Battalion. The Lieutenant inspecting the messes, at one o'clock, and the Ensign will inspect the barrack rooms at half-past twelve, and will take care to enforce the barrack regulations. The same to be mentioned in the report of the senior Officer at dismounting. The Battalion will assemble in the barrack yard, in case of any riots of a serious nature, and will wait the orders of a Field-Officer, who will cause it to move to the Place Louis XV., if it appears expedient. Officers on detached duties will, in case of serious disturbance, likewise move to the Place Louis XV." (*Battalion Order*, Paris, Nov. 3, 1815). The public duties in Paris, found by the two Guards Brigades and by the King's German Legion on the 5th of November, amounted to 1 Captain, 12 Subalterns, 38 sergeants, 55 corporals, 13 drummers, and 587 privates.

‡ Appendix No. II.

Imperialists were allowed to engage after proper examination.* The command was entrusted to Marshal Macdonald, who had remained firm in his allegiance to the King, during the whole of the Hundred Days of the second French Empire; and he replaced Davoût, who resigned.

Immediately hostilities came to an end by the Convention of the 3rd, a large number of English people went over to Paris, on business or pleasure, and settled in that gay capital, almost as if it had been their own. Coaches were soon brought over, and horse-racing introduced, contrasting very much in the disfavour of the native *sport*, which the King endeavoured to encourage, but which was then quite in its infancy. In short, the English made themselves thoroughly at home.

"Going along the *Rue du Faubourg St. Denis*, we saw many of the British privates sauntering with a lazy air of enjoyment, looking at the print stalls where they were caricatured, cheapening grapes with the fruit girls, or treating themselves to a glass of lemonade. Our Officers, too, swarmed about, mounted—some well, some very badly; for those who could not procure a decent animal, put up with almost any creature that had four legs. Contrasting remarkably with the heavy cabriolets and clumsy dirty coaches—the awkward calèches and grotesque voitures—English equipages, complete, light, and genteel, glanced rapidly by, spattering, as foreigners, mortification from their wheels on the vehicles of the country. To estimate this exhibition properly, it is necessary to fancy its counterpart displayed by Frenchmen in London; to imagine a Frenchman of fashion, vested with magnificent amplitude of box-coat and commanding longitude of whip, spanking his four blood greys down Bond Street and St. James's Street, or drawing up smartly, in a knowing style of driving, to talk over the topics of the morning with the Officer of the French Guards, on duty at the Palace of the King of England!" †

All eyes were turned to Paris at that time. Many Sovereigns were living there—the Monarchs of Austria, Russia, Prussia, Holland, Bavaria, Wurtemburg, and France, and several independent Princes of Germany. They were accompanied by some of the most distinguished statesmen and diplomatists of the age; and military leaders were also present who enjoyed a European reputation for their achievements in the field. Events of transcendent importance were taking place in this capital; and the fate of a

---

* Baines, *Wars of the French Revolution*, ii. 519.
† *Paris revisited in* 1815, p. 265.

great and gallant nation, outlawed for a quarter of a century, and now reduced to submission, was being decided. Curiosity urged many to go to France, from all parts of Europe, at this historic juncture; the pleasures of society moved others, and duty took a still larger number there. "All the world's in Paris,"* was indeed true, and crowds flocked to that city; while the discordant elements to be found there, and the strange medley of Frenchmen, Englishmen, and foreigners of almost every nationality, brought together and kept together, at such a time and at such a place, presented at once a scene that was both unique and remarkable.

Paris was gay and dissolute, and the Palais Royal might be called the centre of dissipation.

"Mingled together, and moving about the area of this oblong square block of buildings, might be seen, about seven o'clock p.m., a crowd of English, Russian, Prussian, Austrian, and other Officers of the Allied armies, together with countless foreigners from all parts of the world. Here, too, might have been seen the present King of Prussia" (the late Emperor William I. of Germany), "with his father and brother, the Dukes of Nassau, Baden, and a host of Continental Princes, who entered familiarly into the amusements of ordinary mortals, dining *incog.* at the most renowned restaurants, and flirting with painted female frailty." †

The Palais Royal contained the principal, but by no means the only, gambling hell in Paris, and these constituted the "very fountains of immorality." "There were tables for all classes; the workman might play with twenty sous, or the gentleman with ten thousand francs. The law did not prevent any class from indulging in a vice that assisted to fill the coffers of the municipality of Paris." †

In such a society it was only natural that constant disputes should arise between men who gave way to dissipation, and who, full of life and spirits and of national prejudices, had little to occupy them beyond the mere routine of military duty. Men's minds were in a state of excitement, and all were engaged in defending interests which frequently conflicted with those of their temporary companions. These disputes could only be settled at that time by the sword or pistol. Numerous duels accordingly took place, sometimes between Royalists and Imperialists, and often between Frenchmen and the representatives of the invaders.

---

* Popular song of the day. Gronow, *Reminiscences*, i. 90. † *Ibid.*, i. 87.

It is stated that in almost every case the aggressors were the French; and while the English Officers had sometimes to defend themselves against the insolence of the natives, it appears that the Prussians, who used to congregate at the Café Foy in the Palais Royal, were the principal victims of Gallic fury, and were assailed more pertinaciously than the rest by half-pay French Officers, who went on purpose to pick quarrels with them.

"Swords were quickly drawn, and frequently the most bloody frays took place; these originated, not in any personal hatred, but from national jealousy on the part of the French, who could not bear the sight of foreign soldiers in the capital. . . . On one occasion our Guards, who were on duty at the Palais Royal, were called out to put an end to one of these encounters, in which fourteen Prussians and ten Frenchmen were either killed or wounded."*

France was the possessor of the most extensive collection of works of art ever before known; acquired, not by the genius of her people, but by the grasping policy of her Imperial master. Napoleon, having taken possession of every large city in continental Europe, during the plenitude of his power, had systematically seized all that was remarkable therein, and had transferred his plunder to Paris. The French were inordinately proud of this vast and unique collection, which served to flatter their vanity and to form a lasting monument of their extraordinary military successes. It had been untouched by the Allies in 1814, but in 1815 the disturbers of Europe were to be severely punished, and the stolen property was to be restored to its former owners. Attempts having failed to effect a restoration amicably, owing to the opposition of Talleyrand, forcible possession of the Louvre was taken on the 23rd of September, by a body of British troops, and with the assistance of Austrians and Prussians, the splendid galleries of that palace were stripped of those treasures of art, which belonged principally to Italy and to the Netherlands. Out of fifteen hundred celebrated pictures, it is said that only seventy-four were left in Paris. The restoration of the statuary was not less complete; and the well-known antique Corinthian bronze horses, taken from Venice, to form, in the Place Carrousel, the supporters of the great monument, designed—but not finished—to perpetuate Napoleon's fame, were taken down and conveyed back to that city. Nothing

* Gronow, *Reminiscences*, i. 106.

affected the Parisians so much as this act of strict justice ; for it showed them their own absolute weakness and humiliation, and it wounded their pride in the most sensitive point.*

The policy of revenge and proscription against persons who aided and abetted Napoleon in the early part of 1815, which had been announced in the proclamations issued by Louis at Cambrai before he entered Paris (June 25th and 28th), was not to remain a dead letter ; and we have now to mention some of the saddest incidents which took place at this crisis in French history, and which were witnessed by the British army. Fouché had become Minister of Police. He justified his acceptance of that post by declaring that he wished to save the men who were threatened with vengeance.† Upon him it devolved to carry out this policy, and though he did so with outward reluctance, and told the King that there had been no conspiracy to dethrone him in favour of Napoleon—which appears to have been quite true, for all acted on the wild impulse of the moment,—yet still he was not ashamed to come forward in the odious light of an accuser against his former friends. On the 24th of July, two ordinances, countersigned by himself, were published, by which thirty-two Peers who had joined Napoleon's Upper House, established since the 20th of March, were declared to have forfeited their rights to the French Peerage ; twenty Officers and other Officials were at the same time ordered to be arrested, and brought to trial before a court-martial ; and thirty-nine more were desired to quit Paris in three days, to places pointed out by the Minister of Police, and to remain there under his supervision, until the new Chambers should decide whether they were to be banished, or delivered over for trial to the tribunals.‡

* *Paris revisited in* 1815, p. 312, etc. ; Alison, *History of Europe, from* 1789–1815, x. 969.
† Thiers, *Histoire du Consulat et l'Empire*, xx. 516 (Paris, 1862).
‡ Baines, *Wars of the French Revolution*, ii. 517. It appears that these ordinances did not evoke dissatisfaction from the British Government, for Lord Liverpool, writing to Mr. Canning on the 4th of August, says, "One can never feel that the King is secure upon his throne till he has *dared* to spill traitor's blood : it is not that many examples would be necessary ; but the *daring* to make a few will alone manifest any strength in the Government" (*Supplementary Despatches*, etc., xi. 95). On the other hand, they raised much indignation on the part of the friends of the incriminated persons, and several letters were written to the Duke of Wellington, to implore his powerful intercession in their distress. Apparently he could do nothing for them, except in the case of General Lobau (*ibid.*, xi. 59, 101, 273). Marshal Davoût was not included in the list of proscribed persons, but he wrote to the War-Minister, Marshal Gouvion St.

The first victim put upon his trial was General Labedoyère, who commanded the regiment at Grenoble that deserted its post and joined Napoleon in his famous march from Cannes to Paris. His defection had given the first signal to the universal revolt against the King's authority that followed, and was one of the causes of the Emperor's success; the partisans of the King were therefore more than ordinarily embittered against him. He admitted the facts of his treachery; he contented himself by defending his honour by declaring that, though he might have been misled by illusions, by recollections of his former master, and by a false idea of honour and of what was due to his country, he was no traitor or conspirator, and hoped that his death might atone his error. He was shot on the 19th of August,

Next day Marshal Ney, who had been previously apprehended in the Department of Lot, was examined at the Conciergerie; but his case was adjourned till later in the year. Meanwhile the King's Government was overthrown, in September, and an ultra-Royalist Ministry established, with the avowed intention of showing no clemency to the proscribed. Ney's trial accordingly took place early in November, and he was at first arraigned before a court-martial of four Marshals.* But the latter decided that the prisoner, being a Peer, was entitled to be judged by his peers, and it devolved upon the Upper House to do so. His guilt was

Cyr (July 27th), to protest energetically against the injustice, which he alleged had been done to such men as Gilly, Grouchy, Clausel, Laborde, and others, whose only fault was that they had carried out orders, which he had given them as Minister of War. He maintained that his own name ought to be substituted for theirs, and he drew attention to the assurances given by the King, that if the army made its simple and unconditional submission, His Majesty would show clemency and do more than was desired (*ibid.*, xi. 70). Davoût was then near a somewhat exasperated and only partially converted force of Imperialists, south of the Loire, and, had his arrest been contemplated, the attempt to carry it out might have been accompanied by unpleasant consequences to the ultra-Royalists. Among the proscribed, there appeared the name of Carnot, colleague of Fouché in the Provisional Government, and like him a regicide and a man of the Revolution. Upon what principle Carnot should have been banished, and Fouché should have been made a Minister under Louis XVIII. is difficult to determine; but such was the policy of the reactionary party. Carnot, naturally indignant that he should have been marked out for vengeance by his colleague, wrote to him, "Où veux tu que je me retire, traître?" while the latter replied with equal brevity, "Où tu voudras, imbécile." Fouché did not long survive the fate of those he had betrayed; driven from power in September, he was appointed minister at Dresden, but shortly afterwards he was exiled by a decree which was fulminated against all who had voted for the death of the unfortunate Louis XVI., and thus fittingly terminated his career of intrigue and treachery.

* Marshals Jourdain, Massena, Augereau, and Mortier (Baines, *Wars, etc.*, ii. 525).

clearly established, and it was rendered all the more heinous by the protestations of loyalty with which he quitted Louis when he left Paris to arrest the progress of Napoleon, promising to bring the latter back in an iron cage. For some days he remained true to his duty, but, though a brave man, he was singularly impulsive, and was not endowed with much discretion or judgment. A frenzy of delirium had seized hold of the Royal troops, who were flocking to Napoleon's standards, and Ney began to fear that he had not sufficient force to resist his former master; his moral courage began to fail. Dreading, above all things, a civil war, he resolved that no step of his should precipitate such a calamity; believing that the cause of the Bourbons was irretrievably lost, and, carried away by the violent excitement of the moment, he forgot his promises and the trust reposed in him, and wildly threw in his lot with the Emperor.* Thereby he dealt a final blow to the fortunes of the King. For his defence, it was pleaded that the Military Convention of the 3rd, had guaranteed that no person in the capital should be disturbed or called to account, for his conduct or political opinions; but the Chamber refused to entertain the plea, and he was condemned to death by one hundred and thirty-nine votes against seventeen (December 6th). Strenuous efforts were made to obtain the prisoner's release on account of the Convention, and applications were addressed to the Duke of Wellington, Lord Liverpool, and even to the Prince Regent on the subject. But these high authorities declined to do anything for him, on the ground that the Convention related only to the military occupation of Paris, and that, while the article in question prevented the Allies from adopting measures of severity towards persons in the capital, yet it did not, and could not, prevent the French Government from acting in this respect, as they might deem fit.†

The execution took place in the gardens of the Luxembourg palace, at nine o'clock in the morning of December 7th, when Ney met his death with calmness and courage. It shed a deep gloom over Paris, and did little, as might have been expected, to serve the King. Had Louis shown clemency to the man who had deeply wronged him, and whose reputation had thereby

---

* 1815. Henry Houssaye, *La Première Restauration, le Retour de l'Ile d'Elbe, les Cent Jours*, pp. 301-315 (3me edit. : Paris, 1893).

† *Supplementary Despatches*, etc., xi. 235.

become sullied, instead of proceeding to extremities by violating the Convention of July 3rd, his credit would have been raised. While the justice of such action becomes all the more clear, since it was stipulated that, in the case of difficulties arising, a favourable interpretation was to be given to the claims of the French army and of the city of Paris. Further, as foreign armies have no right to punish the inhabitants of a conquered State for political opinions or conduct, the Convention either bound Louis, on whose behalf the capital was taken, or else it had no value whatsoever.*

The third and last victim selected for vengeance by the ultra-Royal party was General Lavalette, a relation by marriage of the Emperor, and Director of Posts, who was convicted of having misused his power in favour of Napoleon, when the latter reached Fontainebleau in March. Having been in civil employ, he was condemned to death by the guillotine; and the sentence, in spite of appeals to the mercy of the King, was to be carried out on December 21st. In this case, however, the Government were baulked of their prey, and the prisoner made good his escape by the courage and devotion of his wife, with the assistance of three Englishmen. His wife having exchanged dresses with him, Lavalette got out of prison; but he remained in hiding in Paris for more than twelve days, not being able to leave the closely guarded city until the 8th of January; when, by the co-operation of Mr. Bruce, and Captain Hutchinson, Grenadier Guards (afterwards Earl of Donoughmore), he drove to Compiègne in an open carriage, disguised as a British Officer, and accompanied by General Sir Robert Wilson. It was with difficulty that the latter piloted him out of France, but this was at last managed successfully. Sir Robert then returned to Paris on the 10th, and the police, having received information of the facts of the case, he, Captain Hutchinson, and Mr. Bruce were immediately arrested and confined, awaiting trial, till the 22nd of April, 1816, when they were condemned to be imprisoned for three months. That a distinguished Officer of high rank in the British army, and well known in Europe for his personal animosity against Napoleon, should have actively interfered to save the life of one of the latter's best friends, was a sufficient reason to put a stop to further acts of the bloodshed, which cast so unnecessary a shadow over the first months of the restoration of King Louis.†

* Baines, *Wars of the French Revolution*, ii. 527.
† *Ibid.*, ii. 527; Gronow, *Reminiscences*, i. 100. See also *Supplementary Despatches*,

The negotiations which had been going on continually between the Allied Sovereigns and Louis XVIII., ever since they and their counsellors arrived in Paris, terminated at last by a treaty of peace, dated November 20th. There were matters of considerable difficulty to be discussed, before a general agreement could be arrived at between so many independent nations, whose interests were not all identical. The situation, moreover, was somewhat complex, and this is shown by Lord Liverpool who, writing to Mr. Canning, on the 4th of August, says:—

"By demanding considerable sacrifices from France for the security of Europe, we unavoidably lower the character of the Government, which it is our wish to uphold; on the other hand, the stability of that Government, after the Allies shall have evacuated France, is so very problematical, that we should not do our duty to Europe if we looked to no other security than that which the legitimate government of the King of France could in itself hold out to us." *

By the Treaty, the eastern frontier, from the North Sea to the Mediterranean, was restricted generally, to the line that existed in 1790; and thus the French lost a strip of territory which, in 1814, had been ceded to them, including the fortresses of Landau, Sarre-Louis, Philippeville, and Marienburg. France had moreover to pay a war indemnity of 700,000,000 francs, for the expenses of the war. Further, an army of not more than 150,000 men, formed of British, Russian, Austrian, Prussian, and German troops, in about equal proportions, and under a Commander-in-chief appointed by the Allied Sovereigns, was to occupy seventeen fortresses along the northern frontier, from Condé, Valenciennes, Bouchain, and Cambrai, to the *tête de pont* of Fort Louis on the Rhine. The occupation was to continue for three years certain, and might last for another two years. This mixed army was placed under the supreme command of the Duke of Wellington, and all the expenses incurred by it were to be defrayed by the French. It was understood that the primary object of these latter stipulations was to preserve Louis on the throne, and to give time for the consolidation of his government. Lastly, a sum of 835,000,000 francs was exacted by way of compensation to the Powers, for the spoliations and losses which they suffered during the Revolution,

etc., xi. 275, 279, 333, 341; and *Annual Register*, 1816, "Appendix to Chronicle," p. 329.

* *Supplementary Despatches, etc.*, xi. 95.

and to indemnify the minor States for their recent expenses. Thus, the French had to submit to the payment of more than sixty-one million sterling, as the result of their defeat; and this sum did not include the vast amounts which were otherwise taken from them, under the head of contributions for the armies that invaded their country, or that were to be maintained there, for the purpose of inducing them to conform to the new order which had just been established.*

* Baines, *Wars of the French Revolution*, ii. 529, 530, where the text of the Treaty is given; Alison, *History of Europe*, 1789-1815, x. 972.

CHAPTER III.

OCCUPATION OF FRENCH FORTRESSES.

Organization of the Allied army of occupation, under the supreme command of the Duke of Wellington—Return of the remainder to their respective countries—Instructions of the Allied Courts to Wellington—Convention relating to the occupation, attached to the Treaty of Paris—Positions assigned to each contingent on the north-eastern frontier of France—March from Paris to Cambrai—Military precautions—Camps of instruction and field exercises—Reduction of the army of occupation—Difficulties with the French—Congress of Aix-la-Chapelle—Evacuation of France—The Guards Brigade leave Cambrai, after nearly three years' stay there, and embark at Calais—Valedictory Orders—The Coldstream sent to Chatham—Conclusion of military service in French territory.

IN consequence of the Treaty of Paris, November 20, 1815, the capital was to be relieved of the unwelcome presence of the invader, and all the troops not required for the occupation of the north-eastern frontier were to evacuate France as soon as possible, and to be sent back to their respective homes. Of the Allied army of occupation, 150,000 strong, Great Britain, Prussia, Austria, and Russia supplied a contingent of 30,000 men each; of the remainder 10,000 were Bavarians, while Denmark, Saxony, Hanover, and Wurtemburg furnished each a force of 5000 men.

By a General Order, dated the 30th of November, the future organization of the British contingent was notified. It was formed of 3 brigades of cavalry (3 regiments each), 3 divisions of infantry, and 60 guns; the cavalry under the command of Lieut.-General Lord Combermere, and the infantry under Lieut.-General Lord Hill. The First Division (Lieut.-General Sir L. Cole) was composed of 3 brigades (8 battalions); the Second Division (Lieut.-General Sir H. Clinton) of 3 brigades (9 battalions); and the Third Division (Lieut.-General Sir C. Colville) of 3 brigades (8 battalions). The 3rd Battalion Grenadier Guards, and the 2nd Battalion Coldstream Guards, who were ordered to remain in

France, formed the 1st Brigade of the First Division, under Major-General Sir P. Maitland.* The Duke of Wellington, having in the same General Order provided for the return home of the rest of the army, took leave of the gallant troops now about to be dispersed, in these words:—

"Upon breaking up the army which the Field-Marshal has had the honour of commanding, he begs leave again to return thanks to the General Officers and the Officers and troops, for their uniform good conduct. In the short but memorable campaign they have given proofs to the world that they possess in an eminent degree all the good qualities of soldiers; and the Field-Marshal is happy to be able to applaud their regular good conduct in their camps and cantonments, not less than when engaged with the enemy in the field. Whatever may be the future destination of those brave troops of which the Field-Marshal now takes his leave, he trusts that every individual will believe that he will ever feel the deepest interest in their honour and welfare, and will always be happy to promote either." †

The despatch upon which the above arrangements were made was communicated to Wellington by H.R.H. the Duke of York by letter, dated the 9th of November, and is reproduced in an Appendix.‡

---

* Captain Gunthorpe, Grenadier Guards, Brigade Major of the 1st Guards Brigade during the campaign, was appointed to the same post in the 1st Brigade, First Division of the army of occupation (*General Order*, Dec. 2, 1815).

† *Supplementary Despatches*, etc., xi. 248, etc.

‡ See Appendix, No. III. It will be observed therein that the Coldstream Battalion was to be reinforced by 204 men. On the 13th of November a detachment of that strength, from the 1st Battalion, marched from London for this purpose, under Lieut.-Colonel Adams, Captain Wedderburn, and Lieutenants Powys and Kortright, (the first two were to return to the 1st Battalion), and arrived in Paris on the 6th of December. On March 7, 1816, Officers were posted as follows in the 2nd Battalion :—

Captains.	Lieutenants.	Ensigns.	Staff.
Grenadier Company: Lt.-Colonel D. MacKinnon.	Capt. Anstruther. „ Hon. J. Rous. „ „ R. Moore.	...	Assist.-Surg. Smith.
No. 1 Company: Lt.-Colonel J. Macdonell, C.B.	Capt. Sowerby.	Lt. Kortright. „ Montagu.	Adjt. Capt. J. Prince. Quarter-M. Selway. Surg. W. Whymper.
No. 2 Company: Colonel Hon. A. Abercromby, C.B.	Capt. Sandilands.	Lt. Cuyler. „ Short.	
No. 3 Company: Lt.-Colonel Sir W. Gomm, K.C.B.	Capt. Drummond.	Lt. Vane. „ Douglas.	

[*Continued on next page.*

The Prussian contingent was commanded by Lieut.-General von Ziethen, and consisted of 10 infantry regiments (thirty battalions), 1 battalion of Jägers, 9 regiments of cavalry (thirty-six squadrons), and 80 guns, formed into five brigades of infantry, and three of cavalry.

The Austrian corps, under General Baron von Frimont, contained $22\frac{1}{3}$ battalions, $28\frac{1}{2}$ squadrons, and 96 guns, divided into three divisions of two brigades each.

The Russians, under Lieut.-General Count Woronzow,—24 battalions, 6 regiments of cavalry (thirty-four squadrons), and 84 guns: two infantry divisions (of three brigades each), and the cavalry division (also of three brigades).

Prince Frederick of Hesse commanded the Danish contingent,—5 battalions, 4 squadrons, and 20 guns (two brigades). Major-General Sir J. Lyon (relieved afterwards by Count Alten), the Hanoverians,—6 battalions, 4 squadrons, and 6 guns (two brigades). Lieut.-General Baron de Wöllwarth (replaced afterwards by General Count Scheler), the Wurtemburgers,—6 battalions, 4 squadrons, and 6 guns. Major-General von Gablenz, the Saxons,—5 battalions, 4 squadrons, and 8 guns. And Lieut.-General de la Motte, the Bavarians,—3 regiments of infantry, and 2 of cavalry.*

It had already been agreed by the four great Powers (Great Britain, Austria, Russia, and Prussia), on the 22nd of October, that the Allied armies—other than the corps required for the occupation

Captains.	Lieutenants.	Ensigns.	Staff.
No. 4 Company: Lt.-Colonel Hon. E. Acheson, C.B.	Capt. Chaplin.	Lt. Gooch. ,, Gordon.	
No. 5 Company: Lt.-Colonel Hon. H. Pakenham, C.B.	Capt. Walton.	Lt. Powys. ,, Bowen.	
No. 6 Company: Lieut.-Colonel H. Wyndham.	Capt. Lord Hotham.	Lt. Griffiths. ,, FitzClarence.	
No. 7 Company: Lt.-Colonel Sir R. Arbuthnot, K.C.B.	Capt. Cowell.	Lt. Armytage. ,, Hon.W.Forbes.	
No. 8 Company: Lt.-Col. H. Dawkins.	Capt. Girardot.,	Lt. Beaufoy. ,, Hervey.	
Light Infantry Company: Lt.-Colonel Hon. J. Walpole.	Major Bowles. Capt. Shirley. ,, Harvey.	...	Asst.-Surg. Hunter.

* The number of guns is not stated.

—should evacuate French territory as soon as possible, and Wellington was commissioned to make the necessary arrangements for this purpose. Even before that date, the Russians, having a long way to march home before the winter set in, began to move eastwards; and Blücher intimated, as far back as the 8th of October, that, having been desired to withdraw towards Prussian territory, he was giving orders for the purpose of carrying out the intentions of his Government. The evacuation, however, by the British troops, did not begin till the middle of December, when, marching to Calais, they were shipped over to England with the least delay possible under the supervision of Major-General Sir D. Pack; but adverse winds retarded the operation, and it was only completed on the 4th of February, 1816.

When the Allied Sovereigns placed the supreme command of the army of occupation in the hands of Wellington, they gave him instructions to enable him to carry out the duty with which they entrusted him. On the 20th of November, they dealt with the political situation, by reminding him that the objects for which their troops were stationed in France were: (1) to secure the execution of the treaties concluded with that country, and (2) to protect Europe from French violence, and from internal revolutionary upheavals which were liable to take place among the people. They said their hopes of tranquillity were founded upon the system which they had established in the country, and they attached the greatest importance to the maintenance of a legitimate Sovereign, in the person of Louis XVIII. Until such times, therefore, as the forces of the King were organized, it was to be the duty of the Allied armies, in concert with the French Government, to protect the capital and the Royal family from popular effervescence; with this view the Commander-in-chief was empowered to delay his march from Paris until His Most Christian Majesty should notify to him that his presence in the capital was no longer necessary. The Allied Sovereigns, moreover, did not desire their troops to perform mere police duties, or to interfere in the internal administration of the country; but this did not exempt them from the obligation they were under, to maintain Louis on the throne of France, and "to support him against every revolutionary convulsion which might tend to upset by force the order just established, and to compromise the general tranquillity." They did not disguise from themselves that it would be a delicate matter to judge when intervention might become necessary, but they announced their entire confidence in the British Commander-in-chief, to whose discretion they left the matter, should it ever arise. In order, however, to enable him to form a correct opinion upon it, they instructed him to take into consideration the views of the diplomatic Agents of the Powers residing in Paris. Finally, the latter were directed to send him, at least once a week, a united and common report, when he was absent from the capital; and they were also to transmit, in their corporate capacity, any communication which he might think it proper to address to the French Government.*

The military situation had been considered at an earlier date (October 22nd), with the following conclusions: Full authority over the Allied army was given to the Commander-in-chief, who was enjoined to consult, as far as he could, the usages which prevailed in each contingent. The troops of each nationality were to be quartered as much as possible together, and on the lines of communications leading to their respective countries; they were to be under the immediate command of their own Generals, and everything relating to the discipline or to the interior economy of the various corps was to be dealt with by their own Officers. General Officers commanding contingents were formally placed under the supreme command of the Duke of Wellington; they were ordered to send their reports to him, and to obey him in all the dispositions which he might deem it his duty to make. Lastly, the French Government were invited to arrange with him, without delay, all matters affecting the occupation and the maintenance of the troops, as well as the "execution of particular conventions to regulate both these objects." †

Attached to the Treaty of the 20th of November there was a Convention, which was "as valid as if inserted word for word" in the Treaty, and, by Article No. 4,—

(1) The Allied troops were to occupy the Departments of Pas de Calais, Nord, Ardennes, Meuse, Moselle, Lower and Upper Rhine, their line of demarcation being the frontiers of these Departments respectively.

(2) A neutral zone was established between the above-mentioned strip of French territory in foreign occupation, and the remainder of the kingdom, in which neither the French nor the Allies were

* *Supplementary Despatches, etc.*, xi. 240. † *Ibid.*, xi. 208.

to maintain any military force, except for some special reason, and then only by mutual agreement. This zone was bounded on the south and west, by the river Somme to Ham, thence in nearly a straight line to Chalons-sur-Marne, whence it continued to a point between Joinville and Chaumont; from that place it took an easterly direction to Blamont, and then ran south to the Swiss frontier near St. Hypolite.

(3) The French were to have power to garrison certain places within the territory to be occupied by the Allies; but the forces to be quartered there were not to exceed the number which was laid down, and only such war *matériel* and stores as properly belonged to these places were to be kept there, the remainder to be removed into the kingdom west of the neutral zone. Altogether 22,000 men were allowed to garrison these places, the largest number being in the following fortresses, viz. Calais, where the garrison was not to exceed 1000 men; St. Omer, 1500; Arras, 1000; Lille, 3000; Dunkerque, 1000; Douai and Fort Scarpe, 1000; Metz, 3000; Strasburg, 3000; Schelstadt, 1000; Neu Brisach and Fort Mortier, 1000; and Belfort, 1000 men.*

The British contingent was ready to move to its allotted stations by the beginning of the year 1816; but a delay occurred in consequence of the representations made by the Duc de Richelieu, the French Minister of Foreign affairs, who believed that it would be dangerous to leave Paris unguarded until the discussions on the law of Amnesty, which was then being debated, had terminated.† Wellington adds, "From what I have seen and heard likewise of the King's Guard, I don't conceive it is as yet a body in which much confidence could be placed, in case there should be any disturbance in this town." ‡

* *Supplementary Despatches, etc.*, xi. 192.

† The law of Amnesty, as it was called, raised many fierce animosities. It received the Royal sanction on January 12th. By this law, the ordinances against proscribed persons were ratified and extended. Exiled persons might be deprived of their property; the relations of Napoleon were excluded for ever from the kingdom, and were declared incapable of enjoying civil rights or of possessing any property. "Regicides, who, in contempt of a clemency almost boundless, . . . accepted offices or employment from the Usurper, and who, by so doing, declared themselves irreconcilable enemies of France and of the lawful Government, are for ever excluded the realm, and are bound to quit it in the space of one month, under pain of the punishment enacted by the 33rd Article of the Penal Code; they cannot possess any civil right in France, nor any property, title, or pension granted to them of favour" (*Annual Register*, 1816, "General History," p. 107). It was in virtue of this clause, that Fouché was banished by his recent allies.

‡ *Supplementary Despatches, etc.*, xi. 265.

These difficulties, however, were speedily overcome; and on the 24th of January, the Commander-in-chief of the army of occupation wrote to the Ambassador of Great Britain and to the Plenipotentiaries of the other Allied Powers, saying that he proposed forthwith to evacuate the capital. These Ministers having agreed, the troops began their march towards the fortresses on the north-eastern frontier of France, which they were to occupy, and, before the end of the month, Paris was left to the King and to the new system that had been established by the Treaty. No disturbances occurred, and Louis was enabled to maintain his authority without the intervention of a foreign force; but Wellington found that it would be expedient to remain a short time longer in the capital, believing that his presence there was "very useful to the Government and to the King, in a variety of ways, and gives confidence to that party which brought back the King." As he was alone in the capital, and without British troops, Marshal Oudinot sent a detachment of French soldiers to mount guard over his quarters.*

The positions occupied by the Allied contingents were as follows: The British corps had their head-quarters at Cambrai, and were quartered in the Departments of Pas de Calais and Nord, at Cassel, Hazebrouck, Lillers, St. Pol, Bapaume, Cambrai, Valenciennes, etc.; near them, in the Department Nord, the Danes were stationed at Bouchain, the Hanoverians at Condé, and the Saxons at Le Quesnoi. Occupying the eastern portion of the latter Department, as well as nearly the whole of the Ardennes, the Russians placed their head-quarters at Maubeuge, and were quartered in Landrecies, Avesnes, Charlemont, Givet, Réthel, etc. The Prussians were in the Departments of Meuse and Moselle, their head-quarters at Sédan, occupying Mezières, Montmédy, Longwy, Bricy, Thionville, Commercy, Bar-le-Duc. The Baravians were close to them and to the Palatinate, at St. Avold, Sarreguemines (head-quarters), and Bische; the Wurtemburgers at Weissemburg and Lauterburg.† The Austrian contingent took possession of the Departments of Upper and Lower Rhine, head-quarters at Colmar, and the principal

---

* *Supplementary Despatches, etc.*, xi. 301, 296.

† Under Article No. 4 of the Convention of November 20th, Lauterburg and Weissemburg had been allotted to the French, who were permitted to place garrisons there of 200 and 150 men respectively. The French Government, however, consented to give them up to the Allies, in January, and were allowed to occupy Abbeville instead (*Ibid.*, xi. 292).

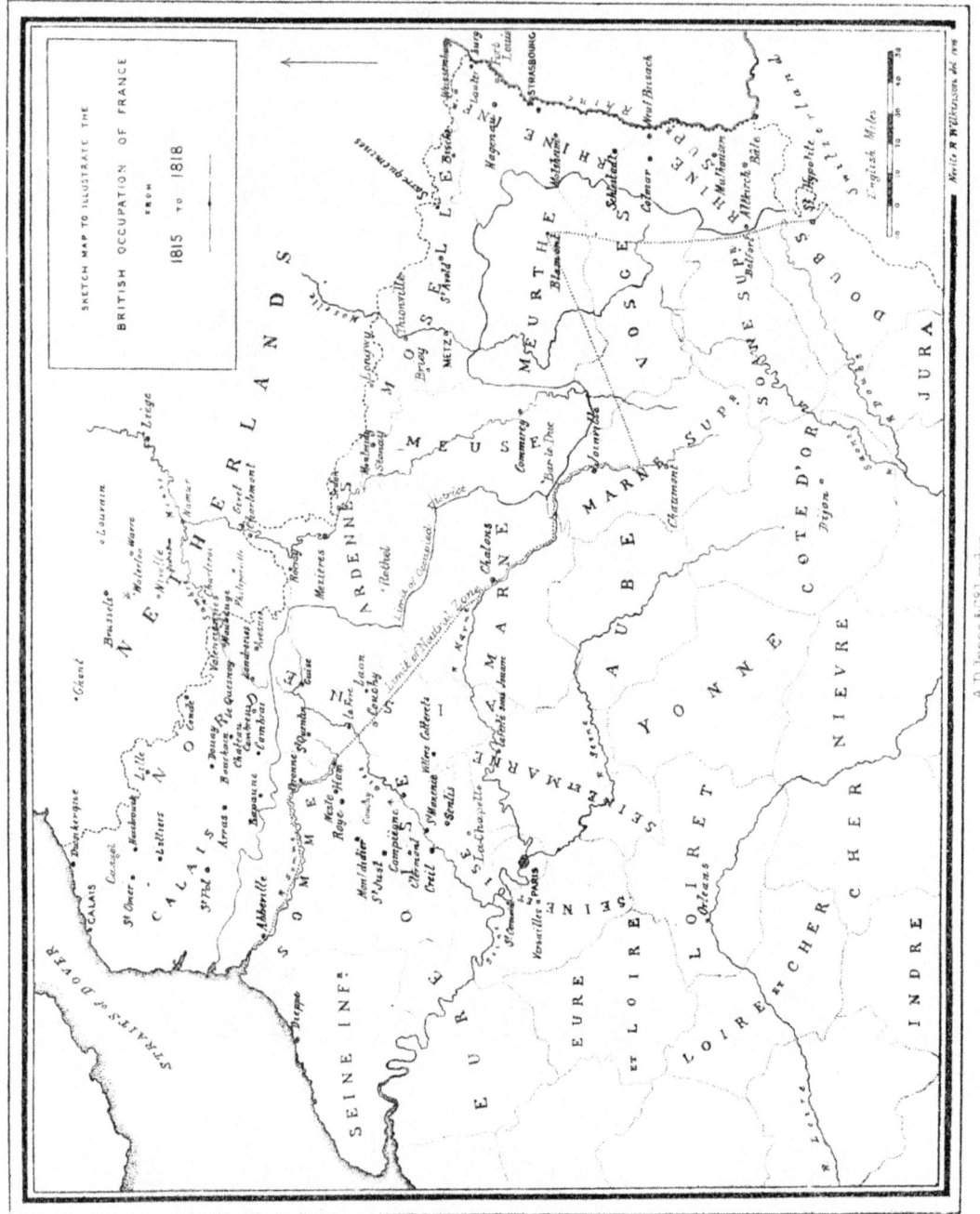

OCCUPATION OF FRENCH FORTRESSES.

garrisons were at Hagenau, Molsheim, Bischweiler, Mulhausen, and Altkirch.*

The Coldstream Guards were the last troops to leave Paris. On the 26th of January all the public duties in the capital were found by the Battalion,† and the 4th and 5th companies, under Lieutenant-Colonel MacKinnon, were ordered to relieve the 23rd Regiment at Montmartre. Next day, the Guards Brigade with Captain Sinclair's brigade (field battery) of Artillery and the Sappers and Miners attached to the First Division, marched off from the barrière de Villette; the Grenadier Guards and the Sappers and Miners to Louvres, the Coldstream and the Artillery to Gonesse. The public duties were collected by Lieut.-Colonel Dawkins at the barrière des Martyrs, where they were joined by Lieut.-Colonel MacKinnon's detachment, and the whole followed to Gonesse after the rest of the troops had left Paris. The march was continued to Cambrai in detachments, the Battalion being billeted at each halt in several villages,‡ and the route taken was by Senlis and Peronne to Cambrai, which was reached by the head-quarters, together with the Grenadier and the 1st companies, on the 6th of February.

The 3rd Battalion Grenadier Guards and the two companies of the Coldstream just mentioned, formed the garrison of Cambrai, while the remainder of the latter Battalion occupied the following villages:—2nd company, Villers Ploich; 3rd and 4th companies, under Lieut.-Colonel MacKinnon, Marcoing; 5th company, Banteau and Bantouzelle; 6th and 7th companies, Gouzecourt; 8th and the Light-infantry companies, Villers Glishain, under Lieut.-Colonel Dawkins, who had orders "to detach an Officer's party to Honnecourt, if he deemed it desirable;" Lieut.-Colonel Macdonell was quartered at Gonnelieu, and took command of the 2nd, 5th, 6th, and 7th companies.§

---

* *Supplementary Despatches, etc.*, xi. 355, 410, etc.

† As the termination of the occupation of Paris approached, the public duties were gradually reduced, and, on the 26th of January, Officers' guards were found at only six of the barriers of the town.

‡ "It is of the utmost importance to the comfort and the discipline of the soldiers, that the Officers of companies should inspect and visit the quarters of their men frequently, and the Commanding Officer trusts that they will see the necessity of extraordinary exertion on these occasions" (*Battalion Orders*, Paris, Jan. 26, 1816).

§ Appendix No. IV. On April 25th, the 2nd and 3rd companies were ordered to march to Cambrai, being relieved by the 8th and Light-infantry companies. On May 14th two more companies were brought into the town, and the remainder rejoined head-quarters on the 3rd and 5th of June, when the Battalion was complete in Cambrai, six companies being quartered in the Cavalry barracks, and four in the Citadel.

Though peace had been concluded, the foreign contingents were kept ready for active service, and the fortresses were held closely guarded, as if an enemy were in the field. Thus at Cambrai, the gates of the town were carefully locked under the superintendence of an Officer of the main guard, and were kept closed from sunset to dawn ; no one was allowed to enter at such times, except under peculiar circumstances, (and then only when the main guard was turned out). Patrols were sent out constantly at uncertain hours ; Non-commissioned officers and men were not permitted to leave their quarters after dark, without a pass ; sentries were relieved hourly, both by day and by night ; and even the Field-Officer of the day was not admitted into the Citadel by night, and the Officer of the guard there had to communicate with him from the ramparts.*

The occupation of French territory lasted three years, until November, 1818, and during the whole of this time, the British troops were kept actively employed on their military duties. It was a period in which the efficiency of the army was maintained at a high standard. The Coldstream were continually exercised in route marching, in drill, in musketry,† and, the Officers and selected Non-commissioned officers and men, in sword exercise. Every detail of interior economy was carefully attended to, under the company Officers, who were held responsible to the Commanding Officer for the arms and accoutrements, for the men's regimental necessaries, for the cleanliness and good order of the barrack rooms, and for the regular closing of the accounts, which at the time was done on the 24th of each month.‡ In the summer as many of the troops as

---

* It was not until April that "soldiers composing the garrison have permission to pass out of the gates, when properly dressed in side-arms, to walk within one mile of the fortress, unprovided with passes" (*Garrison Orders*, Cambrai, April 29, 1816).

† The following are the musketry results of the Battalion in 1816 :—

Two rounds were fired at 60, 85, and 90 yards, and four rounds at 100 yards. Total cartridges issued, 9,448; total shots on the target, 3,785. Of these the Grenadier company fired 852 rounds, and put 436 shots on the target. Fourteen battalion prizes were given. The company Officers offered, in 1817, prizes to their best shots ; and the Commanding Officer gave three prizes to the best battalion shots. The same was repeated in 1818, the Commanding Officer stipulating that the prizes were only to be awarded if the men were of good character (*Battalion Orders*, Nov. 25, 1816; Aug. 20, 1817 ; and June 10, 1818).

‡ "The following certificate being added to the Monthly Return, the Commanding Officer requests Officers commanding companies will forward their reports to him, respecting the settlement of the men's accounts, in good time, so as to enable him to sign the Monthly Return on the morning of the 25th : 'I certify that the company's accounts have been settled by the Captain, or the Officer commanding the company, up to the 24th of ——, and that the balances then due have been regularly paid to the men

could be spared from fortress duty were encamped wherever open spaces were available, the Guards Brigade upon the glacis of Cambrai, for the purpose of carrying out the Field exercises then practised by the army. The Duke of Wellington paid minute attention to the drill of the contingent, and issued repeated orders on the movements in which he desired the regiments to perfect themselves.*

Reviews on a larger scale took place in the autumn of each year, in the neighbourhood of Denain. In October, 1816, the English, Danish, Saxon, and Hanoverian contingents were assembled, 36,000 men and 84 guns strong (of which nearly 26,000 men and 60 guns were furnished by the British army); a detailed programme of the operations to be performed was prepared, a feigned enemy was told off, and the whole concluded by a march past, according to the accustomed forms of the different corps present.†

Their Royal Highnesses the Duke of Kent and the Duke of Cambridge were present on this occasion, and were received by Guards of Honour furnished by the Coldstream Guards. Similar manœuvres took place in the middle of October next year, near Bouchain, at which the King of Prussia and the Prince of Orange assisted, and again the same thing was repeated in September, 1818. Finally, another military display was given on the 23rd of October, 1818, just before France was evacuated by the Allies, near Villers-en-Couchies, in the presence of the Emperor of Russia and of the King of Prussia; 51,000 men and 168 guns were then brought together, of which 23,000 and 84 guns were Russians, 19,000 and 60 guns

in daily proportions, in conformity with the General Orders of June 3, 1815'" (*Battalion Order*, April 25, 1818).

* *Supplementary Despatches*, etc., xi. 426, 501; xii. 31, 538. It may be interesting to remark that the review of infantry in column, not contained in "His Majesty's Regulations" of the day, was ordered and provided for by the Field-Marshal.

† *Ibid.*, xi. 522. The following Brigade Order, dated Cambrai, Oct. 23, 1816, concerned these manœuvres: "The light companies of the Brigade and the three leading companies of the Coldstream marched yesterday through the village of Denain in a soldierlike and exemplary manner. The rest of the Brigade did anything but follow their example. That loose marching, which it fell into, has two effects. The troops either arrive late at their destination, or they arrive harassed and unfit for their operations. Either is an evil of the first magnitude. The principle on which this march originated is pure selfishness. The individual would save himself a little inconvenience at the expense of serious evil to no matter how many of his comrades in rear. The Brigade, with the exception of those companies already mentioned with approbation, and the leading and rear companies of the Grenadier Guards, will assemble every morning at the usual place, the Bapaume gate, at half-past seven o'clock, till they receive an order to the contrary." The latter portion of this order was countermanded on the 25th.

British, 3000 and 10 guns Danish, 3000 and 8 guns Saxons, and 3000 and 6 guns Hanoverians.* The enemy was represented by a detachment of Cossacks and of Russian infantry and artillery, and by the British cavalry, three companies of Sappers and Miners, and three brigades of artillery; the latter under Lieut.-Colonel Sir G. Scovell, and the whole under the general direction of Major-General Narishkin.

"It is supposed that the enemy is master of Bouchain, Le Quesnoi, and Valenciennes, and occupies a position behind the Escaillon. . . . The object of the army is to reconnoitre Valenciennes from the heights of Famars, and for this purpose the enemy's corps is to be forced back upon the place; having been in the first instance dislodged from his position on the Escaillon, the direct attack upon the front of which, is to be facilitated by a movement to turn his left."

The movements to be executed were all published beforehand, and the operations ended by a march past.†

Soon after the British contingent reached its quarters in the Departments of Pas de Calais and Nord, a reduction was effected in its strength by three regiments of cavalry,‡ by drafts of men entitled to their discharge or unfit for service, and by 400 men from the Guards Brigade (200 from each Battalion, so as to bring them to 1000 instead of 1200 men per Battalion). By this means, taking into account some 800 recruits who joined the contingent, the latter amounted to a little more than 29,000 Officers and men in the beginning of May, 1816.§

There were found to be some 60 men unfit for service in the 2nd Coldstream Guards about this time, and the 200 were made up by selecting 15 of the most unserviceable men per company (or 150 from the Battalion). Captain Shirley, and Lieutenants FitzClarence and Douglas, proceeded to England in charge of this

---

* *Supplementary Despatches, etc.*, xii. 783.

† *Ibid.*, xii. 711. The following letter, written by the Duke of Wellington to General Woronzow, commanding the Russian contingent, dated Aix-la-Chapelle, Oct. 13, 1818, just before the review at which the Emperor of Russia was present, is not without interest: "I write you just one line to tell you that, from what the Emperor has said to me, I judge that he thinks, from the reports he has heard, that, in marching in open column your troops do not preserve their distances regularly. You will, of course, attend to those hints, and make them preserve their distances from front rank to front rank" (*Ibid.*, xii. 765).

‡ The three cavalry brigades were, however, still maintained in France, each consisting of two regiments, instead of three.

§ *Ibid.*, xi. 386.

party (April 23rd), which, together with that belonging to the 3rd Battalion Grenadier Guards, was placed under the command of Lieut.-Colonel D. MacKinnon, Coldstream Guards.

In the course of the year, the Duc de Richelieu endeavoured to secure from the Allies a more solid and more general reduction of the army of occupation, in order to lessen the financial strain that burdened France, at a moment when she was oppressed by debt and afflicted by a bad harvest. He hoped thereby to render the King more popular. But he experienced considerable reluctance on the part of the British Government and of Wellington to agree to any such proposition, until the Chambers had proved by their acts that they were prepared to support the rule of Louis XVIII., and so "dissipate all reasonable apprehension as to the fulfilment of the late Treaty."* The Duke, indeed, was at first much opposed to it, and wrote strongly against it from Cambrai even as late as December, 1816, being of opinion that any real reduction of the Allied forces would tend to excite the French malcontents, and do harm to the Royal cause and to good government, and that "we ought to reduce only gradually and in proportion to our casualties." † A little later, however, being in Paris (January 9th), he modified his opinion on account of the successful negotiation of a French loan in London, which might "recall to the recollection of public men in France the obligations they owe to the Allied Sovereigns, and again reconcile them to measures which France herself, and not foreign Powers, rendered necessary." ‡ Under these circumstances, he proposed a reduction of 30,000 men (or one-fifth from each contingent), to be made on the 1st of April, 1817, and to be announced "in the manner most likely to produce a favourable effect on the public mind," as soon as the budget passed and the measures for ensuring the loan were definitely adopted.§ These proposals were accepted by the Allies, and were embodied in an official note, which was presented to the French Government on the 10th of February, 1817.‖

In pursuance of these arrangements, six battalions returned to England, proceeding there by Calais, to which were added detachments of 200 men from each of the Guards Battalions, or about

---

* *Supplementary Despatches, etc.*, xi. 485, 506. † *Ibid.*, xi. 573.
‡ *Ibid.*, xi. 592. § *Ibid.*, xi. 589, etc.
‖ See *Annual Register*, 1817, "General History," p. 103, where the note is given *in extenso*.

6000 men in all. The staffs, moreover, of the Third Division (Sir C. Colville) and of two brigades (Sir R. O'Callaghan and Sir J. Keane) were broken up.*

In June, 1818, Sir P. Maitland having been sent to Upper Canada as Lieut.-Governor of that province, Major-General Sir J. Lambert was appointed to the Guards Brigade at Cambrai; but as he was on leave, Colonel Woodford, Coldstream Guards, remained in temporary command until August. In June, also, Major-General Sir R. O'Callaghan replaced Sir J. Lambert as Brigadier of the 7th Brigade, and Sir C. Colville assumed command of the Second Division, vice Sir H. Clinton.

The Band of the Grenadier Guards had been sent for a few months to Paris, during the autumn of 1815, and left London on the 1st of September, proceeding by Brighton to Dieppe. Next year, the Coldstream Band went to Cambrai, on the 10th of June, by Dover and Calais, and remained there till the following October.†

The health of the troops in France, during the three and a half years succeeding Waterloo, seems to have been satisfactory. By a return, dated Paris, July 15, 1816, it appears that the number of sick amounted to 1060 men in the whole British contingent, of which only 43 belonged to the Coldstream, out of a total strength of 1104 Officers and men belonging to the Battalion at that time.‡ The principal cause of illness arose from the prevalence of ophthalmia, which, beginning in Paris in the winter of 1815, continued to affect the men until they left the country in 1818. Numerous orders were issued to prevent the spread of this evil.

Two Officers belonging to the Regiment died in France during this period, viz. Lieutenant J. Buller, in Paris, in January, 1816, and Lieutenant A. Gordon, killed in a duel with a French Officer, at Cambrai, in April, 1818.

---

* *Supplementary Despatches, etc.*, xi. 622, 638, 657. The order for sending home these detachments from the Guards Battalions "originates in the reduction of the whole establishment of the Guards, and the consequent necessity of the Battalions in France bearing their proportion of the non-effectives. H.R.H. desires me to express his hope that this diminution of 400 Guards may not embarrass you in regard to the amount of reduction" (Major-General Sir H. Torrens to Field-Marshal the Duke of Wellington: *ibid.*, xi. 639). The detachments marched from Cambrai on March 15, 1817, under the command of Lieut.-Colonel Hon. J. Walpole, Coldstream Guards. Captain Sowerby and Lieutenant Hervey were in charge of the Coldstream; and Assistant-Surgeon Smith, Coldstream Guards, accompanied the troops to Calais.

† For a short account of the Band of the Coldstream Guards, see Appendix No. V.

‡ *Supplementary Despatches, etc.*, xi. 439.

OCCUPATION OF FRENCH FORTRESSES.

There were not many incidents of any great importance to mark the occupation of French fortresses by European contingents. France, deprived of her incomparable military Chief, destitute of popular leaders, and exhausted by the wars that drained her resources during the past twenty-five years, settled gradually down, and accepted, though very reluctantly, the government which the Allied Powers had imposed upon her. The alien force did the work which had been contemplated; for, keeping the people under control, and repressing all revolutionary ebullitions, while Louis was consolidating his rule, the occupation did not come to an end until he had established his power in the country. Subsequent events have proved that the settlement thus effected by the will of Europe was not a permanent arrangement; France never consented to it, and we now know that it was overthrown within the brief space of fifteen years.* But when the Allied forces finally returned to their homes, and left the conquered people to their own resources, the Bourbon *régime* seemed, at all events outwardly, to be restored, and the new authority to be unquestioned.

The British troops conformed in every respect to the laws of the country, and to the various and frequently vexatious police regulations that prevailed at the time.† They conducted themselves peaceably in their various cantonments, and contrived to get on well with the

---

* Wellington perceived clearly the weakness of the new system; but he blamed the stupidity of the ultra-Royalist party, who, ruling the King, endeavoured to gain a cheap popularity at the expense of the Allies, to whom they owed entirely their restoration to power. "The descendants of Louis XV. will not reign in France; and I must say, and always will say, that it is the fault of Monsieur" (afterwards Charles X.) "and his adherents. . . . I wish Monsieur would read the histories of our Restoration and subsequent Revolution, or that he would recollect what passed under his own view, probably at his own instigation, in the Revolution. The conduct of the Royalists in joining with the Jacobins against the Moderate party, certainly led to the King's death. There are persons now at Paris who recollect the triumph of these parties when they obtained the vote for excluding from office, and from the Legislative Assembly, all who had been in the Constituante Assembly; and yet it is certain that that vote, more than any other single measure, was the cause of all the subsequent misfortunes, confiscations, murder of the King, etc.; and they could not avoid comparing that triumph with the senseless one over the Government the other day, upon a vital question in the law for regulating the press" (The Duke of Wellington to the Right Hon. J. C. Villiers, Jan. 11, 1818; *Supplementary Despatches*, etc., xii. 213).

† One order may be quoted, illustrating the condition of the rural districts in France at the time: "It having been represented by the Civil Authority that smoking out of doors of houses, in the villages, is contrary to the Police Laws, from the danger to which the houses would be exposed to fire from their being generally low and thatched, Commanding Officers are requested to take measures to prevent it. Smoking can only be allowed inside of the houses" (*Divisional Orders*, Cambrai, May 2, 1816).

population. So generally quiet was the state of affairs, that a liberal allowance of leave could be granted to the Officers of the contingent, soon after their arrival in the north of France.* The same relations existed between the inhabitants and the troops of the other Powers.† But, nevertheless, the occupation raised many controversies,—easily to be accounted for by the temper which the people were ready to display towards the invader, after a crushing military defeat. Irregularities committed by the troops, when they took place, were rectified without delay, and measures were adopted to prevent their recurrence; in this respect, at least, the French had nothing to complain of. On the other hand, there were repeated difficulties with the civil officials of the country, and with the turbulence that moved many of the inhabitants to be disorderly. The French Préfets and Maires too often refused to discharge their functions, the magistrates to convict on the clearest evidence, and the police to repress riots when the natives were found to be engaged in disputes with the foreign troops. Wellington continually protested strongly on this subject to the King's Government, and assured the Ministers that, unless the local authorities did their duty, the troops would be provoked to retaliate and revenge the injuries they had too often to put up with.‡ The irritation felt by a certain portion of the population against the foreign contingents, led to constant brawls, which became a source of danger when they occasioned the people to assemble tumultuously. The danger of frequent collisions was increased by the habit, then adopted by the British Officers, of using their fists for their personal protection, when drawn into scuffles with the natives in the streets. To stop this, the Duke insisted that all Officers should wear "their sidearms . . . . whenever they appeared out of their quarters or tents, except when hunting or shooting." §

* Fifteen Subalterns per regiment (nine in the cavalry), half the Captains, and one-third of the Field-Officers had to be present (*General Order*, Paris, Feb. 27, 1816). By another General Order, dated Cambrai, June 1st, the above rule, relating to Field-Officers, applied to Regimental Captains of the Brigade of Guards.

† "Je suis bien heureux de pouvoir faire rapport à Votre Majesté que le système de l'occupation militaire d'une partie de la France remplit les attentes de ceux qui l'ont adopté plus que l'on pouvait l'espérer. Les officiers et les troupes de toutes les nations se comportent envers les habitants du pays de manière à les concilier ; et je suis bien heureux de pouvoir assurer Votre Majesté que les siennes en donnent le meilleur exemple " (The Duke of Wellington to the Emperor of Russia, April 24, 1816 : *Supplementary Despatches, etc.*, xi. 373).

‡ *Supplementary Despatches, etc.*, xi. 421, 436, 440, 737 ; see also pp. 630, 726.

§ *Ibid.*, xi. 478, 570, 579 ; and xii. 77. "The measure" (the occupation) "has

A grave incident occurred at Cambrai, where a riot took place in June, 1816; hearing which, Wellington wrote to Sir. P. Maitland, then in command of that fortress, as follows:—

"I beg you will tell the Sous-Préfet that I am surprised that after the many examples he has had of our desire to do justice to those who have to complain of our people, the police at Cambrai should have suffered such a riot to take place without noticing it. You have my orders to turn out the troops and fire whenever the people attempt to riot again. I repeat them now, and I beg you will tell the Sous-Préfet that I have reminded you of them; and particularly that the troops are not to be turned out to quell a riot without firing in earnest. I beg you will also tell the Sous-Préfet of Cambrai, that I can no longer allow the Garde Nationale of Cambrai to remain armed. They must be paraded in an hour after you will make this communication, and must lodge their arms in the great square, and go to their homes. You will take possession of their arms; for which you will give a receipt. They are to be lodged in store. Inform the Sous-Préfet that I consider him and the Maire responsible to me that no arms are kept by the individuals of the Garde Nationale. I understand that people from the gaming-houses have been sent down to all the garrisons; and I beg you will tell the Sous-Préfet that I will not allow them to remain; and they had better therefore remove without obliging me to use force." *

The questions that arose out of the peculiar conditions in which the occupied districts were placed, caused difficulties, which differed in certain respects from those arising out of other military occupations. In 1871, for instance, after the peace of Versailles, Germany

succeeded beyond our most sanguine expectations. Not only are there no complaints, but I really believe that the common people of the Departments occupied, particularly those occupied by us, are delighted to have the troops, and the money spent among them. But not so the gentry, particularly the Royalists; not so those employed by the Government, and even the Ministers themselves. . . . All this would be of little importance in the decision of the question of reduction, if the King's Government possessed any real authority and strength, and if the people of the country were not of a character easily disturbed and irritated, and led to acts of violence and outrage whenever they find weakness. I believe that although we, the English, behave better than others, we are on that account the worst treated. There are constant broils between individuals of the middling and better classes, and Officers of the army, particularly at Valenciennes. We can get no justice from the authorities of the country—indeed, that is a general complaint in each of the contingents; and in more than one instance it has happened that a mob has collected with impunity upon the occasion of an assault upon or broil with an Officer" (The Duke of Wellington to Viscount Castlereagh, Cambrai, Dec. 11, 1816: *ibid.*, xi. 572).

* "*Supplementary Despatches*, etc., xi. 420. General Ziethen had previously given orders that all these gambling establishments should be closed in the places where the Prussian contingent were cantoned " (*ibid.*, xi. 409).

occupied some French provinces; and, in this case, the conquering armies had only to deal with the inhabitants—there were no hostile troops in their vicinity. But, in 1816, the Allies were placed in another position, and French soldiers were in their neighbourhood. Europe, moreover, had caused a revolution in France, and had to support the new government, until its power was established. The army of occupation, therefore, was not only exacting redress from the vanquished nation, according to treaty, but it was also in close alliance with the Government of the latter. Hence it was not unnatural that some delicate points should be raised, embarrassing to the French Ministers, who, while they posed as patriotic Frenchmen, had much to fear from the Imperialists and other malcontents that roamed over the country. A question arose in the Prussian districts, regarding the disbanded troops of Napoleon's armies, which is perhaps best explained by quoting an extract from a letter addressed by the Commander-in-chief to General Ziethen, dated February 15, 1816:—

"The soldiers of the Imperialist armies," says Wellington, "are viewed with suspicion, not only by the chiefs of the Allied army of occupation, but also by the King of France and by the French Government. . . . Your Excellency is therefore right to watch these persons, and I am sure that your measures, taken with this object, have the approval of the King of France. But I beg you to be careful that you do not trespass upon those powers which belong to the King or to the legislature. It is true, the King of France has ordered disbanded soldiers to return to their homes, and they do not obey if, having their domiciles elsewhere, they persist in congregating in those Departments, which are occupied by the troops under Your Excellency's command. You are therefore right in obliging these persons to obey their Sovereign's order, and in sending them out of the Prussian districts. But to oblige all these soldiers who inhabit your districts, to be in possession of a card of residence, to be submitted to your Brigadiers, is a step in advance. This is more than a police measure, which in my opinion should be limited to putting the existing law in motion; it is an act of sovereignty, and even of legislation; because it obliges soldiers who are subjects of the King, and who are residing in their homes by the King's command, to furnish themselves with papers for their personal security, which neither the King nor the laws of the country require of them. I think, therefore, that your order ought only to oblige such soldiers who are not domiciled in your Departments to quit them, and to command your Officers to carry out your order, if they find these unauthorized persons. At the same time, in order to clear up the subject, you can demand from the mayors, the Sous-Préfets, etc., a list of the men who have a right to live in your Departments, and you can remove all those, whose names are not to be found on the lists. This you may do, because you would be only carrying out the decrees of the Sovereign authority; but I do not think we should be justified in doing more than this."*

Owing to the arrangement sanctioned by the Convention of the 20th of November, 1815, attached to the Treaty of the same date, by which the French were allowed to maintain garrisons in certain specified places in the Departments under foreign occupation, further complications arose, which increased the tension between the King's Government and the Allied forces. While manœuvres were going on in the summer of 1816, the Governor of St. Omer raised a note of alarm, on seeing British troops in the vicinity of the fortress; and the excitement became such, that Wellington was obliged to write to the Duc de Feltre (the War Minister), a letter of strong remonstrance, in which, having first defended himself against a ridiculous charge that he intended to seize a French fort, he declared that the occupation was a measure calculated to secure the peace of Europe and the consolidation of the Royal power, that the foreign contingents were the allies of the King, and that he would not suffer his soldiers to be disarmed when they had occasion to march through a French garrison.†

---

* *Supplementary Despatches, etc.*, xi. 303. Elsewhere, the Duke of Wellington, writing to the French Government, says: " Je suis très loin d'approuver les mesures de rigueur que je vois adoptées souvent comme mesure de police, mais il n'est pas très facile de les empêcher. L'existence d'une police militaire une fois admise, l'examen par les commandants militaires des passeports de ceux, qui passent par le pays occupé, en est une conséquence, qui ne peut pas être évitée. Il faudrait voir, si en mettant en exécution ces mesures de police, il se trouve des abus. Pour ce qui regarde la demande au maire de Stenay de la liste des militaires qui s'y trouvent ou aux environs, V.E. verra que j'avois suggéré cette mesure dans ma lettre au Général Ziethen. Elle devient onéreuse à cause du nombre de militaires que se trouvent dans ces environs; mais aussi il faut observer, que la nécessité de tenir les militaires en observation, est urgente en proportion de leurs nombres, et le Général Ziethen m'apprend dans une lettre du 20, qu'il n'y a pas moins que 20,000, dans les districts occupés par l'armée Prussienne" (Duke of Wellington to the Duc de Richelieu, Paris, March 2, 1816: *ibid.*, xi. 323).

† " Si on me croit assez fripon pour vouloir m'emparer d'une place occupée par un garnison du Roi, on devrait au moins me faire la justice de croire que je ne suis pas assez bête pour le faire. . . . L'occupation est une mesure de paix; son objet est, en affermissant le trône du Roi, et en donnant au Roi le temps de s'affermir lui-même dans son gouvernement, de maintenir la paix parmi les nations, et d'assurer autant que possible la tranquillité du monde. Les troupes des Puissances étrangères qui se trouvent en France sont donc les alliées du Roi; et quel que soit l'opinion à présent sur le bien ou le mal qu'elles font à S.M., on ne peut pas nier que l'année passée on croyait que leur présence était absolument nécessaire pour assurer les objets que tout homme bien pensant avait

The passage of troops through fortified places had an unfortunate result at Cambrai; for, on the 10th of May, 1818, when a French detachment marched through the town from Paris to Douai, a riot ensued, in which three or four men of the Coldstream were injured. The British garrison behaved well in the emergency, and the following order was published by Colonel Woodford, then in command :—

"Colonel Woodford desires to express his satisfaction at the temperance and forbearance shown by the Non-commissioned officers and soldiers of the Brigade, in the affray between them and the French soldiers and the inhabitants yesterday evening; to this temperate conduct, so highly creditable to brave troops, and to the activity of the Officers and Non-commissioned officers who were present, is to be attributed the early restoration of order and tranquillity throughout the town." *

The Allied forces were now soon to quit French territory. It had been stipulated by treaty that the occupation was to last five years, but it was also expressly stated that it might terminate in three, and all parties by this time wished to bring it to a conclusion as soon as possible. The French naturally pined for emancipation; and the words of the Duc de Richelieu, delivered in the Chambers, that "every heart throbbed at the thought of seeing on the soil of the country, no other banner but that of France," found a responsive echo throughout the length and breadth of the land, and awoke a passionate longing for freedom in the minds of the people, which was very difficult to resist.

en vue. Mais quand des troupes amies ou alliées se trouvent dans un pays, est-ce l'usage que, . . . si on veut faire passer un détachment de troupes par une ville fortifiée (et observez que si on veut marcher en hiver ou en été cette armée-ci, il faut passer par les places fortes), il faut désarmer les officiers et les soldats à la porte, placer les armes sur les chariots, et passer ainsi comme prisonniers ! Vraiment je rougis en écrivant sur cette matière, dont je n'ai appris les détails que dernièrement ; et je m'assure que V.E. verra comme moi la nécessité de mettre fin à de telles absurdités. Je sais bien qu'elles sont contraires aux ordres du Roi. . . . Le principe et les usages militaires exigent qu'il y ait des précautions en admettant une troupe, même de la même nation, dans une place forte ; mais est-ce nécessaire, est-ce l'usage de les désarmer ? Est-ce possible que je puisse m'y soumettre ? N'y a-t-il pas des précautions d'une autre nature qui seraient réelles, et qui sont d'usage, et qui pourraient concilier tous les objets de la sécurité de la ville à passer, avec ce qui est dû au caractère et au respect dû à l'armée d'une autre nation ? Par exemple, ne pourrait-on pas avertir du passage, et convenir du nombre qui pourrait passer par la porte au même moment ? . . . Je ne peux pas, ni ne veux pas, me soumettre au désarmement de mes soldats, en passant par une ville quelconque" (*Supplementary Despatches*, etc., xi. 493).

* *Brigade Order*, Cambrai, May 11, 1818.

MUSQUETEER 1650.

Wellington, also, was disposed to assist them. The Government of the King had been showing increased hostility to the foreign contingents, who were becoming daily more hateful in the eyes of the French nation. He expressed himself clearly on this subject to Lord Bathurst, on the 8th of March, 1818:—

"As soon as the occupation becomes odious to the people, and that we are liable to the attacks which they are daily excited to make upon us, and that, under these circumstances, we are to begin a new lease, as it were, of the occupation, we must close up, and take our real position with our whole force between the Meuse and the Scheldt, and our occupation must become more burthensome to the country in which we shall be placed, and in fact, become one of war. Of course that state of things could not last, and the Powers of Europe must be prepared to support their troops left in such a situation in this country." *

It was apparent to all that this condition of tension must come to an end; and, though there was no certainty that the King could maintain himself on the throne without foreign support, yet it was evident that the cure for the evils to be dreaded, was liable to become a greater misfortune to Europe, than the apprehension itself. The French, moreover, had made great efforts to discharge their financial obligations to the Allies; and in these efforts they were successful, aided by the Duke of Wellington, who, upon the proposal of the Emperor of Russia, was appointed president of the diplomatic and finance committee charged with the regulation of these liabilities.† Added to this, the fortifications of the Netherlands frontier were by this time nearly completed, and as this was done to form a barrier against France, the moment had arrived when the country could be delivered from the burden that oppressed it, as well as from the cause which produced so much irritation.

In the autumn, therefore, of 1818, a Congress was convened at Aix-la-Chapelle, for the purpose of determining the question; ‡ and

---

* *Supplementary Despatches, etc.*, xii. 381.

† Sir Archibald Alison, *History of Europe from the Fall of Napoleon in 1815, to the Accession of Louis Napoleon in* 1852, i. 538 (London, 1852). *Supplementary Despatches, etc.*, xii. 119, 156, 193.

‡ M. de Richelieu, present on the part of France, was instructed only to obtain the emancipation of France. "Make every sacrifice," said the King to him at his departure, "to obtain the evacuation of the territory. It is the first condition of our independence. No flag but our own should wave in France. Express to my Allies how difficult my government will be so long as it can be reproached with the calamities of the country,

an agreement was made, on the 1st of October, by which the foreign forces were to leave the soil of France on or before the 30th of November. To this compact was added an invitation to His Most Christian Majesty to join the four Great European Powers, and to take part in their deliberations, present or future, for the maintenance of peace, and for the mutual guarantee of the rights of nations. The conference, however, did not end there; for a secret convention was also signed, by the four Powers only, stipulating that, in case France should resume her revolutionary ways, and again threaten the tranquillity of the civilized world, British, Prussian, Austrian, and Russian *corps d'armées* were to assemble forthwith at Brussels, Cologne, Stuttgart, and Mainz respectively, for the suppression of these disorders.*

Wellington took early measures to effect the evacuation by the army of occupation, and hastened the operation with all possible despatch. General von Frimont reported (October 23rd) that the Austrian contingent would send the first column across the Rhine on the 1st of November, and that the whole corps would quit French territory on the 11th. The Prussians moved off early in the month, and were directed upon Cologne, Bonn, and Coblentz. The Russians marched in two columns immediately after the review, which had taken place near Villers-en-Couchies on the 23rd of October, the first through the Netherlands, the other following the Prussians to the Rhine at Mannheim. After this latter column, came the Saxons, who left Le Quesnoi on the 7th and 9th, and moved to Forbach. The Bavarians began to evacuate their cantonments on the 12th; while the Hanoverians and the Danes marched northwards, through the Netherlands, the former between the 4th and the 9th, and the latter between the 12th and the 19th. The British troops, who were placed under canvas during their march, were sent to Calais immediately after the review just mentioned, where they were embarked under the orders of Major-General Sir M. Power. The embarkation began on the 29th of October. As soon as the fortresses were permanently evacuated by the Allies, the French, who had been specially authorized to enter the occupied Departments for the purpose, marched into them without delay, and, hoisting the white flag,

and the occupation of the territory. . . . Obtain the best conditions possible; but at any sacrifice, get quit of the stranger" (Alison, *History of Europe*, 1815–1852, i. 566).

* *Ibid.*, i. 568, etc.

under a Royal salute, once more took possession of their own territory, amidst the universal enthusiasm and joy of the military and of the inhabitants. The British stores, which could not be conveyed to Calais, were shipped at Valenciennes, and were taken by water to Antwerp; a portion were sold to the King of the Netherlands.*

The progress of the evacuation being sufficiently advanced, the Field-Marshal commanding the Allied forces, issued, on the 10th of November, a valedictory address, and on the same day similar orders were communicated to the British army. Later, on the 1st of December, a letter from H.R.H. the Commander-in-Chief was published, conveying to the British contingent the thanks of the Prince Regent "for the discipline and good order which have been so successfully maintained, to the honour of the British arms, during the period it has been stationed in France."†

On the 6th of November, a letter was received from the Préfet of the Department of Nord, recording his gratitude and that of his subordinates, for the rigid discipline which prevailed in the army of occupation, "to which has been due the harmony which existed between the troops and the inhabitants." He added that he felt a real satisfaction in testifying to the excellent conduct of the British corps, and to the zeal with which all the Officers carried out the views of the Duke, to alleviate as much as possible the burden of the occupation.‡

The Guards Brigade did not leave France with the rest of the British army, but remained at head-quarters at Cambrai, with the Chief of the Staff, Lieut.-General Sir G. Murray (the Duke being obliged to return to Aix-la-Chapelle after the review of the 23rd of October), until the morning of the 18th of November; when, evacuating the fortress, they moved, at eleven o'clock, to Cantin. The march of the Coldstream was made in six columns, four being composed of two companies; and was continued to Calais, the port of embarkation, avoiding as much as possible all large towns and centres of French patriotism. Marching by Lillers,

---

* *Supplementary Despatches, etc.*, xii. 739–826; Alison, *History of Europe*, 1815–1852, i. 574. It appears that the Russians returned to their native country by sea (C. Joyneville, *Life and Times of Alexander I.*, iii. 276: London, 1875).

† These three documents are to be found in Appendix VI.

‡ *Supplementary Despatches, etc.*, xii. 784. The Duke's answer is given at p. 819, and conveys his acknowledgments to "the first authority of the Department" for his good opinion.

Racquingham, and Louches, the Brigade reached Calais on the 23rd, and immediately embarked for Dover. On this date Sir J. Lambert published the following order of farewell to the Guards, who had completed their service in France:—

"*Calais*, November 23, 1818. Major-General Sir J. Lambert cannot relinquish the command of the Brigade without congratulating the Officers and soldiers on the termination of a service of four years' duration, during which they have acquired to themselves on many occasions the greatest honour and credit. The Major-General requests that the Officers will be assured that he was perfectly sensible of the honour conferred upon him on his appointment to the Brigade, and feels certain, had circumstances permitted that its exertions in the field might have been more efficiently called for, that he should now have had the satisfaction of expressing his admiration of that distinguished conduct which has ever called forth the encomiums of those who have had the good fortune to be in command." [*]

Arrived at Dover, the Coldstream marched to Chatham, where they arrived on the 28th of November, and remained quartered in that garrison till further orders.

Thus ended this stirring drama that began in March, 1815, and in which the Coldstream Guards participated to the fullest extent. During these eventful years, services were not only rendered to King and country, on the field of battle, at one of the most momentous crises of modern history; but duty was also zealously performed, in a less acknowledged sphere, when a warlike nation was induced, with much difficulty, to abate her military ardour, to renounce her menacing attitude, and to resume a pacific policy towards her neighbours. The years spent in France were useful to the British troops quartered there. It was a time when they had to be prepared for every emergency, when they had to cultivate amicable relations with a foreign people who resented deeply their presence among them, when their demeanour towards the inhabitants had to be both firm and conciliatory, and when their military efficiency and discipline could alone enable them to discharge the delicate duties with which they were entrusted.

This chapter must not conclude without recording that, at the end of the occupation, the Duke of Wellington was created a Field-Marshal in the armies of Austria, Russia, and Prussia; and that his services to Europe, which could not be further rewarded by

[*] General Sir F. Hamilton, K.C.B., *History of the Grenadier Guards*, iii. 74 (London, 1874).

his own Sovereign, were acknowledged in simple language, which expressed the difficulties of the situation, and the Royal approbation at the manner in which they had been overcome.

"The command of the army," said Lord Bathurst, "composed of so many nations, and belonging to Sovereigns eminently distinguished for their military exploits, not stationed within any of their own dominions, but in temporary and partial occupation of a given district within the territories of a martial people, with whom His Majesty had so recently closed an almost uninterrupted warfare of more than twenty years' duration, presented difficulties of no ordinary magnitude, which could only be surmounted by no ordinary measure of judgment and discretion. In this command your Grace maintained the British army (divided for the relief of the inhabitants in separate and distant quarters) unimpaired in their discipline, and even improved in their condition. You preserved the several contingents composing the Allied army in the utmost harmony with each other, and in the best understanding with the authorities of the country which they occupied. You won so much upon the esteem and confidence of His Majesty's Allies, that they all spontaneously applied for your arbitration of their respective claims upon France; and you impressed that Government with such a sense of your justice, impartiality, and exertions, that you had the gratification of receiving assurances from His Most Christian Majesty that, but for your intervention, that intricate negotiation could not have been satisfactorily concluded. Amidst, therefore, the signal achievements which will carry your name and the glory of the British Empire down to the latest posterity, it will not form the least part of your Grace's renown, that you have exercised and concluded a command, unexampled in its character, with the concurrent voice of approbation from all whom it could concern." *

[* Earl Bathurst to the Duke of Wellington, Nov. 27, 1818: *Supplementary Despatches*, etc., xii. 851.

CHAPTER IV.

FIRST PART OF THE LONG EUROPEAN PEACE.

Distress in England after the war—Reductions in the Army and Navy—Stations of the Brigade—French Eagles captured, deposited in the Chapel Royal, Whitehall—Reforms in interior economy—Death of George III., and Accession of George IV.—Cato Street Conspiracy—Trial of Queen Caroline—Coronation of George IV.—Guards in Dublin—Distress in 1826—Death of the Duke of York—Changes in uniform—Death of George IV.; succeeded by William IV.—Political agitation at home, revolution abroad; the Reform Act—Coronation of William IV.—First appearance of cholera—Death of the King, and Accession of Her Majesty Queen Victoria—Changes and reforms introduced during the reign of William IV.

THE defeat of Napoleon brought about a period of peace in Europe, which, lasting till 1853, almost entirely undisturbed by the clash of arms, is chiefly conspicuous in history for the internal changes, and for the popular and national ideas that were then developed, both in England and on the Continent. This period, containing necessarily, as far as the Coldstream is concerned, few of those stirring incidents which invest the annals of a regiment with public interest, marks the introduction to our present modern society, and exhibits a rapid growth in the British Empire, and a great improvement in the material lot of the people. But it opened inauspiciously, and was at its commencement tinged with gloom.

The principles of the French Revolution, generating dangerous and violent forces, and threatening Christendom with anarchy and destruction, were at length laid low, and, to outward appearances at least, they were finally crushed and eradicated. The victory rested with England, to whose indomitable energy, national power, and vast financial resources, the result of the gigantic contest had been due. And as men who have conquered in a desperate struggle, look to rest and refreshment as the fruit of their labours, so did Great Britain indulge in the expectation that, the enemy being vanquished, she would at once be compensated for her innumerable sacrifices by the quiet and unalloyed enjoyment of the rewards of her valour. Nor was this an extravagant hope. Even during the war, while the people were oppressed by a crushing taxation, and when the country was in the very throes of an exhausting and terrible conflict, England, thanks to her commanding maritime supremacy, that alone endowed her with extraordinary strength, advanced steadily in riches and in population.* It may, then, be readily conceived that, if such was the case in the hour of darkness, the nation had cause to look forward with confidence, to a rapidly accelerating progress in material prosperity, as soon as the millennium of a general peace should dawn upon the civilized world. But anticipations are frequently disappointed, and in this case they were not immediately realized. The cessation of hostilities, instead of heralding an era of plenty, was the signal of much misery and distress, which cast a dark shadow over the last few years of the reign of George III., and chastened the rejoicings that followed the successful termination of the greatest war of modern times.

Various causes are assigned for this unexpected suffering, into which we cannot enter. Suffice it to record the fact, and to note, that the widespread poverty that then prevailed, led to disorder, which, breaking out in many parts of the country, had to be quelled by the interference of military force. In London there were also disturbances or threats of riots, so that, from the end of 1816 until the autumn of 1817—and, indeed, upon many occasions afterwards—the Guards quartered in the Metropolis were constantly kept ready for the preservation of the public peace; the troops were often confined to barracks, the Officers recalled from leave, the public duties strengthened, and piquets temporarily sent to protect vulnerable points in the city. The rabble, urged by leaders, who endeavoured, as usual, to convert the distress to their own purposes, began to display a rising animosity towards the soldiery; † and schemes were formed for the purpose of burning the barracks in London, and of attacking the Tower, the Bank, and other places of

* The exports, which in 1792 were valued at £27,000,000, amounted to nearly £58,000,000 in 1815; imports rose from £19,000,000 to £32,000,000 between those years; the shipping advanced from 1,000,000 to 2,500,000 tons; and the population of the three kingdoms, from 14,000,000 to 18,000,000 souls (Alison, *History of Europe*, 1815-1852, i. 79).

† Adverting to the insults to which both Officers and men were exposed when mounting and dismounting guard, marshal-men and park-keepers were warned to attend those parades, and to prevent the disorder complained of, and Officers were ordered to report them, if this duty was not properly performed (*Brigade Order*, Oct. 17, 1816).

importance. No actual outbreak occurred until the 2nd of December, when a disturbance took place, known as the Spafield riots, in which the mob, having procured arms, marched into the City and retained possession of the Minories for some hours. After doing much damage, they were dislodged by the troops sent to put them down, and the district was patrolled till order was completely restored.*

The abrupt cessation of hostilities occasioned reductions in the large naval and military establishments which had to be maintained for the vigorous prosecution of the war; and the promptitude with which they were effected, aggravated not a little the general distress that followed. The Government, defeated in their proposal to continue the property tax, and having thereupon voluntarily given up the war duty on malt, found themselves suddenly deprived of £17,000,000 of revenue, and had no option but to discharge forthwith, and in no sparing manner, a large portion of the forces of the Crown. Of the 100,000 men required for the Navy in 1815, only 33,000 were retained in 1816; the military establishment was also fixed during the Session, at 111,756 men, not counting the regiments serving in India, paid by the East India Company, nor the contingent quartered in France and provided for by that nation. To effect the necessary reductions in the land services, some 50,000 of the regular Army, the Militia 80,000 strong, and of course the foreign corps, nearly 21,000 men, were disbanded.† Some of these changes did not take place until 1817, but they affected the Coldstream as early as the 24th of December, 1815, when the Regiment lost 400 men; on the 24th of March, 1817, simultaneously with the reduction effected in the army of occupation in France, another diminution of 200 men was made in the establishment; again, shortly after the 2nd Battalion

* *Annual Register*, 1816, "Chronicle," 190; *ibid.*, 1817, "General History," 7, 12. The following letter from the Adjutant-General of the Forces to the Field-Officer in Brigade Waiting, dated December 4th, and published in Brigade Orders of the 6th, refers to this riot: "I have received the Commander-in-Chief's commands to desire that you will convey to the Brigade of Foot Guards, H.R.H.'s entire approbation during the last two days, of the temper and discipline they have displayed, while rendering the most effectual aid to the civil authorities, by which the tranquillity of the metropolis has been secured."

† Alison, *History of Europe*, 1815-1852, i. 108. "We have had one of the most disagreeable sessions I ever remember; a sour, discontented temper among our friends, considerable distress throughout the country, and endless debates upon economy, whilst everything that has been done by the Prince and his Government, is either forgotten or thrown into the shade" (Lord Castlereagh to the Duke of Wellington, May 13th, 1816: *Supplementary Despatches, etc.*, xi. 401).

FIRST PART OF THE LONG EUROPEAN PEACE. 75

returned from Cambrai (December, 1818), the services of four Lieutenants, sixteen Ensigns, two Assistant-Surgeons, and 200 men were further dispensed with; and lastly, on the 25th of August, 1821, four companies were abolished, twelve Officers were seconded, and 216 Non-commissioned officers and men were discharged.* The sweeping nature of these reductions, rendered necessary by the termination of the war, is perhaps best appreciated by comparing the Regimental establishment as it stood in the spring of 1814, with that which was in force in the autumn of 1821:—

1814.	1821.
22 Companies.	16 Companies.
4 Field-Officers (Colonel, Lieutenant-Colonel, and 2 Majors).	4 Field-Officers (Colonel, Lieutenant-Colonel, and 2 Majors).
22 Captains.	16 Captains.
46 Lieutenants.	20 Lieutenants.
20 Ensigns.	12 Ensigns.
2 Adjutants.	2 Adjutants.
2 Quartermasters.	2 Quartermasters.
3 Surgeon-Major and Battalion Surgeons.	3 Surgeon-Major and Battalion Surgeons.
4 Assistant-Surgeons.	2 Assistant-Surgeons.
1 Solicitor.	1 Solicitor.
2 Drum-Majors.	2 Drum-Majors.
1 Deputy Marshal.	1 Deputy Marshal.†
2 Sergeants-Major.	2 Sergeants-Major.
2 Quartermaster-Sergeants.	2 Quartermaster-Sergeants.
2 Armourer-Sergeants.	2 Armourer-Sergeants.
2 Schoolmaster-Sergeants.	2 Schoolmaster-Sergeants.
176 Sergeants.	64 Sergeants.
176 Corporals.	63 Corporals.
47 Drummers and Fifers.	35 Drummers and Fifers.
2706 Privates.	1344 Privates.
3220 Total.	1580 Total.

* If Officers, not included in the reduction of 1818, wished to retire on half-pay, the difference to be paid on an exchange was fixed at £1000 for a Lieutenant, and at £600 for an Ensign, "to those on the permanent establishment who may be entitled to such indulgence." In the reduction of 1821, the men were allowed to take away their knapsacks, their regimental clothing of the year, and their great coats, if they had been two years in wear; the Officers seconded, were to be re-absorbed into the Regiment, by seniority, as vacancies occurred. (Lord Palmerston to Field-Marshal H.R.H. the Duke of Cambridge, Colonel of the Coldstream Guards, War Office, Aug. 16, 1821.)

† The Deputy Marshal ceased to form part of the Regimental establishment in December, 1828.

In consequence of these changes, the King's Guard and the Buckingham House Guard were reduced to ninety and thirty privates respectively, and the other public duties were lightened (January 1, 1822); very shortly afterwards (February 14th), the guards furnished by the Tower Battalion at the East and West India Docks were also abolished, and the Dock companies were thereby obliged to provide themselves with adequate protection.

During the war of 1815, and the subsequent occupation of Paris, there were only three Battalions of the Brigade in England, and they were all quartered in the West-end of London. In the winter of 1815–16, after the conclusion of the peace, two more Battalions returned home, when Windsor and the Tower were again occupied. On the 20th of August, 1816, a roster was published for the regular half-yearly change of quarters, viz. from the Tower, to Windsor, to Lower Westminster, to Portman Street barracks, to Knightsbridge barracks. This arrangement was slightly altered in December, 1818, when French territory was evacuated, and Finsbury and Chatham were added to the list.* The quarters at these last two places were shortly afterwards vacated, or irregularly occupied, and Holborn and Brighton (or Portsmouth) substituted for them; in the end of 1821, a Battalion of Foot Guards proceeded to Dublin, and six months later the Brigade was stationed as follows:—Grenadier Guards, 1st Battalion, Dublin; 2nd Battalion, Tower; 3rd Battalion, Knightsbridge: Coldstream Guards, 1st Battalion, King's Mews barracks (now known as St. George's barracks); 2nd Battalion, Portman Street: Third Guards, 1st Battalion, Lower Westminster; 2nd Battalion, Windsor.†

As there was not, at this time, sufficient accommodation for a battalion at any of the London barracks, that portion of the men who could not be lodged there were billeted in the vicinity. At Windsor, also, the Foot Guards, though sometimes furnishing detachments at Hungerford, Reading, Kew, and Sandhurst, had not

---

* *Brigade Orders*, Aug. 20, 1816, and Dec. 9, 1818; the latter of which contained a provision to enable the Coldstream and the Third Guards to exchange quarters with a Regiment having two Battalions in London, in the event of both their Battalions being simultaneously out of town.

Knightsbridge barracks occupied a site near St. George's Place, Hyde Park Corner, at the back of the present Alexandra Hotel; Portman Street barracks was situated where Granville Place, Portman Square, is now built.

† The changes of stations, as far as they affect the Regiment, up to January, 1833, are given in Appendix No. 273 of MacKinnon's *Origin and Services of the Coldstream Guards*; after that date, they are to be found in Appendix No. XV.

FIRST PART OF THE LONG EUROPEAN PEACE. 77

enough room in the barracks, and a portion of the men were similarly provided with quarters in the town. The system of billeting was gradually brought to an end, but it does not seem to have entirely disappeared, in London at least, until 1837, when barrack accommodation was provided for the whole Brigade. The discipline of the men in quarters was specially looked after, each company being told off into squads under proper superintendence ; the men were frequently visited, and were efficiently controlled, and reports were made of any complaint either on the part of the soldiers, or on the part of the landlords.* The following appears in the 1st Battalion Orders of the 25th of February, 1820 :—

"Colonel Woodford feels certain, from the excellent conduct of the Battalion throughout the past year, that he may look forward with confidence to a continuance of good order, sobriety, and discipline in quarters, and although many soldiers will be dispersed in the public-houses, he trusts that they will never dishonour themselves by associating with any disaffected or ill-disposed people. The men must be regular and clean in their quarters, and they may expect to be visited frequently and at uncertain times and hours, both by day and in the evening; and any man reported for improper behaviour will be removed to barracks immediately."

From May, 1816, until the summer of 1820, the West-end Battalions supplied a detachment of some 250 men, at Deptford and Woolwich, to protect the Government establishments maintained there. The detachment was relieved every fortnight at first, and afterwards once a month. Later, the Brigade supplied detachments of variable strength, for the same purpose, at irregular periods, to both, or to either of, these places, viz. : April, 1836–April, 1837 ; June, 1847–November, 1847 ; July, 1850 ; March, 1851 ; October 28, 1853–February 8, 1854.

On the 18th of January, 1816, the Eagles captured at Waterloo, were deposited with great solemnity in the Chapel Royal, Whitehall. An escort, consisting of Officers and men of the three Regiments, who had all been present at the battle (of which the Coldstream furnished 1 sergeant, 1 corporal, and 23 privates), marched past the public duties and the rest of the Brigade, assembled on the Horse Guards parade, lowering the Eagles as they approached the

* See *2nd Battalion Order*, Sept. 11, 1819. It appears that the men of the Brigade were at one time allowed to earn money as coal porters, but no record has been found to show when the practice ceased. It is said that a certain number of men on guard were also allowed to do the same thing, provided they joined their posts at the evening roll-call, and that this was the origin of beating the taptoo on the Queen's Guard.

King's Colour, and proceeded thence to Whitehall, accompanied by the band of the Coldstream. Divine Service was then read, during which, the trophies were brought in, and were lodged in the Chapel.

It is perhaps worthy of remark that, as early as 1817, Government granted to soldiers the privilege of sending their own letters by post, at the then very cheap rate of one penny.*

The supply of Regimental necessaries had hitherto not been satisfactorily managed. The Commanding Officer accordingly established stores, from which all the articles required by the men could be procured, of good quality, at the cheapest rate, and at fixed and known prices; and he published an order, January 23, 1817, directing that, for the future, all the men's necessaries should be got for them there, and at no other place.† This order was enforced in the 2nd Battalion, then at Cambrai, on the 9th of February.‡

Increased attention was paid about this time to interior economy, and former orders on the subject, issued piecemeal, were summarized. The method of paying the men and of keeping their accounts, established by the Commanding Officer, was enforced by Regimental Orders of January 19, 1818, and July 28, 1820; the messing was more closely looked after; and the duties of the company Officers, and of the Officer of the day, were better defined. By a Regimental Order of June 20, 1822,§ Officers commanding companies were directed frequently to visit the barrack rooms, and to see the messes, also to inspect the men's necessaries weekly, instead of monthly as heretofore; marching order parades every Sunday morning were then instituted for this purpose, and the custom was not abolished

* *General Order*, Jan. 22, 1817.

† By 1st Battalion Order, October 10, 1819, all articles of necessaries and clothing were to be marked with the Regimental mark previous to their delivery to the men.

‡ The following Battalion Order was issued on this subject, dated Cambrai, February 11, 1817: "The monthly inspection of necessaries is to take place every 24th, if possible. The different articles sealed and approved by the Commanding Officer are to be the patterns for the Battalion, and no necessaries are to be considered as Regimental excepting such as are stamped by the Quartermaster. The Non-commissioned officers and men are to be completed according to the list sent to each company. There will be only one delivery of necessaries in the month from the store-room, as soon after the inspection as possible. The sealed patterns are to be sent to each company with the new articles, to enable the men to compare them, and if they are not equally good, the pay-sergeants are to send them back immediately to the Quartermaster."

§ Repeated and somewhat enlarged by 2nd Battalion Orders of August 2, 1827, and February 25, 1830. By the former, the Officer for the week was directed to inspect the breakfast messes every morning at eight a.m.

until the year 1843, when Saturday was finally substituted for Sunday, as the day upon which the inspection was to take place.

Colonel Sir Richard Jackson, K.C.B. (First Major of the Regiment), having left the Coldstream, Colonel Alexander Woodford, C.B., succeeded him in the command of the 1st Battalion, and Colonel Sir Henry Bouverie, K.C.B., promoted Second Major, assumed the command of the 2nd Battalion (January 18, 1820).

George III., after a long and glorious reign of sixty years, died on the 29th of January, 1820, and was succeeded by the Prince of Wales, who, through the illness of the King, had been Prince Regent, or Monarch in fact, though not in name, ever since the end of 1810. The ten years during which George IV. occupied the Throne, did not differ generally from the five that succeeded Waterloo: they were marked by disturbances and political commotions, which, lasting until the reign of his successor, William IV., brought about important and radical changes in the constitution of the country. During this period, moreover, the power of steam was brought into practical use, and railways and steam-ships began to take the place of stage coaches and sailing vessels. England, in short, was passing through a phase of transition, when a new order was being established both in the political and social life of the people.

The first Battalions of the three Regiments of Foot Guards attended the obsequies of George III., which took place at Windsor, February 16th, and received from General Earl Cathcart, Gold Stick in Waiting, in chief command of the troops, through Colonel Askew, the Field-Officer in Brigade Waiting, "the entire approbation of H.R.H. the Commander-in-Chief of their appearance, attention, and regularity, on that most melancholy occasion, and his sincere thanks for the propriety of their conduct in performing the several services assigned to them." Next day the 1st Battalion Coldstream proceeded for four months to Portsmouth, returning to Windsor in June.

The 2nd Battalion meanwhile remained at Portman Street, and rendered good service on the occasion of the apprehension of the Cato Street conspirators, on the 23rd of February. It was ascertained that the latter, not unlike a modern gang of anarchists, were plotting to murder the King's ministers, and to overturn every form of government; that they were well armed, and were lying concealed in a loft over a stable in Cato Street, the only approach to which was by a ladder and through a trap-door. Some police, accompanied by a detachment of thirty men of the 2nd Battalion, under Lieutenant F. FitzClarence, stormed the loft, garrisoned by twenty-five desperate characters, and a fight ensued in the dark, under circumstances of great confusion. Several conspirators succeeded in making their escape, but nine were secured, and sufficient arms and ammunition for one hundred persons were seized ; not, however, before one of the policemen was killed, and a sergeant of the 2nd Battalion, named Legge, wounded.* A Regimental Order, dated February 25th, was issued, referring to this incident :—

"The Commanding Officer has great pleasure in expressing his satisfaction with the piquet of the 2nd Battalion commanded by Lieutenant Fitz-Clarence, on the night of the 23rd instant. The gallantry and moderation with which they performed their duty, are in the highest degree creditable."

The new reign began with an event that stirred the whole nation to the very depths, and wrought irreparable scandal through every grade of society—the trial of the unfortunate Caroline, Queen of George IV. Happily, the episode is now forgotten, and there is no necessity to revive it. But the trial of a Queen, publicly charged with degrading personal conduct, is unique in modern history, and it created naturally an extraordinary excitement among all classes at the time ; and, as feeling upon the subject ran exceedingly high, and a spirit of disorder and disaffection was widespread, the Brigade had a part to play in it, which cannot entirely be passed over. The trial itself took the form of a Bill of Pains and Penalties, read a first time in the House of Lords, July 5th. On the second reading, evidence was heard, and the proceedings, beginning on the 17th of August, did not end until the 6th of November, when there was a majority of twenty-eight in favour of the measure. At the third reading (November 10th), the majority sank to nine votes, and thereupon Government abandoned the Bill. The populace had ever been the partisans of the unhappy Queen, and, when she arrived in England in June, she met with a reception which could only compare with that which greeted Charles II. on the restoration of the Monarchy in 1660. So, also, when the withdrawal of the Bill was announced,

---

* *Annual Register*, 1820, "Chronicle," 51. Alison, *History of Europe*, 1815-1852, ii. 424.

London was illuminated on three successive nights, and, the results of the inquiry being forgotten, a universal joy manifested itself through the whole country, which almost equalled the unbounded enthusiasm displayed after the fall of Napoleon.

During this trying time, the Battalions of the Brigade quartered in the Metropolis formed the main force for the repression of disorder, and arrangements of the most comprehensive nature were made to prevent an outbreak that was almost hourly expected. A detachment of 350 rank and file was furnished daily, from the 17th of August, for the protection of the House of Lords. For this purpose, 50 men were added to the Tylt, a guard of 50 men was stationed during the trial, in the Cotton Yard behind Westminster Palace, the piquet at Carlton Palace was permanently posted, and a force was held as a reserve in St. James's Park. The guard at the British Museum was doubled, the Tower Battalion was prepared to supply 200 men at any moment, on the requisition of the Lord Mayor, while a Captain's piquet of 100 rank and file was kept constantly ready at each of the three principal West-end barracks—the King's Mews, Knightsbridge, and Portman Street. The usual half-yearly change of quarters took place on the 26th of August, when the 1st Battalion Coldstream proceeded from Windsor to the Tower, and the 2nd Battalion from Portman Street to Knightsbridge barracks, and to that part of Upper Westminster contiguous thereto. The military arrangements made for the trial were sometimes modified during its procedure, now being reduced and again increased. During October, a guard was placed in Westminster Hall, and the Bank piquet remained on duty for twenty-four hours. These precautions were finally discontinued on the 15th of November, and the ordinary leave granted to Officers; though we find, on the 28th, riots were again apprehended, and the 1st Battalion was directed to attend to the Lord Mayor's requisition to the extent of 300 men.

The violence of popular excitement soon subsides, and, the inquiry over, the Queen's partisans lost interest in her cause. The King, too, became more popular with the mob, and it was possible to fix a date for his Coronation. This great event was solemnized upon the 19th of July, 1821, with all the magnificent pomp and quaint ceremonial of past ages, and is more than usually interesting in that it was carefully conducted upon ancient models, and that it is the last pageant of its kind which is ever likely to be seen in England. The Royal procession, in gorgeous and mediæval array, moved from Westminster Hall to the Abbey by a covered platform, 1500 feet long, by 25 broad, fitted with a lower edging three feet wide on each side, and returned by the same route, after the religious ceremony was concluded. The whole of the Foot Guards (except the 1st Battalion Third Guards) were present (the 2nd Battalion Coldstream having been brought up from Windsor for the purpose), and were commanded by Colonel Hon. H. Brand, Lieut.-Colonel of the Regiment. The two Grenadier companies of the Coldstream were stationed in the Abbey with the State Colours. The platform was lined throughout by 1500 men standing in single file on each side, on the lower portions just mentioned. They were divided into three divisions, each under a Field-Officer, with a part of the bands, drums, etc. Forty Officers and 1141 men were employed in furnishing strong piquets, extra guards, and Guards of Honour, in strengthening the public duties, and in patrolling the neighbourhood of Westminster. A portion of the streets was also lined, the Coldstream having its right at the west gate of the Abbey, and extending towards Westminster Hall. The troops got into position at one o'clock in the night preceding the ceremony; and a large force of cavalry, aided by Yeomanry, the Light Horse Volunteers, and the Honourable Artillery Company, were also present under Major-General Lord Edward Somerset, and furnished patrols throughout the Metropolis. These ample precautions were rendered necessary by the apprehension of a riot; for the Queen, whose application to be crowned had been refused, expressed a determination, nevertheless, to appear in person, and serious disturbances were expected to be the result. To such an extent did the panic spread, that, we are told, places to see the procession, which had been selling for ten guineas, were to be had, on the morning of the ceremony, for half a crown.*

The following General Order was published on the day after the Coronation :—

"The Commander-in-Chief has received the King's gracious command to express to the troops employed yesterday in aid of the arrangements for the Coronation, His Majesty's thanks for the orderly, soldierlike, and

---

* Alison, *History of Europe*, 1815–1852, ii. 484. For a full account of the Coronation of King George IV., see *Annual Register*, 1821, "Appendix to Chronicle," p. 324, etc.

exemplary conduct which they have evinced upon the occasion. The Commander-in-Chief has received the King's further command, through the Secretary of State, to convey to the Light Horse, His Majesty's thanks for their services upon the same occasion, and his full sense and approbation of the loyalty and zeal which they have manifested in the offer of them."

Next day, on the appointment of Colonel Brand, C.B., to the rank of Major-General, Colonel Woodford, who had commanded the Coldstream Battalion at Waterloo, became Lieut.-Colonel of the Regiment, and Colonel Macdonell, C.B., promoted Major, was posted to the command of the 2nd Battalion.

On the 3rd of September, the sum of £665 was distributed among the Non-commissioned officers and men of the Brigade who had taken part in the King's Coronation, under the name of "Platform money." The 6 Sergeants-Major received each 14s. 1½d.; 226 Sergeants, 7s. 1½d.; 225 Corporals, 4s. 8¾d.; and 3575 Drummers and Privates, 2s. 11¼d. A little more than £100 was allotted per Battalion, the Coldstream receiving £212 2s. 1½d.

It seems unnecessary to record the various and numerous reviews that have at all times taken place; it would be monotonous to do so, and little interest would thereby be afforded. For the most part, therefore, they will be omitted. It was usual upon these and other occasions, for the inspecting Officer to record publicly his opinion of the state of the troops reviewed; thus very many testimonials exist—speaking of the efficiency which has ever distinguished the Coldstream, and thanking the Officers and men for their zeal and exertions—written by order of the Sovereign, the Commander-in-Chief, the Colonel of the Regiment, the Lieut.-Colonel, Generals under whom a Battalion happened to be serving, and also giving messages from foreign Princes. These communications to the Regiment have also been generally omitted, as their number renders it difficult to reproduce them, and as their repetition would be tedious..

It has been already mentioned that a Battalion of the Foot Guards was sent to Dublin at the end of 1821. The step was rendered advisable by the increasing trouble which afflicted Ireland, where discontent prevailed, and where the recent currency laws had reduced the value of agricultural produce, on which alone the peasants had to depend. Each Battalion was kept there for a year, the change being made in the summer. It became the turn of the 1st Battalion Coldstream to proceed to Dublin in July, 1823, and on the 25th the troops were conveyed in canal boats from Paddington on the road to Liverpool, whence they were sent to their destination. The Lieut.-Colonel of the Regiment thus published his opinion on the manner in which the start was effected from London:—

"*Regimental Order, July* 25, 1823. Colonel Woodford desires to express the satisfaction he felt at witnessing the highly creditable manner in which the 1st Battalion turned out for the embarkation this morning; he has particularly to notice the sobriety of the men, and the activity and propriety with which the Non-commissioned officers performed their duties, and he has made a favourable report to H.R.H. the Duke of York on the subject."

During their stay in Ireland, this Battalion gained the unqualified approbation and praise of the Lieut.-General, the Commander of the Forces, and of the Major-General commanding the District; and this will be best shown by giving two orders issued in Dublin. The first appeared in Regimental Orders of February 19, 1824:

"*Garrison Orders, Dublin, January* 24, 1824. Major-General Sir C. Grant has great pleasure in expressing to the garrison of Dublin, the satisfaction the Lieutenant-General Commanding the Forces experienced yesterday in making the inspection of the Coldstream Guards. The order, cleanliness, and regularity which were so observable, reflect much credit on Lieut.-Colonel Milman and the Officers of this distinguished corps, generally, and the great attention which has been paid to that essential branch of interior economy. As all Commanding Officers in Garrison were present at this inspection, they have had an opportunity of seeing how much can be done, even in very indifferent barracks, by a little care and attention. The Major-General will expect to find all the barracks of the Garrison of Dublin in the same creditable state as those of the Coldstream Guards."

The second was published as follows:—

"*Regimental Order, August* 7, 1824. Colonel Woodford has great pleasure in communicating to the 2nd Battalion, the General Order issued in Dublin, so flattering to the Officers, Non-commissioned officers, and men of the 1st Battalion."

"*General Order, Adjutant-General's Office, Dublin, August* 2, 1824. The 1st Battalion of the Coldstream Guards being on the point of embarkation to return to England, Lieut.-General Lord Combermere feels he cannot in too strong terms, express his approbation of the good conduct and discipline of this fine Battalion, during the time it has been employed in this command. The Lieutenant-General could not but be highly gratified in his recent inspection of the Battalion, by the soldierlike appearance, steadiness, and extreme precision with which the movements were executed. The Battalion has no less claim to merit for the extreme order and regularity which prevail in the barracks, affording ample proof of excellent interior arrangement, unremitting attention on the part of all ranks, and of the zeal and ability with which the command is conducted. In conveying his best thanks to the Battalion generally, Lord Combermere feels desirous to express particularly to Colonel Sir H. Bouverie, the sense he entertains of his zeal and exertion in the performance of every point of duty, and especially during the period he had the superintendence and command of this Garrison."

The Duke of York recorded his appreciation of the conduct of the Battalion, by causing a letter, dated August 12th, to be addressed to Colonel Woodford, which was published in Regimental Orders of the 14th:—

"H.R.H. has learnt with great satisfaction from your letter, as well as from the reports from Ireland, that the conduct of the 1st Battalion of the Coldstream has received the unqualified approbation of the Commander of the Forces, which would offer a confirmation, if any had been necessary, of the favourable opinion he has always entertained of the discipline, and meritorious discharge of every duty."

Alterations in the Regimental Hospital in Vincent Square, established in 1814, were completed in September, 1823, and the building was re-occupied on the 9th; quarters were provided therein for a Medical Officer, under whose care the recruits of the Regiment (then at the Recruit House in London) were also placed.* About the same time, 1824, another Medical Officer took up his residence in barracks, and was made specially responsible for the men, women, and children of the Battalion stationed there. After an inspection made by the Duke of Cambridge, the Colonel of the Regiment, an order was published, dated August 10, 1825, expressing to Dr. Whymper and the Medical Officers His Royal Highness' satisfaction and pleasure at the perfect state, regularity, comfort, and cleanliness of the Regimental Hospital.†

A boat-race against time was got up in 1824, the conditions being, that "six Officers of the Guards belonging to aquatic

* *Regimental Order*, Aug. 16, 1824. † See Appendix No. VII.

clubs" should row in a six-oared wherry from Oxford to Westminster Bridge in sixteen consecutive hours, the crew to choose their own coxwain. The distance is 118 miles; there were no outriggers in those days, and many locks intervene and obstruct the course to be rowed over, which, however, on application to the Thames Commissioners, were kept in readiness to let the boat through without delay. An attempt had previously been made to perform the same feat in seventeen hours, by Lord Newry (the late Lord Kilmorey), with a crew selected by himself from among his own people, but it failed. The present match was looked forward to with considerable interest, and large sums of money were laid upon the event. Captain Short (Coldstream Guards) seems to have been captain of the boat, the other oars being Captains Gordon-Douglas (afterwards Lord Penrhyn), and H. S. Blane (Grenadier Guards), and Captains G. F. H. Hudson, G. D. Standen, and Hon. J. C. Westenra (Third Guards). The wherry left Oxford at 3 a.m. on the 14th of May, and, reaching Bolter's Lock at 11.30, Windsor Bridge at 1 p.m., Teddington Lock at 5.30, Putney Bridge at 6, and Battersea Bridge at 6.30, arrived at Westminster Bridge, at 6.45, "amidst the acclamations of thousands of spectators," with just a quarter of an hour to spare. "They were assisted out of the boat, carried on shore, and put to bed." The average rate was about seven and a half miles an hour, counting stoppages for refreshment and those occasioned by going through the locks, and the feat was remarkable, considering the class of boat that existed at that time. We are told, moreover, that all the crew were in a state of great exhaustion at the conclusion of the race, and that one or two could not stand without support.*

On the 16th of July, 1825, Major-General Woodford, promoted to that rank on May 25th, retired from the command of the Regiment, and was succeeded by Colonel Macdonell, Sir H. Bouverie having also been appointed a General Officer in May. Thereupon Colonel Hamilton became Senior Major (commanding the 1st Battalion), and Colonel Raikes, Junior Major (2nd Battalion).†

---

* *Annual Register*, 1824, "Chronicle," p. 59.

† The distinction between the First and Second Majors, which existed in Regiments of Foot Guards, was abolished by authority, dated, September 11, 1821 (MacKinnon, *Origin and Services of the Coldstream Guards*, ii. 503).

MUSKETEER 1669.

FIRST PART OF THE LONG EUROPEAN PEACE.

In July, 1825, the Regiment contained the following Officers:—

Colonel.—Field-Marshal H.R.H. the Duke of Cambridge, K.G., G.C.B., etc.
Lieutenant-Colonel.—Colonel J. Macdonell, C.B.
Majors.—Colonels J. Hamilton; and W. H. Raikes.
Captains.—Lieut.-Colonels F. Milman; T. Barrow; D. MacKinnon; and H. Dawkins; (*Mounted*).
    Colonel Sir R. Arbuthnot, K.C.B.; Lieut.-Colonel Sir W. Gomm, K.C.B.; Colonel Waters, C.B.; Lieut.-Colonels T. Steele; J. Fremantle, C.B.; W. Walton; A. Wedderburn; C. Shawe; G. Bowles; C. Bentinck; G. FitzClarence; F. Russell.
Lieutenants.—Major J. S. Cowell; Captains J. Drummond; C. Girardot; T. Chaplin; H. Salwey; Hon. J. Forbes; A. Cuyler; W. Kortright; H. Armytage; H. Gooch; T. Powys; H. Bentinck (Adjutant); F. Shawe; F. Buller; J. Montagu; H. Vane; R. Bowen; C. Short; J. Hall; Hon. H. Dundas; W. Cornwall; Hon. W. Graves; H. Murray; B. Broadhead.
Ensigns.—Lieutenants C. Hay; G. Bentinck; W. Northey (Adjutant); J. D. Rawdon; Hon. T. Ashburnham; Hon. E. Erskine; W. J. Codrington; E. D. Wigram; St. J. Dent; Hon. H. Fane; Hon. J. Hope; W. Cotton; Hon. A. Upton; F. Paget; B. Manningham; E. B. Wilbraham; Lord M. W. Graham.
Quartermasters.—T. Dwelly and B. Selway.
Surgeon-Major.—J. Simpson. *Battalion Surgeons.*—W. Whymper, M.D., and T. Maynard. *Assistant Surgeons.*—G. Smith and F. Gilder.
Solicitor.—W. G. Carter, Esq.

The year 1826 was one of distress in England, which led to considerable disorder, especially in the manufacturing parts of Lancashire. The workmen, believing that the introduction of machinery, then beginning to be used, was the cause of their sufferings, committed many acts of outrage, and, during the last week of April, a large amount of property was destroyed by riotous mobs in that county. In order to strengthen the military force required to suppress these disturbances, the 2nd Battalion Coldstream and the 1st Battalion Third Guards proceeded to Manchester (by canal from Paddington) on the 1st and 2nd of May respectively. The 2nd Battalion were stationed there until the end of July, when they were sent to Dublin to relieve the 2nd Battalion Grenadiers, which, on reaching Liverpool, were ordered to remain in the Northern District.

On leaving this District, the following letter was addressed by the Lieut.-General Commanding (Sir J. Byng) to the Commanding

Officer, 2nd Battalion Coldstream, dated July 23rd, and published in Regimental Orders, August 8th:—

"The Battalion of Coldstream Guards under your command, being on the point of its departure for Ireland, Sir John Byng thinks it but due to the Officers and men, to notice to them the very creditable reports which have reached him of the orderly and soldierlike conduct of the Battalion during the time it has been stationed at Manchester—testimonials which, joined to what he has observed himself when on the spot, are the more gratifying to the Lieutenant-General, because, whilst they afford him an opportunity of thanking them for their useful services in the District under his orders, another occasion presents itself of recording his unqualified approbation of a corps which so highly distinguished itself under his command at the Battle of Waterloo; and for whose welfare and high character he must ever feel sincerely interested. In communicating the above to you, the Lieutenant-General requests you will be so good to make it known to the Battalion in such manner as you may judge proper."

Colonel Raikes having retired from the service, June 21, 1826, Colonel MacKinnon became Junior Major, commanding the 2nd Battalion.

It was not until towards the end of the year that the two Battalions of Guards quartered in Lancashire were brought back to London, and then a fresh duty awaited the Brigade. There was trouble between Spain and Portugal, and the Government determined to support the latter Power. The resolution to do so, was hastily formed or tardily published, and on the same day that it was announced in Parliament (December 11th), orders were issued for six companies of the 1st Grenadiers and of the 2nd Battalion Third Guards, made up to 84 rank and file each, to be held in readiness for foreign service; the Brigade so formed, to be commanded by Major-General Sir. H. Bouverie (late of the Coldstream). The expedition, numbering 5000 men, under Sir H. Clinton, started immediately afterwards, and, before Christmas, the troops began to land at Lisbon. As no portion of the Coldstream took part in this service, it is unnecessary to make any further allusion to it in this volume, except to note that it lasted more than a year, and that the two Battalions did not return home until the spring of 1828.

The death of the Duke of York, January 5, 1827, brought to a close the career of an able military administrator who, for twenty-one years of his early life (1784–1805), had been Colonel of the

Coldstream Guards. His unremitting devotion to the best interests of the service, during a period of thirty-two years (broken by a short interval only), in which he served as Commander-in-Chief (1795–1827), earned for him an enduring fame in the annals of the country. When he first was entrusted with this high office, the British army was still afflicted by that inefficiency which caused disaster in North America, and brought ruin and disgrace upon our arms; but, at the end of his life, greatly owing to his vigour and ability, this lamentable state of things was completely changed, and victory and glory once more shone upon our banners.

"It is not on account of his early services," wrote Sir Walter Scott, "that we now venture to bring forward the late Duke of York's claims to the perpetual gratitude of his country. It is as the reformer and regenerator of the British army, which he brought, from a state nearly allied to general contempt, to such a pitch of excellence, that we may, without much hesitation, claim for them an equality with, if not a superiority over, any troops in Europe." *

At the funeral, which took place at Windsor, the Brigade was represented by a force of about 1400 Officers and men, of whom the 1st Battalion Coldstream furnished 12 Officers and 269 Non-commissioned officers and men.

In the summer of this year, the 2nd Battalion returned from Ireland, and was quartered in Portman Street, the 1st Battalion being stationed in King's Mews barracks (August 1st).

Next year, the 1st Battalion marched to Manchester (October 1st),† and remained there for ten months, when they were sent to Dublin, by Liverpool (July, 1829), for a year's service in Ireland, returning to London (Portman Street) in August, 1830. During this period, the Battalion continued to receive the highest commendation for the excellent discipline and good conduct that prevailed among all ranks, and the following extract from Major-General Dalbiac's confidential report, dated May 6th, and sent by order of the Commander-in-Chief (Lord Hill) to the Lieut.-Colonel, for the information of the Colonel of the Regiment, Field-Marshal H.R.H. the Duke of Cambridge, will be read with interest:—

* *Annual Register*, 1827, "History and Biography," p. 460.
† The following Regimental Order was published upon this occasion, dated 20th: "The Commanding Officer of the Regiment cannot withhold his great satisfaction at the reports made to him of the exemplary conduct of the 1st Battalion on the march from London to Manchester."

"It is impossible to speak in terms too commendable of the good order, the interior economy, and the general efficiency of the 1st Battalion Coldstream Guards, which I consider to be a corps of the first value. The body of men is particularly good; the Battalion thoroughly instructed in its duties in garrison and in the field; the conduct of the men very exemplary. The Commanding Officers have severally afforded me much valuable assistance in upholding the discipline of the Garrison." *

In this connection, a Battalion Order of February 11th, published in Dublin, may also be quoted:—

"In consequence of the diminution in the list of defaulters, Lieut.-Colonel Fremantle requests that Officers will set at liberty the defaulters in their respective companies."

On May 15, 1829, Colonel Hamilton having retired, Colonel MacKinnon became Senior Major (1st Battalion), and Colonel Sir W. Gomm was promoted Junior Major (2nd Battalion).

It should be noted here, that, about this time, a mistake began to creep in with respect to the title of the Regiment, which, being placed in the Army List between the First, or Grenadier, and the Third Regiment of Foot Guards, was occasionally described as the "Second Foot Guards." In December, 1829, the Lieut.-Colonel (Colonel Macdonell) protested against this innovation; and, in reply, Sir H. Hardinge, then Secretary at War, had it stopped, and regretted that a clerical error should have accidentally been made.†

Some changes had been made in the uniform of the Officers of

* Deputy Adjutant-General, Horse Guards, to Colonel Macdonell, July 5, 1830. It may be stated that the Regimental standard of height for recruits, was fixed at 5 ft. 9 in. in the autumn of 1828, and was raised to 5 ft. 10 in. three months later.

† There is evidence to show that when the standing army was in its infancy, the designation "Second" instead of "Coldstream" Guards was, upon a few occasions, used in official documents; but this happened through inadvertence, and the Regiment invariably protested against this name, basing the objection on the origin of the corps and its services at the Restoration of King Charles II. The military authorities acquiesced in this protest, and admitted the validity of the objection. Hence the motto "Nulli Secundus" was used; and the motto soon took a wider meaning than is merely expressed by Regimental succession in the army roll. While on this subject, it will not be amiss to note that the modern ungrammatical appellation of "Coldstreams" is incorrect. The Regiment is the "Coldstream," and the men are called "Coldstreamers." Soldiers who handle grenades or fusils may be known as Grenadiers or Fusiliers; but those who are called after one town (Coldstream), cannot be designated by the plural of that town. One or two old documents, dated about 1689, contain the word "Coldstreams." The rest are invariably correct; but if language was, in a very few instances, defective at that period, it might surely be corrected in the present day.

the Brigade after 1815, especially in the beginning of the reign of George IV.; but a more complete and permanent change began to be adopted in the year 1830, and was not finally effected until 1834. It may be sufficient to state here, that blue trousers with gold lace, those of Oxford grey mixture with the red stripe (for winter wear), and the present gold and crimson sashes were then introduced. The gorget, the white pantaloons, or breeches and stockings (worn in the evening), and the cap-lines and tassels of Non-commissioned officers were discontinued; and the bearskin cap became the head-dress of the whole Regiment instead of the Grenadier company only, as was formerly the case. The Rose—one of the distinctive badges of the Coldstream, which has now, unfortunately, entirely disappeared from the uniform of Officers, though still happily to be seen on that belonging to Non-commissioned officers and men—was then retained on the epaulettes, and was not removed until a quarter of a century later. Further, a braided great-coat was allotted to Officers of the Brigade, of the same pattern for the three Regiments, to distinguish them from the Line. Lastly, Field-Officers of the Guards were ordered by the King (*Brigade Order*, March 2, 1831) to wear the same sword belt, as that of a General Officer. Uniform, at that time, seems to have been worn in out-quarters more frequently than is customary at present; and orders exist, which show that Officers stationed in Dublin, were not allowed to appear in plain clothes, unless going to some distance in the country, and remaining absent all night from their quarters. On the other hand, there was no special mess-dress; but uniform at mess was nevertheless the rule, and Officers did not dine in barracks in plain clothes.

The death of George IV. occurred on June 26, 1830, and William IV. ascended the Throne. The funeral of the late King took place at Windsor, and was attended by the 2nd Coldstream (the 1st Battalion was in Dublin). Upon this occasion an order was issued intimating that, "Colonel Macdonell has been honoured by His Majesty's commands to communicate to the 2nd Battalion, in the strongest possible terms, his approbation of their conduct during the ceremonial of the Funeral of His late Majesty King George IV.," adding that "the King has further directed Colonel Macdonell to say that it affords him the greatest pleasure thus to express his satisfaction, on the first opportunity he has had of seeing them since his accession to the Throne." An order couched in similar terms was addressed to that part of the Brigade, employed in the ceremonial just mentioned, viz. 1st Grenadiers, quartered at Windsor, 100 men each from the 2nd and 3rd Grenadiers, the 2nd Coldstream, and the 1st Battalion Third Guards.

During the early years of his reign, William IV. frequently inspected the Foot Guards. The 2nd Battalion Coldstream was the first reviewed (July 19th), and on the same day, the King granted the Regiment the privilege of receiving His Majesty with the Coldstream March instead of the National Anthem. This was communicated by the following Regimental Order:—

"Colonel Macdonell has received His Majesty's commands to communicate to the Officers, Non-commissioned officers and men, his entire satisfaction with their appearance this morning. His Majesty has been further pleased to command that hereafter, when he is received by either Battalion of the Regiment, the band is to play the Coldstream Regimental March instead of 'God save the King.'" *

On the same day, the King commanded that the Field-Officer in Brigade Waiting, accompanied by the Adjutant in Waiting, and an Orderly Sergeant from each Regiment of Foot Guards, should attend His Majesty's carriage on State occasions. The former practice was that the Field-Officer attended the Sovereign, and had a place in a Royal carriage assigned to him.

A few days later the members of the Nulli Secundus Club were honoured by an invitation to dine with His Majesty (July 31st). Upon this occasion, the King was pleased to express the attachment which he felt, especially, for the Coldstream Guards, and the sincere interest he took in the continued prosperity of the Nulli Secundus Club, and he intimated it to be his intention to receive the members at dinner every year.†

---

* The Coldstream March is taken from Mozart's *Nozze di Figaro* ("*Non più Andrai*"), and it used to be called "The Duke of York's March." About fifty years ago, "The Milanollo" was introduced as a Regimental Quick March.

A like privilege to play their Regimental Marches instead of the National Anthem, when receiving His Majesty, was also granted (July 19th) to the other two Regiments of Foot Guards. Two Battalions of the Grenadiers were inspected by the King on July 22nd, when it was ordered that the spears of their Colours should be surmounted by a wreath of oak leaves, and that the whole of the Officers and men of these Battalions, and of the detachments from the Brigade keeping the ground, should wear laurel in their caps, in compliment to the Duke of Wellington, it being the anniversary of the battle of Salamanca.

† See Appendix No. VIII.

On the 22nd of July, Colonel Macdonell, having been promoted Major-General, was succeeded in the command of the Regiment by Colonel MacKinnon; thereupon Colonel Sir. W. Gomm became Senior Major (1st Battalion), and Colonel Milman, Junior Major (2nd Battalion).

The period 1829-1832, will ever be memorable in English history as one of great trouble, anxiety, and difficulty. There was considerable distress among the working classes, especially in 1829,—due, according to some writers, to the currency laws which then came into operation.* But besides this, and far more important, a wave of agitation swept over the face of the country with a terrific force, unknown since the great Rebellion. Violent riots and great disorder were of frequent occurrence; and civil war, though happily it never broke out, was imminent, and was believed by some to be inevitable. During this period, Catholic Emancipation was carried and Reform was passed; the landmarks of the then existing British Constitution were obliterated, and the political principles, which were held by many to be the basis of national prosperity, were uprooted. The death of George IV. at this critical juncture, contributed in no small degree to fan the flames of discontent, and to produce the uncompromising changes in the government of the country, which were effected in 1832. But events abroad also served to shape the destinies of England; for, added to the trouble at home, Europe, too, was convulsed by mighty disturbances, which shook to their foundations some of the principal Continental nations, and influenced the course of agitation in this country. Belgium, at that time subject to the Crown of Holland, rebelled, declared her independence, and succeeded in establishing herself as a separate Monarchy under the rule of a Prince of Saxe-Coburg, who assumed the title of King Leopold I.† In France the spirit of revolution, vainly smothered in 1815, and ignorantly dealt with by the Bourbons, again reared its head, and Charles X. was hurled from his throne. The ancient Monarchy of France was finally and for ever extinguished, and a Citizen-King, surrounded by Republican institutions, was invited

* Alison's *History of Europe*, 1815-52, iv. 214, etc.

† King Leopold I. was a near relation of our Royal Family, being uncle of Queen Victoria, brother of the Duchess of Kent. His first wife, moreover, was Charlotte, only child of George IV., by his Queen, Caroline. Had this Princess lived, she would have become Queen of England, and her husband, like his nephew subsequently became, would have been Prince Consort.

to reign by the favour of the Garde Nationale—the armed representatives of the populace. The insurrection, that succeeded in vesting Louis-Philippe with a semblance of Royal power, and that effectually tore to shreds the constitution fixed by the Allies in 1815, began in Paris on the 26th of July, 1830, just two days after the dissolution of Parliament in London. The general election took place about a month later; and in the excited state of men's minds, when widespread sympathy was felt and expressed for the aspirations of the Orleanist faction in France, the result could not but reflect the movement that was carried on there, and give impetus to an agitation which had already acquired considerable strength.

Parliament opened on the 26th of October, and three weeks later, on the fall of the administration of the Duke of Wellington, Lord Grey was called to office. The winter passed gloomily, and a wild spirit of revolt was abroad. The southern counties around London were "in a state of open insurrection;" the agitators, frequently referring to events in Belgium and France, inflamed the passions of the people; outrages and excesses were committed, and so great was the consternation created by the fear of disorder, that the King's visit to the city (November 9th) had to be given up. It is unnecessary to describe the various vicissitudes which attended the great struggle for Reform. Suffice it to say that the country continued to be the prey to an increasing agitation, unparalleled in modern British history, and that the Bill was finally passed into law by a large majority, June 7, 1832, because those that opposed it were intimidated into silence, believing that further resistance would end by plunging the nation into the abyss of civil war.

The army, taking no part in the effervescence that seethed around, was occupied in the uncongenial duty of preserving the public peace, wherever it was disturbed. In London, a system of Metropolitan Police had just been organized (1829), to replace the watchmen, who up to that time were responsible for good order and for the prevention of crime. The new force had only come into existence, nor was it sufficiently strong to cope with the serious emergency that had arisen. The Brigade, therefore, was frequently held in readiness to aid the civil power, and in November, 1830, all Officers were recalled from leave, while Non-commissioned officers and men on furlough were ordered to rejoin their corps without delay. A detachment of two Subalterns and fifty-seven men were stationed at North Hyde, furnished by each Battalion in turn, the reliefs being made fortnightly, until March 1, 1831, when it was found by the 1st Battalion Coldstream, who proceeded to Windsor on that date.*

The Coronation of the King and Queen took place in Westminster Abbey, September 8, 1831, the day after the Reform Bill had passed the committee stage in the Commons. The ceremony was sufficiently magnificent, but was shorn of much of its ancient splendour, and, in accordance with the economy of the age, His Majesty was prevented from giving the usual Coronation Banquet in Westminster Hall.† The Brigade lined the streets in the vicinity, the 1st and 2nd Battalions Grenadiers and the 1st Scots Fusilier Guards ‡ occupying the west side, the 1st and the 2nd Battalions Coldstream—a portion of which had been brought from Windsor—and the 2nd Scots Fusiliers, the east side, the left of the Coldstream being posted near the Abbey. Piquets were also held in readiness in case of disorder, which happily did not occur. The troops, in review order, wearing white trousers, and Officers in gold sashes, were in position at 7 a.m. The *largesse* of "Platform money" was not distributed upon this occasion, but an allowance of one shilling, to each Non-commissioned officer and private under arms, was made for refreshments, half of which was spent, the remainder being given to the men in the evening.§

The pleasures of political agitation were somewhat marred, and the intensity of the strife was perhaps blunted, by the first appearance in England of the plague of cholera, which occurred

---

* On November 10th, an allowance of ninepence daily per man was made for the purchase of refreshments to the troops assembled on piquet duty, in and near the metropolis. It was ordered that this money should not be spent on spirituous liquors. The following 1st Battalion Order, dated June 7, 1831, was issued: "The Commanding Officer has much satisfaction in making known to the Battalion a communication he has received from the Mayor of Windsor, expressive of the obligation the civil authorities feel themselves under, for the assistance afforded by several soldiers in securing offenders against the public peace during the past week, and particularly on Saturday last."

† For a full description of this Coronation, see *Annual Register*, 1831, "Chronicle," p. 140, etc.

‡ The Third Guards were called by their new title, Scots Fusilier-Guards, in Orders, dated, June 24, 1831.

§ Present at the Coronation, and drawing the shilling: 1st Battalion Coldstream—27 sergeants, 19 drummers, and 526 rank and file; 2nd Battalion Coldstream—14 sergeants, 12 drummers, 266 rank and file.

towards the end of 1831. This terrible disease, having broken out in Bengal in 1817, spread to Persia in 1823, where it remained in a more or less dormant state, until 1830, when it revived, and extended rapidly through Russia, into Austria, and North Germany. In spite of severe quarantine regulations, cases of this fatal illness were reported in Sunderland on October 26, 1831; and before the end of the year many persons were attacked, and succumbed to its violence, in the north of England and in Scotland.

In February, it appeared in the port of London, and from thence it spread through every part of the kingdom, and continued its ravages into Ireland. The panic created by this unknown epidemic was great. Medical men were naturally at a loss to understand, much more at a loss to treat effectively, the new disorder; but, though severe, it was everywhere less fatal than preconceived notions had anticipated, and, when it gradually disappeared in the autumn, surprise seems to have been general that so much apprehension had been entertained.*

The results of cholera were not, however, unimportant, for the visitation served to introduce more sanitary and cleanly habits among the people, and to put an end to the billeting system and to overcrowding in military barracks. Every precaution was naturally taken to preserve the health of the troops, and to guard them against infection. The 2nd Battalion, being at the Tower, in a dangerous quarter, stringent orders were issued to secure this object. Frequent medical inspections took place, certain districts were placed out of bounds, drunken men were isolated until visited by the Surgeon, the water supply was not neglected, and the men were "earnestly desired to report themselves directly they felt unwell, as it is found when remedies are applied in time fatal results seldom ensue." The order (dated March 21, 1832) added that—

"the Commanding Officer has great pleasure in observing the orderly behaviour of the men in general during the last week, and he trusts that by abstaining from absence from barracks, drunkenness, and other excesses, and a strict compliance with the above regulations, they will continue to second his efforts as much as possible, to keep the barracks free from disease."

In February, moreover, Warley was converted into a Depôt for

* *Annual Register*, 1831, "History of Europe," p. 298; *ibid.*, 1832, p. 304.

all Brigade recruits, who were taken from the Recruit House in London; and the Royal Waggon Train, being removed from Croydon, the barracks there, were placed at the disposal of the Foot Guards for the occupation of those convalescents or weakly men, who were unable to perform the usual military duties in town. During the same month, married soldiers and others were sent to Croydon, Chatham, and Brighton—at which latter place there was then accommodation for 336 men. In March, also, certain houses in Hanley Road, Hornsey, were hired for a year, fit to receive five Officers and 463 men. New barracks were constructed, or the old ones improved, and, in November, 1833, the King's Mews were changed into St. George's barracks,* and the Recruit House into the present old wing of Wellington barracks, called at that time, for a few months only, Westminster barracks. On March 1, 1834, the Brigade occupied the following quarters: Grenadier Guards—1st Battalion, Tower; 2nd Battalion, Portman Street; 3rd Battalion, Wellington (Westminster) barracks: Coldstream Guards — 1st Battalion, Windsor; 2nd Battalion, Knightsbridge, Kensington, and the Magazine barracks: Scots Fusilier Guards—1st Battalion, St. George's barracks; 2nd Battalion, Dublin.

It may be stated here, that a company was also stationed in Buckingham House, usually found by the Battalion occupying Knightsbridge, and that the latter barracks were given up in May, 1836, and St. John's Wood substituted for them. The Brigade continued to occupy these West-end quarters until the Crimean war broke out—that is, Portman Street, St. George's, and Wellington barracks accommodated one Battalion each, while the fourth Battalion was divided into detachments, the head-quarters and three or four companies being in St. John's Wood, the remainder in Kensington, the Magazine, Buckingham Palace, and St. George's or Wellington barracks.

In July, 1832, the 2nd Battalion proceeded to Dublin by Bristol, returning to London in the following summer. Ireland was then passing through one of the phases of popular discontent and resistance to law so common in her history, and which have for so long troubled the government of that island. The antitithe agitation was then in full swing, and was accompanied by

* These barracks are now smaller than they were then, a portion having been given up to increase the National Gallery.

incidents very similar to those that occurred during the recent anti-rent struggle, with which we are familiar. As a means of pacifying the disturbed districts, troops were quartered in them, just as was done in 1880. The 2nd Battalion furnished three companies for this duty during the latter end of October, when it appears that this force, under the command of Lieut.-Colonel Hon. J. Forbes, was stationed at Leighlin Bridge, in Carlow, and was quartered there for a fortnight. The Battalion gained the approbation of the military authorities in Dublin, shown by two orders (dated May 23 and August 12, 1833), testifying to the high opinion entertained by them of the "exemplary conduct," and of the discipline of the corps whilst serving in Ireland.

The next two years passed without much incident until 1836, when the Regiment was put into mourning by the unexpected death of the Lieut.-Colonel (Colonel MacKinnon), who, having served in the Coldstream throughout the whole of his military career, from the early age of fourteen to the day of his death, in every rank from Ensign to Lieut.-Colonel, through the Peninsular war and at Waterloo, where he was wounded, may be considered as an Officer peculiarly belonging to the Regiment.* In spite of illness, he remained at his post until the middle of June, when he obtained a year's leave; but he was unable to avail himself of it, for a few days later, on the 22nd, he died, only forty-six years of age, respected alike by the Officers and the men. The public exercises of the Regiment were immediately suspended till after the interment of the Commanding Officer, and, on the 8th of July, the following order was promulgated by Colonel Sir W. Gomm, who succeeded him, on the occasion of an inspection of the two Battalions by Lord Hill, the Commander-in-Chief:—

"The Lieutenant-Colonel feels much pride in communicating to Colonel Milman, Colonel Fremantle,† and the Officers and men of both Battalions of the Coldstream, the marked satisfaction expressed by the General Commanding-in-Chief at the high soldierlike appearance, steadiness under arms, and precision of movement, which they both displayed at the inspection — qualities pronounced by Lord Hill to be so eminently characteristic at all times of the Corps to which they belong. The

---

* Colonel MacKinnon is the author of the *Origin and Services of the Coldstream Guards*, a work remarkable for its research in the early history of the British army.

† Upon the death of Colonel MacKinnon, Colonel Milman became Senior Major (1st Battalion), and Colonel Fremantle was promoted Junior Major (2nd Battalion).

Lieutenant-Colonel, while imparting these gratifying sentiments of Lord Hill to the Regiment, would be greatly wanting in what he feels to be due to his Lordship and to the Corps at large, to the memory no less of its late distinguished Commanding Officer, did he fail to communicate, at the same time, the strong expression of condolence and regret with which Lord Hill adverted to the loss freshly sustained by the Regiment, and the Army in general, in the death of Colonel MacKinnon—a regret which Lord Hill felt assured was so largely and so duly shared with him by all ranks and orders of the Regiment."

Sir W. Gomm did not long retain the command of the Regiment; but, as will be seen, he returned to the Coldstream a quarter of a century after he had left it, when he was appointed Colonel of the Regiment. Becoming Major-General, the Lieut.-Colonelcy devolved upon Colonel Milman, and Colonels Fremantle and Walton succeeded as Senior and Junior Majors respectively (January 10, 1837).

The Coldstream now stood—

Colonel.—Field-Marshal H.R.H. the Duke of Cambridge, K.G., etc.
Lieut.-Colonel.—Colonel F. Milman.
Majors.—Colonels J. Fremantle, C.B.; and W. Walton.
Captains.—Lieut.-Colonels A. Wedderburn; C. Shawe; G. Bowles; and C. Bentinck; (*Mounted*).
    Lieut.-Colonels T. Chaplin; H. Armytage; H. Bentinck; C. Short; W. Cornwall; B. Broadhead; C. Hay; H. Gooch; J. Rawdon; Hon. T. Ashburnham; W. Codrington; E. Wigram.
Lieutenants.—Captains W. Stewart; Hon. J. Hope (Adjutant); G. Knox; Hon. A. Upton; F. Paget; Hon. E. Wilbraham; Lord M. W. Graham; J. Pringle; J. Clitherow; Gordon Drummond; Lord F. Paulet; C. Horton (Adjutant); J. Forbes; R. Vansittart; C. Windham; C. Wilbraham; W. Tollemache; J. Elrington; H. Daniell; Hon. R. Boyle; F. Halkett; H. Dent.
Ensigns.—Lieutenants C. Dundas; R. Hulse; D. Chisholm; S. Conroy; Hon. F. Villiers; H. Brand; G. Herbert; Viscount Alexander; Hon. R. Lambart; G. Johnson; W. S. Newton; Hon. C. Grimston; G. Mundy; P. Bathurst; E. Milman; Hon. L. Hope; Spencer Perceval.
Quartermasters.—T. Dwelly; and W. Morse.
Surgeon-Major.—G. Chenevix. *Battalion Surgeon.*—W. Hunter, M.D.
    Assistant-Surgeons.—F. Gilder; and J. Wedderburn.
Solicitor.—W. G. Carter, Esq.

The reign of William IV. was now drawing to a close, and a few months only elapsed, when, by the death of the Sovereign,

June 20, 1837, our present Gracious Queen, then just eighteen years old, ascended the Throne. The funeral obsequies took place as usual at Windsor, and were fixed for the 8th of July. The 1st Grenadiers were stationed there at the time; and the 1st Coldstream had gone to Dublin in 1836, whence they did not return until August, 1837. About one hundred men from each of the other Battalions of the former Regiment, as well as four companies from each Battalion of the Scots Fusiliers, and the whole of the 2nd Coldstream Guards proceeded to Windsor to take part in the ceremony.

Before closing this chapter, it may be well briefly to record one or two points which affected the Regiment during the reign that has just come to a conclusion. Towards the end of 1829, gratuities, in addition to the pension, were granted, on discharge, to specially selected Non-commissioned officers and men, who, by their length of service and meritorious conduct, were recommended for reward; and on the 30th of July of the following year, the silver medal for "Long service and good conduct" was instituted, and presented to them. Later, in 1836, good conduct badges—or "marks of distinction," as they were then called—were introduced, and worn on their uniform, by men whose character deserved recognition. Each "mark" added a penny a day to the recipient's pay; and, if in uninterrupted possession of it for five years immediately preceding discharge, the same amount was added to the pension.* During this reign, moreover, a Commission inquired

---

* "November 14, 1829. With a view of rewarding meritorious soldiers when discharged, and of encouraging good conduct in others whilst serving, ... a gratuity, in addition to the pension, may, in certain cases, be given to one sergeant or corporal and one private annually in every regiment of an establishment of 700 rank and file and upwards. The men to be recommended, must have completed twenty-one years of actual service in the infantry; they must never have been convicted by court-martial, and must have borne an irreproachable character, or have particularly distinguished themselves in the service. The sergeants must have ten years' service and the corporals seven years' in their respective ranks as Non-commission officers, and must have been discharged as such." The gratuities amounted to: Sergeants, £15; Corporals, £7; Privates, £5.

"August 18, 1836. Whereas it has been represented that it would materially tend to the encouragement of good conduct in the army, if a reward to be attained only by a well-conducted soldier were substituted for the additional pay, now granted to soldiers who have completed certain periods of service, all soldiers who shall enlist on or after September 1, 1836, shall have no claim to additional pay after any period of service; but a reward of additional pay for good conduct shall be granted to such soldiers, under the following rules—

"After seven years' service, 1d. a day, and to wear a 'ring of lace round the right arm,' provided the man's name does not appear in the Regimental Defaulter book for at

FIRST PART OF THE LONG EUROPEAN PEACE.

into military discipline, more especially into the system of flogging, then in force in the army. The final report, dated March 15, 1836, was in favour of retaining corporal punishment, but recommended that "no pains may be spared to endeavour to make its infliction less frequent."* Regimental numbers, identifying soldiers, appear to have been introduced into the army about this time; they were at first applied only to the men's records, but gradually they were more generally adopted (*Regimental Order*, January 2, 1836).

In the summer of 1836 it was ordered that the Battalions of the Foot Guards, and not the light companies only, should be practised in light infantry movements in extended order (*Brigade Order*, July 11, 1836).

We have seen that the Brigade Depôt was transferred from London to Warley early in 1832. It appears, that the recruits of the Coldstream and of the Scots Fusiliers were ordered to Croydon in June, 1833, and the rest followed to the same place next year. A Subaltern Officer was placed in command of the station; but in January, 1837, a Regimental Lieutenant (bearing rank of Captain) was ordered to perform this duty, and he remained there for a fortnight at a time. An Assistant Surgeon, relieved every two months, was also quartered at the Depôt.

The control exercised by the Lieutenant-Colonel over the two Battalions of the Regiment was made somewhat more direct by the introduction of weekly reports, which were furnished to him by Officers commanding Battalions, and which stated what drills, exercises, etc., were performed, and whether there had been ball practice or marching (*Regimental Order*, April 12, 1833). A scale of punishment was instituted, to equalize, as far as possible, awards made for minor offences (1st *Battalion Order*, May 24, 1831). On July 14, 1832, a Regimental Order was issued, which gives some idea of the system then pursued in the Regiment, as regards the discipline of the men:—

---

least two years immediately preceding such claim. After fourteen years', an additional 1*d*. and two rings, if the man has been in the enjoyment of the first 1*d*. for at least two years immediately preceding such further claim. And similarly, a third penny and three rings, under the same conditions, after twenty-one years' service."

* *Annual Register*, 1836, "Public Documents," p. 315. Flogging was finally abolished in the army in 1881; but it was done away with, in 1867, when troops were not engaged on active service.

"Battalions will have evening parades. In London the Battalions will always parade in Guard Order, when finding the public duties. No leave is to be given from church parade, inspection of necessaries, or Surgeon's inspection, unless absolutely necessary. Men unfit for duty, or parade, caused by liquor, to be punished as drunk. When a drunkard appears in a suspicious state at evening parade, and that by leaving barracks he would probably get intoxicated, he must be kept in, and on no account be permitted to enter the canteen. . . . No soldier to have leave all night, and only six men a company to have leave from parade, or till twelve o'clock. To receive leave or other indulgence, the soldier must have been clear of all defaulter's list at least a month. To get a pass or furlough, he must have a good general character, and have been clear of the defaulter's list two months. Soldiers must have been two years in the Regiment, before they can apply for a pass."

Lastly, it may be stated that His Majesty's Commands for the part to be taken by the Brigade, at investitures of the Order of the Bath, were published in 1835 (*Brigade Order*, August 19th), and were to be considered as a Standing Order for the future, when the ceremony should take place in St. George's Hall, Windsor Castle. The Sergeant-Major and fifteen Sergeants from the Windsor Battalion, and the Sergeants-Major and forty-two Sergeants of the West-end Battalions, were stationed in the Hall; the former at each of the doors right and left of the Throne, the latter forming a line from the Throne to the entrance; the whole under the Adjutant of the Windsor Battalion, whose place was near the King. At the subsequent banquet in the Waterloo Chamber, the Colours of the Battalion were crossed over the south fireplace, six Sergeants of the same corps stood at the doors, and the remainder formed a line from St. George's to the Banqueting Hall, as the procession passed to and from the Waterloo Chamber; the Band was placed in the latter room, the Drums at the top of the grand staircase. Additional sentries were mounted, eight in the Quadrangle, and one on Queen Elizabeth's Gate.

OFFICER TEMP. JAMES II.

CHAPTER V.

SECOND PART OF THE LONG EUROPEAN PEACE.

Beginning of the reign of Queen Victoria—Troops during Parliamentary elections—Coronation of the Queen—Fire at the Tower of London, 1841—Rebellion in Canada—Two Guards Battalions sent there, 1838, of which one the 2nd Battalion Coldstream Guards—Return home, 1842—Visit of the Russian Tsar Nicholas I. to England—European revolution—Bi-centenary celebration of the formation of the Coldstream Guards, 1850—Death of the Colonel of the Regiment, H.R.H. the Duke of Cambridge; succeeded by General the Earl of Strafford—Exhibition in London—Death of the Duke of Wellington—Changes and reforms up to 1854—Camp at Chobham.

THE young Queen had only reigned a few months, when it became necessary to send a military expedition to Canada, where for some time trouble had been brewing, and where reinforcements were required to maintain the authority of the Crown, and to settle the difficulties that had arisen. The 2nd Battalion Coldstream formed part of this expedition, and left London March 28, 1838; but before we refer to the events which occurred in that colony, we propose to deal shortly with those that took place at home, until the year 1842, when the Battalion returned to England.

During the General Election that followed immediately after Her Majesty's Accession, the troops quartered at Portman Street and in St. John's Wood, were ordered to march away from the borough of Marylebone. The 2nd Coldstream being at the former station, proceeded, in consequence, to "Hammersmith and adjacents," July 22nd, until the 28th. The system of removing soldiers from the place of an election seems never to have been adopted in Westminster, nor does it appear to have been a usual practice elsewhere in the Metropolis, except in the City, where the Bank piquet was often suspended for two or three days; as a general rule the troops were confined to barracks. On one other occasion, however (June 28, 1841), the 1st Battalion Coldstream vacated Portman Street, and marched to Fulham, Parson's Green, and Walham Green, while an election was taking place in Marylebone; and from thence, on the 3rd of July, proceeded to Hounslow and Twickenham during an election in the county of Middlesex; the Battalion returned to London on the 9th. Upon the same occasion, the recruits at Croydon were marched to London, July 5th, to their respective Regiments, until after the termination of the East Surrey election, July 12th; during the interval, the Assistant Surgeon, the Hospital establishment, and a corporal and an old soldier from each Regiment, only remained in barracks.

On the retirement of Colonel Milman to half-pay, August 8, 1837, Colonel Fremantle succeeded as Lieutenant-Colonel, and Lieut.-Colonel Shawe was promoted Major. Colonel Walton took command of the 1st Battalion, and Colonel Shawe of the 2nd.

The expedition to Canada put an end to the Dublin quarter, which was not again renewed for nearly twenty years; and the 1st Battalion Scots Fusiliers, who had proceeded there in the summer of 1837, returned to London in the following March. Moreover, during the absence of two Battalions of the Brigade in North America, the Tower was not occupied by Guards in 1838, and duty was done in Windsor, 1839-1842, by a regiment of the Line.

On May 6, 1838, the Royal Military Chapel in Wellington Barracks was opened for the first time; and a year later (July, 1839), the three Regiments took it in turn to send their Bands there to attend Divine Service.

The Queen's Coronation, June 28, 1838, was conducted on the abridged model of that of William IV.; but in some respects it was more magnificent and stately than the latter, and it included a public procession to and from Westminster Abbey, which had been absent in former ceremonies of the kind, since the reign of Charles II. As the personality of Her Majesty, moreover, roused enthusiasm among all classes to a far greater degree than had been the case with many of her predecessors, the people, drawn in dense crowds to the splendour of the spectacle, were not slow to display the feelings of genuine loyalty and affection, with which they were filled towards their youthful Sovereign; and the effect produced on the public mind, was even greater than if, under ordinary circumstances, the older forms of mediæval pageantry had been adopted. The streets were lined by troops from Buckingham Palace to the Abbey, the infantry in single rank on either side of the road; the Brigade

SECOND PART OF THE LONG EUROPEAN PEACE.

occupied the distance from Westminster to Marlborough House, and the five Battalions were present. The 1st Coldstream, having been brought up from Windsor, were in Pall Mall, the Scots Fusiliers thence to the Horse Guards, and the Grenadiers took up the remaining ground. On the other side of the Coldstream, in St. James's Street, Piccadilly, and Constitution Hill, there were Marines, Rifles, and the 20th Regiment (then at the Tower). In the Abbey a line was kept by a detachment of the Queen's company, Grenadier Guards, the Ensign of which carried the Royal Standard, and men of the Grenadier companies of the 1st Coldstream and of the 1st and 2nd Scots Fusiliers, under Subaltern Officers of their own corps.*

Her Majesty held her first review in Hyde Park on the 9th of July following, at which the Coldstream was not present, being at Windsor, but a detachment under Lieut.-Colonel Gooch went up to London and found the public duties upon that occasion. It may be interesting to note that each man of the force inspected, was supplied "with thirty rounds blank cartridge, a good flint, and a spare one in his pouch."

Colonel Fremantle having retired December 31, 1839, Colonel Walton became Lieutenant-Colonel, and Colonel Bowles was promoted Major (2nd Battalion), Colonel Shawe assuming command of the 1st Battalion. In the Regimental Order of farewell, Colonel Fremantle, after referring to his services of nearly thirty-five years in the Regiment, dwells on "his proud satisfaction of participating in those fields of honour in which the Coldstream acquired its noble perfection," and continues:—

"Since the peace, I have served in it, with the approbation and protection of our Royal Colonel, and in harmony and good fellowship with my brother Officers. My earnest desire in thus taking leave, is a continuation of the same honour and happiness. However much I may personally regret resigning the command of the Coldstream Guards, I avail myself of the painful occasion to perform a pleasing duty, to express my thanks to Sergeant-Major Lundie, the Non-commissioned officers and soldiers of the Regiment, and to congratulate them upon that system of discipline which, of late years, has tended so much to the diminution of crime and consequent

* One interesting feature of the Coronation was the presence at it, as French Ambassador Extraordinary, of Marshal Soult, the opponent of the Duke of Wellington, in many fields of battle in the Spanish Peninsula, and at Waterloo. It need scarcely be said that the reception of this gallant old soldier, by the English people and by the Duke of Wellington, was most cordial, and that all were glad to welcome warmly a former hostile Commander, who had displayed skill and valour when he fought against us.

punishment. I trust that the same spirit of loyalty which has rendered the Coldstream Regiment 'Second to None,' will ever continue to be prominent in its duty to Her Majesty."

Among the miscellaneous duties performed by the Brigade in London, was that relating to the extinguishing of metropolitan fires,—one even now discharged, but which was of more importance in days when the Fire Brigade was imperfectly organized. In October, 1834, when the Houses of Parliament were destroyed, the exertions of the troops to arrest the flames were warmly recognized by the Home Secretary; and again, in January, 1836, the thanks of Lord Palmerston were published, with the intimation that, but for the timely assistance of the Brigade, the Foreign Office would have been burnt down. On the night of October 30, 1841, a conflagration took place in the Tower, which, having spread with alarming rapidity, completely gutted the Armoury, and destroyed many of the trophies of former wars which had been deposited there. Owing to the exertions of the Battalion quartered in the Tower (1st Scots Fusiliers), and other portions of the Brigade, that hurried to the disaster, the Regalia was saved, and many interesting parts of that historic fortress and prison were preserved.* On the 5th of November the following Regimental Order was issued:—

"Field-Marshal the Duke of Wellington, Constable of the Tower, having brought to the notice of the General Commanding-in-Chief the meritorious conduct of the troops, who assisted in checking the conflagration which unfortunately took place in that fortress on the night of Saturday last, the 30th ulto., I have Lord Hill's command to desire that you will be pleased to convey, to the portion of the Brigade of Guards employed upon that occasion, the gratification which his Lordship feels, at receiving this report of their exertions, and of the great service which they rendered, not only in stopping the progress of the flames, but in saving the public property thus threatened with destruction. Lord Hill anticipates the additional pleasure, which the Guards cannot but experience, from the circumstance of this report of their conduct having emanated from the Duke of Wellington."

Officers who have so often seen the piece of plate, representing the Sphinx, on the table of St. James's Palace, may be interested in knowing, that it was received at a general meeting of the Guards Club, on May 5, 1842. The Duke of Bedford, executor of General

* See *Annual Register*, 1841, "Chronicle," p. 99, for a full description of this well-remembered calamity.

Earl of Ludlow, Scots Fusilier Guards, gave it, in accordance with the latter's will, by which he left "the Egyptian vase, presented to him by the Brigade of Guards in the camp before Alexandria, to the Guards Club, with his grateful thanks."

It is now time to revert to the more serious affairs, which engaged the attention of the 2nd Battalion in North America. Canada at that period was divided into two distinct colonies—the Lower province, inhabited almost entirely by old French settlers, and the Upper province, peopled by immigrants of British nationality. In the former, a simmering of discontent had prevailed for some years; the colonists resented the system by which, under a semblance of constitutional government, their popular representatives were excluded from all control and authority over their own affairs. In the month of November, 1837, things came to a head, and a rebellion broke out, led by one Papineau. Encouraged to violence by this evil example, assisted by free-booters from the United States, and having some grievances of their own to complain of, another insurrection occurred almost simultaneously in Upper Canada. In both cases, the disorder was instantly put down by Sir J. Colborne (afterwards Lord Seaton), with a military force in Lower Canada, and by the local militia in the other province. But the news reaching home, that an actual outbreak had taken place, created the utmost sensation in England. It was immediately determined to strengthen the troops in the colony, and to send out Lord Durham as Governor-General and High Commissioner, with large powers to deal with the difficulty.

On the 23rd of January, the 2nd Grenadiers and the 2nd Coldstream were ordered to be held in readiness for embarkation for Quebec, each to be made up to 800 rank and file; and the Brigade, so formed, was placed under the command of Major-General Sir J. Macdonell, K.C.B. (late of the Coldstream). Captain Arthur Torrens, Grenadier Guards, was appointed Major of Brigade; and Captain J. Elrington, Coldstream Guards, Aide-de-camp to the Major-General. On the 22nd of March this body of men was inspected by Lord Hill, when a congratulatory order was issued upon their appearance, expressing the Commander-in-Chief's conviction that they "would do honour to the high reputation of the Brigade of Guards," and concluding with his "best wishes for their welfare while employed abroad in the service of the country." After the Officers had attended a Levée "to take leave," and had been entertained at dinner by the Colonel, the Duke of Cambridge, the 2nd Coldstream left London for Winchester, in four divisions, on the 28th and 29th.

1st Division, Lieut.-Colonel Hon. T. Ashburnham, Commanding (Nos. 1 and 2 Companies); Captains W. Tollemache, Hon. R. Boyle; Lieutenants Hon. L. Hope, G. Mundy.

2nd Division, Colonel G. Bowles, Commanding (Nos. 3 and 4 Companies); Captains R. Vansittart, C. Wilbraham; Lieutenants M. Tierney, Hon. A. Graves.

3rd Division, Lieut.-Colonel W. Stewart-Balfour, Commanding (Nos. 5 and 6 Companies); Captains C. Windham, R. Hulse; Lieutenants W. Clayton, Lord Alexander.

4th Division, Lieut.-Colonel E. Wigram, Commanding (Nos. 7 and 8 Companies); Lieutenants S. Perceval, E. Milman, P. Bathurst.

Head-quarters, Colonel C. Shawe, Commanding the Battalion; Lieutenant D. M. Chisholm, Adjutant; Quartermaster T. Lee; and Surgeon F. Gilder, and Assistant-Surgeons E. Greatrex and W. Robinson.

The following Officers belonging to the Battalion were allowed to find their own way out to Canada: Lieut.-Colonels W. Codrington, Hon. J. Hope, and T. Chaplin; Captains H. Daniell, F. Halkett, and H. Dent. Lieutenant Hon. F. Villiers was appointed Aide-de-camp to Lord Durham. The Battalion embarked at Portsmouth on the 17th of April, in H.M.S. *Edinburgh* and *Athol*, and landed at Quebec on the 11th of May, a few days before the arrival of the new Governor-General, who reached the Colony towards the end of the month, and was received in state by the newly arrived Guards Brigade.

The situation in Lower Canada was one of outward tranquillity, the rebellion had been crushed, and order was restored; but serious complications still remained to be adjusted. Numerous prisoners were in custody awaiting trial, for their treason; and as it would have been impossible to obtain a conviction by a local jury, Sir J. Colborne, the temporary Governor, confined most of them in prison, 161 in number, until the decision of the High Commissioner could be given. On the 28th of June, Lord Durham issued an Ordinance, by which he granted a complete amnesty to all, with the exception of eight of the principal ringleaders; these men he transported to Bermuda. He also declared that if these men, or if Papineau and other fifteen chiefs of the insurrection—who had absconded and had fled for safety into the United States, directly they were in danger of capture—were again found at large without permission, they would suffer death as traitors. The Ordinance, though humane and calculated to bring about peace without further bloodshed, was adjudged to be illegal or unconstitutional. There was no power to transport offenders nor to threaten, with the extreme rigour of the law, those who had not been tried. It would have been necessary to pass an Act of Parliament to make it valid, and the state of parties at home rendered any such course impossible. Government was weak, a strong Opposition was ready to oust the Ministers from office, and Lord Durham had many personal enemies. Lord Melbourne, the Prime Minister, disavowed the Ordinance, and threw over the High Commissioner, and thereupon the latter resigned his post, and left Canada, November 1st.* But before quitting North America, he committed an act for which he has been gravely censured; for, he announced to the rebels (October 9th), that the general amnesty he granted had been ratified by Her Majesty's Proclamation, and that the exceptions to the amnesty had been disallowed, and he told them that there was no further impediment to prevent them from returning to the colony.† The exiles were not slow to avail themselves of this welcome intelligence, and in the month of October they came back, freed from the consequences of their former guilt, and determined to light afresh the torch of civil war.‡

During the first six months, the troops had little to do beyond their ordinary duties,§ and in the summer leave was freely given to many of the Officers to see the country, on the understanding,

* As upon the arrival of Lord Durham, so at his departure, the Guards Battalions furnished Guards of Honour of 50 men each, with Regimental Colour, under a Lieutenant and Captain and two Ensign-Lieutenants. The streets were lined by the remainder of the Brigade.

† "The Proclamation contained an entire amnesty, qualified only by the exceptions specified in the Ordinance. The Ordinance has been disallowed, and the Proclamation is confirmed. Her Majesty having been advised to refuse her assent to the exceptions, the amnesty exists without qualification. No impediment therefore exists to the return of the persons who have made the most distinct admission of guilt, or who have been excluded by me from the province, on account of the danger to which its tranquillity would be exposed by their presence. And none can now be enacted, without the adoption of measures alike repugnant to my sense of justice and of policy" (Lord Durham's Proclamation, October 9, 1838: *Annual Register*, 1838, "History," p. 322; "Public Documents," p. 311).

‡ Alison, *History of Europe*, 1815-1852, vi. 328, etc.

§ On the day fixed for the Coronation of the Queen, June 28, 1838, the Coldstream fired a *feu-de-joie* in the citadel of Quebec, where they were quartered, at 9.30 in the evening.

however, that none were to enter the United States. But, in spite of the appearance of outward tranquillity, there was a spirit of disaffection abroad, the authorities were resisted, the jury system had broken down, and the population of one nationality were bitterly divided from that of another. The execution of the law was difficult, as a Battalion Order of the 11th of July may perhaps exemplify—publishing the good conduct of several privates of the Coldstream for assisting the Superintendent of Police in the execution of his duty ; " but for them, two prisoners would have escaped, and he would have received a severe beating from the crowd."

Feeling ran high among the loyal inhabitants, at the weakness and timidity of the Home Government, and at the ungenerous treatment their Commissioner had received at their hands. Addresses poured in upon him from all quarters, expressing sorrow at his departure. A farewell dinner was also given to him by the Officers of the Guards Brigade, at which Sir J. Macdonell spoke of him and his policy in eulogistic terms—an incident which raised some comment, as it was supposed by some to be an interference by a military Officer in a political question ; though undoubtedly it testified to the sentiments that prevailed among the well-disposed. It was universally felt in the province, that the welfare of the colony had been sacrificed to the evils of party exigencies.

Already, before the departure of Lord Durham, a rising had been prepared, under the leadership of the returned exiles, and it broke out on the 3rd of November, 1838, in the neighbourhood of Beauharnois, a place on the right bank of the St. Lawrence river, not very far distant from Montreal.

Troops were at once despatched to quell the disturbance. The Grenadiers joined the expedition, and did not return to Quebec till the end of April, 1840 ; but the Coldstream Battalion being ordered to remain in that town to secure its tranquillity during the crisis, did not form part of the column sent forward to disperse the rebels.[*] The outbreak was sudden, and caused considerable alarm while it lasted ; but the operations were of short duration, nor were they of much importance from a military point of view. Volunteer

[*] On November 6, 1838, the following 2nd Battalion Order was issued : "The Piquet Officer is to go round the walls of the citadel (at Quebec) twice at night, and he is not to do so at the same time as the Officer of the citadel guard. He is always to be properly dressed during the night, and to be ready to turn out at the shortest notice. The Captain of the day will go his rounds twice during the night, the second time just before daybreak."

forces also lent their aid to put down the rebellion, and on the 17th of November they were cordially thanked by the Commander of the Forces (Sir J. Colborne, who, since Lord Durham's departure, was also Governor), "for defeating the traitors and invaders" by "their heroic perseverance and devotion to the service of their country, which they have displayed from the first moment of this second revolt." The disaffected made little or no resistance, and, unable to maintain themselves in the field, they soon dispersed or surrendered. The insurrection thus came to an end almost immediately, and many of the prisoners were taken to Montreal, where a Court-Martial sat continuously for six months to try them. The Coldstream, still at Quebec, did not furnish Officers for these trials.

After the suppression of the insurrection, there was still cause for the presence of troops in the colony. First, to protect the loyal portion of the population from the evil influence of agitators, who continued to lurk in the country; and secondly, to maintain order, while reforms were being introduced, calculated to put an end to discontent for the future. Volunteer corps were raised, and Officers appointed to command and organize them. Lieut.-Colonel Hon. James Hope (Coldstream Guards) was placed in command of the "Queen's Volunteers," and reported, Dec. 10, 1839, that this corps was then composed of 2 staff-sergeants, 24 sergeants, 6 drummers, and 432 rank and file, of whom 381 were taking their share of garrison duty.* Captain Halkett (Coldstream Guards), appointed Assistant Military Secretary in Upper Canada, also superintended the formation of another corps.† About the same time, the Royal

---

* *District Order*, Quebec, April 14, 1840: "The Queen's Volunteers having nearly closed the period of their engagement, the Major-General cannot allow that body to separate without recording his perfect satisfaction at the efficient manner in which they have performed their duties. Lieut.-Colonel Hon. J. Hope, in discharge of the important trust confided to him as Commanding Officer, has fully met the expectation naturally formed in his ability and judgment. The Lieut.-Colonel has been ably and zealously seconded by Major Irvine, and well supported by the Officers in general, to all of whom the Major-General makes his acknowledgments; and he begs that Lieut.-Colonel Hope will convey to the Non-commissioned officers and privates his thanks, and the conviction he entertains, that, should emergency arise, Her Majesty's Government may depend on a renewal of their valuable services."

† This Officer died before rejoining the Coldstream. The following order appeared on the occasion of his death: "Toronto, October 26, 1840. It is with the most sincere and poignant regret that His Excellency the Lieut.-Governor and Major-General Commanding has to announce the death of Captain Halkett, Coldstream Guards, Assistant Military Secretary and Colonel in the Militia of Upper Canada. The demise of this lamented and promising Officer took place yesterday. The zeal with which Captain Halkett devoted himself to the duties of his office, and the ability with which he discharged

Canadian Regiment was raised, and some Non-commissioned officers and men from the Guards were allowed to volunteer for service therein. As it appears to have offered special advantages to married men, the latter readily endeavoured to be allowed to obtain a transfer to its ranks.

Although Lord Durham's action in Canada was repudiated by the Government in England, the efforts he made to reconcile the people to British rule were in the end very successful. Before he left North America, he made a masterly and comprehensive report upon the position of affairs in the colony, and he recommended remedies to redress the grievances, which he perceived kept the people in a state of ferment. "As Mr. Mill has said, these recommendations laid the foundation of political success and social prosperity, not only of Canada, but of all the other important colonies. . . . In brief, Lord Durham proposed to make the Canadas self-governing as regards their internal affairs, and the germ of a federal union."* His report was accepted, and it became the basis of the policy which Government now adopted. Mr. Paulet Thompson, created shortly afterwards Lord Sydenham, was sent to North America at the end of 1839, in the capacity of Governor-General of the two Canadas, to carry out the recommendations which he proposed. At the same time, Sir J. Colborne returned to England, being relieved as Commander of the Forces by Lieut.-General Sir Richard Jackson (late of the Coldstream Guards). Early in 1841, the legislative union of the two provinces was carried into execution, and from this act the new system of colonial life, as now understood in the British Empire, may be said to date.

The Coldstream continued all this time to remain at Quebec, nor were they moved therefrom until they left North America in 1842. During these years small drafts were annually sent out to keep up the Battalion to its proper strength, and upon almost every occasion they were inspected previous to departure by the

---

them, could not fail to ensure the high consideration and the most perfect confidence with which he was regarded by the Lieut.-Governor and Major-General Commanding. His soldierlike qualifications and most gentlemanlike character were highly appreciated by his brother Officers, and the kindly spirit with which he conducted business, often of a perplexing nature, and the amiable disposition which he displayed in private life, secured for him the esteem of the community at large."

* Justin McCarthy, M.P., *A History of our Own Times*, i. 77; John MacMullen, *History of Canada*, p. 426 (London, 1868).

Colonel of the Regiment, H.R.H. the Duke of Cambridge. Arrangements for winter clothing were made by the Commanding Officer, who authorized a coat and cap to be worn by the Officers, in cold weather, the former to replace the ordinary red coatee, then used instead of the present tunic. An allowance was made by the Treasury, calculated at £1 10s. for every effective soldier serving in Canada for the first winter, and at 5s. for subsequent winters. This money formed a fund, from which a supply of winter clothing was provided for Non-commissioned officers and men. These articles were to be considered public property, and could, if necessary, be transferred from one man to another.

In the winter, parties were sent out into the woods when snow lay deep on the ground, to be practised in "camping, etc.," or rather, in constructing log huts. The public duties in Quebec appear to have averaged two Subalterns (on guard at the Castle and at the citadel), 10 sergeants, 15 corporals, 2 drummers, and from 110 to 180 men,—besides ten to fourteen men of the Royal Artillery. It may here be mentioned that the stuffed goose's head, adorned with a gorget (to be seen in the Regimental Orderly Room), records an incident which took place at this time. The goose, having attached itself to the Battalion, became the constant companion of one of the sentries in the citadel, and a humble, though faithful friend and follower of the Regiment. While it lived it wore the gorget that now is to be found round its neck; and a picture, also in the Orderly Room, testifies to its never varying attendance on the beat of the sentry it had chosen to follow.

On March 27, 1841, Officers were posted to companies as under:—

Compy.	Lieutenant-Colonels.	Captains.	Lieutenants.
No. 1.	Hon. James Hope.	J. Forbes.	Hon. L. Hope.
		Hon. C. Grimston.	
No. 2.	Hon. T. Ashburnham.	J. Elrington.	Hon. A Graves.
No. 3.	C. Hay.	R. Hulse.	M. Tierney.
			S. Perceval.
No. 4.	H. Bentinck.	P. Bathurst.	W. Clayton.
No. 5.	T. Chaplin.	H. Daniell.	J. Kirkland.
			W. Verner.
No. 6.	W. Codrington.	R. Vansittart.	P. Somerset.
No. 7.	W. Stewart-Balfour.	Earl of Caledon.	G. Whyte-Melville.
No. 8.	E. Wigram.	C. Windham.	T. Wigram.
		E. Milman.	

Sir James Macdonell left Canada (June, 1842), having been promoted Lieut.-General some time before; thereupon, Colonel Bowles, commanding the 2nd Coldstream, assumed the command, as Guards Brigadier, of the two Battalions, until they left for England. Also on the promotion of Captain Torrens (September, 1840), Captain Lord Frederick Paulet, Adjutant of the 2nd Battalion, was appointed to succeed him as Major of the Brigade in Canada, when Captain Forbes became Acting Adjutant.

The reforms introduced by Lord Sydenham produced a speedy and salutary effect in Canada, and the recollection of the period of rebellion soon passed away. Tranquillity, order, and stable government were restored by the new policy, and the improvement effected, appeared to be of a permanent character. The Guards might have gone back to England in 1841, for, as far as affairs in the colony were concerned, their presence was no longer required. But we had still a question with Washington, and, as the two Battalions happened to be in North America, it was naturally deemed advisable to keep them there until this matter should be adjusted. Previous treaties had not properly defined the north-eastern frontier of the United States, nor traced a clear line of demarcation between the State of Maine and the British possessions which lay to the north of it. Both Governments desired to come to an amicable conclusion on the subject, and, early in 1842, Lord Ashburton was sent out to settle it. A Treaty was agreed to and approved at Washington on the 9th of August. Our American cousins were not displeased with the result, for it gave them advantages, which perhaps, in strict right, they had little reason to expect. But in a sense, it was also satisfactory to the British Government, as at least it put an end to a dispute, or to a cause of future trouble, of long standing. The arrangement was therefore ratified without demur, and we were content to abide by it.*

The Brigade had now been for more than four years in North America, and the time had been passed pleasantly and profitably by all ranks. Seldom have the Guards had an opportunity of observing for themselves the life of a thriving British colony, and the development of our national energy across the ocean. The experience was a useful and a novel one, and was very different to that which they are wont to feel, when sent to a foreign country

* The text of the Treaty is to be found in the *Annual Register*, 1842, "Public Documents," p. 498.

to maintain the interests of the Empire in times of war, or of disturbance. In Canada, at least, we were among our own people, among settlers loyal to the British Crown, who form a part of our own commonwealth. Difficulties did exist among them, but these were capable of easy adjustment by the light which the British Constitution will always afford in such cases; and guided by this light, it was not long before statesmen found a remedy for the evils that were complained of. If the troops were necessary to put down the disorder of the few, and to guard the introduction of reforms from the impatience of popular agitation, so is it also true, that the intelligence of the whole colony ranged itself on the side of the authorities and of the soldiers, who saved the Canadian communities from the tyranny, and the rapacity of revolutionary leaders.

Thus did a cordial feeling of respect and of mutual good will spring up between the Guards and the colonists; and the former, adhering closely to their Regimental traditions, that have formed their character, and guided them in every position in which they have been placed, maintained their discipline unimpaired in the midst of surrounding temptations.* Some of our men acquired a taste for colonial life, and wished to settle in the country. For this purpose, it was necessary to obtain their discharge in Canada, and an application was accordingly made to that effect. The order for the return of the Brigade to Europe, was dated August 18, 1842, and, two days later, Sir H. Hardinge, the Secretary at War, agreed that a certain number of men might be allowed to receive their discharge with a modified pension. He specially desired that it should be known "that this extensive indulgence had been assented to, in consequence of the very exemplary manner in which the Guards have conducted themselves, during the time they have performed Colonial service in North America."

The movement towards home took place in the autumn of 1842, the bulk of the Grenadier Guards leaving a few days before the Coldstream. Six companies of the latter, having embarked at Quebec on the 5th of October, on board H.M.S. *Calcutta*, sailed

* The facility with which British soldiers could desert by crossing the border to the United States, and the efforts made by many from the States to induce our men to do so, formed no small a temptation to many young soldiers. It will be seen presently how few of the Coldstream were guilty of this serious military crime.

therefrom on the 6th, and reached Spithead on October 31st, whence they proceeded by train in two detachments to Winchester. After an inspection by Major-General Sir H. Pakenham, on the 1st of November, the Officer Commanding, in communicating the Major-General's "high approbation of the steadiness and appearance" of the men, expressed his own "sense of their soldier-like conduct during the late voyage and up to the present moment, which he will take the earliest opportunity of bringing to the notice of the Officer Commanding the Regiment." The remaining two companies followed from Canada, together with two companies of the Grenadiers, in H.M.S. *Pique*, and left on the 19th of October, arriving at Spithead on the 12th of November. The Battalion, reunited at Winchester, remained there until the 22nd of November, when they were sent to London (St. George's barracks).* On the 30th of November, the Lieutenant-Colonel issued the following Regimental Order:—

"Colonel Walton has much pleasure in congratulating the 2nd Battalion on their highly soldierlike appearance and steadiness under arms at the inspection this morning. In welcoming the return of this fine Battalion to England, the Lieutenant-Colonel takes the opportunity of expressing to Colonel Bowles and the Officers and Non-commissioned officers and privates, the feelings of pride and satisfaction he has experienced, in hearing the good accounts, which have from time to time been received of the conduct and soldierlike feeling exhibited by the Battalion, from the commencement of its period of service in America, so fully borne testimony to by every Officer under whom it served. It is worthy of remark, that, during a period of nearly five years, so few cases of desertion have taken place in a Battalion 800 strong; nine only of which have occurred among the duty men, and this in a country where temptations to the commission of this crime were particularly strong. The Lieutenant-Colonel feels assured that such old soldiers who, for the purpose of equalizing the two Battalions, may shortly be transferred from one to the other, will by their example, impress upon their younger comrades the necessity of a ready submission to discipline, and due subordination to those placed over them, by which

---

* The 2nd Battalion, returning home from British North America, contained 41 sergeants, 18 corporals, and 688 men. The Officers who were present were: Colonel Bowles, Commanding Battalion; Captain Lord F. Paulet, Adjutant; Quartermaster Lee; Assistant Surgeon Robinson; Colonel H. Bentinck; Lieut.-Colonels Codrington and Wigram; Captains Vansittart, Daniell, Hulse, and Earl of Caledon; Lieutenants Kirkland, Somerset, Whyte-Melville, and Verner (with the six companies); and Colonel Chaplin, Captain Bathurst, Lieutenant Ellice, and Assistant Surgeon Munro (with the two companies).

the individual comfort of the soldier is so much advanced, and the credit of his corps firmly established."

On the return of the Brigade from Canada, Windsor was again occupied by the Foot Guards, and Winchester remained an out-quarter until June 24, 1847, when Chichester was substituted for it. A Battalion was stationed at this latter place up to 1854.

Colonel Bowles, who had joined the Regiment in December, 1804, having retired upon half-pay, after nearly thirty-nine years service, on May 30, 1843, Colonel C. Bentinck was promoted Major, and commanded the 2nd Battalion.

As far back as January, 1832, a sergeant and corporal from each of the three Regiments were sent to the Fencing Rooms of Mr. Angelo (at that time in Old Bond Street), to learn a system of bayonet exercise which he had invented, and were inspected the following month by Lord Hill. The latter appears not to have considered the results satisfactory, and nothing more was done in the matter.* But later, in February, 1843, Mr. Angelo's services were again requisitioned, and several Non-commissioned officers were sent to his School of Arms, in St. James's Street, to be instructed in the sword exercise, and with a view to their drilling the men of their Battalions in the use of the bayonet. Mr. Angelo, moreover, held periodical inspections of the Officers and men of every Battalion of the Brigade. He commenced this duty in December, 1843, and continued to perform it until the spring of 1852. The bayonet exercise thus begun in the Brigade, was not extended generally to the rest of the army, until after the Crimean war.

A review took place at Windsor on June 5, 1844, before the Emperor of Russia, attended by the 2nd Scots Fusiliers, then stationed there, and by the 2nd Grenadiers and 2nd Coldstream, who proceeded from London for the purpose. Lord Saltoun commanded the Brigade; the whole, including infantry of the Line, cavalry, and artillery, being under Lord Combermere. It is perhaps of interest to remark that His Majesty the Tsar, who within ten short years, was engaged in a serious war with this country, conveyed his approbation and thanks to the troops, and desired that they should be spoken of as "his comrades in arms." Three years later, another review on a large scale, but of infantry

* General Sir J. Hamilton, K.C.B., *History of the Grenadier Guards*, iii. 108.

only, was held in Hyde Park, June 17, 1847, before H.I.H. the Grand-Duke Constantine of Russia, and was attended by the Duke of Wellington. Five Battalions of the Brigade were present (1st and 2nd Grenadiers, 1st and 2nd Coldstream, and the 2nd Scots Fusiliers), divided into two brigades—the Coldstream in one, under Colonel C. Bentinck,—and a brigade of the Line. The whole under the command of H.R.H. Prince George of Cambridge, who expressed the pleasure it afforded him to command a body of the Brigade of Guards for the first time.

On the retirement of Colonel Walton (May 8, 1846), Colonel Shawe became Lieutenant-Colonel, and Colonel Chaplin was promoted Major (2nd Battalion). A few months later (November 13th), Colonel Shawe being appointed Major-General, Colonel C. Bentinck succeeded to the Lieutenant-Colonelcy of the Regiment, and his brother, Colonel H. Bentinck, became Junior Major. Thereupon Colonel Chaplin commanded the 1st, and Colonel H. Bentinck the 2nd Battalion. It will be remembered that Colonel C. Bentinck had served as Deputy Assistant Adjutant-General at Waterloo; and that Colonel Walton, then Acting Adjutant of the 2nd Battalion, had been appointed Brigade-Major of the 2nd Guards Brigade, June 20, 1815, until the corps was dissolved, after the treaty of Paris, November 20, 1815. Again, in 1848 (April 25), there was another change in the command of the Regiment, when, on the retirement of Colonel C. Bentinck, Colonel Chaplin was promoted Lieutenant-Colonel, and Colonel Hay became Major. According to the rule then prevailing, the latter commanded the 2nd Battalion, and Colonel H. Bentinck was transferred to the 1st Battalion.

In May, 1848, the Regiment stood as follows:—

Colonel.—Field-Marshal H.R.H. the Duke of Cambridge, K.G., etc.
Lieutenant-Colonel.—Colonel T. Chaplin.
Majors.—Colonels H. Bentinck; C. Hay.
Captains.—Colonels W. Cornwall; W. Codrington : Lieut.-Colonels Hon. A. Upton ; F. Paget ; (*Mounted*).
    Lieut.-Colonels Hon. G. Upton ; J. Clitherow; Gordon Drummond; Lord F. Paulet; J. Forbes; R. Vansittart; C. Windham; H. Daniell; Hon. R. Boyle; W. S. Newton; E. Milman; G. A. Vernon.
Lieutenants.—Captains G. Johnson ; Spencer Perceval ; M. Tierney ; Hon. V. Dawson ; H. Cumming ; T. Steele ; W. M. Wood ; W. Eccles ; C. White ; W. Baring ; C. Cocks ; P. Somerset (Adjutant) ; J. Cowell ;

J. Halkett (Adjutant); Sir J. Harington, Bart.; D. Carleton; Lord A. C. FitzRoy; C. Burdett; F. Newdigate; L. MacKinnon; Sir G. Walker, Bart.; G. Warrender; W. Dawkins.

Ensigns.—Lieutenants H. Jolliffe; Lord Dunkellin; F. Burton; Hon. P. Feilding; E. Dering; W. Reeve; Hon. G. Eliot; C. Baring; H. Bouverie; H. Armytage; Hon. H. Byng; C. Morgan; A. Thellusson; T. Rolt; R. Sulivan; H. Cust; D. Williamson.

Quartermasters.—W. Morse; T. Lee.

Surgeon-Major.—E. Greatrex. *Battalion Surgeon.*—W. Robinson. *Assistant-Surgeons.*—J. Munro; J. Skelton.

Solicitor.—W. G. Carter, Esq.

The fever of revolution again attacked the continent of Europe, and the year 1848 was one of confusion and disturbance. Insurrections of a violent character were the order of the day, and convulsed every country. France more especially was affected, where Louis-Philippe, the Citizen-King, was swept away, and a Republic erected. England alone was preserved free from rebellion, in spite of the efforts of a body of malcontents, called Chartists, who sought to involve the country in serious trouble. For some time this body had been at work to undermine the British Constitution by every means in their power. They selected the 10th of April upon which to give a great display of their strength and numbers, and so to "overawe Government into a concession of their demands, as the only means of averting a violent revolution." * But these efforts entirely failed; for the people, firm in their love of order, had no sympathy with agitators, whose sole desire was to disturb the public peace. Preparations on an extensive scale, were made by the Duke of Wellington to resist any unlawful attempts that might be made to coerce the constituted authorities. But the troops, as far as possible, were kept out of sight, as a reserve, to come to the aid of the numerous special constables, who, drawn from every class of society, eagerly enrolled themselves for the occasion. Early in March, when the trouble was brewing, the Guards were confined to barracks, and piquets were held in readiness to assist the civil power; these arrangements continued intermittently during the month. On the 10th of April, however, more elaborate precautions were taken: the 1st Coldstream, then at the Tower, having left detachments in the Mint and Bank, were stationed for the day in Blackfriars; the

* *Annual Register*, 1848, "History," p. 124.

2nd Grenadiers, brought up from Chichester, occupied Somerset House; the West-end Battalions being placed at Wellington barracks, at Buckingham Palace, in the Magazine (Hyde Park), in the Royal Mews (Pimlico), and at St. George's and Portman Street barracks.* The day passed without riot or disturbance; after which, the effervescence gradually cooled down, and the normal state of public tranquillity soon prevailed again.

The year 1850 was the two hundredth anniversary of the formation of the Regiment, and it was celebrated, with due solemnity and much enthusiasm, on the 22nd of May. The 1st Battalion was quartered in Portman Street, the 2nd in St. George's barracks. In the forenoon, the Regiment paraded in Hyde Park, and the men of the two Battalions were formed into one corps of eight companies, those belonging to a company of one Battalion being mixed up with those of the corresponding company of the other. In this order the Regiment, 1400 strong, were marched to Portman Street, under Colonel H. Bentinck. A substantial dinner was then provided for Non-commissioned officers and men in the barrack yard, which had been completely covered with canvas, and suitably decorated with emblems, flags, and banners; and conspicuous among them were the tattered Waterloo Colours wreathed in laurel, presented to the Regiment the day before, by Lieut.-General Sir Alexander Woodford, who had commanded the 2nd Battalion at that battle. Sergeant-Major Hurle presided, and the Colonel and all the Officers were present, H.R.H. the Duke of Cambridge occupying a seat among the privates. After some time spent together, during which the warm relations existing between the various ranks of the Regiment were manifested, the Officers left at four in the afternoon, and dancing and other amusements terminated the day. In the evening, the bicentenary festival was also celebrated by a dinner held in the Banqueting Hall, St. James's Palace, and attended by all the Officers past and present, together with a few guests, among whom was the Duke of Wellington, Colonel of the Grenadier Guards, and then Commander-in-Chief. Altogether 140 persons sat down to table; Colonel Chaplin presided. In the course of the entertainment, many toasts were proposed and honoured, among them "the Marquis of Huntly, the oldest Coldstreamer present," who, as Lord Strathavon, had left the Regiment in 1792, and was now nearly

* Hamilton, *History of the Grenadier Guards*, iii. 146.

ninety years of age. The Duke of Wellington also made a speech, from which, on account of his great military position and authority, it may be interesting to give the following extract :—

"I may well be gratified and flattered at the honour you have done me in inviting me to attend your festival on this occasion. Long before I had the honour of holding a commission in the corps of Guards, I had every reason to respect that corps on account of their display of every military quality as soldiers, in every situation in which they could be placed. I have had the good fortune to see them in the presence of the enemy—in situations of difficulty under every possible circumstance, and on every such occasion they have conducted themselves with distinction, and have displayed every quality which could be expected from the best class of soldiers. Among these, the least distinguished have not been the Coldstream Guards. I see many around me whose conduct I have had occasion to applaud under every variety of circumstance—in the field, in cantonments, and in quarters. Gentlemen, I know also it is impossible to see troops equal to the efficiency of the Guards."

The recollections of the bicentenary celebration were still vividly in the minds of the Coldstream, when the Regiment was plunged into mourning by the death of their veteran Colonel (July 8, 1850), who, appointed in September, 1805, was the oldest soldier in the corps, and "the Father of the Coldstreamers," as he himself delighted to be called. H.RH. Prince Adolphus Frederick, Duke of Cambridge, was born in 1774, and was the seventh and youngest surviving son of George III. He saw active service in Flanders, —where he was twice wounded—in 1793, under his brother the Duke of York and Marshal Freytag, and again in the two subsequent years. Later, he was given appointments in Hanover, and was Governor there until the death of William IV., when the Duke of Cumberland became Sovereign of that State, and when the kingdom was finally separated from the Crown of England.

The funeral took place at Kew on the 16th, and it was attended by both Battalions, each of which furnished a Guard of Honour, the 2nd Battalion at Cambridge House, Piccadilly, and the 1st Battalion at Kew. On the 25th the following Regimental Order was issued :—

"The Commanding Officer is desired by H.R.H. the Duke of Cambridge to express to the Officers, Non-commissioned officers, and privates, his thanks, and those of the Duchess of Cambridge and family, for the feeling manner in which they conducted themselves at Kew, on the occasion of the funeral of His late Royal Highness."

Shortly afterwards (August 15th), the Colonelcy of the Regiment was bestowed by Her Majesty upon General the Earl of Strafford, G.C.B. (late of the Third Guards), and better known in the Coldstream as Sir John Byng, the gallant commander of the 2nd Guards Brigade during the campaign of 1815, and (when Sir G. Cooke was wounded) of the Guards Division at Waterloo.

London, in the summer of 1851, was the scene of the first great Exhibition of the Industry of all Nations—a scheme to promote the peaceable development of commerce, which was conceived, initiated, and organized by the enlightened energy of the late Prince Consort. This splendid display of the arts and sciences created extraordinary interest among all classes, both at home and abroad. The Brigade took its part in this undertaking by guarding the building, and by furnishing a piquet of one Officer and 50 men in case of emergency. The latter were quartered in the disused Knightsbridge barracks, and the usual autumn change of quarters was put off until the end of October.

On the 22nd of August, Colonel H. Bentinck was promoted Lieutenant-Colonel on the retirement of Colonel Chaplin, when Colonel Hon. A. Upton became Junior Major (2nd Battalion).

The year 1852 (September 14th) saw the death of the now aged Duke of Wellington—the great Commander who broke the power of Napoleon, and who, above all other Generals, raised the military prestige of England to that high standard of fame and glory, that made the British nation invincible in the field, and enabled her to stand single-handed against the conqueror of Europe. It is quite impossible in a work of this kind, to attempt to recapitulate a tithe even of the services which this great man rendered to his country. They stand recorded in history, and in the annals of the Coldstream they are partially described in the events which occurred up to 1818, when his active military career, as a General in the field, came to an end. Suffice it here to reproduce the touching General Order which Her Majesty caused to be published to the Army as soon as she learnt that her faithful soldier and servant had breathed his last:—

"The Queen feels assured that the Army will participate in the deep grief with which Her Majesty has received the intelligence of the irreparable loss sustained by herself, and by the country, in the sudden death of Field-Marshal the Duke of Wellington. In him Her Majesty has to deplore a firm supporter of her Throne; a faithful, wise, and devoted councillor; and a valued and honoured friend. In him the Army will lament the loss of a Commander-in-Chief unequalled for the brilliancy, the magnitude, and the success of his military achievements; but hardly less distinguished for the indefatigable and earnest zeal with which, in time of peace, he laboured to maintain the efficiency and promote the interests of that Army, which he had often led to victory. The discipline which he exacted from others, as the main foundation of the military character, he sternly imposed upon himself; and the Queen desires to impress upon the Army, that the greatest Commander whom England ever saw, has left an example for the imitation of every soldier, in taking as his guiding principle, in every relation of life, an energetic and unhesitating obedience to the call of duty." *

The remains of the illustrious dead having been removed from Walmer to London (November 10th), the lying-in-state lasted some days in Chelsea Hospital, when Guards of Honour were furnished daily by the Battalion finding the public duties; and thousands flocked to the scene to pay a last tribute to the memory of the greatest Englishman of the century. The funeral was fixed for the 18th, and the ceremony was on as imposing and magnificent a scale as a grateful country could devise upon so solemn an occasion of universal mourning and public sorrow. The procession started from the Horse Guards Parade, under an escort of six battalions, eight squadrons, and nineteen guns, together with representatives of every available regiment of the British Army,† the whole under the command of Major-General H.R.H. the Duke of Cambridge.

The infantry consisted of two brigades, one of which, under Major-General Shawe (late of the Coldstream), was composed of

---

* *Annual Register*, 1852, "Chronicle," p. 144.

† "The Queen, having been graciously pleased to command that every regiment in Her Majesty's Service shall, as far as practicable, be represented in the funeral procession of Field-Marshal the Duke of Wellington, by a detachment, consisting of one Field-Officer, Captain, Subaltern, Sergeant, Corporal, and six privates, the General Commanding-in-Chief requests you will be pleased to issue the necessary orders for selecting these detachments from the several Battalions of the Foot Guards enumerated in the margin, [viz. from each of the seven Battalions of the Brigade], transmitting the names of the Officers to this Department for Viscount Hardinge's information. In selecting the men for this honourable duty, His Lordship desires a preference may be given to length of service, when combined with good conduct and general orderly habits. The Officers and men to be fully armed and equipped" (*Adjutant-General to the Field-Officer in Brigade Waiting*, Nov. 4, 1852).

the 1st Battalions of the Grenadiers, Coldstream, and Scots Fusilier Guards. The 2nd Coldstream, then at the Tower, was posted near St. Paul's, where the interment took place, while the flank companies of the 2nd and 3rd Grenadiers, the late Duke's Regiment, took up a position within the iron railings there.*

Eighteen months had barely elapsed, after the disappearance of the chief actor in the glories of the great wars that disturbed the beginning of the century, when the long European peace came to an end, and again there was a call to arms, and the nation was involved in the harassing anxieties of a sanguinary struggle in the East with Russia. The Crimean war opens up a new era in the military history of the country, and as the Coldstream participated largely in it, it will be described in the subsequent chapters. Meanwhile, it may be convenient to mention, as briefly as possible, some few of the changes and reforms that affected the army at large, and the Regiment in particular, during the period (1837-54), with which we are now more immediately concerned.

It may be stated that, during the reign of William IV., there was only a sergeant's guard at Buckingham Palace; but in July, 1837, when Her Majesty took up her residence there, it was increased to one Subaltern and forty-four Non-commissioned officers and men. Again, before the Queen's Accession, guard-mounting, attended by the flank companies of the Brigade, seems often to have been held more than once during the year; but since that time, it took place more regularly as a Birthday ceremonial. Moreover, prior to 1841, the public duties mounted, as a rule, all the year round from the Horse Guards Parade; from that date, however, they appear to have paraded there during the summer months only (May 1st–October 1st), when white trousers were worn by the troops. The practice of mounting the public duties from the battalion parades during the whole year, except for about a month, as at present, began about 1849.

As early as 1829, efforts were made to increase the comfort of the men on guard, by providing them with means to cook, or at least to warm, their dinners, which, prior to that date, had been served up to them in a very unsatisfactory manner. Later, other improvements were introduced into barracks. Suitable washing

---

* A full account of the funeral of the Duke of Wellington is given in the *Annual Register*, 1852, "Appendix to Chronicle," p. 483.

and cooking arrangements began to be organized (1838 and 1843), and fuel and light were authorized for a room to serve as a "library" for the use of men (1839). These changes, however, were not finally complete until 1849, in which year also, the new barracks at the Tower (Waterloo barracks) were finished and ready for occupation. It may be interesting to note that, in 1850, by an order from the Horse Guards, all bagatelle tables in barracks were forbidden; and this was interpreted to entail the removal of a billiard table which had been set up at Chichester, as the Field-Officer in Brigade Waiting considered it "in the same light as the bagatelle boards which have been so recently done away with by the Commander-in-Chief" (*Brigade Order*, July 24, 1850).

Regimental Savings Banks were established in the end of 1843, and were brought into operation in the Coldstream by a Regimental Order, dated January 22, 1844.

Considerable attention was paid to the well-being of the Recruit Depôt at Croydon, and it is satisfactory to record a Regimental Order of the 20th of June, 1843, showing that the system then adopted, met the requirements which it was intended to supply.

"The Commanding Officer has not failed to observe the state of efficiency in which the recruits from Croydon have been sent up to join their respective Battalions, so highly creditable to Sergeant Trew and the Non-commissioned officers under his command in the superintendence of that establishment."

In 1849 new school arrangements were introduced there, and a routine of duty, both for the winter and summer, was fixed to enable the recruits to attend the classes regularly.

On the 19th of December, 1845, a medal for "Meritorious Service" was introduced into the army, to be presented, in addition to an annuity not exceeding £20, to sergeants recommended for distinguished service, and to be held while doing duty or together with pension. A yearly sum of £2000 was set apart for this purpose.*

* About the same time, the conditions under which the "distinguishing marks for good conduct" were granted, were made more easy. We have not attempted in this work, to give all the many changes which have been made to better the soldier's lot and to encourage good behaviour in the ranks, being content to indicate only some of the first steps taken to secure these results. It should, however, be understood, that when a reform of this nature was introduced, it very naturally grew to the advantage of the men, until it expanded into the system now in force.

It may be remarked that in April, 1850, a modification was made in the manner of keeping the men's accounts, and Officers were held responsible, as heretofore, to inspect and sign the pay and soldiers' settling books, as well as to see that any balances deposited in the Savings Bank were duly entered. A certificate to this effect was signed once a month.

Events contributed to cause the country generally, to bestow some greater attention on military matters than had been the case for many a long year. The fear that we might become involved in a serious dispute with the French, owing to affairs in Syria in 1841; the increasing hostility displayed by that people; and the revolution that disturbed Europe in 1848-49, induced us to make some augmentations to the regular forces, to reform the system of army service, and to reconstitute the militia.* But the value of these changes would not have been complete unless other means had also been taken to improve the state of the army. It is known, and recognised with gratitude, that H.R.H. the Prince Consort devoted his great talents, with the earnestness that marked his character so strongly, to the well-being of the army, and laboured indefatigably to secure reforms and to increase efficiency.† Lord Hardinge, the new Commander-in-Chief, successor to the Duke of Wellington, also took immense interest in the subject, with the result that the soldier's firearm was improved, and that some system of practical training was at last provided for both Officers and men.

The armament of the Brigade underwent a change during the first sixteen years of Her Majesty's reign. As far back as 1836, the Quartermasters of the 1st Coldstream and of the 3rd Grenadiers received "percussion muskets intended for trial;" but the old flint-lock was still retained, until about the year 1843, when percussion caps were introduced, and the "pickers and brushes," worn by the

---

* *The Army Book for the British Empire;* Lieut.-General W. H. Goodenough, C.B., R.A., and Lieut.-Colonel J. C. Dalton (H.P.), R.A., aided by various contributors, pp. 27, 42 (London, 1893).

Non-commissioned officers and men of the Coldstream were lent to militia regiments for the purpose of drilling them. On November 20, 1852, a Regimental Order expresses the gratification felt by the Lieutenant-Colonel at the reports which he received of their good conduct, and of the manner in which they conveyed the instruction required.

† It must be noted here, that the Prince Consort was an advocate of a system by which men might be allowed to leave the Colours, on furlough, before their army service expired, and so form reserve battalions in case of emergency (Theodore Martin, *Life of H.R.H. the Prince Consort*, ii. 436; 4th edit.: London, 1877).

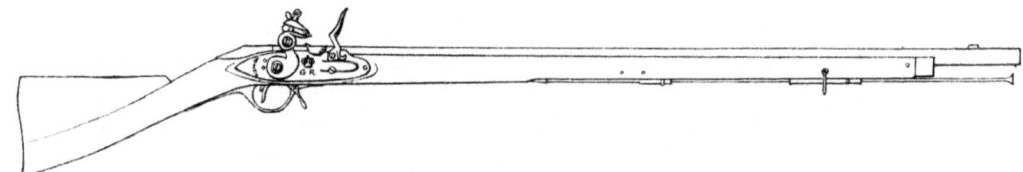

REGULATION MUSKET 1830.

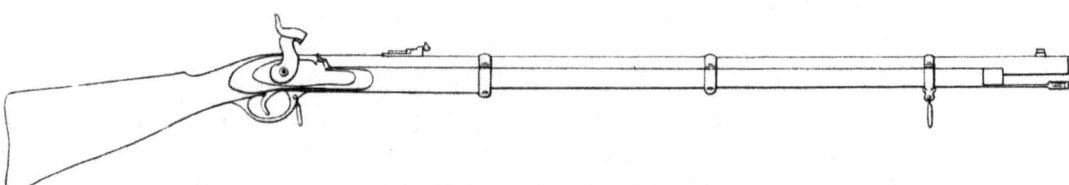

ENFIELD. 1853-1865.

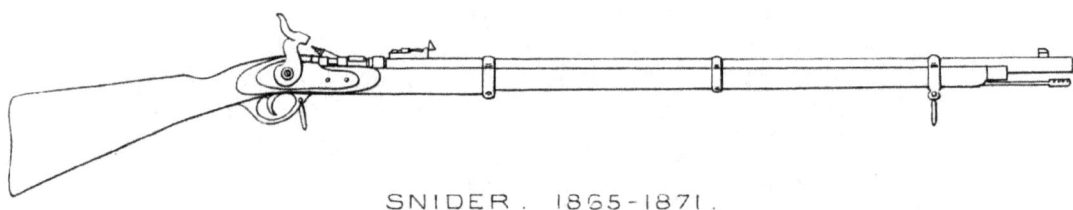

SNIDER. 1865-1871.

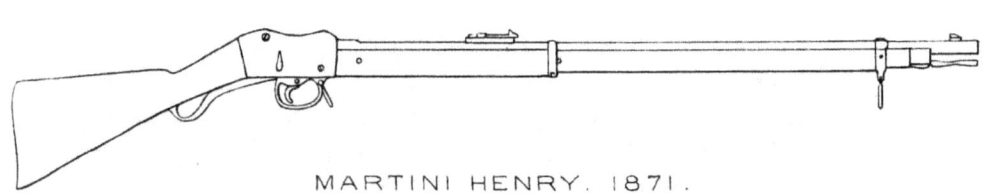

MARTINI HENRY. 1871.

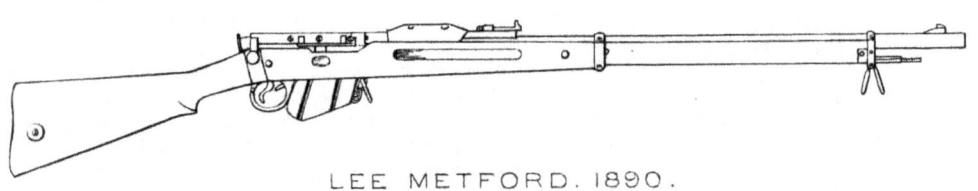

LEE METFORD. 1890.

Scale.

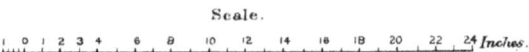

corporals and privates, were discontinued in the Regiment. The Minié musket-rifle was produced in 1851, and Brigade Orders, dated February 26th, and April 1, 1852, directed the seven Battalions of the Foot Guards to send two intelligent Non-commissioned officers to Woolwich, for the purpose of being instructed in its use. Early the following year, a few of these firearms were served out, when each Battalion of the Regiment received 200. A general distribution of the new musket-rifle, however, was not by any means complete when hostilities broke out in 1854, nor had the authorities apparently quite made up their minds upon its value; but, fortunately, sufficient progress had been made in its construction, and the Guards and the greater portion of the British Army, that took the field, were all armed with it before they met the Russians. It may therefore be stated at once, that the weapon which we had in the Crimea, was much superior to that used by the majority of the enemy's troops. Another pattern was adopted in 1853, but it was not issued till later.

Prior to the introduction of the Minié rifle, musketry was imperfectly and irregularly practised. Battalions in out-quarters (Chichester and Dublin) contrived to do so, but in London it was not attempted. Officers took much interest in teaching the men the use of their firelock, and encouraged them to shoot by offering prizes for which they competed. The ranges were, of course, short—100 yards,—the results inferior, and only five or ten rounds per man were fired. The target, some 6 feet by 2 feet broad, was often embellished with a figure of a French Grenadier, to give the men zest in their efforts to hit it. In 1853, a range was procured near Kilburn, and on the 25th of August, the four Battalions in London were ordered to commence ball practice there as soon as possible. The year following, it was but natural that "incessant" musketry should be ordered, and in March a party was sent to the school of Hythe, which appears to have been opened about that time. In May, a return was called for on the musketry as practised at Kilburn, and Captain Le Couteur (Coldstream Guards), "having made himself acquainted with the method of instruction as carried on at Hythe," was ordered to superintend all target practice of the 2nd Battalion which was then at home. It may be added, that drafts going out to the Crimea, were also ordered to practise musketry during the voyage out, and ammunition was provided for that special purpose. The present system of musketry now adopted in the army, appears to have grown out of these beginnings.

In 1852, several detachments, consisting of one Officer and 20 to 25 men of the 1st Battalion, were sent to Chatham for the purpose of being instructed in siege operations, and in the construction of field-works.

The next year was one of considerable military activity, brought about by the efforts of the Prince Consort, and by the fact that other nations, more especially Prussia, were devoting much attention to the training of their troops. A camp of instruction was formed at Chobham, under the command of Lieut.-General Lord Seaton, which lasted for two months, commencing from the middle of June. The Foot Guards proceeded there for their training in two Brigades, each remaining for a month,—the first consisting of the 1st and 3rd Grenadiers, 1st Coldstream, and 1st Scots Fusiliers, under Colonel H. Bentinck; the second, of the 2nd Grenadiers, 2nd Coldstream, and 2nd Scots Fusiliers, under Colonel Godfrey Thornton (Grenadier Guards). Captain Frederick Stephenson (Scots Fusilier Guards) was appointed Major of Brigade of both Brigades.

The instruction was of a practical character, and the troops acquired a knowledge of their duties in the field, which could in no other way be imparted to them. Some 16,000 were altogether present. Being the first peace manœuvres held in England (we should perhaps, in the present day, call them only summer drills), the camp at Chobham evoked much interest among all classes; and as the Queen, accompanied by the Prince Consort, frequently inspected the troops or was present when military exercises were performed, it became a centre of attraction to thousands of spectators, who flocked to see those unwonted displays of mimic warfare.

Thus ended the year 1853, the forerunner of the great war with Russia, which was so soon to try the value of the British army under the cruel test of hardships, difficulties, and privations. The army at that time had passed through a long period of peace; it had little theoretical knowledge of its profession, and was imperfectly served by those departments that are indispensable to its efficiency in the field. But it was a thoroughly disciplined army, one that knew its duty, that respected and obeyed authority, and that bore unflinchingly and without murmur, all the sufferings which it was called upon to endure. This was the army with which England again engaged in a serious European war. Nor was the country disappointed with the work that was performed. For, in spite of many shortcomings in administration and organization, and notwithstanding innumerable trials and difficulties, the troops maintained unsullied the honour of their Sovereign, by the conspicuous display of those pre-eminent and fundamental military virtues,—discipline and fortitude.

CHAPTER VI.

BEGINNING OF THE WAR IN THE EAST.

Position of Russia in Europe—State of the Continent in 1853—British alliance with France—The Tsar's quarrel with Turkey—Commencement of hostilities on the Danube—The affair of Sinope—How it drew England and France into the war—Three Battalions of the Brigade of Guards ordered on foreign service—Concentration of the Allies in the Mediterranean—Guards Brigade at Malta—Thence to Scutari—Want of transport—The Allies moved to Varna—Good feeling between the British and French troops—Course of the war on the Danube—Siege of Silistria—Retreat of the Russians into Bessarabia—Intervention of Austria—The Allies in Bulgaria—Sickness among the troops—Return to Varna—Preparations for the invasion of the Crimea—The organization and strength of the Allies.

THE Empire of Russia—except for the great expansion in Central Asia which has taken place during the last forty years, and which has now brought its frontiers close to India—was scarcely less vast and formidable in 1853 than it is at present. Stretching from Germany on the west, to the Pacific Ocean on the east, bordering the Black Sea, and pressing on Turkey, Persia, and China, it occupies an immense and continuous territory, both in Europe and in Asia, and exercises many and important influences over the civilization of the world. Inhabited generally, by a docile agricultural population who live in the plains, and whose liberties and property are at the mercy of a strong executive power, it is ruled by an Autocrat both in name and in reality, and is governed by a trained army of ubiquitous administrators and officials, who enforce his decrees, and coerce the whole people to spend their existence in the service of the Tsar. The organization of Russia, less adapted, perhaps, to secure the welfare of her subjects than to accomplish the will of her rulers, is skilfully constructed; and the sagacity she displays in the conduct of her affairs, is as conspicuous in the manner she brings fresh conquests within her grasp, as in that by which she controls and assimilates the numerous and heterogeneous nationalities, that are to be found within her borders. But here her advantages end. Russia has no seaboard, and her foreign commerce, incommensurate to her size and importance, is not sufficient to enable her to develop her vast resources, or to consolidate the stupendous forces with which her disciplined intelligence, large possessions, and teeming population should endow her. A glance at the map reveals the disability under which she labours. Fettered in the north by an ice-bound ocean, she has but two outlets through which to reveal her strength, and these are blocked by the narrow channels of the Sound and the Bosphorus.

That Russia is ambitious and greedy of power, few will deny; but her encroachments are not altogether due to the mere love of extending her territories. Her existence, as a nation of the first rank, is menaced by her maritime weakness, and until she frees herself from the shackles that cripple her commercial activity on the sea, she is the ready and easy victim of the Power that holds, and has strength to use, the keys of her house. But, added to this, her statesmen have long perceived that, as soon as they shall have gained the Bosphorus, they will win a commanding supremacy over the destinies of the world. While, therefore, they are impelled to a system of aggrandisement, in order to force their way to the sea and to preserve the life of their Imperial structure, they by no means despise the glorious goal of wide dominion, to which the success of this policy must infallibly conduct them. This, then, is, and has been for many generations, ever since their genius conceived the design, the reason which has urged them relentlessly to enlarge their possessions in Poland, Persia, and in Central Asia, and to exhibit undying hostility towards the Turkish Empire.

The Western Powers have not failed to recognise the danger to which they are exposed by this active and aggressive policy, and Great Britain, having vital interests of her own in the far East, has never been able to view with unconcern the absorption of Turkey by her Northern rival. Hence, it has come about that, when the Sultan has been threatened, many nations of the West have endeavoured to go to his assistance, and to ward off the disaster that seemed to be imminent. But their efforts have been badly directed; for, divided among themselves, pursuing divergent interests, interfering without wisdom, or led away by false conceptions of the real situation, they too often manacled the defensive power of Turkey, and gave victory to the Russians, when the latter had not won it by their own strength. In this way Russia advanced and prospered,—by the ascendency that organized intelligence will ever command over a policy of mere sentimental or unreflective expediency,—until 1853, when another crisis was impending in the East, which produced a great European war, and terminated the long peace that had existed since 1815.

It is not necessary to dwell upon the origin of the war. It arose from a trivial incident—the possession of the keys of the Holy Places in Palestine. The Emperor Nicholas I. reigned at St. Petersburg at that time, and he claimed these emblems of superiority as head of the Greek Church; so also did the French, in virtue of an old Treaty made in the sixteenth century, which, they affirmed, constituted them protectors of the Latin Church in the East. The Sultan adjusted the petty cause of dispute, and thereupon the Tsar made fresh demands, which the Porte resisted. These will be adverted to presently, but a word will be necessary here to describe briefly the position of affairs, that existed on the continent of Europe.

France did not long maintain the Republic set up by the Revolution of 1848. Louis Napoleon, nephew and political heir of the first great Napoleon—in spite of the old decree banishing the family of the late Emperor,—was elected President for four years by a large majority (December 20th). Strengthening his position with the army, by appeals to past glory, and with the people generally, by the maintenance of order in troublous times, he resolved to revive the Empire, and succeeded in December, 1851, in constituting himself President for ten years, with largely increased powers, and with the title of Prince. Twelve months later (December 2, 1852), he was proclaimed Emperor under the name of Napoleon III., and was so acknowledged by Europe. The new Sovereign was not blind to the advantages which a friendship with England would confer upon him; he was even anxious to conciliate a people he had known and respected in the days of his exile. The defect in his title, moreover, was best obliterated by the adoption of a policy of adventure. The appearance of the Eastern cloud furnished him with an opportunity he was glad to seize; and, as it became darker, so did he, the more readily, co-operate with the British Cabinet, in their attempt to disperse it. When it was determined that peace could no longer be maintained, an alliance was cemented between the two countries, and England and France, so often in the past unhappily opposed in war, were at length found side by side in the strife, combating the same foe and loyally supporting each other in the field of battle—rivals only in the honour and glory to be derived therefrom. And yet this union was not without serious drawbacks. Seldom can a confederacy of independent States be satisfactory; for each has different interests to serve, and conflicting opinions too frequently weaken the efforts of those who have banded themselves together to accomplish an object avowedly dear to all. In 1854 the alliance was definitely established; it became *l'entente cordiale*, as it was felicitously termed, and, when the war was in progress, harmony and mutual respect and confidence reigned between the armies engaged. But, as a price, to please Napoleon, England gave up some of her most cherished customs of naval warfare—a sacrifice which the armed forces of Europe had in vain sought to wring from her,—and hostilities assumed a direction which, as will be seen, did the least damage to the enemy, and effected injury to the cause which the British nation had most at heart.

The popular explosion in France in 1848, affected not only that country, but produced widespread results, and its consequences were felt, like the Revolution of 1830, all over the continent of Europe. In Austria the crisis had been peculiarly acute, and the Hungarians and Italians rose in rebellion against the authority of their Sovereign. The latter was able to re-assert his power in Lombardy by his own resources; but in Hungary the resistance was so strong that, when the Tsar offered the assistance of his troops, the proposal was accepted, and Russian bayonets reduced the Magyars to obedience, and placed them once more under the Austrian Emperor (1849). In Prussia and in the petty States of Germany less difficulties had been experienced; but the temper of the people had been aroused, and they clamoured for reform and a greater control over their own affairs. The German Princes were alarmed; they distrusted their subjects, and relied for counsel and aid upon Russia—the only Power whose government, like theirs, was despotic, but who, unlike them, had no fear of a popular ebullition. In truth, the credit of the Tsar was in the ascendent in Central Europe: he ostensibly saved Austria from disaster, if not from dissolution; he intervened in the question of the Danish Duchies,* which then agitated the whole of Germany; and he mediated successfully between Austria and Prussia, when they became rivals and jealous of each other, on account of the efforts of the latter to restore in her own favour the Imperial Constitution of Germany, which had come to an end in 1806. In short, the Emperor Nicholas controlled the German nations; he arbitrated in their differences; and could involve them in serious trouble should they see fit to dispute his pleasure.

When Russia, therefore, not content with the settlement effected with respect to the Holy Places, determined still to provoke a quarrel with Turkey, the Western Powers were not united upon the problem that invited their attention. England and France alone resolved to resist her pretensions, while the others—Austria, Prussia, and the minor States of Germany—practically ranged themselves on her side. The demands made upon the Porte are of little importance; any pretext is good, where an object is to be gained. The Sultan was required to accept the protection of Russia over his Christian subjects, and he refused to submit (May 23, 1853). In this determination England agreed; indeed, it is clear that it would have been impossible for him to deliver over a very considerable section of his people into the hands of his hereditary enemy. Thereupon a Russian force, under Prince Michael Gortchakoff, crossed the Pruth (July 2nd), occupied the Principalities (now the kingdom of Roumania), and established itself upon the Danube. The Turks immediately made great efforts to meet the emergency, by collecting troops and despatching them both into Asia Minor, and into Bulgaria. But no declaration of war took place, for the Western Powers persuaded the aggrieved party to have patience, while they sent representatives to Vienna to try to avert hostilities by the arts of diplomacy.

These endeavours failed entirely, not to say ridiculously. An Instrument was drafted, called the Vienna Note, to which both the Tsar and the Sultan were to consent, as a basis for a future arrangement. The former did so readily, but the latter peremptorily refused his adhesion to it. That he was right, is shown by the fact that the Note was so loosely drawn, as to be capable of an interpretation, whereby the full demands of Russia would have been agreed to by Turkey; and in the negotiations which followed, it became apparent

* Schleswig and Holstein, torn from Denmark in 1864.

that this was the only interpretation which the Emperor Nicholas had adopted! So the intervention projected at this centre of Russian intrigue, came to an end with the full concurrence of the British and French Governments, who were obliged to recognize that they had been duped. In October, the Porte formally called upon General Gortchakoff to evacuate the Danubian Principalities, and ordered Omar Pasha, the Turkish Commander-in-chief in Bulgaria, "to commence hostilities if, after fifteen days from the arrival of his despatch at the Russian head-quarters, an answer in the negative should be returned." After the stated interval, towards the end of the month, the war commenced, not only on the Danube, but also on the Armenian frontier in Asia.

Interesting as is the campaign that now began, to the student of military history, it will be impossible to describe it at any length in these pages. It must suffice to say that, at the end of the year, the results in Asia were unimportant. There were victories on both sides, but no great progress was achieved by either of the combatants. It was different in Europe, for there, thanks to the skill and energy of Omar Pasha, and to the gallantry of his troops, the Turks gained many and considerable advantages. Crossing the Danube at Turtukai, they secured a position on the northern bank of the river at Oltenitza, in the face of superior forces, and repulsed every attempt to dislodge them. Again, having established themselves firmly at Kalafat, opposite Widin, they attacked and dealt a crushing defeat (early in January, 1854) on a strong corps, which had entrenched itself in their vicinity near Citate. The Ottoman troops were everywhere victorious in this theatre of operations; the Russians, on the other hand, were beaten and disorganized, their *morale* shaken, and their losses, on their own admission, amounted to 35,000 men.

While these successes were being won, an incident occurred which caused the war to spread, and drew England and France into its meshes. A small Turkish squadron of a few frigates and smaller vessels lay at anchor at Sinope; whereupon, a far more powerful Russian fleet, consisting of heavily armed and large ships, approached under cover of a fog, surprised them, and completely destroyed them (November 30th). The attack was conducted under circumstances of considerable barbarity; no quarter was given, the ships were sunk, the wounded and the helpless were not spared, and 4000 men were slaughtered or drowned. When the news of this action reached Europe, indignation, already aroused by previous events, could not be restrained in England, and so strong was the feeling evoked in the country, that war could no longer be avoided. At first sight it may appear strange, that the story of useless butchery, perpetrated in war time, should produce so violent a resentment; but when events are reviewed, the reasons for it will be perceived. It is necessary to glance at these events, in order to understand some features connected with subsequent operations.

The guiding line of thought that influenced the statesmen of the two Powers, interested in curbing the aggression of St. Petersburg, was the conviction that Russia was at that time overwhelmingly powerful, and that the Ottoman Empire was in the last gasp of impotence and decrepitude. The Emperor Nicholas had for long fostered this idea, and had carefully instilled it into our Government. With this object, he made a journey to this country as early as 1844, and he pressed it upon our Ambassador at his Court, in secret communications held in the spring of 1853, before the actual crisis had taken place. We were then told that Turkey was "a sick man—a very sick man" who might at any moment "die upon our hands," and that it was therefore advisable to divide his inheritance; and our cupidity was tempted by the offer of Egypt, and even of the island of Crete, if we would take these bribes, and give Russia a free hand. We believed these assertions of omnipotence on the one hand, and of prostration on the other, though needless to say we had no desire to share in the spoils. Our minds instantly recurred to the campaigns of 1828-29, when the Russians crossed the Balkans, and forced a disastrous treaty upon the Sultan at Adrianople. We dwelt upon these results, showing only Russian victories and Turkish defeat, and we drew our conclusions therefrom. But we forgot a few historical facts connected with that war.

We forgot that the Russians could only undertake a successful invasion of Turkey, when they had the command of the Black Sea, and that we ourselves had secured this for them, in 1828, by annihilating the Turkish fleet the year before (August, 1827), at the unfortunate victory of Navarino. We forgot, also, that the Balkans do not form the last line of defence, but that the difficulties of an invader increase materially as he approaches the Sea of Marmora. In 1829, the Russian army had achieved a great deal, but it had not attained to victory. It was exhausted, and unable to maintain itself at the end of a long line of communications; while Turkey, on the other hand, was gathering her forces together. We surely, then, failed to recollect, that we seized the opportunity at that very critical moment to force the Sultan to make a shameful peace; thereby saving the aggressor from disaster, and securing to him advantages which otherwise he could never have hoped to gain.

As a consequence of the exaggerated dread inspired by the great Northern Power, the Turks were not allowed to act in their own defence in 1853; they were obstructed by severe diplomatic pressure, and harassed by vexatious interference. At last, after the *fiasco* at Vienna, they could no longer be restrained by their timid friends, and, in spite of them, they at length declared war, in the autumn of 1853. Now, when the Emperor Nicholas ordered an advance into the Ottoman Empire (viz. the Danubian Principalities), in July, and when the Porte, dissuaded from using force to repel the invasion, was obliged to allow her enemy quietly to consolidate himself therein, Russia, to appease Europe, made an announcement that she intended only to seize a material guarantee, and would engage in no further offensive operations. She would only meet any assault directed against her. England and France had sent their ships to a port near the Dardanelles (September 11th), and, as soon as the Sultan commenced hostilities, they ordered them up to Constantinople, to protect Turkey from Russian aggression (October 22nd). Conscious of the dangers surrounding the small Turkish squadron in the Black Sea, very urgent requests were made, that the friendly fleets should pass through the Bosphorus, to prevent its falling into the power of the enemy. But these applications were all peremptorily refused.* To make the matter very much worse, and, indeed, to render the whole course of action unintelligible, *the Turkish fleet itself,* by the strong representations of the Sultan's Western advisers, was also kept back idly in the Bosphorus, and was prevented from sailing to the support of the exposed squadron! †

* "Our last information from St. Petersburg, still represents Russia as desirous to treat, and as determined, above all, to assume the offensive in no quarter. This confidence explained why our fleets did not move" (*M. Drouyn de Lhuys to Count Walewski,* Paris, Dec. 15, 1853).

† See *Correspondence respecting the Rights and Privileges of the Latin and Greek Churches in Turkey,* part ii., pp. 248-258. Writing from Therapia, November 5, 1853, to Lord Clarendon, Lord Stratford de Redcliffe, the British Ambassador at Constantinople, says, "I have succeeded in dissuading the Porte from sending a detachment of line-of-battle ships and sailing frigates into the Black Sea at this moment" (*ibid.,* p. 250).

Hence the disaster at Sinope became inevitable. When this state of affairs was realized in England,—when it was seen that our diplomatic skill was again at fault, that the assurances of Russia were not to be relied upon, and that our naval demonstrations were held in contempt,—then the natural consequences followed, and the British people, their Government notwithstanding, determined that the disturber of the peace of Europe should be punished.

Early in 1854, the English, French, and Turkish fleets entered the Black Sea; but the Russian flag had everywhere disappeared. The victorious Admiral at Sinope,—never dreaming that our extreme caution and fear of giving offence to his Imperial Master would prevent us from taking some action, or from giving the Sultan leave to pursue and capture him,—had betaken himself back to Sevastopol with the utmost speed; he only waited to make the necessary repairs to secure a safe passage, for "the Russian squadron had suffered considerably." Nor was the Emperor Nicholas cast down by recent events, except for the fact that Omar Pasha was steadily destroying his military prestige on the Danube, and was revealing to the world the real weakness of his supposed power in the field. He ordered his Ambassadors in London and Paris to demand their passports, and they left those capitals on the 6th of February. Meanwhile the tedious and fruitless negotiations continued at Vienna, and Russia, far from showing any conciliatory disposition, increased her demands. But these conferences came to nothing, and on the 13th the British Ambassador was invited to quit St. Petersburg.* An Ultimatum followed, calling upon the Tsar to evacuate the Principalities, and the formal declaration of war was issued on the 28th of March.

Before this date, preparations for the coming strife had already been made. Treaties of alliance were concluded with France and Turkey, and the expeditionary force was sent to Malta. On the 10th of February a Brigade Order was issued, whereby a Brigade of Foot Guards, consisting of the 3rd Battalion Grenadiers and the 1st Battalions Coldstream and Scots Fusilier Guards, were to be held in readiness to proceed on foreign service by the 18th, each Battalion to be completed to 40 sergeants, besides the usual Staff-sergeants, and 850 rank and file. The 1st Coldstream, then quartered at St. George's barracks, were sent on the 14th of

* The French Ambassador in Russia thereupon applied for his passports.

BEGINNING OF THE WAR IN THE EAST.

February to Chichester, where the 2nd Battalion were stationed,* there to be made up to field strength, and to transfer weakly or unfit men to the latter. This was the first movement of the troops in London, and the people, eager for war to commence, and ever ready to welcome their brave defenders, hailed the appearance of the men with unbounded enthusiasm. A contemporary writer thus describes the scene:—

"It was just noon when the Battalion left, . . . the whole line of streets, from the barracks, along the Strand, over Waterloo Bridge, to the terminus of the South Western Railway, was literally blocked by multitudes, all eager to show some token of sympathy. Many a hand was stretched out to the brave fellows as they passed, which they had never clasped before—men of the humblest station grasped hands in which the best blood of England flowed. 'Fair women and brave men' waved their parting adieus. The windows and even the housetops were peopled with spectators, whose cheers, and waving of hats, and kerchiefs, testified their interest in the scene. Many of the Officers were young-looking men, and the rank and file seemed to be in the very bloom of youth and manhood, and to have attained that soldierly bearing which only a perfect discipline, united to professional pride, ever thoroughly forms." †

The Battalion, having been inspected at Chichester on the 17th, proceeded to Southampton, and, amid the hearty cheers of a dense crowd, embarked on board the steamship *Orinoco* (22nd) for Malta. Arriving there after a prosperous voyage, on the 4th of March, they were stationed at Fort Manoel (4 companies), Fort Tigne (1 company), and in the Lazarette (3 companies). The strength was 35 Officers, 919 men, and 32 women, the average age and service of the men being twenty-nine and seven years respectively.‡ The following Officers embarked:—

Colonel C. Hay (*Commanding Battalion*).
Colonels W. Codrington; and G. Drummond (*Mounted*).
    Lieut.-Colonels W. S. Newton; Hon. V. Dawson; M. Tierney; T. Crombie; and H. Cumming.
Captains C. Cocks; J. Cowell; L. D. MacKinnon; W. Dawkins; H. Jolliffe; C. T. Wilson; Hon. A. Hardinge; Hon. Percy Feilding (Adjutant); Charles Baring; Hon. G. Eliot; H. Bouverie; H. Cust; H. Armytage; and Hon. H. Byng.

* The 2nd Battalion proceeded to Windsor, and on the 28th to Wellington barracks.
† Nolan, *History of the War against Russia*, i. 92.
‡ John Wyatt, Battalion-Surgeon, *History of the 1st Battalion Coldstream Guards during the Eastern Campaign, from February*, 1854, *to June*, 1856, p. 1 (1858).

Lieutenants A. Thellusson; P. Crawley; Sir James Dunlop, Bart.; G. Goodlake; Lord Bingham; F. Ramsden; H. Tower; Hon. R. Drummond; and P. Wyndham.
Battalion Surgeon J. Skelton. Assistant Surgeons F. Wildbore; and J. Wyatt.
Quartermaster A. Falconer.

The three Guards Battalions reached Malta about the same time, and were commanded by Colonel Bentinck (Coldstream Guards), who was appointed Brigadier-General, February 21st. There they remained for about seven weeks, awaiting events; while other troops, all infantry, poured into the island, without General Officers, Staffs, or Departments, wherewith to form an army. At first it seemed somewhat doubtful whether they would go further. Our Government at home still dreamt of peace, and could not make up their minds that war was upon them; they even seemed to have thought that, though a naval demonstration had signally failed at Constantinople, a military display in the Mediterranean might frighten the Russians! The interval, however, was not misspent; it was utilized in preparing the men for active service, principally in the exercise of musketry, which was practised without interruption. With reference to this important subject, the following, written by a Coldstream Officer (Colonel Wilson), who was present with the Battalion, will be of interest:—

"When the Household Brigade was ordered abroad, the military Court of Chancery had come to no decision relative to the suitableness of the Minié rifle for the general use of infantry. As yet that amazing tool was in the possession of only a few *select* men in every regiment.* Hence, Lord Hardinge, who, it must be confessed, did much for the improvement of English small arms, judged it expedient that the Guards should take 'Brown Bess' to Malta; but, at the same time, he despatched thither cases of Miniés, under the charge of a competent instructor of musketry, Captain Lane-Fox [now General Pitt-Rivers, late Grenadier Guards]. . . Thanks to Captain Fox's exertions in favour of modern betterment, and a few experiments, a right verdict was at length delivered. At Scutari, old Brown Bess was marched off ignominiously to the Ordnance stores, and

* The Battalions of the Brigade proceeding on foreign service, started with 200 stand of Minié rifles and 650 percussion muskets (*Brigade Order*, Feb. 21st). Even as late as February, 1854, the respective merits of these two firearms were so little determined, that we find parties from each Regiment of the Brigade, ordered to fire 100 rounds "of the common balls out of the old musket," and to report upon the comparative accuracy of the fire (*ibid.*, Feb. 8th).

the Minié maiden became the faithful consort of every foot soldier. How completely have subsequent events substantiated the truth of Fox's arguments!" *

Towards the end of March our French allies, already formed into fighting units, began to appear in Malta on their way to Gallipoli, when they fraternized freely and cordially with their British friends. A few days later, Lieut.-General Sir George Brown reached the island, and started for the same destination, where he was joined by five battalions of infantry. Shortly afterwards, Scutari, opposite Constantinople on the Asiatic side of the Bosphorus, was occupied by our troops, and the British forces in the East began to collect there. The Guards Brigade left Malta on the 21st of April, in three ships, seven companies of the Coldstream embarking on H.M.S. *Vulcan*, the eighth accompanying the Grenadier Guards on board the *Golden Fleece*; and, landing at Scutari on the 29th, they encamped there. Next day a General Order was issued, which announced to the troops the arrival and appointment of General Lord Raglan, G.C.B., to the command of the army in Turkey,† whose composition into divisions and brigades, "to replace the provisional arrangement hitherto made by Lieut.-General Sir G. Brown," was also notified. The organization and strength of the Allies will be given later, when they were more complete, but it may be stated here, that Captain F. Stephenson (Scots Fusilier Guards) was appointed Brigade-Major of the Guards Brigade, and that the following Officers belonging to the Coldstream were placed upon the Staff: Lieut.-Colonel T. M. Steele, Military Secretary, and Lieut.-Colonel P. Somerset, Aide-de-camp to Lord Raglan; Captain Hon. A. Hardinge, Deputy Assistant Adjutant-General, First Division; Captain Hon. H. Byng, Aide-de-camp to Brigadier-General Bentinck; and Lieutenant Lord Bingham, extra Aide-de-camp to Major-General Earl of Lucan.‡

---

* "A Regimental Officer" (Colonel C. T. Wilson, late Coldstream Guards), *Our Veterans of* 1854, *in Camp and before the Enemy*, p. 15 (London, 1859). The exchange of these firearms was not effected in the Battalion till the end of May, 1854.

† See Appendix No. IX.

‡ The following also eventually served upon the Staff as Coldstream Officers: Lieut.-Colonel Lord Burghersh, Aide-de-camp to Lord Raglan; Lieut.-Colonel J. Airey, A.Q.M.G. Light Division; Captain Hon. H. Campbell, Aide-de-camp to Major-General Codrington.

"The army, or rather the infantry element of an army," writes Colonel Wilson, "accumulated apace. Most mornings saw leviathian steamers letting go anchor in the Bosphorus; and an evening seldom passed without a fresh uprising of tents. But cavalry, artillery, military stores of all sorts, were yet afar off, tossing somewhere in sailing transports. In too many quarters, indeed, there were indications that the administration still clung to the fatal hallucination of peace, when there could be no peace,—still tried to believe that a demonstration within a mile of Constantinople, must be successful. 'Floriana and its parades failed,' some said, 'because Malta is so distant from the Pruth; but this concentration of ours at Scutari has a real business look, which *must* tell!' Unluckily, the Tsar knew that the government of England was built up of incoherent materials. He had faith in his old familiar friend, '*ce cher* Aberdeen.' His Greek spies informed him, how on the heights of Chalcedon stood no army ready to combat, only a stout corps of the unrivalled British Foot; therefore, he stayed not his hand. Old birds are not to be caught with chaff." *

The six weeks spent at Scutari passed pleasantly enough. The scenes around them were new to the rank and file, and many, in the Household Brigade certainly, had never dreamt of the East and its marvels. There was much to excite the interest of the men, and little to mar their enjoyment. British sports and pastimes were freely indulged in; the food was good; stores of groceries and other material comforts were provided; no hardships were endured; the heat was not too oppressive; the military authorities even relaxed some of their old-fashioned and most cherished regulations, and the dog collar, called the stock, which then throttled our soldiers, was happily discarded. Cavalry and artillery began, moreover, to arrive in camp, and we seemed at length to be consolidating into a field army. The troops were turned out on the Queen's birthday, and again on the 31st of May, for the inspection of the Sultan; and, as usual, they presented a splendid appearance, both in physique and discipline; moreover, they also began to look like an organized force. Still there was no transport, and the medical service left much to be desired. With no efficiency in these departments, how was war to be conducted? And as the deficiency was absolute, did our Government really mean that we should take the field? At last a makeshift was proposed, which is best described in Colonel Wilson's words:—

* *Our Veterans, etc.*, p. 20.

"The utter insufficiency of means of land-transport greatly perplexed the authorities, and, judging from the ever-varying complexion of the memoranda, orders, and notifications on the subject, which issued continually from the bureaux of Selimnieh, it was unlikely a satisfactory solution of the problem would be promptly reached. At one moment, we were assured that the commissariat (hapless institution! doomed from the very beginning to be the scape-goat of every administrative failure or shortcoming) would provide for the conveyance of tents, sick, baggage, and the like; an hour afterwards, it was noised abroad that that department declined to engage in such duties, that the poor Treasury camel, starved and cuffed about as it was, had quite enough to do to provide the troops with daily bread, without undertaking any fresh burdens. Then did a public-spirited man in authority, hit upon the policy of making the Captains responsible for the carriage of the *impedimenta* of their respective companies; naturally enough, this scheme was unfavourably received by those so seriously menaced in that delicate point—the pocket. The intended victims remonstrated, inquiring whence the purchase-money of so many horses and mules was to be derived? how losses were to be indemnified? meekly adding, that the project was unprecedented in military finance. These objections silenced the prescriber of the nostrum. The alarmed centurions heard no further about the matter." *

After this, orders were issued to all Officers to provide themselves with bât-horses.† Twenty-one were allotted to each battalion, of which two belonged to every company for the transport of tents (*General Order*, June 1, 1854). Baggage parades frequently took place, to instruct the men how to pack the loads, and to accustom the animals to carry them.

During the stay at Scutari, the question arose as to what further should be done, and, to resolve it, the British and French Commanders-in-chief proceeded to visit Omar Pasha in Bulgaria. The latter naturally desired to have the Allies at his back, and he urged that they should occupy Varna. This was agreed to, and the armies of England and France were at last to be transferred to the seat of war. On the 29th of May, Sir G. Brown's division began to move, and a fortnight later (June 13th), the Guards and Highland Brigades, forming the First Division, steamed up the Bosphorus for their new destination. The Coldstream were conveyed there in the steam-transport *Andes*. The

---

* *Our Veterans*, etc., p. 23.

† *Battalion Order*, May 25, 1854: "Officers are to provide themselves with animals for the conveyance of their baggage without delay."

men started in light order; a reduced kit was carried in the knapsacks, the great coats, smock frocks, and blankets rolled on the top, but the rest of the clothing and necessaries were packed in the squad bags and left behind.*

It may strike the modern reader as strange, that a proportion of women were allowed to accompany their husbands belonging to the force destined for the East. In Scutari they were lodged in huts in the camp, and though inadequately provided for, badly housed, and subject to inconveniences which could not be permitted in the present day, their existence still was tolerable. But seeing how incomplete were the transport arrangements, our astonishment must be extreme, when we learn that the British army, about to take the field in a quarter where no depôt or base of operations existed, was to be accompanied by these women, whose presence under such circumstances, could not fail to be a misery to themselves, as well as a serious burden to our defective military organization. Yet this was done, and we find two tents per battalion, making a total of ninety-six, allotted for their accommodation. In the subsequent operations these unfortunate women, as might have been easily anticipated, suffered considerably. They remained in camp until the embarkation for the Crimea took place. A few were even allowed to sail with the army to that coast, and during the passage the wife of a sergeant of the Coldstream gave birth to a daughter, who was appropriately christened "Euxina." Fortunately they did not all land.† They were sent back to Scutari, where the main depôt and primary base of operations of the army in the East was formed, of which a Brevet Major of the 30th Regiment was appointed Commandant.‡

Arriving at Varna (June 14th), the 1st Coldstream landed late

---

* *General Order*, May 25th. "There will be no store of any kind at Varna. Everything not intended for the field must be left here in store" (*Battalion Order*, 26th).

† At least some of the men's wives (none belonging to the Brigade, as far as can be ascertained) accompanied their husbands into the Crimea, and remained there, during the course of the campaign. When we come to the winter of 1854-55 (Chapter X.), it will be seen what hardships they had to suffer. In mid-winter a letter, dated December 31st, was published in Orders, stating that some women's clothing had arrived, and would be issued upon the production of a certificate that the women applying were fit persons to receive it.

‡ *General Order*, June 8, 1854. Subsequently a smaller depôt was also formed at Varna, under command of a Captain of the 50th Regiment (*General Order*, June 30, 1854).

in the evening, and had to pitch their camp in the dark. The site was unfortunately selected, both for the Brigade and for the rest of the British army, being situated on a slimy flat, close to a large lake of stagnant water, three-quarters of a mile from the town. Before a week elapsed, the intense heat, bad water, indifferent and insufficient food, and the monotony of inaction began to tell upon the men; they were afflicted with diarrhœa and other ailments, so that the health of the troops, hitherto entirely satisfactory, rapidly deteriorated. The French, on the other hand, had taken greater care of themselves; they occupied higher ground, and they suffered less. During the stay there—about a fortnight, for, on the 1st of July, an advance was made to Aladyn, some ten miles in the interior—the masses of the allied soldiery met each other for the first time, and the warmest good-fellowship existed between them. The French Chiefs, Marshal St. Arnaud and General Canrobert, often rode through our camps, and the men invariably turned out and cheered them with the utmost heartiness and good will—a welcome which was always much appreciated. In spite of the sickness that oppressed our troops, the Officers amused themselves, as they are always sure to do, in various ways, not least of which was a hunt, extemporized (but without hounds), after the wild mongrel dogs that were driven out of the town, and infested the district. In the month of June, the armies continued their concentration in Bulgaria; and by the 21st the bulk had arrived there, when, in addition to the detachments of Turkish and Egyptian troops that were stationed in the neighbourhood, they mustered some 60,000 men.[*]

Meanwhile the forces under Omar Pasha were seriously engaged with the enemy, and a few words will be necessary to explain briefly the military events that took place. After the victory at Citate, there was a pause in the operations till the middle of February, owing to the severity of the winter and to the temporary illness of the Turkish Commander. The Russians made strenuous efforts to repair their failures and their losses sustained in 1853, and they poured large reinforcements into the Principalities. In March, the Ottoman troops gained several successes. On the 4th, they crossed to the northern bank of the Danube and made a raid on Kalarashi; they repulsed an attack at Kalafat on the 11th, and on the 15th they prevented a

[*] Nolan, *History of the Russian War*, i. 201.

passage at Turtukai, while a like attempt upon Rustchuk was also defeated. But the enemy, under General Luders, succeeded about the same time in crossing the river lower down, near its mouth, at Galatz, and invaded the Dobrudsha—an unhealthy district, full of swamps, and badly suited to military operations. Overjoyed with this advantage, Gortchakoff now reinforced Luders. After a series of well-contested engagements, at the price of great losses, the principal fortresses of the province, as far as Trajan's wall (which extends from Rassova to Kustendji, on the Black Sea), were reduced; while Omar left them to their fate, and took no steps to retrieve the fortunes of the campaign in this quarter. These reverses, however, were partially compensated by another victory near Kalafat, and, as the Russians retired before the Turks in this direction, Krajova was occupied by the latter. This retreat was in reality a change of plan, for the enemy moved a portion of his forces to the east, and pressed on the right of Omar's line, with the design of establishing himself between Varna and Silistria.* His design was now to lay siege to the latter place, which interposed, and which he had to take, if he meant to try and establish a footing in Eastern Bulgaria.

The protracted siege of Silistria has become famous in the annals of the war, indeed in the history of military achievements. Space does not allow a proper description of the gallant and desperate resistance, which was then made by the Turks against overwhelming odds; but the principal points connected therewith may be glanced at in this work, if only because the British Officer, Major Butler, to whom, with Major Nasmyth, great glory is due for the defence, was transferred to the Coldstream Guards, as a reward for his brilliant services, though he never belonged to the Regiment, for his death occurred before he was actually gazetted.†

Silistria was attacked on the 14th of April, but it was three weeks later before a partial investment of the place was effected. The Russians were determined to take the place at any cost, and they made desperate efforts to accomplish their object; they brought up all their available forces, and placed their most

* Nolan, *History of the Russian War*, i. 127, etc.

† Captain J. A. Butler, from half-pay, Ceylon Rifles, was gazetted Lieutenant and Captain Coldstream Guards, July 15, 1854; he was promoted Brevet-Major; and, on the 28th following, Lieutenant Ramsden was appointed Lieutenant and Captain, *vice* Brevet-Major Butler, "died of his wounds." His death took place on June 22nd, but his appointment was never cancelled.

renowned and capable Officers in command. During the siege, the war seemed almost everywhere else to stand still in Eastern Bulgaria, and all eyes were fixed on the memorable drama, that was being enacted in this part of the theatre of operations. The garrison was weak, and the indifferent works were only hastily repaired and strengthened; but the defenders were well led, while the matchless bravery and the military virtues of the Turk were fully displayed. Among the leaders, Mussa Pasha, the Commander, stood pre-eminent for intrepidity and firmness. He was admirably supported by the two British Officers, Captain Butler and Lieutenant Nasmyth, whose scientific knowledge, ardent valour, and cool judgment made their services of the utmost value, and gained for them undying renown. The enemy having drawn his lines as close as possible to the fortifications, resorted to every art to carry them. His principal efforts were directed towards an open work, called Arab Tabia, whose fall would have disconcerted the whole defence. Time after time, during the month of May, the besiegers bombarded the stronghold, sapped up to it, tried to mine it, and assaulted it both by day and by night. All to no purpose; every attempt was repulsed with slaughter and disgrace. The Turks held fast to their entrenchments, repaired them, met the enemy underground by countermines, and made continual sorties, which they always pressed home. Nowhere was a lodgment made; the troops of the Tsar gained no single advantage, but were harassed and beaten. During this time Omar Pasha was at Shumla, only some fifty miles distant, at the head of a formidable corps. Contrary to his well-known character and to his previous conduct in the war, he unaccountably remained inactive, and his subordinates near him followed his example. But in the beginning of June, he broke loose from the fetters that seemed to numb his faculties, and once more began to display something of his wonted energy. He ordered attacks to be made on various points of the Danube, which were successful; and he pushed a brigade to Silistria, which entered it and reinforced it. The Russians were now thoroughly disheartened, and, under cover of a final assault, they raised the siege on the 23rd of June, and fled in disorder from the scene of their disaster. In the siege alone they lost as many as 12,000 men, and all their principal leaders were severely wounded. Of the Turks, 4000 to 5000 men fell, but among them were counted the brave Mussa and the heroic Butler, who succumbed to his wounds on the 22nd, the day before victory crowned his noble deeds.*

Nor was this the only success gained by the Ottoman troops. During May, the Turkish army based on Western Bulgaria, and operating from Kalafat, was not idle, and defeated the enemy in several engagements, pushing him back towards the east. By the end of the month, this advance began to have some effect on the fortunes of the siege, and to be inconvenient to the communications of the Russians. When, therefore, the latter gave up all hope of taking Silistria, and left it in despair, they also soon after evacuated all the strong places they had taken in the Dobrudsha, and, re-crossing the river, they abandoned that province. This event was followed by an attack on Giurgevo, opposite Rustchuk, where the Russians still endeavoured to maintain a position; but the Turks drove them out, and forced them to fall back towards Bucharest, in the middle of July. Shortly afterwards, the enemy made a disorderly retreat towards the Pruth, pursued by the victorious Turks, who entered the Roumanian capital in triumph on August 8th.

"The retreat of Gortchakoff was neither dignified nor skilful; his whining appeals to the inhabitants for mercy, and his haste to get his troops beyond the reach of their enemies, contrasted ludicrously with the braggart bulletins and proclamations which were so profusely scattered, when there was no armed foe to dispute the seizure of the 'material guarantee.'" †

About this time another element was introduced into the tangled web of Eastern affairs, which had great influence over the course of events, and over the future conduct of the Anglo-French Allies. Austria now intervened; and her action at this juncture led to important results. This action must be taken briefly into consideration before we can understand the causes that led to the invasion of the Crimea. The geographical position of this Empire necessarily exercises a deciding control over the communications of an army entering the Ottoman territory from the north. Austria, in short, commands the lid of the Turkish box; she can open it, and she can shut it, and prevent the hand of Russia from trying to snatch the prize—Constantinople—which lies at the bottom. In 1853, she held the lid wide open; but in 1854 another course was adopted,

* Nolan, *History of the Russian War*, i. 214, etc.; Alexander W. Kinglake, *The Invasion of the Crimea*, ii. 48, etc.

† Nolan, i. 236.

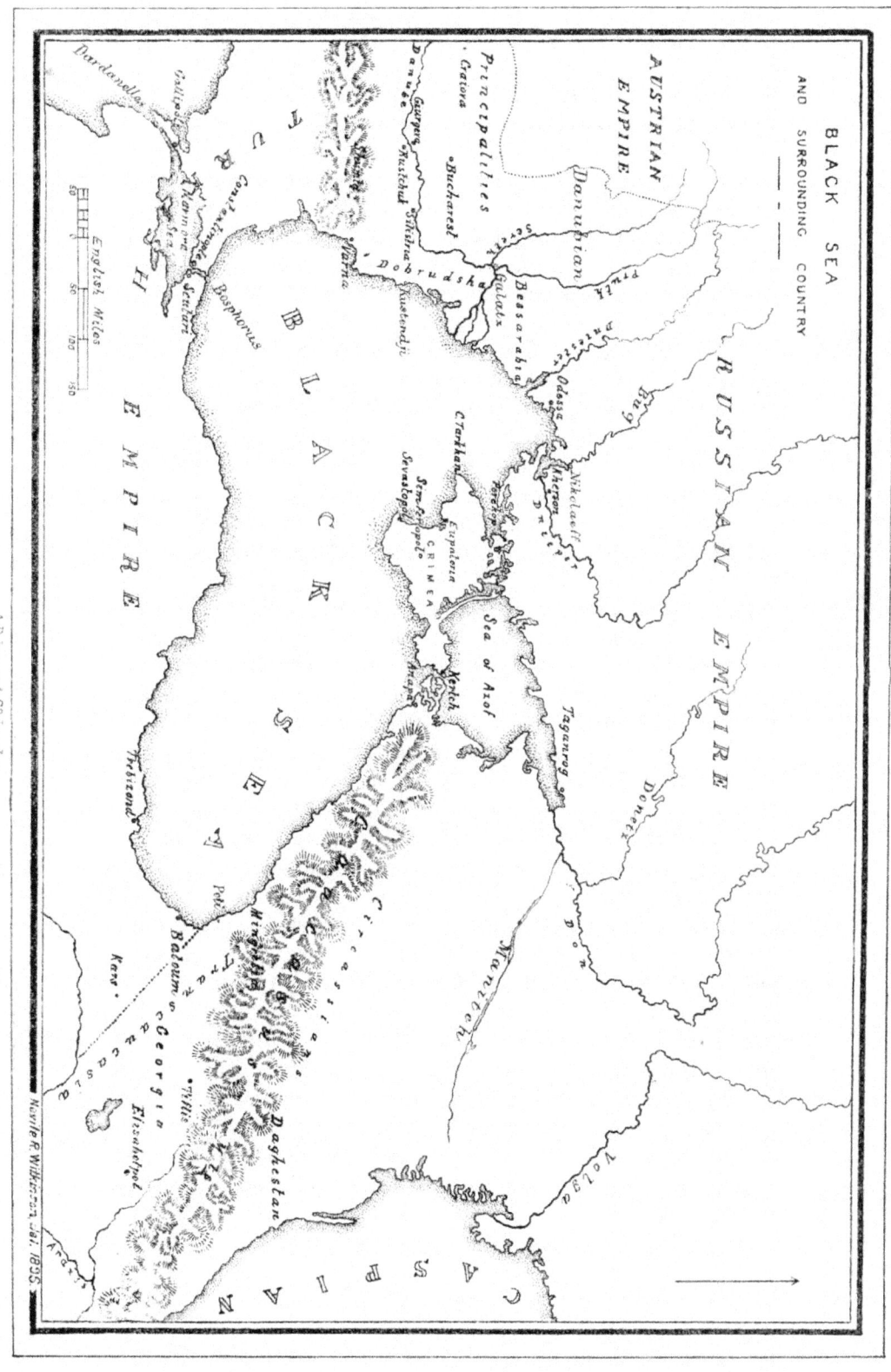

more pleasing to the Allies, though not less gratifying to the Tsar. It would not have suited the Government of Vienna to run directly counter to the two maritime Powers of Europe, and to declare themselves openly on the side of Russia; a diversion in Italy might have been serious to their prosperity. So the plain policy of opening the lid could no longer be maintained with safety. They therefore concentrated a force of observation on the south-eastern frontier early in spring, and, having prudently made an offensive and defensive treaty with Prussia, whom they did not trust, they calmly awaited events; and nothing was done till the summer. Austria then prepared for future contingencies, by inducing the Porte to sign a convention (June 14, 1854), by which she undertook to make Russia evacuate the Principalities, and to occupy them herself while hostilities lasted. Still she avoided any dispute with the Emperor Nicholas; she remained inactive, until the fortunes of the war should decide which of the belligerents was going to win in the field. On the 20th of August, however, when victory had declared itself entirely on the side of the Ottoman armies, then, and then only, her forces entered the Principalities, under the agreement that had been already signed, and thereby she rendered several important services to the Russians. She protected their retreat, saved them from disaster, and enabled them to proceed undisturbed into the Crimea, by preventing the Turks from pressing upon them, during their unfortunate march to the Pruth. She became a barrier in the way of the Allies should they deem it necessary to invade Bessarabia, and take a "material guarantee" for the repression of future encroachments in Turkey. And, lastly, she upheld the false prestige of the Tsar's omnipotence, by making it appear that the Russians had evacuated the Danubian Principalities, not because they were forced to do so by the unaided valour of the Turks, but because the strategic position of the Austrian Empire had obliged them to retire.

Meanwhile, little or nothing had been done by the Allies. Their fleets, indeed, found no enemy to oppose them. Except, therefore, bombarding Odessa (April 22nd) to avenge an outrage on a flag of truce, and destroying batteries erected at the mouth of the Danube, there is nothing of interest to record. It is to be noted that we neither utilized, nor assisted the Turks to utilize, this great and important river—over which our naval superiority gave us considerable power—for the purpose of the war; but if our Ministry had the intention of remaining inactive in Bulgaria, the want of all enterprise is easily understood, and was the natural result of the policy pursued in London. In the military sphere, a few squadrons, under Lord Cardigan, were sent, in the end of June, when the fighting was all but over, to reconnoitre towards the Dobrudsha, and returned about the 10th of July. They acquired no information that could be of service, but, owing to the heat, exposure, and insufficiency of food, many of the horses perished or were disabled, and our small body of cavalry was uselessly weakened. After their return, a large French force was pushed forward from Varna as far as Kustendji. There was obviously nothing to be done in this quarter at this period, so no advantage was or could be gained; but cholera attacked the expedition, causing enormous loss, and they, too, were needlessly weakened.*

We left the Guards Brigade at Aladyn, close to Varna, which they reached on July 1st. Here a halt was called, and the humdrum of camp life was resumed. In the morning, the men were drilled, they practised musketry, made fascines and gabions, or threw up earthworks; in the heat of the day they lay about and slept; in the evening, the more energetic endeavoured to obtain some addition to the ordinary scanty and insipid supper. The peasants were conciliated, and a bazaar was established, under the auspices of Colonel Gordon Drummond of the Coldstream, which was fairly successful. It may be also noted that, after some discussion, the old-fashioned regulations were further relaxed at this time, and, shaving being dispensed with, beards were at length allowed to be worn in the field.†

The Brigade was inspected by Omar Pasha on the 6th of July, and his presence inspired the men with genuine admiration. Here at last, was a General who had really seen the Russians, who had fought against them, and who had beaten them. The sight of such a leader gladdened our gallant soldiers not a little; for they were sadly disappointed with their forced inaction in Bulgaria,—so close to scenes of martial glory. Now at last they buoyed themselves up with hope; they would move to the front and take

* On August 8th it was computed that 10,000 lay dead or were stricken down by sickness (Kinglake, *Crimea*, ii. 133).

† This change had probably a wider bearing, if we may judge by the following Regimental Order (London, July 25, 1854): "The moustache will be taken into wear by the Coldstream, commencing to-morrow morning."

the field in earnest against the enemy. But this, alas! was not yet to be, and before their warlike ardour was to be satisfied, many trials were still to be endured.

Next day, the Brevet, dated June 20th, arrived in camp, and made considerable changes in the Coldstream. By this gazette, Brigadier-General Bentinck and Colonels Hay and Codrington were promoted Major-Generals. The first of these Officers continued to command the Guards Brigade in Turkey; the second, appointed to the Mauritius, returned home; while General Codrington remained at the seat of war, and shortly afterwards obtained a brigade there;* and before the peace, he became Commander-in-chief of the British army in the Crimea. Owing to these changes, Colonel Hon. A. Upton became Lieutenant-Colonel of the Regiment, while Colonel Hon. G. Upton was posted to the command of the 1st Battalion, and Colonel G. Drummond to the 2nd Battalion. The latter accordingly, as soon as he was relieved, was ordered to proceed to England, as also were the following Officers, who were transferred on promotion to the home Battalion: Lieut.-Colonel Newton, Captains Halkett, Cowell, and Lieutenant Thellusson. By Brigade Order (London, June 6th) a draft of 150 men for each Battalion in Turkey, was held in readiness to proceed to the East on the 1st of July. The Coldstream detachment, under the command of Colonel Hon. G. Upton and nine other Officers, including a Medical Officer, embarked in H.M.S. *Vulcan* on the 27th, and reached Aladyn on the 20th of July. About the same time, on the promotion of Captain F. Stephenson, Captain Hon. P. Feilding temporarily took his place as Brigade Major, and Captain Hon. G. Eliot became Acting Adjutant of the Battalion.†

---

* Vacant by the appointment of Major-General R. Airey as Quartermaster-General on Lord Raglan's Staff, *vice* Major-General Lord de Ros, invalided home.

† The Officers of the Battalion were posted as follows: Commanding Officer, Colonel Hon. G. Upton; Acting Adjutant, Captain Hon. G. Eliot; Quartermaster, A. Falconer; Medical Officers—Battalion Surgeon, J. Skelton; Assistant Surgeons, F. Wildbore, J. Wyatt, J. Trotter.

Company.		Lieutenants.	Ensigns.
No. 1.	...	Capts. H. Jolliffe.	Lts. F. Ramsden.
		C. Baring.	
No. 2.	Colonel Lord F. Paulet.	L. D. MacKinnon.	Hon. R. Drummond.
			Hon. W. Wellesley.
No. 3.	Lt.-Col. T. Crombie.	H. Armytage.	H. Tower.

[*Continued on next page.*

The camp at Aladyn was placed near the lake of Devna in a singularly beautiful spot, "the seventh heaven of the artist;" but it was terribly unhealthy, and entirely unsuited to a military station.* Sickness, in the shape of typhus, dysentery, and ague, was not long in appearing among the troops. It assumed increasing and alarming proportions, and it was found very difficult to restore the strength of those who were once attacked. During July, about a fifth of the Battalion were admitted into hospital; the men lost their elasticity, and their spirits drooped. On the 27th of the month, it was determined to move to a higher situation near Gevreklek, a village about three miles away. It was hoped that the change would produce an improvement, and everything was done to endeavour to stay the disorders that had broken out; but without avail, and cholera appearing, added its ghastly horrors to the general distress. In spite of the efforts of the military authorities, and the devotion of the doctors, the medical department was unable to bear the strain thus suddenly put upon it, and the sick, placed in small bell tents, and unprotected from the scorching heat, suffered terribly. The rest, weakened by disease, awed by the plague that burst upon them, and doomed to passive inactivity, were depressed and nerveless.

"A heavy torpor hung about the camp, voices rarely to be heard, except when the sergeants warned the duties, or summoned a funeral party to turn out. The poor men lounged about pallid, gloomy, depressed, and, worst of signs, their appetites were remarkably affected; not half of their daily portion of pork or beef could they consume; and yet, with strange perversity, the authorities chose this moment as the apt time for superadding an extra half pound of meat to the rations—the original allowance being overmuch for our feeble digestions, we were to get still more!" †

Company.		Lieutenants.	Ensigns.
No. 4.	Lt.-Col. Hon. R. Boyle.	Capts. W. Dawkins.	Lts. Sir J. Dunlop, Bart.
			Percy Wyndham.
No. 5.	Lt.-Col. C. Cocks.	H. Bouverie.	P. Crawley.
			A. J. Fremantle.
No. 6.	Lt.-Col. M. Tierney.	C. Strong.	H. Cust.
			E. A. Disbrowe.
No. 7.	Colonel W. Trevelyan.	Lord Dunkellin.	G. Goodlake.
No. 8.	Lt.-Col. Hon. V. Dawson.	C. T. Wilson.	
		Hon. G. Eliot.	

* This remark does not apply only to this camp, but to every camp occupied by the British army in Bulgaria at this time. The evils that befell the Brigade of Guards were reproduced with greater or less intensity, at each of our military stations in this Turkish province.

† *Our Veterans*, etc., 81.

BEGINNING OF THE WAR IN THE EAST.

At length the stricken troops were moved out of the pestilential place in which they were stationed; a new decision was made, and the British army was to be taken back to Varna. The Brigade left Gevreklek early on the 16th of August, and such was the condition to which they were reduced, that three days were required to accomplish a distance of less than fifteen miles; the health of the men was so entirely broken down, that they were unable to carry their packs during the short stages of five miles each.

"Seldom has there been a more dismal march. The men, very ghosts of the rosy giants who, but six short months before, had stepped so cheerily across Waterloo Bridge, now plodded along in gloomy silence. Not the most tremulous version of a song, not the feeblest effort at a joke proceeded from the haggard ranks; and, worst sign of all, even tobacco had fallen to a discount; . . . and yet 'twas the flesh alone that ailed, the spirit was willing as ever; ay, that it was!"*

During the period the Battalion was stationed in Bulgaria, 57 men died in the camp hospital, 28 of them from cholera and 25 from typhus fever. The chief mortality occurred among the men lately arrived from England, who appear to have been very young, with an average age and service of $21\frac{3}{4}$ and less than 2 years respectively. Many Officers were also affected by the pestilence, and the Regiment had to mourn the loss of two among them—Colonel Trevelyan, and Lieut.-Colonel Hon. R. Boyle, M.P. Five others were invalided.†

Arrived at Varna, the sea breezes, the prospects of at last getting a glimpse of the enemy, and possibly the new site selected for encampment—away from the influence of the plague-breeding lake, in the position which Omar Pasha had originally advised before the British army left Scutari—produced beneficial effects upon the men. Though they were still sickly and weak, and cholera lurked among them, their health improved, and their spirits revived.‡ On the 29th of August, the Brigade embarked

---

* *Our Veterans, etc.*, p. 91.

† Wyatt, p. 15. Lieut.-Colonels Tierney and Crombie, Lieutenants Wyndham and Fremantle, and Assistant-Surgeon Wildbore. Lieut.-Colonel Cumming had been invalided from Scutari in May, and Captain Hon. H. Byng, Aide-de-camp to General Bentinck, was sent home in July, on account of ill-health.

‡ "At last the order to embark for the Crimea arrives. We are wild with delight at the prospect of being shot at instead of dying of cholera!" (Colonel Tower, late Coldstream Guards, *Diary*, Aug. 28, 1854).

for the much talked of invasion of the Crimea, but the start was not made till some days later. The Coldstream, 26 Officers and 737 men, were divided into two wings; the left wing and head-quarters on board the *Tonning*, the right in the *Simoon* with the Grenadier Guards. From the latter, to prevent overcrowding, two companies, under Colonel Lord F. Paulet, were subsequently trans-shipped to the *Vengeance*, and, on the 4th of September, to H.M.S. *Bellerophon*. The sick of the Battalion, 89 in number, and 30 convalescents, were left behind in the camp hospital, in charge of Assistant-Surgeon Trotter; shortly afterwards they were sent to Scutari with the same Medical Officer, who rejoined the Battalion on the 9th of November. A Brigade detachment, more-over, consisting of three Officers (under a Captain and Lieutenant-Colonel), four sergeants, and 100 rank and file, selected from convalescents and those unfit for active service, were left behind at Varna; of these the Coldstream furnished a sergeant and 33 rank and file, under Captain MacKinnon, who rejoined the Battalion in the Crimea, on the 4th of October.

The fleet weighed anchor on the 7th of September, and, getting into communication with our French and Turkish allies, the united armada started on its errand to the Crimea. The events that now took place will be described in the next and subsequent chapters, but, before concluding this one, it will be necessary to give some idea of the forces and organization of the Allied hosts that sailed on this memorable occasion to invade the Empire of the Tsar of All the Russias.

The British army, under the command of General Lord Raglan, consisted of five infantry divisions and of one cavalry division, each of two brigades. The First Division, under Lieut.-General H.R.H. the Duke of Cambridge, consisted of the Guards (3rd Grenadiers, 1st Coldstream, and 1st Scots Fusilier Guards, Major-General Bentinck), and the Highland brigades (the 42nd, 79th, and 93rd Regiments, Major-General Sir Colin Campbell), and of two field batteries of artillery. The Second Division, under Lieut.-General Sir de Lacy Evans, consisted of Major-General Penne-father's (30th, 55th, and 95th Regiments), and Brigadier-General Adams' brigades (41st, 47th, and 49th), and of two field batteries. The Third Division, under Lieut.-General Sir R. England, con-sisted of the brigades of Brigadier-Generals Sir J. Campbell, Bart, (1st, 38th, and 50th), and Eyre (4th, 28th, and 44th), and of two field batteries. The Fourth Division, under Lieut.-General Hon. Sir G. Cathcart, was still incomplete, as two battalions had not yet arrived; the remainder was formed of the 20th, 21st, 63rd, 68th Regiments and the 1st Battalion Rifle Brigade, together with one field battery; the brigades being commanded by Major-Generals Arthur Torrens and Goldie. The Fifth or Light Division, commanded by Lieut.-General Sir G. Brown, was formed of the brigades of Major-General Codrington (7th, 23rd, and 33rd), and of Major-General Buller (19th, 77th, and 88th), also of the 2nd Battalion Rifle Brigade, and of one troop horse artillery, and one field battery. The Cavalry Division, under Lieut.-General Earl of Lucan, was formed of the Light (4th and 13th Light Dragoons, the 8th and 11th Hussars, and the 17th Lancers, Major-General Earl of Cardigan), and of the Heavy brigades (4th and 5th Dragoon Guards, and 1st Royal Dragoons, the Scots Greys, and 6th Inniskilling Dragoons, Major-General Hon. J. Scarlett), also of one troop of horse artillery. General Scarlett's brigade left Varna later than the rest of the army, and reached the Crimea in October. A siege train had also been provided; but it was temporarily left behind. Each division was about 5000 men strong, and the English army numbered altogether some 26,000 infantry, nearly 2000 cavalry, and 60 guns.*

The French, under the command of Marshal St. Arnaud, were formed into four infantry divisions, each about 7000 strong, commanded by:—Generals Canrobert 1st Division; Bosquet, 2nd; Prince Napoleon, 3rd; and Forey, 4th Division. At first they brought no cavalry with them to the Crimea, but they had 68 guns. They were also accompanied by some 7000 Turks, who, commanded by Suleiman Pasha, were attached to the French Marshal's army.

* General Sir Edward Hamley, K.C.B., *The War in the Crimea*, pp. 31, 112 (London, 1892).

CHAPTER VII.

THE INVASION OF THE CRIMEA.

Small results gained by the Allies—Sudden determination to attack Sevastopol—Russian position in the Trans-Caucasian provinces—Conditions under which the Crimea was invaded—The allied Armada sails from Varna to Eupatoria—Landing effected at "Old Fort"—The move to Sevastopol; the order of march—The enemy on the Alma river, opposes the advance of the Allies—Description of the field of battle; strength and position of the enemy—Commencement of the battle of the Alma—Advance of the Light and the Second Divisions—Deployment of the First Division—Advance of the Guards and Highland Brigades—Defeat of the Russians—No pursuit—Losses—Bravery and steadiness of the British troops—The Allies lose valuable time after the battle—Arriving at last before their objective, Sevastopol, they refuse to attack it—General description of Sevastopol.

HITHERTO the Anglo-French Allies had done nothing in the great struggle, which had been raging between Russia and Turkey since the autumn of 1853, though they had been officially at war with the former for more than five months, and were preparing for the strife before hostilities had been declared. There was much cause for disappointment at this inglorious result; and it was humiliating to the gallant armies of the two foremost nations of Europe, to be sent to the East, merely to eat out their hearts in inactivity, when feats of valour against the enemy were performed almost within earshot of their camps. Nor was the excuse put forward for this apathy—the want of transport—of any value; for every member of the Government knew that transport is indispensable to an army's motion, and that without it no campaign is possible. That it could have been obtained is not to be denied; and the conclusion is irresistible, that the intention of taking the field in earnest, did not enter into the calculations of our Cabinet. But now, when the enemy, driven out of the Principalities, effected his escape under the friendly cover of an Austrian force, when the Tsar, moreover, in no mood to sue for peace, still breathed defiance, our Government were placed in a difficulty. They had undertaken to make Russia submit; but their diplomacy was unsuccessful, and their demonstrations were disregarded; added to these failures, valuable time had slipped away, and the season was wasted. Something, then, had to be done at once to retrieve the past, for the country was losing its patience, and would brook no further vacillation. Hence a change in policy became inevitable.

The Government had been cautious, not to say timid; but they now entirely altered their demeanour. They suddenly became bold to the verge of rashness, and resolved at any price to take Sevastopol by a *coup de main*. It is true they were in complete ignorance of the strength, defences, armament, and capacity of that fortress; they knew little of its position, and nothing of the peninsula in which it is situated; and, while the transport of the army was more than defective, the commissariat and medical services were not in a much better condition. But these things seem to have pressed them lightly. Their opinion was strong, that Sevastopol was sure to fall, directly the Allied forces appeared before its ramparts; and its destruction, they doubted not, would bring about a peace, and cause the Tsar to relinquish his arrogant pretensions. As soon, therefore, as the raising of the siege of Silistria put an end to the war on Ottoman territory, they hastened to frame a despatch to Lord Raglan, dated June 29th, directing that an expedition against Sevastopol should be prepared. The despatch was so worded, that it left the British Commander little option but to comply. He therefore accepted the arduous undertaking which was pressed upon him, though he did so very much against his better judgment, and he announced his intention to the Government in a letter, dated July 19th.* It was early in September, as we have seen, before the armada was ready to sail from Varna.

There can be no doubt, that it was anomalous and very inconvenient to send out a military expedition to check Russian aggression with no rational plan of action. In the beginning of the

* Kinglake, ii. 115, etc. It is not without interest to observe, that the draft of the despatch of June 29th, was submitted to the Cabinet the day before, and that it passed without modification or even comment. Mr. Kinglake tells us that the Ministers, upon whom devolved the momentous duty of directing the course of military operations at this critical time, "were overcome with sleep; . . . the despatch, though it bristled with sentences tending to provoke objection, received from the Cabinet the kind of approval which is often awarded to an unobjectionable sermon" (*Ibid.*, 94).

year, the terror which the supposed omnipotence of the Emperor Nicholas inspired, made us believe that all our efforts would be required to save Turkey from certain and swift destruction. We even imagined that Constantinople was in imminent danger; and the French rushed to Gallipoli, to take up a flanking position against the hostile columns, which were almost immediately expected to assault that city. This was our only plan, and we trusted to events to develop another for us, should it be required. When, therefore, we found that the result of the war on the Danube had overturned all our preconceived ideas, we were unprepared for such an event; and we drifted towards the first plausible scheme put forward, irrespective of ways and means. Hence, the descent on Sevastopol was in the nature of an afterthought: a crude design, hastily proposed and rashly adopted, without reflection or calculation, and concerted without reference to the Commanders at the seat of war, who, nevertheless, were forced to accept it, and were held responsible for its execution.

After the collapse of the campaign in the Principalities, the urgent question naturally arose—where was Russia to be attacked, and how was she to be coerced by the Western Powers? There were vitally delicate joints in the armour of that Empire, not inaccessible to our resources, in Poland and in Finland. But the resuscitation of the oppressed northern nationalities formed no part of our policy; they were held to be beyond the scope of our aspirations. So we confined ourselves to a few inconclusive descents on the coast of the Baltic, and the enemy had no serious cause of disquietude in this important portion of his dominions. Our intervention, therefore, in these quarters need not further be discussed.*
The army being in the Levant, principal operations were to be conducted there.† The Crimea, no doubt, occupies an important position in the Black Sea, and its conquest would necessarily cramp the future plans of Russian aggrandisement. But who

---

* The overwhelming catastrophe that overtook Napoleon I. in 1812, when, in spite of his military genius, he lost his whole army of 500,000 and his great power in Europe, calmed the impetuosity of those who might have hoped to invade Russia, as if she were an ordinary European nation. Yet the object-lesson could have been, and it is feared was, pushed too far. Napoleon's disaster was due to his own perversity and to his military pride; for had he been content to re-organize and emancipate Poland, and avoid the snow-covered and barren steppes of the interior, his success, in destroying the sources of the power of Russia, could not have failed to be complete, and the tide of her encroachments must have rolled back for generations.

† See Map No. 2, p. 149.

was to hold it, if it were taken? Sevastopol, also, situated in the peninsula, is a land-locked harbour, and a base of naval operations, defended from the sea, and, in 1854, it was partially protected, on the land fronts, by some indifferent works. If there were a good prospect of rapidly capturing it, the design to do so had much to recommend it. Such an event would injure the prestige of Russia, on which she greatly relies for acquiring power; it would temporarily put an end to a secure harbour suitable to maintain her fleet in the Black Sea, and it would be one step towards the conquest of the Crimean Peninsula. But was the chance—the slender chance —of prompt success worth the risk? Why enchain our whole forces before the walls of a single and isolated fortress, if the *coup de main* were to miscarry, and a lengthened siege became necessary? Was not the Euxine in our sole possession, and, as long as this remained so, was not Sevastopol outside the sphere of military operations, and entirely innocuous?

Austria had been allowed to close the western theatre of operations against the belligerent Powers. But it never seemed to have occurred to them to cast a thought on that other theatre of war, which still lay open to their attack in Asia. During 1854, the Turks were in disorder there; acrimonious quarrels broke out among the leaders of their forces, and, though the Russians made no great progress, the fortunes of the war were deciding against our allies, to the detriment of the cause we had undertaken to defend. In this quarter, moreover, we had every prospect of success; we should have exposed ourselves to the least risk, and, if victory crowned our efforts there, we should have secured the most brilliant results. This field of operations, not distant from the Crimea, offered ample scope for our energies, and, as we approached it in 1855, though we did not avail ourselves of its advantages, a brief allusion to it must here be made.

The Caspian Sea is connected with the Euxine by a chain of lofty mountains (the Caucasus), which runs from Baku, on the former, to near Poti, on the latter, and then, taking a northwesterly direction, skirts the shore as far as Anapa, close to the straits of Yeni-kale. The Caucasus forms the natural southern limit of Russia, but, in the course of years, by the incomparable ability and, perhaps, by the unscrupulous character of the policy pursued at St. Petersburg, the frontiers of the Empire have been pushed south of these mountains, pressing upon Persia on the

Araxes, and on the Ottoman Empire in Armenia. Now, communications with these Trans-Caucasian provinces (Mingrelia, Georgia, etc.) were insecure in 1854; for, inhabiting the northern slopes of the great range were vigorous, unsubdued races of hardy mountaineers, called by the general name Circassians, who for years had preserved their liberties and independence, in spite of the efforts of the Tsar to enthrall them. This eastern Switzerland had some claim upon our sympathy, if not because of the cause of freedom for which the people struggled, at least on account of the peculiar position they occupied on the Russian line of communications. Nor should it be forgotten that the subjugation of these mountaineers affected, in no slight degree, the tranquillity and the future security of India; for, until they were overcome, the systematic advance of Russia into Central Asia was not easily accomplished. Operations to support the Circassians and the kindred tribes in the Caucasus, had the advantage, then, of directly protecting, in the far East, those interests, to secure which, we had embarked in the war; and, if they had been successful, as they could not fail to be successful, even by the employment of a moderate force, the enemy must have lost Trans-Caucasia. The Russian Empire, considered to be safe from attack, was very vulnerable in this quarter, at a time when the mountain region was still unsubdued; and a blow struck there, making the Allies masters of the situation, would necessarily have enabled them to settle the Eastern Question as they thought best for the welfare of Europe. But the influence which was exercised over the Tsar's aggressions in Turkey, by the brave races, who for so long held the passes against tremendous odds in defence of their homes, was scarcely recognized and hardly noticed in the West in 1854.*

We have already seen that, owing to the benevolence displayed by Austria to the Russians, the latter were enabled to retire from the

---

* Major-General Sir Henry Rawlinson, K.C.B., *England and Russia in the East*, p. 272 (2nd. edit.; London, 1875). The writer doubts if the fall of Circassia has ever been properly understood. He alludes to the great efforts made by Russia immediately after the Crimean war to subdue these tribes; she practically accomplished this difficult task in 1859, when Shámil was taken prisoner. A year or two later, the extinction of the Circassian nationality was achieved. This " was the turning-point of Russian Empire in the East." The regular and successful advance in Central Asia took place after this event, beginning in 1863. Since then, but only since then, this advance has been rapid, and has proceeded without a check, until, in spite of " neutral zones " and "buffers," the present commanding position has been gained in Asia, almost within sight of our Indian frontiers.

Danube into Bessarabia unmolested by the pursuing Turks. This act on the part of a Power regarded as a friend by Great Britain, cost us dear shortly after this time. Its immediate consequences were, however, not unnoticed, and it was plain both to the allied Governments and to the Commanders, that the enemy would push his forces into the Crimea, without delay, if he got an inkling that an attempt on Sevastopol were imminent. Unfortunately the enemy got more than a hint as to our intentions. In order to prepare for the success of a *coup de main* on a position, it is evident that one essential condition to be observed is secrecy; nor is it immaterial to mislead the enemy by false attacks, alarms, and reports. But exactly the reverse took place. No demonstrations were made, and we blazoned our design to the whole world; the English press spoke of it freely and openly, since the end of June; and Marshal St. Arnaud had the imprudence to issue a vainglorious proclamation to his army, on the 25th of August, which ended with the following inflated words: "Bientôt nous saluerons ensemble les trois drapeaux réunis flottant sur les remparts de Sévastopol de notre cri national, Vive l'Empereur!"

A plan, previously concerted with the Officers who were to carry it out, upon so difficult a subject as the operation in hand, could not have been matured and adopted, unless the means of isolating the Crimea from the rest of Russia, had also been considered. There are two principal lines by which the peninsula is fed from the main land. The isthmus of Perekop and the Sea of Azof. The former, unconnected with the great river system of the Empire, was of service mainly to bring portions of the army of Bessarabia to the neighbourhood of Sevastopol. The latter, however, receiving the waters of the Don, served to take down reinforcements and supplies from the interior to the new seat of war. The despatch of the 29th of June already alluded to, contains a passage on this matter: "As all communications by sea are now in the hands of the Allied Powers, it becomes of importance to endeavour to cut off all communication by land, between the Crimea and the other parts of the Russian dominions." It would have been fortunate if, in accordance with these instructions, we could have seized the narrow isthmus of Perekop, but we did not do so, and it remained open to the enemy. On the other hand, a small body of troops could have gained a footing near Kertch, and have maintained itself there; for, the Allied naval resources were more than ample to support it, to occupy and dominate the Sea of Azof, and to cut the Crimea off completely from the supplies sent down the river Don, from the large depôts and magazines established in its vicinity. Such an expedition, moreover, would have served to blind the enemy as to the intentions of the invaders with regard to Sevastopol, and have made him uncertain whether the ultimate aim was not to operate in the neighbourhood of the Caucasus. Having much to lose in this quarter, he was all the more sensitive to pressure there, and greater deception could thus have been practised on his fears.

That these expeditions did not take place at that time, is probably to be ascribed to the belief of the Commanders that the whole force was little enough, in order successfully to carry Sevastopol by storm. The orders they received from home did not contemplate a lengthy operation. Not for an instant did any one suppose, that it could last through the winter. It was late in the year; barely six weeks, or at least two months, of good weather could be expected to continue. It was known that the winter in the Black Sea region was intensely severe and cold; there was no provision made for the army against the terrible hardships which the snow, frost, and hurricanes of the Crimea must entail. The plan proposed to the allied Commanders was a short operation, and by them it was so accepted; it was a descent upon a coast, a march, and an assault. Fixing their eyes intently upon this plan, the importance of attacks on the enemy's communications, dwindled in their estimation, and lost much of its value. Expeditions of this nature, were fitted rather to a regular siege, which might be expected to last for many months, and were scarcely essential to carry out the object which was then in hand, viz. to bring up every available battalion to the point, where a ready-prepared and decisive victory was to be gained.

These preliminary observations are necessary to a Regimental history, as an introduction to the events which are now to be recorded. For if they were not stated, it would be impossible for the reader to understand the reasons for the hardships, which our troops had soon to suffer, or to appreciate the glorious part they played in a calamitous war, where their fortitude and courage not only saved, but enhanced, the military greatness of Great Britain, and stood out in bright relief to so much that was unfortunate and damaging to our reputation as a nation of the first magnitude in Europe. It may in truth be stated, that to the British soldiers, and to the Officers who led them, the country owes it that a national catastrophe did not occur. Their discipline and dogged resolution never wavered for an instant, and they carried England unscathed through the ordeal. A history dealing with the actions of a Regiment engaged on that memorable occasion, would be sadly incomplete, if it failed to show this truth, or to describe the false positions in which the vital interests of this country became unhappily involved, and from which it was extricated solely by the manly bearing, and unflinching self-sacrifice of the army.

The armada, which left the shores of Bulgaria on the 7th of September, did not immediately sail to its destination; part of the Allied fleet had started before that date, but the whole met together on the 8th, and next day the British portion anchored in deep water some miles east of the Isle of Serpents. Lord Raglan now left to reconnoitre the coast, and to select a landing-place. His French colleague was ill, and could not accompany him. Proceeding from Balaklava to Eupatoria, he finally selected a stretch of sandy beach, covered by lagoons, at a spot marked on the maps as "Old Fort," situated some twelve miles south of the latter town, and about twenty-five from Sevastopol.* Meanwhile, the Allied flotilla again got into communication, the slower sailing ships coming up to the *rendezvous*. On the 12th, the magnificent and orderly array of the united fleets, occupying nearly nine miles of sea room, approached the Crimea, and converged on Old Fort; and then our men got a first welcome glimpse of the strange and unknown country they were about to invade. Next day, Eupatoria was summoned, and surrendered without a shot being fired; and on the 14th, exactly the forty-second anniversary of the triumphant entry of Napoleon I. into Moscow, the Allies began to land, the Turks on the right, then the French, and the British on the left.

The sea voyage braced up the health of the men; they were fast losing the lassitude and despondency that so lately oppressed them, and were regaining their usual strength, elasticity, and good spirits. "Notwithstanding there is no casting loose the foul fiend—cholera," and many casualties were reported; but the Coldstream seem to have been spared by the scourge during the passage, though eight sick were unable to disembark, and were sent to the *Simoon*. A foretaste of cold weather was also unexpectedly experienced, for on the 12th, there was a hail-storm "abundantly accompanied by snow." †

* See Map No. 3, p. 165. † *Our Veterans, etc.*, p. 102.

Before leaving their ships, the troops had the temporary character of the expedition brought strongly before their imagination. The bât-horses, collected with difficulty at Scutari, were left behind in Bulgaria; there was no transport for regimental baggage, except an animal to carry the medicine-panniers. Officers loaded their haversacks and their persons with three days' salt pork, biscuit, and such indispensable articles, that a short campaign required. Dressed in tight-fitting swallow-tailed coatees, resplendent with gold lace, now sadly tarnished, their clothing was scarcely adapted to the harsh trials of actual warfare; added to which, they were weighted and encumbered, and had the appearance of "animated lumps of undigested packages, all cloak, bundle, and hairy cap." Nor did the men fare any better. It appears that the only heavy part of the knapsack was its wooden frame, and this had been discarded some weeks before; when this was done, it served as a light and fairly good valise in which to carry the necessary kit safely and secure from rain. At the last moment, however, it was feared that the men were still too weak to carry even their lightened packs. But, instead of reducing the articles to be taken therein to a *minimum*, this *minimum*, in the shape of a pair of boots, a pair of socks, a shirt, and a forage cap, was ordered to be wrapped in the blanket and great coat; while the knapsack itself, designed to hold them, was left behind on board ship, together with all other articles of private property brought from Varna. Thus an unsightly and most inconvenient bundle was formed, ill-adapted to its purpose, and a doubtful place for the safe keeping of the few articles that were considered indispensable to the soldier's welfare.* Three days' rations, some cooking utensils, wooden water-kegs, and sixty rounds of ammunition completed the personal equipment brought into the enemy's country.

From the 14th to the 18th, the disembarkation of the Allies continued, observed by Cossack horsemen until driven away, and interrupted only by the rolling waves, which, tumbling on the beach, made it sometimes unsafe to land the horses and guns. The Light and First Divisions were on shore on the 14th; the Guards Brigade, remaining in formation till the afternoon, marched inland for about three miles, after the Light Division had started, where

* It appears that the two companies of the Coldstream which were on board H.M.S. *Bellerophon*, under the command of Colonel Lord F. Paulet, retained their lightened knapsacks (Wyatt, p. 19). The reader will be interested to learn that the men left Varna dressed in white trousers; the order to take cloth trousers into wear, is dated Sept. 15th.

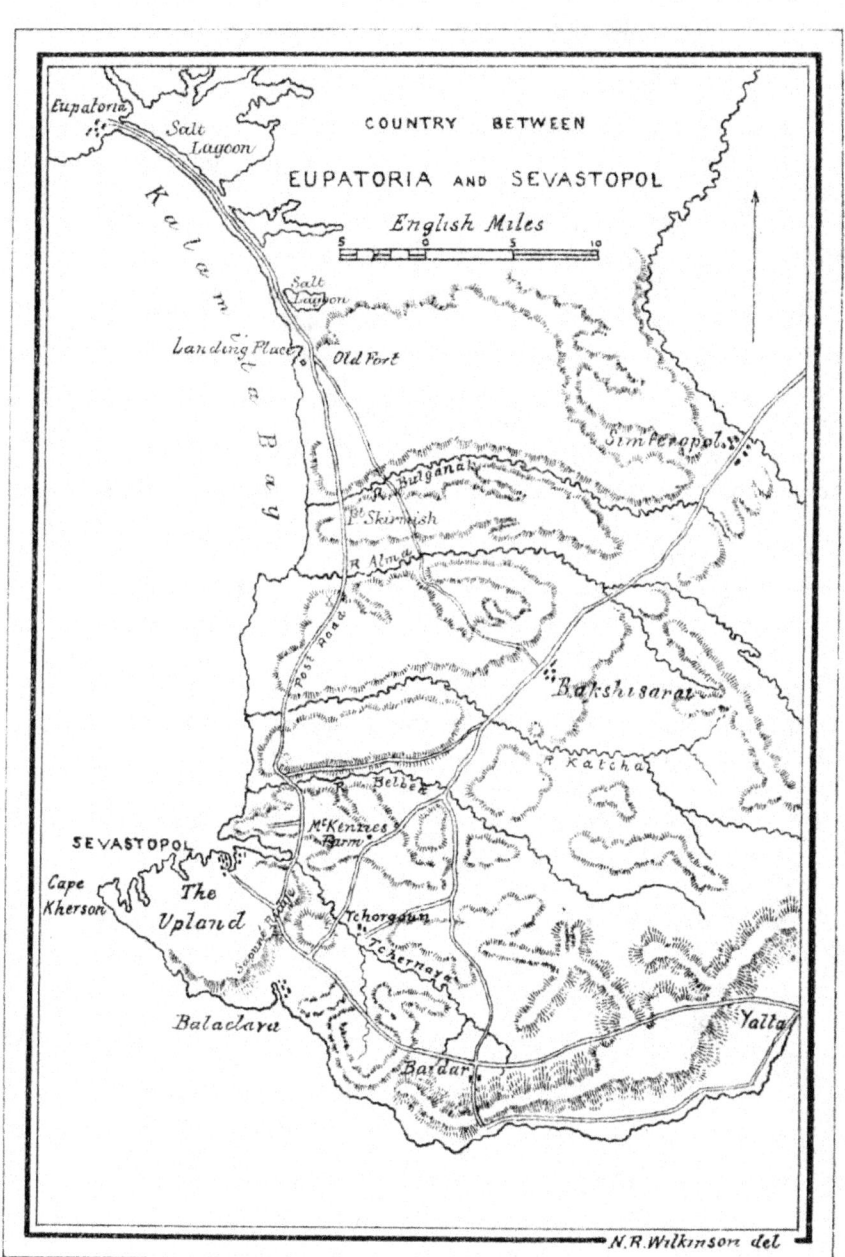

they bivouacked for the night. The morning was fine, but the evening turned very cold, the wind rose, and the rain came down in torrents, drenching all ranks and conditions, from the Divisional Commander, H.R.H. the Duke of Cambridge, to the youngest drummer. It was an inhospitable welcome that awaited our first night on the Crimean coast, but the men were in good heart, and made light of their misfortunes. On the 16th, a few tents were landed, but, for want of transport, they had to be returned on board the following day,—except one, which was retained for the sick, and was to be carried between the medicine-panniers on the hospital bât-horse. The story of the halt near Old Fort, would not have been complete had there been no "scare" to record. Was it ever wanting among troops, who for the first time await the approach of an enemy? Here it took place about midnight on the 16th, when an alarm was raised of the approach of Cossacks, and the troops turned out hurriedly; nor was it unlikely that the Russians would endeavour to attack the Allies, before they were ready to advance from the coast. Upon this occasion, however, a false report only had gained credence; there was no enemy in the vicinity, and the occurrence, though startling for the moment, doubtless, eventually served to steady the nerves of men who had never yet heard a shot fired in anger. In one way, things went smoothly enough, at all events in the camp of the Brigade, who, placed near a friendly Tartar village, bought small sheep at two shillings each, and fowls for fourpence or fivepence; but the dreaded cholera still hovered about, and one man of the Battalion died, after a few hours' sickness, on the 17th.

At last, early on the 19th, all arrangements being completed, the troops, horses, and guns landed, a small number (250) of country carts collected, and some cattle, sheep, and other supplies procured from the neighbourhood, the Allies began their march to Sevastopol, supported by the fleets that steamed slowly along the coast in the same direction. They numbered rather less than 60,000 men and 128 guns, and as the French and Turks had no cavalry with them, the united army had only one brigade (Lord Cardigan) to rely on. Marshal St. Arnaud marched near the sea; Bosquet's division was in front, followed by Prince Napoleon on the left, by Canrobert on the right, and by Forey in rear; and, lastly, the Turks and the baggage and reserve ammunition, were in the open space which was surrounded by these four divisions.

The British army moved on the left of the French, and were thus placed on the exposed flank; the Second and Light Divisions leading, the former nearest our allies, followed respectively by the Third and First Divisions, the Fourth marching after the First. The guns were on the right of their divisions, the infantry in double column of companies from the centre of battalions, and the cavalry divided, two regiments on the left flank, two covering the advance, and one in rear. This formation was adopted, because, the left of the Allies being undefended, it was not improbable that the enemy might venture to make an onslaught upon that flank from Simferopol. The weather was sultry, and the advance lay across a vast rolling plain, destitute of trees and shrubs, and swept bare of inhabitants and supplies by the Russian cavalry. After two hours, the heat affected some of the men, and, the ever-recurring plague of cholera still dogging their footsteps, victims to its ravages began to fall out.

"And now an astounding fact became patent to all—we had no ambulance! We had invaded an enemy's country without means of transporting the sick and wounded, beyond a few stretchers in the hands of bandsmen and drum-boys! The sick and wounded of 27,000 British soldiers were to be carried bodily over burning steppes, where water was not, by drummers and fifers! These lads being physically unequal to the duty expected of them, we endeavoured to supply their places with files of the heavy-weighted soldiery: but of course this hard expedient broke down too; the work could not be done by human muscle, in fact; hence, tall fellows, not a few, were left behind, to take their chance of being picked up—God help them!" *

But in the afternoon the attention of the troops was diverted from these scenes of suffering; shots were heard in the front. The enemy was expected to take up a position near one of the rivers that flow at right angles across the Eupatoria post-road, on both sides of which the Allies were advancing; and here, at length, on the Bulganak, the divisions in rear thought that they were going to try conclusions with the enemy. In a very short time, however, the firing proved to be but a skirmish; for, after the expenditure of a few rounds, the Russians—6000 infantry, 2000 cavalry, and two batteries—moved back, before they had made us deploy

* *Our Veterans*, etc., p. 122. Kinglake tells us that, in the evening, a force was sent to bring in the stragglers, who were very numerous during the march (*Invasion of the Crimea*, ii. 209).

much of our force, and left us in possession of the stream without further resistance. There we bivouacked for the night, in the full assurance that a great action would be fought on the following day.

According to an estimate of the enemy's forces in the Crimea, made by the Foreign Office at home, it was computed that there were some 45,000 men near and in Sevastopol, excluding troops which might be drawn from the Caucasus and Bessarabia. Of this estimate Lord Raglan had been informed, but it seems he placed no great reliance upon it. He knew, however, that the Russians were relatively strong in cavalry, and that their army was commanded by Prince Menshikoff.

It was between nine and ten before the Allies moved from their bivouacs on the morning of the 20th, the British army bringing their left shoulders up, to get into closer communication with the French. On reaching the top of a grassy ridge which looks over the valley of the Alma, the position taken up by the enemy on the heights above that stream, first came into sight, and immediate preparations were made to dislodge him. The field of battle is a sloping plain from the north to the river, which is fordable in summer, from whence springs abruptly on the south bank, to a height of 300 to 400 feet, a commanding range of hills overlooking the plain, and running from the sea, for a distance of five miles, to a bluff called Kurgané Hill.* The river makes a trifling bend, forming a slightly re-entering angle towards these heights, on the western side of the Kurgané; and here the post-road crosses the stream, close to the village of Burliuk, by a wooden bridge, which had not been destroyed. This point marked the junction of the English right and the French left. On the French section of the field, the heights press close and cliff-like to the river, but they recede and become more accessible for a mile to the west of the angle mentioned. Roads available for guns ascend the hills at the mouth of the Alma, at the village of Almatamak, at a farm a mile further up, and again close to Burliuk, where, on the Russian side, the ground is more practicable; this last road leads to a height known as the Telegraph Hill. On the English section, the heights are further from the river, and the ascent is everywhere easy for all arms; but on that very account it was the more difficult to storm, for here the ground could be swept with fire, and the defenders had every facility for

* See Map No. 4, p. 174.

making counter-attacks. The tops of the hills form a wide plateau, stretching southwards towards the Katcha river, indented only near the angle, by a depression between the Kurgané and Telegraph Hills, through which the post-road rises, as it proceeds to Sevastopol.*

The Russian army, numerically weaker than the Allies, being 33,000 infantry, 3400 cavalry, and 120 guns, occupied the plateau. The main portion, 21,000 infantry, 3000 cavalry, and 84 guns, was placed on Kurgané and on the post-road, opposite the English section; the remainder, 12000 infantry, 400 cavalry, and 36 guns, near the post-road and on Telegraph Hill, were opposed to the French. The cavalry took post on the enemy's right and rear, supported by horse artillery; but no troops were further to the west, where the ground was under fire from the war-ships. Menshikoff, however, forgot, though he had time at his disposal, to block the roads which ascend the cliff and the rough precipitous hillsides opposite the French position. Nor did he construct fieldworks on his front and right flank, contenting himself with only two gun-epaulments on Kurgané, one of which, about 300 yards from the river, was armed with 14 heavy guns of position.

There was a pause when the Allies approached the position they were about to assail, during which the troops refreshed themselves with cold pork and biscuits, after their march on a warm and glorious morning. In the interval, all eyes were turned to the heights that frowned in front, and saw in the distance the hostile sharpshooters extended along the river, in the vineyards and gardens, through which the advance was about to be made. Nor were we unconscious that the whole of our force was easily to be discerned, and our intentions to be divined by our antagonist; for we halted boldly on the sloping plain, in full view of the enemy, who, perched on the higher ground, was enabled to make his observations and to conceal much of his own order of battle from our anxious gaze. Meanwhile, the two Commanders-in-chief were concerting their plans. They had met before, but this was their final consultation. St. Arnaud had fixed and strong ideas on the situation; he was voluble in expressing them, and, though zealous and brave, he was somewhat shallow and self-opinionated. Lord Raglan's first care was to insure a good understanding with his impetuous colleague. He was hampered by the alliance; and there was no supreme Commander to give a decision at this

* Hamley, *War in the Crimea*, p. 47, etc.

moment when unity of action was indispensably necessary. The Chiefs parted, and came to no definite conclusion; unless a hazy understanding can be called so, that the French were to try and turn the Russian left, but that the British could not do the same thing on the other flank "with such a body of cavalry as the enemy had in the plain." *

At one o'clock Bosquet's division advanced. One brigade with the artillery, pushed through Almatamak and up the road there; the remainder, and the Turks, some 10,000 men, crossed the Alma near its mouth, and, ascending the pathway that leads thence to the cliff, found themselves far from the battle-field, and never fired a shot during the action. Canrobert took his division along the road at the farm, and debouched on the plateau a mile to the west of Telegraph Hill; but his own artillery followed that of Bosquet, and were with the latter's left brigade, a mile still further to the west. Prince Napoleon's division was on Canrobert's left, and made for Telegraph Hill; while Forey was in second line, in reserve. As the Turks were 7000 strong and the French 28,000, Marshal St. Arnaud had only 25,000 men and 68 guns in action.

The original formation of the British army had not been altered: the Second Division was on the right, the Light on the left, both in the first line, followed by the Third and First in the second line, the Fourth Division in reserve; four regiments of the cavalry covered the left, one followed in rear. The whole, 23,000 infantry, 1000 cavalry, and 60 guns—for part of the Fourth Division were still on the road from Old Fort—covered by the Rifles, now moved forward straight for the enemy's strong position on Kurgané, the right being directed upon Burliuk. The Russian skirmishers retired, setting fire to that village as the first line approached; while the latter, coming nearly within range of the hostile artillery, deployed. But too little ground had been taken up, and, in spite of every effort to rectify the mistake, the battalions overlapped, and were dangerously crowded. Lord Raglan, in pursuance of the arrangement already made with St. Arnaud, now delayed the attack until the French had time to complete the movement they had begun; but the Marshal was impatient, and before his troops could produce any impression on the enemy's left, he urged his colleague to wait no longer. In response to this strong request, Lord Raglan ordered his first line to advance.

* Kinglake, ii. 239, etc., 250.

The Second Division (Sir De L. Evans) was delayed by the conflagration raging in Burliuk; but the Light Division (Sir G. Brown), breaking through the vines and fording the river, gained a footing on the south bank, disordered by the obstacles they met, by the want of space, and by the hot fire poured upon them. General Codrington, heading his brigade and two battalions that joined him—one of Buller's and one of the Second Division—led them boldly up the slope under the fire of the battery behind the epaulment; while the rest of Buller's brigade covered his left flank from a threatening movement observed in that direction. On his right were three of Evans's battalions; the other two, under Adams, having crossed the Alma, below the burning village, pushed into the space to the west of the post-road. The Russians, seriously alarmed at Codrington's impetuous onslaught, withdrew their heavy guns from the epaulment, except two, which they could not get away, and which were captured. Cheered by this retreat, the British gained the breastwork, and took possession of it; but they now found themselves face to face with large masses of the enemy's infantry and cavalry, supported by field-guns. The gallant rush in the face of a tremendous fire had come to an end; it was the moment for supports to arrive; but as they were not close enough to be available at this critical moment, the attacking brigade was soon afterwards forced back to the foot of the slope.

Meanwhile, the First Division (Duke of Cambridge) deployed and halted just beyond effective range, watching with enthusiastic animation and breathless interest, the movements of their comrades in front of them. There was more room for them, as they were not overcrowded by the Third Division (Sir R. England), which took up a position somewhat in rear. On the right stood the Guards Brigade in their usual order—Grenadiers on the right, Coldstream on the left, and Scots Fusiliers in the centre; the Highlanders were formed on the left of the division. While they waited, spent round shot came bounding through the ranks like cricket balls. The men, longing to take part in the fray, were in exuberant spirits; the least trifle amused them, and a little Maltese terrier called "Toby," belonging to the Coldstream drummers, drew loud laughter from the light-hearted soldiery as it gave chase to the Russian round shot which rolled slowly along the smooth ground.

At length Lieut.-Colonel Steele brought the order to advance.

and never was it obeyed with greater alacrity and spirit, the whole division moving forward with admirable precision. Approaching the vineyards, the enemy directed his artillery upon our men; but they quickly pushed their way through the tangled shrubs, and over a low wall obstructing their path up to the Alma, which they immediately crossed, and here they found shelter from the fire of the Russians. As it had been impossible to reconnoitre the ground, each regiment had to take its chance of finding a favourable spot, or the reverse, for its passage; and it happened that the Coldstream reached the river, where it makes a large S-shaped bend, so that the greater part of the Battalion had to go through the water three times. Owing to the many obstructions in their way, all three Battalions were in considerable confusion when they arrived at the foot of the southern bank, and they at once began to reform their ranks. Colonel Upton, having halted the Coldstream, called out the markers to the front, quickly assembled the companies upon them, and then wheeled the Battalion into line, before making any further advance, in a manner that would have satisfied the most exacting drill-sergeant on parade in Hyde Park.*

Meanwhile Codrington's brigade were still in front, clinging to the epaulment they had captured, and engaged in a very unequal struggle with the enemy. Their distress was apparent from the river, and General Bentinck immediately ordered the Scots Fusilier Guards to hurry to their relief before there had been sufficient time to reform their line, and while their ranks were still disordered and their companies mixed up. As they moved forward, they met General Codrington's Aide-de-camp, who was sent to beg them to hasten to the front as quickly as possible, and they eagerly complied. Just at this moment a series of untoward circumstances occurred. The backward rush of some of the Light Division struck them with tremendous force; an order intended for the 23rd Fusiliers, "Retire Fusiliers!" was heard in the field, and was believed by many of the Fusilier Guards to apply to them; the enemy was close, and in hot pursuit, and his artillery was firing furiously upon them. It was a critical moment, and one that would have been fatal to any but the best troops; but in spite of the gallantry of the Officers, who, running forward, endeavoured to

* See *The Crimea in 1854 and 1894* (by General Sir Evelyn Wood, V.C., G.C.B.), p. 55 (London, 1895).

rally the men, two or three companies were swept back by the retreating brigade, and were carried away with them towards the river, while the remainder halted, opened fire, and held their ground.*

As this was going on, the other two Guards Battalions, now completely reformed and in proper order, advanced steadily forward up the hill. Coming into alignment with the Scots Fusilier Guards, and perceiving the hot engagement that was still raging, the left company of the Grenadiers was wheeled back, and fired across the front, while the Coldstream, without changing position, opened upon the Russians as soon as they got the opportunity, and the latter retired. Though there was a gap in the Brigade which could not be immediately closed, the Guards—

"continued to advance in lines absolutely unbroken, except where struck by the enemy's shot; such French Officers on the hills on the right as, in an interval of inaction, were free to observe what our troops were doing, spoke of this advance of the Guards as something new to their minds, and very admirable." †

Soon they reached the epaulment, firing as they advanced, the enemy giving way before them, and as they came up to the crest of the hill the three companies, previously mentioned, rejoined their Battalion, and the whole Brigade was again complete.‡   To

---

* The following extract of a letter written by General Codrington, on September 27th, will be read with interest: "We were borne back, and when I saw we could not long bear up in these groups (from which I could not get them), I sent young Campbell [now Lt.-Col. Hon. H. Campbell, late Coldstream Guards] to the rear to the Battalion of Guards which I saw, to beg them to hurry their advance, otherwise we must lose all we had gained. . . . I saw the line of Guards coming up, though they were further off than I wished, and than they ought to have been in such a crisis; it was the Fusiliers in my rear to whom I sent, and I tried hard to keep our position, though in our irregular order, till they came; but I could not, the fire was heavy, the men collected in instinctive heaps and were borne back on the advance of the left wing of the Fusiliers, carrying, in fact, three or four companies back with them down the slope to the rocky shelter. . . . When the two or three companies of the Fusiliers were borne back with us, the right wing went on gallantly." The losses of this Battalion were very heavy, and amounted to 11 Officers and 170 men during the day. Among the many acts of bravery performed by Officers and men during the crisis, Lieutenant R. Lindsay (now Lord Wantage) gained the Victoria Cross for his intrepid conduct.

† Hamley, *War in the Crimea*, p. 59.

‡ A point connected with this phase of the battle may be noted. The British soldier had never been trained to advance firing, and at first there was some difficulty in preventing him from halting to load, especially as the repeated cheering of the men drowned to a considerable extent the orders of the Officers. Many of the latter, however, springing to the front, showed by their example that the advance was on no account to

our left, protecting the left flank of the British army, were the Highlanders in echelon of battalions from the right; and this magnificent corps, handled with great ability, fired into the hostile columns that passed them on their way to the epaulment (round which the fight centred in this quarter of the field), and contributed in no small degree, to lighten the task of the Guards.*

Nor had the British artillery been inactive; pressing forward, they took up positions wherever they were to be found, whence they fired either upon the enemy's guns or into the solid masses of his infantry. At the moment when the Duke's division appeared upon the slope, three of Evans's battalions were engaged near the post-road; two more, under Adams, were further to the right, moving up the hill; England's Division was crossing the river, and the Fourth Division (Sir G. Cathcart) was still in rear, as a reserve. The first onslaught of the Light Division had shaken the enemy; and now, when opposed to the steady advance of the Guards and Highlanders, he did not long maintain the contest. The Russians were unable to fight in line; they remained throughout the whole day in dense columns.† This faulty formation, adopted to suit the quality of their troops, gave them greater weight had they been able to come to close quarters with their antagonist, but it prevented them from using their muskets, and offered a large target to our fire. On the other hand, the fire of the two British brigades was fully developed. Moving as if on

---

be checked, and the line thereafter did not halt. Sir Colin Campbell drilled the Highland Brigade to advance firing, the morning after landing at Old Fort, and instructed them to open out, so that they should not crowd upon each other or interfere with each other's movements when loading and firing.

* Of the Coldstream, it is written that the Battalion was "drawn up in line with beautiful precision; because of the position of the ground on which it advanced, it had been much less exposed to fire and mishaps than either of the other Battalions of the Brigade, and it had not been pressed forward, as each of the other two Battalions had been, to meet any special emergency occurring on its front. Therefore it was that it fell to the lot of the Coldstream to become an almost prim sample of what our Guards can be in the moment which precedes a close fight. What the best of battalions is, when, in some Royal Park at home, it manœuvres before a great princess, that the Coldstream was now on the banks of the Alma, when it came to show its graces to the enemy. And it was no ignoble pride which caused the Battalion to maintain all this ceremonious exactness; for though it be true that the precision of a line in peace time is only a success in mechanics, the precision of a line on a hill-side with the enemy close in front, is the result and the proof of warlike composure" (Kinglake, ii. 426).

† "They had a curious formation of close column, with swarms of skirmishers on each side; they seemed to run out of the ranks to fire, and then take refuge in their columns again; they would have been much safer outside altogether" (Tower, *Diary*).

parade, the Guards in line kept up a continuous and well-aimed stream of lead, at short ranges, into the masses in front of them, while the Highlanders in echelon succeeded in striking the right flank of the enemy.* Unable to bear down on the thin lines that opposed them, the Russians wavered, and, with a ringing cheer, our men charged home, and drove them from the field. The English army had cleared the formidable position held by the enemy on Kurgané, as well as from that hill to the eastern slopes of the Telegraph, where the French had now arrived. Menshikoff's troops fled from the field, and their retreat was so precipitate that it was not even covered by cavalry or artillery. For a short time our batteries played upon their ranks; but Lord Raglan's request that Marshal St. Arnaud might complete the rout by sending forward his comparatively fresh troops, was met by a frivolous excuse, and there was no pursuit.

The British losses amounted to 106 Officers, 121 sergeants, and 1775 rank and file, total 2002, of whom were killed 25, 19, and 318 respectively. The French, who played a minor part in the action, exaggerated their casualties, which really numbered only 60 killed (including three Officers), and 500 wounded. The Russians put their losses at nearly 6000, but this was probably less than the truth. The Coldstream and the Highlanders had been protected to a great extent by the folds of the ground, and they were fortunately not under the direct fire of the Russian guns, as the other two Battalions of the Division had been. The casualties of the Scots Fusiliers have been already given; those of the Grenadier Guards amounted to 4 Officers and 137 men; the Highland Brigade (three battalions) lost 90 of all ranks. In the Coldstream there were two Officers and 27 men wounded,—of the former, Captain Cust, who succeeded Captain Byng as Aide-de-camp to Major-General Bentinck, died of his wounds immediately after the action; the other, Captain C. Baring, had his arm amputated.

Military critics are disappointed with this battle, and condemn

---

* "Scarcely a man had seen a shotted musket fired before, except at a target, and yet they looked as cool and self-possessed as if 'marking time' in an English barrack square" (*Our Veterans, etc.*, 133). "We soon drove the enemy before us up the hill and through the epaulment, but the guns had been taken out [except the two previously captured], and a regiment was retreating out of the rear of the work in very tolerably good order, firing at us, and in no confusion or disorderly haste. We gave them two or three steady volleys before they were out of shot; our men fired wonderfully steadily all the time. We fired sixteen rounds going up the hill" (Tower, *Diary*).

BATTLE OF THE ALMA

Scale

- English troops
- French "
- Turkish "
- Russian "

A Prince Napoleon
B Canrobert
C Bosquet
D Bosquet and Turks
E Forey in Reserve

both sides for displaying little tactical knowledge or talent. Menshikoff left almost everything undone, to enable him to make a stand on the ground he had himself selected for barring the march of the Allies. The influence of St. Arnaud, who at this time was in bad health, seemed to damp the usual ardour of the French; and on this occasion they hardly maintained the high standard of their brilliant military reputation. We have seen that Lord Raglan and the Marshal had formed no definite plan of action before the fight began. If they intended to turn the enemy's left, and drive him off the road to Sevastopol into the interior, the English attack was too soon delivered; and if they hoped to push him towards the sea, they took no measures to effect that object. They pursued neither of these courses, and a mere frontal attack was undertaken, which resulted in dislodging the Russians, but which, in the absence of a vigorous pursuit, involved them in no serious disaster. Lord Raglan, moreover, having ordered the first line to advance, took up a position well in front of his own army, within the ground occupied at that time by the enemy; in this exposed place he watched the course of the battle, but he ceased to be able to control it. Hence the co-operation between his divisional commanders, necessary to the attack, was wanting, and we missed the opportunity of inflicting a greater defeat upon the enemy than we succeeded in doing. Of the bravery of both the Officers and men, of the steadiness and discipline under fire of the rank and file, who for the first time were in action, but one opinion has ever been expressed.

"All, therefore, that we had to be proud of was the dash and valour of the regiments engaged. These were very conspicuous, and worthy of the traditions of the Peninsular days. A French Officer, who was viewing the field, where our men lay, as they had fallen, in ranks, with one of our naval Captains, observed to him, 'Well, you took the bull by the horns—our men could not have done it.'" *

As has been said, there was no pursuit after the battle, and the enemy was allowed to leave the field unmolested. This was the more unfortunate, since the retreat of the Russians degenerated into a rout. But worse followed, for the morning of the 23rd dawned before we stirred from the scene of our success, and two of the most valuable days of the campaign were irretrievably lost

* Hamley, *War in the Crimea*, p. 65.

to the Allies. The fault was St. Arnaud's, whom nothing could shake in his determination to remain where he was. Happily the strain of the alliance touched not the troops of either nation, and among them existed warm feelings of an honest *camaraderie*. Just as the First Division was about to fall in, a French brigade passed by on its southward march, and friendly expressions of mutual recognition and of good will were heard; from us, by lusty cheers and waving of bearskins and bonnets, and from them by hearty cries of "Vivent les Anglais! Vivent les Montagnards!"

Leaving the Alma, the approach to Sevastopol was made by easy stages. On the 23rd a halt was called at noon on the Katcha, where we had the mortification of learning that the heavy field-pieces, which had done us so much damage on the Kurgané heights, had left but four short hours before our arrival. Next day, we reached the Belbek, thirteen miles from the late field of battle, and within striking distance of Sevastopol, the goal of our ambition. And now a strange thing happened. Far from attacking the very position we had come to assail, we even refused to make a reconnaissance to ascertain the nature of its defences, and the force and quality of the enemy holding it.

The expedition, we have seen, was expressly designed to be a speedy operation, and every step taken with respect to it was governed by that one idea; otherwise, it would never have been undertaken in the autumn of 1854. Hence, a coast destitute of secure harbours wherein to form a base of operations, was not considered unsuitable as a landing-place; communications between the Crimea and the rest of the Russian Empire were not intercepted; a line of advance exposed to attack by a relieving army was not rejected; a late season of the year did not put an end to the enterprise; and hence, also, there was no provision made for the winter. These conditions were none of them in accordance with sound military science or practice; but they were accepted, and they led the army to the north side of Sevastopol—to the objective which the Allies designed to reach when they landed at Old Fort. Arriving there, the Anglo-French armies came face to face with an obstacle, some works loomed in the haze before them, and they began to deliberate. Counsellors, not consulted when the expedition was planned, were now admitted as advisers, and they naturally viewed the problem without reference to the past. We had lost touch with the defeated Menshikoff, and it was thought that he probably had his army safe behind the entrenchments in front; the attack might not succeed, a delay might occur, and at any rate it was dangerous to wait when we had no secure base in our rear. In short, the hazardous nature of the expedition which had been forced upon the allied Commanders from home, suddenly burst upon them with a vivid light never experienced before, and they had to recognize, although unfortunately they did not yet acknowledge, that the surprise had failed, that a lengthened siege was inevitable, and that the descent on the fortress, as originally conceived, was a snare and a delusion.

And yet, had the position been reconnoitred, some interesting facts would have been revealed. We should have found the defences weak, imperfectly armed, and garrisoned only by 11,000 men, whose weapons for the most part were antiquated flint-locks, while others were only provided with pikes or cutlasses.* The field-force that fought on the 20th was not there at all; it had hastily retired to the south side to re-organize itself after the disaster it had suffered.

The possession of the north side of Sevastopol offered the Allies considerable advantages.† The town, barracks, dockyards, and arsenal are built on the south side of an extensive creek, deep enough to float the largest ships of war, which runs from the sea in an easterly direction four miles inland, 1000 to 1200 yards in breadth. This inlet, forming the roadstead or harbour of Sevastopol, is defended at its mouth by several strong forts, some of those on the north side being perched on cliffs 100 feet high. The northern bank entirely commands the south side, and rises from the water's edge more abruptly than the latter. These things were known to the Allies before they landed in the Crimea. It is obvious that, if the invaders could have established themselves on this northern bank, they would have taken the town and some of the forts in reverse; and that, if they could have brought up sufficient guns of the requisite calibre, the fortress itself would have been untenable, and the destruction of the ships in the harbour ensured by the force of plunging fire directed upon them.

While we lingered on the Alma, General Menshikoff had not been idle, and he determined to secure all the advantages which the Russian fleet of the Black Sea might be able to confer. It was hopeless to suppose that this fleet could cope with our own

* Kinglake, iii. 43.   † See Map No. 5, p. 182.

magnificent ships which lay outside the harbour; and indeed, ever since the battle of Sinope, it had been carefully kept out of harm's way. The only use to which it could be put, was to convert it into an addition to the land defences of Sevastopol; but even then, it would be exposed to danger, for the enemy had a wholesome dread of what the historic daring of British seamen is capable of achieving when directed by an enterprising commander. On the night of the 22nd, therefore, he effectually barred the entrance of the roadstead by sinking seven vessels, and by constructing a boom across it, and thus he secured his shipping from any direct attack which our navy might have contemplated. Hence, the Russian war-ships became stationary floating batteries, and their function was to play their guns upon the ground that bordered the roadstead. For this device, also, the Allies must have been prepared, and might have taken it into consideration before even they started on the expedition. Now, the plateau on the top of the heights overlooking the town from the north, was much less (if at all) exposed to the enemy's naval artillery than the ground over which the invaders must advance, if they meant to deliver their attack from the south; and the fire directed upon this plateau would be uncertain and inefficient, since considerable portions of it were out of sight of the ships below.

The British Admiral, Sir Edmond Lyons, at that time second in command, never lost sight of the original plan of invasion: he advocated strongly an attack upon the north side, and was prepared to take a prominent part in the action he expected to follow. If successful, the closing of the harbour was of trifling moment. This powerful co-operation was impossible on the south side. Lord Raglan agreed with the Admiral, and was also in favour of striking a blow from the north, as had always been intended. But he was in a position of great difficulty. Some of his own advisers were against the proposal, and the French Marshal, always unfavourable to activity in this quarter, was sinking under a disease that carried him off before the end of the month. The question whether this attack from the Belbek river would have brought about the immediate fall of Sevastopol, need not be further discussed; no attempt was made to ascertain whether it was practicable. Suffice it to say that General Todleben, who defended Sevastopol, afterwards expressed his deliberate opinion, and elaborately argued it out, that the northern plateau was untenable by the Russians, and that operations conducted against it would have led the Allies to a speedy success. Nevertheless, it is important to notice that the original design of taking Sevastopol by a *coup de main* under the effects of a surprise, was given up before even a reconnaissance was made to ascertain the strength of the objective, to which the Allies were committed by that very design. We shall now see that, refusing to pursue their plan, on account of the serious military errors it disclosed, the Allies were forced to adopt another plan, which equally, if not in a greater degree, violated the canons of the science of war.*

* The late Sir E. Hamley holds that General Todleben was wrong, and writes: " But he [Todleben] says the enemies' [allied] ships, approaching the shore, could batter the fort almost with impunity, [*i.e.* the Star-Fort, or the principal work on the north side of Sevastopol, which the Allies would have had to attack]. The impossibility of this is best shown by the fact that, in the subsequent engagement between the fleets and forts, one of the batteries on the cliffs (100 feet high) of the north side disabled several of our ships without receiving a shot in return, although they made it the object of their fire, and that the Star-Fort is distant inland from this battery 1000 yards. Thus, according to Todleben, the ships, while themselves under the fire of the coast batteries, which they could not injure in return, were to bombard a fort 1000 yards beyond these batteries, and which would be invisible from the sea" (Hamley, *War in the Crimea*, p. 71).

The bombardment spoken of, in which the English ships were injured, was only directed against the forts situated at the entrance of the harbour. From that point, no doubt, the Star-Fort could not be seen; but still Todleben made no puerile suggestion with respect to the geography of a place every inch of which he had good reason to know intimately. The Russian entrenchments on the north plateau could be reached by the guns of our fleet, from another spot off the coast, just round the promontory on which the coast batteries were built, and where our ships would be to a great extent (if not entirely) sheltered from the fire of the latter.

CHAPTER VIII.

BEFORE SEVASTOPOL.

Predicament in which the Allies found themselves—Flank march round Sevastopol—Occupation of Balaklava by the British and of Kamiesh Bay by the French—The Allies refuse to assault Sevastopol; they prefer to bombard it—Depression of the Russians, who fear a prompt assault—Description of the defences round the south side of Sevastopol; successful efforts of the enemy to strengthen them—Description of the upland of the Chersonese, occupied by the Allies; their position and labours—First bombardment and its results—No attack; a regular siege inevitable—Draft of Officers and men to the Coldstream arrive in the Crimea—Establishment of the Regiment—Russian reinforcements begin to arrive—Battle of Balaklava; Cavalry charges—Sortie of the Russians against the British right flank; its failure.

THE Allies, at this juncture, found themselves placed in a strange predicament. Their plans had hitherto been successful, and nothing remained to be done except to justify their first resolutions by standing firm to their original purpose. The critical moment at length arrived, and then, in the very presence of the enemy, they changed their minds. They would not operate against the north of Sevastopol; they would attack it from the south, and form a secure base in the harbours of Balaklava and Kamiesh, that indent the coast of the upland plain, called by the ancients the Chersonese. In order to accomplish this new design, they had to march the united armies from the Belbek to the south-west corner of the peninsula, quite close to the fortress they intended to capture. Added to this, the ground over which they had to pass was unknown; they left behind them the broad, open, and treeless plains, where they could march in battle array, ready for emergencies; they now approached a woody, difficult, and intersected country, and had to adopt long columns of route in moving across it. According to the information in their possession, moreover, a hostile army was sheltered somewhere within the lines of Sevastopol; it was believed to be securely posted behind the entrenchments on the northern plateau. They did not wish to meet it there, and, to avoid doing so, they were obliged to have recourse to the only alternative, and to commit a bad military error. They exposed the right of their long columns and their rear to imminent danger, and, courting disaster, invited the Russians to fall upon them, in a position where partial defeat must prove fatal to their existence.

On the 25th the main body, preceded by a regiment of cavalry, a troop of horse artillery, and a battalion of Rifles, left the Belbek, and the perilous flank march commenced. It was carried out in a manner which would have given the fullest advantages to the enemy had he availed himself of them. The general direction was kept, often by consulting the compass; but the difficulties of the country, the thick woods, and the haste which urged us forward, disarranged the order of the troops. At one moment, indeed, the head-quarters, leading the whole advance, were followed by a long procession of thirty guns without supports, and offered a tempting and easy reward to Russian enterprise. But, slow though we may be to recognize it, a miracle does sometimes take place, and in this case it showed itself in the fact, that the extraordinary march proceeded onwards without the slightest mishap. Not only this, but the British even captured some twenty carts from the enemy, though they failed to get hold of the horses, which were cut away directly we came into sight. This meeting came about in a curious way. It happened, as we have seen, that Prince Menshikoff, far from taking post on the north plateau, was refitting his defeated army in the town of Sevastopol south of the roadstead. He came to the conclusion that he ought to preserve his communications with the interior of the Crimea, and support the advance of the reinforcements he expected to come from Bessarabia. At dawn on the 25th, therefore, he, too, emerged from his retreat, crossed the Tchernaya at Traktir Bridge, and, advancing to Mackenzie Farm, marched towards Bakshiserai. Thus it came about that the two contending armies, moving on the same day, and for some time advancing towards one another by the same road, crossed each other's path, and that neither had the least conception of what the other was doing. It was fortunate that, in this curious game of blind man's buff, Menshikoff did not strike our columns of route full in the flank; as it was, we ust happened to drive our ram into the tip of his tail; for, as the head-quarter Staff, stumbling suddenly on the last portion of the enemy's baggage train as it passed unconsciously by, stood wondering at the sight, a few of our guns hurried up to the rescue, unlimbered, and secured some of his unhorsed carts. Among the booty was a carriage belonging to one of the Russian Commanders, in which were stars, crosses, medals, uniform, French novels, and a portfolio "of coloured prints, the morality of which will not bear discussion."

The experiences of the First Division on this march should not be omitted. After waiting ready equipped for two hours, the men at length moved off, at 8.30 in the morning, and plunged almost immediately into the forest.

"Everybody who has seen beaters pushing their way through a thick cover, may form a faint idea of the difficulties which beset, and the obstacles which retarded our progress. The heat was overpowering, not a breath of air percolated the dense vegetation. You scrambled on with arms uplifted to protect the face against the swinging back-handers dealt by the boughs; now your shakoe was dashed off, now the briars laid tenacious hold on your haversack, or on the tails of your coatee. It was as much as you could do to see the soldiers immediately on your right and left. For the time, military order was an impossibility, brigades and regiments got intermixed. Guardsmen, Rifles, and Highlanders straggled forward blindly, all in a ruck. There was much suffering, and some stout soldiers dropped involuntarily to the rear, to be heard of no more." *

After four hours or more, the troops emerged on a lane blocked by the cavalry and baggage, and squeezed through. A little later they heard an explosion, and, pushing forward, they came upon the scene of the singular meeting that took place between the head-quarter Staff and the rear of the enemy's army. Continuing along a tolerably good road, they approached the valley of the Tchernaya after dark, and, crossing it at Traktir Bridge, they finally bivouacked near the village of Tchorgun, at ten o'clock at night, "completely exhausted, parched with thirst, and their clothes much torn by struggling through the wood." Indeed, they were fortunate, for it was one in the morning before the last British division reached its halting ground. The French, who followed their English allies, remained for the night midway on the wooded heights near Mackenzie Farm, where they suffered much from want of water. Next day the movement continued;

* *Our Veterans, etc.*, p. 163.

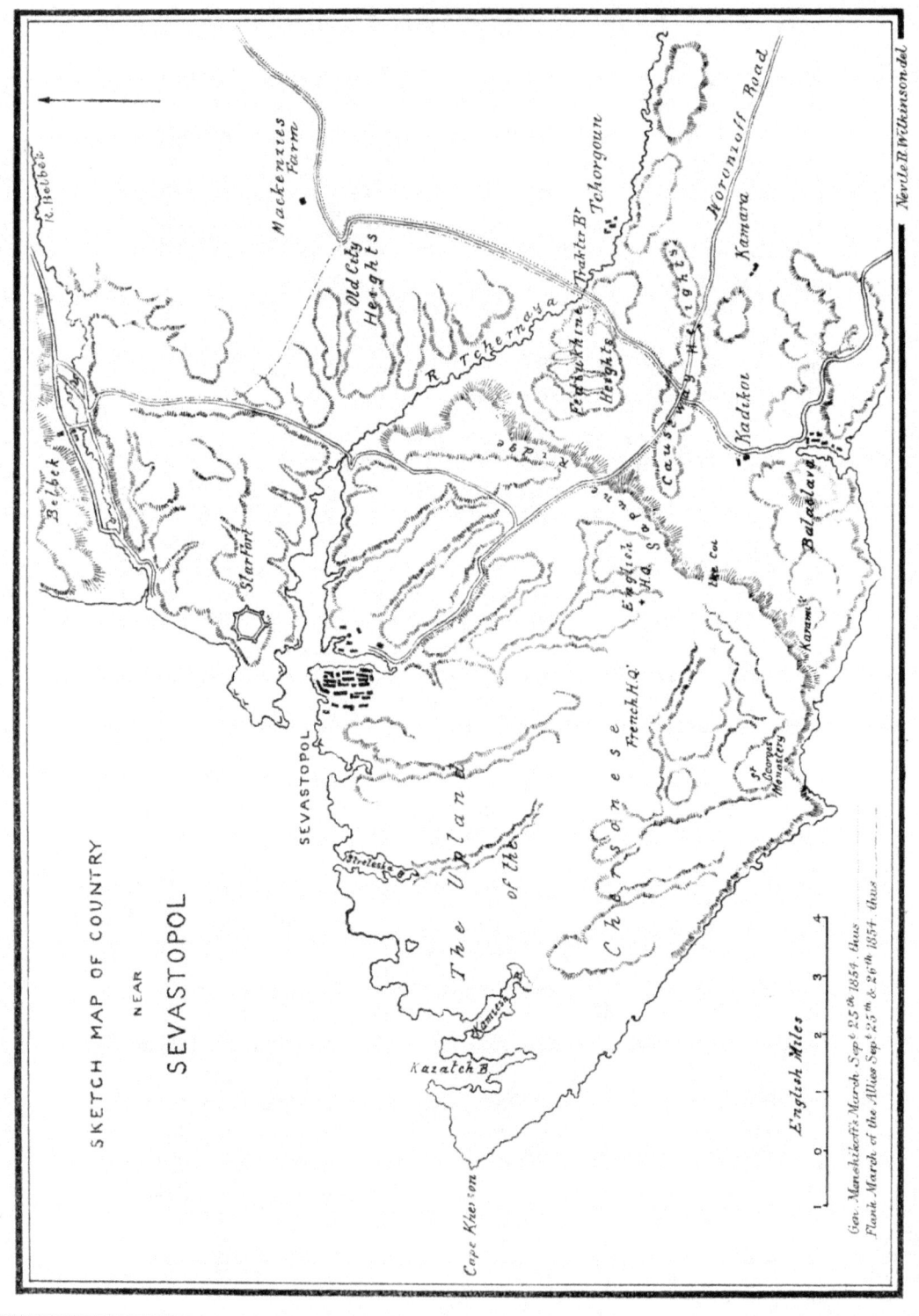

and the cholera, that accompanied our troops without intermission, burst out with renewed malignity, and struck its victims down on the roadside along our line of march. After three hours, the division reached Kadikeui, about half a mile from Balaklava; while our ships, approaching, threw a few shells into an old Genoese fort, which commanded the harbour, and which was held by a handful of Greek troops in the Russian service; after a mere show of resistance, they surrendered without difficulty. The French also moved forward on the 26th, and established themselves on the Fediukhine heights near the Tchernaya. The Fourth Division, under Sir G. Cathcart, had been left behind on the Belbek, to embark the sick that remained there; on the same day (26th) he, too, started from his bivouac on the north of Sevastopol, and, following the track of the Allied armies, arrived on the Tchernaya without misadventure.

Thus the flank march was completed, and during the whole of the difficult and dangerous operation, lasting two days, the Russians stood by absolutely passive, and the Allies were entirely unmolested. Not a company was cut off, nor was a gun taken. This was the more remarkable since, perceiving the movement from a high tower in Sevastopol, they were accurately informed of our plan at midday of the 25th; General Menshikoff must also have known it, from the meeting that took place between the hostile armies near Mackenzie Farm. It was, indeed, fortunate that we had so forbearing an enemy.

Communications having now been fortunately re-established with the fleet, the British occupied the Bay of Balaklava, the French that of Kamiesh, where their respective bases of operations were formed. Thus we were placed on the right of the new line fronting northwards, and we were again posted upon the exposed flank. About this time, an event of importance occurred to the French. Marshal St. Arnaud got so ill, that he was obliged to give up his command, and to leave the seat of war. He was to be taken to Scutari, but he died on the passage. General Canrobert succeeded him—a valiant, honourable, and straightforward soldier, but one little fitted to take upon himself the onerous responsibilities of his new position.

The Allies now found themselves occupying a fertile country, almost entirely denuded of inhabitants, who fled at their approach, covered with highly cultivated gardens, orchards, and vineyards, which teemed with vegetables and fruit in great abundance. Never were troops so amply supplied as during the first few days of their stay in this land of plenty; but the good things did not last, they were soon exhausted, and could not be replaced. The men were not easily restrained from enjoying to the full the luxurious feast which lay before them, after the fatigues of the forced flank march; though it is to be feared they suffered from its effects, and from the fact that they were still without tents. Cholera continued, and diarrhœa (its pilot-fish) increased considerably.*

The idea seems to have been pretty general among the troops that the flank march was intended to shift the position of the united armies from a strong front of Sevastopol to a weaker side, and that the attack was only delayed until we got close to the southern defences of the town. It was confidently expected that the assault would be soon delivered, and the landing of the siege-train did not put an end to that hope. As days went by, however, it began to be realized that operations of a slower nature were to be begun, and that a siege, not an assault, was to be undertaken. This surmise was entirely correct; though the Chiefs of the armies still held to the belief that, when a bombardment by siege guns had taken place, the defences would be destroyed, and the town would then fall before the winter set in. Lord Raglan personally seems to have been disposed to make an immediate attempt against the enemy's lines, without incurring this further delay; and this view was certainly shared and supported by Sir George Cathcart, and was also advocated by Sir Edmond Lyons. It was urged that the Russian fortifications were slight and weak at the end of September, when the Allies got within striking distance, and, though we should be stronger against them as soon as the siege batteries were constructed and armed, yet the time required to do so could be utilized by the defenders in so strengthening their works, that the advantages of a delay would accrue to them, and to our detriment. General Canrobert, however, was cautious, and was disinclined to run any risks just as the supreme command was vested in him by the French Emperor. Others, among the British advisers at head-quarters, held the opinion that it was dangerous to deliver an attack unless prepared

* Of 76 cases of sickness that occurred in the Battalion in the month of September, 30 were fever, 24 diarrhœa, and 7 cholera (Wyatt, p. 24).

by artillery fire; they feared that the attempt might cost us 500 men, which loss they hoped would not occur if a siege were opened in the regular manner. Lord Raglan was forced to concur.

During this time the Russian commanders, left in Sevastopol after General Menshikoff's departure, were in a state of great depression, and believed that the town could not hold out against a vigorous assault. The entire garrison amounted to 35,850 men, made up of heterogeneous elements—one single battalion of regulars (750 men), militia, gunners, marines, seamen, and workmen. Of the latter, there were 5000—a useful body to create a fortress, if time were granted, but useless to repel an immediate attack. Of the sailors set free from the imprisoned fleet, there were 18,500, of whom a fourth part only were well trained or even decently armed.* The south side, moreover, does not lend itself easily to a good defence.† A creek, hardly half a mile broad, called the inner harbour, runs inland for nearly two miles from the main roadstead, terminating in three ravines which ascend the upland of the Chersonese. This inlet divides the town from a suburb, called the Karabelnaya, and as both had to be held against the Allies, there was a formidable obstacle obstructing communications between them. The French, based on Kamiesh Bay, were opposite the western portion of Sevastopol, that is the town itself, from the sea to the head of the inner harbour. The British army on the right, faced Karabelnaya, and were responsible for the ground from the inner harbour to Careenage Bay,—another inlet, half a mile long, which also terminates in a ravine indenting the upland,—where the enemy's defences ended. The line held by the Russian garrison was about four miles in length: two miles from the sea to the head of the inner harbour, and the same distance onwards to Careenage Bay. On the 25th of September, this long line was imperfectly defended. On the French section, the gorges of the Quarantine and Artillery Forts had been closed, and three bastions or redoubts had been constructed between them and the head of the inner harbour, where the Flagstaff bastion stood, connected, with but little interruption, by a naked loopholed wall. On the British section, there were four works, which were unconnected by wall or entrenchment, known as the Redan, the Malakoff Tower, the Little Redan, and

* These numbers are taken from Hamley's *War in the Crimea*, p. 86. Todleben says there were but 16,000 "combatants" (excluding artillery) available for the defence of the south side (Kinglake, iii. 195).

† See Map No. 6, p. 194.

No. 1 Battery, near Careenage Bay. Of these the Malakoff was "a mere naked tower, without a glacis, exposed from head to foot, unsupported by the powerful batteries which were destined to flank it, and uncovered as yet by the works which afterwards closed up round its base." The whole of the south side of Sevastopol, moreover, was armed with 172 guns, of which by far the greater number faced the French, and only a few the British position.*

The serious and very reasonable apprehension entertained by the Russian chiefs did not, however, prevent them from taking every measure to fortify their position, directly they understood that the Allies were approaching the south side in force. The greatest activity prevailed day and night in the garrison and among the inhabitants, the women and children taking their share of the labour, and thus the works designed by the Russian Engineer Officer, Todleben, were rapidly thrown up. The Anglo-French Commanders never interrupted these operations, nor did they make any demonstrations to try the quality of the defences; they contented themselves with distant reconnaissances, so that in a short time the entrenchments were greatly strengthened, especially the Malakoff, and began to look more formidable than had been the case before; the armament also was being changed, the lighter guns giving place to heavier ordnance drawn from the ships and arsenal.

The upland of the Chersonese, on which the Allies had established themselves, is a sloping plain, trending from a line of hills called the Sapuné Ridge, 500 to 700 feet high, that bounds it on the east, from the head of the roadstead of Sevastopol to a point on the coast some four miles west of Balaklava. The upland is scored by numerous ravines, running from the ridge in a general north-westerly direction to the town and coast; but on the eastern side of the ridge the ground falls abruptly and almost in a cliff-like manner into the valley of the Tchernaya river, which discharges itself into the roadstead. The distance from Balaklava to Sevastopol is nearly eight miles. Of the two roads connecting them, one, the Woronzoff road, was metalled, and, proceeding along the Causeway Heights, formed the main communication with the south of the Crimean peninsula; the other, a

* Kinglake, iii. 123, etc., 194, 347. Sir Edmond Lyons urged the immediate assault of the Malakoff hill, "then unoccupied, and advised the immediate construction of a battery there, which would make it necessary for the fleet to take care of themselves" (*Ibid.*, iii., Appendix, p. 491). The capture of the Malakoff in September, 1855, caused the immediate fall of Sevastopol.

mere cart-track or pathway, more to the south, ascended the ridge over the "Col de Balaklava," three miles from that place, and joined the Woronzoff road two miles further on, on the upland.

This extended position had to be defended from attacks that were to be feared from Menshikoff's army. The latter, having left Sevastopol, was in easy communication with the town and was securely posted on very defensible ground, from whence it could advance upon the right of the Allies or upon our base at Balaklava. Moreover, the Russians would, before long, be strongly reinforced by troops which, as we have seen, were hurrying without opposition from Bessarabia into the Crimea; but when this event would take place was still uncertain. The Allies had lost all touch with the enemy's army they had defeated at the Alma, and their hesitation to assault the weak defences that covered Sevastopol directly after the flank march, was in a measure due to their ignorance of what their opponent was doing. In reality he was then many miles away, and had no intention of resuming hostilities without further assistance; he was re-organizing his men, and waiting for the fresh forces he expected from the north.* Only for the moment, therefore, was the right flank of the invaders free from danger, and under no circumstances could it have been left unguarded.

The French divided their army into two Corps. The 3rd and 4th Divisions, under General Forey, formed the besieging force, and took post before Sevastopol, their right on the great ravine which runs into the inner harbour, their left on Streleska Bay. The 1st and 2nd Divisions, together with the Turkish contingent, constituted a Corps of observation, under General Bosquet, and were entrenched on the Sapuné Ridge, facing the east, between the Woronzoff road and the Col previously mentioned. The whole of the British army was engaged in the siege, before the suburb of Karabelnaya, the left on the ravine, in communication with the French, the right upon ground not far from the Sapuné heights. The defence of Balaklava was provided by the 93rd Regiment (withdrawn for the purpose from the Highland Brigade), 1,000 Marines, a battery of Artillery, and a body of Turks (3,500 of whom had been recently despatched to the Crimea, the remainder, two battalions, being lent by the French). These troops, which included a provisional battalion formed of 25 to 30 weakly men drawn from every regiment, were placed under the command of Sir Colin Campbell, who was detached

* Kinglake, iii. 215.

from his brigade. In front of them, in the valley, was Lord Lucan's cavalry division.

These measures did not, however, secure the right flank of the British siege-works. At this point, the cliff-like appearance of the heights overlooking the Tchernaya partially disappears, and the upland falls towards the roadstead and the river, in numerous spurs, intersected by ravines. This broken country was known to the Allies by the name of Inkerman, and along its foot there ran a road from Balaklava, which, skirting the Tchernaya to the roadstead, proceeded to Sevastopol along the southern shore of the latter. The river, moreover, was crossed at its mouth by a bridge and a causeway, over which another road led to Bakshiserai. This was a vulnerable point in the line adopted by the Allies, who far from being able to invest the place they intended to besiege, were too weak even to establish themselves upon the head of the roadstead, and prevent an irruption from the town, or an attack from the direction of Bakshiserai upon the right of their position. To guard this vital point, only a strong piquet was employed, and a battery of two guns of position, called the "Sandbag battery," constructed to strengthen it, had soon to be disarmed, as it was found impracticable to support the guns by infantry. The flank, in short, was left undefended, because the whole of the British army was required to undertake the siege, and because Bosquet's corps had entrenched themselves on an inaccessible position on the ridge, where no enemy could attack them, and where they could neither give efficient support to the defences of Balaklava, nor be of any immediate use should an onslaught be made on the unguarded spurs of Inkerman. In other words, we suffered from the effects of a divided command.*

We left the Guards Brigade, on the 26th of September, near Balaklava, at the end of the flank march. For the first few days there was little done. "Troops passive and grape-gorging, with the exception of strong fatigue parties engaged in the slow and laborious office of landing the siege guns from the transports, which now cram the harbour of Balaklava."† On the 2nd of October, the First Division marched to the front, and about this time the British army was thus bivouacked before Sevastopol. The Second Division on the right, with the First in support, nearly

---

* Kinglake, iii. 291 ; Hamley, *War in the Crimea*, 124.
† September 29th (*Our Veterans*, etc., p. 177).

a mile in rear; next came the Light Division, separated from them by the Careenage Ravine. These three divisions manned the British Right Attack. The Fourth and Third Divisions were posted south-west of Cathcart's Hill, and continued the line to the west, in rear of the Left Attack, to the ravine, on the other side of which lay the French siege corps, near Mount Rodolph. The work of bringing up the battering train continued without interruption, and some heavy guns from the ships were drawn to the batteries by sailors, who, forming a brigade under command of Captains Lushington and Peel, took part in the operations which were soon to commence.

It was fortunate that tents were at last issued, on the 5th of October; for the men, having been constantly bivouacked since the disembarkation at Old Fort, nearly three weeks before, were again attacked by sickness. Cholera reappeared on the day after the troops stood on the upland plain before Sevastopol, and an Officer of the Coldstream, Captain Jolliffe, died of it on the 4th. It seems that the delay in providing shelter, even of an indifferent nature, was due to the want of transport, which still failed us; nothing apparently could induce our Government to give the army this indispensable requirement. The boon of again having a tent to cover them in the chilly autumn nights of the Crimea, was keenly appreciated by Officers and men; but comfort is a relative term, and, judged from the ordinary standpoint, the slight shelter which was supplied, was inadequate and insufficient.

On the 4th, Captain MacKinnon and a small detachment of convalescents, who had been left behind at Varna, reached the Battalion.

The constant labour which the Russians devoted to the improvement of their fortifications became apparent to regimental Officers, as they anxiously scanned the enemy's works during their leisure time.

"Within the last few days," writes Colonel Wilson, on the 7th, "an amazing change has taken place in the aspect of the town. The base of the Great Tower (the Malakoff) is now 'shored up' with earthworks; and defences of similar construction—some far advanced towards completion—are being thrown up along the entire line commencing at Careenage Bay on the east, and terminating near the cemetery on the west [near the Flagstaff bastion]. Hence, in the course of a week, if not sooner, Sevastopol will have assumed the likeness of a vast entrenched camp."

On the same day, it seemed to leak out, that "the place looked so much stronger than had been anticipated, that perhaps we might not take it this winter;" and it was devoutly hoped that precautionary measures would be taken in time, against "the onslaughts of Generals Rain, Frost, and Snow, no matter how great soever may be head-quarter confidence in the overwhelming efficacy of our opening fire." *

It was, however, still officially considered that the projected bombardment would shatter the Russian defences, and that the speedy capture of Sevastopol would be the result. This opinion was also shared by many of the Officers of the British army, and every nerve was strained to make the operation a success. On the 10th we broke ground, and began the construction of three batteries. Two, known as Chapman's and Gordon's, called after the Engineer Officers in charge, were some 1400 yards from the Redan, and the trench connecting them became eventually the first parallel. Chapman's battery, 41 guns, was placed on Green Hill, between two ravines that descend into the inner harbour, viz. the valley of the Shadow of Death and the Woronzoff ravine. Gordon's battery, 26 guns, stood on Mount Woronzoff (also called Frenchman's Hill), between the Woronzoff and the Docks ravines. On the next hill, between the Docks and the Careenage ravines, the Victoria or Lancaster battery was built, armed with 6 guns (5 of the Lancaster pattern), more than 2000 yards from the enemy's lines. The French began their siege-works on the 9th, on Mount Rodolph, and placed 53 guns in battery, 1000 yards from the enemy's fortifications. Thus the Allies had 126 guns in position, not counting the field artillery. The enemy had 118,—64 facing the French, and 54 the British,—besides 223 of lesser calibre.

The Battalion, in common with the other troops stationed before Sevastopol, took their full share in the construction of these batteries, by supplying working parties and covering guards to resist sorties. The operation was new to all ranks, who had received little training in these special duties, the greater part of which had to be performed at night. But any confusion incidental to the circumstances of the case speedily passed away, and from start to finish the men stuck to their work, and did it thoroughly, under a heavy and unreturned fire, that constantly poured upon them from dawn to dark from the Russian lines.

* *Our Veterans, etc.*, p. 191, etc.

"On the 14th October," Colonel Wilson writes, "the duties grew very hard. For myself I have been at work four nights out of five, and so have many others. . . . But in this respect, of course, the rank and file are the principal sufferers. To what insignificance do our hardships sink when compared with theirs! In the case of the private, downright manual labour—picking, shovelling, dragging, lifting—is superadded to watching. In his instance, no little dainties . . . vary the nauseous salt junk, and the wish-wash of green coffee. In his instance, the tatters—which were a uniform once—only cover the wearer's nakedness imperfectly: that ragged patchwork has long ceased to combat with the wind and rain. . . . Oh! what painful illustrations of the cheap and nasty principle, are those filthy dangling shreds and bursted seams! How one's heart yearns toward the unflinching British 'common soldier' so sternly superior to privation, so proudly reckless of his life! Brave heart! unconquerable soul! Crimean hero, whom we cannot glorify too much!" *

The excellence of the work performed by the Brigade is thus described in a recent publication, already alluded to:—

"The spade work of the soldiers varied considerably, but from the Royal Engineers' journal of work done in Bulgaria, and from what I saw early in the siege, that of the Guards Brigade was undoubtedly amongst the best. This may have arisen from the memory of instruction at Chobham camp in 1853, or from regimental pride, or from both causes. . . . By the end of August the infantry had made six thousand gabions and seven hundred fascines; for every one of these passed as serviceable, the soldiers received 14d. and 7d. respectively, which included the labour of cutting and carrying the brush-wood which was close at hand. In the Guards Brigade each section of three men produced three gabions daily; in the Line the average did not exceed one gabion daily per section. Throughout the long ensuing siege, the working parties in the trenches did well or badly in proportion to the efficiency of the Officers. When they sat and smoked, paying no attention to the men, the sergeants followed suit, and but little progress was made. On the other hand, when the Officers, keen and sympathetic, knew how to get cheerful work out of their men, the spirits of the directing Engineer Officer rose considerably." †

The following extracts from Colonel Tower's diary, give,

* *Our Veterans, etc.*, p. 211.
† Wood, *Crimea in* 1854 *and* 1894, p. 87. As the training at Chobham camp lasted but a short time, and amounted in reality to very little, and as the work performed in Bulgaria and before Sevastopol afforded more practical instruction than could possibly have been given at Chobham, does it not seem probable that the excellence, attributed to the Brigade, arose much more from what is called regimental pride, from the character of their system, and from the efficiency of their Officers, than from any other cause?

moreover, an idea of the nature of some of the duties discharged by the men, and the conditions under which they were performed :—

"*Oct. 14th.* Paraded at 3 a.m. for a covering party in rear of Chapman's battery. The enemy annoyed us very much all day, throwing shot and shell, but, by dint of creeping about and keeping well under the parapet, we all got safe back to camp at 6 a.m., after twenty-seven hours in the trenches.

"*Oct. 16th.* On covering party in rear of the sailors' battery. There was a large heap of stones, two to three feet high, behind which we laid down as flat as we could; about 10 a.m. a red flag was hoisted on the Redan, and immediately every gun they had mounted commenced pitching into our battery, . . . for about half an hour, evidently to try their range. Every sort of missile they could cram into their guns came whistling over us and knocking our heap of stones about. We lay as still as mice, and the shot rattled about like hail, and went bounding away over the hill in our rear towards the camp; Goodlake and self, Francis Baring and Bob Lindsay were our party. In the middle of the *jeu d'enfer*, old Gordon the Engineer appeared walking over the open towards the battery, the shot striking the ground all round him; he never quickened his pace, and seemed perfectly unconscious of his imminent danger: but fortune favours the brave, and although he ought to have been struck fifty times, he coolly walked up the hill with the utmost indifference."

In preparation for the bombardment, fixed to commence at 6.30 a.m. on the 17th of October, the troops were held in readiness in their camps to fall in at a moment's notice, arrangements were made in case the army was ordered to move forward to assault the Russian position, scaling ladders, tools, etc., were collected, and a body of sharpshooters was specially organized. In the First Division, the latter were placed under Captain Goodlake of the Coldstream, whose gallant services soon earned for him the Victoria Cross.[*] But the first onslaught on Sebastopol failed to

---

[*] By *First Divisional Order*, Oct. 16th, ten men and a Non-commissioned officer from each battalion, good shots, volunteers preferred, were selected to act as sharpshooters, under a Captain and a Lieutenant of the Brigade of Guards, and a Lieutenant of the Highlanders. "The sharpshooters will have to approach within 400 or 500 yards of the enemy's works, there to establish themselves in extended order (by single men) under cover of anything which may present itself to afford protection. They will endeavour to improve their cover behind any obstacle by scraping out a hollow for themselves in the ground, and they will carry with them provisions so that they will be enabled to remain, being once under cover, for many hours (even twenty-four) without relief. Whilst so established, they will endeavour to pick off the enemy's artillerymen in the embrasures. The approach of the sharpshooters to the spot they must occupy, must be rapid, in a scattered order; each man acting for himself, and exercising his intelligence to the utmost of his ability. Each man will select the spot which suits him best, and be guided only in that choice by the cover he may find and the command it

produce the results that were expected from it. The Allies found the enemy placed in far other circumstances than had been the case when they first presented themselves before the south side on the 26th of September. At that date the advantages gained by the battle of the Alma had not been entirely dissipated: the Crimean field army, under Menshikoff, was beaten, and was far away from the scene of hostilities, refitting and awaiting reinforcements; the garrison of Sevastopol—composed of a mere medley of details, imperfectly armed, and many of whom could scarcely be called "combatants"—was physically and morally weak; the entrenchments were slight and incomplete; the guns to oppose an attack were light. On the 17th of October a great change had been effected. The forces from Bessarabia were arriving; the Russians had been able to reconnoitre the valley of the Tchernaya, and to threaten our exposed right flank and our base of operations; they spared as many as 25,000 of the regular army to strengthen the garrison of the town; the *morale* of the latter had been raised; the defences were much improved—they assumed the appearance of genuine fortifications; the armament was greatly increased, and had been rendered formidable.

Nevertheless, the operation was an affair of great importance and magnitude. The Allied fleets took part in it in full force, though it was not possible for them to produce any real effect; for the land defences were out of their reach, and the sea forts were extremely strong. Still all the artillery the invaders could muster, discharged their thunders upon the fortifications which covered the south side of the town and the entrance of the roadstead. The French, subjected to a hotter and closer fire than we, suffered severely, and between ten and eleven in the morning, two explosions having occurred in their batteries, their guns were silenced. The British, on the other hand, were very successful. Directing their fire upon three of the enemy's works, they inflicted considerable damage on the Flagstaff battery, silenced the Malakoff, and almost demolished the Redan, the salient of which was blown to pieces by the explosion of a powder magazine. The defences of the Karabelnaya were completely paralysed, an immediate assault was

---

may give him of an effectual fire into the embrasures." It is to be noted that the Officers ordered to perform this important duty were in no way "selected" for it, but were taken by "roster." In Crimean days, as well as during the Peninsular war, it was considered that all Officers were fitted to discharge the ordinary duties which their profession required of them.

expected, and the troops to oppose it being demoralized, fell back in confusion.*

But no attack took place. The French were unable to advance against the lines which had silenced their siege guns. It was too much to ask them to allow us to go on, under cover of their friendly co-operation and support. The enemy, in a word, gained by the Anglo-French alliance, and the common interests were obscured under the pressure of inter-national courtesy. Thus a severe strain was still to weigh down the resources of the two Great Powers of Europe; an insignificant fortress was to baffle their united efforts; their armies were to be destroyed on the upland of the Chersonese by cold and famine; and, while our British Engineers alone could survey with complacency the results of their skill, evidenced by the speedy destruction of the defences around Karabelnaya, the Allies were not one whit nearer the accomplishment of their object than they had been before the bombardment began. Still the Chiefs of the invading forces were sanguine that their fire at last would tell, and would allow them to storm the place together, at points where each had breached the defences opposed to them; but in this expectation they were, as they deserved to be, disappointed. The bombardment was continued on the 18th, and the British batteries alone took part in it—for the French were not ready, and were improving their earthworks after the disaster of the day before,— not, however, against the wreck which we had created by the evening of the 17th, but on renewed and freshly armed defences that were repaired in the night by the ceaseless energy of the garrison, whose labours were undisturbed by any countermove on our part. Again, on the 19th, the united artillery fired on the hostile batteries with complete success on our side, but once more the French guns were silenced. The bootless bombardment continued till the 25th, ever with the same result: the lines covering the Karabelnaya were open to attack, but the forts opposite Mount Rodolph were unsubdued. Thus no advantage was gained, or indeed could be gained, under the rule which the Allies had imposed upon themselves to the benefit of the enemy, who, not slow to perceive the situation, took every advantage therefrom. A great display, therefore, was all that took place, which cost the Russians nearly 4000 men, while the Allies lost less than a fourth part of that number.

* Hamley, *War in the Crimea*, p. 105.

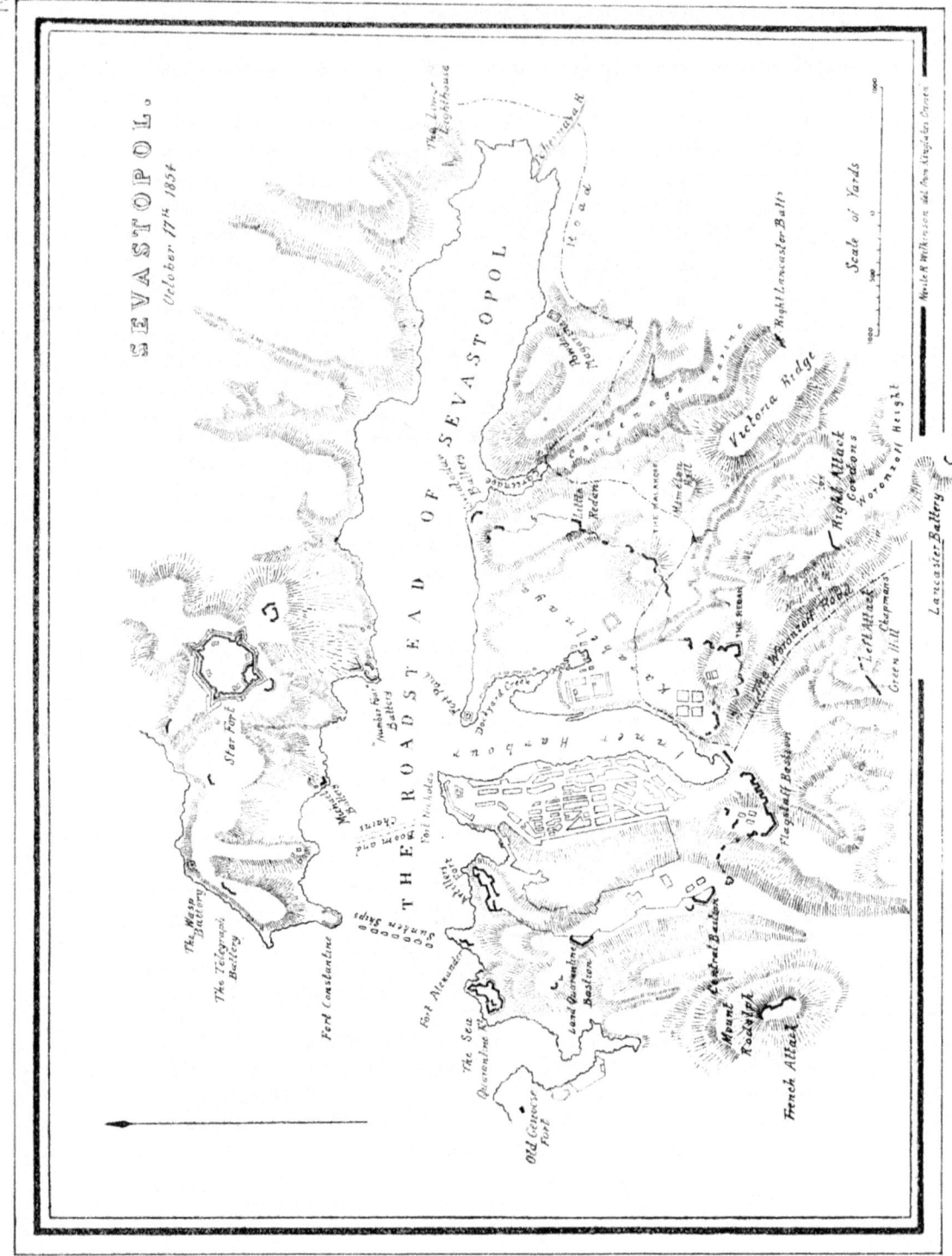

As the fire proceeded from day to day, the attention of the First and Second Divisions was directed to their right flank.

"Started an hour before daybreak on outlying piquet on the heights to our rear, and was kept the whole day in a state of excitement by a large force of Russians, cavalry and artillery, in the plain below; some took up a position on the hills in front of Balaklava, and some remained near where we bivouacked at the Tchernaya bridge, evidently threatening Balaklava. Some of them advanced towards us, and brought some artillery and opened fire. Presently a battery of ours unlimbered in the bushes by my piquet, and got ready for action; the 2me Zouaves were also sent, and there was a report that the enemy was advancing up the Inkerman gorges; in short, we thought we were in for a scrimmage. But after a short time the Zouaves and artillery were sent back to their quarters, and I was left face to face with the Ruskis. After dark their fires blazed all over the plain, but nothing occurred. I was with my sentries all night. They evidently intend making an attack on Balaklava when we assault the town, which doubtless must take place soon." *

The enemy, seen upon this occasion, was again observed by a piquet of the Coldstream on the 20th, among the Inkerman ruins (beyond the Tchernaya), mounting guns. Towards evening he opened fire, and directed his aim upon the camp of the Second Division, until the Sandbag battery, previously mentioned, was constructed, and armed with two 18-pounders. The British fire soon drove away the guns from the ruins, but the 18-pounders had to be removed to a less exposed position.

Nine Officers reached the Crimea and joined the Battalion on the 17th, the first day of the bombardment, viz. Lieut.-Colonels Newton, Cowell, and Halkett (who had left Bulgaria on promotion in July), Lieut.-Colonels Mark Wood, Dudley Carleton, and Lord A. Charles FitzRoy, and Lieutenants Heneage, Hon. W. Amherst, and Greville.

It should be stated here, that, on account of the war, the Regiment received an augmentation, first on the 13th of February, and again a little later. The establishments were as follows:—

	Colonel.	Lt.-Colonel.	Majors.	Captains.	Lieutenants.	Ensigns.	Adjutants.	Qr.-Masters.	Surgn.-Major.	Surgeon.	Assist.-Surgns.	Solicitor.	Sergeants.	Drummers.	Rank and File.	
Feb. 1st, 1854	1	1	2	16	20	12	2	2	1	1	2	1	72	37	1280	2 Battns. 16 Cos.
Mar. 1st, ,,	1	1	2	16	20	12	2	2	1	1	3	1	88	37	1600	2 Battns. 16 Cos.
Aug. 1st, ,,	1	1	2	20	24	16	2	2	1	1	4	1	118	46	2200	2 Battns. 20 Cos.

* Tower, *Diary*, Oct. 18th.

Of the twenty companies, twelve were at home and eight at the seat of war, but the latter were strong companies on paper, and the former weak; it was further ordered that the service Battalion was not to bear upon its strength less Officers than were required for 10 companies, the Adjutant not included.* Hence the two mounted Officers who, before the receipt of this order, were posted to companies in the field, were placed upon the 1st Battalion establishment, and nominally belonged to companies at home.

During the first few days of the operations against Sevastopol there were several casualties among the Officers of the Grenadier Guards. On the 16th, Captain Rowley was killed, and, two days later, the same fate overtook Colonel Hood, the gallant Commanding Officer who had greatly distinguished himself by his coolness and intrepidity at the Alma. The losses of the Coldstream at this moment were happily less. It was not till the 20th, that the first man was wounded in the trenches; but next day, Lord Dunkellin was unfortunately captured. Commanding a working party without arms—for at that time the men told off to dig were sent to the front unarmed,—he lost his way in the darkness, and, stumbling upon a piquet which he thought was English, he went forward by himself to ask where he was. As it happened, he found himself within the enemy's lines, and was taken; his men, however, luckily escaped under cover of the night.†

Prince Menshikoff so far recovered from his defeat on the 20th of September, that he occupied the hills in the neighbourhood of Mackenzie Farm, and took possession of the roads leading therefrom into the valley of the Tchernaya on the 7th of October. He had good reason to be proud of the achievements of the garrison of Sevastopol, and to rejoice at his own singular good fortune. The town was fast growing into a powerful fortress, sufficiently strong to resist any sudden assault, and likely for months to occupy the energies of a far more numerous force than stood before it at that time. He himself was placed in an unassailable position. Secure as regards his communications with the interior of Russia

---

* *Brigade Order*, London, Sept. 5, 1854.

† This incident does not appear to have modified the rule by which working parties were sent to the trenches at night, across an unknown and intersected country, without arms or an escort, if we may judge from the following General After Order of the 22nd: "The Commander of the Forces directs that all parties, whether armed or on fatigue, which may be ordered to the front, may be accompanied by a Staff Officer competent to guide them." On the 11th of November, however, it was ordered that all working parties were to take their arms with them (*First Divisional Pass Order*).

and with Sevastopol, he not only received without difficulty the fresh forces that were hurrying to his assistance; but he also hemmed the invaders into a small corner of an exceedingly inhospitable country, restricted their enterprise, and threatened them with destruction in case a reverse were to happen to them. History, indeed, fails to record any great genius in this Russian General, nor were his troops of that high order to account for the immense advantages he gained at this moment. He was simply fortunate in the Governments and in the leaders of his antagonists, who, unable to combine to carry out any single plan, continually changed their intentions, until a surprise on the north side was converted into a lengthy siege (without investment) of the south side.

The Bessarabian reinforcements began to reach Simferopol early in October, and on the 15th, General Liprandi arrived there. A few days later it was determined to make an attack on our base at Balaklava, with some 25,000 troops (22,000 infantry, 3400 cavalry, and 78 guns) commanded by that Officer. The attack took place on the 25th, a day immortalized in our military history by the bravery of the British cavalry, particularly by the charge of the Light brigade, "one of the most brilliant ever remembered in the annals of war," though it resulted in the destruction of that corps.*

Balaklava was covered by two defensive lines, the outer and the inner. The outer line, more than two miles in length, running along the Causeway Heights and near the Woronzoff road, had the support of a few small earthworks, "mere scratches with the spade, a donkey might have been ridden into some of them," armed with only nine 12-pounder guns in all, and occupied by about two battalions of Turks. The inner line, near Kadikeui, was 3000 yards in rear, and was held by the 93rd Regiment, a few invalids, the Marines, and the rest of the Turks. The Russians, advancing in force at dawn on the 25th, brought 30 guns (some of them of heavy calibre) against the earthworks on the Causeway Heights,—which were isolated, entirely unsupported, and commanded by neighbouring ground,—and captured two of them on the right of the line, after a stubborn resistance; a third soon after fell into their hands. They then pushed forward their cavalry, of which

* General G. Klapka, *The War in the East, from the year* 1853 *till July*, 1855 (translated by Lieut.-Colonel A. Mednyansky), p. 96 (London, 1855).

four squadrons reconnoitred towards Kadikeui; the latter came within range of the 93rd, drawn up in line, who received them with a volley, and with such determination that they quickly wheeled about and fled to the rear. The rest, a solid column, nearly 3000 strong, supported by 32 guns, moving in somewhat the same direction, came suddenly close to the British Heavy cavalry brigade, who, without the slightest hesitation, charged, and in a few moments routed them, and sent them back in confusion, past the front of the Light brigade. Unfortunately Lord Cardigan did not fall upon the flying mass and complete their discomfiture; so they got away down the valley that lay between the Fediukhine and Causeway heights, both of which were held by the enemy's infantry and artillery, and took up a position about a mile and a quarter away, behind some Russian guns. And now "some one blundered," and the Light brigade made their famous charge, over this dangerous ground, flanked on each side by well-posted artillery, straight into the guns and the cavalry at the end of the valley. The story of this gallant deed is well known. The Russian gunners and cavalry were swept away, and forced to retreat before the impetuous onslaught of our weak squadrons, but the brigade was broken, and indeed destroyed. It numbered 670 sabres at the commencement of the action, and at the conclusion its mounted strength was only 195. The enemy was quite unable to cut off the retreat of the remnants of our light horse, as they rode back after their desperate expedition, very few prisoners were taken, and the French, making a spirited and successful charge upon the Fediukhine Heights, prevented the Russians from harassing our men from that quarter, as they emerged from the deadly and unequal conflict.

Heavy firing had been heard in the British camps before Sevastopol at dawn, and, when the serious nature of the attack was perceived, orders were sent to the First and Fourth Divisions to march down to meet the danger. Two of Bosquet's infantry brigades, as well as the French cavalry, which had by this time reached the seat of war, were also brought to the field of battle. When our troops got to the Sapuné Ridge, and looked on the plain beneath, they saw with breathless interest the first encounter between the contending horsemen.

"The Heavy cavalry charge," says Colonel Tower, "was just going on as we came in sight of the Turkish redoubts; we could indistinctly see the grey horses and bearskin caps [the Scots Greys] swallowed up in a dense mass of grey-coated Russians, their sabres flashing in the sun." *

The subsequent charge of the Light brigade was not so apparent to our infantry :—

"The threatened attack of Balaklava," continues Colonel Tower, "turned out to be nothing; and when it appeared to be all over, the Light cavalry started on their suicidal expedition, we could see them over the line of hills of the Turkish redoubts, and then they vanished to be seen no more. When the remnants returned, I got leave to fall out, and walked up to the Turkish redoubts, and almost the first thing I saw was poor Nolan's body, his chest knocked to pieces by a round shot; the whole plain was dotted about with men and horses, some struggling on the ground, some loose horses galloping about without riders; a great many Russian cavalry were lying about where the Heavy cavalry had driven them back,—our men had used their sabres with good effect."

Despite the glorious conduct of our troops upon this occasion, we lost a good deal and gained very little. The eastern portion of an unsupported advanced line of redoubts on the Causeway Heights was captured by the weight of numbers, and the outer defences of Balaklava were occupied by the enemy; but his further movements towards Kadikeni were crushed by a handful of our Heavy cavalry, and our Light brigade proved their superiority over him by a useless feat of daring which is unparalleled in warfare.

Thus, though Balaklava was still safe, we were deprived of the use of the Woronzoff road as a means of communication between our base of operations and the upland, and we had only the unmetalled path which led over the Col to rely on. We shall see that this result of the battle of the 25th was a serious one for the British army besieging Sevastopol. There was, indeed, some idea of turning Liprandi out of the Causeway Heights; but had it been definitely formed, the infantry would have descended from the ridge on which they stood by the Woronzoff road, whence the object would have been more easily accomplished. Instead of this, however, they were moved onwards to the Col, and remained during the day covering Balaklava. No forward operation was

* *Diary*, Oct. 25th. Readers of the late Sir Edward Hamley's *War in the Crimea*, p. 113, will remember the vivid description which he has given of this brilliant cavalry charge, as it appeared to him and to the troops (among them the Coldstream) standing on the heights above.

undertaken, and it was probably considered that we had not sufficient troops to hold the outer line efficiently. So the main road was placidly given up to the enemy, and at nightfall the Guards Brigade and the Fourth Division returned to camp, while the remaining two Highland regiments were left at Balaklava to strengthen the garrison at that important place.*

The vulnerable point on the right flank of the British position has already been adverted to, also the position taken up by the French Corps of observation under General Bosquet. We have seen that this force could not help the Allies to retain possession of the Woronzoff road, nor could it, as we shall see, secure the right of their siege-works from serious attack. The first attempt to disturb this flank was made at noon on the 26th, when a force emerged from Sevastopol, of which 700 men advanced up the Careenage Ravine, while the remainder, 4300 men and four guns, crossed that obstacle, and directed themselves upon Shell Hill, in front of the camp of the Second Division. The former column was met by the sharpshooters of the Guards, under Captain Goodlake, who, drawing up his insignificant detachment behind a ditch that ran across the ravine, held the hostile column in check, and barred its further advance,—even capturing several prisoners,—until, a little later, some men of the Rifles appearing upon the scene, the enemy was driven back.†

The main column, endeavouring to reach Shell Hill, met the outposts of the Second Division, some 250 strong, who, instead of retiring before so superior a force, stubbornly resisted it, and held it at bay, until, outflanked and pressed back by numbers, they retreated slowly and in good order. But the Russians gained nothing, for the divisional artillery, reinforced by a battery of the First Division, had time to come into action, and when the enemy

---

* The battle which deprived us of our principal road, cost the Allies—
English, 40 Officers; 386 sergeants, rank and file; 426 total
French, 2 ,, 50 ,, ,, 52 ,,
Turks, 9 ,, 250 ,, ,, 259 ,,

Total, 737 men, and 409 horses. The Russians lost some 600 men, of whom the greater number fell before the British Heavy cavalry. The latter suffered but little in that superb charge, though they had many casualties when shielding the recoil of the Light brigade (*Our Veterans, etc.*, p. 255).

† This was one of the acts of gallantry performed by Captain Goodlake during the war, for which he was awarded the Victoria Cross.

appeared upon the crest of the hill, he was met by the fire of our guns, which speedily repulsed him, and made him retire precipitately to the fortress, pursued by the piquets, and under fire of the Lancaster battery. In this combat, where the Russians acknowledge the loss of 270 men and 80 prisoners, as against 12 killed and 77 wounded on our side, Lieutenant Conolly, of the 49th Regiment, greatly distinguished himself. He was promoted Brevet Major, obtained the Victoria Cross, and a commission in the Coldstream. The Brigade was not employed in this action; they stood in reserve out of musketry fire, and watched the fight, ready for emergencies, but their services were not required.*

This sortie was intended, according to Todleben, to distract our attention from Balaklava; and it may well be that Liprandi, knowing its importance, was under grave apprehension lest the Woronzoff road might be wrested from him. It has also been thought that the Russians were endeavouring to effect a lodgment on Shell Hill, preparatory to the attack they meant soon to deliver on our right flank at Inkerman, and this is very likely. But, if so, they had an inadequate force to accomplish such a purpose, and by this time they had ample experience of the fighting qualities of the British troops, who, man for man, were immensely superior to their own. Indeed we had every need of the sterling bravery of our gallant soldiers, for a great crisis was at hand. The strength of our Crimean army was becoming alarmingly weakened, not only by the wear and tear of active service and losses incurred on the field, but through the unusual amount of sickness that prevailed, and the arduous nature of the campaign in which we had become engaged. In the Coldstream there were 190 more admissions into hospital in October than there had been in September.† On the other hand, the actions of the 25th and 26th increased the confidence of our men when opposed to the enemy. They felt themselves more than a match for him if they could only get leave to be at him; but they little knew how severe the trial would be that awaited them in a very few days.‡

---

* The Russians appear, upon this occasion, to have understated both their strength and their losses.

† Wyatt, p. 28.

‡ Colonel Wilson, describing the excellent tone that prevailed among our men at this time, notes the behaviour of the wounded on the 26th, as they limped or were carried on stretchers past the Brigade. He says it was "wonderful, the very reverse of what might have been looked for. Far from drooping in spirits, most of them were in buoyant

On the night of the 28th, many of our camps were alarmed, and believed they were about to be attacked. The outposts watching the plain of Balaklava heard cavalry approaching, and a great deal of firing in the dark took place—the sentries blazing away whenever they saw, or fancied they saw, the phantom horsemen, "who seemed perpetually galloping, but never coming any nearer. Staff Officers kept arriving to know what the commotion was about. Of course I could give them no information." A regiment of Zouaves and the guns in a French redoubt poured volleys into imaginary columns coming to storm our position. "The Russian drums all along the Fediukhine heights beat to arms; and I sat down quietly on a stone in advance of my sentries, and could hear nothing more, but made up my mind Liprandi intended to give us a benefit in the morning." When the morning broke the mystery was cleared. It was found that a number of Russian horses had stampeded from their lines, and that no enemy was near. A hundred or more were caught, and served to mount a few of our cavalry, while the remainder scampered back across the plain to their legitimate owners.*

The weary monotony of the siege continued after the sortie of the 26th, the troops being largely employed in the trenches, constructing approaches or batteries, or acting as covering guards, generally under a heavy fire from the fortress in front of them.

"The enemy is barricading the streets, and we shall have to fight every inch of ground. I fear we have a great many of our sorrows to come, more especially wintering here; too horrible to contemplate! An army of 30,000 men in our rear with a large force of cavalry, and Sevastopol, which seems to be getting stronger every day, in our front. Any number of general actions is better than a siege. In the trenches for twenty-six hours at a time (we used to mount now at 2 a.m., with nothing but biscuit and salt pork to eat), shells constantly troubling one's life, and showers of dirt covering you every time a shot strikes the parapet."†

The French were sapping up towards the Flagstaff Battery with the greatest energy. They were becoming strong enough to

spirits. Sometimes a fine youth with a badly fractured arm, hurraed lustily as he passed; another, whose thigh a round shot had smashed, would—faint as he was—raise himself up a little on his litter, and brandish his rifle triumphantly. I observed that nearly every man, whether slightly or sorely hurt, still clutched his musket. . . . A bullet through the heart alone conquers such soldiers" (*Our Veterans, etc.*, p. 266).

* Tower, *Diary*, Oct. 28th. † *Ibid.*, Oct. 27th.

withstand the guns of the garrison, and to retrieve their failure of October 17th–25th. Another bombardment, to be followed by an assault, was contemplated, and the allied Commanders had full confidence that this time, at least, the effect would be decisive. They even agreed to meet on the 5th of November to arrange the details of their projected operation. But neglected opportunities too often rise in judgment against a General in the field. The 5th was the day of Inkerman, and all our plans were completely frustrated.

CHAPTER IX.

THE BATTLE OF INKERMAN.

Large Russian reinforcements reach the Crimea—Position and strength of the enemy; of the Allies—Description of the field of Inkerman—Commencement of the battle, 5th of November—The progress of the first part of the fight—The Guards Brigade advance to the scene of action—The struggle round the Sandbag battery—Arrival of the Fourth Division under General Cathcart—The manœuvre of the latter, and its failure—The arrival of the French—Successes of the British artillery—Repulse of the Russian attack; the retreat of the enemy; there is no pursuit—Operations of the garrison of Sevastopol and of the Russian force in the Tchernaya Valley during the day—Great losses incurred on both sides—Reaction among the soldiery after the battle.

THE Russian reinforcements which, as we have seen, began to arrive in the month of October, continued their advance upon the Crimea, so that early in November the hostile forces at the seat of war amounted, all told, to more than 120,000 men capable of taking part in the operations of the campaign.* The moment had now come when the enemy determined to deliver his well-prepared attack upon the invaders, and hoped to rid the Crimea for ever of their presence. It must be confessed that he had a good opportunity of accomplishing his object, and that every advantage was on his side. He could choose his own time and place of attack; his forces were far more powerful than those of the invaders, both in numbers and in position; and, by the reconnaissance or sortie of October 26th, he found out (if he did not already know it) that our vulnerable right flank was unsecured by any fieldworks to make up for our other deficiencies. The onslaught, then, that was to drive us away from Sevastopol, and to sweep us into the sea, was to be directed upon this flank, upon ground which our soldiers called Mount Inkerman, and Sunday, the

* Sir E. Hamley, in his *War in the Crimea*, p. 129, estimates these forces at 110,000 to 115,000, including the enemy's sailors. He has, however, apparently omitted to include men whom he previously counted as part of the garrison at the end of September (see *ante*, p. 185).

5th of November, was chosen as the day upon which to put the design into execution.*

On the evening of the 4th, Prince Menshikoff established his head-quarters near the mouth of the Tchernaya, and his troops were posted as follows: The garrison was not increased beyond the numbers it contained towards the end of October. General Dannenberg, head-quarters on the Old City Heights, midway between Mackenzie Farm and the head of the roadstead, commanded a corps of 50 battalions, 1 squadron, and 134 guns (of which 54 were guns of position). This corps was divided into two columns, namely, General Soimonoff, 19,000 infantry and 38 guns (22 of position), whose troops were temporarily sheltered in the lines of the fortress in the Karabelnaya; and General Pavloff, 16,500 infantry and 96 guns (32 of position), concentrated on the Old City Heights. To the left of Pavloff, there was another force of 16 battalions, 62 squadrons, and 88 guns (15,000 infantry), composed mostly of Liprandi's column, but now under Prince Gortchakoff, whose head-quarters were at Tchorgun. Lastly, there was a body of 4000 infantry and 36 guns guarding the road to Bakshiserai, somewhere near Mackenzie Farm. Thus, besides the garrison which amounted to nearly 60,000 men, placed in what was now a secure stronghold, amply covered and well armed, there was a force of 54,500 infantry, a powerful body of cavalry, and 258 guns available to operate against the undefended flank of the Allies.

The latter, on the other hand, had received a few reinforcements, but not sufficient to compensate for the immense losses to which they had been subjected. On the evening of the 4th, they numbered but 58,000 infantry,—16,000 British, 31,000 French, and 11,000 Turks; and this small force was further weakened by the fact that the allied Commanders, totally unacquainted with the warlike qualities of their Ottoman auxiliaries, would not allow them to develop their value, and left them no chance to assist in the approaching battle. So far did Lord Raglan's prejudice go, that the 6000 attached to the British army, were not suffered to take part as combatants, and when Omar Pasha proposed to send him a further contingent he refused the offer.† Hence there were practically

---

* See Map, No. 7, p. 216. Properly speaking, Inkerman was on the other side of the Tchernaya, called by us Old City Heights.

† Hamley, *War in the Crimea*, 128; *Kinglake*, v. 33, 34 note, 41 note. Sir Evelyn Wood says, in his recent publication, that he has "never understood why these

only 47,000 British and French infantry left to meet the grave crisis which now confronted us. These troops were disposed on an irregular curve which stretched from Streleska Bay (north of Kamiesh Bay) along the front of the enemy's lines of Sevastopol to the heights of Inkerman, thence southwards on the Sapuné Ridge to the Col, where it ran more to the east, near Kadikeui, and covered Balaklava. This line measured twenty miles in length, it was unsupported by any central reserve, and was everywhere in contact with powerful masses of the enemy.

Menshikoff's onslaught was to be delivered as the first gleam of light appeared at dawn on the 5th, when his forces were to be before our outposts, ready to press the advance home. The principal attack was confided to Dannenberg's corps, whose two columns were to converge upon the British unguarded position at Inkerman, —that of Soimonoff, issuing from the Karabelnaya by the road that skirts the south bank of the roadstead, that of Pavloff marching down to the Tchernaya and crossing the river by the causeway and bridge near its mouth. Gortchakoff was to support this operation, and endeavour "to seize one of the ascents to the Sapuné Ridge;" and the garrison was to "cover by its fire the right flank of the assaulting columns, and, should there be confusion in the enemy's batteries, to storm those batteries." The Russians were elated by the bright prospects before them. "Future times, I am confident," wrote their Chief, "will preserve the remembrance of the exemplary chastisement inflicted upon the presumption of the Allies. . . . Heaven visibly protects Holy Russia. Have the kindness to bring this to the knowledge of our august Sovereign for the great satisfaction of his magnanimous heart." Two of the Grand-Dukes, sons of the Tsar, arrived in the Crimea, to encourage the Muscovite troops, and to bear witness to the "exemplary chastisement" about to be inflicted; but the "magnanimous heart" was not to be satisfied, for Menshikoff forgot to take into account, what a handful of British soldiers are capable of doing when sorely pressed, and when protecting the honour of their Queen and country, even against overwhelming odds.

A general description of the ground known as Inkerman (or Mount Inkerman) has already been given. The Lancaster battery, now nearly dismantled, and holding but one gun, had been planted

Moslems, who came out so grandly at Silistria, were considered unfit to fight alongside the English and French troops" (Wood, *Crimea in 1854 and 1894*, p. 199).

on the Victoria Ridge between the Docks and Careenage ravines, and more than a mile in rear, stood the camp of General Codrington's brigade of the Light Division. To the east, another main spur, jutting out from the upland, fills up the space between Careenage Ravine and the Tchernaya, broken by water-courses which descend into the ravine, the roadstead, and the river. Into the ravine, there is one water-course, the Wellway, which joins it 400 yards in rear of the Lancaster battery ; and into the Tchernaya there is another, the Quarry Ravine, through which a post-road runs connecting the upland with the head of the roadstead. Between the Wellway and the Quarry Ravine, the main spur is some 1300 yards broad, and supports a rise, called Home Ridge, that bends to the north under the name of Fore Ridge, and thence slopes away towards the Tchernaya, in two spurs, which overlook the valley, and which are divided by St. Clement's Gorge, viz. Inkerman Tusk and the Kitspur. On the Kitspur the Sandbag battery had been erected on commanding ground : it was a mere short wall of earth, only eighteen paces in length, too high to shoot over except where cut by two embrasures ; it was unprovided with a banquette, and at this moment it was vacant and unarmed. Astride the post-road the Second Division was encamped, immediately behind Home Ridge, in front of which the main spur is contracted to 250 yards in breadth. But at a distance of 1400 yards from the ridge, the main spur again widens out considerably, and here there is another rise, called Shell Hill, flanked on each side by buttresses, West and East Jut, which the enemy had vainly tried to capture on October 26th. About a mile in rear of the Second Division, and always on the same main spur, near a ruined windmill, stood the camp of the Guards Brigade, the Coldstream being somewhat in rear, and separated from the rest by a narrow ravine. Thus, in the first instance, available to resist an attack on Inkerman, there was one division, viz. the Second, of 3000 men and 12 guns ; supported in rear by the Household Brigade, 1300 men, and 12 guns of the First Division, and, on the left, though with a great obstacle intervening—the Careenage Ravine—Codrington's brigade, 1200 men. To the rear, some two miles from the Guards, lay the northern portion of Bosquet's Corps of observation, which at this time was in closer communication with the Highlanders and Marines, at Balaklava, than had been the case before October 25th. To the left, were Buller's brigade of the Light, and the Fourth and the Third Divisions, distant respectively from

Home Ridge, 1½, 2½, and 3 miles. These latter troops were covered by the defences which the trenches and batteries afforded, as was also Forey's French siege corps, which, as already mentioned, took up the line from the British Left Attack to Streleska Bay. But no such protection was available for the division and the two brigades more immediately threatened in the vicinity of Inkerman.

Though both Commanders of the Allied armies felt anxiety on account of this exposed flank, nothing was done to make it secure. General Canrobert paid us the compliment of placing extraordinary reliance on our troops,—especially the *bonnets de poil*, as he called the Guards; on the other hand, Lord Raglan, weak in numbers, thought he could not spare any of his men from the trenches. Still, the omission to safeguard this vital position with earthworks has never been explained, for as Turks could have been obtained for this purpose, and as Engineer Officers were available, the excuse given, like many others put forward to cover our deficiencies in this extraordinary war, can hardly be deemed satisfactory. Of the value of works of defence to be occupied in case of attack, it is sufficient to point out that, if we were victorious without them, we should have been far stronger with them, and the battle (if it had taken place at all under these circumstances) could not have failed to result in greater disaster to the enemy, and in much less loss to ourselves.

The Guards furnished piquets to watch the flank and rear of the British army. On the 1st of November a stronger force was considered necessary to accomplish this object, and the Brigade supplied eight piquets daily. Six (numbered 1 to 6) mounted an hour before daybreak for twenty-four hours, under the Field-Officer of the day while the other two (Nos. 7 and 8) were posted as a reserve from sunset until an hour after sunrise, the whole during the night being placed under the command of a "full Colonel of the Brigade."* Besides finding three working parties in the trenches, each 40 to 50 men strong under an Officer, the Coldstream furnished, on the 4th, piquets Nos. 5 and 8, and again on the 5th, Nos. 3, 5, and 6. Thus before dawn on the morning of the battle, the Battalion had two piquets (Nos. 4 and 5 companies) coming off, and three (Nos. 6 and 7 companies) going on duty; so that four companies were absorbed, and when the first alarm was given, only half the Battalion (Nos. 1, 2, 3 and 8 companies) were in camp. The Colonel on duty, during the night 4th–5th, should have been

* *Brigade Order*, Nov. 1, 1854.

Lord F. Paulet, but as he was incapacitated by illness, Colonel Upton took his place; moreover, Lieut.-Colonel Newton, detailed Field Officer of the day for the 5th, had left long before daylight began to appear. The next senior Officer was Lieut.-Colonel Dawson, and, when the first alarm was given, he quickly formed up what remained of the Battalion, and immediately marched them to the front where the battle was heard, to the support of the Second Division, who were then seriously engaged with the enemy.

"MacKinnon, Ramsden, and I," writes Colonel Tower, "were all three living in one tent, and were awakened at daybreak, or soon after, by firing in the direction of Inkerman; we thought little of it, as we were accustomed to alarms, and the piquets constantly fired; but presently a big gun or two told us it was more than piquets. The bugles sounded in the camp, and 'fall in directly' was echoed by the sergeants along the line of tents. We hurried on our arms, as we always slept in our clothes, and found the Battalion falling in. Vesey Dawson was in command, on a chestnut horse; Granville Eliot, Adjutant, on his old grey arab, Bashi-Bazouk. It rained a great deal during the night, and that memorable Sunday morning dawned a nasty damp foggy day; the mist was rising from the ground and the brushwood was quite wet; we could only see a few yards before us, but we could hear the pattering of musketry, and the firing had been going on fully half an hour before we came on the scene of action. We left camp in column of fours, but before we got to the Second Division tents one or two round shot came right through our ranks, and we began to have an idea how close the enemy was, and of the serious nature of the business. We formed line, and advanced through the Second Division tents, many of which were knocked down and shot through. . . . We were the battalion on the extreme right of the army, and my company (No. 1) was on the extreme right of the Battalion."*

Meanwhile, what had happened was this. Although we knew that an attack was imminent, we were unable to tell the precise day on which it was to take place. The night 4th–5th passed quietly, there was no firing, no alarm, no spies came to warn us. The sentries on outpost, and the piquets, heard a rumbling noise in the valley, but the sounds were deadened by the heavy rain that fell during the 4th and throughout the night, and they were not sufficiently distinct to induce us to concert any definite arrangements to meet the emergency. In so far the enemy acted with caution and ability; the attack came upon us as a surprise, even

* Tower, *Diary*, Nov. 5th.

though we expected it. He failed, however, to marshal his immense masses to the best advantage. The orders given to Dannenberg's forces were vague, and there was a confusion as to whether both Soimonoff and Pavloff were to operate on the eastern side of the Careenage Ravine, or whether the former was to advance along the Victoria Ridge and the latter against Inkerman. Obviously, had this plan been adopted, Codrington's brigade and Evans' division would both have been in imminent danger ; and had either been driven in, the results must have been disastrous. Fortunately, the two unwieldy Russian columns jammed themselves together on the broken ground east of the ravine, and interfered by their numbers and proximity with each other's movements.

Soimonoff, arriving on the ground a little before his colleague, commenced the attack with his powerful column. Advancing cautiously and silently in three lines covered by skirmishers, he had 6000 men in the first line, followed by 3300 and his heavy guns, and 9000 with the light artillery in reserve. The latter was the first hostile body perceived by the British advanced piquets ; who, though they could then see nothing, heard their approach. On discovering them, they opened fire, and these volleys were heard by General Codrington, who, according to his usual practice, was near the Lancaster battery reconnoitring to the front with his relieved piquets, before the day broke. He at once got his brigade under arms, moved them to the edge of the ravine near the battery, and lost no time in conveying the alarm to head-quarters and to the left. Buller then moved out towards the threatened point, and the Fourth and Third Divisions were in readiness to march.

The enemy soon pressed back the outposts of the Second Division, and the camp being aroused, the troops formed on Home Ridge ; while the 22 heavy Russian pieces establishing themselves on Shell Hill, opened on the ridge and on the ground in rear of it : by this means the Russians hoped to crush the British supports that were supposed to be in their ordinary place. But, as a matter of fact, we had none there, a single thin line held the crest, and the fire beyond it succeeded only in destroying the camp and the horses left behind. While this was going on, the twelve field guns of the division were neither silent nor inefficient, and General Pennefather (in command, Sir De Lacy Evans being at Balaklava, on the sick list *) now pushed forward bodies of 200 to 500 men to

* He came up later, but refused to take the command out of Pennefather's hands.

reinforce the piquets, who were slowly retiring before the advance of the masses opposed to them. One of these detachments, 500 strong, under General Adams, moved to the right, towards the Sandbag battery; and another, hurrying to the left, soon came in contact with a huge hostile column which bore down on them in the mist. The Officer in command had just time to sing out, "Fire and charge!" and the men obeying with loud cheers, the enemy was driven back, right through the line of his guns on Shell Hill, before the impetuous onset could be arrested. The result of this hand-to-hand encounter between a thin line of red-coats and a strong column of the Russians, was often repeated during the day. The battle, in short, resolved itself into a series of personal combats between small British detachments and dense masses of the enemy; the former, under the nearest Officers, dashing boldly, without supports, against the latter wherever opportunity offered or danger pressed. There was no central control, nor were manœuvres attempted; both were impossible. But the activity, intelligence, and courage of the few—to be counted by hundreds against thousands—never flagged for an instant, and the unwieldy forces opposed to us, though so much more powerful in point of numbers, were shattered and driven back in confusion.

"No doubt the mist was favourable to the fewer numbers, hiding from the Russians the fact that there was nothing behind the English lines, which came on as boldly as if strong supports were close at hand. It needs some plausible supposition of this kind to account (however imperfectly) for the extraordinary combats which ensued, where the extravagant achievements of the romances of chivalry were almost outdone by the reality." *

Soimonoff, leaving 10,000 men in rear of his guns on Shell Hill, made his first real assault with 9000 infantry, who, to avoid our artillery fire, moved along the eastern slope of the Careenage Ravine. Part of Pavloff's corps, 6000 men, had by this time arrived on the scene, and they got into the Quarry Ravine, and, bearing across Inkerman Tusk, made for the Sandbag battery. Thus the narrow flat of the main spur, connecting Home Ridge with Shell Hill, was swept with fire from the enemy's guns, and on one side of it (our left) were 9000 Russians advancing, while 6000 more were threatening our right front at the head of the Quarry Ravine and on the spurs in the vicinity overlooking the Tchernaya. General

* Hamley, *War in the Crimea*, p. 141.

Buller reached the field at this juncture, with 600 men and a battery from the Fourth Division. To meet the onslaught of 15,000 men suitably supported by artillery, against both our flanks, Pennefather, therefore, had just 3600 men and 18 guns. Soimonoff's advanced troops on our left met with a transient gleam of success; they captured three guns, which were hurrying into action, and they managed to push into the Wellway. Had they been able to emerge on the plateau near Home Ridge, they would have taken the British position in reverse.* But this column was quickly discomfited by a gallant charge of a few men of the 77th Regiment, and by a piquet of the Grenadier Guards under Lieut.-Colonel Prince Edward of Saxe-Weimar, posted close by. Nor did the remainder of Soimonoff's corps hold their ground, for they also gave way when met by the steady line of British infantry, and the whole attack upon our left was soon repulsed; indeed, one of our groups, having driven in immensely superior forces, pursued them, and halted not until Shell Hill was reached. The three English guns taken by the enemy were speedily recaptured, and were found to be uninjured; the Russian General, Soimonoff, moreover, was killed at this period. Nor did Pavloff's 6000 men fare any better, though they were confronted by only 700 to 800 Englishmen. At the head of the Quarry Ravine, the leading hostile battalions were charged by 200 men of the 30th Regiment, and were routed; while the rest, attacked by General Adams and the 41st Regiment near the Sandbag battery, were also driven back in confusion.

It was now nearly 7.30 in the morning, and everywhere the struggle had resulted in our favour. But the battle was only in its infancy. Soimonoff's reserve, 10,000 strong, was intact, and the remainder of Pauloff's corps, 10,000 men, had arrived, together with his long train of artillery, which, placed on commanding ground, prolonged the line of guns from Shell Hill to the end of East Jut. Dannenberg now assumed command of these 20,000 infantry, and of the columns whose first attack had failed. He determined to employ his masses against our right, and so cooperate more closely with Gortchakoff, who, as we have seen, was manœuvring in the valley, with orders to seize the Sapuné Ridge. This latter corps had very early assumed a threatening attitude

* Apparently this advanced column was composed of sailors or marines, not reckoned in Soimonoff's corps; they were, therefore, additional to it (Kinglake, v. 117).

as far north as the heights for which the Guards Brigade were responsible, and this fact somewhat delayed their advance to the front; * but it was soon perceived that the enemy in this quarter was making a mere empty demonstration, that the real crisis was round Home Ridge, and that the piquets were sufficient in the present emergency to guard the hills overlooking the Tchernaya. The Grenadier and Scots Fusilier Guards, encamped closer to the scene of action, were therefore moved forward to take their share in it, followed soon after by the Coldstream (four companies strong, under Lieut.-Colonel Dawson, as we have seen), and the whole came into action about 7.30, when the introductory phase of the fight was over, and just as the new attack was developing itself. Shortly after the departure of the Regiment, the two relieved Coldstream piquets (Nos. 4 and 5 companies), having been kept out somewhat longer than usual, on account of Gortchakoff's movements, came into camp, and, finding it empty, advanced to the front, as did also Colonel Upton. The strength of the Brigade was as follows:—

	Officers.	Sergeants.	Drummers.	Rank & File.	Total.
Grenadier Guards ..	22	24	17	438	501
Coldstream (6 companies)	17 †	34	14	373	438
Scots Fusilier Guards ..	20	23	17	332	392
Brigade Staff		3 (Major-Gen. Bentinck; Capt. Ellison, Bde. Maj.; & Capt. Visct. Balgonie, A.D.C.)			3
Total	62	81	48	1143	1334

Dannenberg's advance was directed against the Sandbag battery,

* See Kinglake, v. 70.

† The names of these Officers are: Colonel Hon. G. Upton, commanding Battalion; Captain Hon. G. Eliot, Acting Adjutant; Lieut.-Colonels Hon. V. Dawson (commanding the four companies that first left camp, viz. Nos. 1, 2, 3, and 8), Lord C. FitzRoy, J. Cowell, and J. Halkett; Captains L. MacKinnon, C. Strong, C. Wilson, H. Bouverie, P. Crawley, F. Ramsden, and H. Tower; Lieutenants E. Disbrowe, Hon. W. Amherst, and C. Greville; lastly, Captain Hon. P. Feilding (Acting D.A.A.G. First Division) is here reckoned as a Regimental Officer, since early in the day his horse was shot, and he then joined and fought with the Battalion.

Belonging to the Regiment, and also actively engaged with the enemy, were Lieut.-Colonels T. Steele and P. Somerset on the head-quarter Staff; and Captain Hon. A. Hardinge, D.A.A.G. First Division.

On piquet, and holding the heights over the valley against Gortchakoff's demonstrations, were Lieut.-Colonels Newton in command, Wood, and Carleton; Captains H. Armytage, and Sir J. Dunlop; and Lieutenant Heneage; with Nos. 6 and 7 companies.

Of the Medical Officers, the Battalion Surgeon, J. Skelton, had been invalided home, November 1st; Assistant-Surgeon Wyatt was present, also Quartermaster Falconer.

a work, although quite unfit for defence, and worthless when gained, yet served as a rallying-point, which the enemy endeavoured to capture, and which we determined to defend. Round it and near it, therefore, there surged the bloody and lengthened contest in which the Brigade was about to take a leading and conspicuous part. The attack was of a far more fierce and formidable nature than those which preceded it, and which were almost as child's play compared with what followed. Instead of yielding to an impulse to fly when the heads of their columns recoiled before our impetuous charges, as had invariably been the case in the early morning, the Russians, still assailed by the same dauntless and romantic British courage, now fought with greater determination; they worked round our flanks and rear, and refused to be carried back by the retreating bodies which our men repulsed. The advance, in short, was better regulated, better fed, and better covered by artillery.

Adams was still holding the Sandbag battery, and had received reinforcements after his first success; our troops were also at the head of the Quarry Ravine, where a short wall of loose stones, called "the Barrier," blocked the post-road. Little breathing-time was allowed them after the repulse they had just inflicted on the enemy, and a desperate struggle recommenced at these points. The small British detachments, overpowered by numbers and threatened in flank, were forced back; they retired fighting, and in good order, losing many men, among them General Adams. Three guns, under Captain Hamley (the late Sir Edward Hamley, whose book has been so frequently referred to), effectually checked any desire the Russians might have indulged in to harass our retreat. At this juncture the Guards Brigade arrived on Home Ridge; and it will be useful to take a rapid glance at the position as it was at that moment.

On the left, General Codrington was chained to the slopes near the Lancaster battery, and could not move therefrom without endangering the whole line. He received, though unwillingly, slight reinforcements, and his force then amounted to 1400. Later, additional troops reached him from the Third Division, and some artillery, but the latter were overpowered by heavier fire, and the one gun in the Lancaster battery could not be used till near the conclusion of the battle. During the day he held the ridge, maintained a heavy fire upon the enemy in Careenage

Ravine, and stood ready to oppose any hostile advance that might have been contemplated up its course. His casualties amounted to about 180 men. Next, in and near the Wellway and in front of it, were the various groups who had repulsed Soimonoff's first attack, including the company of Grenadier Guards previously mentioned; in all, about 1000 men—that is, allowing for losses, less than a third of the whole force that held Inkerman during the preliminary stage of the battle. It was not known that the enemy meant to concentrate all his efforts on our right, and to leave the other flank practically unmolested, so these men were also chained to the places where they stood, expecting fresh adventure, and, if any of them had to be moved to meet an emergency elsewhere, others replaced them in the position they held. Of the rest, a proportion were men exhausted or unrallied after their previous exertions, and it is calculated that some 1400 men only remained to defend Home Ridge and the Kitspur, 700 on each. As we have seen, those holding the latter were slowly retiring. Of reinforcements arriving, the Guards, 1300, had just reached the ridge, as well as 12 guns of the First and 6 of the Light Divisions. The Fourth Division, 2000, under Sir G. Cathcart, was approaching, so that some 4700 men and 36 guns might be reckoned upon for immediate purposes, while 1600 French and other of Canrobert's troops were moving forward. On the other hand, the enemy was still very strong, though he had lost part of the 15,000 troops that first attacked, some of whom, indeed, were streaming away from the field panic-stricken, down the Careenage Ravine into Sevastopol, and over the Tchernaya bridge. But he had his powerful and numerous artillery securely posted on West Jut, Shell Hill, and East Jut, and, besides the greater portion of the 15,000 men, there were 20,000 fresh troops. Of these latter, 10,000 were in reserve, and the other 10,000 in the Quarry Ravine, in the neighbouring glens, on the post-road, and in the Sandbag battery which they had just captured.*

* According to the theory of Mr. Kinglake (whose excellent work on the Crimean War has been largely drawn upon, in preparing this part of the present volume), the 15,000 men who attacked in the early morning in two columns, one 9000 strong on our left and the other 6000 on our right, were so completely shattered by their first encounter with the detachments of the Second Division, that they *all* fled away, and not a man of them took any further part in the battle. Also that, of the 20,000 infantry remaining to the Russians, practically only 10,000 were engaged, the reserve of 10,000 being most of it kept back. Thus, while 15,000 were dispersed into space with the utmost ease, in

The enemy had secured a footing on the plateau of the Inkerman main spur, and the Guards Brigade, coming up at that instant, were launched against him, the Grenadiers in front, then the Scots Fusiliers, the Coldstream following a short distance in rear. The leading Battalion charged, and drove the Russians back to the crest; the next formed on its left, and Dawson prolonged the line to the right.

"Thus the narrow strip of height on the beak of which arose the two-gun work [the Sandbag battery] was thinly edged by the *Tria juncta in uno*, ranged two deep: the Duke of Cambridge and General Bentinck in command." *

Many of the rifles at first missed fire, for the incessant rain had saturated everything; but by snapping off caps to dry the channel and by other means the arms were got to work.† The failure to use their weapons at this crisis caused great confusion, as may well be imagined, for there was a dense mass of Muscovite grey coats and flat caps in front, advancing against the Brigade.

"We were almost among them *at once*, we were certainly not twenty-five yards from them. . . . They yielded ground and we advanced a little, showing a most decided front, but they kept pouring a most deadly fire into our ranks, which began to tell fearfully. The enemy's artillery were

an hour, by very few opponents, almost as if by magic, the 10,000 made so good a resistance that they were with difficulty vanquished, in three hours and a half, by the 4700 Englishmen who were on the scene at this moment, aided by 1600 French, who appeared soon after, and by the Algerines, Zouaves, and other troops of the same nation, 4000 strong, who reached the ground between ten and eleven o'clock. Nor is it alleged that the early attacks of the enemy were delivered by worse troops than those who came into action at 7.30 a.m. This theory was evidently not believed by some who fought at Inkerman, and Colonel Tower is of opinion that when the Guards first entered into the struggle, they met the Tarutin and Borodino regiments; that is, the eight Russian battalions which formed the main portion of the first attack made by the enemy with 6000 men on the Kitspur, and which, by Kinglake's account, were not only repulsed, but clean driven from the field never to appear there again, by the bold onset of 700 to 800 Englishmen.

The losses during the day of the two Russian columns, that took part in the first attack, before 7.30, amounted to some 5000 men; and this fact seems to show conclusively that the 15,000 men continued the fight, as stated in the text, long after the hour when Mr. Kinglake says they disappeared from the battle-field. The casualties of the 10,000 men under Pavloff, who came into action at 7.30, were somewhat greater, proportionately, than those of the first two columns. The losses of the reserve (10,000 men), which to a great extent was kept back out of the struggle, were proportionately much less. (P. Alabine, *Notes of the Expedition in* 1853-5, published in the Russian language, at Viatka, 1861, gives the losses by Russian regiments.)

* *Our Veterans, etc.*, p. 287.
† Some of the nipples had even to be unscrewed (Tower, *Diary*).

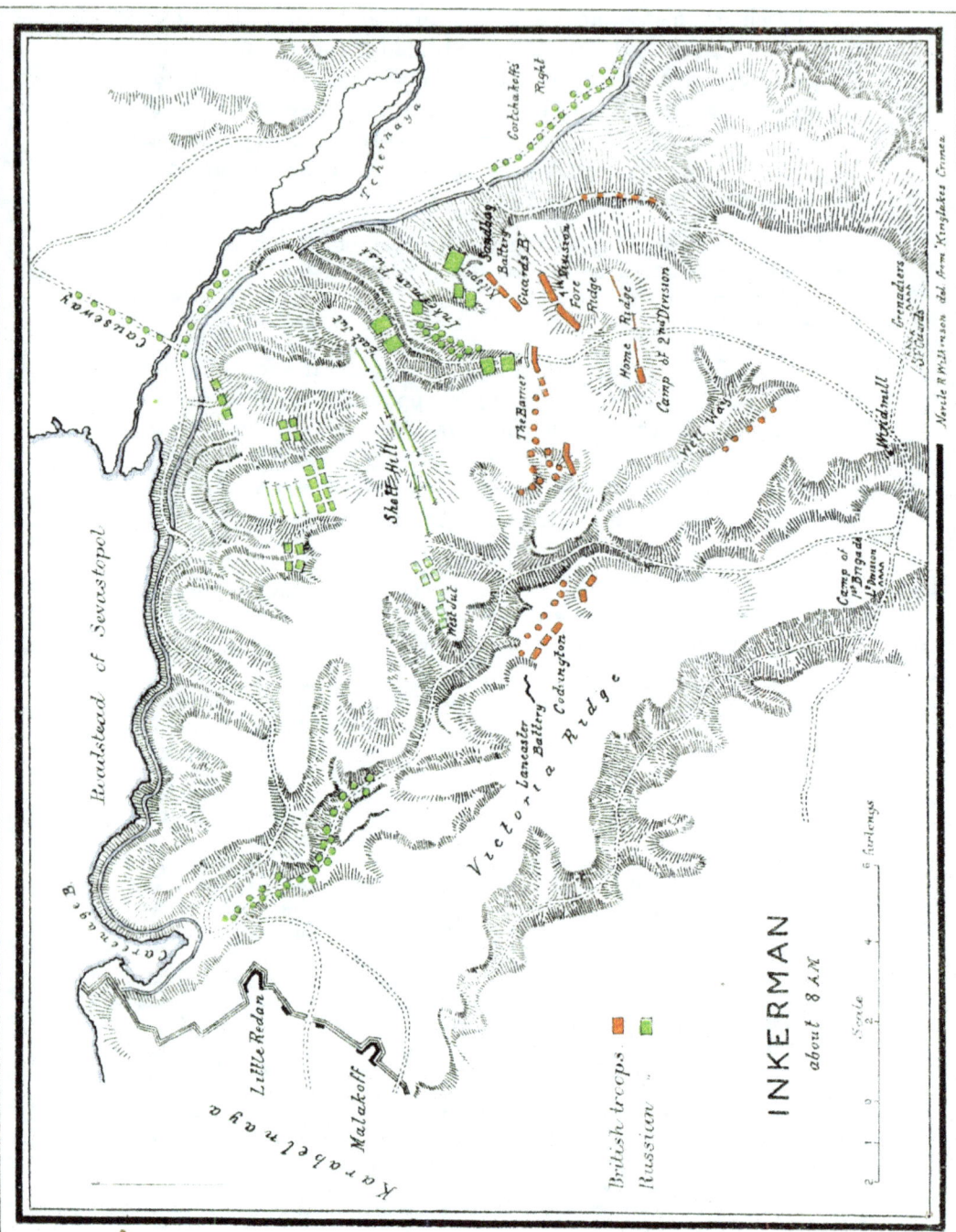

posted on Cossack and Shell hills, and they had seventy or eighty guns at least, but the mist prevented their laying their guns properly for our lines, and they worked the Second Division heights whilst we were far in advance of that; the road was also a point on which they concentrated their fire. Big gaps began to be visible in our line, our dark great coats and bearskin caps towering above the bushes made our men conspicuous in the grey mist. . . . Several times I saw heads of Russian columns coming swarming through the bushes, the Officers in front waving their swords and shouting to the men; but directly they saw us there was a hesitation, a huddling together, an indecision, and a decided tendency *not* to come on. They fired quickly and nervously, and generally over our heads; they were so close to us before they saw us, and they were on lower ground than we were; if they had advanced in anything like a decided manner, we *must* have been entirely swamped and annihilated. But our fellows stood their ground manfully, and the more the Ruskis came up, the quicker our fellows rammed down their cartridges and blazed into them. . . . Our men were getting very few and far between; our poor company, No. 1, suffered terribly, but we yelled and screamed and fired at the columns we saw in our front; they were immensely superior to us in numbers, ten to one at least, and seemed now to stand their ground very well; they pressed us *hard*. But determination and dogged courage kept them back, and not a yard would we yield. The numbers in front of us increased every second, and we were really hand to hand with them; the bushes were full of English and Russians mixed up together. The groans of the wounded, Officers yelling and screaming at their men, the soldiers shouting at one another, and (I have no doubt) using their favourite expressions, and the firing almost deafened one.

"The Brigade was getting very much mixed up now. . . . Several other regiments and men of the Second Division piquets furnished us with stragglers who were of the right sort. Our Brigade line, or remnant of our line, was the rallying-point of everybody who was animated with a right spirit. Oh, for breechloaders at this moment, how we could have swept them off as they came up the hill! . . . I kept taking ammunition out of dead men's pouches to feed the pouches of the living, screaming if I saw any fanatic Ruski that required shooting. . . . Some one behind or in the ranks hallooed out, Charge! Granville Eliot galloped forward right at the mass in front of him, Cowell, Bob Lindsay (Fusilier), young Greville, and myself were all close together, and we ran forward with all the men that were near us. It really was a critical moment in the battle, at least in our *local* part of the battle. Eliot fell from his horse, shot through the head; Cowell staggered and fell by the same bush; young Greville was shot through the body. The enemy was frantic at this moment; the few men who charged with us were all shot, and I found myself entirely surrounded by flat caps. . . . I could see no one but

Russians anywhere near; one fired at me, the powder almost singed my cap. I could see some bearskins on my right through the bushes, and accordingly made for them as hard as I could lay legs to the ground, and I suppose Bob Lindsay and the men who were with us did the same.

"There was a small two-gun sandbag battery on the crest of the hill, into which the remnants of the Brigade were retiring; the Grenadier Colours were already there: the Russians had been driven out of it just before.* There were perhaps a hundred men of the three Regiments in the little battery, and crowds of Russians hemmed us nearly all round; we extended men on the left and rear to prevent their cutting off our retreat and getting in behind us. Column after column kept pouring up the hill, and every moment our chances of retreat looked worse and worse. The parapet in front of us was too high to fire over, and the enemy kept climbing into the embrasures and up the exterior slope of the parapet; but one after another they fell, shot by our men as they showed. . . . We could see lines of bayonets outside the parapet, and could hear them howling and cheering one another on; it was now *fearfully* exciting. . . . We kept them at a respectable distance; our line extended some way in the rear and left: but they kept getting nearer, and our men fell very thick. . . . Vesey Dawson I saw shot by a Russian creeping into the embrasure; Sir R. Newman of the Grenadiers was also killed, and some other Grenadier Officer fell wounded. Our ammunition was beginning to fail, some of the men had not had a round of their own for a long time: the dead furnished the living; but now even that began to fail, and the men in their excitement threw stones, lumps of earth, anything they could see, over the parapet among the Russians, and they came back again amongst us with interest. One of the most remarkable things about Russian troops is the noise they make in action, and I think it is catching, as I never heard our men make such a yelling as they did all this day; I know I was as bad as the rest, because I could not speak for hoarseness that evening and the next day. How long the game of throwing stones lasted I cannot say, but it seemed a long time. There was a visible diminution of bayonets outside the battery, and we had really driven the enemy back a great deal on our left; it was more that they ceased coming on than that we were driving them back. We were still surrounded by them, and they were firing into us as hard as they could.

"Of course we could do nothing but retire; this we accordingly did, the Grenadier Colours being our rallying point: but in our weak state, with only a handful of men, *very* few Officers, and very little ammunition, retiring in the face of a body of the enemy was no easy matter, although the enemy were not in the same strength they were, nor did they seem to be animated with the same spirit they had shown previously. They retired from outside the Sandbag battery certainly; because I remember

---

* For their gallantry upon this occasion, Colonels Lord Henry Percy and Sir Charles Russell, Grenadier Guards, got the Victoria Cross.

going outside the battery with several men and pursuing, or rather firing into the enemy, as there were large bodies of them below the battery amongst the bushes; I very nearly got killed for my pains, as I got too far down the hill, and found the top above me lined with Ruskis, and had to run the gauntlet through the bushes along the side of the hill to rejoin the remnants of our Brigade with the Grenadier Colours. . . . At this moment the *Indigènes* [the Algerines] came into action; they were the first individuals that appeared on the stage, and well do I remember their black faces and blue uniform coming tearing through the bushes. . . . When we got to the Second Division heights we were given ammunition. . . . As to what occurred in the front after this I cannot pretend to say, I only know firing went on with considerable vigour for some time; but the battle *had* turned in our favour.

"The French troops advanced in masses down the road and over the Second Division heights [Home Ridge], but the *real* fighting all along the line was over when we retired and when the *Indigènes* advanced. Some heavy guns on the Second Division hills had cut up their artillery on Cossack and Shell hills very much; the distant rumbling of musketry was going on and some heavy firing still, but it got further off. . . . I am *perfectly certain* the brunt of the battle was over when we were retiring out of Sandbag battery: the sun then came out, and it was perfectly clear; our heavy guns began to tell upon the enemy's artillery on Cossack Hill. The fog having lifted, I saw the whole battle for the first time when we retired out of the Sandbag battery; before then, we had been entirely enveloped in mist and fog. I put this period at about 8.30 or 9, perhaps a little later, but no Frenchman appeared on the right of the battle till after this time, 9.30. . . . I am perfectly confident the Russians were in retreat when Bosquet's *Indigènes* came into the action. . . . When the *Indigènes* came through the bushes, some of our men joined them to have a last shot at the Ruski, and they probably formed along the hill in our old position, and peppered into the retreating columns as they went down the hill." *

This account of the fierce struggle between the Brigade and overwhelming masses of the Russians, written in the private diary of an Officer of the Regiment, gives a few of the confused events that took place immediately near him. Colonel Tower belonged to No. 1 company, and as Colonel Wilson was with No. 8 company, a few words describing what occurred about him may be also reproduced.

"Amid a dense fog raged wholesale murder; the mortal strife was hand to hand, foot to foot, muzzle to muzzle, butt-end to butt-end. It must not be supposed that we always stood rooted on our ground, that we never

* Tower, *Diary*, Nov. 5, 1854.

budged. No, the fight rested not steadfast for an instant. It was now backward, now forward, now sideways. Here, a Grenadier party, after a frantic tussle, would be forced by overwhelming swarms out of the battery; there, a knot of Coldstreamers would arrest the advance of an entire Russian battalion; in another place, a cluster of Fusiliers, rallying after a repulse, would fling themselves upon a column, and with the sheer might of strong hearts, arms, and steel, send it slap-dash over the height's crest. This ceaseless wrestling to and fro accounts for the Sandbag battery being occupied alternately by men of the different Guards Regiments (or, more properly speaking, by mixed parties of the three Regiments larded with brave Liners). Whenever Pavloff succeeded in ousting one band of defenders from the work, a comrade batch would rush in, and, by a combination of bullet, bayonet, and gun-stock, thrust forth the intruders. . . .

" Time marches so marvellously fast in battle, that it is utterly impossible for men, plunged in the *mêlée*, to form an idea of how they stand with the clock. I have therefore no notion at what period reinforcements reached us. All I know is, that towards the end of the fight I saw many Linesmen fighting intermixed with Guardsmen. . . . Despite melting ranks, despite fresh regiments which continued to stream up the hillside, despite the growing scarcity of ammunition, the English clung to their battery with the grip of despair. If, by chance, the bull-dog's hold was for an instant shaken off, the next moment his teeth closed tighter than ever on the sandbags. . . .

"The Russian Officers behaved like true soldiers. They ever were in front of their less adventurous rank and file, urging them on with voice and uplifted sword; nay, they rushed freely on certain death, with the view of inflaming the sluggish spirit of their followers. . . . And now half the Brigade—a grandiose title for 1300 men—strewed the ground; some slain outright, others bleeding to death, others vainly imploring to be carried off the field. Oh! that I must write ' vainly,' but in the devilish turmoil not a man whom God had shielded could be spared to carry away the wounded. The honour of England, nay, the very safety of the army, demanded that all living should be breast to breast with the Russians. . . . Meanwhile the Guards seemed at their last gasp, every minute found them less able— not a jot less willing—to repel the enemy. Hardly a man tasted food that morning, hence individual strength began to flag; where companies contended now only subdivisions struggled, hence collective power was ebbing fast. Nor was this all, ammunition had become frightfully scarce; in many cases, indeed, the soldiers had none left, so they were reduced to rifling the pouches of their fallen messmates; and when that resource failed, to pounding away at the ugly Calmuck visages with stocks and stones." *

It is unnecessary to proceed further with this account, for

* *Our Veterans, etc.*, p. 290, etc.

the writer now gives his experiences, when his excited men, having forced a superior number of Russians into hurried flight down the hillside into the valley, rushed after them in pursuit, in spite of their Officer's efforts to call them back. It is sufficient to say that any description of the struggle between the Guards and the masses which Dannenberg brought against them is impossible. The combatants were in close proximity, the contest was fought out in a thick fog, and on broken ground covered with tough hornbeam bushes and oak scrub, so that our men were speedily dispersed into groups, and few could really say what their neighbours were doing.*

But the main features of the contest are fairly clear. The Russians, securely posted in the Quarry Ravine, St. Clement's Gorge, and on the eastern slopes of the Kitspur, made their main attack against the latter, and as their assaulting columns were

---

* The following extract, from an account furnished by a Coldstreamer present at the battle, will be read with interest: *Sergeant W. Wilden, No. 1 Company*, writes:—"Suddenly the alarm came, 'fall in,' every man rushed for his rifle and ammunition; the order was so sudden many had not turned out, and several took their places in the ranks only partly dressed; poor Captain Ramsden was killed in his brown shooting-suit. . . . During the early part of the day, I should think about 8 or 8.30, the atmosphere became so thick with fog, rain, or mist, and the smoke from firing on both sides, I was not able to see more than eight or ten of my comrades, and scarcely able to distinguish the enemy, although within a few yards of him. At this juncture an alarm ran through our shattered ranks that the enemy was surrounding us. This turned out to be true, for he was working round our right flank to obtain possession of the small Sandbag battery. . . A terrible struggle took place for possession of this battery; the enemy pushed his columns to the front in great numbers, and at the same time his left flank was gradually working round and attacking our right. At this time I should think about two companies of our Battalion held the battery. Here our losses were very heavy. We held it apparently for some time, and kept the Russian massive columns in check, until an unfortunate crisis happened; our ammunition was exhausted, and, as our ranks were so terribly shattered, we were compelled by superior numbers to retire from the battery, or, in other words, we were driven out, and left it in the hands of the enemy; but only for a short time, for we rallied and charged the enemy at the point of the bayonet and recaptured the battery. Here a dreadful struggle ensued, a hand-to-hand fight took place, in which bayonets were freely used on both sides, and at one period stones were resorted to to beat the enemy back from the north-western embrasure. . . . Although several bayonet charges were made upon the enemy, we were unable any longer to hold our ground against overwhelming numbers, and greatly exhausted, we were compelled gradually to retire, at the same time disputing every inch of ground. Here the enemy gradually advanced, and many of our wounded comrades were bayoneted or killed by the enemy. At this moment, the welcome sound of the bugles of the gallant Bosquet's division of Zouaves reached our ears; their numbers enabled them to force the enemy back and regain the position we were gradually losing. We then retired . . . Two long 18-pounder guns were about this time drawn by hand to replace those dismantled, and were used until the close of the battle."

driven from the crest, they rallied again in the hollows beneath, and kept surging upwards, and renewing the strife. For some time the Brigade drove back the successive waves of the advancing enemy unassisted, except by the broken fragments of Adams' men; but a little later, when Cathcart's division approached, some 500 of his troops were pushed forward, and joined in the fray, while another portion moved to the head of the Quarry Ravine, and regained the Barrier. The latter, reinforced from time to time, remained there during the rest of the battle, and though the enemy passed them by, now as he advanced and again as he retired, it seems he never closed in on their rear or reconquered the post. Colonel Upton, reaching the ground some time about 8 a.m., with No. 5 company and a company of the Scots Fusilier Guards, also coming off piquet,* endeavoured to close an undefended gap which existed between the Sandbag battery and the Barrier, and he prevented the enemy from seizing its advantages at that moment. But his force was insufficient to hold it for more than a brief space, and his men were most of them drawn into the vortex of the principal fight. Hence, it was not difficult for the Russians, pressing through the gap, to work round the left flank of the Brigade, and to penetrate to their rear. Most of the Fourth Division, having been split up into fractions, were sent wherever the pressure of the battle required their presence; but a residue of 400 men under General Torrens remained, and with this force Cathcart hoped to relieve the Brigade in their arduous struggle, and assail the enemy in flank by descending the slopes on our right. The attempt, though successful at first, was not fortunate, and it failed to accomplish the results that were expected from it. The men soon dispersed in groups, were almost surrounded, and had to fight their way upwards with the Russians above them. It was here, moreover, that the valuable life of Cathcart was lost, and that Torrens (some time in the Grenadier Guards) was severely wounded.

This manœuvre appears to have changed the principle on which the Brigade had been resisting the hostile columns, and many who hitherto never pursued the beaten bodies of the enemy beyond the crest, now rushed after them down the slopes into the hollows beneath. In this way the group near Captain Wilson got out of hand, and pursued far down into the valley of the Tchernaya, where they

* It appears that No. 4 company moved forward separately, and joined the main body of the Battalion.

were met by shots from Gortchakoff's riflemen, "who sprang up among the bushes, and blazed full in our faces." Meeting some stray groups of Cathcart's submerged detachment, the whole party reascended the heights, and lost heavily as they climbed up. Here they found themselves between two fires, and ascertained that the enemy was really above them, for at first they thought they were mistaken for Russians, and were being shot at by English soldiers. Avoiding this danger, by taking an upwards direction to the left, they stumbled upon a dead ammunition mule, and eagerly replenished their pouches, as for some time they had not had a round among them. Having at last reached the top, they found that the fog had lifted, that the Brigade was not where they had left it, and that Zouaves and Algerines (the *Indigènes*) were approaching the ground, and were driving the enemy back, as Colonel Tower has already told us. Wilson and the last of his men joined this attack, and many fell; he finally attached himself to the French 50th of the Line as they advanced, and then finding he could do nothing more, he sought the Coldstream, eventually falling in with them near Home Ridge, which he reached before the shattered remains of the Battalion got there.

From the moment our men began to descend the slopes their means of maintaining their post on the Kitspur seemed to diminish. Under any circumstances, the struggle of the few against the many was gradually exhausting the power of the former, and reinforcements were urgently required. It was fortunate, therefore, that our allies now appeared upon the scene. Bosquet, who for some time in the early morning had been observing Gortchakoff, came speedily to the conclusion that that General meant to remain quiescent; he therefore sent forward some of his troops without delay, to Home Ridge, where the danger was most pressing. Two Battalions, 1600 strong, arrived first; and one, the French 6th of the Line, pushing towards the Kitspur, struck in flank the Russians, who, advancing through the gap, which was ever getting wider, were endeavouring to operate against our rear. This French battalion, however, soon got into difficulties, and the other, the 7me Léger, was sent to its support. But before this was effected another crisis occurred; for, the enemy, urging forward his numerous forces up the ravines which he occupied, brushed past the Anglo-French then on the Kitspur, and made a very determined onslaught on Home Ridge itself. This serious manœuvre was repulsed by the gallantry of a few British detachments present on the spot, and of the 7me Léger; the defeated column was driven back, so that the two French battalions were brought together. It was now 10 a.m., and another French force, a brigade with some artillery, led by Bosquet in person, reached the battle in two columns: in the first, some rifles, a battalion of Algerines, and one of Zouaves (1900); in the other, more Zouaves, and the French 50th of the Line (2200). There was still a good deal of difficulty in forcing the enemy to recede; for as the first column pursued him, they advanced too far, and fresh hostile forces were able to move up the ravines leading to the main spur, thereby threatening our allies in rear. But on the arrival of the second column, the Russians, now thoroughly broken by their losses and by the stubborn resistance which held them in check, gave up the contest. They were finally driven off the Kitspur and out of the ravines which had been so useful to them during the struggle, by enabling them to re-organize after so many repulses inflicted by our slender forces. Kinglake thus speaks of a band of the Coldstream during this phase of the fight:—

"The Zouave battalion was advancing . . . when the bearskin all at once reappeared. It was from the wooded steeps of the hillsides that the spectre uprose. Since the time when last we observed it, the small band of Coldstream men collected by Wilson had remained in the brushwood below, watching always for some such occasion as the one that now offered. Amid a roar of joy and welcome—for the Zouaves and the Guards were close friends—these Coldstream men joined the advance, aligning on the right of the French. . . . What followed was slaughter." *

Meanwhile we had already gained an immense superiority over the enemy's artillery. As early as about 9.30, two 18-pounder guns of position had been brought on Home Ridge, and after a short space of time the power of the hostile batteries began to wane. The French guns, coming up, posted themselves on our right, and the bombardment continued with increasing advantage on our side, though the number of our pieces was not half that of our opponents. Some of our men on the left and centre of our line also advanced, and added to the misfortune of the gunners on Shell Hill. The battle was really decided at eleven, though the artillery continued to fire till much later. As soon as the bulk of the Household

* Kinglake, v. 402.

Brigade returned to Home Ridge, and after ammunition had been served out, the men were reformed, and were moved up to protect the guns against any sudden assault. This duty was "worse than fighting the infantry, for we got no revenge for the men we lost," and we incurred casualties not a few.*

The retreat of the Russians commenced about one o'clock, and was covered by a column of their reserve; which, attempting to advance, was quickly dispersed by a few rounds of the 18-pounders. There was no pursuit. The enemy slipped away, and "seemed to melt from the lost field; the English were too few and too exhausted, and the French too little confident in the advantage gained, to convert the repulse into a rout." Our allies, deducting losses, numbered at the end of the engagement some 7000 infantry, for, besides the troops already mentioned, three battalions (2400) arrived on the ground at eleven; they also had 700 cavalry and 24 guns present. Lord Raglan was anxious to complete the victory by falling on the rear of the flying Russians, but his cautious colleague would not consent; for he still feared an attack from Gortchakoff's untouched forces, and was unwilling to expose his men to the fire of the ships that were moored in the roadstead.†

While the battle was going on, the garrison of Sevastopol kept up so poor a demonstration, that we were able to denude our camps of men, and push them to Inkerman. Besides the men on duty in the trenches, the greater part of the Third Division watched the

---

* Letter of Mr. Taylor, late Quartermaster Somersetshire Militia, then in the Coldstream; one shell killed and wounded eight men. Colonel Upton was wounded at this period. See, also, *Our Veterans, etc.*, p. 299.

The action of the Guards at Inkerman seems to be imperfectly described in Kinglake. According to that writer, the bulk of the Brigade came out of action at 8.30; though he notes that the force under Wilson joined the last attack undertaken by the French about 11 o'clock, and allows that the companies which followed Upton were in the field as late as 10. Giving Bosquet's impressions of the scene presented to his observation at that hour, he says, "High above on the right, where there sauntered a red-coated Officer with the *bonnet de poil* and a singularly unconcerned air (Colonel Upton), some men of the Guards could be seen lying down among the brushwood" (Kinglake, v. 382). Yet Tower and Wilden, whose accounts have been given, state that they were relieved on the Kitspur by the Algerines and Zouaves—that is, after 10 o'clock; and Wilson who, according to Mr. Kinglake, was on that portion of the battle-field later than any other Guardsman, tells us himself that he got back to Home Ridge *before* the bulk of the Brigade reached it. Some isolated groups, separated during the fierce struggle in the fog and brushwood from the main body, possibly found themselves on Home Ridge before; Taylor says he helped to pull up the two 18-pounders, which, as we know, took place about 9.30.

† Hamley, *War in the Crimea*, p. 157.

fortress, and they were subjected to no further inconvenience than that which the fire from the place, intensified on this day, entailed. About 9.30, however, the enemy made a sortie against Forey's siege corps, under General Timofeyeff, with 5000 men and 12 guns. The blow, though it met with some success at first, failed, and the Russians were pursued by our gallant allies back under the shelter of the fortress. Thus little was done by the garrison to assist Dannenberg, and that little was of trifling value. Gortchakoff's operations during the day were still less effective. He made a few feints, fired upon the Sapuné Ridge, and, it is said, did lose 15 men. He thereby gave the companies on piquet (among them, Nos. 6 and 7 companies of the Coldstream) the opportunity of engaging him with distant volleys, without apparently causing much, if any, loss to our side. In short, he did nothing, when by attacking Bosquet, he would have prevented that General from advancing to our assistance at Inkerman. His orders were "to support the general attack, to draw the Allied forces upon himself, and to try and seize one of the ascents to the Sapuné Ridge." Mr. Kinglake, however, tells us that these written orders were explained away by "oral communications" into something different,* and makes us believe that there is a mystery which has never been explained, hanging over the operations of this Russian Commander, who held so much power in his hands on that day. What we do know is that Dannenberg, in spite of his overwhelming numbers, was unable to secure a footing on the Kitspur, that this was due to the manner in which it was defended by our scanty forces, and that in this defence the Household Brigade played a glorious part, and suffered much in consequence.

The losses were very great on both sides: those of the enemy, who moved in heavy columns, being more than those of the Allies, though relatively, in proportion to numbers at the seat of war, he suffered less than we did. The Russians had 10,729 killed, wounded, and prisoners, including 256 Officers. The English 2357 of all ranks, of whom 130 were Officers (or 39 Officers, and 558 men killed, and 91 Officers and 1669 men wounded). The French 929, among them 49 Officers (or 13 Officers and 130 men killed, and 36 Officers and 750 men wounded).† The Brigade lost nearly half its effective strength, viz., out of a total of 1334:—

* Kinglake, v. 59 (note), 69.
† The above were the losses on the field of Inkerman. The total casualties on the

Killed	12	Officers,	9	Sergts.,	1	Drumrs.,	177	Rank & file,	Total	199
Wounded	20*	,,	20	,,	4	,,	357	,,	,,	401
Missing	—	,,	—	,,	—	,,	4	,,	,,	4
Total	32	,,	29	,,	5	,,	538	,,	,,	604

The Coldstream suffered in like proportion, but the casualties among the Officers far exceeded those that occurred in the other Regiments. In fact, almost all the Officers were swept away. Out of seventeen present, four only escaped uninjured, viz. Captains Strong, Wilson, Crawley, and Tower. Of the rest, eight were killed or died soon after of their wounds, viz. Lieut.-Colonels Dawson, and Cowell, Captains MacKinnon, Bouverie, Eliot, and Ramsden, and Lieutenants Greville, and Disbrowe. The remainder were wounded; viz. Colonel Upton (slightly), Lieut.-Colonels Halkett, and Lord C. FitzRoy, Captain P. Feilding, and Lieutenant Amherst (all severely). The losses of the Battalion amounted to—

Killed	8	Officers,	3	Sergeants,	73	Rank & File,	Total	84
Wounded	5	,,	11	,,	107	,,	,,	123
Total	13	,,	14	,,	180	,,	,,	207

The principal casualties were in the flank companies. No. 1 entered the action with 50 to 60 men, and No. 8 was slightly stronger. The former lost one sergeant and 43 rank and file, and the latter two sergeants and 41 men. No. 2 came next, losing 37 men. Where a Battalion has so freely shed its life-blood in the stubborn defence of the position assigned to it, it may seem strange that no official notice should be taken of the death of the Officer who led it into action, and who directed its movements until he fell, and more especially when in the Brigade to which the Battalion belonged, no other Commanding Officer lost his life. Yet this is what occurred with respect to the memory of the gallant Colonel Dawson, and the feelings of his brothers in arms were not inadequately expressed in the following lines, written by Colonel Wilson:—

"The despatch which informed England of this dearly bought victory, commended the services of many of the living and blazoned the merits of

5th of November amounted to: Russians, 11,959; English, 2573; and French 1800 of all ranks (Kinglake, v. 443, 457).

* Counting Major-General Bentinck, who was severely wounded. Of the Coldstream Officers serving on the Staff on that day, none were wounded; Colonel Somerset, however, had a horse shot under him.

many of the dead; but from that encomiastic scroll there was at least one remarkable omission. To the memory of Colonel Vesey Dawson, shot through the heart while in command of the Coldstream Guards, was conceded not a passing word of eulogy or of regret. It is melancholy to reflect that on this humble page should stand the only record of how as brave a soldier as ever drew a sword, as noble a gentleman as ever earned the respect of his fellow-men, fought and died." *

We are told that this great victory caused no outward elation among our troops. A reaction succeeded the excitement of the struggle; the danger now past began to be realized for the first time; and the men, though hardened to the miserable scenes which war creates, were almost awed by the terrible carnage and devastation that met their eyes on the hard-fought field. The Second Division camp was laid flat, the tents uprooted and scattered, canvas saturated with blood carpeted the ground. Our own camp swarmed with the wounded and the dying, and the sight sent a chill of depression through the few survivors as they returned to their bivouacs. Everywhere on the narrow space of the battle-ground the victims lay thick, some killed, others groaning in agony, and nowhere thicker than in and around the Sandbag battery, where the contest raged the fiercest. Here the dead were literally piled up on one another as they fell.

"The whole battle-field, which could all be seen at a glance, except where concealed by brushwood, looked perfectly *covered* with bodies; between the Second Division hills and the crest of the Inkerman hill is a very short distance, and the entire action having been fought on that limited space, there was an awful scene of carnage upon it. . . . Before evening we got all our wounded off the field; the dead, of course, remained there, and the poor wounded Ruskis who were a great deal too numerous to take off. . . . From the heights I could see the Russian army winding up the road; the whole country was covered with troops straggling over the causeway over the Tchernaya marsh; they were a long time crossing. Arabas full of wounded, guns, etc., lumbering up the way, but they had quite enough of it. . . . Our hospital was a most piteous sight. . . . Our poor fellows were all dying or dead. . . . The camp was miserable, and I could only thank God I was not lying in the hospital tent with half my limbs smashed to pieces, or lying on a stretcher ready to be buried." †

Saddest of all, was the cruel thought surging in every mind that many of our brave wounded had been basely bayoneted as

* *Our Veterans, etc.*, p. 306. † Tower, *Diary*.

they lay helpless on the ground, by an uncivilized enemy, who, unable to drive off the few that held the plateau against him, wreaked his vengeance on the defenceless, as soon as they fell into his hands. We had ample evidence of this savagery—established, moreover, by a special inquiry—that cast so black a stain on the Russian army, for, when our men hurled the foe from a corner from which he had driven us, we found our wounded stabbed to death.

Thus was the battle of Inkerman fought and won by small bodies of the British and French armies, over an overpowering hostile force of more than 35,000 infantry, amply supported by artillery; who, having stolen in during the night up to our outposts, endeavoured to break through the Allied line round Sevastopol, at a point where we were weakest, and where we had absolutely no defences.* The result proved the immense superiority of our arms over those of Russia; so also does it give us some indication of what would have happened if we had boldly attacked Sevastopol at the end of September, before, or immediately after, the flank march, or even during the bombardment in October. The British fought with a valour and constancy that surpassed even the glorious traditions of the past. Led by Officers who hurled themselves like the old Knight Errants into the thick of every danger, they nobly followed on with that unflinching steadiness produced by constitutional bravery, by devotion to their leaders, and by the splendid discipline that was the predominant characteristic of our Crimean troops. Their bold extension and their courage in maintaining it, even without supports and when opposed to heavy columns, made the Russians think that the line of red-coats was but a fringe of our strength, and they hesitated when they ought to have acted boldly. We were, moreover, provided with a superior rifle, and so when the enemy, emerging from the ravines, found himself met by a heavy and shattering fire, his columns were brought to a standstill, and he lost the advantage which his solid formation might have given

* It cannot be insisted too often that the Sandbag battery was a battery only in name; and that its importance consisted in the fact that it served as a rallying-point, on account of its being a conspicuous object, round which the main struggle on the Kitspur raged. Russian exaggerations have given it a wholly fictitious value; even Todleben, describing the fight a little after eight o'clock, says that the Okhotsk regiment (3000 strong) attacked the Sandbag battery held by their "worthy rivals—the intrepid Coldstream," that they expelled the latter, and that nine guns were the reward of this brilliant feat of arms! (see Hamley, *War in the Crimea*, p. 160).

him. He was far from being imbued with the spirit that animated our men, and he lacked the determination to close with them.

"Had he, at the commencement of the battle, pushed these columns resolutely forward, it follows nearly as a matter of course that, by sheer momentum of his heavy masses, the British lines would have been broken through and trampled down utterly. It would have been a question of weight alone. As it was, no devotion, no exertions on the part of the Russian Officers, could at the outset spur their battalions to one grand combined rush. Time was frittered away in a series of persevering but desultory attacks, which were invariably repulsed, thanks to English valour and English firearms." *

* *Our Veterans, etc.*, p. 309. It is proper to add that the Russian Rifle corps, 1800 strong, were armed with as good a weapon as our Minié, also that some of the British battalions (the 20th Regiment, for instance, who distinguished themselves greatly in the battle) carried the old smooth-bore musket, known as "Brown Bess" (see Kinglake, v. 475).

PRIVATE 1742.

CHAPTER X.

THE WINTER OF 1854-55 IN THE CRIMEA.

Prostration of both sides after the battle of Inkerman—Sevastopol not to be taken in 1854—Tardy arrangements to enable the army to remain in the Crimea during the winter—Violent hurricane of the 14th of November; stores scattered and destroyed—The winter begins in earnest—How the Government at home attended to the wants of army at the seat of war—Absence of a road between the base at Balaklava and the front—Miserable plight to which the army was reduced—Indignation in England, and the measures taken to relieve the troops—Admirable manner in which the misfortunes were borne by the British soldiers—Operations on both sides during the winter—The Turks occupy Eupatoria; successful action fought there—The Guards Brigade sent to Balaklava.

THE battle of Inkerman exhausted the energies of the combatants, and for a few days they recoiled from each other, stunned by its effects. The Allies had gained a Pyrrhic victory; another such victory, and their forces must be annihilated. The enemy also had received a crushing defeat, which shattered his military prestige and ruined the *morale* of his army. Neither side was in a condition to operate against the other, and each faced his opponent listlessly, almost helplessly. But Menshikoff, though disgraced in the field, deserved the gratitude of his Imperial Master, and had every reason to be content with what he had achieved; for, he had gained an advantage of supreme importance. He had put it out of the power of the Anglo-French invaders to finish the war during the year 1854, and thus, while chaining them fast to the bleak and narrow upland of the Chersonese, he had the satisfaction of knowing that they would be exposed to the rigours of the approaching winter. This result was all the more disastrous to us, since, not having foreseen it, we were in no position to meet it, and were unprovided with the means of maintaining our troops in the inhospitable region to which we had become committed. In short, the Allies were about to be handed over to foes far more destructive and terrible than those they had hitherto met. Instead of contending against Russian weapons, they were now also to struggle with the forces of nature and the fury of the elements. On the 6th of November it was finally determined to put off the bombardment, and to winter in the Crimea. The Commissariat Department, informed of this decision, was then, and then only, ordered to make such preparations as would enable the army to remain on the upland. But the tardy order came too late, for in less than ten days the winter began in earnest, and nothing could then be got ready to save the troops from the cruel trials that awaited them.

On the day after the battle, the Allies were engaged in burying the dead, in removing the Russian wounded who still lay on the ground, and in clearing the field of the traces of the struggle. An invitation addressed to General Menshikoff to agree to a truce, and to send out his men to bury their own dead, was refused, for that prudent commander was naturally disinclined to give his troops so sombre and depressing an object-lesson of their utter inefficiency in the field. His army, however, met this invitation in another fashion, and, whether in error or by design, they answered it by firing upon our burying parties. As another attack was feared, the front was cleared of incumbrances as soon as possible, and the wounded were promptly taken to Balaklava. Their sufferings were considerable; there was a scarcity of hospital comforts and appliances at the seat of war, and the ambulances in use were unfitted for the purpose of conveying injured men.

Much affected by the heavy losses sustained by his "First Brigade," the Duke of Cambridge came early into the Guards camp, where the few men present turned out to cheer him.

"Accompanied by his Aide-de-camp, the brave and popular Macdonald, the Royal General was assiduous in his attentions to the wounded Guardsmen, sympathizing in cheering tones with the livid wretches that still breathed, and shedding tears of manly sorrow upon the mangled clay of those who had completed their last tour of earthly duty." *

The funeral of the numerous Coldstream Officers formed a most sad procession. Seven—Dawson, Cowell, MacKinnon, Eliot, Ramsden, Disbrowe, and Greville—were laid to rest in one grave, in a small rocky ravine near the Windmill. Bouverie's body was

* *Our Veterans, etc.*, p. 314.

only recovered late on the 6th, and he was buried by the side of Lieut.-Colonel Hunter-Blair of the Scots Fusilier Guards, who survived the action twenty-four hours.

"It was really enough to unman anybody; poor fellows! far away from all their friends and relations; poor Greville, whose death killed his mother, everybody loved him; we laid them side by side, and I remember the earth pattering on their poor bodies with dull hollow sound." *

Colonel Upton, though badly hurt, was able to remain at his post till the middle of November, and he assumed the command of the Brigade, *vice* General Bentinck, wounded, and of the First Division from the 7th, when the Duke of Cambridge was sent to Balaklava, on the sick list. The command of the Battalion thus devolved upon Colonel Lord F. Paulet. The Coldstream was, in truth, a mere skeleton of the fine body which embarked at Portsmouth in the spring of 1854. It only mustered now 11 Officers and 307 men, while no draft,—except a small one of 58 men, which, having left London on the 26th of October, reached the Crimea on the 22nd of November,—was on the road to compensate for this serious deficiency of strength in the field. When news of the battle arrived in England, strenuous efforts were made to fill up the attenuated ranks of the army, by sending out fresh battalions and reinforcements to those already at the seat of hostilities. But the campaign, ever since July, when we were first encamped near the pestilential lake of Devna, had sadly drained our resources— far more rapidly, indeed, than the home authorities had anticipated, —and though recruiting had been actively going on, the large demands which this war created could not be satisfied. In this way, the next draft sent to the Coldstream only amounted to 153 men, and could do little to restore our depleted ranks to an efficient state. This draft started on the 24th of November, and arrived in the Crimea on the 18th of December.† In France,

* Tower, *Diary*. All the Guards Officers were buried in this spot. During the winter of 1855, more than a year later, their bodies were exhumed, and were properly interred on Cathcart's Hill, where they now lie.

† The average age of the small draft of 58 men reaching the seat of war in November, was twenty-one, and their service nearly two years. The averages of the next draft arriving in December, were twenty-one and a half years and eight months, respectively. Lieutenants Whitshed and Julian Hall accompanied the first; and Lieut.-Colonel C. Burdett, Captains F. Burton and J. Le Couteur, and Lieutenants G. Wigram, A. Lambton, G. Rose, and G. Ives the second. Assistant-Surgeon C. V. Cay reached the Crimea on November 28th.

however, there was not such a dearth of fighting men as seems to have been the case in England, and considerable reinforcements were despatched to the east, so that somewhat later (in February) our allies were able to extend the siege-works that surrounded the south side of Sevastopol.

We have seen that the omission to strengthen the unguarded flank at Inkerman by earthworks had led to serious consequences. The critical nature of the battle made this so clear, that, when the fight was over, though we had fewer men to spare than were available before, this vital position was at once placed in a state of defence. English, French, and even Turks—held hitherto to be an incumbrance—were set to perform this duty, and Fore Ridge and Shell Hill were soon crowned with works, commanding the approaches to the scene of the recent struggle, and securing it at last, as far as possible, from further molestation.*

The ordinary routine of siege life had hardly recommenced after the rude shock which interrupted it on the 5th, when the winter burst upon the Crimean peninsula with a suddenness and violence that marked a distinct feature in the story of the war, and brought innumerable troubles upon the Allies engaged in it. The weather lately had been cold and stormy, varied upon occasions by short gleams of sunshine and partial warmth. At daybreak on the 14th, however, a violent hurricane, accompanied by a deluge of rain, unexpectedly arose, and swept with terrific force over the country, and not only blew away every tent standing on the upland, scattered the stores upon which the army depended, and stopped all communications, but also dashed to pieces or disabled much of the shipping laden with supplies that were then very urgently needed.† The ground was speedily converted into a deep and impassable sea of sticky mud, which flew about in large quantities; the temperature fell, and snow

---

* Recent events having opened the eyes of authority, the shoulder was put vigorously to the wheel. Hence the fortification of an all-important point which, previous to the battle, had either been considered unnecessary, or had been pronounced impossible of achievement with the means at disposal, was actually executed with sorely straitened means after the battle. In a word, few hands contrived to do what comparatively many hands had been judged incapable of doing. "Where there's a will there's a way" (*Our Veterans, etc.*, p. 325).

† It is said that only three tents remained upright in the English camps (Nolan, i., p. 650). But a fourth, belonging to Lieut.-Colonel Carleton, also survived, and it was the only one that did so in the Guards camp. The Turkish tents, placed in a sheltered position, made a better resistance than ours, and comparatively few were swept away.

came down. The men of the various regiments huddled together like sheep, behind bushes or rocks, or wherever they could find some protection against the violence of the elements. The condition of the houseless troops was miserable in the extreme, both during the day and long afterwards, for they had nothing wherewith to repair their losses; but it was worse with the sick and wounded, who were exposed to the full force of the cyclone, and to the cold and the rain. A considerable amount of shipping had been left outside the harbour of Balaklava, instead of being safely berthed inside the landlocked bay. Of the vessels anchored in this dangerous position, many went to pieces on the rocks forming the iron-bound coast; altogether twenty-one were sunk, and their valuable cargoes were all lost. H.M.S. *Retribution*, with the Duke of Cambridge on board, narrowly escaped destruction. On that fatal first day of a severe Crimean winter, the troops were deprived of vast quantities of ammunition, food, clothing, and forage, and there was no reserve at hand from whence they could be replaced.

The difficulties and sufferings that now overwhelmed the army began with this storm, but they are clearly to be traced to the aimless manner in which the campaign had been conducted. The original intention had been to surprise Sevastopol, but it soon disappeared out of sight, and no step was taken to capture the town in accordance with the conditions under which the expedition landed on Russian soil. On the contrary, a regular siege was gradually commenced, and a completely new plan was thereby adopted. But the change was never recognized, its bearing upon the fortunes of the war was not appreciated, and no stores were accumulated at the base of operations to meet the requirements of the lengthy proceedings into which the invaders had drifted. This was the more unfortunate, since, when the allied Commanders undertook the flank march, and shifted their ground from the north to the south side of Sevastopol, they found themselves obliged to operate upon a barren upland which afforded no supplies, and very soon they even lost the advantage of drawing forage from the valley of the Tchernaya. Thus, after the 25th of October, if not before, nothing whatsoever was to be obtained from the land in which the army was established, and every single article had to be transported by sea from a distance. The battle of Inkerman at last revealed the true position in which we stood; but it was then too late, and when the storm destroyed the vessels lying outside the harbour, which contained considerable addition to our scanty stores, it must be acknowledged that this position was indeed deplorable.

Nor should it be forgotten that requisitions put forward were imperfectly attended to by the authorities in England, and that there was often confusion at the base (Scutari and Balaklava), which appears to have been incompletely organized. Owing to these circumstances, many misfortunes overtook the British army, some of which may be cited. Though a request was made early in September for 2000 tons of hay, only 228 tons were received in the Crimea by the 1st of February, 1855.* In November an application was forwarded for 3000 tents, and for a steam mill and bakery, but more than six months elapsed before they arrived at the seat of war.† Again, we have seen that a substantial portion of the kits were left behind in the squad bags, at Scutari, at the end of May; also that, on landing at Old Fort, the packs were taken away from the men. The former seem to have been allowed to remain where they were stored. But an effort was made in the middle of October, just a month after they had been left on board ship, to recover the knapsacks, though apparently with very indifferent success; and the troops remained, exposed to the severe inclemency of the weather, without any change of clothing, in the worn-out and tattered garments that had uninterruptedly done duty day and night from the beginning of June, when they landed at Varna. Lastly, biscuit and salt pork formed the usual, indeed the never-varying ration served out to the British soldier. This diet was his only food, and it produced scurvy, as was only to be expected. To counteract this plague, limejuice and vegetables were thus urgently required, but neither was available. It is true that small quantities of vegetables were sometimes to be had, but then they were sold to the starving men at famine prices.‡ A tardy requisition was made in October for limejuice, and half the quantity demanded (20,000 lbs.) reached Balaklava on the 19th of December; but there it remained almost unnoticed, and

---

* Kinglake, vi. 128, note. † *Ibid.*, pp. 98, 138.
‡ *General Order, Memo.*, Nov. 1st: "Commanders of divisions will send to-morrow at 9 a.m. to the Quartermaster-General's office, on the wharf at Balaklava, for potatoes. . . . They must be paid for at the spot at the price of £1 1s. per cwt." *Ibid.*, Nov. 6th: "Those corps or divisions which desire potatoes should send to Balaklava for them; the price is £1 1s. per cwt. . . . The money required to pay for them

this antidote against the scourge of scurvy was only unearthed on the 29th of January following; nor was it apparently ordered to be issued to the troops as a ration, until the middle of February.*

Arising directly out of the incomprehensible manner in which this extraordinary war was conceived and carried on, another circumstance, more powerful for evil than the apathy with which the necessities of the army were regarded by the Government, caused famine and distress to oppress our troops. We had no road between Balaklava and the front; and hence, when supplies reached the former place, we were without means of conveying them to the spot where they were to be consumed. And yet the distance to be traversed was under eight miles. It has been shown that, of the two roads connecting the English before Sevastopol and the base, one, the Woronzoff road, was metalled; the other, over the Col, was but a mere pathway or cart-track: also that on the 25th of October, we lost the use of the former, and were restricted to the latter. During the autumn this pathway was serviceable; indeed, so firm and open was the country, that waggons and guns could easily move across it anywhere. But when the torrents of rain flooded the ground on the 14th of November, the whole aspect of the upland became altered, and the track as well as the plain were converted into a deep morass, over which communications were rendered almost impossible. The French, with proper forethought, constructed a good road between Kamiesh Bay and their camps, directly they occupied the Chersonese; but as all the British troops were required to push forward vigorously the siege-works, and as we indulged in the misplaced confidence that Sevastopol would fall immediately after the bombardment of

must be sent at the same time." It appears that later, after December 10th, whenever vegetables were available they were supplied to the men gratis; but as they had to fetch them from Balaklava under circumstances of extreme difficulty (as will presently appear), it is scarcely to be wondered that the wearied troops did not always avail themselves of the boon (see Kinglake, vi. 138, note). It should further be stated here, that Lord Raglan, "in consideration of the length of the siege operations, the constant labour the men have been called upon to perform, the inclemency of the weather, and the cheerfulness and good will they have manifested in discharge of their duty," granted the unusual issue of working pay to the troops employed in digging, etc., in the trenches, at the rate of, for Non-commissioned officers as overseers, one for every twenty men, 1s. by day, 1s. by night; for rank and file, 8d. by day, 10d. by night (*General Order*, Nov. 14, 1854).

* Wyatt, pp. 41, 55. Limejuice, after February 16th, was issued three times during the month.

the 17th of October, we never even thought of securing our communications, until after the 5th of November, when it was decided to winter in the Crimea. The rejected Turks, offered by Omar Pasha, might certainly have performed this important service while the weather was clear and dry, but the prejudice against them has already been mentioned, and their assistance was refused. After the battle of Inkerman we took measures to construct the road, and we acted as we did with respect to the defences near Home Ridge; tools were hastily procured from Constantinople, and Turks were at last employed. But it was then too late. The unfortunate men were unprovided with food and shelter, and the weather was severe; they died so rapidly that the living were all required to bury the dead, and in a short time this ill-fated contingent disappeared altogether.

The scarcity of forage and the want of a road acted and reacted on each other, and formed the principal causes of the winter troubles. The horses and mules died of starvation, and it was useless to replace them, as there was not wherewithal to feed them. The transport, miserably insufficient as it always had been, dwindled into nothing, and all but disappeared; troop horses of the cavalry were impressed into this service, but they too perished. Carriage traffic soon ceased, and an attempt was then made to convey supplies on the backs of the wretched beasts that survived. This expedient also failed; the quagmire of tenacious clay intervening between the port and the front, the famine, and the exposure to cold and wet, all operated together, and the animals could work no more. Thenceforward there was nothing for it but to make the men themselves wade through the deep mud, and fetch up such things from the base as they required, to keep body and soul together. The duty was no inconsiderable addition to their ordinary toil, for while they were decreasing fast in numbers, the labour in the trenches did not abate. The journey also sometimes took twelve hours to accomplish, and during the time it lasted they were without food, shelter, or rest.* This miserable makeshift was, of course, entirely inadequate to supply the troops, and the more bulky or heavy articles, however necessary to the well-being of the army, could not be brought to camp at all. The serious error by which magazines had not been established in time at the seat of war, was repaired quickly by the great energy

* Hamley, *War in the Crimea*, p. 170.

displayed at head-quarters, and in December considerable quantities of every kind of stores were available at Balaklava, but there most of them remained unused, because, as Government would not supply forage (and it seems it was not easily procured out of England), there was no transport, and as there was no road to span the morass, means did not exist of crossing it and of reaching the front.

The winter all through Europe was a peculiarly severe one, and there was no exception to its inclemency in the Crimea, where the season was specially cold. All the combatants suffered from its effects; even the Russians felt it acutely, though housed and provided with a tolerably fair transport service from their well-stored magazines on the Sea of Azof. Our French allies also underwent many privations, due to the general difficulties that affected the invaders established on the barren upland and exposed to the wind, the snow, and the rain; but more especially on account of the small *tente d'abri* which sheltered them at night, and which was not so useful as our bell tent. But the British army suffered most. Like the French, our men were sent to trenches filled with water, where they remained wet to their knees for many hours during the day and night; but, unlike them, these hardships were of constant recurrence. Reinforcements were rapidly sent to General Canrobert, and his force was strong enough to enable him to give his soldiers rest when their tour of service in the siege-works was finished. But the British had no such exemption; their numbers were insufficient for the purposes of the campaign; and they practically were always at work. Lord Raglan computed that they were "on duty five nights out of six, a large proportion of them constantly under fire."* If we add, that they were seldom dry; that they had little or no fuel except brushwood and roots; that they could not cook their food; that the coffee served out was in the form of the green unroasted berry;† that the ration of rice failed from the 15th of November to the end of December; that the boots were defective and bad; and that there was no warm clothing available until

---

* Letter to the Duke of Newcastle, Dec. 26th.

† Many of the men now existed almost entirely upon the biscuit and ration of spirit; the camp was often strewed with portions of uncooked salt meat, and partially roasted or green coffee (Wyatt, p. 40). The green coffee ceased on February 22nd, and compressed vegetables were supplied for the first time on the 26th (*ibid.*, p. 56).

the beginning of the latter month ;—it will be readily seen that the hardships undergone were of no trivial character.*

Nor did the men's sufferings end here, for when exhausted by toil and privations there was no alleviation to those whose health and strength had given way. So badly organized were the hospital arrangements, that we are told the climax of misery was only reached in the places set apart for the sick. Circumstances necessarily made the field-hospitals in the front rude habitations for numerous patients seized and tormented by painful complaints.† The transport of invalids to Balaklava was, moreover, a difficult proceeding and an agonizing ordeal; but arrived at the port, their troubles should surely have come to an end. It was not so, however, for such was the confusion prevalent at the time, so great the number of the sick, that they were subjected, if possible, to worse treatment during the voyage across the Black Sea and in the great hospital established at Scutari. In short, this hospital was a loathsome lazarette, "crammed with misery, overflowing with despair," until Miss Nightingale and a number of Nuns and Sisters, having arrived on the scene early in November, acquired such influence and acted with such admirable prudence and energy, that gradually—the evil was too great to be arrested at once—order was restored, sanitary conditions were introduced,

---

* In the Coldstream some warm clothing and blankets were issued to the men early in December, more were obtained later, and in January a further supply was procured. Lord Raglan directed (January 6th) that each soldier should receive a pair of boots gratuitously (*General Order*). The following is the clothing served out to the Battalion (including the Regimental hospital) between the 6th of December and the 28th of February: Great coats, 392; trousers, 100 pairs; sheepskin coats, 459; tweed coats, 29; fur caps, 503; flannel shirts, 147; jersey frocks, 861; pairs of socks, 1527; flannel drawers, 994; mitts, 993; boots, long and short, 532; comforters, 446; gregos, 55 (Wyatt, pp. 41, 45, 57). The long boots appear to have given little satisfaction. On account of the cold—the thermometer sometimes ranging from eleven to fifteen degrees Fahrenheit,—it was not easy to make the men take off their boots at night; their wet feet often being swollen, were pressed by the leather, and thus frost-bite was induced (*ibid.*, p. 42).

† The indefatigable Surgeon of the Coldstream in the Crimea, Dr. Wyatt, tells us that a marquee was applied for (November 17th) to replace the ill-ventilated bell tents used as a Regimental hospital. It arrived next day, but without ropes, and these, though repeatedly demanded, were only obtained a fortnight later, through Colonel Steele, Lord Raglan's Military Secretary, who at last procured them from a man-of-war. On the 18th of December another marquee was required (the sick were becoming very numerous), and it arrived on the 29th, also without ropes and deficient of five pieces of canvas; in this case the error was only rectified on the 30th of January.

and the sick were well tended and cared for by the gentle and able nursing of kindly ladies.*

The British forces before Sevastopol were rapidly melting away in consequence of the combination of misfortunes that overwhelmed them. Diseases of a violent type broke out, and cholera, typhus, diarrhœa, dysentery, scurvy swept away the ranks; frostbites were common, and even men reported fit for duty, were so weakened as to be scarcely able to continue their labours under the hard circumstances that surrounded them. The drain was excessive upon our strength in the field, and the small army was in truth threatened with extinction. Between the 1st of November and the 28th of February we lost as many as 22,506 men, not including the killed in action; of whom 8898 had died in hospital, while the remainder, 13,608, were lying there sick on the latter date. In spite of fresh regiments and drafts which reached the Crimea after Inkerman, the total effectives all told at the seat of war, reckoning the troops at Balaklava, amounted then to only 17,311 men. In January there would have been about 3000 to 4000 men of the infantry available to repel another attack of the enemy, had he attempted to repeat the operation of the 5th of November.† The British would have had a smaller force at the end of February.

The Coldstream shared to the full the calamity which has just been so imperfectly described. Taking part in the constant duty which exhausted the army, exposed to the cruel suffering that the winter brought about, and conspicuously displaying the virtues of strict discipline and of uncomplaining fortitude which enabled our men to preserve a bold and defiant front against the Russians, the lot of the Battalion can scarcely be separated from that which afflicted and honoured its brethren in arms standing before Sevastopol. Its fate was the same as theirs, its sorrows were equally acute, its bearing likewise was proud and dauntless, its glory bright and lasting. But its losses were heavy, as the following table will show:—

* Hamley, *War in the Crimea*, p. 172, 179, etc. After the battle of Inkerman, the depôt which had been established at Scutari early in June, was re-organized and placed under the able command of Colonel Lord William Paulet (November 23rd), through whose energy many improvements in the hospitals were effected (see Kinglake, vi. 437). An acting Sergeant-Major (Sergeant White of the Coldstream) was appointed there (November 19th).

† Kinglake, vi. 202, etc.

	Regimental Hospital.		Sick Transferred to Scutari.	Remarks.
	Admissions.	Deaths.		
Nov. (including wounded at Inkerman)	277	22	153	Eight died of cholera and eleven of wounds.
December	221	17	99	
January	186	37	91	The average daily sick was more than sixty-three per cent. of strength present.

On the 1st of November the effective strength of all ranks in the field was 600 Officers and men; 1st of December, 451; 1st of January, 353; 1st of February, 173; and at the end of February there were fewer than 100.*

But there was an end at last to these mournful circumstances that oppressed our forces fighting in the Crimea; and with the first peep of spring a new era of hope dawned upon the army. The news of the winter troubles roused a strong feeling in England, and the nation was stirred to its depths with sympathy for its brave and suffering soldiers, of whom no country had more reason to be proud, and with resentment against the supposed delinquents who were accused of bringing about the disaster. Greater activity and energy were displayed at home, and a railway was begun to connect Balaklava with the front, so that by the end of March it reached the Col on the edge of the upland, at a time when the road, constructed by ourselves and the French, was made to the same place. A Land transport service was also at length organized. Subscriptions were collected, and clothing, food, stores, and even luxuries poured into the Crimea, and into the hospitals established at and near Scutari. The Government was overturned, and a Commission of inquiry was instituted, both in England and at the seat of hostilities, to report upon every circumstance connected with the war. The result of these investigations, as well as the conclusions arrived at by another that sat later (in 1856), need not be alluded to in this

* Wyatt, p. 58. It should not be forgotten that the two drafts which reached the Battalion on November 22nd and December 18th, numbered together 211 men. It appears that there was considerable sickness and mortality among the young and unseasoned soldiers who composed the drafts. Of the Officers invalided during the winter (November to February), were Captain Wilson (November 22nd) and Captain Strong (January 1st); Captain Hardinge, moreover, had to leave the Crimea on account of his health (December 24th), and returned the following May.

volume. But one point cannot be omitted which deals with the conduct of the troops, who, in the dark hour of trial, did honour to their Queen, to their country, and to their noble profession.

"Great Britain," says the report of the Commissioners sent to the Crimea, "has often had reasons to be proud of her army, but it is doubtful whether, the whole range of military history furnishes an example of an army exhibiting, throughout a long campaign, qualities as high as have distinguished the forces under Lord Raglan's command. The strength of the men gave way under excessive labour, watching, exposure, and privation; but they never murmured, their spirit never failed, and the enemy, though far outnumbering them, never detected in those whom he encountered any signs of weakness. Their numbers were reduced by disease and by casualties to a handful of men, compared with the great extent of the lines which they constructed and defended, yet the army never abated its confidence in itself, and never descended from its acknowledged military pre-eminence. Both men and Officers, when so reduced that they were hardly fit for the lighter duties of the camp, scorned to be excused the severe and perilous work of the trenches, lest they should throw an undue amount of duty upon their comrades; yet they maintained every foot of ground against all the efforts of the enemy, and with numbers so small that, perhaps, no other troops would even have made the attempt. Suffering and privation have frequently led to crime in armies as in other communities, but offences of a serious character have been unknown in the British army in the Crimea . . . intemperance has been rare. Every one who knows anything of the constitution of an army must feel that, when troops so conduct themselves throughout a long campaign, the Officers must have done their duty and set the example." *

The Russians, on the other hand, except for the great labour and care expended on the fortress, remained almost quiescent during the winter months. Restricting their energies to the defences of Sevastopol and to the annoyance of the besiegers, they made the fortress exceedingly strong, and pushed advanced works in front of the line they had already occupied. The greater portion of their field army was brought into the town to reinforce the garrison, the remainder being quartered in the neighbouring villages, or in the Tchernaya Valley. But no offensive operations were undertaken, notwithstanding their immensely superior numbers; and this was the more fortunate, since in the midwinter our forces were so weakened that the English trenches were guarded by only 350 men. This extraordinary inactivity on the part of the enemy has excited astonishment, and it may well be asked—

* First Report, 1855, pp. 2 and 3.

" how it was that an enemy who possessed such enormously superior forces in men and material, and who could, at any time during a period of months, have directed on some selected point of the siege-works thousands of troops that would have found only hundreds to meet them, did not muster the courage for such an enterprise, when it promised deliverance to the fortress and ruin to their foes." *

On the part of the Allies, the approaches to the fortress were pushed forward with considerable activity, both by ourselves and by the French, but there was little actual fighting except what was brought about by the siege operations. In the beginning of February, the French, who, thanks to the liberal supply of men sent to the seat of war, were growing in numbers, undertook to extend the siege-works on our right;† thus continuing the line of trenches towards the roadstead of Sevastopol. Bosquet's Corps was employed for this purpose. Another element of strength was brought into the field during the winter, to which brief allusion must be made. It was at last determined that Omar Pasha's army should be removed to the Crimea from Bulgaria, where it was unable to influence the course of hostilities; the concentration was effected at Eupatoria, and, on the 17th of February, before the movement was complete, the Turkish force there amounted to 23,000 men. The Russians, having reinforced the troops they had in this part of the peninsula to 20,000 men, attacked the

* Hamley, *War in the Crimea*, p. 194. Whether the Russians were destitute of the necessary courage to take advantage of the obviously favourable chances that the winter offered them of sweeping away the feeble residue of frozen and plague-stricken Englishmen that still survived before Sevastopol, or whether their conduct was the result of a deliberate design, may perhaps be revealed at some future time, when eventual consequences of the Crimean war have been fully developed. It may easily be imagined that the Government of St. Petersburg shrank from converting the existing war of cabinets, hitherto purely local, into a general struggle of nations and principles (Klapka, *War in the East*, p. 101). For had Great Britain been driven from the Crimea, she would surely have taken her revenge, and have removed the contest from a barren and useless fortress, where unhappily she became involved, to a vital point in the armour of her foe. If there were to be a war at all, it is obvious that the struggle for Sevastopol was the least expensive and the most advantageous form of hostilities that the Tsar could engage in; he lost comparatively little if the contest should prove adverse to his arms, more especially if he could prolong his resistance against the united efforts of the two great Powers of Europe. The more he succeeded in doing this, the more he gained a fictitious prestige, the more he exhausted our resources, by the dissolving process which the winter must surely effect, and the more he made the Western nations beware for the future how they again attempt to thwart his plans.

† Our allies had 56,000 men in the Crimea in November, 65,000 in December, and 78,000 in January (Hamley, *War in the Crimea*, p. 176).

place on that date, and were repulsed with a loss of some 800 men. This success seems to have been decisive, in so far that the Allies now held firmly a point within striking distance of the enemy's communications through the isthmus of Perekop; but its value was considerably lessened by the following fact. In the autumn of 1854, General Menshikoff was dependent upon this line to draw reinforcements from Bessarabia, and, as he found it open, he advanced freely along it, and reached Sevastopol before the 5th of November, as has been already related. This advantage gained, the road through Perekop became of comparatively minor importance, and the enemy thenceforward relied upon the line from the Sea of Azof. His communications in this quarter could, of course, only be threatened by a force based somewhere in the neighbourhood of Kertch; but that place was avoided, and Eupatoria was selected. Hence the achievement of the 17th of February, while it might have been followed by satisfactory results had it taken place early in October, was, to a certain extent, a barren victory, and served only to show that our Turkish auxiliaries were capable of performing some service in the war.*

The Guards Brigade, having suffered so severely at Inkerman, and being the only infantry force in the front composing the First Division (the Highlanders occupied Balaklava since the 25th of October), it was necessary to reinforce that division by adding thereto the 97th Regiment (November 23rd). This regiment was armed with the old smooth-bore musket, but as sickness diminished the ranks, the Minié rifles of non-effective Guardsmen were handed over to the survivors of the 97th and of other corps similarly situated. On the 22nd of November the position of the camps of the Grenadiers and Scots Fusiliers were moved to the spot where the Coldstream was established. Two days later, a new disposition of the piquets was ordered; of the eight furnished by the division, six were found by the Brigade and two by the 97th. The strength of these piquets, 50 men each, allowed a double sentry every fifty paces of the entire front; three piquets were placed in reserve, and all were "to be encouraged in making fires, as it is desirable that our full strength should be estimated."†

---

* Colonel (now Field-Marshal Sir Lintorn) Simmons was present with Omar Pasha as British Commissioner with the Turkish army. He served in that capacity from the summer of 1853, until the end of the war.

† *Divisional Memo.*, Nov. 24, 1854.

On the 25th of December the piquets were reduced to 30 rank and file each.

During Colonel Upton's absence at Balaklava on sick-leave, Colonel Lockyer commanded the Division until the 15th of January, when the former returned to the front; the senior Guards Officer present commanded the Brigade during this interval. Colonel Lord Frederick Paulet was also away on the sick-list until the 16th of January, and the Battalion during this time was under Lieut.-Colonel Newton; Captain Armytage was appointed acting Adjutant, vacant by the death of Captain Eliot. On the 17th of January the Brigade lost the services of their Paymaster, Captain South (late 20th Regiment), who, having been present with them ever since they left England, was obliged to leave the Crimea through ill-health. His duties were undertaken by a committee, composed of Colonel Hamilton (Grenadiers), president, and Lieut.-Colonel Stephenson (Scots Fusilier Guards), and Captain Sir J. Dunlop (Coldstream), members.

On the 26th of November the Household Brigade furnished a detachment of 200 men, under a Captain and Lieutenant-Colonel, to the neighbourhood of the monastery of St. George, on the coast west of Balaklava, for the purpose of making gabions, which were required for the siege-works. Of these, the Coldstream provided 70 men with Officers, and Non-commissioned officers in proportion. The detachment was relieved by a similar party on the 21st of December, and again on the 20th of January by 150 men, each Battalion finding a Subaltern Officer and 50 men, with the usual number of Non-commissioned officers.

Major-General Lord Rokeby arrived in the Crimea on the 2nd of February, and assumed the command of the First Division and of the Brigade, when Colonel Upton reverted to the Battalion. But not for long, for, owing to the promotion of the Lieut.-Colonel of the Regiment (Colonel Hon. A. Upton), he was gazetted to that command (February 20th), and left soon after to take up his duties in London.* By this change Lord Frederick Paulet

* In parting from the Battalion when it was still before the enemy, and after having held the command during a very eventful period, Colonel Upton issued an order of which the following is an extract: "He has known their gallantry and firmness before the enemy, their endurance, and their discipline under every trial and pressure. . . . To the young soldiers one word at parting: let them ever hold in view the conduct and bearing which have characterized their older comrades, that they in their turn may pass them on to others, and so uphold and carry forward the name of the distinguished Regiment of which they now form a part."

became Major of the 2nd Battalion, and Colonel Gordon Drummond obtained the command of the 1st; at the same time Lieut.-Colonels Daniell and Perceval were posted to the latter, and Newton to the former (Acting Majors, mounted).*

When the sick of the Battalion left the front for Scutari, no information regarding them was obtained by the Regimental authorities, and to correct this serious inconvenience, a Captain and Lieutenant-Colonel from each Battalion of the Brigade was sent to inspect the hospitals where Guardsmen were treated, and to arrange a more proper system for future adoption (February 16th). Lieut.-Colonel Dudley Carleton, who represented the Coldstream, reported that the admission of men into hospital, as well as the patients' death or discharge, were imperfectly registered:

"their kits were either stored or condemned without regular authority, or were left in the hold of transports, carried up and down during many voyages, and not unfrequently plundered. When a man died, no regular record was kept or transmitted to his regiment, although professedly done. No returns whatever had been sent to the Battalion of men dead, invalided home, or otherwise employed." †

Colonel Carleton remained absent six weeks, and during this time he established a system of fortnightly returns, which thenceforward were regularly despatched to the Crimea, and he placed a sergeant of the Coldstream on the staff of the hospital at Scutari to carry it out.

It has already been mentioned that the winter troubles added to the losses incurred at Inkerman, and, in the absence of sufficient reinforcements from home, had destroyed the efficiency of the Brigade at the seat of war. At the end of January the three Battalions could hardly muster a tenth of their proper strength, and numbered only some 312 men able to do duty.‡ Lord Rokeby seems to have been so struck with their exhausted appearance, that he endeavoured to obtain for them an exemption from trench duty for a time; but as the Order book shows them to be still continually at work, it is evident that it was not possible to comply with the proposal. Towards the end of February, however, it was found

---

* Lieut.-Colonel Stepney, Captains Markham, Blackett, and Caulfeild, and Lieutenant Lane-Fox, joined the Battalion in January, February, and March.

† Wyatt, 53. The three Officers were, Lieut.-Colonels Hon. C. Lindsay, D. Carleton (now Lord Dorchester), and Hon. S. Jocelyn (now Earl of Roden).

‡ Kinglake, vi. 204, quoting from the *Report of the Sevastopol Commission*.

absolutely necessary to make a complete change, and to move them to Balaklava, there to rest and to recruit their strength after the very arduous labours in which for so long they had been engaged. Accordingly, on the 22nd, the Grenadiers marched there, followed by the Coldstream on the 24th, and by the Scotch Fusilier Guards about the same time. In the Regiment there were less than 100 men of all ranks on parade. For some time previously it had become manifest that, if the men continued to live under existing conditions, it was but a question of time how long the Battalion could survive except on paper. Of the sick left behind, 41 followed on the 27th, and 75 were conveyed next day by French mule transport (the usual conveyance lent us by our allies, and indeed the only transport procurable, since our own arrangements had broken down), but the last detachment was not removed to Balaklava until the 28th of March.* The Guards remained at the base till June, 1855, and though absent more than three months from the front, they missed little chance of performing any useful military service.

* Wyatt, pp. 54, 65.

CHAPTER XI.

THE FALL OF SEVASTOPOL.

Stay of the Brigade at Balaklava—Improvement in the condition of the men—Return of the Guards to the front, June 16th—Changed aspect of affairs before Sevastopol—Review of events during the time spent at Balaklava—Second bombardment—Interference by Napoleon III. in the course of the war; operations paralysed—General Canrobert resigns, and is succeeded by General Pélissier—Energy displayed by the latter—Third bombardment—Fourth bombardment; assault on Sevastopol—Its failure—Death of Lord Raglan; succeeded by General Simpson—Siege operations continued—Battle of the Tchernaya—Fifth bombardment—Sixth bombardment; second assault—The Malakoff is captured—Fall of the south side of Sevastopol—The Russians evacuate the town, and retreat to the north side—State in which the Allies found Sevastopol.

THERE are few incidents of Regimental interest to record during the stay at Balaklava. The men were lodged in huts, but as these were situated near a burial ground and close to the stables of the Land Transport Corps, the advantages gained by a change from the fatigues and hardships of the siege to the base of operations were sadly diminished, and several cases of maculated fever for the first time appeared. In March, another site having been selected on the west side of the harbour, in a more favourable and sanitary position, and huts having been constructed, the Battalion moved there towards the end of the month. The better food, the shelter, the increased comfort, and the rest now enjoyed by the men, produced a satisfactory effect upon their health, to which the improvement in the weather also contributed; for, the short, though terribly severe winter had passed away, and with the spring the temperature became warm and pleasant. During March, 101 men were admitted into hospital, of whom 24 were suffering from typhus, and the mortality amounted to 10; while next month, 53 men only were admitted, and but 5 deaths occurred.*

* Wyatt, p. 65.

The Battalion were employed principally in the ordinary duties performed at the base of operations, guarding the stores and buildings or other places set apart for the use of the army, and unloading the ships that arrived in Balaklava. Drills were carried out, and the troops practised, in occupying the trenches at night, to meet any sudden attack which the enemy might contemplate. The danger of such an attack was lessened by the fact that the enemy had relaxed his hold, as far back as the end of December, upon the heights on the left bank of the Tchernaya, captured by him on the 25th of October, though he continued to occupy the line of the river. It was still necessary to restrain his activity in this quarter, and several reconnaissances took place to prevent his advance. As was only natural, the Officers at Balaklava, when off duty, rode frequently to points where operations of interest were being undertaken, but the Brigade itself was not engaged at this period.

The gabion-making detachment was continued near Balaklava, to supply the siege-works before Sevastopol.

Early in March, convalescents from Scutari, wounded at the Alma and at the Inkerman, returned to the Battalion, but the next draft did not arrive until the 1st of May, when 7 Officers and 307 men, whose average age and service were $22\frac{1}{2}$ years and 7 months respectively, landed in the Crimea.* Owing to the Regimental promotion which had taken place, Colonels Lord F. Paulet (commanding the 2nd Battalion) and Newton, and Lieut.-Colonel Wood were now ordered home to the 2nd Battalion; while Colonel Gordon Drummond assumed the command of the 1st Battalion, Colonels Daniell and Perceval being Acting Majors (mounted), as has already been stated. About this time, also,† Officers were posted to companies as follows :—

No. 1 Company: Captains F. Burton, H. Tower, and C. Blackett. (Subsequently Lieut.-Colonel Lord C. FitzRoy.)

No. 2 Company: Lieut.-Colonel C. Burdett; Captain M. Heneage; Lieutenant St. V. Whitshed.

No. 3 Company: Lieut.-Colonel Herbert Stepney; Captain Le Couteur; Lieutenant Rose.

---

* The Officers were: Colonels Gordon Drummond, Daniell, and Perceval; Lieut.-Colonel Cocks; Captain Thellusson; and Lieutenants Adair, and Lane. Shortly afterwards Lieut.-Colonel Lord C. FitzRoy (wounded at Inkerman) and Major C. Baring (wounded at the Alma) reached the seat of war; Assist.-Surgeon T. Rogers arrived on June 15th.

† *Battalion Order*, May 4, 1855.

No. 4 Company : Lieut.-Colonel W. Dawkins; Captain Hon. R. Drummond; Lieutenant H. Lane.
No. 5 Company : Major P. Crawley ; Lieutenants A. Lambton, Lane-Fox.
No. 6 Company : Captain Sir J. Dunlop ; Lieutenant A. Adair. (Subsequently Major C. Baring.)
No. 7 Company : Lieut.-Colonel C. Cocks; Captain J. Caulfeild; Lieutenant G. Ives.
No. 8 Company : Lieut.-Colonel Dudley Carleton ; Captains A. Thellusson, Gerald Goodlake; Lieutenant Godfrey Wigram.

As the summer approached, the weather became extremely hot, and towards the middle of May, 90 degrees were registered in the shade. Cholera again broke out among the troops, but, warned by the visitation of this plague in the previous year, every precaution then known to medical science was taken to avert it. The number of sick increased during May and June, the admissions into hospital being in the first month 134, and the deaths 5, and in the second month 267 and 36 respectively ; of the latter, 24 men died of cholera.

On the 16th of June, the Brigade returned to the front to join in the operations which were intended to be undertaken by the Allies on the 18th, the anniversary of the battle of Waterloo.* The Battalion was 488 strong (excluding Officers). Three Officers and 61 men were left behind sick, as well as 15 convalescents ; altogether 111 men were abstracted from the effective strength. On reaching the upland the old positions were scarcely to be recognised by the rank and file who had remained more than three months at Balaklava. The French having already extended the British Right Attack, occupied the ground in front of the Karabelnaya from the Dockyard Ravine, past the Carcenage Ravine, and along Mount Inkerman to the heights overlooking the roadstead. Innumerable siege-works cut up the plateau, the lines were pushed further forward,

* The Highland Brigade marched up with the Guards, and thus the First Division, under Lieut.-General Sir Colin Campbell, was once more complete before Sevastopol. Shortly afterwards the following changes were made in the British army. The Highlanders were separated from the Guards, and having several battalions added to them, formed the "Highland Division," commanded by Sir Colin Campbell. Lord Rokeby, promoted locally Lieut.-General, commanded the First Division, formed of the Guards Brigade, under Brigadier-General Craufurd; and of the 2nd Brigade, viz. a battalion of the 9th, 13th, 31st Regiments, and of the Rifle Brigade, under Colonel Ridley. About the same time, the Second, Third, Fourth, and Light Divisions were commanded by Major-Generals Markham, Eyre, H. Bentinck, and Lieut.-General Sir W. Codrington respectively. The Cavalry, under Lieut.-General Sir J. Scarlett, was divided into three brigades : the Heavy, Light, and Hussar brigades.

a large force was concentrated on the spot, and the face of the country—so bleak and barren in February—was now covered with the green carpet of a luxuriant vegetation.

We must now take a hasty glance at the state of affairs prevailing before Sevastopol and elsewhere, which controlled the war, while the Guards were at Balaklava. In spite of the united efforts of the British and French occupying the ground before the Malakoff, the enemy succeeded in extending his works to his front, and in materially strengthening the lines that covered the Karabelnaya. The fact was becoming more apparent that General Canrobert, gallant soldier though he was, was not disposed to risk the chances of making a bold move against the Russians; and that the latter, under the distinguished leadership of Colonel Todleben, were enabled thereby to prolong the struggle.

But Canrobert was not entirely his own master in this matter, for towards the beginning of the year 1855 the Emperor Napoleon interfered with the conduct of the operations in the Crimea, in a manner to impede seriously the progress of hostilities. Declaring himself to be dissatisfied with the course pursued, the Emperor conceived the idea of delaying the siege until he could isolate Sevastopol from the rest of the peninsula; and he even proposed to go himself to the Crimea to carry out his design. He was happily dissuaded from undertaking this latter part of the project—dangerous both on account of his inexperience in war, and because of the instability of his authority in Paris,—and it was finally abandoned, after he had been received as a guest at Windsor (April 25th); but he still adhered to his determination to enforce some hazy plan which his vanity had formed, and thereby he increased considerably the difficulties of the Allies.

Added to this, there was a renewal of negotiations at Vienna. The Tsar Nicholas died early in March, and though his successor Alexander II. was clearly in the hands of the war faction, some feeble attempt was made to patch up a peace. The negotiations failed; but the events alluded to could not but exercise some influence over the fortunes of the war, by fettering the action of the French army engaged in it.

This appears to be shown by the results that followed the second bombardment of Sevastopol, which commenced on the 8th of April. Immense preparations had been made to ensure its success, and it was confidently expected by the Allied hosts that this bombardment would at last lead to an immediate and triumphal assault of the fortress.

"Ten days did the terrific storm of iron hail endure; ten days did the Russian reliefs, holding themselves ready to repel attack, meet wounds and death with a constancy which was of necessity altogether passive. On the 19th they saw the fire of the Allies decline, and settle into its more ordinary rate; they saw too, that the sappers were again at work with their approaches, and reading in this the signs of a resumption of the siege, and the abandonment of the policy of assault, they once more withdrew their sorely harassed infantry to places of shelter and repose. Then they began to reckon their losses, which amounted for the ten days, in killed and wounded, to more than 6,000 men. The French lost in killed and disabled, 1,585 men; the English, 265.*

All this expenditure of lives and of war *matériel* effected just nothing, nor was anything even attempted against the enemy; for the French, though having an opportunity to assault, not possessed at that time by their British allies, were "kept waiting for Louis Napoleon, and were restrained from engaging in any determined attack." †

In order to accomplish the views of the Emperor Napoleon, a French army of reserve was being collected near Constantinople, and as it was expected soon to reach the Crimea—to undertake the plans which had been sketched out in Paris,—two important operations against the enemy were delayed. First, a further bombardment, arranged to take place at the end of April, and to be followed by an assault, was put off; and secondly, an expedition, at last agreed to, against the Russian communications in the Sea of Azof, and which had actually started to Kertch (May 3rd), was recalled.‡ Both these events caused much embarrassment to Lord Raglan, who, understanding imperfectly even then the Emperor's proposals, found his own plans thwarted by the supine and unintelligible conduct of his colleague. The confidence reposed in the latter was naturally shaken; and when, a few days later, Napoleon's scheme was fully revealed to the allied Commanders, was discussed, and was found to be impossible of execution, General Canrobert felt

* Hamley, *War in the Crimea*, p. 212.
† Kinglake, vii. 195; compare Hamley, *War in the Crimea*, p. 225.
‡ "I merely record that both armies were certainly, if not discontented, amazed, when an expedition which started on the 3rd of May to Kertch, to destroy Russian magazines and stores, was recalled three days later, on the receipt of a telegram from Paris" (Wood, *Crimea in* 1854 *and* 1894, p. 264).

his position to be intolerable, and he resigned the chief command of the French army. It is right to add that, though Canrobert's character unfitted him to direct the difficult operations which lay before him, he was well suited to assume the lower functions of a commander of a division or army-corps. Being of a loyal and soldierlike disposition, and unwilling to leave the seat of war, he begged that he might revert to the position he originally occupied in the French army when the war broke out, and recommended that General Pélissier (who had reached the Crimea in January) should be appointed the new Commander-in-chief. These proposals were sanctioned in Paris by telegram, and were immediately carried into execution (May 19th).

The change in the French command completely altered the state of affairs in the Crimea. The vacillating weakness of Canrobert and his subserviency to the foibles of his Imperial Master, were at last replaced by the hardy daring of Pélissier and by his manly disregard of an ill-timed interference in the conduct of the war, which could only end in disaster. The forces fighting against Russia, moreover, were increasing; while the strength of that Empire was ebbing fast. In April nearly half of Omar Pasha's Turks, about 45,000 strong, were taken from Eupatoria to the Chersonese, and next month a compact division of 15,000 Sardinians —who had joined the confederacy against Russia—landed in the Crimea, under the command of General La Marmora. The enemy about this time, by reason of his immense losses, had little more than 100,000 men in the peninsula; the Allies were more numerous, and could dispose of about 180,000 men.* Thus, it was becoming apparent, that by vigorously pushing on the siege, Sevastopol must fall, and that the resources of Russia—so fatally allowed to accumulate in the early stages of the war—were beginning to fail.

Immediate arrangements were made to storm the advanced works which Todleben had constructed, to occupy the Tchernaya and the plain of Baidar that lay beyond it, and to attack Kertch and the Russian base of supplies formed on the coast of the Sea of Azof. On the 23rd of May, after severe fighting, the French gained an important advantage over the enemy near Quarantine Bay; and, two days later, he was also attacked on the Tchernaya

* English, 28,000; French, 100,000; Turks, 45,000; Sardinians, 15,000 (Kinglake, viii. 7).

and driven out of Tchorgun. About the same time, the expedition to Kertch, composed of 15,000 English, French, and Turks, started for its destination. Operations in this quarter were entirely successful, and by the middle of June the Allies, having struck deep into the resources of the Russians, cut their chief line of supply, and in no small degree carried out practically the policy of investment which the Emperor professed to desire.*

The allied Commanders now directed their efforts to the Russian advanced works covering the Karabelnaya, and, determining to attack them, they prepared for the assault by a fierce canonade (the third bombardment), which opened on the 6th of June with tremendous violence and effect, and lasted until the 10th. On the evening of the 7th, the French advanced against the White works (situated on Mount Inkerman, to the east of Careenage Ravine), and the Kamskatka Lunette (on the Mamelon, covering the Malakoff and some 500 yards in front of it) ; and the English moved against the Quarries (covering the Redan and about 400 yards from it). These attacks were successful, and the enemy, driven from all these outworks, was restricted to his main line of defence. The captured positions were occupied and held by the Allies. Between the 6th and the 10th the Russians lost altogether, in killed, wounded, and prisoners, 8500 men and 73 guns ; the Allies nearly 7000 men.

These advantages were now to be pressed home, and a great effort made to assault the main line round the Karabelnaya; the Malakoff and the Redan were to be attacked, and the fortress so long besieged was at last to fall. The final act of the long drama was fixed for the 18th of June, when the Anglo-French allies, having shared so many dangers and hardships in common, might reap the

* Hamley, *Crimea*, p. 242. Established now at last on the shores of the Sea of Azof, the Allies might even at this late period have inflicted a crushing blow on the enemy in the direction of Circassia, and so have brought about the end of the war, and a severe check to Russia's advance through Central Asia and towards India—the objects that Great Britain had in view when she undertook to curb the Tsar's pretensions in the East. It appears that the attention of the Foreign Secretary (Lord Clarendon) was directed at that time to this most important point ; but there was a difficulty with the French, who, conceiving that they would be giving assistance to a purely English policy, would not concur in any such scheme (see Rawlinson, *England and Russia in the East*, 272 note). It must not be forgotten that Louis Napoleon disapproved of the expedition to Kertch—the one operation in the war which was crowned with complete and immediate success, and which cost the Allies nothing,—and that he peremptorily ordered Pélissier to take no part in the attack on Anapa on the Circassian coast (Kinglake, viii. 79).

reward of their arduous labours, and obliterate the memories of the day of Waterloo.

The fourth bombardment opened on the 17th, and the fleets once more joined their fire to the numerous great siege guns planted before Sevastopol. The devastating force of the artillery soon obtained a mastery over that of the fortress, and the usual results followed : the enemy's works were knocked to pieces, his defences ruined, and he lost 4000 men. Now, therefore, was the time for the assault to take place, and, as we have seen, the Guards Brigade were brought up to the front from Balaklava to participate in the operations about to ensue. But the ardent expectations of the besiegers were not yet to be realized, and the attack ended unfortunately. Neither in the Malakoff nor in the Redan, were the French or ourselves able to effect a lodgment ; the only consolation was the capture of a position in front of our Left Attack. Among the blunders that occurred to account for the failure, perhaps the most unfortunate was that of Pélissier himself. It had been settled that the bombardment was to continue for two hours after dawn on the 18th, so as to shatter the repairs which the Russians invariably made to their works during the night, and that then the assault was to commence at about 5.30 in the morning. But this plan was altered at the last moment, by Pélissier, who wished the advance to begin at dawn, without any previous preparation by artillery fire. Lord Raglan was not consulted, and, when he heard of it, he submitted to the change most reluctantly. The enemy, therefore, was ready, behind parapets hastily renewed and armed with field guns during the night, and thereby he was enabled to repel the attack. That this was probably the main cause of the failure, may perhaps be inferred from the fact that when, after the assault, the bombardment recommenced, the soldierlike spirit of the Russians gave way, and many of them, unable to stand against the terrific fire poured upon them, fled to the harbour, and endeavoured to escape to the north side of Sevastopol.* The Guards Brigade were not engaged upon this occasion ; they remained in reserve, and were not brought forward. In fact, the attack had failed, and further expenditure of lives had to be avoided. The losses were great on that fatal day ; that of the English amounted to 1500, of the French to 3500, and of the enemy only to 1500.

* Hamley, *War in the Crimea*, p. 261.

Two Officers occupying very conspicuous positions in their respective armies disappeared from the scene of their labours about this time. General Todleben was slightly wounded on the 18th, and more gravely hurt a few days later, so that he had to leave Sevastopol, and the Russians lost the services of that master mind to whose conspicuous ability, energy, and courage the prolonged and successful defence of the fortress was primarily due. The Allied armies also were plunged into mourning by the unexpected death of Lord Raglan, who never recovered from the grief and disappointment which oppressed his mind after the events of the 18th. This reverse, added to the labours and anxieties of the previous fifteen months, during which time he discharged his high but onerous duties without intermission, undermined his constitution, and he died on the 28th, surrounded by his personal friends and his military staff. He was succeeded by General Simpson.* His body was removed to England, and was taken to the Bay of Kazatch with full military honours, on the 3rd of July; and, in accordance with General Orders, the troops not engaged in the funeral or on duty in the field, remained in their tents during the afternoon. While the ceremony lasted, the Allied forces before Sevastopol were passive in the trenches, and, whether owing to chance, or to a graceful act of courtesy on the part of the Russian Commander, the guns of the garrison also kept silence.†

The siege was pushed forward with great activity after the 18th, and in this portion of the weary operations the Guards Brigade took their full share. Seeing the mistake committed by advancing over open ground for a distance of 400 to 500 yards, against the *enceinte* covering the Karabelnaya, General Pélissier now proposed to sap up close to the fortress. The soil near his own siege-works favoured such an undertaking; but not so, that which lay in front of our positions, where a thin layer of earth only covered the solid rock. Thus, while the French were able to get close to the ramparts of the Malakoff, the British were prevented from pushing through the ground much beyond the Quarries, or from lessening to any considerable extent the distance that separated them from their objective—the Redan.

These siege operations lasted without intermission until early in September. On the night of June 18th, the Brigade found 30 Officers

---

* See Appendix No. X., containing General Orders on Lord Raglan's death.
† Kinglake, viii. 299.

and 1000 men for the trenches, of which the Coldstream, furnished 8 Officers and 263 men; and so on, from day to day, in varying numbers, according to the requirements of the moment. It was ordered on the 21st, that "in future the proportion of Officers and men in the trenches will be one Captain and one Subaltern to every 100 men;" and also "should any part of the guard of the trenches be called upon to work, they are positively forbidden to take off their accoutrements or to go far from their arms."* Commencing July 10th, the duties were found by divisions —the First, Second, and Light in the Right, the Third and the Fourth in the Left Attack,—and during that night the Battalion furnished 7 Officers and 312 men, also 21 men more as a special working party.†

* *First Divisional Morning Order*, June 21st.

† Special and other working parties and shot-loading fatigues in the trenches were frequently ordered at this time. The following, relating to the duties in the trenches, may be of interest:—

Head-quarter Memo., July 10th: "General Officers of divisions will be so good as to detail not less than a Brigadier-General, three Field Officers, and two Adjutants for duty in the trenches on the days that their divisions furnish the guard, Right Attack."

Divisional Order, July 12th: "The troops will be told off to their places in the trenches before they leave their camp, and they will move off from the parade in front of the camp, after being so told off, at 6.15, so that they may all be in their places in the trenches and the relief completed by 8 o'clock, according to the General Order on the subject."

Head-quarter Memo., July 24th: "Until further orders the guard in the trenches by night, will be 2400 men, under a General of the day with three Field Officers; of this number 600 men will work if required by the Royal Engineers, from 4 to 8 a.m., and return to their camp at 8 a.m. if it should seem prudent to the senior Officer in the trenches to dispense with them. . . . The remainder of the guard will furnish working parties as usual during the day, when required by the Royal Engineers. . . . There will be a special working party, consisting of 400 men under a Field Officer, independent of the guard of the trenches, except in case of an attack, when they will be available to be called upon by the Officer commanding in the trenches. . . . General Officers of divisions furnishing the guards in the trenches are to consider the remainder of their division as a support ready to reinforce the guard, with which they will proceed in case of alarm, and resume the command of the whole force in the trenches."

Later, in the middle of August, a reserve of 600 men was ordered "to remain in the trenches the twenty-four hours, and will be planted during the day in such spots in the 1st parallel or other places of security as may be pointed out by the Generals of the Attacks. Troops not on duty are to remain in camp till further orders" (*Head-quarter Memo.*, Aug. 16th).

Head-quarter Memo., Aug. 17th: "A steady fire of musketry, by riflemen and good shots, must be kept up during the night, from the advanced trenches of both Attacks on the Redan and works in rear and flank. The object being to prevent the enemy from repairing the damage done to their works. The artillery should assist this as much as possible by throwing light balls."

Colonel Tower says that, on August 21st, he was in the 5th parallel, and that he was

It should be noticed here, that the Guards Brigade, on August 31st, exchanged the whole of their arms and ammunition for the new Enfield rifle then introduced, and that, at this time, there were two patterns in use by the troops of the British army standing before Sevastopol.*

Notwithstanding the interest which the operations undertaken between June and September excited, and the high hopes generally entertained that the fortress would soon fall, the little-varying duty in the trenches became monotonous in the extreme, and all wished earnestly that this phase of the war might quickly pass away. Some cricket matches served to while away a few of the weary hours; but the weather was extremely hot and oppressive, and the season was sickly. There was, of course, much to distract the minds of men who, for the first time, found themselves in the presence of an enemy; but it was different for those who had been almost constantly at work for many months on the same spot and at the same object, and thus even these distractions lost much of their novelty and interest.

"The siege was really getting too fearfully tedious now," writes Colonel Tower, about August 28th. "The weather was hot and sultry; our camp was a long way from the works. We used to parade about 5 p.m., having crammed in all the victuals we could get. We toiled down three miles in the sun, carrying great coat, haversack, revolver, and defiled into the zigzags before sundown; all night (if in the advance) we were straining our eyes over the parapet, momentarily expecting a sortie, being graped and shelled the whole time, and losing a good many of our party. The sun got up very early, and often a breeze with it, and from sunrise to sunset we had to sit in a dusty ditch, being shelled, our food—salt pork and biscuit—covered with dust and sand. The men could not show their noses over the parapet. . . . The deep blue sea stretching away, dotted

---

ordered to keep up a heavy fire all night on the embrasures. 75,000 rounds were fired from the trench in which he was stationed. He also says that the custom in the middle of August, was to withdraw the guards of the trenches to a position in rear, and to leave an Officer and small party in the advanced line to watch the enemy's works, and to fire at the embrasures when any one showed himself (Tower, *Diary*).

Towards the end of August, and during the beginning of September, more men were employed. There was a party for the trenches 2800 strong, the guard as before 2400, and the special working party, 400 men. During this period, more than one division furnished the necessary daily number required.

* "After 5 p.m. on the 28th inst. the small-arm ammunition magazine on the right of the eight-gun battery in the Right Attack will contain only Enfield rifle ammunition, pattern 1853, bore ·577; the three other magazines will still be supplied with Minié rifle ammunition, pattern 1851, bore ·702."

with ships coming in and going out, looked so cool and nice in the distance, I used to think of home far away, and long for the siege to be over. It really seemed now as if it were drawing to a close. The bridge across the harbour had been constructed some time, and could be for no other purpose than as a means for the enemy to retire. The French pressed the enemy at the bastion Du Mât [the Flagstaff Battery] and the Malakoff; I used to spend a good deal of time in the French trenches, and knew the whole position as well as any one in the army."

The casualties in the Battalion were not very severe during these three months, and amounted to 47 wounded, of whom 6 died of their injuries. Besides this number, an Officer of the Regiment, Captain Hon. R. Drummond, was wounded, on August 25th, in the trenches, having been shot through the chest; he left the Crimea on September 6th, but died before he reached England, unfortunately, indeed, just before the steamer anchored at Spithead. The general health of the Battalion may be seen from the following table:—

	Admissions into Hospital from		Deaths from	
	Disease.	Wounds.	Disease.	Wounds.
July	138	20	8	1
August	132	15	5	3
September	65	12	2	2

Between June 20th and September 21st, 78 men returned to duty from the hospital at Balaklava; but, *per contra*, 95 men were sent down from the front for treatment during the same period.*

The Russians could do little to resist the formidable preparations made by the Allies to bring about the capture of Sevastopol. They lost heavily every day, even under the ordinary fire which the besiegers poured upon them, and, perceiving that the end of the long struggle was imminent, they resolved to make one final effort to free themselves from the forces that were closing nearer and nearer to their defences. After much consideration, General Michael Gortchakoff† determined to bring down the field army,

---

* Wyatt, p. 86.

† General Menshikoff had been replaced in his command in the Crimea by General Gortchakoff in the spring of 1855; the same who fought on the Danube, and whose curious movements, on the day of Inkerman, have already been adverted to.

which was established on the Mackenzie heights and on the Belbek, into the valley of the Tchernaya, and to attack the French, Sardinians, and Turks holding that portion of the field. On August 15th, accordingly, a general action took place in that quarter, known as the battle of the Tchernaya, between a Russian army of 48,000 infantry, 10,000 cavalry, and 272 guns, and a somewhat smaller force of the Allies, who, though they massed as many as 60,000 men, did not deploy their whole strength upon that occasion. The enemy displayed much bravery, but showed little skill; he was routed, and fell back slowly towards Mackenzie Farm, losing 69 Officers and 2300 men killed, 160 Officers and 4000 men wounded, and 31 Officers and 1700 men missing—total 8260. The French had 1500 killed and wounded, and the Sardinians 200.* The besieging armies expected that this battle would be accompanied by a general sortie from Sevastopol; but it did not take place, for, the Russians were getting exhausted, and their resources were almost entirely at an end. In order to prevent any such attempt, and also to enable the French to sap up quite close to the defences of the Karabelnaya opposite to them, the Allies opened another, though only a partial, bombardment (the fifth) on August 16th, and continued their fire for some days with great violence; but no assault followed, for they were not yet ready to enact the final scene that was soon to begin.

General Gortchakoff might now have yielded the fortress which had been held so tenaciously and gloriously by the armies of the Tsar; but, after a full inspection of the town, of its ruins, and of the miseries and horrors it contained, he came to the resolution that it was to be held to the last extremity, and that the honour of his Sovereign prevented him from either evacuating it or capitulating. He determined, therefore, to bring into Sevastopol all he could spare of his field army, and to resist to the end. Hopeless as the outlook was at this moment, he still professed to believe that he could hold out for another month.

The last and sixth bombardment commenced on September 5th, and continued, if possible, with even greater fierceness and intensity than before, till the 8th, the day set apart for the grand assault. Pélissier guarded himself this time against advancing at dawn; and, having observed that at noon the Malakoff was usually more weakly occupied than at any other hour of the day or night,

* Hamley, *War in the Crimea.* p. 271.

he resolved to take advantage of this circumstance, and to deliver the attack then. At noon therefore, the French, under Bosquet, were to storm the Malakoff, the Curtain near, and the little Redan; while the English, under General Codrington, were to attack the Redan. The town defences, moreover, were to be assailed by the French opposite to them, aided by a Sardinian brigade under General Cialdini; but this movement was subject to further orders.

A very fierce fight took place at all these places, of which one alone was successful; for the French, having entered the Malakoff, secured a firm footing there, and gained that important position in the enemy's main line. Their losses were immense, not less than 3087 in killed and wounded out of 7446 men engaged in this portion of the battle-field. Everywhere else the assaults were beaten back, and the Allies could only believe at first that they had but gained an indecisive victory.

The attack on the Redan was made, as has been seen, under very difficult—almost impossible—circumstances; but, if it was only undertaken to relieve the pressure which the enemy brought to bear upon our allies near the Malakoff, our purpose was fulfilled. It is, however, difficult to believe that a diversion was all we intended to effect, since this assault was to be the final act of the great military drama which had been going on for a whole year in the Crimea, and which riveted the eyes of Europe upon Sevastopol. The troops engaged comprised the Second and Light Divisions, 6200 strong—1700 in the first line, 1500 in support, and 3000 in reserve in the 3rd parallel; the Third and Fourth Divisions formed a main reserve; but neither the Highland nor the First Division, to which the Guards Brigade belonged, was called up to share in the action. The Brigade was posted in rear, about half a mile from the Malakoff, where a splendid view of the fighting was obtained. There was much regret among all ranks composing it that they were not allowed to advance and take part in the attack; more especially since, when the French (according to Colonel Tower) asked General Simpson to send some of his troops to help them to hold the Malakoff, the request was refused, and the First Division, or, at least, the Guards, who were close by, were not told off to perform this duty. If this is more than camp gossip, it is, indeed, to be regretted that no British troops were enabled to participate in the glory of inflicting a final reverse upon the enemy's position in the Karabelnaya.

General Simpson explains that he determined to give the honour of leading the assault to the Second and Light Divisions, because they had defended the trenches and approaches to the Redan for many months, and because of the intimate knowledge they possessed of the ground. Military critics believe that this was a "cruel kindness to the army." The two divisions were exhausted by the siege, and the knowledge of the ground is considered upon this occasion to have been a positive disadvantage, "for, in acquiring it, the troops generally lost the dash which is essential to success." Moreover, these divisions were now filled with young and only partially trained soldiers, "who paid no attention to the orders that were given;" "the companies lost all formation and cohesion from the irregular manner in which they ran forward, and they stood in confused groups behind the parapets;" "the battalions got mixed up;" in fact, "the young, raw recruits failed to follow their leaders in the way in which the soldiers had done at the Alma and Inkerman."[*] On the other hand, there were fresh troops available; the Guards had only shortly before come up to the front from Balaklava, where they passed three and a half months, and the Highlanders had been there between October and June. Neither, as we know, were employed in the assault, much to their disappointment and chagrin.

But all this is only one side of the story. The task before the British was, under any circumstances, most difficult to fulfil. They had to advance over the open for a considerable distance, against a strong work, covered in front by obstacles, whose rear was unenclosed, and whose fire was unsubdued. It had been impossible to construct *places d'armes* in our trenches, owing to the rocky nature of the soil, and hence the reserves could not be concentrated in suitable positions whence to push forward at the proper moment and feed the attack. Nevertheless, the leading British troops advanced with the utmost gallantry and spirit, notwithstanding the furious fire to which they were exposed; they penetrated into the Redan, and clung to the position they had gained. But they could not maintain themselves there; for, the Russians, hurrying up in immense numbers, forced them to retire before the reserves—hampered in the narrow trenches—were able to advance to their support. The French, moreover, having spiked the guns they found in the Malakoff, had none to turn

---

[*] Wood, *Crimea in 1854 and 1894*, pp. 370-378.

upon the enemy as he entered the Redan in force to drive out our storming parties. After this failure, the attack was put off to the following day; our losses amounted to 2271 Officers and men, those of the French to 7567, and of the Russians to 12,913.*

But there was no necessity to renew the combat; for the enemy, aware of the strength of the Malakoff position, which commanded the whole of the defences of Sevastopol, evacuated the south side during the night of the 8th–9th, and withdrew to the northern bank of the roadstead, blowing up their magazines, and firing the town in several places. The Allies had thus early intimation of the impending fall of the fortress which for so long had withstood their valour; but the full extent of the victory was scarcely appreciated before the morning of the 9th, when the enemy's retreat became known to the armies engaged. The evacuation of the Redan was first ascertained by some Highlanders in the trenches in the night, who, stalking up to the ditch and abatis that was near it, found the work tenanted only by spiked guns and by dead men.

"N——, who knew my wandering tendencies, came to me in the middle of the night before daybreak, and told me to get up at once, that some one had come out of the trenches, and that the Redan was evacuated. I got on Bono Johnnie and galloped off about daylight. I arrived at our trenches, which I found occupied by the Highland Division; they were fast putting out a line of sentries to prevent any one going over to the Russian works. . . . I went across the hill towards the Malakoff, the ground literally paved with iron; the great high parapet was already broken down, and in the afternoon the ditch was filled in with gabions and a regular road made into the work. Dead and dying inside the work; such a scene of devastation and confusion impossible to conceive: guns broken and upset; powder in the embrasures, two or three inches deep, all loose on the ground; wounded men, French and Russians, still crawling about, and the trenches full of Russians who had crept in. . . . From the top of the parapet our trenches were spread out like a map. I was wild with delight at thinking the siege was over, and all the country opened to us. I posted off to the White barracks, and ransacked the whole place, coming back through the Redan." †

The Allies did not enter the town on the 9th, for Sevastopol was a blazing mass of ruins, and the frequent explosions showed the place to be undermined: the garrison having escaped under

---

* Hamley, *War in the Crimea*, pp. 278-285. The 23rd Royal Welsh Fusiliers, in support, lost, in killed and wounded, 15 Officers out of 18, and 197 men out of five companies (Wood, *Crimea*, loc. cit.).

† Tower, *Diary*, Sept. 9, 1855.

cover of the night, when we were unaware of their intention, could not be further pressed at that moment, so there was no object to serve by sending the troops into a fire-trap. A terrible conflagration raged, and to this was added the burning and the final destruction of the Russian Black Sea fleet. The minds of our men could be well filled with awe and joy at the wonderful sights that met their gaze—awe at the fiery furnace the enemy kindled to mark his departure from the stronghold he had held so audaciously and bravely, and joy that the protracted siege was at last concluded.* Early on the 10th, the fires had ceased, and the conquerors, advancing to secure their prize, found one great building intact. Having penetrated into it, they were amazed to discover that it was a hospital containing no less than 2000 dead and dying men, who had been left to their fate without food or treatment for two days and nights, in the midst of the dire confusion and chaos that prevailed in the town; among them were three English Officers.† At midday on the 13th, a fatigue party of 500 men of the First Division, under Major Ponsonby, Grenadier Guards, were ordered into the town to help to cleanse it, and to bury the numerous dead. The duty was a disagreeable one, as may well be imagined; it was well performed, as can be seen from the following Divisional Memorandum, dated September 15th :—

"The General Commanding the Forces expresses, through Lieut.-General Lord Rokeby, his regret at being obliged to employ the Brigade on the disagreeable fatigue duty of Thursday last, but which, for the health of the army, was absolutely necessary; and he was fully satisfied with the manner in which that duty was performed."

The French now occupied Sevastopol, and the English the Karabelnaya, where regular guards were established. The British troops (500 each day from the Brigade) were employed, with a working pay of 1s. 6d. a day, in making a main road from Balaklava to the front, and others in the neighbourhood, under the superintendence of Lieut.-Colonel Hon. A. Hardinge, Coldstream Guards.

It should be stated here, that, on the 27th of August, Lord Stratford de Redcliffe, Ambassador at Constantinople, reached

* The Battalion Order dated the 9th, "The Battalion will parade for inspection of necessaries at 9 a.m. to-morrow, Officers in blue coats, etc.," shows that the ordinary routine of military duty was never relaxed.
† Hamley, *Crimea*, p. 286; Nolan, ii. 473.

the Crimea for the purpose of investing several Officers with the Order of the Bath. The ceremony took place at the British headquarters, in the presence of General Pélissier and his Staff. The Guards Brigade furnished a Guard of Honour; the Coldstream, the Queen's Colour, the Ensign and Lieutenant (Lieutenant Whitshed), and 50 men; and the Scots Fusilier Guards, the Captain and Lieutenant-Colonel, the Lieutenant and Captain, and 50 men. Among those on whom the honour was conferred, connected with the Regiment or to be connected with it, were Lieut.-Generals Sir Colin Campbell, Sir H. Bentinck, and Sir W. Codrington.

The Brigade paraded in review order on the 20th of September, for the purpose of receiving medals and clasps, which were distributed to the Officers, Non-commissioned officers, and men who had landed in the Crimea before the 1st of October, 1854.

Early in October, 1855, new reinforcements reached the Battalion. On the 2nd, 24 convalescents arrived for duty from Balaklava, as against 7 invalids sent to England next day. On the 4th, the fifth draft landed from home, consisting of 8 Officers and 207 men, whose average age was 24 years, and service 15 months. "They were principally volunteers from the Militia, and a remarkably fine body of men, not so tall as the original Guardsmen, but in every way better adapted for the exigencies of active service." * Officers were posted to companies as follows, October 7th:—

No. 1 Company: Major C. Baring, Captain H. Tower, Lieutenant Rose.

No. 2 Company: Lieut.-Colonel C. Burdett, Major Lord Bingham, Lieutenant Julian Hall.

No. 3 Company: Lieut.-Colonel Herbert-Stepney, Captain C. Blackett, Lieutenant Adair.

No. 4 Company: Captain Le Couteur, Captain Lord E. Cecil, Lieutenant Whitshed.

No. 5 Company: Captain Sir J. Dunlop, Lieutenant A. Lambton.

No. 6 Company: Lieut.-Colonel F. Newdigate, Captain W. Reeve, Lieutenant H. Lane.

No. 7 Company: Major H. Armytage, Captain Hon. W. Feilding, Lieutenant Godfrey Wigram.

No. 8 Company: Lieut.-Colonel Lord Dunkellin, Captain Heneage, Lieutenant Hon. W. Edwardes.†

* Wyatt, 86.

† A few days later, Majors Baring and Armytage were invalided to England, and Captains Hon. H. Byng and Jervoise joined the Battalion—the former from home, the latter by transfer from the 42nd Highlanders.

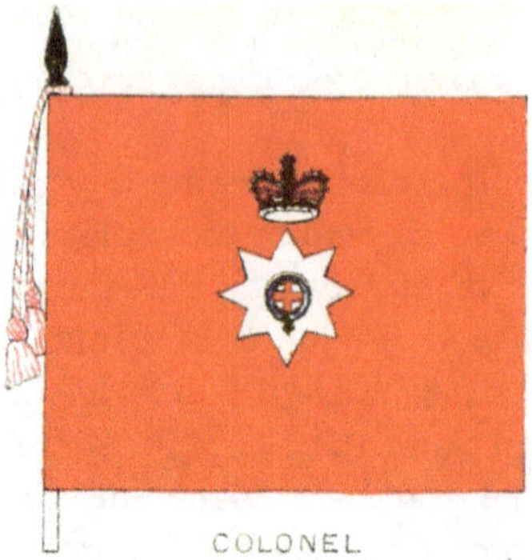

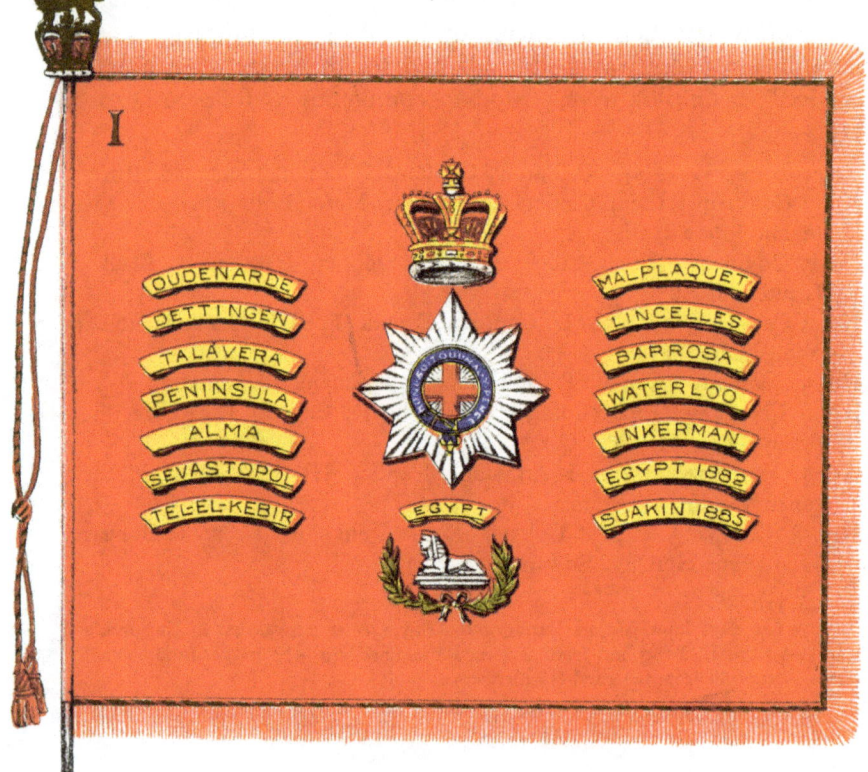

COLONEL

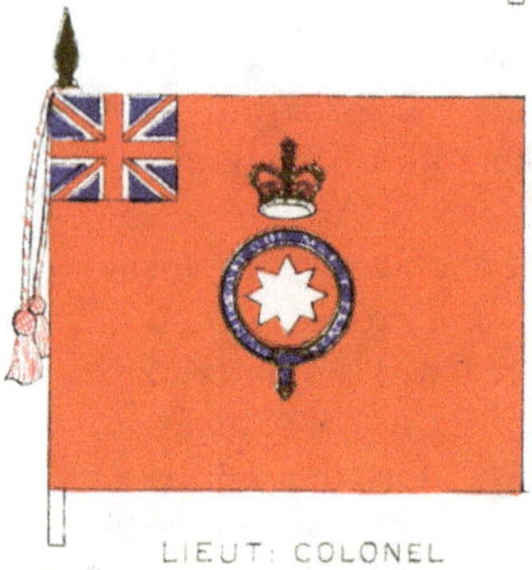

LIEUT: COLONEL

1750

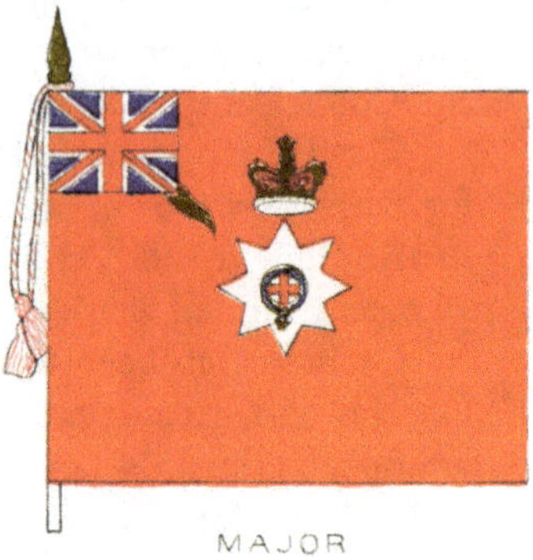

MAJOR

QUEENS COLOUR 1ST BATTN 1893.

N.R.Wilkinson del. A.D. Innes & Co London Mintern Bros Chromo.

CHAPTER XII.

THE END OF THE RUSSIAN WAR.

Home events during the war—Sympathy of Her Majesty with her Crimean soldiers—Badges of distinction added to the Colours—Inactivity of the Allies after the fall of Sevastopol—Expeditions against the Russian coast—Sir W. Codrington succeeds Sir J. Simpson as Commander of the Forces—The winter 1855-56—Negotiations for a peace, which is concluded, March 30th—Events after the cessation of hostilities—A British cemetery in the Crimea—Embarkation and return home—The Crimean Guards Brigade at Aldershot; visit of Her Majesty the Queen—Move to London, and cordial reception there—Distribution of the Victoria Cross—Summary of events connected with the war—Losses—Appointment of H.R.H. the Duke of Cambridge as Commander-in-Chief, and of Major-General Lord Rokeby to command the Brigade of Guards.

THE details of the great struggle in the Crimea have necessarily occupied so much of the space of the last few chapters, that there has been little opportunity to allude to the occurrences connected with the Regiment which took place at home during this eventful period. It will therefore be well to pause in the narrative of the war, and to devote a few lines to that subject.

As soon as the Guards Brigade started for Malta in February, 1854, the public duties in London were reduced; and later in the year, when the requirements of active service necessitated a still further reduction, they were fixed at 1 Captain, 4 Subalterns, 9 sergeants, 10 corporals, 6 drummers, and 144 men, to furnish the Queen's Guard, Buckingham Palace, the Tylt, the British Museum, and the Magazine Guards; and at 1 Subaltern, 2 sergeants, 2 corporals, and 20 men, to furnish the Bank piquet.*

The principal duty of the home Battalion was naturally at this moment to train and supply men to the 1st Battalion in the Crimea, and we have already seen something of the quality of the drafts that were sent out to the East.† But as the ordinary

---

* *Brigade Order*, Nov. 23, 1854. † See Appendix, No. XI.

recruiting was not sufficient to maintain the forces at the seat of war in a proper state of efficiency, the militia—the true reserve of the British army at that time—was called upon to perform its functions in the emergency. Not only was a portion of the militia embodied and employed as garrisons in those places where regular troops were not available, but volunteers were obtained from its ranks to fill up the gaps which the war created in the active army fighting before Sevastopol. In this manner men of good physique and trained to military service were obtained, and were drafted into the regular army. In April, 1854, the Non-commissioned officers and men of the Brigade told off to assist in training militia regiments, were ordered to use their best exertions to induce men to volunteer for their Regiments.* In December, 1854, Officers of the Brigade were employed to superintend recruiting from the militia. Men were also obtained from the Irish Constabulary, and it was settled, December 18, 1855, that volunteers to the Guards from that corps might reckon their previous police service as military service.

It appears that there was an intention to form a Brigade depôt at Malta, in March, 1855, the companies to form which, were to be borne on the strength of the Battalions in the East, from the date of embarkation. But this plan was not carried out, and the home Battalions remained all through the war with twelve companies, as against eight companies belonging to the service Battalions; the drafts to the latter were always furnished direct from London.

As soon as the three Guards Battalions had left England, the other four were stationed in the West-end (St. George's, Portman Street, and Wellington barracks), and there they remained (subject to the ordinary half-yearly change of quarters) until January, 1855, when the Tower was again garrisoned by the Brigade. In May, room had to be found for 500 men of the Line passing through London, and a portion of the 2nd Battalion Grenadier Guards then in Wellington barracks, were put into billets in Westminster, for four days. This probably is the last time that any men of the Brigade have been billeted in London. On the 13th of June, the 2nd Battalions of the Coldstream and Scots Fusilier Guards proceeded to Aldershot Camp, then newly established, until the 27th of August, when they were relieved by the two Grenadier

* *Brigade Order*, April 1, 1854.

Battalions, left in England.* The latter remained there until the middle of December, when Windsor was again occupied by a Battalion of Guards, and there were then less than three Battalions of the Brigade stationed in the West-end, the head-quarters of one being in the Tower, with a detachment only, in Portman Street.† During the absence of a portion of the Brigade in Aldershot, the Depôt of the 66th Regiment furnished a part of the public duties in London; but at the end of August, most of these men having been moved out of town, temporary reductions in the duties were made (September 16th, and October 9th) until the return of the Grenadiers.

It has been already stated that the Emperor Napoleon visited England in April, 1855, where a cordial welcome awaited him and the Empress, who accompanied him. A detachment of a Subaltern and 25 men from each Battalion, under a Captain and Lieutenant-Colonel of the 2nd Grenadier Guards (with the Queen's Colour belonging to that Battalion), proceeded to Windsor on the 14th, and were stationed there until the 19th, during the period of the French Sovereign's visit to the Queen. Numerous Guards of Honour attended upon His Majesty, two of which were found by the 2nd Battalion, both at Bricklayers' Arms Station, on the 16th and 21st, on the arrival at, and departure from London, of the Imperial guest. On the 19th, the Emperor went to Guildhall, and the streets were lined by the two Grenadier Battalions as he went to the City and returned back to the West-end. Another Royal visit of one of Her Majesty's Allies took place on the 1st of December, when the King of Sardinia, Victor Emanuel, arrived in London, and went to Windsor. Of the Guards of Honour furnished upon that occasion, the Coldstream found four—two on the arrival of the King at Bricklayers' Arms Station and at Paddington Station on the 1st, one at Lord Palmerston's house in Piccadilly on the 4th, and one at Bricklayers' Arms Station on the 6th, in the early morning.

The dress of the Brigade occupied the attention of the military authorities at this time. The white summer trousers were exchanged

* The following order was published upon this occasion, Aug. 27th: "The Major-General Commanding, [at Aldershot] desires to express to the Commanding Officer his sense of the general good conduct of the Battalion and the attention they have paid to their drill during the time they have been under his command, and to request them to accept his thanks accordingly."

† For stations occupied by the Coldstream, see Appendix No. XV.

for another pattern made of a light grey stuff; the coatee was done away with, and the tunic was introduced (April, 1855). Epaulettes ceased to be worn, and thereby the badge of the Rose, still worn by the men, disappeared from the uniform of the Officers of the Coldstream. The tunic at first was a double-breasted garment, but a year later (March, 1856), when Officers required new red coats, they were ordered to supply themselves with single-breasted tunics, such as are still worn in the Brigade. The bearskin caps had been cut down early in 1854, to nine inches in height, and the plume was not to exceed six inches. Also, by an order dated October 7, 1854, peaks to caps were to be discontinued by sergeants, and were only to be worn by the Sergeant-Major, the Quartermaster-Sergeant, the Armourer Sergeant, the Regimental Clerk, the Drill Sergeants, and the Drum Major—a custom which still prevails in the Brigade.

A curious means taken to test beer may be gathered from the following Brigade Order, dated April 18, 1854, and shows the practical, though perhaps unscientific, manner in which our predecessors went to work when they wished to ascertain a matter of sanitary importance to the men :—

"Each Battalion will send to Wellington barracks on Thursday morning, to receive from the Quartermaster of the Scots Fusilier Guards some beer, which is to be delivered to six sergeants, who must undertake not to taste any other malt liquor during the time (10 days) they will be supplied with it, the object being to test its wholesome qualities. The Field Officer requests to be furnished with a report from each Battalion at the expiration of the period specified above."

We find that a few days previous to this order (April 13th), a committee of Officers was appointed to consider the question of the general introduction of gas into barracks.

Later (July 17, 1855), a Field Officer of the Brigade (Lieut.-Colonel Wood, Grenadier Guards) was sent to the "end of Commercial Road, Pimlico, near to the projected Chelsea Bridge, there to view, in conjunction with a Medical Officer, a site for a barrack." It will be seen that this was the first step taken to construct Chelsea barracks, which, when completed, removed the Foot Guards from the cramped quarters in Portman Street and St. George's barracks, which they occupied at this time.

The Enfield rifle (pattern 1853), issued, as we have seen, to the Brigade in the Crimea at the end of August, 1855, was served out to the Guards Battalions on home service on the 26th of October of the same year. Nine hundred and one stand constituted the armament of the 2nd Battalion, and "on their receipt the smooth bore now in possession, including the sergeants' fusils, are to be returned into the Ordnance stores."

It is well known to all her subjects that Her Majesty the Queen followed the varying fortunes of the Russian war with the utmost attention, interest, and concern; and that to none was her warm sympathy more heartily and graciously expressed than to her gallant army, who, amid unparalleled privations and difficulties, maintained intact the glory of the British Crown and of the country. Frequently did Her Majesty, surrounded by the Royal Family at Buckingham Palace, personally see such of her wounded soldiers as were able to be brought into the presence of their Sovereign, and there praise them for their merit, and condole with them on their sufferings. This honour was freely bestowed on the men of the Brigade, and on many occasions the Commanding Officers of Regiments were ordered to furnish lists of Guardsmen who were well enough to participate in it. In 1855, the Queen's birthday was celebrated on the 18th of May, and on the Horse Guards parade, Her Majesty presented medals for service in the Crimea to all Officers and to three Non-commissioned officers and twenty privates per Regiment of the Brigade, entitled to receive them. Next day the following Order was published:—

"The Field Officer in Brigade Waiting is commanded to express to the Officers and soldiers of the Brigade of Guards who were present yesterday at the ceremony of the presentation of medals, Her Majesty's solicitude as to whether they have suffered from the effort which evidently many of them made, at the cost of much suffering and inconvenience, and requests that Officers Commanding Battalions will make the necessary inquiries, and forward the result of them to him with as little delay as possible."

When the fall of Sevastopol was known in England, there was much rejoicing that the Allied arms had captured the enemy's stronghold and great naval arsenal in the Black Sea. But hostilities were not at an end, nor was an immediate peace in prospect. Nevertheless, certain distinct stages in the war were concluded, and victory had more than once smiled upon our standards. A General Order, therefore, was issued on the 16th of October, 1855, giving authority to inscribe the words "Alma," "Inkerman," "Balaklava," and "Sevastopol" upon the Colours of the regiments taking part in these actions and in the siege. On the following December 28th the three badges of distinction, "Alma," "Inkerman," and "Sevastopol," were inscribed upon the Colours of the Regiments of Foot Guards.

The Allied armies, having captured the fortress that so long resisted their skill and courage, found themselves placed in considerable embarrassment. The question naturally arose as to what should now be done. But that question was not readily answered, because no steps had been taken beforehand to decide it. The northern side was still held by the Russians, and their forces there were closely united to their field army, which occupied defensive positions on the Mackenzie heights. The undertaking to clear the two banks of the Sevastopol roadstead of the enemy, and to drive him out of the peninsula had the outward appearance of a difficult operation, and no measures had been concerted to proceed with it.* The Anglo-French armies made no attempt to follow up the victory of the 8th of September, but hung listlessly on the ground they had won, deliberating as to their future movements, and doing nothing to secure success. In short, though the capture effected brought prestige to the besiegers, and placed in their power the fleet, the docks, and most of the forts at Sevastopol, no further advantage seemed likely to accrue, and we found ourselves almost as far as ever from exercising a coercive control over the councils of the Tsar.

As a matter of fact, General Gortchakoff was by no means as strong as he was supposed to be, and could scarcely have maintained himself in the Crimea had he been vigorously attacked by the brave forces that had invariably beaten his troops whenever they met them in the field. His position, indeed, was very precarious—so precarious was it, in the opinion of his own Government, that he had the fullest liberty given him to evacuate the peninsula if he found it necessary to do so. But he was not obliged to resort to this painful and humiliating measure; for the Allies never pressed him. Far from making any effort to dislodge him, or from even manœuvring against him to ascertain how he was

* It will be remembered that the north side of Sevastopol commands the south side. The capture of the former would have jeopardized the latter; but the fall of the south side left the other intact.

circumstanced, they kept almost entirely aloof, and they left him alone in peace.

The British Government, sincerely desirous to achieve a more important success than had been gained, urged that the war should be vigorously prosecuted. They poured troops into the Crimea, so that our army there in November numbered as much as 51,000 men, of whom 4000 were cavalry, and 96 guns, besides a Turkish legion, raised by England, of 20,000, and a German legion of 10,000. The transport was now completely re-organized, and the medical service in good working order; and, added to this, the fleet, always overwhelmingly strong, was more powerful than it had been before.* A campaign was now at last possible against an enfeebled enemy under far better conditions than had been the case in the same season of the previous year, when we invaded Russia, whose resources then were practically unimpaired. The English people, also, were at one with their Government, and were anxious for a vigorous prosecution of hostilities, if the enemy could not be otherwise subjugated. But they and their rulers could effect nothing, for our allies would not move, and above all things was it necessary that the alliance should be cordially maintained. Hence, our political relations with the French interfered with our national interests, and controlled our military operations against the enemy: and, as has happened in the past, and will again happen, in wars conducted by several nations, the common foe reaped no inconsiderable benefit by having a confederation of Powers ranged against him.

In short, the fall of Sevastopol practically brought the drama to a close. The efforts of the besiegers to take the town, after they had allowed it to grow into military importance, seemed to exhaust the further zeal and ardour of the Emperor Napoleon: it was impossible for us to re-kindle them into activity. Nor could Marshal Pélissier be roused to action; his enthusiasm for the success of the struggle had now grown cold, and his former energy had evaporated. His troops had taken the Malakoff, the key of the fortress, and, proud of their victory over the enemy, the French

---

* Hamley, *War in the Crimea*, p. 296. These forces continued to increase, and by Christmas, 1855, the British army in the Crimea was still more numerous than is stated in the text, and there were 120 guns; besides, a reserve force was collected at Aldershot, and amounted to over 18,000 men in April, 1856; at which time it appears we had in the East about 60,000 men (excluding transport, etc.).

were content with the glory their army had achieved. So, also, had the Emperor gained all he wanted to secure; and, the war having established him firmly on the throne, he was anxious for peace with Russia, and for some new and more profitable adventure.

And yet something had to be done to preserve the semblance of war. The Turks, already at Eupatoria, were therefore reinforced, and some successful reconnaissances were effected in that important quarter: operations were, moreover, continued on the shores of the Sea of Azof, with advantage to the Allies; and lastly, after threatening Odessa, a descent was made upon Kinburn and its neighbourhood. These desultory expeditions served to keep up the illusion that the fight was still earnestly maintained. But they led to no permanent results, and they need not be further described; because, under the circumstances and conditions in which they were undertaken, they only exercised, and could only exercise, a very minor influence on the war. Omar Pasha had at last (end of September) been allowed to take a portion of his hitherto inactive army—chained for no useful purpose in the Crimea—to attempt the relief of Kars, a Turkish stronghold in Armenia, then besieged by the Russians. He was only barely supported by the Allies, if indeed he was not hampered by them, and he failed to accomplish his object. Kars fell on the 28th of November, and the victory gained there by the enemy compensated him not a little for the reverse he sustained at Sevastopol. The French might view the incident with unconcern; but to England, having vital interests in Asia, the loss of this place was of far greater moment.*

Officers of the 1st Battalion were posted to companies as follows on December 17, 1855:—

No. 1 Company: Lieut.-Colonel Hon. P. Feilding; Captain H. Jervoise; Lieutenant G. Rose.
No. 2 Company: Lieut.-Colonel C. Burdett; Captain Whitshed; Lieutenant Hall.
No. 3 Company: Major Thellusson; Captain Blackett; Lieutenant Adair.
No. 4 Company: Captain Reeve; Captain Heneage.
No. 5 Company: Captain Hon. H. Byng; Lieutenant A. Lambton.

* While this important event was taking place, the bulk of the British army was engaged in improving the communications of the Chersonese—a work which cost us much labour and was of little use to us, though shortly afterwards, when the peace was signed, it was of great value to the Russians.

No. 6 Company: Lieut.-Colonel F. Newdigate; Captain Lord E. Cecil Lieutenant Lane.
No. 7 Company: Major Le Couteur; Lieutenant Hon. W. Edwardes.
No. 8 Company: Lieut.-Colonel Lord Dunkellin; Captain Hon. W. Feilding; Lieutenant Wigram.

Colonel Gordon Drummond still commanded the Battalion, while Major Lord Bingham was appointed Adjutant about that time (21st December).

The Brigade remained on the upland of the Chersonese, with the bulk of the British army, guarding the Karabelnaya, constructing roads, drilling, practising musketry, and performing the ordinary duties of camp life.* A tent had been converted into a Crimean Guards Club, "where we used all to meet, read the newspapers, talk, and smoke," and there the first anniversary of the battle of the Alma was duly celebrated by a dinner. There were races at Kamara on the 17th of October, shooting expeditions, and other expedients to pass away the time. Occasionally an interchange of shots took place across the roadstead that divided the hostile armies; but they were rather signals to show that the war had not yet officially come to an end than anything else, and they never produced any important results.

The monotony of these proceedings during an inactive campaign, and in the presence of an unsubdued enemy, was one day electrified into new life by a terrible explosion that occurred in the lines of our allies. On the 15th of November, 100,000 lbs. of powder blew up in the French artillery park, and kindled a fire that placed one of the principal English magazines in imminent danger. Looking from the British camp, a huge column of smoke was seen to ascend high in the air; it then spread out like a tree,† broke, and sent down a shower of iron, stones, rubbish, broken side arms, guns, gun carriages, and every conceivable appurtenance of war; shells burst in all directions, and other combustibles added their flames

---

* The duties in the Karabelnaya district were composed of seven guards, amounting all told to 2 Captains, 4 Subalterns, 12 sergeants, 2 drummers, 12 corporals, and 249 privates.

At first the Brigade supplied 500 men daily for road-making; but later in the year these parties were frequently double that strength. It also furnished large fatigue-parties of several hundred men to bring up huts from Balaklava, wherein to lodge the troops.

Musketry was carried out with considerable energy during the winter months, and special orders on the subject were issued by the Commander of the Forces.

† Pliny describes the great eruption of Vesuvius which overwhelmed Pompeii, as having at first the appearance of a gigantic pine tree emerging from the volcano.

to the conflagration. Happily the fire was got under without further mishap, but many Officers and men, mostly French, were killed and wounded.*

On the 11th of November, a few days before the accident just mentioned, General Sir James Simpson having resigned, Lieut.-General Sir William Codrington was appointed by Her Majesty the Queen to the chief command of the British army in the Crimea. This Officer, a Coldstreamer, served in the Regiment from 1823 until July, 1854, when, as junior Acting-Major of the 1st Battalion, and present with it in Bulgaria, he was promoted Major-General. Remaining at the seat of war, he very soon obtained the command of a brigade in the Light Division, as has been previously recorded. At the head of this gallant brigade he greatly distinguished himself at the battle of the Alma by his cool and intrepid bearing; the part he played at Inkerman has already been mentioned. He was with the army from start to finish of the war against Russia, being present on the upland before Sevastopol throughout the whole of the first severe winter (except once for the space of a very few days, when on the sick list), and engaged in all the fights (usually in executive command) that took place round and in the Redan. Few Officers in the British army were more exposed to the dangers and the privations of this war than Sir W. Codrington, and he survived both without a scratch and without even a temporary illness of a serious nature.

The second winter was now approaching, and hostilities, while

---

* Nolan, ii. 638. Assistant-Surgeons Wyatt and Trotter of the Coldstream gained the special thanks of the French authorities for the assistance they afforded to the wounded upon that occasion.

It appears that our troops had cause to be somewhat accustomed to this class of misadventure. Under date Nov. 14th, Colonel Tower writes, "On guard in the Redan; as I was walking about inside the works, I met two of my men who were off duty, with pipes in their mouths, wandering about. I cautioned them, and told them there had been many accidents. A short time afterwards my sergeant came rushing up to me with all his eyebrows singed off, to tell me Goodram and Bates (the two men) were buried alive in a Russian magazine. I got Engineers, and we dug for a long time in smoking ruins; at last we came upon them, burnt to cinders, and hardly a bone in either of their bodies that was not broken. . . . They died soon after we got them out. Goodram was a most gallant fellow, and would have got the V.C. for going into the Redan with the assaulting party on the 8th of September. They had trodden on a fougasse left, probably on purpose, by the enemy when he evacuated."

Private Goodram, it appears, slipped out of camp at night, September 7th–8th, crept close to the Redan in the dark, and joined the leading files of the storming party. He greatly distinguished himself during the assault, and is said to have been the first man to reach the parapet of the work.

they showed no sign of coming to an end, still languished. But it was passed under very different conditions to those which prevailed during the terrible season that overtook us in 1854–55. The autumn was fine and enjoyable, and the real cold weather was not felt until the end of November. We were then quite prepared for it, so that the army did not suffer. The health of the troops was excellent, and for some time prior to the end of 1855 there was such an abundance of every kind of supply, that scarcely any requirement remained for the Medical Officer in charge to suggest.

"During the six months which ensued from the commencement of January, 1856, until the period of embarkation from the Crimea to England, the condition of the men, in every respect, both as regards amount of sickness and duties performed, was so much allied to a similar period passed in any garrison, that a detailed notice would be useless, except so far as it would display an almost unprecedented amount of good health, compared with a period passed at any of the out-quarters at which the Guards are stationed in England, and far better than obtains in the close and confined barracks of the Metropolis." *

Both in respect to the comfort and the good administration which our men now enjoyed, we contrasted very favourably with the French, who, though they were better off than we had been in the winter 1854–55, did not improve their services as we had done; they consequently fared worse than the British army in the cold season of 1855–56, and suffered considerably in the spring of 1856.

When Sevastopol was in the power of the Allies, they destroyed its value, as much as they could, as a naval arsenal, and thus the docks, all the forts in their possession, the barracks, and the aqueducts that led into the town were demolished. These tasks were accomplished in the mid-winter.

On the 1st of March the sixth and last draft reached the 1st Battalion, consisting of 8 Officers and 263 men, whose average age and service amounted to $23\frac{1}{2}$ years and 18 months respectively. The men were stout and robust, and, like the preceding draft, well adapted for all the possible requirements of active service.†

* Wyatt, 91. Written in 1858, before the small barracks in Portman Street and St. George's ceased each to contain the head-quarters and the main portion of a Guards Battalion.
† *Ibid*, p. 91.

Next day Officers were posted to companies as follows:—

No. 1 Company: Lieut.-Colonel Hon. P. Feilding; Captains Tower; Jervoise; Lieutenant Rose.
No. 2 Company: Lieut.-Colonel Burdett; Major Crawley; Captain Hall.
No. 3 Company: Lieut.-Colonel Newdigate; Captain Hon. H. Byng; Lieutenant A. Adair.
No. 4 Company: Lieut.-Colonel Reeve; Captain Lord E. Cecil; Lieutenant Sir W. Forbes, Bart.
No. 5 Company: Lieut.-Colonel Dawkins; Captain G. FitzRoy; Lieutenant S. Mainwaring.
No. 6 Company: Captain J. Caulfeild; Lieutenants W. Seymour; Hon. E. Legge.
No. 7 Company: Majors Armytage; Thellusson; Lieutenant Hon. W. Edwardes.
No. 8 Company: Lieut.-Colonel Lord Dunkellin; Captain Hon. W. Feilding; Lieutenant Lane.

Ever since the capture of Sevastopol, the work of diplomacy had again been active at Vienna; and with some additional advantage this time to the Russians, for it succeeded in partially alienating the Emperor Napoleon from the alliance. In form that Sovereign remained true to Great Britain; but it was clear that, as far as he was concerned, the war was at an end, and that the Tsar had no more to fear from his animosity. This facilitated the action of Austria, and under her mediation a project of peace was accepted by the Russians on the 16th of January, 1856. A month later a Conference sat in Paris to settle an immediate armistice and to conclude a general peace. The Treaty of Paris was accordingly signed on the 30th of March, and it put an end finally to the war that had lasted two years. By the terms of this agreement, which yielded back to their original Sovereigns all territories in possession of either of the combatants, an important article was included, viz. the Black Sea was neutralized, its waters and ports were "formally and in perpetuity interdicted to the flag of war," naval arsenals on its shores were not to be maintained, and ships of war were forbidden to enter or pass through the Dardanelles and the Bosphorus. It is of interest to record the fact that this article, to gain which England had expended so much blood and treasure, was infringed by Russia in 1859, who, with no one to interfere in the neutralized sea, blockaded the Circassian coast, and at last overcame the stubborn resistance of the liberty-loving tribes of the Caucasus that for so long checked her progress in Central Asia. Having accomplished this work, she then boldly repudiated the article, with scarcely a protest on our part, in the beginning of 1871, when we were at peace with her, just fifteen years after the conclusion of the Crimean war; and again she prepared her forces to effect another development of the Eastern Question.

On the 2nd of April official tidings of peace were communicated to the several armies engaged in the struggle, by a salute fired upon the upland. Thenceforward the contending forces, drawn together by that mutual respect and esteem with which brave men regard one another, looked upon each other as friends, and all traces of hostility vanished as if by magic. British and Russian soldiers were to be seen in scores on their respective sides of the Tchernaya, conversing as best as they could, and exchanging presents. The thoughts of our men, however, were now naturally turned towards home; but two months were still to elapse before the Coldstream quitted the soil on which they had for so long lived and suffered, and where their military virtues had been so conspicuously displayed.

About this time the French appointed a special mission to inquire into the relative sanitary conditions of the English and French field hospitals in the East, and Assistant-Surgeon Wyatt was sent to aid in the investigation made.

"The whole of the Field hospitals," says Dr. Wyatt, "were inspected, and the most satisfactory conclusions drawn by the Inspector in favour of the detached system of Regimental hospitals in the English army, compared with the congregated ambulance arrangements of the French; he was very favourably impressed with the Field hospitals of the Guards, which he examined most minutely in all their details."

Added to this, British Sanitary Commissioners made an inspection of the hospitals in the Crimea, and it is with satisfaction that portions of two paragraphs of the report are recorded here.

"The best example of a marquee hospital was that belonging to the Guards, after they went to the front in June 1855. . . . Among the best examples of a winter camp which came under the notice of the Commission during the winter of 1855, was that of the Brigade of Guards on the plateau, in laying out of which great care and intelligence had evidently been bestowed. There was plenty of space for allowing the air to circulate;

the arrangement of the huts was good, the ground was well trenched and drained, and many of the huts were raised on stone foundations."*

Shortly before the conclusion of the peace an event of great interest to our allies took place (March 16, 1856)—the birth of a son to the French Emperor, an heir destined, it was confidently hoped, to preserve the Napoleonic dynasty, and to hand down to posterity the glory of the great founder of the Imperial House. Rejoicings were unstinted in Paris and in London; and in the former place, where the peace Conference was sitting, the representatives of all the Powers, not excluding Russia, added their congratulations to the happy Emperor. Nor was the auspicious occasion forgotten in the Crimea, where it was celebrated by a ball on the 1st of April.† And yet how fickle is Fortune, and how she decided against this unfortunate prince! He did not ascend the French throne, and was but fourteen years of age when he was condemned to fly from his native land, never to return to it. Napoleon III., overwhelmed by the united might of Germany, was driven from his capital in 1870, and a few years later he ended his days an exile in England. Living in our midst, his son, the Prince Imperial, served in the British army, and lost his life, when only twenty-three years of age, in a small skirmish in South Africa; and thus he died before any new phase among his unstable countrymen could recall him in the character of a pretender to the French Imperial crown. *Sic transit gloria mundi.*

The interval between the conclusion of hostilities and the departure from the Crimea was eagerly seized by many to visit their late enemy and the places of interest to be found in the peninsula. A few extracts from the diary of Colonel Tower will perhaps give a fair example of these experiences.

"*April 8th.*—Rode to Mackenzie Farm to visit the Russian camp; the Russian Officers were extremely civil, and showed us all round their camp. The men lived in excavations in the ground, like cellars, two or three steps down, with a roof of branches or anything to make it waterproof;

* Wyatt, 92, 93.
† "A ball will be given to-morrow, in honour of the birth of the Imperial Prince, by the Officers of the 1st Division of the Corps of Reserve French army, in their camp on the Woronzoff road, near the Sardinian army, to which all the English ladies and the Officers of the English army are invited. Officers attending the ball will appear in full dress uniform, but without swords and spurs" (*Head-Quarter Memo.*, March 31, 1856).

fusty little holes, and the usual Russian soldier's smell. This is very peculiar, the tan of the leather is the chief ingredient, and the sour smell of the black bread is another powerful ingredient. They are decidedly unclean in their persons, and never appear without their long brown coats and high boots. . . . They seem to be always fetching water in their tins. The Officers seemed as pleased as we were that the war was over, and regaled us with whatever liquor they had, generally champagne.

"*April 13th.*—We all went in a body to the Mackenzie heights [*i.e.* with Sir W. Codrington and his Staff], and were received by Luders [the Russian General then in command] and his Staff. A capital luncheon with every sort of delicacy was prepared for us, Pélissier and his Staff also being there. About 10,000 Ruskis passed us in review, as they were being sent away northwards. It was very interesting, as we saw specimens of almost every branch of the Russian service. . . . A great many Officers of the Guards who had volunteered for service in the Crimea, marched past with the regiments to which they were attached; also cavalry Officers with their sabres and spurs in the infantry. They point their toes as they march past, like the Prussians.

"*April 17th.*—Luders returned Codrington's and Pélissier's visit, and came down to have an exhibition of the English and French armies. We were in line of contiguous columns, nearly 30,000 strong and 86 guns (no cavalry), all in the most perfect order; I never saw anything so well as our troops looked. The men had their best clothing on; regiments all made up to their full strength; artillery with new harness, horses in first-rate condition. I saw one of the Russian Generals separate himself from the Staff, and ride down between the Grenadiers and our Battalion, to see the size of the men and depth of the column; he kept muttering exclamations of surprise and admiration, and well he might. I think 30,000 puts it under the mark. The French were in line with big intervals between their regiments, which made a line extending almost to Kamiesh, and it must have been very tiring riding all along such a line, but I suppose they thought it would make them appear stronger. It would have looked much better if they had also been in contiguous columns.

"*April 25th.*—Rode with General Craufurd [Commanding Guards Brigade] and Percy Feilding to the Alma; we got there easily in the mid-day, and spent all the afternoon stepping the distance from the river to the epaulment, clambering up where the French ascended the steep bank, looking for Horace Cust's grave. We found the field of battle exactly as we left it, not a spade was put into the ground in the valley, not a vine cultivated or a house rebuilt. It had quite the appearance of a 'Field of blood.

"Next day, off at daybreak to Bakshiserai—a good big town, full of soldiers and Officers who were quartered there. We went by appointment to our friend Trubetskoi, who had a very good house and put us up famously; he introduced us to a set of Ruski Officers, who were the most rollicking and debauched set I ever came across. They had a tremendous orgie in our honour, drinking, singing, etc.; they mix every liquor they can get together. . . . Percy and I rode back to our camp that evening (the 27th), after taking leave of Trubetskoi, who really did all he could to make our expedition pleasant."

So the days passed on, varied, besides duty, by *fêtes* of pleasure, excursions, cricket matches, and races, until the embarkation took place, and the Battalion returned to England. But, prior to this event, a solemn duty was performed, and a resting-place for the dead was prepared, where the remains of those who had fallen in the war might be laid. A site selected on Cathcart's Hill was enclosed, and a portion of it was devoted as a burial place for the Brigade. A number of masons from the Guards were employed, early in April, to build a suitable wall, and fatigue parties were furnished to finish the work. The bodies of most of the Officers and others, killed at Inkerman and elsewhere in the vicinity, were exhumed, and reverently interred in the new cemetery. The masses of the dead, however, could not then be removed there, so, instead, the places where they lay were carefully fenced in. But this arrangement did not last, because the enclosures became dilapidated through time, and the graves were liable to be desecrated. A few years ago this was remedied, and the bones of the departed, together with the monuments erected by the care of their comrades, were taken to Cathcart's Hill, and are there preserved in perpetuity within the cemetery which had been first laid out in the spring of 1856.

The welcome news that the Battalion was to be sent back home, published on the 3rd of June, was preceded by a Divisional Order of Lieut.-General Lord Rokeby, commanding the First Division, dated the 2nd:—

"As the embarkation of the various regiments will shortly cause the dissolution of the First Division, Lieut.-General Lord Rokeby wishes to permit himself the pleasure of expressing the grateful thanks he entertains of the support he has received from all ranks during the period he has had the honour of being in command. Every one has at all times endeavoured to meet his wishes, and the Lieut.-General confidently believes that the record of the army will afford proof of the good results which have emanated from the cheerful spirit of obedience which has characterized the conduct of the noble regiments and corps of which it was formed. The state of the hospitals and the general health of the regiments, under God's blessing, speaks for and forms the best reward of the Divisional and Regimental Medical Staff, and the Lieut.-General requests Dr. Williams, and all junior to him in that Department, to accept their full share of the thanks he presumes to offer to all ranks, and the wishes he forms for their prosperity and happiness."

On the 4th of June, the Battalion embarked at Kamiesh Bay, and sailed from the Crimea in H.M.S. *Agamemnon*, arriving at Spithead on the 28th, whence they were sent by train to Aldershot camp. They had been absent on foreign service for 2 years and 126 days (856 days), which time was passed in the following places: Malta, 48 days; Scutari, 45 days; Bulgaria, 75 days; Crimea, 627 days; and at sea 61 days.

The strength on embarkation from England (February, 1854) had been 35 Officers and 919 Non-commissioned officers and men, and during the period of duty in the East, reinforcements amounting to 1141 men were sent out in six drafts, making a total of 2060 men who served in the war. The number of primary admissions from all causes into the Regimental and general hospitals was 3101, of which 2785 were from disease, 243 from wounds, and 73 from accidental injuries. Death reduced the Battalion by 699 men, of whom 81 were killed in action, 54 died from wounds, and 564 from disease: 65 men were invalided home by wounds, and 187 by disease; and 111 men were finally discharged the army on account of disabilities contracted during active service—59 from the effects of wounds, and 52 from those of disease.* Total loss of Non-commissioned officers and men, 810. Ninety-one Coldstream Officers were employed in the Russian war.† Of these, nine were killed in action, viz. Lieut.-Colonels Hon. T. Vesey Dawson and J. C. Cowell, Captains L. D. Mac-Kinnon, H. M. Bouverie, Hon. G. Eliot, Horace Cust, and F. Ramsden, and Lieutenants E. A. Disbrowe and C. H. Greville; one died of wounds, viz. Captain Hon. R. Drummond; three died of disease, viz. Lieut.-Colonel Hon. R. Boyle, Colonel Trevelyan, and Captain

---

* Wyatt, 97; see Appendix No. XII. 3.

† Five more were transferred to the Regiment (during the war) after they had left the Crimea, viz. Majors Hon. W. Boyle, Conolly, V.C., and Maxse (the two last wounded), Captain Hedworth Jolliffe, and Lieutenant W. Stirling. The latter fought against the Russians in the Navy, as did also Lieutenant W. F. Seymour (who, however, joined the Coldstream in the Crimea). Naval-Cadet J. B. Sterling, moreover, served in the war, but he was not gazetted to the Regiment till 1861.

Hylton Jolliffe: total loss of Officers, thirteen. Seven were wounded, viz. Major-General Sir H. Bentinck, Colonel Hon. G. Upton, Lieut.-Colonels J. Halkett, Lord C. FitzRoy, Hon. P. Feilding, and C. Baring, and Captain Hon. W. Amherst. Seventeen were invalided on account of illness, of whom seven were unable to return to the Crimea. Several were obliged to leave the seat of war on promotion, and altogether twenty-two seem to have done duty at least twice before Sevastopol.

The Crimean Guards Brigade, concentrated at Aldershot, remained there a few days, and during that time the Battalion was inspected by the Colonel of the Regiment, Field-Marshal Earl of Strafford, whose presence, as a Coldstream Officer, formed a connecting link between the glories of Waterloo and those achieved in the Russian war.

On the 8th July, Her Majesty the Queen appeared at the camp, and was received by the troops quartered there who had lately come back from the East. After the march past, a representative body of Officers and men, who had been under fire, from each regiment, was formed up in a hollow square round Her Majesty's carriage, to listen to the gracious address of welcome pronounced by the Queen herself to her brave men just returned from an arduous and protracted war. The address was thus published in Orders:—

"Officers, Non-commissioned officers, and soldiers, I wish personally to convey through you, to the regiments assembled here this day, my hearty welcome on their return to England in health and full efficiency. Say to them, that I have watched anxiously over the difficulties and hardships which they have so nobly borne, that I have mourned with deep sorrow for the brave men who have fallen for their country, and that I have felt proud of that valour which with their gallant allies they have displayed on every field. I thank God that your dangers are over, whilst the glory of your deeds remains. But I know that, should your services be again required, you will be animated by the same devotion which in the Crimea has rendered you invincible."

Colonel Tower, who was present upon this interesting occasion, throws light upon it by recording in his diary that Her Majesty "made us a capital speech, full of gratitude and good feeling, and got quite eloquent; at last she quite broke down, and burst into tears when she talked of the poor fellows that were not there to receive her thanks." He adds, "If she had seen us in the trenches in July, 1855, or in Bulgaria in July, 1854, she would not have recognized her Brigade; we were now [July, 1856] all so nice and smart."

Next day the Crimean Battalions of the Brigade, 3200 strong, left Aldershot to make their public entry into London. Parading at 5.30 in the morning, they were conveyed to Nine Elms Station by train, where the three bands met them. The day was observed as a general holiday; the route taken was densely thronged by an enthusiastic crowd; the houses were decorated with flags; and the church bells rang out a joyous peal of welcome. On passing the Horse Guards, H.R.H. the Duke of Cambridge met the column, and as soon as the men perceived their former Commander, who had been with them at the hard-fought battle of Inkerman, "their stern gravity gave way, and they honoured him with the heartiest cheers." As they defiled through Buckingham Palace, the Queen, accompanied by the Royal children, by her mother the Duchess of Kent, her uncle the King of the Belgians, and by other illustrious persons, came to the balcony to greet her gallant troops with her gracious presence. Arrived in Hyde Park, they found the other four Guards Battalions, with the Colonels at the head of their respective Regiments, formed up in a line of quarter columns, facing Park Lane, with sufficient interval between them to receive the Crimean Battalions in their proper places on parade; and while the latter marched into their positions under the orders of Generals Lord Rokeby and Craufurd, their comrades presented arms. The three Regiments, now complete, were then handed over to their respective Colonels, to H.R.H. the Prince Consort, Field-Marshal Earl of Strafford (seated in a carriage, because he was too infirm to head his Regiment on horseback), and H.R.H. the Duke of Cambridge. The Prince Consort having proceeded to join Her Majesty, the Duke of Cambridge assumed command of the whole. On the arrival of the Queen the bands played the national anthem, and the seven Battalions marched past Her Majesty, to the air, "See, the Conquering Hero comes." The Brigade then advanced in Review order to the flagstaff; another Royal salute was given; and the pageant came to an end.

On the same day the following Brigade Order was issued:—

"H.R.H. the Duke of Cambridge has received Her Majesty's Command, through the Adjutant-General, to express to the Brigade of Guards Her Majesty's entire satisfaction and approval of the appearance of the Brigade this day in the Park, which he requests the Commanding Officers of Regiments to make known to the several Battalions under their command."

After the review, a complete change of quarters took place in the Brigade: The 1st Grenadiers proceeded to Aldershot, 2nd Grenadiers to Dublin (which was again occupied by the Household troops), 3rd Grenadiers to Wellington barracks, Buckingham Palace, the Magazine, and Kensington; 1st Coldstream to the Tower and St. John's Wood, 2nd Coldstream to Windsor; 1st Scots Fusilier Guards to Portman Street and St. George's barracks, 2nd Scots Fusilier Guards to Aldershot. A few days later the Battalions of the Regiment were equalized, in that each was formed of ten companies, instead of twelve and eight, as had been the case during the war; two companies belonging to the 2nd Battalion were therefore transferred to the 1st, and the Officers were posted as follows:—

Colonel.—Field-Marshal the Earl of Strafford, G.C.B., G.C.H.
Lieut.-Colonel.—Colonel Hon. G. Upton, C.B.

1st Battalion.	2nd Battalion.
Majors.—Colonel Gordon Drummond.	Colonel Lord F. Paulet.
Captains.—Colonels W. S. Newton; T. M. Steele, C.B. (*Mounted*).	Colonels S. Perceval; W. Mark Wood (*Mounted*).
Lieut.-Colonels C. L. Cocks; D. Carleton; A. St. G. Herbert-Stepney, C.B; J. Airey, C.B.; C. S. Burdett; F. W. Newdigate; Lord Dunkellin; W. G. Dawkins.	Lieut.-Colonels J. Halkett; C. W. Strong; Lord Burghersh, C.B.; Hon. A. Hardinge; Hon. P. Feilding; W. Reeve; C. Baring; Hon. H. Byng.
Lieutenants.—Majors J. H. Le Couteur; H. Armytage; A. Thellusson; P. S. Crawley; Sir J. Dunlop; G. L. Goodlake; Lord Bingham; Captains H. Tower; Hon. W. Wellesley; Hon. W. Feilding; Major M. Heneage; Captains Lord E. Cecil; C. Blackett; G. FitzRoy; Hon. R. Monck (Adjt.).	Captains A. Fremantle (Adjutant); J. Caulfeild; Majors Hon. W. Boyle; J. Conolly; H. Maxse; Captains Hon. W. Amherst; C. Greenhill; H. C. Jervoise; St. V. Whitshed; Hon. H. Campbell; Julian Hall; G. Wigram; A. Lambton; G. Rose.
Ensigns.—Lieutenants Sir W. Forbes, Bart.; Hon. W. Edwardes; H. J. Lane; A. Adair; W. F. Seymour; S. T. Mainwaring; Hon. E. Legge; Hon. W. Ogilvy; G. Cameron.	Lieutenants E. S. Burnell; W. Stirling; F. Seymour; R. Thursby; N. Burnand; F. Buller; W. Wynne; E. Reeve; H. Bonham-Carter; H. Fortescue.

DRUMMER 1745.

1st Battalion.	2nd Battalion.
Quartermaster.—A. Falconer.	A. Hurle.
Surgeon-Major.—J. Munro, M.D.	
Battalion-Surgeon.—J. Skelton, M.D.	
Assistant-Surgeons.—J. Wyatt; T. Rogers; F. Bowen, M.D.	C. V. Cay; J. W. Trotter.
Solicitor.—W. G. Carter, Esq.*	

Where four allies were conducting a war in common, it was only natural that there should be an interchange of medals and of decorations, and this was done with no ungenerous hand. A new medal, more coveted than any other by soldiers and sailors, was established early in 1856, both for Officers and men in the Naval and Military services, who had distinguished themselves before the enemy "for valour." The distribution of the Victoria Cross did not, however, take place until the 26th of June, 1857, when all the claims for that most conspicuous honour had been fully investigated. The day appointed for the ceremony was observed as a general holiday, and a review was held in Hyde Park before Her Majesty the Queen, who affixed to the breast of each man entitled to it, the bronze cross he had won in the field by his personal bravery. In the Coldstream the recipients of this proud distinction were Majors Goodlake and Conolly, and Privates Strong and Stanlock.†

This event, though it took place more than a year after the

---

* The difference made in the Regiment by the war will be seen by comparing the above with the following, giving the list in February, 1854:—

Lieut.-Colonel.—Colonel H. Bentinck.

Majors.—Colonels C. Hay; Hon. A. Upton.

Captains.—Colonels W. Codrington; Hon. G. Upton; J. Clitherow; G. Drummond; (*Mounted*). Lieut.-Colonels Lord F. Paulet; H. Daniell; Hon. R. Boyle; W. Newton: Colonel W. Trevelyan: Lieut.-Colonels S. Perceval; M. Tierney; T. Crombie; Hon. T. V. Dawson; T. Steele; H. Cumming; W. M. Wood.

Lieutenants.—Captains C. Cocks; P. Somerset; J. C. Cowell; J. Halkett; D. Carleton; Lord A. C. FitzRoy; C. Burdett; F. Newdigate (Adjutant); L. MacKinnon; Sir G. Walker, Bart.; W. Dawkins; H. Jolliffe; C. Strong; Lord Dunkellin; C. Wilson; Hon. A. Hardinge; F. Burton; Hon. P. Feilding (Adjutant); W. Reeve; Hon. G. Eliot; C. Baring; J. H. Le Couteur; H. Bouverie; H. Armytage.

Ensigns.—Lieutenants Hon. H. Byng; A. Thellusson; H. Cust; P. Crawley; Sir J. Dunlop, Bart.; G. Goodlake; F. Ramsden; Lord Bingham; H. Tower; Hon. W. Wellesley; Hon. R. Drummond; P. Wyndham; E. Disbrowe; A. Fremantle; C. Greville; M. Heneage.

Quartermasters.—A. Hurle; A. Falconer.

Surgeon-Major.—J. Munro, M.D. *Battalion Surgeon.*—J. Skelton, M.D. *Assistant-Surgeons.*—F. Wildbore; J. Wyatt.

† See Appendix, No. XIII.

conclusion of peace, is connected with the Crimean struggle, and may be said to terminate the history of the protracted hostilities that troubled our relations with Russia. Thenceforward the war became a thing of the past, and its memories were merged into or overshadowed by other events which occurred elsewhere.

We have seen how the struggle shaped itself; how disastrously it was directed; and how devotedly our army maintained it, under very adverse and wholly exceptional circumstances. We allied ourselves to a Potentate whose tenure of power was precarious, whose interests were not our interests, and who only wished to adopt a foreign policy of adventure to reconcile his new subjects to his rule. His armies loyally supported ours in the field, and there we happily formed a sincere respect for the brave French troops who fought by our side. But the Government of Paris,—objecting always to transfer the theatre of war to Asia, where the enemy was really vulnerable,—restricted our field of operations to Europe; and as Austria protected the Russians on the Bessarabian frontier, we were forced at a late period of the year to make a descent upon the Crimea. Unhappily we had made no preparations for such an expedition, and had formed no plan for carrying it out; in fact, such an invasion had not seriously entered into our calculations when we declared war against the Tsar.

Thus, we landed fortuitously at a point where the road led to the north side of Sevastopol, but where no harbours near that town, were at hand to form a base of operations. Hence, without a base, we advanced to our objective, and, in due course, and after a successful battle, we arrived before it. But, on reaching this point, the Commander of our allies was indisposed to carry out the plan to which we had committed ourselves. We therefore shifted our forces by a strange flank march to the south side, in the hope that we might there at least be enabled to bring the campaign to a speedy conclusion. Sevastopol was at that time guarded by a small garrison, composed of a medley of indifferent and badly armed troops; it was imperfectly defended towards the land, and in this direction it was an insignificant stronghold. Still, as long as it remained in that state, we hesitated to make any or even the least move against it; we preferred to wait to bring up our siege-train, and to open regular approaches, with the expectation that the town would fall before the cold weather should set in, and put an end to all field operations.

But we had miscalculated. We did not take into account what a patriotic and energetic garrison might achieve during the unexpected respite granted them, nor did we perceive that we were altering, just as winter was approaching, the whole plan of invasion from an expedition of surprise to the more lengthened process of a regular siege. Thus, under the direction of an Engineer Officer of genius, did Sevastopol assume the proportions of a fortress, while the English and the French were looking idly on ; and before they could batter down simultaneously the new works in front of each,—which they allowed the enemy to construct,—the Russian forces, drawn from the Danubian Principalities, were hurried by forced marches into the Crimea, to the support of the scanty troops that were then to be found there. The very moment we had meant to deliver our final blow, the enemy's arrangements were complete, and we had to fight the unequal battle of Inkerman. Although we were victorious there against tremendous odds, the result obliged us to spend the winter on the barren and snow-swept plain of the Chersonese.

For this emergency we were entirely unprepared, and an intensely cold season having begun early, our troops, as we have seen, suffered in consequence. We then hung on to our positions before Sevastopol with strong tenacity of purpose, and with a resolution which is above all praise. But we could not resume the siege till the spring of 1855, and it was early in September before the south side fell. Taught by disaster, we then made every arrangement to continue the struggle with the best prospects of success ; but the French, having gained the objects they had in view, became inactive ; they clamoured for a cessation of hostilities ; and thus, to preserve an alliance into which we had permitted ourselves to be drawn, we signed a peace of little value, and so put an end to the war.

The successes gained were not due to the skill of the Government that directed the struggle ; they were solely due to that indomitable bravery, discipline, and power of endurance which have ever characterized our soldiers, as well as to the admirable system which made the British regimental Officers and men second to none that existed at that time in the other European armies.

The results of the war were dearly purchased. According to a return presented to Parliament, 390 Officers and 20,425 Non-commissioned officers and men were killed or died of wounds or of disease in the Crimea, and 14,718 men were invalided at the conclusion of the war, bringing the total casualties up to 35,533 of all ranks. But this return omits to include casualties in the Naval brigade and in the Marines (doing duty on land), and in the Commissariat, Transport, and Hospital departments; nor does it seem to give our losses incurred during the disastrous stay in Bulgaria, etc.: so that the figures do not represent the entire losses to which even our Land forces were subjected.* On the other hand, it was computed that the Russians lost as many as half a million men. But this is a surmise, and the facts have never been known. The estimate is probably exaggerated, though it is certain that the enemy's casualties were exceedingly great; but loss of men is not the greatest calamity that could befall an Empire like Russia.

Two events must be noted here which took place about this time, one of which affected the whole army, and the other the Brigade only. On the death of Lord Hardinge, who had succeeded the Duke of Wellington as Commander-in-Chief in 1852, H.R.H. the Duke of Cambridge was appointed to that high office, and assumed his new functions July 15, 1856—an office which he held without interruption until the 31st of October, 1895, for a space of nearly forty years.

The day before, the following Brigade Order appeared:—

"July 14, 1856. Her Majesty has been pleased to appoint Major-General Lord Rokeby, K.C.B., to serve on the Staff of the army, with a view to his exercising a general supervision over the Battalions [of Guards] in England, including those at Aldershot; all communications having reference to the Brigade of Guards will be addressed to him in future, instead of the Field-Officer in Brigade Waiting as heretofore."

It may be well to explain that, previous to this appointment, orders to the Brigade had been issued by the Field-Officer in

* Appendix XII. It will be observed that the losses mentioned in the text do not take into account those of the Navy incurred on board ship. On the 8th of May, 1856, Lord Panmure made a statement in the House of Lords, to the effect that from the 19th of September, 1854 (that is, the day before the battle of the Alma), 270 Officers and 19,314 men were killed, or died of wounds or of disease, and that 2873 men were discharged the service as incapacitated for further service by war; total, 22,457 casualties,—excluding, apparently, soldiers who died on board ship, sailors and marines serving on shore, and departmental troops. It seems strange that this imperfect statement should be sometimes quoted, instead of the return above mentioned, even though the latter is far from being satisfactory, and does not complete the tale of the losses to the Naval and Military Forces of the Crown during the war with Russia.

Brigade Waiting—a Commanding Officer of a Guards Regiment or Battalion, taken by roster—who is always an Officer of the Sovereign's Household. The effect of the order just quoted, was to place a General Officer in actual command of the Brigade, while the Field Officer in Brigade Waiting was still retained to fulfil the Court duties, he being, as formerly, the direct medium of communication between the Court and the Household Infantry.*

* For some years, after 1856, it appears that the Field-Officer in Brigade Waiting continued to exercise considerable control over the military affairs of the Guards. The Major-General Commanding issued general orders, the details of which were carried out by the Field-Officer. Between 1856 and 1868 the Foot Guards were called a Division; but April 27th of the latter year, the old term Brigade was again restored, and it was directed that the General's orders should be called "Brigade Orders," while those emanating from the Field-Officer should be termed "Sub-brigade Orders." The "Sub-brigade Office" was abolished February 28, 1873. The Home District, created in 1870, was placed under the command of the Major-General Commanding the Brigade of Guards, and this arrangement still prevails.

CHAPTER XIII.

A PERIOD OF WAR, 1856–1871.

Reductions after the war—Comparison between the situations in Europe, in 1815 and in 1856—Fresh troubles and complications imminent—Many wars and disturbances—Scientific instruction introduced into the army—Practical training of the troops carried out—The material comfort of the soldier attended to—Military activity in England in 1859—The Earl of Strafford succeeded by General Lord Clyde—Death of H.R.H. the Prince Consort—Misunderstanding with the United States of America—Chelsea barracks completed—Marriage of H.R.H. the Prince of Wales—Death of Lord Clyde; succeeded by General Sir W. Gomm—The Brigade of Guards Recruit Establishment—Public duties in London—Fenian troubles in Ireland; the 1st and 2nd Battalions succeed each other there; the Clerkenwell outrage—Reforms in the armament of the British infantry.

THE termination of the Crimean war, though it entailed considerable reductions in the army, was not accompanied by the acute distress that marked the close of the great struggle with France in 1815. In the latter case, the country had been seriously engaged with a formidable enemy for twenty years, and was constrained to devote all its resources to crush him. For nearly a generation, Great Britain had been a nation standing in arms, and thriving, so to speak, upon the success of her operations by sea and by land. The sudden cessation of hostilities, and the no less abrupt and violent change from a strong war footing to a small peace establishment, caused a temporary dislocation in trade, and this contributed in no small degree to create an unfortunate effect upon the economic conditions under which the people were then living. Whereas, in the more recent case, we were engaged for a relatively short space of time, and were not involved in efforts which could bear comparison with those we had been obliged to make earlier in the century. Hence we were able to diminish our armaments without incurring the same difficulties that had previously oppressed the industry of the country ; and arrangements could be safely made to reduce the regular army by 50,000 men, and to disband all those other forces that were brought together for the purposes of the Russian war. On the 1st of November, 1856, the establishment of the Regiment was diminished by some 600 men, and was fixed on the following scale:—

Colonel.	Lt.-Colonel.	Majors.	Captains.	Lieutenants.	Ensigns.	Adjutants.	Qr.-Masters.	Surgn.-Major.	Surgeon.	Assist.-Surgns.	Solicitor.	Sergeants.	Drummers.	Rank and File.	
1	1	2	20	24	16	2	2	1	1	5	1	92	34	1600	2 Battalions, 10 Cos. each.

Another difference between the peace of 1815 and that of 1856 is also of sufficient importance to require a notice. The final defeat of Napoleon at Waterloo found Europe exhausted by the long wars of the French Revolution; and the Congress of Vienna effected such a settlement among the civilized nations, of apparently so stable a character, that all Governments believed in the certainty of a protracted period of international tranquillity. Nor was this expectation disappointed, and for forty years there were no complications to disturb the political order that had then been established. But the assurance of peace led many to suppose that the era of war had come to an end, and we in this country were inclined to adopt that view—to such an extent, at least, that we deprived the army of some of the departments which are necessary to its existence in the field. So to say, we hid the remnant of the standing army away from the sight of the nation, as an institution almost out of harmony with the spirit of the age, and as an instrument of offence which would scarcely be again required for practical use. The warlike traditions of the past, however, remained in full vigour among the British troops, between 1815 and 1854; nor was there any relaxation of the strict principles of soldierlike bearing and conduct which had been inaugurated and enforced by the Duke of York and by the Duke of Wellington. No troops were more highly disciplined than those that belonged to the British army; among none had the military spirit and tone been so carefully fostered and so fully developed: and it was due to the splendid qualities which had been instilled into them, that the achievements of our men in the Crimea commanded the respect and the admiration of the world. But the knowledge of even elementary military sciences failed us; no instruction beyond drill was given;

we had little organization, no warlike grouping or cohesion of units, no transport, no real power to take the field or to utilize there the magnificent troops which their Officers had formed. The struggle with Russia had revealed these defects; and, taught in the bitter school of adversity, we were naturally slow, when the peace was signed, to destroy entirely those auxiliary services which had been so painfully created in the midst of war.

Now, the year 1856 was not like its predecessor, the end of a disturbed period; it marked the very commencement of a new era of European complications. The statesmen of the day were filled with no illusions, and were well aware of the unsettled state of affairs which the peace of 1856 had inaugurated. The Italian question was directly raised; Austria lost credit by her weak and vacillating action, and had become despised and isolated; steps to secure the aggrandisement of Prussia were already prepared; the policy of Napoleon III. was obscure and uncertain. Changes in the old landmarks of the Continent and serious trouble loomed in the near future. The threatening aspect of the coming storm, in short, was easy to be discerned: it was only too manifest that England might have to defend her rights, and could not afford, at such a moment, to neglect the affairs of her army and navy.

As events turned out, the war-cloud hovered over the whole world, and oppressed humanity with more or less intensity until 1871. Great Britain had to contend against many difficulties; but they were not of serious importance, except the Indian Mutiny,—which, breaking out unexpectedly in 1857, was not crushed finally until 1859,—and except the rapid advance of Russia across the barren steppes of Central Asia towards the frontiers of our Empire of India. Of our minor troubles, we may note: the Persian war, in 1856-57; the expedition to China, in 1857-61; the subjugation of the Maori natives in New Zealand, 1864; the invasion of Abyssinia, 1867-68; and the threatened dispute with the United States, 1861. In none of these, except the last, was the Brigade of Guards concerned. On the borders of Europe, the Caucasian Switzerland of Circassia was finally overpowered and assimilated with Russia, and the one barrier to her progress in the East was at last swept away, 1859. Nor was America free from disturbance. The United States, torn by dissensions, fought a fratricidal war of secession, 1861-64, that ended in re-establishing the authority of the Northern States over the revolted South: while that political stormy petrel,

Napoleon III., took part in a policy of adventure, by attempting, though unsuccessfully, to establish French influence, under cover of an Austrian prince, in Mexico. But in Europe itself the trouble was greater: France and Sardinia attacked Austria in Lombardy in 1859, and forced her to relinquish her possession of that province; Italy also rose in rebellion against the Princes that then ruled her States, and was consolidated into one kingdom under Victor Emanuel, our late ally in the Crimea. In 1859, also, Napoleon III. showed considerable animosity against England, and it was thought by many that there would be war with France. In 1864, Austria and Prussia joined to wrest the Duchies of Schleswig Holstein from Denmark: and two years later, having quarrelled over the booty, they came to blows, when Prussia defeated her rival hopelessly in the short and sharp campaign of a few weeks' duration in Bohemia, and acquired a complete ascendency over Germany. Italy, at the same time also, was enabled by foreign aid, to compel Austria to surrender her hold on Venetia. Then came the great war of 1870–71, when France and Prussia, regarding each with mutual jealousy and international hatred, engaged in deathly strife, that resulted in the fall of Napoleon, in the signal defeat of France, and in the refounding of the German Empire under the autocracy of Prussia.

The results of these constant contests upon our own army were not, of course, immediately apparent, nor could they produce a decided effect all at once upon the course of our military administration. But sufficient has been said to show that there were obvious reasons why the lethargy which affected the vital concerns of the forces of the Crown in 1815, was not reproduced in 1856, and how it came about that the nation began to take an increased interest in these most important affairs.

The Officers of the British army formed at that time a competent body. Taken from a class where the best leaders of men might be expected to be found, trained in the manly school of field sports and of outdoor exercises, brought up to early habits of obedience and of discipline, and endowed with the faculty of commanding the respect and the confidence of their subordinates, they were as well qualified to manage the rank and file placed under them in peace time, as they were conspicuous for their bravery and for the good example they set when danger pressed, or when difficulties were to be overcome in war time. One thing only did they lack—they had little scientific knowledge of their profession. To remedy this grave deficiency, a Council of Military Education was appointed in May, 1857, to superintend the system of education introduced among the Officers, and the examinations of candidates for admission to the service. It cannot be stated that this subject had been entirely ignored in the past, but it had been little regarded. After 1857, however, considerable attention was given to it, and the new system eventually expanded to its present dimensions—adding, in fact, to the army, as part of itself, a military University, where degrees are bestowed upon graduates, in their various ranks, who pass its examinations. These degrees attesting the scientific and theoretical proficiency of the candidates then became a necessary qualification for promotion in the service, at first to the rank of Captain only, but subsequently to a higher grade. In this respect, the policy has rather been to form an examining Board, for the purpose of testing the acquirements of Officers, than to institute something more akin to a teaching University, with the result that what is called "cramming" (or hasty learning of special subjects) has been largely increased, to the detriment perhaps of a more solid system of instruction. At any rate, whilst the old leaven of manhood and of common sense which has ever characterized the body of British Officers has not been weakened, a form of education calculated to teach technical and scientific duties in the field has been accepted with gratitude and satisfaction.

This important reform was supplemented by H.R.H. the Duke of Cambridge, the new Commander-in-Chief, who carried on the work, initiated by his predecessor, Lord Hardinge, which had been strongly urged by H.R.H. the Prince Consort. The camp of instruction established at Chobham in 1853 was moved to Aldershot, in the midst of a wide extent of heather country; the Crimean huts were erected there, and the head-quarters of a new military district were formed, where manœuvres could be undertaken by large bodies of troops, and where the men could be taught practically their numerous duties in the field. As will be seen, Guards Battalions were often sent there for this purpose. Nor was musketry neglected. Officers were told off as instructors in the art of correct shooting with the rifle that had been introduced into the service; every soldier was trained individually in its use, in a systematic way and in accordance with the regulations laid down at the School of Instruction established at Hythe;

parties, moreover, of Officers, Non-commissioned officers, and men were constantly sent there to undergo a course of musketry, and receive a certificate of efficiency in that very necessary branch of their military training.*

It has been noted that General Sir W. Codrington utilized the time when warlike operations practically ceased in the Crimea, by directing that all British soldiers should be put through an efficient course of musketry. After the war, the Guards continued to shoot on the range at Kilburn, but in 1859 a camp was formed for them at Ash, where rifle practice was carried out by companies, sent there in succession from the Battalions in England during the spring and summer months. Next year a Mounted Officer with a regular staff took command of the camp. Though Ash and Aldershot were the usual places selected for the Guards' musketry, companies were also sometimes sent to Eastbourne and to Gravesend for this purpose.

In the winter months marching was practised, and great gun drill was taught.† In 1861, gymnastic training was introduced,

---

* *Brigade Order*, August 20, 1856: "H.R.H. the General Commanding-in-Chief appoints Captain Instructors of Musketry, Brevet-Major Thesiger, 3rd Grenadier Guards; Major Le Couteur, 1st Coldstream; and Capt. Hon. R. Mostyn, 2nd Scots Fusilier Guards." But it was not until the 30th of April, 1857, that regular Instructors of Musketry appeared in the Army-list in the Coldstream, when Captain Blackett and Major Conolly, V.C., were appointed in that capacity, in the 1st and 2nd Battalions respectively.

February 7, 1857. "The Major-General has much pleasure in promulgating the following, received from the Adjutant-General, dated Horse Guards, February 4, 1857: 'The General Commanding-in-Chief, having received a most satisfactory report of the result of the various practices in shooting and judging distances by the parties lately attached to the school of musketry, by which it appears that they have, in the aggregate, attained a higher figure (38·98) than any batch of parties hitherto under instruction at Hythe, I have it in command to request your Lordship will make known to the Division of Foot Guards the satisfaction with which the said report has been received by His Royal Highness.'"

† The reader may perhaps be interested in knowing that one of the first orders given by the Duke of Cambridge on succeeding to the supreme command of the army related to marches. *Brigade Order*, November 17, 1856: "In compliance with instructions received from His Royal Highness, Commanding Officers will march out their Battalions at least once a week, in complete marching order, not less than eight to ten miles; the system prescribed in General Craufurd's regulations for conducting a march to be adhered to." His Royal Highness had at Scutari, in 1854, when in command of the First Division, drawn the attention of the latter to these regulations. It must not, however, be supposed that marching in peace time was unknown before 1856. For instance, by Regimental Order, dated September 12, 1838, it was laid down, "Whenever weather permits, the Battalion" (*i.e.* the 1st Battalion; the 2nd was then in Canada) "is to be marched once in four days."

and in September of that year, sergeants from the Brigade were sent through a course, so as to qualify as instructors. A gymnasium was about this time first constructed at St. John's Wood barracks, and companies were required to go there for a few weeks at a time. The gymnasium at Chelsea barracks was ready in 1865, and another at Windsor in 1870. The physical development of their men had before this been a special interest to the Officers of the Brigade, who endeavoured to introduce a system of outdoor gymnastics in the Guards, as far back as 1843. The practice, however, on being objected to by the Duke of Wellington, was given up.*

It should be mentioned here that signalling courses were not introduced into the army until 1869. Much attention was then immediately given to this subject in the Brigade, and the Battalions of Foot Guards were frequently complimented upon the efficiency they displayed as signallers.

While military training in many of its various important aspects was eagerly attended to, and was put upon a basis from which it could receive its proper development, the material comforts and welfare of the men were not neglected.† The cooking arrangements of the men in the Crimea had been signally defective, as much on account of the conditions under which they were placed, as by reason of the very little knowledge which they had of the subject. This, no doubt, was a serious want, and it militated against the health of the soldier. A school of cookery was established at Aldershot in 1862, and Non-commissioned officers were sent there to be trained in the new system then adopted. Considerable interest was taken in this matter in the Brigade, reports were frequently called for, and experimental stoves set up to secure the best results combined with economy. Sergeant Cooks were appointed in the Coldstream—in the 1st Battalion, December, 1863, and in the 2nd Battalion, in the following March; but it was not until May, 1868, that the establishment of the Regiment was increased by two sergeants for this purpose, nor was it until May of the year before, that the assistant cooks were

* See Hamilton, *History of the Grenadier Guards*, iii. 145.

† It may be of interest to observe here that a Committee of Officers (nearly all belonging to the Brigade), under the presidency of Colonel Ridley, Scots Fusilier Guards, assembled in London early in 1862 to consider the question of the employment of men in trades.

struck off other duties. As part of the same subject, it may be noted that the Commissariat Store at Chelsea barracks for the bread and meat to be issued to the troops in London, was established December 1, 1865, and an inspecting board of three Officers met daily to examine and to report upon the supplies furnished by the contractors.

Reforms in the canteen system were introduced shortly after the Crimean war. In conformity with instructions contained in the Quartermaster-General's letter of the 30th of November, 1857, boards of Regimental Field-Officers were assembled quarterly to revise the prices of articles sold, and to report upon the canteens inspected by them. The accounts were examined more frequently, and suggestions were invited as to the management of these institutions. In 1864, groceries began to be supplied to the messes, so that the men might only pay wholesale instead of retail prices, and married soldiers were encouraged to take advantage of the low cost of articles sold there. As the management became more efficient, the profits rose, and with this fund at the disposal of Commanding Officers, a great deal was done for the benefit of the men,—books and newspapers supplied at the various metropolitan Guards, extra food provided on long field days, being some of the items of expenditure that first appear to have received the sanction of the authorities.

Nor should we omit to draw attention to the encouragement given to outdoor games and amusements. Officers have always been inclined, naturally, to introduce among their men the healthy exercises which they themselves were taught at school, and which they continued to indulge in after joining the service. Thus cricket was well known, and we have seen that during the Russian war it was not neglected. Football, however, was not as common then as it is now, nor had some other forms of athletic sports taken a firm root in the public schools forty years ago. But as they became better known there, so did they grow in popularity among the troops—as also did boating at Windsor,—until at last they have become well recognized institutions, to the great benefit of the men, and to the immense advantage of the army. Hunting has always been a favourite pastime among Officers, and where it is not sufficiently available they often establish a drag hunt of their own. This was done at Windsor, in the winter of 1856-57, mainly by the Coldstream, whose 2nd Battalion was then quartered there. This institution flourishes to the present day. When the Brigade had the out-quarter at Shorncliffe, as will be seen further on, another drag hunt was also established there, but on leaving that station it had to come to an end.

On the 17th of July, 1856, at the suggestion of the Major-General Commanding the Brigade of Guards (Lord Rokeby), the Battalions who had just returned from the Crimea applied for new Colours, and, on the 27th of February following, the old Colours which had seen service in Russia were deposited, escorted by Guards of Honour of the usual strength, in the Royal Military Chapel at Wellington barracks.

Owing to the death of Colonel Gordon Drummond, Colonel Newton was promoted Major, and took command of the 2nd Battalion, November 18, 1856.

On the 3rd of March, 1857, the 1st Coldstream relieved the 2nd Scots Fusilier Guards at Aldershot (the 1st Grenadiers having been removed to Town from that camp in December), and returned to London at the autumn change of quarters (September 1st), when the 2nd Coldstream proceeded to Dublin, and the 1st Scots Fusilier Guards to Portsmouth. On the return of the latter (November 20th) the Brigade was again quartered in their usual stations, viz. four Battalions in the West-end and the other three in the Tower, Windsor, and the out-quarter (Dublin).* After this time, Battalions were frequently sent to Aldershot for the purpose of receiving practical instruction, but not to be stationed there for merely general duty.† About this time also—that is, between the 1st of September and the 7th of December, 1857—the Brigade furnished a detachment of about 200 Officers and men at Deptford, where occasional duty had been done by it, as we have seen, between 1815 and 1854.

While the Indian Mutiny obliged Government to strengthen

* The new wing of Wellington barracks was ready for occupation about this time; and it appears the present Kensington barracks replaced the old buildings there, April, 1858.

† The periods when the Coldstream were stationed in Aldershot are to be seen in Appendix No. XV. "In compliance with the directions of H.R.H. the Senior Colonel of the Brigade, the roster for casual home service, and for the regular training of Battalions at Aldershot in the summer, will in future be kept separately. The Major-General accordingly desires that the three Lieutenant-Colonels will be so good as to confer together with a view to preparing another roster as soon as they are agreed upon the subject; their proposals will be forwarded to this Office for approval" (*Brigade Order*, Feb. 24, 1866).

OFFICER 1795

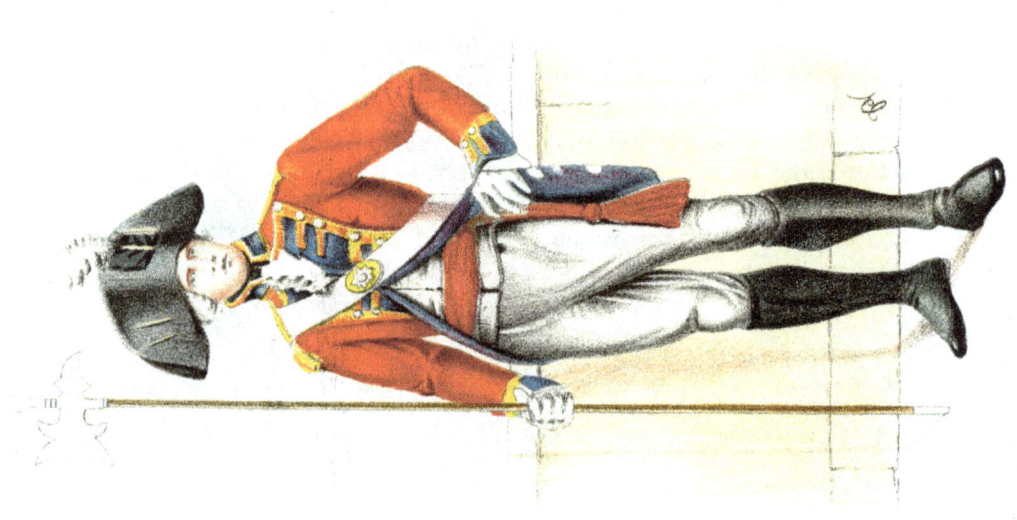

SERGEANT 1775

the army in India, drafts were collected at Colchester and Canterbury to be sent out to the East as they were required. In April, 1858, fourteen Ensigns of the Brigade (three from the 1st Coldstream) were sent to these places to look after the men that were assembled there. The following letter, dated July 3rd, from the Adjutant-General to Lord Rokeby, was published and ordered by the latter to be entered in the Regimental records :—

"The Inspector-General of Infantry having reported to His Royal Highness, that, in consequence of the embarkation of numerous drafts for India, there is no necessity for retaining the services of the Officers of the Guards at Colchester and Canterbury, orders will consequently be sent to those stations directing the Officers of the Guards to return to their respective Battalions. In communicating this decision to your Lordship, I am commanded to acquaint you that His Royal Highness has much gratification in stating that he has received from all quarters assurances of the excellent manner in which these Officers have conducted the duties assigned to them, reflecting as it does great credit on themselves and on the Regiments in which they have been instructed."

The 2nd Coldstream, returning from Dublin to London, September 1, 1858, brought a record of services performed in Ireland which was embodied in a Garrison Order, dated Dublin, August 30, 1858 :—

"The Major-General Commanding the District, in directing the departure of the 2nd Battalion Coldstream Guards, is unwilling to allow them to pass from his command without acknowledging his unqualified approbation of their conduct during the twelve months of their being in Dublin, and his sincere regret at losing them. Possessed of all the attributes which constitute excellence in a regiment, whether as regards the zealous and strict attention to their duty on the part of the Officers, the activity, intelligence, and trustworthiness of the Non-commissioned officers, the obedient conduct, soldier-like appearance, and respectful demeanour of the men, or the order and regularity of the parade, the general cleanliness of the barracks, the comfort of the hospital, the large attendance of the adults at school, the comparative absence of crime, and the pervading system of the corps, the Battalion has stood forth in the garrison as a model of regimental discipline, to excite the emulation and stimulate a generous rivalry. The Major-General, therefore, begs to offer his thanks to Colonel Newton and his Officers for the support they have at all times afforded, and to assure the Battalion that he will always retain a lively recollection of the satisfaction he derived in having it as a part of his garrison."

Colonel Hon. G. Upton, C.B., appointed Major-General, October 26, 1858, was succeeded by Colonel Lord Frederick Paulet, C.B., as Lieutenant-Colonel of the Regiment; thereupon Colonel Newton assumed the command of the 1st Battalion, and Colonel Spencer Perceval, promoted to the rank of Major, was posted to command the 2nd Battalion.

As previously mentioned, events in the year 1859 produced the impression that Napoleon III. was about to declare war against us, and visions of invasion began to haunt us. Considerable military activity was displayed at this time. Second battalions to twenty-five regiments of the Line, and third and fourth battalions to the two Rifle regiments, the 60th and Rifle Brigade, were raised and incorporated into the army: we find also that, early in the year, the Brigade was called upon to furnish Non-commissioned officers that could be spared, as drill instructors to train the men of some of these new corps. Of these, the Coldstream supplied four to the 2nd Battalion, 21st Regiment, at Newport, February, 1859. Nor was the condition of the Militia neglected, and Field-Officers of the Guards, who had been sent to inspect the regiments when embodied, were more frequently employed on this duty about this time. Now, in 1803, when Napoleon I. threatened to make a descent upon our coasts from his great camp at Boulogne, bodies of Volunteers were raised to watch our shores. The same thing happened in 1859, and, although our danger was scarcely real, yet so strongly impressed were the people with the facilities of transit across the narrow channel, which steam would give an invader, and so convinced were they of the power and of the evil designs of the French Emperor, that they began spontaneously to form rifle corps for the defence of the country. This was the commencement of the Volunteer movement which has now developed into an important auxiliary branch of the forces of the Crown intended for service at home. Its usefulness in the field has not yet been practically tested, and we may well pray that the day when it must meet an enemy on our own soil, may never come. But the influence it commands, by strengthening the ties that bind the military and the civil elements, by rendering the regular army popular, and by therefore facilitating the recruitment of a good class of man, is well known; while the self-sacrifice of many who devote their leisure to martial exercises, without prospect of reward, is creditable to the British character, and tends to spread a wider interest in military affairs than was formerly the case.

In the summer of 1859, many of the Officers of the Brigade were employed in reporting upon the numerous ranges which had been proposed as suitable sites for rifle practice. This duty did not cease until the beginning of 1862, when facilities for musketry existed in almost every district, and when the exercise became a popular pastime throughout the country. A National Rifle Association was formed, and a Volunteer camp established at Wimbledon (1860), where shooting competitions took place. The meetings continued year after year with ever-growing popularity, and detachments of Guardsmen were sent from London to perform the military duties in camp and on the ranges. Colonel Tower (Coldstream Guards) was the first Field-Officer selected to command these detachments, in 1865, and since then the Brigade has regularly furnished an Officer of that rank for this purpose, to attend the Rifle meetings, and, later (from 1874), to command the camp.

As far back as 1860, the drill of Officers of the Militia and Volunteers was often superintended by Officers of the Brigade of Guards. In October, 1870, moreover, schools of instruction were established at the Tower and at Wellington barracks, which were eventually consolidated into one, where Officers of the auxiliary forces, having passed a practical course in drill, can obtain a certificate to that effect. Colonel Hon. R. Monck (Coldstream Guards) was the first Commandant of the school at Wellington barracks.*

The Coldstream, having lost their Colonel by the death of Field Marshal Earl of Strafford, the chief command of the Regiment was bestowed upon General Lord Clyde, G.C.B., June 22, 1860, better known by the men in the Crimea, as Sir Colin Campbell. After the war with Russia, this very distinguished Officer was employed in India, where, appointed Commander-in-chief, he took a conspicuous part in the suppression of the

* The following order appeared, dated December 13, 1870, when the Schools of Instruction in London closed for the first time, for the Christmas holidays: "The Secretary of State has recorded his sense of the zeal and discretion which the Officers and Non-commissioned officers attached to and in charge of these schools have exhibited, which is proved by the success which has attended their duties, and the results that have been directly and indirectly obtained, and which reflect great credit upon the Commandants. H.R.H. the Field Marshal Commanding-in-Chief is much pleased at receiving so satisfactory a recognition of their services."

Mutiny. Several other changes occurred in the Regiment about this time. On the promotion of Colonel Lord F. Paulet, C.B., to the rank of Major-General, Colonel Newton became Lieutenant-Colonel, whereupon Colonel S. Perceval assumed the command of the 1st Battalion, and Colonel Steele, C.B., appointed Major, of the 2nd (December 13, 1860). In a few months, however, there was another change; Colonel Perceval was promoted Lieutenant-Colonel, when Colonel Steele was posted to the 1st Battalion, and was succeeded by Colonel Wood in the 2nd (July 2, 1861).

On the 1st of April, 1861, Major-General Lord Rokeby retired, and the command of the Brigade devolved upon Major-General Craufurd. Shortly afterwards (June 27th) a Major of Brigade was appointed in the Foot Guards, and the new post was given to the senior Adjutant, Captain and Adjutant Gordon, Scots Fusilier Guards.

In December, 1861, the whole country was plunged into deep mourning by the premature death of the Prince Consort. It is less than the truth to say that all hearts were moved with profound grief for the Queen in this, the greatest of domestic afflictions; and at the decease of a patriot Prince, whose sage counsels had so often ably directed Her Majesty in many important matters, and who had done so much for the intellectual elevation and the material advancement of her people. The sorrow of the nation was felt nowhere more strongly than among the Guards, who thereby lost their Senior Colonel, and whose inalienable privilege it is to share, as part of the Sovereign's Household, the trials as well as the joys that visit the Royal Family.

This most sad misfortune happened at a moment of a misunderstanding with the United States of America, when it was apprehended that war might break out between the two countries, and when an expedition was being fitted out to defend Canada should the crisis assume an acute stage. It is scarcely necessary to go into the details of the dispute, well known as the "Trent affair," for the Coldstream took no part in the operations which followed. Suffice it to say that two Battalions of the Brigade (1st Grenadiers and 2nd Scots Fusilier Guards, under Major-General Lord F. Paulet) were shipped to British North America, December 19th, and remained there until the autumn of 1864. Fortunately peace was preserved, and the expedition, while watching proceedings during the civil war that was then raging in the States, assumed the character of a movement of troops from one part of the British Empire to another, for ordinary purposes.*

The 1st Battalion Coldstream, having gone to Dublin in October, 1861, did not return to London until the next change of quarters in April following, and so, for the first few months of 1862, there were but three Battalions in the West-end, while the Tower was occupied by a Line Regiment (the 1st Battalion of the 3rd Buffs). To lighten the duties, the latter furnished a detachment at Wellington barracks, which occasionally supplied the guards at Kensington Palace, the Magazine, and at the British Museum. In April, 1862, the full complement of four Battalions did duty in the West-end, and Dublin was given up as a Guards station. On the return of the Canadian expedition the Tower was again occupied by Guards, and the out-quarter was transferred to Shorncliffe. Chelsea barracks, designed as we have seen in 1855, were ready for occupation in the autumn of 1863, and an entire Battalion and a few companies of another were stationed there. Subsequently, the head-quarters of the latter, transferred from St. George's, were also placed in these barracks; while Portman Street had been given up in September, 1863. The new wing of Wellington barracks had been occupied prior to this date, and was opened shortly after the Crimean war, as we have seen.† Thus considerably more space was obtained for the Brigade in London, which was distributed almost as is the case in the present day.‡ It is only necessary to add that the small barracks at the Magazine were vacated, and handed over to the police authorities on the 21st of December, 1866; that those at St. John's Wood ceased to be occupied by the Foot Guards about the year 1876; and that Windsor barracks, which was a crowded and unsuitable

---

* In order to drill and organize Canadian Militia regiments, five corporals of the Guards Battalions not sent to Canada, were selected to proceed with the expedition, and the following terms were offered to them : (1) to have the rank and pay of the next grade above that they then held, from the date of landing ; (2) to be supernumerary on the strength of their Regiments, and to rejoin them on their return ; and (3) an allowance to be given to their wives during their absence from home, or until the latter rejoin their husbands (*Brigade Orders*, Dec. 6 and 14, 1861).

† See footnote *, p. 300, *ante*.

‡ *Wellington barracks*, one entire Battalion, and another having detachments at Kensington and Buckingham Palace barracks ; *Chelsea barracks*, one entire Battalion, and another with a detachment at St. George's barracks ; *Tower*, one Battalion ; *Windsor*, one Battalion ; an Out-quarter, one Battalion.

building for a whole Battalion, were greatly improved and enlarged, and were ready for occupation in 1868.

On the 9th of November, 1862, Colonel Steele, was promoted Lieutenant-Colonel of the Regiment, *vice* Colonel S. Perceval, appointed Major-General; the command of the 1st Battalion then devolved upon Colonel Mark Wood, and that of the 2nd Battalion upon Colonel Dudley Carleton.

Many remember the marriage of H.R.H. the Prince of Wales to the Princess Alexandra of Denmark, March 10, 1863, and the enthusiasm and joy evoked throughout the length and breadth of the land at the auspicious and popular event. Her Royal Highness arrived in London on the 7th, and proceeded to Windsor, where the ceremony was performed, and the following military arrangements were made for her reception in the Metropolis. The 3rd Grenadiers furnished a Guard of Honour at Bricklayers Arms Railway Station, the remainder of the Battalion being in column of wings in front of St. James's Palace; the 1st Battalion 60th Rifles, then at the Tower, were formed outside the station; the 2nd Coldstream Guards in Waterloo Place lining the streets, with a Guard of Honour (the Queen's Guard strengthened to the usual complement) near the Palace, and at right angles to the Grenadiers. The 1st Scots Fusilier Guards were in line near Hyde Park Corner; the Park was occupied by some 17,000 Volunteers; and the 2nd Grenadiers were stationed at the Marble Arch, and had a Guard of Honour at Paddington Station. The 1st Coldstream, then quartered at Windsor, sent a Guard of Honour to Slough. At the Royal wedding on the 10th, the Brigade was fully represented; the 2nd Grenadier Guards (in which Regiment His Royal Highness had served) found a Guard of Honour at St. George's Chapel; the 1st Scots Fusilier Guards furnished another at the railway station on departure; and the 1st Coldstream, besides providing two Guards of Honour, one at the State Entrance of the Castle, and the other at the Chapel, were also present. The Berkshire Volunteers, moreover, had a Guard of Honour outside the gates of the Castle. The Guards Battalions quartered in London celebrated the occasion by parading in Hyde Park, where the 2nd and 3rd Grenadiers and the 2nd Coldstream fired a *feu de joie*, while the 1st Scots Fusilier Guards kept the ground. The day was observed as a general holiday throughout the country, and all classes joined to express their heart-felt congratulations on the happy alliance which had been made by the Heir Apparent of the Throne.*

Nor ought we to forget to mention that a ball was given by the Brigade in the Exhibition buildings, June 26th,† to the Prince and Princess of Wales, in honour of the Royal marriage that had just taken place; the Guard of Honour to receive Their Royal Highnesses was furnished by the 1st Scots Fusilier Guards.

Several changes occurred in the command of the Brigade and Regiment during this same year (1863). On the 25th of June, Lord F. Paulet, having returned from Canada, was appointed Major-General of the Brigade of Guards *vice* Lieut.-General Craufurd.

At the death of General Lord Clyde, General Sir William Gomm, G.C.B., succeeded him as Colonel (August 15, 1863), and was thus again posted to the Coldstream Guards, which he had joined as a Captain and Lieutenant-Colonel just before the battle of Waterloo, and with which he had served up to the rank of Lieutenant-Colonel of the Regiment, until January, 1837, when he was promoted Major-General. Colonel Steele, moreover, relinquishing the command of the Coldstream (November 24th), the Lieutenant-Colonelcy devolved upon Colonel Wood, when Colonel Carleton was posted to the command of the 1st Battalion, and Colonel Stepney, C.B., to that of the 2nd Battalion.

Just at this moment, also, the Regiment lost their Bandmaster, Mr. Charles Godfrey, who died much regretted in December, having joined the Coldstream fifty years before (in 1813). This excellent musician had efficiently conducted the Band ever since 1825.‡

We have seen that hitherto, when promotion took place, and when the Senior Major either left the Regiment or was appointed Lieutenant-Colonel, the Junior Major was invariably transferred

---

* For an account of the Royal wedding, see *Annual Register*, 1863, "Chronicle," p. 36, etc.

† Interested in the success of the first great International Exhibition of Arts and Sciences in 1851, one of the last works of the lamented Prince Consort was to promote a second Exhibition of the same kind in London; but he did not, unfortunately, live to see its completion. It was opened on May 1, 1862, when the ceremony was attended by a deputation from each of the Guards Regiments, who formed part of the opening procession. The buildings were not removed in 1863, and were utilized, as above stated, on the occasion of the Brigade ball. The Albert Hall has now been erected upon this site.

‡ See Appendix, No. V.

to command the 1st Battalion, and the Captain and Lieutenant-Colonel, promoted Major to fill up the vacancy created, was posted to that of the 2nd Battalion. The same rule prevailed as regards the Acting-Majors (Mounted Officers), so that the senior and the third senior always belonged to the 1st Battalion, and the second and fourth seniors to the 2nd. It had also prevailed among the Adjutants up to the first Canadian expedition in 1838, but then it seemed to lapse as far as they were concerned, in the Coldstream at least. This custom was abolished on the 19th of January, 1864, when the following Order was issued:—

"In compliance with instructions from H.R.H. the Duke of Cambridge, no alteration in future is to be made in the posting of Majors Commanding Battalions; these Officers are to remain in the Battalions in which they were originally promoted, the Senior Major to receive the difference in allowance which may be attached to the command of the 1st Battalion. By the same rule, Acting Majors will not change Battalion except for promotion or on appointment to be Senior Acting Major."

The following list shows the Officers belonging to the Regiment in January, 1865:—

Colonel.—General Sir William Gomm, G.C.B.
Lieut.-Colonel.—Colonel Mark Wood.
Majors.—Colonel Dudley Carleton; Colonel A. Herbert-Stepney, C.B.
Captains.—Colonels J. Airey, C.B.; W. G. Dawkins; C. W. Strong; Hon. H. Hardinge, C.B. (*Mounted*).
    Lieut.-Colonels Hon. P. Feilding; W. Reeve; C. Baring; J. H. Le Couteur; H. Armytage; G. Goodlake, V.C.; H. Tower; A. Fremantle; Colonel Hon. W. Feilding; P. Crawley; M. Heneage; C. Blackett; G. FitzRoy; J. Conolly, V.C.; Hon. R. Monck; Hon. W. Boyle.
Lieutenants.—Captains C. Greenhill; H. C. Jervoise; Hon. H. Campbell; Julian Hall; G. Wigram; A. Lambton; Hon. W. Edwardes; H. Lane; W. F. Seymour; Hon. E. Legge (Adjutant); E. S. Burnell; Hon. G. Windsor-Clive; R. Thursby; N. Burnand; FitzRoy Fremantle; F. Buller; E. Reeve; H. Bonham-Carter; Hugh Fortescue (Adjutant); J. F. Hathorn (I. of M.); H. Herbert (I. of M.); H. Brand; Denzil Baring; Hon. F. Howard; R. Cathcart; C. Lee-Mainwaring.
Ensigns.—Lieutenants Hon. V. Dawson; E. Chaplin; Sir E. Hamilton, Bart.; G. FitzRoy Smyth; Lord Wallscourt; H. R. Eyre; J. B. Sterling; G. G. Macpherson; C. Thomas; Hon. J. Vesey; Hon. F. Wellesley; Hon. H. Legge; R. Hall; A. Farquhar; C. Alexander; W. Ramsden.

Quartermasters.—A. Hurle; and A. Falconer.
Surgeon-Major.—J. Wyatt. *Battalion Surgeon.*—C. V. Cay. *Assistant-Surgeons.*—J. W. Trotter; R. Farquharson; A. B. R. Myers.
Solicitor.—R. Broughton, Esq.

To persons living in the present day it may perhaps seem strange to hear of the rigid social laws which were current in our fathers' time against smoking. This indulgence was regarded, only a few decades ago, as a more or less uncivilized habit, which might be enjoyed on occasions in the privacy of a man's own apartments or in some far-away room of a country house, out of sight of all general society, but never to be countenanced in public. Hence, Officers on any sort of duty were not allowed the use of tobacco even during hours of relaxation, and there were stringent rules against the practice on the Queen's Guard. In 1838, for instance, attention is drawn to orders on that subject there, and again in 1844:—

"The Lieutenant-Colonels of the three Regiments of Guards have observed with great regret that the regulations for the Guard table at St. James's Palace are not attended to, particularly as to smoking. . . . The Captain of the Guard in St. James's Palace will have the goodness to add to his report that there has been no smoking in the Officers' apartments in St. James's Palace, during the twenty-four hours he has been on Guard." *

Nearly six years later the rule was modified, in that the prohibition only applied to the mess room in the Palace, and the Captain's certificate was altered accordingly.† The Crimean War, no doubt, did a great deal to destroy the old prejudice which existed on the subject; for British Officers learnt the advantages of the weed in the trenches, and were in close quarters with habitual smokers, the Turks and the French. Still tobacco was not permitted in the barrack rooms, and, early in 1859, the Medical Officers were seriously called upon to report whether smoking there would be likely to prove deleterious to the health of the men. It was not until October 28, 1864, that leave was given to soldiers to smoke in the barrack rooms from the dinner hour to tattoo.

It has already been mentioned that the recruit establishment of the Brigade had been transferred to Croydon in 1833, and there it remained for thirty years, except only that the Grenadier section was moved to St. John's Wood barracks during the war

* *Brigade Order*, March 6, 1844.   † *Ibid.*, Nov. 26, 1849.

with Russia, from March, 1854, to the 18th of June, 1856. On the 1st of April, 1863, the recruits of the three Regiments were taken to St. John's Wood, for the purpose of receiving gymnastic training, until the 2nd of August, 1865, when they proceeded to Warley.* During all this time the establishment was under the command of a resident Officer (Lieutenant and Captain), who took the duty there for a fortnight (at St. John's Wood for a week). Considerable responsibility rested upon the Regimental Drill-Sergeant for the training of the men, and several orders attest the fact that these Non-commissioned officers did their work faithfully and efficiently. In 1870, a permanent Commandant was appointed, when Lieut.-Colonel Moncrieff, Scots Fusilier Guards, assumed the new post (November 28th), and, soon after, another Officer was told off to perform the duties of Adjutant, the resident Subaltern still remaining for a fortnight as Piquet Officer. Besides the Medical Officer, and a Quartermaster who was added later (in 1885), this staff of Officers was all that looked after the Depôt until 1893, when it was again enlarged. On the 12th of April, 1875, a board was assembled at Caterham to view and report upon a site for the Guards Depôt, and this new quarter was occupied on the 23rd of October, 1877. The Senior Drill-Sergeant,† appointed Acting Sergeant-Major, May 5, 1881, was promoted Sergeant-Major on July 1st following. The Depôt then contained a Sergeant-Major, a Quartermaster-Sergeant, an Orderly Room Clerk, four Colour-Sergeants, four Sergeants, twelve Corporals, and two Drummers; and these men remained "on the rolls of their respective Battalions for promotion and married leave."

In 1866 the public duties in London were reduced, and in July they stood as follows:—

	Capts.	Subaltns.	Sergts.	Corpls.	Drums.	Prvts.
Queen's Guard	1	2	2	2	3	36
Buckingham Palace Guard	0	1	2	2	1	27
Tylt Guard	0	1	2	2	1	18
Kensington Guard ..	0	0	1	1	0	15
Magazine Guard ..	0	0	1	1	0	9
Total	1	4	8	8	5	105‡

* The Grenadier section occupied Kensington barracks from the autumn of 1864 until the following March, when they went to Warley.
† Drill-Sergeant Barrell, Coldstream Guards.
‡ There was, in addition, a small guard at Southwark military prison, at St. John's

The years 1866 and 1867 are chiefly marked in the domestic history of the country by the troubles in Ireland, and by the efforts of a secret society, called the Fenians, to stir up rebellion and serious disturbances, not only in that island but in England also. The Fenian body, born and nurtured in the United States, had for some years been endeavouring to infect the mass of Irishmen distributed throughout the whole of the United Kingdom with their pernicious doctrines; and in a sense they accomplished their object by intensifying a feeling that had existed for many a generation between the Celtic and Saxon populations, into one of extreme bitterness and animosity. Beyond this, however, they achieved no immediate success; the illegal and violent measures they advocated, while they caused a momentary panic among the peaceably disposed, soon recoiled upon those who perpetrated them. Hence, the movement speedily dwindled into insignificance, though it left behind a residue of secret organization, which at no distant date was to support another agitation, that again was destined to disturb the country.

In the beginning of 1866, the usual spring change of quarters in the Brigade had been ordered to take place on the 1st of March; the 1st Coldstream was to move from Chelsea to another station in the West-end, and the 2nd Battalion from the Tower to Shorncliffe. But the troubles in Ireland were then giving cause for much anxiety, and the order was not executed. It was known that some few men belonging to Line Regiments had secretly joined the Fenians; it was feared that an armed rising might take place; an attempt to seize Chester Castle had just been frustrated (February 13th), and a Battalion of the Scots Fusilier Guards had been hurriedly despatched there to protect the place. A Guards Battalion was thus urgently required in Dublin, and on the 20th of February the 1st Coldstream were sent there at twenty-four hours' notice, "the sick, boys, and men unfit for active service" being attached to the 2nd Battalion. Shorncliffe was therefore given up as the Guards' out-quarter.

The stay of the 1st Battalion in Ireland during the year, cannot

Wood barracks, when unoccupied by Battalions, and at the Royal Academy, when open. The British Museum guard seems to have been done away with about 1864. The Bank piquet remained as before. The strength of the public duties during the Crimean war has been given in the last chapter (p. 267); in March, 1835, it appears to have amounted to, excluding the Bank piquet,—1 Captain, 4 Subalterns, 14 sergeants, 18 corporals, 5 drummers, and 302 privates.

be termed a pleasant one. Preserving the public peace against the machinations of a secret band of conspirators who succeeded temporarily in deluding a portion of the people, and in partially alienating them from their legitimate rulers, is a duty too nearly allied to the police service to be a favourite one with soldiers. The work, however, was well performed by the Battalion, and this is attested by the following order, which was issued by the Major-General Commanding the Brigade, on the 6th of March, 1867, when their tour of duty was completed in Dublin, and when they returned to London:—

"The Major-General has much pleasure in publishing a Memorandum issued by General Lord Strathnairn upon the 1st Battalion Coldstream Guards leaving Dublin. It reflects the utmost credit on all ranks for having earned so distinguished a compliment. The Major-General notices the favourable mention of Captain Hon. E. Legge, his close attention to his duty as Adjutant proves his zeal in the interest of his Battalion. The Major-General directs that Lord Strathnairn's Memorandum with this Order be read to each Battalion of the Brigade. In a corps constituted as the Brigade of Guards the character of any one Battalion reflects upon the whole."

Lord Strathnairn's Memorandum ran thus:*—

"*Memo.*—The Commander of the Forces has every reason to be pleased with the excellent discipline of the 1st Battalion Coldstream Guards during the twelve months they have been under his Lordship's command. The requisitions of the Government have often during this time necessitated extra duties for the preservation of the public peace, all of which the Coldstream Guards have performed with strictness and cheerfulness. The promptitude with which Lieut.-Colonel Le Couteur, the Officers, the Non-commissioned officers and men of the Battalion gave effect to the wishes of Lord Strathnairn for a thorough organization of the Reading, Recreation, and Refreshment rooms which tend so much to promote discipline, was very creditable to them. Lord Strathnairn cannot record this favourable opinion of the 1st Battalion Coldstream Guards without mentioning his high sense of the unvarying zeal and ability displayed by the Adjutant, Captain Hon. E. Legge, who during the twelve months has never been absent from his post."

The 2nd Coldstream relieved the 1st Battalion early in 1867, and also remained in Ireland for twelve months under conditions nearly similar to those that existed in 1866. At the end of this period,

* Lord Strathnairn, as Colonel Rose, had been British Commissioner with the French army during the Crimean War.

the Lieutenant-Colonel was able to express to the Regiment the high opinion entertained by the General Commanding the Forces of the 2nd Battalion, and his own gratification at this good opinion "during trying times, and when the men were exposed to mischievous temptations." *

Nor had the Battalions of the Brigade stationed in London an easy time during these two years (1866–1867), for they too were harassed by popular effervescence. A reform bill was before the country, and many demagogues, attended by their followers, found it easy to disturb the public peace. Towards the end of July, 1866, the troops were confined to their quarters; a wing of the 2nd Coldstream occupied Knightsbridge barracks during the day; the Major-General took post at the Magazine, to receive reports should anything extraordinary happen; the piquets were increased; a magistrate was placed in every London barrack, and for a few days all Officers on leave were recalled. Next year, the fear of riots still haunted the authorities, and on several occasions the public duties were doubled. But this was little when compared with the excitement produced by the explosion at the Clerkenwell House of Detention on the 13th of December —an outrage of a vile type, perpetrated by the Fenians for the purpose of terrorizing the Government. Immediate steps were taken to defend the Metropolis from a repetition of another such dastardly attempt upon the lives of innocent persons, and for nearly a month the troops were busily engaged, while the ordinary military exercises, marches, gun drill, and gymnastic courses were suspended. A guard was immediately sent to Clerkenwell, of 100 rank and file, under three Officers; sentries carried their rifles loaded; strong piquets, of 100 men under a Captain and Lieutenant-Colonel, were mounted daily in the principal barracks; half the Officers doing duty were held available for any sudden emergency, from five in the afternoon till eleven o'clock at night; the Captain of the Queen's Guard was made responsible for calling upon the nearest piquet to turn out in case of disturbance; a guard was furnished at Millbank prison, and over the small-arm factories in London; signal communication by rockets was established between

* *Regimental Order*, Jan. 21, 1868. On the return of the 2nd Coldstream, the following order, relating to duty in Ireland, was published, March 19, 1868: "H.R.H. the Senior Colonel of the Brigade of Guards has approved of changes in the roster for change of quarters and casual services, by which Dublin remains in a special Irish roster."

the barracks and where an attack might be expected; a party of the 2nd Scots Fusilier Guards was despatched to Cowes and to Osborne; the Bank piquet remained on duty for twenty-four hours on Sundays and on Christmas day, and all leave and furloughs were suspended. At the Tower, moreover, where the 1st Coldstream were quartered, the Officer of the main guard patrolled round the ditches and wharves during the night. These arrangements were not relaxed till the 11th of January, 1868, and things did not resume their normal course until somewhat later. But as a net result of the Clerkenwell outrage, it may be mentioned that the metropolitan barracks were put in telegraphic communication with the Horse Guards, and the work was completed in March, 1868. By an order of the 31st of December, 1867, also, two Non-commissioned officers per Battalion were told off to be instructed in the duties of telegraphist.

In 1867, the Sultan of Turkey came to England, and in 1869 his nominal vassal, the Khedive (the Viceroy of Egypt), did the same thing. There were reviews upon these occasions in their honour, and other martial displays; but these visits, though of political importance, need not further be alluded to here, since, in a military sense, they entailed only the ordinary duties performed by the Brigade when a foreign Sovereign is received in State by Her Majesty the Queen.

Between 1866 and 1871 the following changes took place in the command of the Regiment. In May, 1866, Colonel Wood having retired, Colonel Dudley Carleton became Lieutenant-Colonel, and thereupon Colonel Airey, promoted Major, assumed the command of the 1st Battalion, under the rule of the 19th of January, 1864, already quoted; while Colonel Stepney remained with the 2nd Battalion, until the 14th of August, when, retiring on half-pay, he was succeeded by Colonel Strong. The latter also shortly afterwards (March 15, 1867) went on half-pay, and the command of this Battalion devolved upon Colonel Hon. A. Hardinge; on the 23rd of October following, Colonel Hon. Percy Feilding was promoted Major, commanding the 1st Battalion, Colonel Airey having left the Regiment. Colonel Hardinge succeeded Colonel Carleton as Lieutenant-Colonel, September 2, 1868, when Colonel C. Baring was posted to the command of the 2nd Battalion. Shortly afterwards the establishment of the Regiment was reduced by one Major, and the following Brigade Order was issued on the 29th of May, 1869, to direct how this reduction should be brought about—

"In conformity with a letter from the Military Secretary under date, May 28, 1869, the Major-General notifies to the Brigade that Her Majesty has been pleased to approve of the proposal of the Secretary of State for War, that one Major in each Regiment of the Brigade of Guards be gradually reduced, retaining the Lieutenant-Colonel, who will take command of a Battalion in addition to that of the Regiment. In accordance with the above arrangement, the vacancy in the Grenadier Guards, caused by the promotion of H.S.H. Prince Edward of Saxe-Weimar to be Major-General, on the 23rd of February last, will not be filled up; and the command of the 3rd Battalion Grenadier Guards, vacated by such promotion, will devolve upon the Lieutenant-Colonel of the Regiment, Colonel Bruce, from the above date."

The opportunity to give effect to this order did not come in the Coldstream until January 4, 1871, when, on the retirement of Colonel Hardinge, Colonel Hon. P. Feilding, C.B., was promoted Lieutenant-Colonel, and still retained the command of the 1st Battalion. Colonel C. Baring remained in command of the 2nd Battalion until the 13th of August, 1872, when, retiring on half-pay, he was succeeded by Colonel Goodlake, V.C.

In the Brigade, Lord Frederick Paulet, C.B., was succeeded by Major-General Hon. J. Lindsay (January 29, 1867), and during the period of his command the Guards Institute, near Vauxhall Bridge Road, was opened by H.R.H. the Duke of Cambridge, July 11, 1867, as "a convenient place of refreshment, resort, amusement, and occupation for Non-commissioned officers and men stationed in London." This club only flourished a few years, and was closed in 1872, when the building was bought by Cardinal Manning, and was converted by him into the present residence of the Archbishop of Westminster. General Lindsay also promoted a military industrial exhibition, which took place in Chelsea barracks on the 9th of July, 1868; but on that date Major-General Hamilton, C.B., had already succeeded him in the command of the Brigade, having assumed it on the 1st of April. The latter, promoted Lieutenant-General, left, April 1, 1870, and Major-General, H.S.H. Prince Edward of Saxe-Weimar, C.B., was then appointed in his place.

Of changes in the uniform of the Regiment, the following may be noted: On the 6th of December, 1859, it was ordered that the chin-straps of the bearskins were to be worn under and not on the chin; but this method, apparently, was not long maintained in force. A mess dress was authorized for the Officers of the Brigade, January 30, 1864. Silver stars on the forage cap, and sling belts were to be worn by the Sergeant-Major, Quartermaster-Sergeant, Bandmaster, Sergeant-Instructor of Musketry, Drum-Major, Band-Sergeant, Drill Sergeants, Regimental Orderly Room Clerk, Assistant Regimental Clerk, Battalion Orderly Room Clerk, Hospital-Sergeant, Armourer-Sergeant, Master-Tailor, and the Sergeant of Cooks, April 25, 1870. Lastly, on the 28th of June, 1872, gold cords on the shoulders of the Officers' tunics were substituted for the red silk cord which was worn on one side to secure the sash.

A Regimental Order, dated April 18, 1871, possesses an interest to the Coldstream, which requires a place in this account of their services :—

"A communication having been received by Field-Marshal Sir William Gomm, G.C.B., from the Secretary of the Royal Cambridge Asylum for Soldiers' Widows, to the effect that, at a meeting of the General Committee held March 9, 1871, a resolution was agreed to, according a presentation in perpetuity to the above asylum to the Colonel of the Coldstream Guards, the Regiment of H.R.H. the late Duke of Cambridge, the fact is here noted as a Regimental record."

In October, 1871, the names of the Officers posted to the two Battalions were :—

Colonel.—Field-Marshal Sir William Gomm, G.C.B.
Lieut.-Colonel.—Colonel Hon. Percy Feilding, C.B.

1st Battalion.	2nd Battalion.
Majors.—Vacant.*	Colonel C. Baring.
Captains.—Colonels G. Goodlake, V.C.; Hon. W. Feilding (*Mounted*).	Lieut.-Colonels A. Fremantle; C. Blackett (*Mounted*).
Lieut.-Colonels G. FitzRoy; G. Wigram; Lord William Seymour; Hon. E. Legge; E. Burnell; N. Burnand; F. C. Manningham-Buller; J. Hathorn.	Colonel Hon. R. Monck; Lieut.-Cols. H. Jervoise; Julian Hall; A. Lambton; FitzRoy Fremantle; Lord Cremorne; E. Chaplin; G. FitzRoy Smyth.

* Colonel P. Feilding commanded the 1st Battalion as well as the Regiment. Instead of 16 Ensigns, there were 13,—7 in the 1st Battalion and 6 in the 2nd Battalion. Vacancies were not filled up, owing to the changes that were about to be introduced into the Brigade of Foot Guards.

1st Battalion.

Lieutenants.—Captains H. Bonham-Carter; H. R. Eyre (I. of M.); Hon. F. Wellesley; Hon. Heneage Legge; H. Aldenburg-Bentinck; Hon. H. Corry; Hon. E. Boscawen; R. Goff; Waller Hughes; H. Bruce; E. Boyle; Hon. Ronald Campbell (Adjutant).

Ensigns.—Lieutenants F. Graves-Sawle; Hon. M. Stapleton; R. Pole-Carew; Cyril Fortescue; Hon. C. Cavendish; A. Clark-Kennedy; F. Arkwright.

Quartermasters.—A. Falconer.

Surgeon-Major.—J. Wyatt.

Battalion Surgeon.—

Assistant-Surgeons.—A. Myers; Whipple, M.D.

2nd Battalion.

Captains J. B. Sterling; C. D. Thomas; Hon. J. Vesey (Adjutant); R. S. Hall; C. Alexander; W. Ramsden; Hon. E. Acheson; Hon. L. Dawnay; Hon. E. Digby (I. of M.); W. Turquand; R. Follett; Amelius Wood; Hon. R. Greville-Nugent; Hon. G. Bertie.

Lieutenants A. Moreton; J. G. Montgomery; F. Manley; Hon. Alfred Charteris; Lord Ossulston; L. MacKinnon.

J. Birch.

Surgeon-Major C. V. Cay.

J. Trotter.

This chapter should not conclude without making some mention of the new armament introduced into the British infantry during the period under review. The Danish war, 1864, and more especially the Austro-Prussian struggle of 1866, revealed the immense superiority possessed by troops in the field who were supplied with the breech-loading rifle, over those that still retained the muzzle-loader. In the campaigns which have taken place between the two Germanic Powers, it has been remarked that Prussia has more than once been provided with better war *matériel* than her antagonist. In the Seven Years' War, Frederick the Great had an iron ramrod, the Austrians a wooden one, and the advantages he gained thereby were not inconsiderable. So in the Bohemian campaign of 1866, the Prussians were armed with a breech-loader, and the mass of fire they were able to develop on the battle-field was much greater and far more effective than their enemy could return against them. The great importance of this military question had not been neglected in England, and the object-lesson caused by the struggle in Central Europe stimulated the authorities to greater exertions. While, therefore, we were considering what pattern of breech-loading rifle we should finally adopt, immediate steps were taken to hurry on the conversion of the Enfield into the Snider breech-loader, so that by the end of 1866 Commanding Officers of Guards Regiments were directed to send in requisitions for the new converted weapon (December 19th). The rifle eventually adopted was the Henry-Martini, which was served out to the Coldstream in October, 1874. In time, the latter was discarded for the small-bore magazine breech-loader (the Lee-Metford .303 Rifle), and this was issued to the Regiment early in 1890. Immediately afterwards, the ordinary black powder, which had been in use for many centuries, was replaced by the present cordite, a smokeless nitro-explosive.

N R Wilkinson del.

OFFICER 1839

OFFICER 1849

A D Innes & Co London.

Modern Bros Chromo

CHAPTER XIV.

ARMY REFORM, 1871–1885.

Effect produced in England by the military successes of Prussia—Short service and the reserve system introduced—Abolition of army purchase—Abolition of the double rank in the Foot Guards—Substitution of the rank of Sub-Lieutenant for that of Ensign or Cornet—Manœuvres and summer drills—Changes in the drill-book—Illness and recovery of H.R.H. the Prince of Wales—Death of Surgeon-Major Wyatt, and of Field-Marshal Sir W. Gomm—General Sir W. Codrington appointed Colonel of the Coldstream Guards—Death of Captains Hon. R. Campbell and R. Barton—Company training—Pirbright Camp established—Medical service in the Brigade—Change in the establishment of the Regiment—Death of Sir W. Codrington, and appointment of General Sir Thomas Steele as Colonel—Troubles in Ireland—Alarm in London—The Royal Military Chapel.

THE wars that disturbed the Continent could not fail to rouse the serious attention of every thinking man in this country, and to make all look closely into the causes which had brought about very unexpected results. Englishmen were not surprised at the ease with which the great Germanic Powers overcame the resistance of Denmark, in 1864: nor yet, indeed, to see Austria driven from Lombardy when Napoleon III. set himself to the task, in 1859; because the alliance which we had contracted with the French in 1854, taught us to respect their army, and to believe they possessed a system and organization which placed them at the head of the military nations of Europe. But the struggles of 1866 and 1870–71 were of a very different nature. In the first case, we saw Prussia suddenly emerge from a small peace to a strong war establishment, strike swiftly and surely the minor States of Germany, and swoop down on Bohemia, where, meeting an enemy apparently worthy of her steel, and of about equal numerical strength to herself, she annihilated his forces in a few weeks, and obliged him to conclude a peace almost before he knew that fighting had commenced. In the second case, we again saw Prussia, in union this time with the smaller Germanic States, arm herself with even greater rapidity than before, concentrate her large armies on the frontier of France, invade the territories of her formidable rival, and lock up the bulk of the hostile forces in the fortress of Metz, while she captured the remainder at Sedan. These astounding successes occurred when scarcely two months had elapsed after the declaration of the war, and the course of hostilities was so favourable to the invader that, in less than seven months, France lay prostrate at the feet of Prussia, and was obliged to sue for terms of peace, humiliating to her national pride and derogatory to her great position in Europe.

No statesman could neglect to examine the causes of these stupendous events, and the institutions which had rendered them capable of realization: no soldier could abstain from studying the new conditions under which hostilities in the future must be conducted, and the numerous questions of warlike interest which modern science had introduced. It is not surprising that the Prussian system should speedily have become our model in the affairs relating to the army, and that the British nation should determine to make a searching inquiry into its military concerns.

It is not necessary to attempt to give a description of all the matters that claimed the earnest attention of the country at that time. Some of them did not affect the Coldstream, or did so only in a slight manner, and their discussion in this work may be omitted, or need receive but a passing notice. Among them, however, the two following should be mentioned: (1) the more efficient training of both Officers and men in their duties, and in the new system of tactics which had to be adopted in the field in consequence of the increased power of artillery, and of the great development of the fire of the breech-loader; and (2) the recruitment of the men, and the term of service during which they should remain with their corps.

We have seen that, as early as 1856, considerable interest had been taken in the first of these points, though it is also true that the reforms introduced were merely in their infancy, and had not by any means gone far enough. This was a natural result, because to effect a change of a salutary character, the expenditure of money is necessary, and public opinion must be moved before it can be obtained. The successes of Prussia had not then thrown light upon the requirements which a state of war in the present day exacts; and it was after these victories had been achieved, and not before, that the country acquired the faculty of realizing the advantages to be gained if all ranks are efficiently taught the details of the military profession.* Later in this chapter, an occasion will present itself to refer to some of the methods undertaken to accomplish this object, and we now pass to the second point, which, having a peculiar interest of its own, exercises a special influence on the fortunes of every regiment that forms part of the army.

Up to 1847 military service had been unlimited, and men who enlisted might be held to remain with the Colours for life.† The system was not satisfactory, and a change was then made by which men contracted to serve for ten years only, with the power of remaining on eleven more, should they be permitted to do so, and, at the end of that period, to receive a pension. In 1867, the first term of service was raised from ten to twelve years, and soldiers were encouraged to continue their service for twenty-one years for pension.‡ The advantage of having a reserve to fill up the ranks of the army in war time had, for some years, occupied the attention of the authorities, and, before 1867, two small attempts had been made to secure this object; but, though the principle was admitted, very little was done in this direction. The war of 1866, however, made the country realize the importance of a rapid mobilization; and the Prussians, having practically

---

* The army authorities have ever been alive to the necessity of professional instruction. Examples are to be found in the handbooks issued by Lieut.-General Lord Frederick FitzClarence (late Coldstream Guards, who helped to arrest the Cato Street conspirators in 1820) and by "A Field Officer" (Colonel Torrens, afterwards Major-General Sir Arthur Torrens, late Grenadier Guards), issued in 1850 and 1851, and if the reader can procure these publications, he will perceive they are as up to date, of their time, as our best text-books of the present day. It is a mistake to accuse the military authorities of slackness, in respect to the training of soldiers. The blame rests on the country which alone could supply funds, and which took no interest in these affairs. During the continuance of the present phase in the world's history, when every Continental nation is armed to the teeth, it is not likely that Parliament will withdraw its annual expenditure upon the army any more than on the navy. But it is right to add that, while the country can provide the money, public opinion will of itself never be able to foster military efficiency, nor instil into the army those qualities which make a man a soldier.

† During an emergency, men had been allowed to enlist for limited periods of service, varying from two to seven years (in the infantry), or while hostilities lasted. This was notably the case in the reign of Queen Anne, in 1745, 1759, 1775, and 1806-1829; but unlimited service for life also ran concurrently in the army at the same time (*The Army Book for the British Empire*, pp. 17, 22, etc.).

‡ *The Army Book for the British Empire*, p. 54. See also pp. 49-67.

Y

shown how, with a reserve at hand, they could, in a short space of time, convert a small peace establishment into a fully equipped army ready to take the field, we also desired to follow their example. In 1867, therefore, we strengthened the reserve; but, as a matter of fact, we still merely nibbled at the question, until 1870, when it at last received a more thorough consideration. In that year the Enlistment Act was passed, introducing "short service" and a more efficient reserve into the army.

By the new system, recruits enlist for twelve years, and engage to serve the whole time with the Colours, or part of the time with the Colours and the rest in the reserve, according to the conditions laid down by the Secretary of State. At first, it was proposed that the two periods should be equal; but this was soon modified to seven years in the ranks and five in the reserve, and in the Guards (since 1883) to three and nine, for such recruits who might prefer those terms. Hence, in the Brigade, men may now enlist for three or seven years with the Colours, and spend nine or five in the reserve; three-years men may, with the consent of their Commanding Officers, extend their service in the ranks to seven years, and from seven to twelve years, after which, still under the same conditions, they are able to re-engage for some years more up to twenty-one, with a view to obtain a pension.

Thus the present system is elastic, and has the merit of training a larger proportion of the population to the use of arms than was formerly the case; of enabling the nation to maintain a relatively small force in peace time, which can be rapidly expanded into an army when hostilities break out; and of reducing the pension list. It also increases the domestic comfort of the men, for it definitely disposes of the question of marriage of the rank and file, which, with long service, was difficult, indeed impossible, to solve. The practical utility of the plan has not yet been tested under the strain of war, and, until it has been so tried, it is manifestly premature to unduly praise it; nor are we yet in a position to judge whether the fighting material we now possess, is as well endowed with the fortitude, virtue, and cohesive force, which discipline bestows, as was the case in so eminent a degree in the past. We can point to this, however, that Continental nations who have tried their reserves in the field consider them to be fully equal to any other troops they have in their ranks; and we, too, have had experience of the noble qualities of comparatively untrained men in some very critical situations and emergencies. But, of one thing, at least, we may be sure: the reserve men will loyally come up when their presence is required. Englishmen have never failed to respond to the call of duty, and it is notorious, when even a fear arises that British interests may be attacked, how quickly the manhood of the country rises to the occasion, and offers to come forward to defend them. It cannot be forgotten that, in 1878, when the then existing reserve was called out, 13,684 men, out of a possible of 14,154, reported themselves; and, in 1882, when 11,642 reserve men were summoned, 11,032 appeared.*

The Prussian model, upon which we based our army reform, was departed from in two important particulars. In one, the departure was fully acknowledged and thoroughly explained in public; but not so the other. In the first, we repudiated the idea of inflicting the evils and the tyranny of universal service upon the country, and deliberately declined to make the people liable to a blood tax, that wastes their wealth and attacks their liberty and independence. Our military forces, hence, are smaller than they would otherwise have been, and our means of mobilization less rapid than those which exist on the Continent, because our reserve men, living where and as they like, are not localized and controlled in the manner which obtains among the Powers of Europe. Nevertheless, we willingly gave up these advantages for the sake of preserving our freedom, so dear to the mind of every Englishman, and the foundation of our national prosperity. As we inhabit an island, and hold the command of the sea by an overwhelmingly powerful navy, there was no valid reason to press for any alteration in our time-honoured custom of recruiting the army by voluntary enlistment.

The second departure from the Prussian organization seems to have been as carefully hidden from the public gaze as the other was ventilated and discussed. The system we chose to copy approached our own, in that the Sovereign was the direct and immediate Chief of the army, and from a purely military standpoint it is easy to

* *The Army Book*, etc., p. 119. We have not paused to inquire how the new system is suitable or the reverse to the requirements of small wars, in which Great Britain is so constantly engaged, because this question depends rather upon the manner in which the home battalion of a regiment serves as a depôt to its colleague abroad; and as this portion of the present army system does not affect the Guards, it is obvious that its consideration is not necessary in this volume.

perceive that such an arrangement—adopted moreover, by every great Power that has a Sovereign, and that aims at real military strength—is the best adapted to produce the most efficient results. Our reformers, however, completely ignored in this respect the model they announced they would follow, and as Englishmen have never been a military race properly so called, they scarcely saw or appreciated the change that was brought about, when the Supreme Command, still vested in the Crown, was exercised through the political channel of the Secretary of State (1870). The historian is bound to record this vitally important alteration in the constitution of the army—a change rendered desirable, perhaps, for reasons that are outside the scope of this work,—for, it affects and must affect the life of every regiment that composes it, and subjects many of the details of purely military interest and of the military profession, to the fluctuations and necessities of party strife.

Nor was it long before the army was made the victim of a political dispute. The war of 1870-71 had roused the people to fever heat, and army reform became the universal cry. Politicians, not gifted with military instincts or knowledge, soon led their followers into those points of the subject that best suited the interests of their party; and as the "abolition of purchase" offered just such an advantage in the parliamentary struggle then going on, it was eagerly seized upon as the most urgent question of the hour. It cannot be said that army reform was impossible without abolishing purchase, for every improvement introduced could have been as easily effected, whether purchase had been retained or not. But it is also true that the practice of buying and selling a commission was an anomaly quite indefensible in itself, which deserved to come to an end, and which was scarcely likely to survive for long. If so, its abolition, safeguarding the interests of all concerned by it, would have benefited the army more than can be said was the case, when it was achieved in 1871, and thereby increased the influence of the political party that carried it.

The purchase system had the disadvantage of checking the rise in their profession of men of very moderate fortune, who entered the infantry or cavalry;[*] and this without doubt was an evil which required reformation, for it excluded from these branches of the army some whose service there might have been of value to

[*] Purchase only existed in the infantry and cavalry, and not in the artillery and Royal Engineers.

the country. On the other hand, this defect was more theoretical than practical; and the system had the advantage of keeping up a flow of promotion, and of keeping down the pension list. It was not an arrangement by which any purchaser could buy his steps; to be allowed to spend money for this purpose was a privilege to which any conditions could be attached. So was it also a cheap means of keeping up the supply of Officers, for the sale of a commission was the only pecuniary reward that was expected, and Parliament was not asked to spend money to provide gratuities, retired pay, pensions, and the like, that now have to be given. Officers, in short, tendered security for their good behaviour, and proved their devotion to their profession by offering their service for a smaller return in the shape of pay than they now receive.

The Bill to do away with this system passed the House of Commons, and went in due course up the Lords, where it was read the first time. On the second reading, a demand was made for further information on the proposals that were then contemplated, and a resolution to that effect was carried. Thereupon a Royal Warrant, July 20, 1871, was immediately issued, which abolished purchase without the aid of Parliament, from the following 1st of November.

On October 31, 1871, another Royal Warrant was published, which contained two points that affected the Brigade: (1) it abolished what has been called the "double rank," and (2) it substituted the new rank of Sub-Lieutenant for that of Ensign in the infantry, and of Cornet in the cavalry, both of which had existed ever since the formation of the standing army.

The abolition of the "double rank" is of too recent a date, and concerns the Officers of the Brigade too intimately and personally, to be able easily to discuss it at the present moment. It will be time enough to do so at some future date, when war on a large scale has tested the quality of the modern army, when it has been practically shown where the military virtues are most plentifully to be found in it, and when we shall have emerged definitely from the transition state in which the reforms of 1871 has placed us. Guardsmen do recognise, and have for a long time recognised, that the advantage which the double rank conferred upon them was an anomaly which deserved to be swept away, for they have ever been anxious to possess no purely military privilege which the rest of their comrades did not enjoy, and have been eager to see removed anything that might savour of favouritism, or give cause for jealousy. Nevertheless, it is well to remember that the double rank was an institution which had obtained the sanction of two centuries, and that it was the survival of an ancient system which possessed some merit. In the infancy of the British army, shortly after the Restoration of King Charles II., brought about by General Monck and his Coldstreamers, there was much debate over the vexed question of "precedence of command." This precedence, in some regiments, not all of them Guards regiments, was fixed, not by seniority of commission, but by seniority of corps, and this arrangement appears to have developed into the institution of the double rank for the Foot Guards, and of Brevet rank for all.*

Now, it seems evident that the object in view, when these things were arranged, was to maintain efficiency in the army; to keep up a flow of promotion; and to prevent Officers from ranking low down in the army list, when, by length of service or for other reasons, it was desirable that they should rise with others in their profession. The regimental system, being the basis of military advancement, then, as it is now, it is obvious that unless some such means were adopted to accelerate the promotion of an Officer, who belonged to a corps where men were unwilling to leave the service, no efforts on his part could secure his rise. Nor can it be forgotten that promotion stagnates in proportion as Officers generally are attached to their profession and to their corps,—that is, in not the least distinguished regiments of the army; and if the regimental system have any value (and that it has a value is evident, while the promoters of army reform showed their opinion of it by retaining it), it becomes clear that relief is most required in those regiments where duty is well performed, and where a high standard of military efficiency is maintained. The principle laid down was neither unwise nor unfair; and if in the case of the Foot Guards it was applied with too generous a hand, it must still be remembered that this was done, not less on account of their services in the field, than by reason of the position they occupied in the army.

The sudden abolition of the double rank in 1871, put the Foot

* Colonel Clifford Walton, C.B., *History of the British Standing Army*, A.D. 1660–1700, pp. 441, etc. (London, 1894). The reader should remember that a form of the double rank still exists in every regiment of the service; the Colonel of each being either a General Officer or a Field-Marshal. Further on in this chapter it will be seen, moreover, that the double rank was practically revived in the infantry in 1881, when it suited Government to do so to serve their own purposes.

Guards in a worse position than if it had never existed; but they still have the honour of occupying a unique position in the army, for, while before 1871 they held the first place, after that date they sank immediately down to the lowest place in their profession. The following table will illustrate this fact:—

PROMOTION TO THE RANK OF CAPTAIN;* AVERAGE NUMBER OF YEARS' SERVICE.

	Brigade of Guards.		Cavalry.	Infantry of the Line.
	To Regimental Lieutenant, bearing Army Rank of Capt.	To Regimental Captain, bearing Army Rank of Lt.-Colonel.	To Regimental Captain, bearing no extra Army rank.	
Between 1838 and 1871 †	Years. $4\frac{5}{12}$	Years. $14\frac{8}{12}$	Years. $7\frac{3}{12}$	Years. $9\frac{11}{12}$
	To Regimental Captain, bearing no extra Army Rank.			
	Years.			
In 1884 ‡	12		$7\frac{1}{2}$	$8\frac{4}{12}$
In 1894 ‡	$12\frac{1}{12}$		7	$8\frac{5}{12}$

The substitution of the rank of Sub-Lieutenant for that of Ensign led to some curious results. By the rules established in October,

---

* The rank of Captain has been principally insisted upon, as it is the decisive step in an Officer's career. Once a Captain, an Officer who distinguishes himself can obtain Brevet rank. As a Lieutenant, he is unable to advance in his profession, except by regimental promotion.

† In calculating the figures of this part of the Table, the promotions have been taken which actually occurred in the years 1838, 1841, 1846, 1851, 1855, 1865, and 1870, in the whole of the Brigade of Guards, and of the Cavalry, and in every fifth Regiment (5th, 10th, 15th, 20th, etc.) of the Infantry of the Line.

The period $4\frac{5}{12}$ years, in the Table for the Brigade of Guards, would have been $5\frac{1}{12}$ years, had the average length of service required to promote an Officer of the Coldstream to Regimental Lieutenant, between 1838 and 1871, been given.

‡ These figures have been taken in the same way as under Note †, but for the years 1884 and 1894.

The year 1884 has been selected because promotion of Officers of the Brigade of Guards, who do *not* enjoy the double rank, began then generally to take effect. The first Coldstream Officer (without double rank) took 13 years to become Regimental Captain; the second, $13\frac{3}{12}$ years.

It may be stated, that, in 1896, the senior Second-Lieutenants in the Coldstream have all but six years' service—that is, nearly as much service as it takes the average Cavalry Officer to attain to the rank of Captain.

1871, a Commission as a Sub-Lieutenant might be given to a successful candidate who had passed certain examinations; and in order to qualify for the rank of Lieutenant, a Sub-Lieutenant was required to serve satisfactorily for twelve months in a regiment, and after such service to go through a course of study, and to pass a professional examination, fixed from time to time by the Secretary of State.

The position of the new Officer was unprecedented, and no one at first knew exactly what he was. Accordingly, on March 5, 1872, we find that he was forbidden to present himself before his Sovereign, because he was "not positively confirmed as a Commissioned Officer;" but then, on the 21st of May following, he was stated to be a "regularly Commissioned Officer, and, when qualified by a knowledge of his work, he was eligible for Courts-Martial and all other military duties performed by Subaltern Officers;" and at last, February 24, 1873, it was announced that he would be received at Court. The trials of the aspirant to serve in Her Majesty's army did not end here. The new civilian chief who assumed the direction of every military detail, determined that the stage of initiation into the most glorious profession the world has produced should be thorny, painful, and difficult. The Sub-Lieutenant, just as he emerged from school and opened the first and brightest page of a happy youth, was allowed to spend a year full of liberty among his new companions in arms, and to enjoy to the uttermost the sweets of life as they unfolded themselves before his vivid imagination. But the bright holiday was brief, and when it ended, the hapless lad was to experience a very different treatment. The year of enjoyment was over, and, giving up his freedom, he was sent back to the rigid discipline of school, (in this case even more severe than that to which he had been accustomed in his boyhood). Here he was tutored, controlled, corrected, and crammed. The power of a Secretary of State is great; but, just as he cannot make water run uphill, so can he not alter the ardent character of a young English gentleman, and the latter, we regret to say, rebelled at the indignities heaped upon him! Solemn indeed were the warnings which his sympathetic military superiors gave him. But they did more than this, for they persuaded the political chief to avoid running counter to human nature, and the rule was changed, and a more rational one substituted for it. The Sub-Lieutenant went first to school, and then he joined his Regiment.

It is pleasant now to leave these matters, and to turn once more to the solid and effective improvements that were introduced about this time. In 1871, manœuvres on an extended scale were, for the first time, held in England, when a successful endeavour was made to conduct operations which should, as far as possible, imitate those that have to be undertaken in war time. Aldershot and its neighbourhood was selected for these exercises, and they lasted for about seven weeks, commencing early in August until the end of September. The Guards Brigade present, was formed of the 1st Grenadiers, 2nd Coldstream, and 2nd Scots Fusilier Guards. Next year similar manœuvres took place in Salisbury Plain, which were even more successful than those of the year before. They lasted about a month, beginning in the middle of August, and were attended by the 3rd Grenadiers, 1st Coldstream, and 1st Scots Fusilier Guards. In this year, also, Regimental transport was introduced, and, in June, one Non-commissioned officer and twenty men of the battalions just mentioned were sent to Woolwich to be trained as drivers. In 1873, parties of the same strength, from the 2nd Grenadiers and 2nd Coldstream, again proceeded to Woolwich for a similar course, this time under the command of a Subaltern Officer from each Regiment, and manœuvres, lasting a month, took place at Cannock Chase, in Staffordshire. The two Battalions, above mentioned, formed the Guards Brigade upon that occasion, each made up into eight companies (25 Officers, 641 Non-commissioned officers and men, exclusive of the Regimental transport detachment). With this year the mimic war undertaken to exercise every part of the army, the fighting units as well as the transport, commissariat, medical services, etc., came to an end: manœuvres cost money, and the recollection of the great struggle between France and Germany was beginning to fade from the memory of those whose privilege it is to pay taxes and return members of Parliament. Henceforward summer drills were substituted for the larger and more instructive operations.

Concurrently with these reforms, and, indeed, during a longer period than is above indicated, the drill-book was often revised, and a system of tactics introduced, calculated to satisfy the conditions under which troops have to move when opposed to modern arms of precision. The space allowed to each man in the ranks has been increased, the rigid structure of the British line has given way to a looser formation, and, greater independence of individual action being deemed desirable, the intelligence of the private soldier has been raised and cultivated. The principles of the science of tactics remain constant, but the system adopted necessarily varies as new weapons are invented; the problem before us, therefore, was how to apply the principles to modern conditions. Our forefathers resolved the question satisfactorily, as far as their generation was concerned. They inculcated a stiff and rigid discipline into the British army, and they endowed the rank and file with a moral stamina sufficient to enable them to maintain themselves on the field of battle in line, and thus develop to the fullest extent the fire of their muskets. Our enemies, not so highly trained, could only fight in column; and, hence, in no small degree, our victories and their defeats. That the closest attention has been unremittingly given to this great problem, all know already; but, as we have not yet had the experience of a great war under new conditions, the results of our labours are not yet practically tested.

It will be remembered that the Prince of Wales fell grievously ill in the end of 1870, and that, hoping against hope, it appeared only too likely that the august patient could not recover. The whole of the English people, at home and abroad, were deeply agitated with anxiety for the life of His Royal Highness, and great was the joy, sincerely felt and universally expressed, when it pleased Providence to spare him to the country, and to raise him up again in vigour and in health and strength. Full of gratitude for this signal favour, the Queen commanded a thanksgiving service to be held in St. Paul's Cathedral, and proceeded there, accompanied by His Royal Highness and the Royal Family (February 27, 1871). It need scarcely be said that all classes of Her Majesty's loyal subjects eagerly seized this opportunity of joining their prayers to those of their Sovereign and of the Princess of Wales, and, as the Royal procession moved to the Cathedral, the people made a demonstration of sympathy, which showed how acutely they had felt the danger as long as it existed, and how great was their happiness now that it was past. The army was fully represented at this ceremony; small deputations from every regiment in the British Isles had assigned to them a place in St. Paul's. The Brigade lined the streets; the 1st Coldstream, occupying a portion of Oxford Street, near the

Marble Arch, represented the Regiment, as the 2nd Battalion was then at Windsor.

In the summer of 1873, the Shah of Persia visited England (June 18th) and remained for a few days. It was the first time that the Monarch of this distant Asiatic kingdom had ever come to Europe, and his reception in this country was conducted on a scale of much magnificence. There were, as usual, numerous Guards of Honour, the streets were lined by the Brigade when he entered the Metropolis, and a review was held at Windsor on the 24th, at which the whole of the London Battalions were present, the public duties being found by the 2nd Battalion, 4th Regiment. The Shah was also taken to the Tower on the 25th, when the 2nd Coldstream, being quartered there, received him with two Guards of Honour.

The marriage of H.R.H. the Duke of Edinburgh to a Princess of Russia, the only daughter of the Tsar Alexander II., and granddaughter of our late antagonist, Nicholas I., took place at St. Petersburg early in 1874, and was an event of some importance and novelty; for never before had the reigning Houses of England and Russia been directly united by the close ties of a family alliance. The marriage was looked upon as a happy augury for the future, and strong expectations were entertained that any past estrangement between the two countries might henceforth cease, to the benefit, it was hoped, of both. On the occasion of the public entry of Their Royal Highnesses, March 12th, a warm welcome awaited them on the part of the people; the streets were lined by the Brigade, both Battalions of the Regiment being present. In the following May, the Tsar came to England, and proceeded first to Windsor (13th) for two days, and was received by the 1st Coldstream, who were stationed there. When His Majesty went to Guildhall, on the 18th, the streets were again lined by the Brigade, and next day a review in his honour was held at Aldershot, attended by the four West-End Battalions.

It may be interesting to note that the power, then vested in the Colonel of the Regiment, to reduce a Non-commissioned officer summarily to the ranks was exercised, in 1874, for the last time:—

"*Regimental Order*, 11th May. Sergeant Moss is reduced to Private by order of Field-Marshal Sir William Gomm, G.C.B., for misconduct whilst attached to the Lincoln Militia."

In the same year, the Coldstream lost a distinguished Officer, Surgeon-Major Wyatt, whose report, on many important Regimental details connected with the struggle in the Crimea, has been frequently consulted in the preparation of the account given of the war in this work. The event stands thus recorded in Regimental Orders, and requires no further comment on our part:—

"April 4th. *Death of Surgeon-Major Wyatt, C.B.* In announcing to the Regiment the sad news of the death of Surgeon-Major Wyatt, C.B., the Commanding Officer feels sure he will express the feelings of every member of the Coldstream Guards when he says that a severer loss could hardly have befallen the Regiment; nor can he record so melancholy an event without bearing some tribute to the untiring zeal and brilliant talents of an Officer who, during a service of nearly twenty-three years, has won for himself a reputation almost as widespread in France as in his own country. Few men stood higher in the profession to which Surgeon-Major Wyatt belonged, and it is unquestionable that the energy which he displayed during the siege of Paris, and the great professional skill which he then had an opportunity of showing, reflected no small credit on the corps of which he was such an ornament. Considering the impaired state of his constitution he would undoubtedly have been justified in declining to undertake the arduous duties at the siege for which he was specially selected by the Secretary of State for War, and it is certain his death was hastened by the hardships and privations which, in his unflinching zeal, he so voluntarily and nobly underwent."

The two Battalions were both represented at the funeral, the 1st finding the firing party, and the 2nd the escort.

But this was not the only loss that the Regiment had to experience about this time, for a greater cause for mourning was in store for them, when their veteran Colonel, Sir William Gomm, died, March 15, 1875, in full vigour of an unimpaired intellect, though more than ninety years of age. Having entered the army as Ensign, in the year 1794, at an early age, this distinguished Officer had served his Sovereign for more than eighty years, and thus the last link which connected us with the past glories of the great wars of the French Revolution was severed. The Lieutenant-Colonel only expressed the universal feeling of sorrow that prevailed in the Coldstream, when he issued the following short sympathetic order upon this melancholy event:—

"March 15, 1875. *Death of Sir William Gomm.* The Commanding Officer has the painful duty to perform of announcing to the Regiment the sad news of the death of their gallant and distinguished Colonel, Field-Marshal Sir William Gomm, G.C.B., which took place this morning. A notice of his distinguished services, which included more than one battle during the last century, can hardly be recorded within the limits of a Regimental Order, but the present occasion cannot be allowed to pass without expressing the respect entertained by all ranks for the example set to us by one of the most honourable careers ever passed in the British army. The lively interest evinced by our late Colonel in the welfare of the Regiment has been unceasing ever since his first connection with it, and in him the Coldstream Guards lose as kind and generous a friend as has ever been entrusted with its interests. The Band and drums will cease to play in or out of barracks until after the funeral; a band of crape will be worn by the Officers on the left arm until after the appointment of a new Colonel shall have been gazetted. A rosette of crape will be attached to the Colours until after the funeral."

The Bands and drums of the Brigade ceased to play while the Coldstream was in mourning, until after the funeral, which took place at Rotherhithe, and was not accompanied by any military display; but all available Officers of the Regiment were, of course, present upon so sad an occasion.

General Sir William Codrington, G.C.B., the late Commander of the Forces in the Crimea, now succeeded as Colonel of the Coldstream, and issued an address to the Regiment:—

"*Regimental Order*, April 5, 1875. The Commanding Officer has much pleasure in promulgating the following notification received by him from General Sir W. Codrington, G.C.B., and feels sure that the Regiment will be gratified to learn that a renewal of that distinguished Officer's connection with the Coldstream Guards is as keenly appreciated by himself as it is by all ranks of the Regiment.

"Her Majesty has been pleased to confer upon me the Colonelcy of the Coldstream Guards, in succession to the late Field-Marshal Sir W. Gomm, whose distinguished services were appreciated by the army and by the Regiment in which he served so long and so well. The position in which I am now placed by Her Majesty's favour renews my former services of thirty years in the Regiment, and although separated from it in 1854, yet service in the field with another portion of the army did not separate me so far from the Coldstream Guards as to prevent my seeing and valuing, on many difficult occasions of war service, the action of the Brigade of Guards of which the Coldstream formed part. Twenty years have passed since these occurrences, but the recollection of them has not passed away, nor the interest diminished in the well-being of the Regiment with which Her

Majesty has again connected me by a duty which it will be a pleasure and an honour to carry out."

From 1871, as we have seen, there had been but one Lieutenant-Colonel and one Major in the Coldstream, the former being in command of the Regiment and of one Battalion, the latter having the command of the other Battalion. In 1875, however, the original establishment of one Lieutenant-Colonel and two Majors was restored, and Colonel A. Lyon Fremantle (son of a former well-known and distinguished Coldstream Officer), being promoted Major to fill up the vacancy, was posted to the command of the 1st Battalion (April 28th). The reason for this change was that the Lieutenant-Colonels of Guards Regiments were to be employed, in addition to the command of their own Regiments, in the capacity of Brigadiers of the metropolitan Volunteer Corps, which were then incorporated into three separate brigades. In order to discharge these duties, Regimental Adjutants were shortly afterwards (1881) also appointed, and these Officers, besides performing the ordinary work attached to that position (carried out up to this date by a Battalion Adjutant), acted as Brigade-Majors of the Volunteer brigades so created. Captain and Lieut.-Colonel Hon. E. Digby was the first Regimental Adjutant of the Coldstream.

Just before Colonel Goodlake, V.C., left the service (August 7, 1875), Colonel Fremantle was transferred to the command of the 2nd Battalion, and Colonel Hon. William Feilding succeeded the former Officer as Major Commanding the 1st Battalion. On September 5, 1877, Colonel Hon. Percy Feilding, C.B. retired upon half-pay, and the Lieutenant-Colonelcy devolved upon Colonel Fremantle, who was replaced in the command of the 2nd Battalion by Colonel FitzRoy. Only a few days later, Colonel William Feilding also went on half-pay (September 29th), and Colonel Julian Hall, promoted Major, was posted to the command of the 1st Battalion.

The Regiment then stood thus (December, 1877):—

Colonel.—General Sir William Codrington, G.C.B.
Lieut.-Colonel.—Colonel A. Lyon Fremantle.
Majors.—Colonels G. FitzRoy ; Julian Hall.
Captains.—Lieut.-Colonels G. Wigram ; A. Lambton ; Lord W. Seymour (Staff); E. Burnell ; FitzRoy Fremantle ; (*Mounted*).
F. Manningham-Buller ; G. FitzRoy Smyth ; H. R. Eyre ; J. B. Sterling ; C. D. Thomas ; Viscount de Vesci ; Hon. F. Wellesley ;

R. S. Hall; W. Ramsden; Hon. E. Acheson; H. Aldenburg-Bentinck; Hon. L. Dawnay; Hon. E. Digby; Hon. H. Corry; R. Follett.

Lieutenants.—Captain Hon. E. Boscawen (Adjutant); Major R. Goff; Captains Waller Otway; H. Bruce; Amelius Lockwood; Hon. R. Campbell (Adjutant); Hon. G. Bertie; F. Graves-Sawle; A. Moreton; Hon. M. Stapleton; R. Pole-Carew; J. G. Montgomery; Cyril Fortescue; F. Manley; R. Barton; F. Arkwright; L. MacKinnon (I. of M.); Lieutenants V. Dawson (I. of M.); Hon. E. Dawnay; Hon. H. Monck; Lord D. Gordon; A. FitzRoy; J. Ross-of-Bladensburg; A. Codrington; Hon. H. Legge; J. Gladstone; D. Dawson; C. Brand; Hon. F. Lambton; Hon. G. Gore; H. Stopford; Hon. H. Gough; Hon. A. Henniker-Major; Lord Sandhurst; A. Clarke-Jervoise; G. V. Boyle; Viscount Lambton; Hon. A. Dawson; Hon. H. Amherst.

Sub-Lieutenant.—H. Surtees.

2nd Lieutenants.—Edgar Vincent; W. Corbet.

Quartermasters.—J. Birch; W. Reynolds.

Surgeon-Major.—C. V. Cay, M.D.   *Battalion-Surgeon.*—Surgeon-Major C. Read.

Surgeons.—A. Myers; J. Whipple, M.D.; J. Magill, M.D.

Solicitor.—R. Broughton, Esq.

As the aspect of affairs in Ireland had improved, and as the disturbances that distracted the people had entirely ceased, it was found unnecessary to continue to keep a Guards Battalion any longer in Dublin. At the spring change of quarters of the year 1876, therefore, the Battalion there was not replaced, and the occupation of Shorncliffe camp was again resumed as the out-quarter of the Brigade. The 1st Coldstream accordingly went there at that time, and lost then, with sincere regret, an Officer of much merit in Quartermaster Falconer, who, having been in that position ever since 1853, left the Regiment in 1876. This excellent Officer was born in the town of Coldstream; he had been present with the Battalion during the whole of the war with Russia, and had gained for himself, during his long period of service in the Regiment, the sincere respect and the hearty good will of all ranks.

Major-General Prince Edward of Saxe-Weimar retired from the command of the Brigade of Guards, and was succeeded by Major-General F. Stephenson, C.B., August 1, 1876, who retained that appointment until July 31, 1879, when Major-General G. Higginson C.B., replaced him.

A second change was made in the course of this century in the title of the Scots Fusilier Guards, and on April 4, 1877, it was promulgated for general information that this Regiment would in future be designated by the name of Scots Guards.

During the period under review, from 1871–1885, the country was engaged in some minor wars. An expedition to Ashanti took place 1873–1874; hostilities were undertaken on the North-West frontiers of India, notably in Afghanistan, to keep out the influence of Russia, which we feared, and to counteract the rapid advance of her forces towards our borders; and operations were conducted against various native tribes in South Africa, principally against the Zulus, and against the Transvaal Republic in the same quarter of the world. In none of these were the Coldstream employed;* but some of the Officers of the Regiment were engaged in them in different capacities, and of them three lost their lives. Lieutenant Hon. Alfred Charteris, Aide-de-camp to the General Commanding the Ashanti expedition (Sir Garnet Wolseley), was attacked by fever, contracted in that unhealthy climate, and died, deeply regretted, on board ship when on his way home. The other two, Captains Hon. Ronald Campbell and Robert Barton, fell the same day in South Africa, on March 28, 1879. The high estimation in which these two brave Officers were held by their brothers in the Regiment, and the promise they gave of future distinction, have never been forgotten by their companions; their loss is still mourned, and their memory

---

* After the battle of Isandlwhana, January 22, 1879, in which the Zulus succeeded in overwhelming several companies of the 24th Regiment, some Officers and Non-commissioned officers of the Brigade of Guards, under Colonel Davies, Grenadier Guards, were sent to take charge of drafts proceeding to South Africa to join that Regiment. The Coldstream furnished one Officer (Captain Hon. G. Bertie) and two sergeants (one of them, the present Superintending Clerk, Sergeant-Major W. Johnson). The drafts were wrecked on their way out, but fortunately no loss of life occurred. Arrived at the seat of hostilities, the Guardsmen did duty with the 24th Regiment until the end of the war. The following Brigade Order appeared in London, October 3rd :—

"In congratulating the detachment of Officers and Non-commissioned officers sent to the Cape under the command of Colonel Davies, Grenadier Guards, the Major-General has much pleasure in publishing, for the information of the Brigade, the following order, issued by Colonel Glyn, C.B., commanding 1st Battalion, 24th Regiment, dated s.s. *Egypt*, October 1, 1879: 'The Officer Commanding cannot allow the Officers of the Brigade of Guards and Militia who have been attached to the 1st Battalion, 24th Regiment, during the late campaign in South Africa, to leave the Battalion without recording his appreciation of their services, and thanking them most sincerely for the willing and energetic manner in which they have performed their duties. Colonel Glyn assures them that they will always be held in kindly remembrance both by himself and his Officers. To the Non-commissioned officers of the Brigade of Guards, the Commanding Officer also tenders his best thanks for the assistance they have rendered when serving with the drafts and, subsequently, with the Battalion in the field."

is preserved and cherished, for they recall to the mind of those who knew them the type and embodiment of the Coldstream Officer. Of the details of their services it is not necessary to say more than this, that Captain Campbell, Chief Staff Officer to Colonel Wood, V.C., C.B., (now General Sir Evelyn Wood), lost his life while performing an act of daring gallantry, for which, had he lived, he would have received the Victoria Cross; an Officer and a soldier who followed him (Lieutenant Lysons and Private Fowler, 90th Regiment), and who fortunately escaped unhurt, were both awarded that high order of military merit. Captain Barton, in command of the Frontier Light Horse, was also killed in the same neighbourhood. In Colonel Wood's despatch, the following sentences are worthy of record in these pages.

"Camp, Kambula, Zululand, March 30, 1879.

"I directed Colonel Weatherley to dislodge one or two Zulus who were causing us most of the loss" [the enemy being concealed behind rocks or in caves], "but as his men did not advance rapidly, Captain Campbell and Lieutenant Lysons and three men of the 90th, jumping over a low wall, ran forward and charged into a cave, where Captain Campbell, leading in the most determined and gallant manner, was shot dead. . . . His Excellency" [Lieut.-General Lord Chelmsford, Commanding] "knew Captain Hon. R. Campbell: he was an excellent Staff Officer, both in the field and as regards office work, and, having shown the most brilliant courage, lost his life in performing a gallant feat; and though he fell, success was gained by the courageous conduct of Lieutenant Lysons and Private Fowler, 90th Light Infantry. Captain Barton, commanding the Frontier Horse, was always most forward in every fight, and was as humane as he was brave. On the 20th January, one of Umsabe's men, whom Captain Barton wished to take prisoner instead of killing him, fired at Captain Barton within two yards, the powder marking his face. When last seen on the 28th, he was carrying on his horse a wounded man." Lieut.-Colonel Buller (now General Sir Redvers Buller, V.C.), commanding the mounted troops of Colonel Wood's column, and who himself gained his Victoria Cross on that day for his own gallantry, writes as follows:—"Captain Barton is also a great loss; active, energetic, and intrepid, he was an excellent Officer, and devoted to his profession." *

The grave outlook of foreign affairs in the spring of 1878, when Russia, after a successful war with Turkey, forced a disastrous

* *Supplement, London Gazette*, May 7, 1879. See Appendix XIII. Sir E. Wood has written an account of Captain Campbell's heroism in *Pearson's Magazine* (Feb., 1896), "One of the Bravest Deeds I ever saw." See *Brigade of Guards Magazine*, ix. 164.

treaty upon the Sultan (treaty of San Stefano), led many to think that England would again become involved in further hostilities in the East, and for a time there was serious anxiety on the subject. But, warned by the Crimea, we were hardly inclined to embark in another quarrel with the Tsar. A European Congress then assembled in Berlin to modify the Treaty of San Stefano, and to conclude a new international agreement, known as the Treaty of Berlin (July 13, 1878). As a demonstration, and indeed also to take advantage of the opportunity to test the system introduced into the army by short service, the reserves were called up in April, and, as we have already seen, the summons to attend was well responded to by the men. The Coldstream reserves were posted to the 2nd Battalion. The three Guards Battalions first on the roster for active service (viz. the 2nd Grenadiers, 2nd Coldstream, and 1st Scots Guards), each selected thirty-two men to go to Aldershot to be trained as stretcher-bearers. The Regimental transport was re-organized, and proceeded later to Aldershot with the Battalions above-mentioned, to take part in the summer drills; shortly after which (September 11th) its establishment was fixed at one Officer, one sergeant, six drivers, three waggons, and one small-arm ammunition cart. Later (January 25, 1879), this transport was kept together as one corps, and the three Officers took it in turn, for four months at a time, to have it in charge.

The efforts to extend and improve the training of Officers and men, which have been already alluded to, were still continued, and in 1883, it was ordered that Company Commanders should give personal attention to the subject, and be responsible for the efficiency of the men placed under their immediate command. Before this date, however, the Brigade had already availed themselves of the advantages which Pirbright offered for some of these purposes. A Guards camp having been opened for musketry in 1881, it was soon utilized as a place where practical instruction in military exercises (other than ordinary drill), could be given by the Company Officers. In April, 1882, Commanding Officers were enjoined to carry out a series of minor tactical operations in conjunction with the course of musketry practice, and to examine their Battalions by companies, and by double companies, in outpost duty, attack formation, shelter-trench exercise, etc. The Battalions were also to stay at Pirbright for fourteen days, five to be devoted to minor tactics, four to preliminary drill, and five to musketry. Afterwards, they remained a longer time in camp, and were thus enabled to do all their company training there, besides their musketry.*

Following the example set us by Continental armies, we added sectional and field firing to the course of target practice which was annually carried out, and increased the number of rounds to be expended by the trained soldier from 100 to 150 (1882). Musketry had received considerable attention from the authorities, and it was held imperative that the men should not only be able individually to shoot with accuracy, but that they should also be trained to fire together, under conditions that prevail in the field, and against objects similar to those which present themselves to the aim of troops in war time. A Siege Operations Committee having been appointed to conduct experiments at Dungeness early in 1880, a detachment of the 1st Coldstream, then at Shorncliffe, was told off to assist them in their labours. The following Brigade Order (March 11, 1880) relates to this service:—

"The Major-General has great pleasure in noticing the highly favourable report of the conduct of a detachment of the 1st Coldstream Guards under the command of Lieut.-Colonel Otway, employed under the Siege Operations Committee at Dungeness. The President of the Committee remarks upon the cheerful endurance and steady discipline of the men, as well as the watchfulness and judgment of the Officers, and the ability and energy with which Captain Fortescue carried out the daily arrangements."

We have already had occasion to remark that, on the introduction of signalling, great interest was taken in the subject in the Brigade, and frequent allusions were made to the efficiency of the Guards in this respect. An extract of an order, dated March 11, 1884, may be quoted:—

"His Royal Highness's attention has been drawn to the energetic action of Lieut.-Colonel Bonham, which is deserving of praise, as also to the attention paid by the other Officers specially named, viz. Lieutenant Lloyd, 1st Grenadiers, and Lieutenant Lovell, 2nd Coldstream. Will you please convey an expression of His Royal Highness's satisfaction to the 1st and 2nd Coldstream Guards, the Royal Horse Guards, and the 3rd Grenadier Guards, who have taken such good positions in the list of relative efficiency."

* Guards being stationed in London, have no ground near their barracks suitable for many of their military exercises.

In the last chapter some notes were given upon the improvements which were made in the canteen system after the Crimean war. In 1879, the "coffee bar" was separated from the canteen proper, and thus two shops were established in barracks for the soldiers' use, in one of which no alcoholic liquor could be bought; this change was completed in London in 1880 and 1881. We may also state here that, through the instrumentality of Officers of the Brigade, early in the latter year, a coffee tavern was set up outside barracks in Buckingham Palace Road, for the use of the Non-commissioned officers and men of the Guards; the arrangement that was then made did not, however, continue for any great length of time, and though the tavern still exists, its connection with the Brigade is now severed.

A few changes in uniform since 1872 deserve a passing mention. Shoulder straps were added to the Officers' tunics and blue coats (end of 1880), and the gold cords on the former garments were then abolished. New badges were put on these straps to show the military rank of the wearer. Previous to this, although the rank of an Officer was indicated on the collar of the tunic, no such distinction was to be seen on the blue coat. In the following March, the dark grey cloth, adopted for the trousers of Officers in the Brigade in 1830, gave place to a blue tweed. Up to 1874 Non-commissioned officers and men wore buttons on the skirts of the tunic, but they were then removed on account of the new valise equipment which was introduced at that time, instead of the old knapsack. Since that date the valise has been always carried by the soldier, though the pattern has more than once been changed.

Some alterations were effected in the medical service of the Brigade. Up to the year 1865, the Surgeons belonged exclusively to their respective Regiments as much as any other Officer of the Guards, and their promotion took place therein when vacancies occurred in their own corps only. Forming a small body in each, it is evident that their advancement was always uncertain, and too frequently was it exceedingly slow. To relieve this stagnation, the Medical Officers of the Brigade, though still belonging to and wearing the uniform of their respective Regiments, are now placed upon one list according to seniority, and are promoted in their turn into whatever corps the vacancy occurs. A better flow of promotion is thus obtained, though the Medical Officers are subject to the inconvenience of being sometimes obliged to change their Regiments when they gain a step. Another change, made in April 2, 1881, was the appointment of a Brigade Surgeon in the Guards to act as Principal Medical Officer. This system replaced the old arrangement by which the three Regimental Surgeons-Major took it in turn to do duty in Brigade Waiting, and to act as the medical adviser to the Major-General. Lastly, in 1881, the three Regimental hospitals were converted into station hospitals, for the general use of all troops quartered in the London garrison.

The grade, created to supplant the old military title of Ensign, met with some vicissitudes. Sub-Lieutenants ceased to be so called in 1877, and the name Second-Lieutenant was then substituted for it. In 1881, however, the rank was altogether abolished, and Second-Lieutenants were promoted Lieutenant, while young Officers joining the army were gazetted Lieutenants. But this arrangement did not last long, and again there was another change, for in 1887 Second-Lieutenants were re-introduced into the army; but there appears to be no tendency to restore the old traditional rank of Ensign.

One of the consequences of the abolition of purchase, clearly foreseen by the authors of army reform, was to produce a state of complete stagnation in promotion. To relieve this evil, a device was resorted to, whereby Officers, their qualifications or inclinations notwithstanding, were not allowed to remain in certain positions in their regiments for more than a definite period or after attaining a specified age. For instance, Commanding Officers of regiments and battalions were limited to five years command (reduced to four in the case of the latter, 1881), and all Captains were forced to retire from the service if not promoted to Major before the age of forty. The relief thus afforded was not of great advantage to the bulk of the juniors, and it constituted a well-founded grievance to many who, while able and willing to serve, were thrown out of their profession through no fault of their own.* Now, in 1881, a large number of Captains were doomed to be ejected,

* The automatic system of facilitating a flow of promotion at no cost to the State, which purchase produced, may perhaps be illustrated by the fact that, from 1814 to 1871, or during fifty-seven years, the Coldstream had twenty-one Lieutenant-Colonels; or each, on an average, served in that capacity for a period of about two years and nine months. Whereas, between 1871 and 1895, there have been five Lieutenant-Colonels, whose average period of command has nearly reached the full five years allowed by the new regulations.

whereat it appears the Secretary of State got seriously alarmed, Nor is it surprising that he should fear the prospect of having between 3000 to 4500 vigorous and educated men going "up and down the country," and pointing out in every constituency the grievances to which they were subjected by the hasty introduction of political army reforms that his own party had effected in 1871.* He was constrained to save these men, and the only way to do this was to promote them *en masse* to the rank of Major. Hence all Majors in the infantry below a Mounted Officer, (since 1893, below the Second in command), are "Captains and Majors," fulfilling the duties of the former, and dignified with the rank of the latter. They therefore enjoy the "double rank," which was held to be so objectionable, in 1871, when it prevailed in the Foot Guards. The advantage, however, does not go on, for on becoming "Second in command," an Officer performs the duty of Major, but has no extra rank given to him.

The introduction of Warrant-officers into the army was brought about at this time also; and the Sergeant-Major and Bandmaster (and later the Regimental Clerk) were so promoted.

These things were effected in July, 1881; and then the following changes were made in the establishment of the Coldstream: The companies were reduced from 20 to 16 (8 per Battalion, instead of 10, as had been provided during the Crimean war). The Lieutenant-Colonel remained in command of the Regiment, but instead of two Majors Commanding Battalions, the designation of these Officers was altered, and they were called Lieutenant-Colonels Commanding Battalions. Of the Captains there had been twenty, or one to each Company, and the four seniors used to be called Acting-Majors, or Mounted Officers; instead, there were now eight Majors in the Regiment (the four seniors being mounted,† and the four juniors unmounted), and nine Captains. Lastly, the rank of Second-Lieutenant was abolished, and instead of 20 Lieutenants and 20 Second-Lieutenants, there were 36 Lieutenants. The differences in the two establishments are to be seen in the following table:—

* See *The Army Book for the British Empire*, p. 57.
† The dismounting of two "mounted" Majors took place in 1893; and now there are in the Regiment two "mounted" (or a "Second in command" per Battalion) and six "unmounted" Majors,

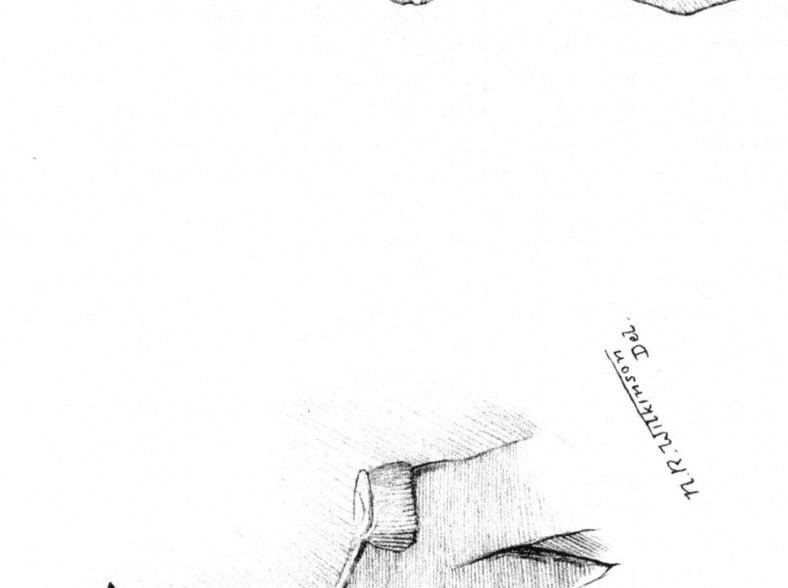

OFFICER 1849

UNDRESS CAP PRIVATES
ABOUT 1850.

May, 1881.	July, 1881.
20 Companies.	16 Companies.
1 Colonel. ⎫	1 Colonel. ⎫
1 Lieut.-Colonel ⎬ Field-Officers.	1 Lt.-Col. Com. Regt. ⎬ Field-
2 Majors ⎭	2 Lt.-Cols. Com. Batns. ⎭ Officers.
20 Captains.	8 Majors.
20 Lieutenants.	9 Captains.
20 Second-Lieutenants.	36 Lieutenants.
2 Adjutants.	3 Adjutants.
	(1 per Battn. and 1 Regtal).
2 Quartermasters.	2 Quartermasters.
2 Surgeons-Major.	2 Surgeons-Major.
3 Surgeons.	3 Surgeons.
1 Solicitor. *Total Officers* 74.	1 Solicitor. *Total Officers* 68.
2 Serjeants-Major.	2 Sergts.-Major. (Warrant-officers).
	1 Staff Clerk.
2 Quartermaster-Sergeants.	2 Quartermaster-Sergeants.
1 Bandmaster.	1 Bandmaster. (Warrant-officer).
2 Sergt.-Instructors of Musketry.	2 Sergt.-Instructors of Musketry.
2 Drum-Majors.	2 Sergeant-Drummers.
2 Armourer-Sergeants.	2 Armourer-Sergeants.
2 Orderly Room Sergeants.	6 Orderly Room Sergeants.
2 Pioneer Sergeants.	2 Pioneer Sergeants.
20 Colour-Sergeants.	16 Colour-Sergeants.
2 Sergeant Cooks.	2 Sergeant Cooks.
60 Sergeants.	48 Sergeants.
	Total Warrant-officers, Sergts.
Total Sergeants, etc., 97.	*etc.*, 86.
32 Drummers and Fifers.	32 Drummers and Fifers.
Total 32.	*Total* 32.
80 Corporals.	80 Corporals.
1420 Privates.	1420 Privates.
Total Rank and File, 1500.	*Total Rank and File*, 1500
1703 *Total*.	1686 *Total*.

On the 10th of November, 1880, Colonel Fremantle having left the Regiment, Colonel FitzRoy was appointed Lieutenant-Colonel, when Colonel Wigram, promoted Major, assumed the command of the 2nd Battalion. On the completion of five years period of command, Colonel Julian Hall retired on half-pay, September 29, 1882, and was succeeded in the command of the 1st Battalion by Colonel Arthur Lambton, who thus became

Lieutenant-Colonel of a Battalion in the Coldstream, and who was appointed to serve for four years in that capacity. Colonels FitzRoy and Wigram, C.B., finished their periods of five years simultaneously, November 10, 1885. The latter, placed on half-pay for a few weeks, was brought back as Lieutenant-Colonel of the Regiment (December 16th), and the command of the 2nd Battalion devolved upon Colonel Sterling (November 10th).

By the death of General Sir William Codrington, G.C.B., on the 6th of August, 1884, the Coldstream lost their Colonel, who had served as such for more than nine years. The following Regimental Order was published:—

"*August* 7, 1884. The Commanding Officer has the painful duty to perform of announcing to the Regiment the sad news of the death of their gallant and distinguished Colonel, General Sir William Codrington, G.C.B., which took place yesterday afternoon, 6th inst. A band of crape will be worn by the Officers for a month; the Band and the drums and fifes will not play until after the funeral."

The funeral was accompanied with military honours, and took place at Woking Cemetery on the 9th. All Officers attending it were dressed as for Guard, and, including the firing party of 50 men, there was a detachment present of the 1st Battalion, consisting of 100 Non-commissioned officers and men under three Officers.

Sir W. Codrington was succeeded by General Right Honourable Sir Thomas Steele, K.C.B., at that time Commander of the Forces in Ireland, whom Her Majesty appointed the new Colonel of the Regiment.

In the same year, Lieut.-General Higginson, C.B., vacated the command of the Brigade of Guards, and was replaced by Major-General R. Gipps, C.B., April 1, 1884.

The 1st Coldstream was first on the roster for duty in Ireland, and at the end of 1880 was quartered in Chelsea and St. George's Barracks. Serious troubles once more affected that country, and Government was sorely perplexed how to deal with them. The presence of the Guards was again required, and the Battalion was despatched there at a few days' notice, by two special trains from Victoria Station, *via* Holyhead (December 6th). Upon this, the 2nd Grenadiers, then at Shorncliffe, were brought to town, and that out-quarter was given up. On the 15th of December, a detachment of 100 men from the 2nd Battalion joined the 1st in

Dublin, and five days later the 1st Scots Guards left London for the same destination. The Coldstream were quartered in Richmond Barracks, but the Scots Guards were scattered through the town, their head-quarters in Ship Street, with detachments in Richmond, and in Linen Hall barracks.

A novel procedure was now adopted with respect to the command of these two Battalions, which shows how critical the authorities conceived the situation to be. Shortly after their arrival in Dublin, the Major-General Commanding the Brigade and the Home District proceeded there accompanied by his Brigade Staff, and left Colonel Gipps, Scots Guards (the senior Officer) with the District Staff to command the Home District; but the arrangement did not last long, and the latter, temporarily promoted Brigadier General, took General Higginson's place in Ireland, who thereupon returned to London, February 15, 1881.*

The stay of the Battalion in Dublin, lasting until March, 1882, was not more pleasant then than it had been during the Fenian troubles of 1866; but the duties assigned to the troops were everywhere cheerfully undertaken and zealously discharged. Among these duties two may be specially mentioned. In the first place, such was the violence of the mobs that collected to interfere with the due administration of the law, that a collision was apprehended every time a writ was served, a seizure made in a farm, an eviction put into execution, or any other legal process carried out. To avoid the danger, the Irish authorities established the rule that the force protecting the sheriff or other officer employed, should be so overwhelmingly strong, as to put an end to all thoughts of resistance, on the part of those who assembled to frustrate the course of justice. The Royal Irish Constabulary were, of course, always employed on these occasions, but it was also believed that the presence of red-coats would have a greater effect with the excited populace, and for this purpose numerous military posts covered the disturbed districts; but the Guards in Dublin, occupying a central position there, were not obliged to furnish any of these detachments.

Soldiers, therefore, were often requisitioned to escort the civil authorities, and the two Guards Battalions (as well as those that

* On the 7th of December, 1881, Colonel FitzRoy, Coldstream Guards, temporarily promoted Brigadier-General, proceeded to Dublin to relieve Colonel Gipps, appointed Major-General.

succeeded them in Dublin during the troubles), were often employed in this manner—generally by despatching small parties of some fifty men under an Officer. On one occasion, however, the 1st Coldstream had to do more than this. There was a series of evictions near New Pallas, in the county of Limerick, and the whole Battalion, together with a portion of Scots Guards, were sent there for two days to guard the sheriff, who had to execute the judgment of the Court. It was, at least, an uncommon service for so large a force to perform; and the Battalion was in all conscience powerful enough to prevent any breach of the peace!

The other duty to which allusion has been made, refers to what was called "personal protection." Many landlords, and indeed others, were in danger of their lives from the outrage-mongers that infested the land. In order to afford adequate protection to these persons, soldiers were told off to reside in their houses, to accompany them in all their movements, and to be responsible for their safety. The Coldstream and Scots Guards furnished a number of men to perform this duty, and an Officer from each Regiment was appointed to inspect them frequently, and to satisfy himself that this novel service was efficiently discharged. That this was the case may be gathered from the following order, issued in London, dated March 17, 1882:—

"By desire of the Field-Marshal the Commander-in-Chief, I have the honour to transmit to you the enclosed report on the conduct of the Coldstream and Scots Guards, while employed on protection duty in Limerick and Clare under the order of Clifford Lloyd, Esq., Resident Magistrate at Tulla, and to request that you will be so good as to express to all concerned, His Royal Highness's approbation of their conduct in the performance of the duties they have been called upon to undertake, and which are quite unusual with soldiers. His Royal Highness has much pleasure in recognising the valuable services rendered by Captain Fortescue, Coldstream Guards, and by Lieutenant Romilly, Scots Guards, which have been brought to the notice of His Excellency the Lord-Lieutenant."

But the Coldstream had some further experiences. It will be remembered that Mr. Parnell, the leader of the Irish agitation, was arrested as a suspect, October 13, 1881, under an Act of Parliament which had been passed in the spring of that year. The authorities, expecting some resistance, made every military preparation in Dublin to prevent a riot; and their precautions being sufficient, and their resources ample, the capture was very easily accomplished without mishap. Still, the quick-witted Irish very soon realized that the Government in London were afraid of them. They had early perceived that the Cabinet, instead of facing the difficulty boldly, dallied with it, and failed to support the Chief Secretary, Mr. Forster, in his strenuous efforts to cope with it. Hence, seeing no strength in the authority that should have protected them, the people were constrained to obey those who did wield power in the country, by setting its laws at defiance and by oppressing it without mercy. The winter, 1881-82, was disturbed and troubled. The No-rent conspiracy was in full swing; murder clubs, under the name of Moonlighters, kept the land in terror; juries were intimidated, and refused to discharge their functions; and the executive was all but paralysed. It was, moreover, known that a gang of assassins, called "the Invincibles," had bound themselves together to murder Mr. Forster, and it was afterwards ascertained that they had made numerous desperate attempts upon his life, all of which were happily unsuccessful.

Meanwhile, in January, 1882, the 2nd Grenadiers were sent to Cork, and for two months there was the unprecedented number of three Guards Battalions in Ireland, until March, when the 2nd Coldstream relieved the 1st Battalion, who returned to England, and were soon after followed by the 1st Scots Guards. So the gloomy spring passed, when a new complication arose. Mr. Forster had remained at his post with steadfast courage, and scorned the imminent personal danger that surrounded him, with which he knew he was threatened. But he was unable to stand by a leader of whose policy he disapproved, or to follow him in the tortuous intrigue, which became known in history as the "Kilmainham treaty." He resigned, and the then Lord-Lieutenant (Lord Cowper), having also withdrawn from office, Lord Spencer was appointed in his place, and arrived in Dublin, May 6, 1882, accompanied by his new Chief Secretary, Lord Frederick Cavendish.

On that very afternoon, in broad daylight, while walking through the Phœnix Park, which was then full of people, Lord F. Cavendish and Mr. Burke, the Under-Secretary, were murdered by the Invincibles, who had for so long unsuccessfully lain in wait to assassinate Mr. Forster. The event sent a thrill of horror through the United Kingdom, and effectively and at last forced the Government to open their eyes to the true nature of the conspiracy with which they had to deal. The miscreants got away, and for a time there was little information to be obtained as to the perpetrators of this foul deed, and twelve months had to elapse before the conspirators were convicted and punished. The 2nd Coldstream, quartered in Dublin when this tragedy took place, were not called upon to act in the emergency. There was nothing, indeed, for soldiers to do at the crisis, except to redouble their vigilance ; for it soon became clear that the Irish were as much the victims of the agitators and outrage-mongers who had mastered them, as were the officials who suffered by their violence.

In less than three months both the Guards Battalions, quartered in Dublin and in Cork, were required to proceed on active service to Egypt, and left the scenes of internal discord and disorder to meet the open foes of their country. The 3rd Grenadiers replaced them in Dublin (August 8th), and since that time there has been only one Battalion in Ireland. The Coldstream did not return there till the autumn of 1887, when the agitation had assumed a new phase, although the crisis had by no means passed away, nor the difficulties come to an end. Thanks, however, to the vigour of Government, to the remedial measures introduced, to the disappearance of Parnell, to the absence of another leader of character, and to the quarrels that have split up the Nationalist party into hostile fragments, the people are now steadily quieting down ; and, eschewing agitation, they are improving their material prosperity under the new laws which have been enacted for their benefit.

In February, 1881, that is, shortly after the two Battalions went in haste to Ireland at the end of the previous year, the Tower was vacated by the Foot Guards, and was occupied by a Line regiment until November, 1882. There were then four Battalions in the West End, and this continued to be the force maintained there—excepting for the two months, January 25th–March 22nd, 1882, when, as we have seen, three Battalions were stationed in Ireland—until the departure of a Guards Brigade of three Battalions for Egypt. During this war, Dublin was still occupied by a Battalion, but Windsor was vacated, and, until the return of the Brigade from active service in November, the 2nd King's Royal Rifle Corps furnished the Kensington Palace and the Magazine guards. In the following year, 1883, London was the scene of dynamite outrages, perpetrated by the agents of the same secret societies, of American origin, which financed and supported the agitation in Ireland. "For a time the air was dense with rumours of plots and explosives," and all minds were filled with vague alarms. A measure to punish dynamiters was passed in haste through all its stages in both Houses of Parliament, in one day (April 9th), and received the Royal assent next day at noon.* The garrison of the Metropolis also required strengthening, and a Line regiment being brought to the Tower, there were then five Guards Battalions in the West End. Extra guards were mounted on Somerset House, the Royal Courts of Justice, and Millbank prison, the London duties were increased, the public offices protected, and other precautions taken. The panic was considerable while it lasted, but it passed away in about six months, and in the summer the garrison of London assumed its normal strength and condition.

This ends the history of the Coldstream up to 1885, as far as affairs in the United Kingdom are concerned; and we now turn to events that occurred in Egypt and in the Sudan, 1882-1885. Before doing this, however, we may briefly allude to a subject which possesses much interest to all Guardsmen. Some members of the Coldstream may perhaps be unaware that the exquisite decorations that adorn the interior of the Royal Military Chapel in Wellington barracks have been scarcely twenty years in existence. Before that time the walls were cold and bare, and the building contained little to show how zealously the Brigade guard the great traditions of the past,—traditions which they have inherited,—and how warmly they cherish the memory of the Officers, Non-commissioned officers, and men who, ever since the formation of the standing army, have faithfully and bravely performed their duty to the Sovereign of this realm. Numerous are the monuments placed in the Chapel to record the military virtues of departed Guardsmen of every rank, and their deeds on many a hard-fought field of strife; while these memorials furnish a proof of the solid union which knits the three Regiments of the Household Infantry together, in love for their profession and in devotion to their Queen and country.

* *Ann. Reg.*, 1883, part i., p. 84.

CHAPTER XV.

THE WAR IN EGYPT, 1882.

Origin of the war—Emancipation of Egypt from Turkish rule; introduction of European control—Deposition of Ismail Pasha—Tewfik becomes Khedive—Military revolts—Disorganization of the country—Joint action of the English and French; its failure—Naval demonstration—Bombardment of the forts of Alexandria—The French withdraw and leave Great Britain to act alone—British troops sent to Egypt—The Suez Canal seized—Base of operations established at Ismailia—Action of Tel el-Makhuta—Clearing the communications—Actions at Kassassin, August 28th and September 7th—Character of the Egyptian army—Night march on Tel el-Kebir—The enemy is overwhelmed, September 13th—Pursuit; losses—End of the war—Return of the Coldstream to England.

THE hostilities conducted by England in Egypt in 1882 have been described as a mere bondholders' war. This, in a sense, is true, for our intimate relations with that country, which eventually led to military operations, were ostensibly due to our desire to protect the financial interests of those who had lent money to its ruler. But this is far from being the whole truth, because other and higher motives induced Great Britain to intervene in the internal affairs of the native government. Facing alike the Mediterranean and the Red Sea, and containing within its limits the isthmus of Suez, Egypt, besides being the key of the valley of the Nile, commands the most convenient water communications to India, to the further East, and to Australia. Having interests of a vital nature to defend in this far-distant quarter of the globe, it is evident we could never remain unconcerned if anarchy were to prevail in a region through which the main lines pass that connect together portions of the British Empire. Nor was the problem a new one. At the close of the last and at the commencement of the present century, England was struggling with the French for supremacy in India, and at that time Napoleon—then in the beginning of his great career—made a descent upon Egypt to secure a road to that Empire for his own nation. We were then obliged to drive his soldiers out, and, having succeeded in doing this, we prevented the French from forming an Asiatic dominion. Still the trouble continued, in a minor degree, until 1809, when we took the island of Mauritius from them, on which they depended, to base their operations against our possessions. From this date their power in the East declined ; and England, relieved from rivalry, has thenceforward been able to exercise an undivided influence in India. If in the beginning of this century it was necessary to prevent France from interfering with our national expansion ; so was it also the more necessary to restrain the Egyptians from obstructing (as we apprehended) our communications in 1882,— when the Suez canal having been opened (1869), nearly all our Eastern commerce was squeezed through that narrow passage, and when the importance of African exploration was adding greater value to the valley of the Nile.

Egypt has passed through some vicissitudes during the last sixty years. Still considered in theory to be a portion of the Turkish Empire, it was formerly ruled directly by the Porte, until Muhammad Ali, the Governor-General, or Vali, rebelled, and wrested concessions from the Sultan. In 1841, the Governorship was vested in him and in his heirs, and subsequent Firmans having been granted in his favour, Egypt became practically an independent principality. The last privilege accorded to his successors was the right to contract foreign loans without the previous consent of the Porte, and this right to run into debt was freely indulged in by Muhammad Ali's grandson, Ismail Pasha. The latter, after becoming Viceroy—or Khedive, as the title is called—embarked in wild speculations, and indulged in unbounded extravagance. Desiring, like his grandfather, to erect an independent state by the adoption of European civilization, he failed to understand how this civilization was to be brought about. He hastened to produce its effects by an immense expenditure of money, but he omitted to establish an efficacious administration to curb peculation, or to introduce order into his affairs. Numerous speculators of every nationality rushed forward to help him to dissipate his fortune, and it was not long before he involved the people in financial ruin. As the import of alcohol corrupts a barbarous tribe, so did the influx of foreign gold demoralize this Muslim government.

Now, even if England had been prepared to let the bondholders shift for themselves in this crisis, so were not the other European nations; and to prevent so important a country from falling into the hands of any one of them, all agreed to intervene and regulate the evil that had been brought about. Thus Ismail, emancipated from the rule of Turkey, fell under the domination of European control. It is scarcely necessary to describe the various steps taken to secure reform in the financial concerns of Egypt. England and France were more interested in the matter than any other of the Powers. They acted harmoniously together, assumed a joint direction over the affairs of the country, and gradually tightened their hold upon the government. Thereupon the Khedive became restive, and as he would not fall in with the new order established to correct his maladministration, he was removed from Cairo. The authority of the Sultan, as Suzerain, was now requisitioned by Europe: Ismail was deposed, and his son, Tewfik Pasha, reigned in his stead, by favour of the Western Powers (June 26, 1879).

It was easy to see that such an undefined condition of things was not likely to last long. However beneficial to the people an honest administration might be, the interference of foreign officials in the internal affairs of another state, to whose ruler they owed no allegiance, could not but produce friction, and lead to trouble. It is true, Tewfik was pliant, and submitted without difficulty to the unprecedented constitution that was forced upon him; also, that there was little or no public opinion in the country, and apparently no centre of resistance to thwart the action of England and France. Nevertheless, the new Khedive soon lost his authority over his subjects, and resistance did arise, sooner than might have been expected. It originated where it ought least to have been found—in the army, where insubordination showed itself as soon as the native government was weakened and became contemptible in the eyes of the people, and when economy was introduced into the war department. Early in 1881, a military rising was threatened, and with difficulty was it appeased; but, later, a more serious event occurred (September 9th), when the Colonel of one of the native regiments, named Arabi Bey, took the lead, and, surrounding the Khedive's palace with 4000 men, demanded, with arms in his hands, the redress of grievances from his Prince. Destitute of all real power, Tewfik was unable to crush this revolt; he met the mutineers, tried to conciliate them, and gave in to their demands. A change of government took place, and the Chamber of Notables was convened. From that moment Arabi's influence grew stronger, the army became devoted to him, and around him rallied all groups of the people who were dissatisfied with foreign interference. "Egypt for the Egyptians" was now the cry, and the newly appointed Chamber, far from allaying the trouble, added fuel to the flames of discontent that were already kindled. It was evident the crisis could not be much longer deferred.

The French urged the British Government to take active measures to support the Joint Control which then existed in Egypt, and the latter were quite willing to carry out this advice. On the 6th of January, 1882, an Identical or Dual Note was presented to the Khedive, expressing the determination of the two nations "to ward off by their united efforts all cause of external or internal complications which might menace the *régime* established in Egypt." The Notables answered this challenge by claiming the right of regulating the national budget, and Tewfik's action became somewhat uncertain. It could not be accurately ascertained whether he meant to stand by his European allies who had placed him upon the throne, or whether he was about to throw in his lot with the national party. At any rate, Arabi, advanced to the dignity of Pasha, became still more powerful, and was appointed Minister for War.

Now, in England, there was a certain feeling in favour of the Egyptians, and this might be expected to find expression among the supporters of the Liberal party then in power, who claim, perhaps with greater emphasis than others, to respect the liberties of mankind, and to listen to the grievances of all who complain. It is against our custom to stifle the voice of an assembly, however feebly it may be supposed to represent the wishes of a people, and in this crisis there were not wanting some who hesitated to sanction the use of coercive measures. Nor was there a total absence of a *primâ facie* cause of discontent; for the European officials of every nationality had multiplied in Egypt, and in 1882 there were as many as 1324, receiving salaries from the taxes that amounted to a considerable proportion of the revenue,—to £373,704 per annum.* It is possible that if we had not deferred

* *Annual Register*, 1882, pt. i. 361 (note). See, also, D. Mackenzie Wallace, *Egypt and the Egyptian Question*, p. 135 (London, 1883).

to the French at this juncture, we might have put an end to the commotion without resorting to war, and that, had we been the sole trustee for European interests, we might have found some satisfactory solution to the difficulty. But, as had happened before, we were fettered by our alliance with the French, which was not defined, and in order to maintain our relations with them, we followed their lead.

The Dual Note having only intensified the trouble, our Government despaired of maintaining order unless some vigorous action were taken to disperse it. They believed that the best course under the circumstances was to resort to the only legal means which then existed: viz. to revive, in some shape, the dormant rights of suzerainty which the Sultan claimed, which in theory had never been abrogated, and which had been made use of, as we have seen, less than three years before, with the consent of all the European Powers. It was therefore contemplated to utilize the Turks, under certain conditions and restrictions, to put an end to the deadlock, and to prevent Egypt from becoming the prey to the anarchy that appeared to be imminent. Whether the remedy would have proved efficacious and satisfactory need not now be discussed; for the French objected to any such arrangement, and, to please them, we acquiesced in the objection. Then they proposed that the Anglo-French fleets should make a demonstration before Alexandria, and in this we readily concurred without any agreement as to subsequent action. The plan was therefore put into execution (May 20th). But far from appeasing the tumult, this step only aggravated it. The authority of the Khedive was now completely effaced, and Arabi became dictator. The excitement of the people increased, a serious riot occurred in Alexandria (June 11th), and earthworks for the defence of the town began to be thrown up. It was not easy to recede before this defiance. The British Admiral demanded that the construction of fortifications should be stopped, and, later, that they should be surrendered to him. The demand was resisted. It was then deemed necessary to take them at any risk, and to destroy by force the power of Arabi, who was proclaimed a rebel against his Prince.* And now

---

* The precise date, says a writer of the day, on which the Khedive's troops became rebels could be no more accurately ascertained than that of the discovery that the "military tyranny" imposed by Arabi, received the cordial sympathy and support of nearly every class throughout Egypt (*Annual Register*, 1882, i. 369). It was not until

a strange event occurred. The French, though they succeeded in inducing our Government to defer to their wishes, were not bound to us in any way. Having gone just far enough to ensure an armed intervention, they refused to take their share in it, and, when hostilities were imminent, their fleet sailed away from the scene where they must commence.

The bombardment of the earthworks followed on the 11th of July, and it is needless to say that our navy soon reduced the enemy's guns to silence, and drove him out of Alexandria. Arabi's troops having retired, blue-jackets and marines were landed to restore order in the town. Meanwhile a force, drawn from Malta and Gibraltar, had been concentrated at Cyprus, and was commanded by Major-General Sir Archibald Alison, Bart., K.C.B., who arrived in the island, July 14th. These troops were speedily moved therefrom, and, reaching Alexandria on the 17th, they took up a line fronting the Egyptian army at Kafr-ed-Dauer, that lay a few miles south of the coast covering the road to Cairo.*

Preparations were now actively pushed forward to follow up the first blow struck by the British fleet for the purpose of restoring the authority of the Khedive. A vote of credit was agreed to in Parliament, troops were ordered to be got ready to proceed to the seat of war, and a portion of the reserves were called up to serve during the emergency (July 25th). The French also at last plainly expressed their intentions, by declining definitely to take part in the expedition which had now to be undertaken. The decision was made on the 29th of July in their Chambers, by a majority of 416 against 75 votes. Thus Great Britain was obliged to act alone, and if this was the result, it may seem to be a pity that she had not been allowed to have a

---

the 16th of July, after the war began, that the Khedive issued an order dismissing Arabi from his post as Minister of War (*Military History of the Campaign of 1882 in Egypt*, p. 16; prepared in the Intelligence Branch of the War Office, by Colonel J. F. Maurice, Royal Artillery). As we have frequently drawn from this work, in future it will be referred to as "Maurice, *Official Account*."

* See Maps No. 9, p. 379, and No. 8, p. 360. Some future historian may perhaps consider what the result would have been if the fleet had been provided with a land force when the war was begun by the bombardment of the 11th, and whether the revolt against foreign interference could have been strangled in Alexandria, before it grew and required a regular invasion to suppress it. Into these matters we do not propose to enter; it is sufficient to say that no means were prepared to take military advantage of the peculiar nature of the communications which join Alexandria with the rest of the country, and that Arabi's troops got away unhurt.

free hand from the beginning. Be this as it may, she gained the advantage of being at least unfettered in the military operations that followed, and hence the dangers and inconvenience of a joint occupation were happily avoided.

As early as the 3rd of July, General Sir Garnet Wolseley, G.C.B., appointed to take command of the expedition in case hostilities were undertaken, confidentially traced the plan of operations to be pursued. Soon the field army was organized, among which a Guards Brigade was included; and on the 30th of July, the first troops, the 1st Scots Guards (Colonel Knox), left England on board the *Orient*.* The other two Battalions of this Brigade, the 2nd Grenadiers (Colonel P. Smith), and the 2nd Coldstream (Colonel G. Wigram), being at Cork and Dublin respectively, left these stations for the seat of war as soon as they received drafts from London to fit them to take the field. For this purpose, the 2nd Battalion obtained from the 1st Coldstream, one Colour-sergeant, 9 sergeants, and 204 rank and file (28th); and on the 1st of August, having proceeded to Kingstown from Richmond Barracks, Dublin, they embarked, about 750 strong, on board the *Iberia*, and started for Alexandria. They reached their destination on the 13th, and moved immediately to Ramleh, where the Brigade was collecting under the orders of Major-General H.R.H. the Duke of Connaught, K.G.†

The following Officers formed part of the Battalion:—

Commanding the 2nd Battalion.—Colonel G. Wigram.
Mounted Majors.—Colonels A. Lambton; F. C. Manningham-Buller.
Dismounted Majors and Captains.—Lieut.-Colonels J. B. Sterling; Viscount de Vesci; R. S. Hall; W. F. Ramsden; Hon. E. Acheson; R. W. Follett; Hon. E. Boscawen.
Lieutenants.—Captains R. Pole-Carew; J. G. Montgomery; F. C. Manley; L. D. Mackinnon: Lieutenants Hon. E. Dawney; Hon. H. Monck; J. R. Gladstone; D. F. R. Dawson; G. V. Boyle; W. O. Corbet (in command of Regimental transport); G. P. Bouverie; Hon. A. Fortescue; P. A. Lovell (Signalling Officer); D. J. Hamilton; Hon. Alan Charteris; and H. G. Shute; also H. Somers-Cocks (who left Portsmouth for Egypt, August 16).

---

* Lieut.-General Willis and Major-General H.R.H. the Duke of Connaught, with their Staffs, were on board the *Orient*.
† Captain Ivor Herbert, Grenadier Guards, was appointed Brigade Major; Major R. Lane, Rifle Brigade, Aide-de-camp to His Royal Highness.

Adjutant.—Lieutenant Hon. A. Henniker-Major.
Quartermaster.—W. Webster.
Medical Officers.—Surgeon-Major G. Perry; Surgeon J. Whipple, M.D.

The following Officers, also belonging to the Regiment, served upon the Staff:—

Lieut.-Colonel Lord William Seymour, attached to the British Admiral.
Captain Pole-Carew, Orderly Officer to H.R.H. the Duke of Connaught.
Lieutenant A. Codrington, Aide-de-camp to Lieut.-General Willis, commanding the First Division.

Before this date, Sir A. Alison had been covering the concentration of the army at Alexandria, and, by means of strong reconnaissances, he endeavoured to make the enemy believe that the invaders meant to attack him from the north. But this was not the intention of Sir G. Wolseley, whose object was to seize the Maritime Canal, and, basing himself upon Ismailia, to advance thence to the capital of Egypt. In this manner, the main water-way between the Mediterranean and the Red Sea would be secured from any attempt which Arabi might make upon it, and the invading army would obtain the best route into the interior. The route, it is true, was far from being a good one, for it lay in a desert of deep sand; but none of the communications of the country, other than by rail or canal, are good, and, in fact, roads, as we understand them, may be said to have no existence. The one selected, however, besides the strategical advantage it offered, of enabling an army to turn the Delta, and to proceed by the shortest way to Cairo, had along its course a fresh-water canal, where drinking water was to be obtained, and a railway; and both of these served as easy lines of supply. Arabi, indeed, had done his best to render these communications useless, but he could only obstruct them temporarily; and, though he thereby impeded our advance, he was not able to arrest it.

The British Commander had from the beginning believed that the enemy would make a stand at Tel el-Kebir, some thirty miles from Ismailia, on the road to Cairo; and if this were to prove to be correct, he determined to deliver a crushing and effective blow there, and so bring the campaign to a speedy and prompt conclusion. We shall see that he was entirely right in the opinion he had formed, and successful in carrying out his plan. To ensure this success, it was necessary to push advanced troops, of sufficient strength, from Ismailia to a point within striking distance of Arabi's position, behind which the water and rail communications could be restored, and where the main army could be concentrated for the final battle.

The forces massing at Alexandria from the middle of July came, as we know, from the Mediterranean stations, and from the United Kingdom; but troops, native and British, also were despatched to the seat of war from India; and these, beginning to arrive on the 20th of August, landed at Suez, and, later, at Ismailia. The whole formed an Army-Corps, under the command of General Sir G. Wolseley (who landed in Egypt on August 15th), and was made up of a cavalry division, two infantry divisions, corps troops, and an Indian contingent. Each division was formed of two brigades and divisional troops.

The Cavalry Division, 23 squadrons, mounted infantry, and 6 guns, under Major-General Drury-Low: the 1st Brigade (Brigadier-General Sir Baker Russell) contained, among others, three squadrons of Household cavalry, under Colonel Ewart, 2nd Life Guards;* the 2nd Brigade (Brigadier-General Wilkinson), Indian cavalry. The First Division, 8 battalions, 2 squadrons, and 12 guns, under Lieut.-General Willis: 1st Brigade (three Guards Battalions), Major-General H.R.H. the Duke of Connaught; 2nd Brigade (4 Battalions), Major-General Graham, V.C. The Second Division, 9 battalions, 2 squadrons, and 12 guns, under Lieut.-General Sir E. Hamley: 1st Brigade (4 battalions), Major-General Sir A. Alison; 2nd Brigade (4 battalions), Major-General Sir E. Wood, V.C. The Corps troops contained one battery of Royal Horse Artillery, and three batteries of Field Artillery, 24 guns. The Indian contingent, under Major-General Sir H. Macpherson, V.C., 4 battalions (of which 2 were native), 1 company Beluchis, 6 guns (mountain battery). Total force, including a reserve at Aden of 2 native battalions, not brought into the field, amounted to 23 battalions, 27 squadrons, and 60 guns, besides Engineers, Marines, Marine Artillery, siege trains, etc.; or to 1180 Officers, and 28,300 men.†

Although all this army had not landed, yet a sufficient force had been collected to seize the Suez Canal, and to begin the real business of the campaign. Ample preparations had already

---

* One squadron from each Regiment of Household Cavalry.
† Appendix No. XIV. contains the order of battle.

been made by the Navy for this operation. The final details having been settled, a simultaneous landing was effected by blue-jackets and marines at all the important places from Port Said to Suez; and the water-way was cleared from end to end by 4 a.m. on the morning of the 20th of August.* Meanwhile, those portions of the Cavalry and First Divisions that were at Alexandria were embarked on board ship, while those of the Second Division were left behind to protect the town, and to keep up the delusion that Egypt was to be invaded from the north. In order to give the greater currency to this idea, it was further given out that the troops on board ship were destined to make an attack on Abukir. The 2nd Coldstream, which since their arrival at Ramleh had been facing south towards Kafr-ed-Dauer, re-embarked on the *Iberia* on the 18th of August, and the whole fleet, consisting of 8 ironclads and 17 transports, left in the direction of Abukir at noon on the 19th, and approached Port Said next day, in the early morning. As soon as possible the ships entered the canal, and, piloted by Officers of the Royal Navy, were concentrated at Ismailia. They grounded occasionally as they steamed through the difficult passage, and delayed the procession; but these accidents did not materially check the movement, which was not confined merely to the fleet that sailed from Alexandria, but included also transports, conveying troops direct to the seat of war, from England by Port Said, and from India by Suez. General Graham, having landed with a small force of infantry on the evening of the 20th, pushed forward to Nefisha early next day; and the Guards Brigade, arriving at their destination late on the 21st, disembarked on the 22nd. For two days they were busily engaged in fatigue duties at Ismailia, during which time the concentration of troops continued with unabated energy, so that on the evening of the 23rd about 9000 men were on shore.†

The invaders were dependent for drinking water upon the fresh-water canal previously mentioned, that runs from the Nile near Cairo to Ismailia; and now a fear seized the military authorities that Arabi might be able to destroy its banks, and stop the greater portion of our supply, not only at Nefisha and Ismailia, but also as far as Suez. It was therefore determined to send forward a small force on the 24th, under General Graham,

* Three ships, one French and two English, delayed the operation for a few hours.
† Maurice, *Official Account*, p. 36. See Map No. 8, p. 360.

to occupy El-Magfar, where the danger was most to be apprehended, and to prevent the occurrence of any such calamity. The force (1 battalion, 3 squadrons, and 2 guns) was not a large one; but it met with no resistance, and soon accomplished its object, not, however, without causing the enemy to show that he was concentrating a formidable body of men in a position further up the canal, at Tel el-Makhuta. It was evident that the British advanced detachment, if attacked with energy, might be unable to hold its own, and be obliged to fall back; but it was also clear that an initial advantage could be gained if we could bring up a sufficient force to cause the Egyptians to evacuate the ground they were engaged in taking up. Accordingly Sir G. Wolseley, who was present, sent back immediately to direct that the Guards Brigade at Ismailia and a battalion of infantry at Nefisha should move to the front without delay.

Meanwhile, the advanced troops became engaged, and a very unequal fight, as far as the numbers of the combatants were concerned, took place under the orders of General Willis. But the large Egyptian forces showed no disposition to close with the small body opposed to them, and the latter maintained their position until reinforcements, consisting of all the three arms, arrived to their support. Just before sundown the Guards Brigade appeared on the scene, the Coldstream leading; the Battalion then coming into the advanced line, under shell fire which happily was not effective, occupied an extended line of outposts during the night. The day had been exceedingly hot and oppressive, and the operations as well as the want of water had greatly exhausted the men, both those who fought and those who marched to their support under a scorching sun and through the burning sand.

"A scarcely less trying task had fallen to the lot of the Brigade of Guards. A march over the two miles of heavy road between Ismailia and Nefisha, difficult at any time, was, during the burning hours of the midday sun of an exceptionally hot day, a very serious task indeed. Throughout all the rest of the campaign, both before and after this, troops were ordered to march in the cool hours of the early morning, or of the late afternoon and evening. The sudden necessity for taking advantage of the enemy's stand at Tel el-Makhuta alone made this severe task imperative. Even for troops in presence of the Egyptians, the direst enemies all that day were the sun and the parching glare of the desert sand. But at least they had the excitement of actual fighting, and were able at all times to

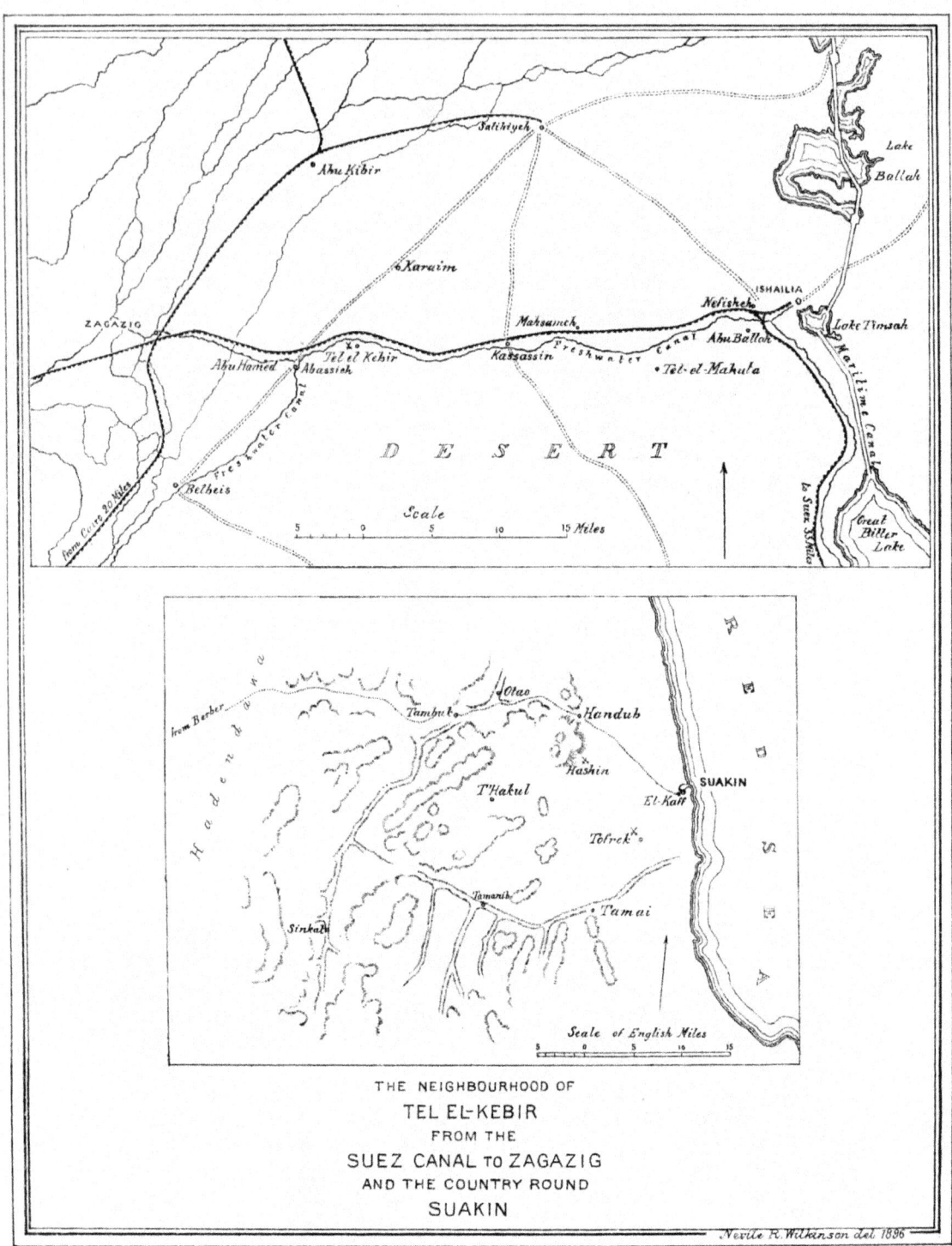

THE NEIGHBOURHOOD OF
TEL EL-KEBIR
FROM THE
SUEZ CANAL TO ZAGAZIG
AND THE COUNTRY ROUND
SUAKIN

take advantage of any shade that waggons and hillocks afforded, and they had not during those hours of fierce heat the additional labour of plodding over sand, burning to the feet and ankle deep. Man after man during the march was knocked down by the severity of the strain, and by stroke of the sun. All who were physically able pushed on with honest pride and steady discipline, but it was not until 6.20 p.m. that the march was over, and that H.R.H. the Duke of Connaught was able to bring up his Brigade to the support of the troops engaged." *

At daybreak (25th), an advance was made by the First Division, General Graham in front, followed by the Guards Brigade in support, and, protecting the right flank, the King's Royal Rifles and Marine Light Infantry, who had just come up, in second line; the Cavalry, under General Drury Low, on the extreme right front. Tel el-Makhuta was found to be abandoned by the enemy; but the Cavalry, still pushing on, found him at Mahsama, where, after a short struggle, they not only dislodged him but captured his camp, seven Krupp guns, and a large quantity of ammunition, stores, and provisions. Next day we took possession of Kassassin, and it was occupied by General Graham, the Guards being left at Tel el-Makhuta.

Meanwhile the disembarkation of men, horses, guns, and stores of all sorts still continued at Ismailia. As the English advanced troops had reached Kassassin,—within striking distance of Tel el-Kebir, where Arabi was known to be entrenching, with the object of making a definite stand against us,—it was now necessary to bring up all available forces for the assault of his lines. General Sir E. Hamley was therefore ordered round to Ismailia from Alexandria with the Second Division (except Sir E. Wood's brigade, which was directed to remain there for the defence of the town and neighbourhood); so also was the Indian contingent moved up from Suez. While the concentration was in progress, communications were restored as rapidly as possible between the base and Kassassin. The line of railway was repaired where it was torn up, and where embankments of earth had been found to block it; and rolling stock brought out from England was landed and placed upon it. The fresh-water canal also was cleared by removing the dams, which had been constructed across it at Makhuta and Magfar. The Guards Brigade remained at Makhuta

---

* Maurice, *Official Account*, p. 49. One man of the Coldstream, struck down by sun apoplexy, died at Nefisha next day (25th).

until the 9th of September, busily engaged in digging away the obstructions that impeded the traffic on the railway and on the canal at these two points, and partly in throwing up redoubts to strengthen the lines of communications. It was a laborious work ;—

"for the skilful dam-makers . . . had so wattled in reeds, telegraph wires, and other binding materials into the mass of the earthworks, that our men, standing in the muddy canal without any convenient foothold, had the greatest difficulty in removing the obstacles." *

Supplies also ran short, on account of the impossibility of conveying them across the deep sand, through which lay the only road to the front, until the railway or canal could be used.

"But the most trying circumstance which the rapid movement had entailed was the absence of tents and camp equipage. These were pushed on by rail and canal as rapidly as the condition of both permitted, but for some days the necessity of depending for chance shade upon the shelter of the trees and villages under that glaring sun called for much endurance on the part of the troops so employed. It was the price paid for the rapid successes of the 24th and 25th. The tents reached the troops at Tel el-Makhuta on the 28th. The valises of the men reached them on the following day." †

Nevertheless, in spite of the difficulties to be overcome, the scorching heat, and the shadeless glare, the work was well and expeditiously performed. The following communication from Colonel Drake, Commanding Royal Engineer of the First Division, refers to what the Brigade did at this period of the campaign :— ‡

"*Tel el-Makhuta*, August 30, 1882. I wish to bring to the notice of the Lieutenant-General Commanding, the excellent work which has been done by the Brigade of Guards on the important work, of opening the communications on the railway and canal. Engineering work, always fatiguing to troops fully employed on military duties, has been especially harassing in this climate ; but in consequence of the great interest shown in the work by the Guards Officers in charge of parties, it has been executed by the men cheerfully and well, and it is my opinion, that had this spirit not been shown by Officers and men, the progress of the army must have been for several days delayed."

Once, on the 28th of August, this labour was interrupted for

---

* Maurice, *Official Account*, p. 55.   † *Ibid.*, p. 57.
‡ An extract of a report upon the signalling performed in Egypt by the Coldstrea is reproduced in Appendix No. XIV.

a brief space. On that day the enemy attempted to make an attack on Kassassin, which, owing to the fact that it was commanded by hills in his possession, was not a strong military position. Having made a demonstration in the morning, which resulted only in a distant artillery fire of little value, Arabi ordered a more vigorous attack upon General Graham in the afternoon, and this produced some fighting, and a charge conducted in moonlight by the three squadrons of the Household Cavalry. The Egyptians then retired, and the action came to an end; but as soon as it was perceived that the enemy was endeavouring to recapture Kassassin, the Guards Brigade were hurried forward from Makhuta to the threatened point, and were placed in reserve. The three Battalions did not return to their quarters until midnight.

On the 7th of September, communications were cleared, a railway service was established, the main bulk of the supplies and stores—of which large quantities had already been despatched to the front—were ready to be sent forward, and the remaining troops, hitherto kept back at Ismailia, were awaiting to be moved to Kassassin. Orders to concentrate the army there were given, when Arabi made one more attempt to defeat the advanced troops opposed to him at that place, before the rest came into position (September 9th). His previous efforts had failed; and it was scarcely likely that, having effected so little before—although in contact with a small portion of the British forces only—he would now be able to achieve a success at this late stage of the war. The attack was nevertheless a formidable one in point of numbers, and almost the whole of the hostile forces, supported by a powerful artillery, were employed in it. But it was easily repulsed, and the enemy was pursued towards Tel el-Kebir, where he ran for shelter.* During the action, the Guards Brigade were once more moved forward from Makhuta to remain in reserve should their services be required; but they were not brought into action. It seems probable that, had the advance of the First and Cavalry Divisions, who were then present, been continued, Arabi would then and there have been driven out of his entrenched position. The pursuit, however, was not pressed home. Instead of returning to their former camp, the Guards remained for the next few days on the ground they occupied on the evening of the 9th.

* Our losses amounted to 3 killed and 77 wounded.

The Egyptian army could scarcely be considered a very formidable foe. The Generals had shown little military capacity, the native Officers no enterprise or power of leadership, and the men in consequence had displayed but a small amount of valour. Drawn principally from the fellaheen, or the peasantry of the country, the ranks of the forces opposed to us were filled with men who had no desire to excel in the profession of arms; and during the first combats of the campaign we gained ample proof of their inefficiency in the field.* As regards their numbers, we are informed that at the date of the bombardment (July 11th), the Egyptian army consisted in all of about 9000 men, 288 field guns, and only 750 horses. Of these, 5000 were in Alexandria, the rest being dispersed over the country. The reserves were called in afterwards, and the 9000 expanded to 60,000, by the 20th of August; when 15,000 were before Alexandria, 12,000 at Tel el-Kebir, 11,000 at Cairo, and 22,000 were distributed in remote garrisons unmolested by the invaders; besides this, there were 6000 Beduin Arabs, half at Tel el-Kebir and the remainder before Alexandria. Again, later, 40,000 raw recruits without training were enlisted, and the total of the army reached the high figure of 100,000 men, not counting the Beduins. For all these men, it appears, arms were available, and 11,000 untrained draft horses were procured.† These vast numbers of undisciplined and unorganized men could do little to serve Arabi's cause, and they seem to have been rather a source of weakness to him. Unable to fight, they were liable to panic, and their presence was more calculated to unsteady the few soldiers who alone possessed some knowledge of their duties than to augment the strength of the army.

By the evening of the 12th of September, the whole available British forces were at Kassassin, some eight miles from Tel el-Kebir, and numbered 634 Officers, and 16,767 Non-commissioned officers and men, 61 guns, and 6 gatlings. Previous to this date, several reconnaissances had been undertaken towards the enemy's entrenched position to examine his works, and to observe his strength, disposition, and habits. The knowledge so gained could only confirm the poor opinion in which the enemy deserved to be held.

* Arabi's force contained a few battalions of Sudanese, or black troops; the latter were his best soldiers, and fought well.
† Maurice, *Official Account*, p. 40, etc.

His lines were continuous, stretching from the canal for a distance of some 6000 yards; but they were not apparently protected by any advanced works, nor provided with efficient inner entrenchments. They seemed to present little difficulty to storming parties, nor were any formidable obstacles visible.* The left (north) flank, moreover, was entirely open and unguarded; and, lastly, no outposts secured the front during the night. Thus feebly did Arabi venture to oppose the army of one of the great Powers of Europe; and if he was unable to bring civilized science to his aid, so also were his troops incapable of displaying the wild heroism that belongs to the barbarian. In short, he invited a night attack either on his left flank or in front; with the certainty that, if the invaders could reach unseen the position he endeavoured to fortify, they could turn it or penetrate it, before he was ready to meet them; and the whole of his defences would be rendered useless. This would bring about his complete defeat, and the dispersal of his raw levies, who eagerly watched for an early opportunity to desert and fly to their homes.

It is, however, one thing to perceive after the event, what ought to be done, but quite another thing to determine beforehand, the best line of action, and to ensure a result as successful and decisive as the assault on Tel el-Kebir proved to be. The night march across the desert was by no means an easy operation. It entailed the bringing up the whole army in battle array, through the dark, close to a given position at a given time. Careful arrangements to prevent confusion had to be therefore made on the part of the leaders, from the Commander-in-chief downwards; and attention and rigid discipline were more than ever required on the part of the men who were thus led to the assault. It is needless to say that all ranks vied with one another in discharging correctly the important functions that every man had to perform during that night; and in this manner was the difficult operation carried through without hitch, and even without temporary delay. It should be added here, that fortune also favoured us in no small degree. Arabi had, in fact, constructed one, and only one, advanced work in front of his lines of defence; but it had not been discovered during our reconnaissances, and we were ignorant of its existence.

* The lines were afterwards found to consist of a parapet from 3 to $5\frac{1}{2}$ feet high, with a ditch in front, about 4 feet deep; they were stronger in the south, near the canal, than on the north, where, in fact, they died away, as it were, into nothing in the desert.

By good luck that work was avoided by our columns, as they went forward in the dark to the attack. Thus we managed to cross the desert unperceived by so dangerous a tell-tale of our movement, and arrived at dawn before the hostile lines, close enough to storm them before the Egyptians even knew that we were in their vicinity.

A conspicuous point in the lines had been selected upon which to direct the march of the Second (Hamley's) Division; Sir A. Alison's Highlanders in front, followed by a brigade formed of the two Divisional battalions of the infantry divisions, under Lieut.-Colonel Ashburnham, C.B., King's Royal Rifle Corps. The First Division was on Sir E. Hamley's right, with an interval of 1200 yards; General Graham's brigade in front, supported by the Guards 1000 yards in rear. Forty-two guns were placed between the two divisions, in line with the Guards Brigade. The Cavalry Division with 12 guns Royal Horse Artillery were on the extreme right. The Indian contingent and the Mountain battery, on the south of the canal, with orders to move off an hour after the rest of the army.

The troops began to strike their tents when dusk set in, and marched to their various rendezvous not without difficulty. It was, of course, imperative that every corps should reach its starting-point in proper order, and there was naturally some moving backwards and forwards in the dark before the masses were correctly formed and aligned. The Brigade took post in their usual formation, the Coldstream on the left, and each Battalion was in columns of half battalions. Everything was ready at 11 p.m.; the men then lay down till 1.30 a.m. of the 13th of September, when they arose in silence, and commenced the advance. We had the advantage of meeting no obstacles in the way; the trackless gravelly soil everywhere afforded an easy passage, and, guided by the stars alone, the army maintained the direction of their march,

At night, however, men are always somewhat under the influence of a vague and undefined feeling. The absence of sound, the inability to see for more than a few feet, the sense of isolation which every group experiences, the strange surroundings, the uncertainty of the future, the idea that some untoward event may happen,—all contribute to produce a suppressed excitement almost akin to nervousness.* The principal danger lay in the fact that

---

* "It is impossible adequately to convey an impression of the absolute silence which prevailed, and of the entire absence of any indication of the existence of a moving army at only a few yards from each of the columns" (Maurice, *Official Account*, p. 82).

should the centre halt, the wings would continue to move, and so wheel inwards, until one flank faced the other. This actually occurred in the Highland Brigade; but the mishap went no further, and was very speedily rectified by the vigilance, discipline, and intelligence of all ranks. The First Division moved more slowly than the Second, and its leading brigade appears to have executed some changes of formation during the night; the Guards, following in support, made no change in this respect, but marched in the order in which they had originally started. Just before reaching the enemy's position, the British army was in an irregular *echelon;* the left was forward and nearest to the enemy, and the right was about 800 yards back.

The Egyptians say their forces at Tel el-Kebir amounted to 20,000 men and 75 guns; but there seems reason to believe that they have under-estimated their numerical strength, and that they had from 25,000 to 30,000 men present.*

As the enemy had no outposts to cover his front; and as we had been fortunate enough to pass by the only advanced work he had constructed, without coming in contact with it,—though our left was at one time unpleasantly close to it,—he had no sort of warning that our whole army was approaching his defensive position, and would assault it at daybreak. He was completely surprised. At 5 a.m., when the first gleam of light was beginning to appear, the Highlanders were close to Tel el-Kebir, and, dashing forward, they carried, after a brief but sharp struggle, the defensive lines in which Arabi apparently had placed so much confidence. While this fight was proceeding, General Graham's brigade hurried up, and penetrated the Egyptian lines, where they presented a smaller obstacle than did those which faced the Second Division. The battle lasted scarcely half an hour. By the end of that time, the enemy was entirely overpowered, and his forces were annihilated and completely dispersed. The Guards followed, and got into the works as soon as possible, but the short action was then practically at an end.

* Maurice, *Official Account*, p. 92. If there is no exaggeration in the total numbers which, we are told, the rebel government collected after the bombardment of the 11th of July, and in the number of guns which were at their disposal at that date, it would appear likely that at least 30,000 men instead of 20,000 men must have been present at Tel el-Kebir; and it is somewhat a surprise to find that Arabi had only so small a force of artillery defending his lines, as 75 guns, when as many as 288 were apparently available at his orders.

"The first of the enemy's shells landed in the middle of some vedettes, about eighty yards to our left front; nearly all the rest fell about one hundred yards in rear of us. As we advanced the Egyptians did not seem to alter their elevation. The bullets were falling all around us; but firing ceased at about 6 a.m., except our guns blazing at the flying Arabs." *

The cavalry was ordered immediately to pursue the enemy to Cairo, the infantry advancing into and occupying the Egyptian camp and the bridge at Tel el-Kebir. The former pushed boldly on to a suburb of the capital, whence Lieut.-Colonel Herbert Stewart went forward with a small force of fifty men, and secured the capitulation of the town and the surrender of Arabi (September 14th). Egypt now lay at the mercy of the British army.†

The losses of Arabi's forces at the battle of the 13th of September can scarcely be reckoned by the killed and wounded; for such was the extent of the disaster he experienced, that he had no further troops at the end of the action. Many fled to their homes, many rushed wildly onwards panic-stricken; all idea of further resistance had come to an end; every man only thought how he could best make his submission, and welcome the conquerors with demonstrations of joy. The Egyptian casualties are reckoned at 2500, and 58 of their guns were captured. The British lost 9 Officers and 48 men killed, 27 Officers and 355 men wounded, and 30 missing, total 469. Of these the Highlanders lost 45 killed, 180 wounded, and 6 missing; General Graham's brigade 9 killed, 119 wounded, and 24 missing; the Guards Brigade 1 man killed, and 2 Officers and 20 men wounded; in the Coldstream, 1 Officer (Lieut.-Colonel J. B. Sterling), and 7 men were wounded,—of the latter, one man subsequently died of his wounds.‡

The victorious forces pushed on towards Cairo after the battle, and secured all the railway centres which communicated with the Egyptian garrisons, still held by the enemy. There was little trouble in causing these garrisons to submit, and by the 24th the whole country was pacified and disarmed. General Willis, with his 2nd Brigade and Divisional infantry, remained at Tel el-Kebir

* Captain Shute (Coldstream Guards), *Diary*.

† See Appendix No. XIV., giving Her Majesty's message to the British army, and Sir G. Wolseley's General Orders, issued after the battle of Tel el-Kebir.

‡ Lieut.-Colonel Balfour, Grenadier Guards, reckoned among the wounded, died of his wounds; as did also two Officers of the Highland Brigade.

for a short time longer, while Sir G. Wolseley, with the Duke of Connaught, and a company of the Scots Guards as escort, went by train, on the afternoon of the 14th, to the capital, followed by the rest of the Scots Guards, by the Coldstream, and by the Grenadier Guards. Owing to obstructions on the line, the Commander-in-chief did not reach his destination until the morning of the 15th; and the Coldstream, starting the same day, reached Cairo that afternoon. The Battalion were then quartered in the Abdin barracks.

The rebellion had now been crushed, and the Khedive's authority having been completely restored, Tewfik entered his capital in state on the 25th, and resumed his place in the government of the country. British troops, and among them the Guards, lined the streets, which were gaily decked with triumphal arches and inscriptions of welcome. If it is allowable to compare a small event with a great one, the scene was in a very minor degree (in principle, at least), not wholly unlike that which attended the return of the Bourbons to Paris in 1815. The "Usurper" in this case was not redoubtable, nor had he scourged Europe as had his proto-type; but he had interfered with the legal gains of European bondholders, and withstood the wishes and designs of the Western nations. The people, also, in the two cases, not having much will of their own, like many others in a similar position, were influenced by one very simple and burning desire—to give their hearty applause to the strongest party.

A draft from England left for the Battalion, under Lieut.-Colonel F. Graves-Sawle and Lieutenant E. Wigram, September 11th; but they were too late to take part in any of the hostilities that marked the campaign, and they went no further than Malta.

There is little more to record. The six weeks spent in Cairo passed agreeably enough, and many eagerly availed themselves of the opportunity to see the sights and the remains of an ancient civilization that makes Egypt one of the most interesting countries in the world. Nor was a race-meeting forgotten, held on the 28th of September, even though other national sports and pastimes had to be discarded on account of the heat. A serious accident, that occurred the same day at the railway-station of Cairo, may also be mentioned. An accidental explosion took place in a waggon laden with ammunition, near the platform, and, as the flames could not be got under, the station buildings were soon destroyed, and much rolling stock and a considerable amount of stores were burnt. Troops were at once sent to the spot, and amongst them the 2nd Coldstream assisted to clear away the *débris*, and guard the place; several smaller explosions continued even during the night.

On the 30th of September a review was held before the Khedive, and the spectacle was made as imposing as possible to impress the natives, not only by the appearance of English troops, but also by the presence of the Indian contingent—Mussulmans like themselves—in the service of Her Majesty. Two days later, the Khedive gave a garden party at the Gezireh palace, to which all Officers were invited in "full dress," the latter being defined for the occasion, "red serges, swords, and forage caps." Lastly, there was the famous procession of the "Sacred Carpet," carried through Cairo on its way to Mecca, and escorted by British troops—an incident which gave rise to some comment in England.

"I had a good deal of difficulty," writes Captain Shute in his diary, "to find the camel with the carpet, as it had gone another way to the station so as to avoid the British escort. Tremendous procession of Arabs with banners; behind the camel with the carpet came several more camels bearing pilgrims to Mecca, and their baggage."

The health of the troops gave some cause for anxiety on account of fever and other illnesses, which broke out among them; and, in consequence, several Officers and men of the Battalion had to be sent home invalided. But the sickness was not abnormally great, considering the fatigues and the privations to which the men were subjected during the campaign; the losses of the Battalion in this respect amounted to eighteen men, of whom twelve died of fever.

Soon after the Carpet incident the war organization of the invading army was broken up, and Sir A. Alison, being left in Cairo with a British force, while the re-settlement of Egypt was being accomplished, arrangements were made to send the remainder home to England, and the Indian contingent to India. The Coldstream, leaving their quarters in Cairo on the 31st of October by train for Alexandria, embarked there, the next day, on board the *Batavia*, and, reaching Portsmouth on the 16th, proceeded thence to Chelsea barracks.

It only remains to record that, in recognition of the services of the army in Egypt in 1882, Her Majesty was graciously pleased to augment the honourable distinctions upon the Colours of the regiments engaged in the campaign by the words "Egypt, 1882," and "Tel el-Kebir."

Thus was the war in Egypt conducted, and thus did the British army conquer Arabi Pasha, and subject the country once more to the rule of Tewfik. A new period now commenced, when Egypt was placed under the protection of England—a temporary protection only, as the Foreign Secretary of the day eagerly announced,—who assumed the responsibility of forming a pure administration out of discordant elements, and of educating the people to respect the system which was introduced for their benefit. The success that has attended our efforts, under difficult circumstances, is an interesting subject; so also is the resentment which the French pretend to feel—because we are obliged to stay in a land we conquered and saved from what might have been anarchy, when they would not move themselves to put an end to the trouble. But the consideration of these matters does not enter into the scope of this volume, as the Coldstream was not employed in the work of Egyptian reconstruction. A question, closely connected with our intervention, did, however, still remain to be settled, and it very speedily involved us in further military operations, in which the Regiment took its share. We must therefore devote the next two chapters to the causes and conduct of this war.

CHAPTER XVI.

FIRST PART OF THE WAR IN THE SUDAN, 1884-85—EXPEDITION UP THE NILE.

General description of the possessions of the Khedive in 1882—Rebellion in the Sudan; rapid rise of the Mahdi—Policy of the British Government—General Gordon sent to Khartum; he is cut off and besieged there—General Lord Wolseley goes to Egypt—Formation of a Camel Corps, of which the Guards compose a Regiment—Problem how to effect the rescue of Gordon—The Nile route selected—Advance to Korti—News from General Gordon—Two columns advance from Korti: one across the Bayuda Desert, the other up the river—Battles of Abu Klea and Abu Kru—The Nile reached near Metemmeh—Sir C. Wilson's effort to proceed to Khartum—Death of General Gordon—Change of plan entailed by this event—Battle of Kirbekan—Retrograde movement of both columns—Troops placed in summer quarters.

EGYPT proper is generally a long and narrow strip of land formed by the valley of the Nile.* Outside the influence of that river, there is nothing but desert, and it is due to the fact that the stream branches out into a Delta at Cairo, that there is any breadth at all in the country. This great water artery receives no affluents for more than 1500 miles from its mouth—the Atbara River, meeting it above Berber, being the last tributary that joins it,—and throughout a considerable portion of its lower course, reckoned from the Nubian Desert northwards, the people can only live by congregating close to its banks. A great part of the soil, in fact, which is situated a few miles from the Nile or from the canals that are fed by it, constructed for purposes of irrigation, is a mere barren waste, covered by sand, and unfit for habitation. To the south of the Nubian Desert there is the fertile province of Dongola, and, separated from it by another desert, a rich country, which, owning Khartum as its chief town, is watered by the tributaries of the great river that flow down from the Abyssinian mountains. This large region, usually called the Sudan,—which

* Map No. 9, p. 379.

includes the seaboard from Suakin to Massowa, and extends to about the line of latitude eleven degrees north,—was for many a century overrun by wild tribes of nomad Arabs, until 1820, when the Egyptians, having begun then to invade it, gradually brought it under their rule. Later, the territories lying still further to the south, were opened up to the energy of the Khedives; and at the time of the war in 1882, Tewfik's sway, outside Egypt proper, stretched to the great water reservoirs in the heart of the African continent close to the equator, where the Nile takes its rise. In the government of these enormous dominions the Khedives had been assisted by more than one Englishman, who succeeded in partially checking the evils of the slave-trade that prevailed among the natives, and in introducing some form of civilization in their midst. By far the most celebrated of these administrators was Colonel, afterwards Major-General, C. Gordon, C.B., whose illustrious name is now a household word in England.

In 1881, a rebellion broke out in the Sudan, and this calamity was mainly brought about by two causes. In the first place, the Egyptians misgoverned the country, and had been obliged to relax their hold upon it, on account of the troubles that eventually involved them in war with England. Their administration, always corrupt, became weak, and as a matter of course the Arabs grew discontented with it. But, in the next place, the people were deeply stirred by a tradition that fixed this time—the completion of twelve centuries from the Hegira, November 12, 1882—as the moment when a great chief was to arise, to regenerate Islam, and to restore the Mussulman world to its former power, glory, and magnificence. Nor had the Sudanese to wait for the exact date fixed in the prophecy; for a native of Dongola, named Muhammad Ahmad, proclaiming himself to be the long-expected Mahdi, enrolled his followers, whom we call Dervishes, headed a serious revolt, and preached a "Jehad," or a "Holy War," against the authority of the Khedive. By October, 1882, when the British were in possession of Egypt, the struggle had begun in earnest, and the rebels had obtained some important advantages. To meet the danger, 10,000 men of Arabi's late army were despatched during the winter to the south; and in March, 1883, General Hicks Pasha, a retired British Officer who had served in India, reached Khartum to direct military operations against the enemy. It is sad to relate that he was poorly supported at Cairo; that, in endeavouring to drive the Mahdi from his head-quarters at El-Obeid, he cut himself off from his communications; and that his whole force was surrounded and entirely destroyed. General Hicks and his Staff died with arms in their hands on the field of battle, and none survived to tell the tale of their misfortunes (October 7, 1883).* With this disaster, the bulk of the Egyptian forces were annihilated; the dervishes acquired an immense addition to their former strength, both material and moral: Khartum was in danger, and there were only some 2000 men left to defend it.†

Nor was this the only trouble, for the dervishes of the Eastern Sudan, led by one Osman Digna, also raised the standard of revolt, and gained several successes over the Egyptians in the autumn of 1883. In order to save so important a port as Suakin from the ruin that seemed imminent, a force of nearly 4000 men was despatched to oppose the rebels, under a former British Officer, General Baker Pasha, who had rendered distinguished service in the Turkish army during the war with Russia in 1877. But all his efforts were of no avail, for his troops also were overwhelmed and destroyed, February 4, 1884.

These events showed how impossible it was for the Khedive to cope single-handed with the Mahdi; so also did they put the British Government in no small difficulty. Our intervention in Egypt had weakened the military resources of the country, and had imposed responsibilities upon us which had not been foreseen when we began hostilities by the bombardment of the forts of Alexandria. We little imagined then, that we should not only have to guard the frontiers from the irruption of savage hordes of Arabs, but also be obliged to try to save the Egyptian garrisons in the Sudan from the perils that menaced them, and to prevent that slave-dealing region from relapsing into the darkness and barbarism that oppressed it in the past. And yet little was done. The revolt was not met at once, and it had time to grow into formidable proportions. The power of the Mahdi increased with great rapidity; the native tribes were unsupported,

* Colonel Arthur Farquhar (late Coldstream Guards) accompanied this ill-fated expedition, and perished in it. Some account of the good services rendered by this Officer is given in Slatin Pasha's recent publication (*Fire and Sword in the Sudan*, 1879-95, by Rudolf C. Slatin Pasha, C.B.; translated by Major F. R. Wingate, C.B., D.S.O., R.A.; London, 1896; chap. viii.).

† *History of the Sudan Campaign* (compiled at the Intelligence Department of the War Office, by Colonel Colvile, C.B., Grenadier Guards), part i. p. 16 (London, 1889).

and had to submit to the terror he inspired. It was then too late to act, unless we were prepared to re-conquer the huge provinces which had already been devastated. It is indeed a calamity that the first-fruits of the regeneration we determined to effect in Egypt, should thus have been unfortunately coupled with the abandonment of many of the Khedive's troops to a merciless foe, and with the obliteration of the work of civilization in an immense tract of country, by the most cruel form of a hateful tyranny.

It was determined to evacuate the Sudan; and General Gordon was requested by the British Government to accomplish this difficult and perilous mission. Accompanied by Lieut.-Colonel Donald Stewart, 11th Hussars, he cheerfully accepted it, and reached Khartum unattended by any force, February 18, 1884. He immediately placed the town in a state of defence, infused new life and hopes into the panic-stricken garrison and inhabitants, and took early measures to carry out his instructions. But it was not long before he perceived the impossible nature of the task that had been allotted to him. He had no soldiers available to secure the withdrawal of the many for whose safety he was responsible, and soon the Mahdi surrounded him, intercepted his supplies, and cut off his communications with Egypt. In March, the enemy threatened Shendi. The month following, he established himself in the vicinity of that place. And towards the end of May, Berber fell. Gordon was thus shut out from the rest of the world, and he was little more than a prisoner in Khartum—besieged there, and fighting for his life and for those entrusted to his charge. Retreat was impossible, and the end must infallibly come, as soon as his powers of resistance were exhausted, unless an expedition were sent to his relief.

Meanwhile Major-General Sir G. Graham and a British field force of some 5000 men had been landed in the neighbourhood of Suakin, to defend that seaport and coast from the inroads of Osman Digna (February 28, 1884). In less than a month, he had inflicted severe losses upon the followers of that chieftain, and had pacified the district. But this was all; and these successes bore no fruit. Graham was not ordered to advance in force upon Berber to guard that important town and the communications thereto with the Red Sea.* Instead of this, he was withdrawn from Suakin

* A proposition had been made at this time to send 200 or 300 cavalry to Berber, which probably they could have reached. But the General Commanding in Egypt

on the 3rd of April, leaving only a small garrison behind him. Hence, just at this critical moment, when it was obvious that the nearest and the ordinary road to Khartum should have been secured and made easily accessible by a light railway, the opportunity of approaching General Gordon was neglected, and the means of enabling him to accomplish his mission were denied him.* On General Graham's departure there was a pause for several months, during which no further operations took place as far as we were concerned,† though the Arabs continued to advance northwards; and, unopposed, they re-occupied their former positions in the Eastern Sudan from which they had just been expelled.

During this interval of inaction in the field, the British Cabinet deliberated on the situation, and, having asked for advice, considered the merits of the various schemes relating to the invasion of the Sudan that were placed before them by the military authorities at home and on the spot. As a result, they at length announced their determination in a despatch, dated August 8th, when Khartum had been already beleaguered and hidden from their view for many months. In this paper ‡ they expressed their opinion that "General Gordon, acting on his instructions," might still "secure the withdrawal from Khartum, either by the employment of force or of pacific means, of the Egyptian garrisons and of such of the inhabitants as may desire to leave;" they announced their intention "to undertake operations for the relief of General Gordon, should they become necessary, and to make certain preparations in respect thereof;" and they further indicated their resolution that the expedition—"whose general scope" was to enable Government "to give directions at

---

(Lieut.-General Sir F. Stephenson, K.C.B.) opposed it, on the grounds that it was undesirable to fritter away our troops in small detachments, that so weak a force in the Mahdi's country and unsupported there, could achieve no success, and must only add to the numbers who had to be rescued from the Sudan.

* The reader will presently see that a strong force was landed at Suakin in the spring of 1885, to construct a railway to Berber, *when it was too late*.

† Except some battalions pushed to the frontier of Egypt to guard it against invasion, that appeared to be threatening; also the first preparations for laying a line of railway from Suakin to Berber, but which was stopped at the end of August. Major-General A. Lyon Fremantle (late Coldstream Guards) assumed command at Suakin at the end of July.

‡ Given in full in Colvile's *History of the Sudan Campaign*, part i. p. 45. Hereafter referred to as "Colvile, *Official Account*."

a very short notice for the despatch of a brigade of troops of all arms to proceed to Dongola,"—was to advance, "should the necessity arise," along the valley of the Nile.

In order to produce an early moral effect upon the enemy, and to facilitate a prompt advance into the Sudan, which every one knew was imperative if Gordon was to be saved, Sir F. Stephenson, on the receipt of this despatch, was anxious to send up troops without delay to Dongola. But such a proceeding did not at once commend itself to Government, and they still hesitated before venturing so far, even though the movement could have been made with perfect safety. At the same time, 400 boats, each suitable for the conveyance of 12 men and 100 rations per man up the Nile, were ordered in England on the 12th of August, and a further number of 400 were also put in hand on the 22nd. But it was not till a month later (September 20th) that the first British battalion entered Dongola, and it was also only then decided (on the 21st) that, "if necessary," the expedition might proceed beyond that place.*

Meantime, General Lord Wolseley, having been sent to Egypt to take command, reached Cairo on the 9th of September, and two days later he wrote home to request that a special Camel Corps might be immediately placed at his disposal, in addition to the troops whom he proposed should take part in the campaign. The new corps, 1200 strong, was composed of detachments of 40 men, with one or two Officers, taken from every Battalion of the Foot Guards (280 men), from the 16 Regiments of Cavalry at home (640 men), and from two Battalions of the Rifle Brigade (80 men); also 100 men from the three Regiments of Household Cavalry, and a similar number from the Royal Marines. The corps was divided into three sections, viz. the Guards (to which the Marines were eventually attached), the Heavy, and the Light Camel regiments. The detachments were quickly got together; they left England on the 26th of September, and landed at Alexandria on the 7th of October.

The command of the Guards Camel regiment was assigned to Lieut.-Colonel Hon. E. Boscawen, Coldstream Guards; the Adjutant being Lieutenant C. Crutchley, Scots Guards; the Signalling Officer, Lieut.-Colonel Bonham, Grenadier Guards; and the Medical Officer, Surgeon J. Magill, Coldstream Guards. The following

* Colvile, *Official Account*, part i. p. 53.

Officers, two from each Battalion, also formed part of the corps : *—

Lieut.-Colonels C. Rowley and I. Herbert; Captain E. Crabbe; Lieutenants Count Gleichen, D'Aguilar, and R. Wolridge-Gordon : Grenadier Guards.

Lieut.-Colonel F. A. Graves-Sawle ; Captain Vesey Dawson ; Lieutenants Douglas Dawson, and Hon. H. Amherst : Coldstream Guards.

Lieut.-Colonels M. Willson, and Sir W. Gordon-Cumming, Bart. ; Lieutenants A. Drummond, and B. Baden-Powell : Scots Guards.

The rest of the British troops required for field operations were drawn from our force already in occupation of Egypt.† Of these, 3½ battalions of infantry, and one of Marines, one squadron, most of the artillery, and a portion of the Royal Engineers were left in garrison at Alexandria, Cairo, and Suakin. The remainder, 9 battalions, 3 squadrons (of the 19th Hussars), the Mounted infantry, a Camel battery, and Royal Engineers took part in the expedition, and were disposed along the Nile to guard the communications, and to form the fighting force.‡ In addition, the Egyptian army was also utilized, but all, except a Camel battery which was pushed to the front later on, were left upon the lines of communication, not further south than Hannek.

Khartum, inaccessible from the south, is cut off from all ordinary communications with the north by large tracts of almost waterless desert, that lie between the town and Egypt and the Red Sea. The determination, therefore, to relieve Gordon entailed a military problem of considerable difficulty, relating to the manner in which he should be reached in time, by a sufficient number of troops and quantities of food supplies, and thus be enabled to retreat from the Sudan together with those he was pledged to save. This problem has been enunciated as follows: How to "place a force of about 5000 fighting men at or near Shendi, at the latest by the end of the year, and to carry with them, not only

---

* The detachments furnished by the Coldstream amounted to: from the 1st Battalion, three sergeants, two corporals, one drummer, and 38 privates ; from the 2nd Battalion, two sergeants, three corporals, one drummer, and 38 privates. Total, 92 of all ranks.

† Except one Battalion, which came from India, and some 390 Canadians (called "Voyageurs"), under Lieut.-Colonel Denison, brought to Egypt to help our men to pilot the boats up the Nile.

‡ The numerical strength, together with the Camel corps, appears to have been about 10,000 men and 6 guns, and eventually 6 additional guns, belonging to the Egyptian army. Subsequently Dongolese troops fought with us against the enemy.

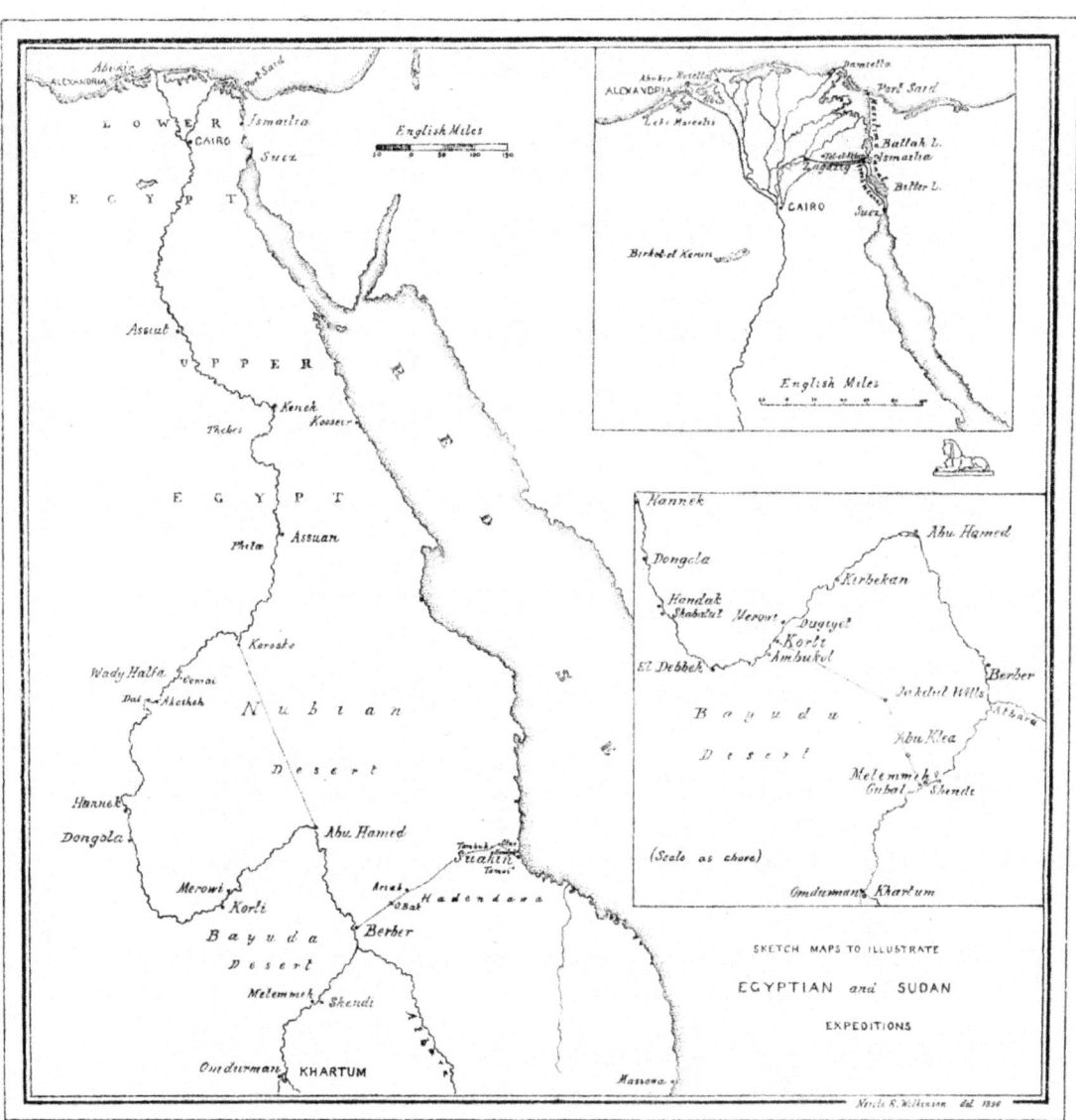

supplies for themselves, but also for the inhabitants and garrison of Khartum."* Two proposals had been made to solve it:—

1. By taking the Nile route, and advancing to the neighbourhood of Dongola, to continue either along the river by Abu Hamed, or else to strike across the Bayuda Desert to Metemmeh, situated on the Nile opposite Shendi. There were many difficulties attending this proposal. The distance from Cairo to Shendi, or Metemmeh, is as much as 1527 miles, and the navigation of the river is greatly obstructed by cataracts, so that frequent disembarkations of men and stores would be necessary to surmount these obstacles. Hence much time, which was an essential element in the problem, would be consumed. Between Cairo and Dongola (1033 miles), and indeed for quite 100 miles further on, no enemy was to be expected; but beyond this point it was uncertain where he might be met. The desert road from Korti, some 100 miles above Dongola, to Metemmeh, had the advantage of avoiding the loop of the Nile that passes round Abu Hamed, and of thus saving a distance of more than 200 miles. But it was likely to be occupied by the enemy; a distance of 24 miles, in the face of the dervishes, would have to be traversed without water from station to station; and even if the route were opened up, it did not offer facilities for the transport of stores, which was a far more serious difficulty to be overcome than the mere conveyance of the troops. The desert, in short, was only suited to enable the British Commander to take a short cut towards Khartum, and to make a dash forward to Gordon's relief, should his position become critical; and it was in view of this consideration that he requested (September 9th) to have a Camel corps allotted to him, as we have just seen. But under any circumstances the expedition would have to proceed forward across many obstacles, for more than 1100 miles from Cairo, before he could avail himself of the services of that corps.

2. The other plan was to base the army of relief at Suakin, and to push therefrom to Berber, a comparatively short distance of 245 miles. But this project, though it contained several important advantages, also presented no small difficulties. Instead of having to form a fighting base at so very remote and inaccessible a place as Dongola, or Korti, it would have been established at Suakin,

* Colvile, *Official Account*, part i. p. 58. Shendi is about one hundred miles north of Khartum.

in easy and direct communication with the centre of our national resources, and where men, and stores of even the heaviest description, could be readily accumulated as they were required. Owing to the fact that Osman Digna had been unmolested since the spring of the year, he had again taken up an offensive attitude in the Eastern Sudan; Berber also was occupied by the enemy, and hence it was hopeless to suppose that there would be any less fighting upon this route than there would be on the other. This, however, taken by itself was not of great moment. But another circumstance of the utmost importance has to be mentioned. There appears to be a more serious dearth of water in one section of the desert, between the Red Sea and the Nile, than in the worst place on the road from Korti to Metemmeh; and a greater distance to be traversed from well to well in the former (58 miles) than in the latter (24 miles). Herein lay the main difficulty of the Suakin-Berber route. To overcome it, a light railway was necessary to span the whole distance; and it had been calculated that it would have taken three months to achieve such an undertaking. If successful, the advance from Berber to Shendi (95 miles) would have been easily accomplished.

It is not our intention to compare these two methods of solving the problem that had to be faced—rendered exceedingly difficult, and perhaps not in any manner to be solved, within the short space of time allotted, by the unfortunate way in which the Mahdi had been allowed to consolidate his power, and to become a formidable foe. An effort has rather been made to give, as clearly as it is possible in a few words, a short acount of the obstacles which beset both these routes, of the conditions which surrounded the two proposals, and to explain some of the considerations that had to be weighed when the Nile route was adopted.

The first stage of the campaign is the history of the advance over more than a thousand miles to Dongola, and across the many obstacles, formed by rapids and cataracts, that interfere with the navigation of the river. The most troublesome obstructions blocking the passage did not begin till Gemai was reached, just above Wady Halfa, and about 780 miles from Cairo. Up to this place, progress was made by rail and by river steamers; though even in this section, the journey entailed five disembarkations. Here the boat service began, and the first serious difficulty had soon to be met; afterwards many others had to be surmounted, always at the expense of much labour and of valuable time.

"To write a detailed account," says Sir H. Colvile, "of the prolonged struggle between man and nature which the ascent of these cataracts by six hundred English boats involved,—how company after company, and battalion after battalion, unloaded and loaded, rowed and tracked, day by day, and hour by hour, under a blazing sun, against that ever-rushing, ever-changing torrent, between unchanging walls of burning basalt,—to tell all this in detail would be to tell an unequalled tale of pluck, determination, and endurance, but one which would be of little practical use in a military history." *

The boats ordered in England had been despatched to Egypt with the utmost promptitude, and such was the energy displayed that the first troops embarked in them at Gemai on the 1st of November.† Assisted by the Canadian "Voyageurs," nearly three-fourths of the fighting force were past that station on the 18th, struggling forward; though only some 1300 men were as far as Dongola. The Guards Camel regiment marched from Assuan (547 miles from Cairo), and on this date were south of Dal. Korti having been selected as the point of concentration instead of Dongola, it was now calculated that the first infantry battalion should arrive there by the middle of December, and the last on January 22, 1885.

The Mounted infantry, provided with camels, had throughout the advance been near the head of the column, and early in December were as far forward as Shabatut (some 40 miles above Dongola). The Guards Camel regiment reaching that place on the 4th, was brigaded with them under the orders of Brigadier-General Sir Herbert Stewart, and until the 10th, the force was practised in their new formations and drill.‡ On the 11th, the whole advanced to Korti, and arrived on the 15th; the Marines detachment joined the Guards here. Shortly afterwards a portion of the Heavy Camel regiment marched into that camp, and two battalions and a squadron of the 19th Hussars also reached it.

While these operations were in progress, some news had been received from General Gordon. On the 17th of November a

* Colvile, *Official Account*, part i. p. 117.
† The last left Gemai on December 19th.
‡ Article in the *Nineteenth Century*, Nov., 1885, by Lieutenant Douglas Dawson, Coldstream Guards.

letter, dated the 4th, announced that he could "hold out forty days with ease," but "after that it will be difficult;" also that there were at Metemmeh five of his steamers with nine guns, awaiting orders.* Again, on the 31st of December, a diminutive piece of paper had reached Lord Wolseley at Korti, bearing the words, "Khartum all right, 14/12/84.—C. G. GORDON," but supplemented by a verbal message to the effect that the garrison were in great straits, that provisions were running low, and would therefore be exhausted before long.†

Before the arrival of this last communication, however, arrangements had already been made to advance in two directions from Korti: one column, called the River column, under Major-General Earle, was to push along the Nile through Abu Hamed towards Berber, while the other, under Brigadier-General Sir H. Stewart, was to march across the desert and seize Metemmeh.

Now, it was known that there were no supplies to be obtained at the latter place; and as a sufficient number of camels do not seem to have been procurable, it was found impossible to convey the Desert column, with the whole of its stores, to its destination in one journey. The distance to be traversed (176 miles) is, moreover, so great, that it was imperative to establish one or two posts on the route. The principal station was fixed at Jakdul wells, where water was plentiful, 98 miles from Korti. Owing, however, to the scarcity of camels, it was necessary, before the final advance could be made, to occupy that place and to make several journeys to it, in order to victual it and organize it as a depôt for future requirements. This preliminary operation took some days to accomplish, and was not completed until the 14th of January, upon which date Sir H. Stewart was enabled to start for Metemmeh.

The orders he received were to attack and occupy that town, to leave there a portion of his force, and to return with the remainder to Jakdul. Colonel Sir C. Wilson, R.E. (the Chief of the Intelligence Department), and Captain Lord C. Beresford, R.N., with a small party of seamen, accompanied the column, and both had special instructions given to them. The latter was to take over one or two of the steamers which were known to be at Metemmeh, and, when he had reported them to be ready, the former was to proceed in them to Khartum, and to deliver a letter to General

* The letter is given in Colvile's *Official Account*, part i. p. 121.
† *Ibid.*, i. 138.

Gordon. Sir C. Wilson was to be accompanied by a small detachment of infantry; he might march the men through the city, and show them to the garrison; but they were not to sleep there; and they were to return with him to Metemmeh. Further, he was only to stay long enough to confer fully with General Gordon, and, having done so, he was to get back to Korti with all convenient despatch.* Lastly, he was supplied with an estimate showing the approximate dates upon which the troops were calculated to arrive at the different stations along the route to Khartum. According to this estimate, General Earle was to reach Abu Hamed about the 10th of February, Berber the 22nd, and Shendi the 5th of March; while the remainder "will commence to reach Metemmeh the 16th of January, and should be concentrated there with sixty days' supplies by the 2nd of March," adding, "If we hire many camels this date may be anticipated." †

Sir H. Stewart started from Korti on the 30th of December, with 78 Officers, 1029 men, 221 natives, 2206 camels, and 45 horses, among them the Guards Camel regiment. Marching in the afternoons and at night, he reached Jakdul, without opposition, early on the 2nd of January, and the same day returned, leaving the Guards and Royal Engineers behind, under Lieut.-Colonel Boscawen. He was again in Jakdul on the 12th. During the interval, the water arrangements were improved, and the post strengthened. In respect to this duty, Sir H. Stewart reports as follows on the 14th January:—

"The post at Jakdul has been vastly improved by Lieut.-Colonel Hon. F. Boscawen and the Guards Camel regiment, during the eight days they have been quartered there. . . . I think it right to state that nothing but extreme hard work on the part of Officers and men could have effected so complete a metamorphosis in this post, and I venture to submit that it reflects the highest credit on the Guards Camel regiment."

Leaving a garrison behind of 150 men of the Royal Sussex Regiment, the force started from Jakdul at 2 p.m. on the 14th, consisting of two squadrons of the 19th Hussars, the Naval division, half a Camel battery, Royal Engineers, Guards, Heavy, and Mounted infantry Camel regiments, a wing Royal Sussex (on

* Colvile, *Official Account*, part ii. p. 6, etc., where the full text of all these orders are given.
† Colonel Sir Charles Wilson, K.C.B., R.E., *From Korti to Khartum*, p. 3, where this paper is given in full. (London, 1885.)

camels), Medical and Transport details; approximately, 115 Officers, 1687 men, 351 natives, 153 horses, 2888 (of whom 860 transport) camels, 3 guns, and one Gardner. Next day, evidence of the enemy's proximity became apparent, and on the 16th the cavalry, which had been pushed well to the front, reported that he had taken up a position to bar our access to the Abu Klea wells. The advance was continued, and in the afternoon, when it was too late to attack, we got into close touch with him. A zeriba was then constructed, strengthened by a hastily made wall and by mimosa thorn; and during the night the Arabs fired into it, but without doing much mischief. Early on the 17th, a small garrison was placed there, and the remainder emerged in square, with skirmishers in front and on the flanks. The formation was as follows:—Front face, Coldstream on the right, Royal Artillery in the centre, Mounted infantry on the left; Right face, Scots Guards on the left, then Grenadier Guards, Marines, Sussex Regiment; Left face, Mounted infantry on the right, then Heavy Camel regiment; Rear face, Heavies on the right, then Naval division, with the Gardner gun, and Sussex; the 19th Hussars were outside on the left. We soon became engaged, and several casualties occurred, the dervishes firing, and apparently being driven back behind the folds of the ground. Our progress was slow, for the cumbrous square formation had to be maintained, and the camels, carrying the wounded, to be prevented from straying outside.*
We were making for a line of flags that was to be seen in front of us, and many now believed that the enemy was in full retreat.

"Just at this moment, when about 450 yards from the flags, as if they had risen from the earth, up rose a line of spearmen all across the wady, [gully], and at the same moment the whole wady behind appeared black with them." †

"The skirmishers at once retired, but as they did so directly in the line of advance of the enemy, they screened him from the fire of the square during the first stage of his charge, and it was not until the spearmen were within 200 yards of the square that the fire could be developed." ‡

The sudden and fierce onslaught of some 5000 fanatics, who

* Nevertheless, some did lag behind, and would have been cut off, but for the courage of Lieut.-Colonel Rowley, Grenadier Guards, who drove them into the square, just as the Arabs began the attack which is about to be described.
† *Nineteenth Century*, loc. cit.
‡ Colvile, *Official Account*, part ii. p. 18.

held death in contempt, was eventually directed against the left rear corner; and such was the impetus of the rush, that the Heavies were pressed back by sheer weight of numbers into the centre of the square, where the camels were, and almost as far as the front and right faces. The square was practically broken, and a desperate hand-to-hand fight followed, but it happily was only of brief duration. The Guards and Marines had been unmoved by the shock; and keeping up a steady fire with the front rank upon the masses of the Arabs, who were hovering near to complete the victory should the rush be successful, they turned about the rear rank to assist in the struggle that was going on behind them.* In a few minutes the violence of the dervishes had expended itself, and they fell back, slowly and sullenly, until we got our guns to play upon them, and they left us in possession of the ground. The cavalry then pushed forward to the wells, and, when the square was reformed, it followed slowly on, the men elated by success, but suffering agonies from thirst. At 5 p.m. the water was reached, but it was not until early on the 18th that the zeriba was transferred to Abu Klea, and the post there was then established and strengthened.

Our losses, which fell principally on the Heavies and the Naval division, were very great, and amounted to 9 Officers and 65 men killed, and 9 Officers† and 85 men wounded; total 168 of all ranks. Of the former, Colonel Fred Burnaby (Royal Horse Guards) fell, well known for his travels and for his adventurous character. Of the Coldstream detachment 2 men (one a sergeant) were killed; Surgeon James Magill and 10 were wounded, of whom one died of his wounds. The strength of the enemy is not accurately known; it is supposed to have been from 9000 to 11,000: his losses were considerable, and 800 lay dead in the open ground close to the square.

In the afternoon of the 18th, the column started for the Nile, and continued to move throughout the night. The troops, the native drivers, and the animals were becoming exhausted by the toil they had undergone; the men found it difficult to keep awake; the camels, insufficiently fed, and at work incessantly for

---

* "I was much struck by the demeanour of the Guards Officers. There was no noise or fuss; all the orders were given as if on parade, and they spoke to their men as if nothing unusual was going on" (*From Korti to Khartum*, p. 36).

† Two subsequently died of their wounds.

nearly three weeks, lagged behind, or got off the track. The line of advance led through a thick mimosa scrub; there was no moon, and, on account of the enemy's proximity, bugles could not be sounded to keep the column together. During the darkness, therefore, there was much confusion, and it was not until dawn that order could be restored. In a short time the river came into sight, some four miles away. To the left front appeared a large and well-built town, now recognized to be Metemmeh, and looking far more important and strong than was represented on our maps or indicated in our reports. As the British column, from its position near Abu Kru, gazed on the fertile valley beneath, they perceived large crowds of armed men issuing from the walls of Metemmeh, and it soon became clear that no water was to be obtained without a fight.

A zeriba was at once formed, wherein to guard the stores and baggage, before a force could advance to cut its way through the enemy. But as this was being accomplished, the latter, creeping up through the long grass and scrub, opened fire from concealed positions, and several casualties occurred. Sir H. Stewart at this moment was severely wounded, and the command devolved upon Sir C. Wilson.

At 2.30 the zeriba was ready, and garrisoned by half the Heavies, the Cavalry, Artillery, and Naval division, while the remainder, under Sir C. Wilson, emerged therefrom in square, the executive command of which was entrusted to Lieut.-Colonel Boscawen. An important duty now devolved upon this Officer, viz. to lead the square past the enemy in the bush to the river, and to keep it as much as possible on the open ground. That the losses at this particular period of the day were comparatively few, may be ascribed to the manner in which the column was directed and manœuvred at this time. Warned by the tactics of the dervishes at Abu Klea, no skirmishers were extended; but as long as the enemy kept up his fire from the scrub, our men, unable to reply with effect, were at a disadvantage. Fortunately this did not last long; for the Arabs, unable to restrain their fiery ardour, charged the square with fury, and were met by the steady and withering fire of our soldiers. In less than five minutes the fight was over.

"The seething mass of fanatics who had headed the charge were now a heap of lifeless bodies, their comrades in rear had melted away into the distance, and the British troops (sadly reduced in numbers since their first fight at Abu Klea) made the echoes ring with a loud cheer."*

There was no more resistance that day, and Sir C. Wilson, having gone forward to select a bivouac, the column was halted on the river as dusk began to fall.

The joy of being once more near a plentiful supply of water, and the sense of relief that the march across the desert had been at last successfully accomplished, now filled the minds of our men, and atoned in some degree for the hardships and privations they had just undergone; but rest was also required, for not only the labours, but the excitement and the dangers of the last few days had told severely upon them, and a much-needed sleep was only partially obtained during the night of January 19th-20th. Next day the bivouac was shifted to the village of Gubat, which was placed in a state of defence; and the zeriba, formed the day before, having been evacuated, the wounded and stores were brought there.† The enemy was hovering near, but made no attempt to interfere with our operations. In view of the orders given to the Commander of the Desert column, and to secure our position at Gubat from attacks which could be easily organized against us in Metemmeh, Sir C. Wilson determined to capture that place, if this could be accomplished without serious risk. On the 21st, therefore, he advanced against it with the greater part of his force, but found it stronger than he anticipated. During the day, Gordon's steamers appeared on the scene, and assisted in the attack; but they also brought news that another horde of Arabs might be soon expected from the direction of Khartum, and orders were therefore given to fall back upon Gubat.

The casualties during the 19th, 20th, and 21st, amounted to one Officer and 22 men killed, and 9 Officers and 93 men wounded; total, 125: added to this, two war correspondents to London newspapers (the *Morning Post* and *Standard*) also lost their lives. Among the severely wounded, belonging to the Guards Camel regiment, were Lieutenant Crutchley, Scots Guards, and Major H. Poë, Royal Marines; in the Coldstream detachment

---

* Colvile, *Official Account*, ii. 27.

† The horses had all been fifty-eight hours, and some even as many as seventy-five hours, without water (*Nineteenth Century*, loc. cit.). The camels had not received anything to drink for six or seven days, having been previously accustomed to be watered every second or third day (*From Korti to Khartum*, p. 95).

two men were wounded. It is extremely sad to have to relate that the brilliant Commander of the column, Sir H. Stewart, never recovered from his wound, and died on the 17th of February, before he could be taken even as far as Korti, deeply regretted by all who served under his command, as well as by every one who knew his kindly, generous, and manly character.

Directly the Queen learnt that the column had reached the Nile, and heard of the pluck and endurance exhibited by her soldiers, Her Majesty caused the Secretary of State to signify by telegram "her satisfaction and warm thanks to her brave troops, and her deep concern for their losses and sufferings, but especially for General Stewart's severe wound;" and in consideration of that Officer's gallant service, Her Majesty was also pleased to promote him to the rank of Major-General. The Khedive, moreover, telegraphed his congratulations and thanks to the men for the success they had achieved.

Sir C. Wilson had now a double function to discharge. His original mission was to communicate a letter to General Gordon, and to give him that moral support which the appearance of a few red-coats for a day or two in Khartum might confer upon him.* But a new duty also obliged him to provide for the safety of the small and sadly diminished force which had just been unexpectedly placed under his command. To this most important task he therefore applied himself. It was reported that enemies were closing about him from Berber and from the south; Metemmeh also was too strong to be taken by a *coup de main*. Thus it was essential that he should see for himself the extent of the Arab resources which might be brought to bear upon Gubat; and while he sent the cavalry up the river, early on the 22nd, he embarked in a steamer, and made his way down the stream. The results of these reconnaissances were satisfactory, and he returned convinced that the dervishes were not in such numbers as he had been led to believe. Meanwhile, the position we occupied was strengthened, and communications with the Nile were secured; Gubat, situated on a height about half a mile from the water, could not be evacuated, and it was garrisoned by the Guards; and another fort, connected with an island by a *tête de pont*, was constructed near the river.

* Three British Officers were, moreover, to accompany Wilson to Khartum, and to be left there with Gordon.

Then a vexatious delay occurred. The steamers required repair, and it was not until the afternoon of the 23rd, when too late to start on that day, that they were reported fit to move. Accompanied by 20 men of the Royal Sussex and 240 black troops, Sir C. Wilson left for Khartum on the morning of the 24th. The passage up the river was rapidly made, in a falling Nile, and on the 28th the beleaguered city was approached. It would be outside the scope of this volume to give any account of the numerous thrilling adventures and hairbreadth escapes that marked this perilous journey. It is sufficient to say that Khartum had fallen on the 26th, and Gordon was killed. The whole place was in the hands of the Mahdi, and the little band of Englishmen ran the gauntlet past the enemy right up to Khartum, and under its guns, until they made sure that the end had indeed come, and that there was no further use in remaining where they were.* We now know that Gordon had been starved out, and that his food ran short on the 3rd or 4th of January, when the last issue of rations took place; that Omdurman, having fallen soon afterwards (January 15th), the dervishes drew closer round Khartum; that they could have entered it any day they chose, as the falling Nile laid bare the weak points of the defences of the city; that at dawn on the 26th this helpless quarter was stormed; and that the place fell after a few minutes' fighting. The expedition had been sent a month too late, and the "game was played out before the British troops reached Gubat; at that period nothing could save Khartum." †

Little occurred to the small British force near Metemmeh during this interval. Convoys, under Lieut.-Colonel Hon. R. Talbot (1st Life Guards), of about a thousand camels and 300 to 400 men, started for Jakdul, to bring up supplies to the Nile, on January 23rd and on February 2nd. Sir C. Wilson,

---

* An account of this journey is to be found in Colvile's *Official Account*, part ii. p. 33, etc.—how the steamers ascended the river with difficulty and advanced to Khartum in the teeth of hostile batteries and under fire from the city; how the fall of the place became undoubted; how the native crews of the steamers showed signs of disaffection; how both steamers were wrecked on the return journey, and how the small British party were exposed to imminent danger; how Lieutenant Stuart-Wortley was sent down the river in an open row-boat, and succeeded in reaching Gubat; and how a rescue party was immediately organized under Lord Charles Beresford, who went to the relief of Sir Charles Wilson, and those with him, in another steamer, amid many difficulties, and in spite of the opposition of the dervishes.

† Major C. M. Watson, C.M.G., R.E., *Royal Engineers' Journal*, June 1, 1892. See *Fire and Sword in the Sudan*, p. 342.

also, after his gallant effort to reach Khartum, left Gubat on the 6th, with an escort of twelve men of the Coldstream, under Captain V. Dawson, and reached Korti on the 9th. These and other movements took place without opposition on the part of the enemy, and thus it appeared that the desert had been effectively swept of Arabs; but they were still to be feared, and rumours were not wanting to the effect that they were concentrating and were converging upon our advanced position on the river. When Lord Wolseley heard of Sir H. Stewart's wound, he decided to send his Chief of the Staff, Major-General Sir Redvers Buller, to replace him, and to despatch some infantry to reinforce the Desert column. Accompanied by six companies of the Royal Irish Regiment, who marched on their feet the whole way from Korti, the new General reached Gubat on the 11th, and assumed command there.

The fall of Khartum, reported at head-quarters on the 4th of February, made a change in the conduct of the war, and the object of his mission being no longer possible, the British Commander was left without instructions as to his future proceedings.* He was thus unable to send any precise orders to Sir R. Buller, who had already left Korti before the death of General Gordon was known there, until he had ascertained the views of Government upon the new situation that had arisen. But these views were not at once forthcoming; for, the first telegram, dated London, February 6th, gave no indication of the policy to be pursued in the Sudan, and it was only after a more explicit statement had been requested, that he was informed that "the power of the Mahdi at Khartum must be overthrown." Orders were then despatched to the Desert column to hold on to the Nile, and, when Metemmeh was taken, to combine with General Earle in an attack upon Berber. But before this message was received, arrangements had been already taken for the evacuation of Gubat. This determination had been rendered necessary because the camels were insufficient in number, and were too much reduced by hard work, to perform the transport service across the desert; supplies were liable to run short; and a hostile force was reported to be marching from Khartum.

Accordingly, the last of the wounded left the Nile on the 13th under escort, commanded by Colonel Talbot, consisting of portions

* Colvile, *Official Account*, part ii. p. 57.

of the Guards, Heavy, and Mounted infantry Camel regiments. Early next day the enemy showed signs of renewed activity, by attacking the convoy, which, encumbered by wounded, many of whom were carried on stretchers, and by Egyptian soldiers and camp followers who had come from Khartum in the steamers, was not advantageously circumstanced to ward off a serious attack. After keeping the enemy at bay by some sharp fighting, the Light Camel regiment, which was luckily in the vicinity, came up to the support of the convoy, and with their assistance the Arabs were soon driven away. Our losses were two killed and six wounded, of whom one belonged to the Coldstream.* On the same day, the 14th, Gubat was finally evacuated by our troops. Abu Klea was reached on the 15th, and, in order to reduce the consumption of water, for the wells were only capable of supplying a moderate force, the Hussars, Guards, Heavies, and the Sudanese who manned the steamers, were sent to Jakdul on the 16th.†

The River column, under Major-General Earle, had meanwhile started on its way to Berber by Abu Hamed (January 24th), and found the ascent of the Nile, through a hostile and practically unexplored country, by no means an easy operation. The physical difficulties of the route seemed to increase day by day, but by dint of hard work and perseverance the troops continued to push on slowly. On the 10th of February, meeting the enemy at Kirbekan, where he attempted to make a stand, they attacked and defeated him; but the victory was unfortunately accompanied by the death of the General—killed by a bullet fired from a stone hut, in which some Arabs had taken refuge. The advance was immediately resumed, and was continued until the 24th, when a point, 26 miles from Abu Hamed, was reached. Here the troops were stopped by a message, dated head-quarters 20th, which ordered the column to return. A retrograde movement was therefore at once commenced. The cause of this fresh order has now to be briefly explained.

On receiving instructions directing the overthrow of the Mahdi's power at Khartum, Lord Wolseley decided that the first step was to reduce Berber, and he therefore wished, as we have seen,

* This man, Lance-Sergeant Leaning, who died of his wounds, was noted for his gallantry upon this occasion.
† Owing to the amount of hard work done, the Guards were now without boots; and this seems to have been the reason why they were selected to go back.

to combine both the River and Desert columns to secure that object. But insuperable difficulties presented themselves to the execution of that design. In the first place, the absence of all means of rapid communication between Korti and the two columns was a serious obstacle to any form of combined operations. Supplies for immediate and future use had, moreover, to be carried along with the troops, over the formidable obstructions which everywhere opposed our progress. The camels of the Desert column had completely broken down, and there was no transport available; the men's boots were also worn out, and their marching powers were in consequence diminishing day by day. The River column, moreover, though able to move forward,—but only slowly, on account of the physical difficulties in the way and the low condition of the Nile,—had not sufficient carrying power to store Berber with the supplies which it would have been necessary to place there.*

These difficulties entailed a change of plan, and both columns were therefore ordered to return. Sir R. Buller had been annoyed by hostile demonstrations against him near Abu Klea since the 16th, and on that day and on the next he lost three men killed, and 4 Officers, and 23 wounded. As soon as this advanced position had no longer to be held, he evacuated it on the 23rd and 24th, in the face of a large number of Arabs, estimated at not less than 8000 men, with such skill and judgment that, having deceived them, they made no effort to interfere with his movements. The retirement was everywhere continued, the Guards reaching Korti on the 9th of March, and the last troops leaving the desert on the 16th. From Korti, the Guards went to Dongola on the 16th, and remained there for some months; while the rest of the army also took up summer quarters on the Nile, not further forward than Merowi,—to await the coming of the autumn, when a fresh advance was to be made to free Khartum from the despotism of the Mahdi.

* Colvile, *Official Account*, part ii. p. 72.

SERGEANT-DRUMMER 1895.
A.D. Innes & Co. London.

CHAPTER XVII.

SECOND PART OF THE WAR IN THE SUDAN, 1884-1885—SUAKIN CAMPAIGN.

Reasons for the expedition to Suakin—Departure of the Coldstream—Orders to Lieut.-General Sir G. Graham—Position of the enemy—Advance against Hashin—Engagement at Tofrek—Attack on a convoy, escorted by the Coldstream and Royal Marines—Advance to Tamai—Construction of the railway—Attack on T'Hakul—Abrupt end of the campaign—The Coldstream proceed to Alexandria, and thence to Cyprus—Evacuation of the Sudan; how the Mahdi took advantage of it; how the Dongolese were treated—Position taken up south of Wady Halfa—Defeat of the Arabs at Ginnis—Return of the Guards Camel regiment—Return of the Coldstream from Cyprus—Honourable distinctions added to the Colours—Officers of the Regiment in December, 1885.

WHEN the British Government made up their mind, early in February, 1885, to put an end to the devastating tyranny of the dervishes, at all events in Khartum, and sent instructions to the British Commander to that effect, they also consulted him as to whether a strong expedition should be despatched forthwith to Suakin. Under the impression that his instructions to overthrow the power of the Mahdi at Khartum were intended really to produce that result, Lord Wolseley gladly accepted the offer that Osman Digna might be dealt with, without further delay. We must refer the reader to the current history of the day to seek the causes of the awakened energy which roused the Government to action at this moment. Very few years have elapsed since 1885, and the events which then took place can scarcely be forgotten. Suffice it to say that the country, justly proud of General Gordon, was roused to indignation when it was realized that, in spite of warnings from the military authorities, the Government had delayed to take proper measures to rescue him and those for whom he was responsible, until the season was too far advanced, and until rescue was impossible. So also, the large and unstinted sums of money, freely lavished upon the tardy expedition that was at last despatched up the Nile, had failed to accomplish the object which the nation had so much at heart. Under all these circumstances, it was clearly judicious to propitiate the popular wrath that began to manifest itself; and how could this be more efficaciously done than by the public announcement that summary punishment was about to be inflicted upon the murderers of the British hero, whose death was so universally deplored? Hence it came about that a railway to Berber was immediately to be commenced; that another expedition to protect it was to be sent to Suakin; and that a still more extravagant expenditure of treasure was to be wasted, now when it was too late, and when the necessary outlay had been curtailed up to the summer of 1884,— that is, as long as there was time to save the garrison of Khartum.

In January and February, 1885, Major-General Lyon Fremantle, in command, as we have seen, at Suakin, since July, 1884, had been reinforced by a squadron of cavalry, two battalions of infantry, and a battery of Royal Horse Artillery, brought from Lower Egypt, and amounting to some 2500 men. With these he engaged in defensive operations against Osman Digna, who had again begun to give trouble in the district. Prompt measures were now taken to make them capable of assuming the offensive by raising them to a total of about 13,000 men. The field force, so augmented, was commanded by Lieut.-General Sir G. Graham, V.C., K.C.B., under the general orders of Lord Wolseley, who was responsible for all operations against the enemy; and composing it, there was a Guards Brigade, troops of the Line, an Indian contingent, and, lastly, an Australian battalion and battery furnished by the Government of New South Wales. This Colonial corps of fighting men, and that provided by the Dominion of Canada for the service of the boats on the Nile, form a new feature in our military history, which we should be sorry to pass over in silence; for they show the patriotic feelings which urge our brethren over the sea, gallantly to take their share in any struggle in which the interests of our Queen and Empire may be involved.

The following organization was adopted at Suakin: A Cavalry Brigade (Colonel H. P. Ewart, C.B.), two squadrons of the 5th Lancers, and two of the 20th Hussars, and a battalion Mounted infantry (4 companies). Three batteries of artillery (one Royal Horse Artillery), and eventually one battery New South Wales.

The 1st or Guards Brigade * (Major-General A. J. Lyon Fremantle), 3rd Grenadiers (Colonel Hon. W. Home), 1st Coldstream (Colonel A. Lambton), and 2nd Scots Guards (Colonel Hon. W. Trefusis). Subsequently, when they arrived, the New South Wales Battalion, under the command of Lieut.-Colonel Richardson, were attached to this Brigade. The 2nd Brigade (Major-General Sir J. C. McNeill, V.C., K.C.B.), three battalions of infantry (of the East Surrey, Shropshire, and Berkshire Regiments), and one of Royal Marines. The Indian Brigade (Brigadier-General J. Hudson, C.B.), one regiment of cavalry (9th Bengal), three battalions infantry (15th Sikhs, 17th Bengal, and 28th Bombay), and one company Madras Sappers. Royal Engineers (one Railway and two Field companies, two Telegraph sections, and one Balloon detachment). And four, eventually five, companies of the Commissariat and Transport Corps.

The 1st Coldstream were made up by a draft from the 2nd Battalion to 1 Warrant-officer, 80 Non-commissioned officers, 16 drummers, and 710 privates, out of which a detachment of 50 men was told off to form a Mounted infantry company. Officers were posted as follows:—

Commanding Officer.—Colonel A. Lambton.
Mounted Majors.—Lieut.-Cols. J. B. Sterling; and R. S. Hall.
Adjutant.—Lieutenant Hon. H. Legge.
Quartermaster.—H. Folson.
Medical Officer.—Surgeon A. Alexander.

Compy.			Lieutenants.
No. 1.	Lt.-Col.	C. Fortescue.	C. Frederick; and F. Maude.
No. 2.	„	F. Manley.	G. Sebright; and C. Holland.
No. 3.	„	R. Follett.	Earl of Wiltshire; and G. Milligan.
No. 4.	„	L. D. MacKinnon.	H. Shute.
No. 5.	Capt.	Hon. H. Monck.	R. Winn (subsequently in command of Regl. Transport).
No. 6.	Lt.-Col.	Hon. E. Digby.	G. Wyndham; and J. Drummond-Hay.
No. 7.	Lieut.	J. Gladstone.	D. J. Hamilton.
No. 8.	Lt.-Col.	Hon. H. Corry.	Hon. Alan Charteris; and R. Grenfell.

The following Officers served on the Staff: Lieutenants Earl of Wiltshire, and Hon. Alan Charteris, Aides-de-camp to Major-General Sir J. McNeill; and Lieutenant Gladstone, Orderly Officer

* Captains Hon. N. Dalrymple, Scots Guards, and the Hon. F. Stopford, Grenadier Guards, were respectively Brigade-Major of the Guards Brigade, and Aide-de-camp to Major-General Fremantle.

to Major-General Fremantle. The detachment of mounted men was placed under the command of Captain Ross-of-Bladensburg and Lieutenant G. Sutton, but until the ponies were obtained, which did not take place before the 5th of April, these Officers did duty with the Battalion, the former commanding No. 7 Company. It should also be stated that the Brigade furnished upon this occasion a company of Army Signallers, under command of Lieutenant F. Lloyd, Grenadier Guards, composed of 12 men from the 3rd Grenadiers, 12 from the 1st Coldstream, and 6 from the 2nd Scots Guards; the corps was attached to the 3rd Grenadier Guards. Further, a Field Hospital was also formed, of which Surgeons-Major C. Read (Coldstream), Lawrence (Grenadiers), and A. Myers (Scots Guards), and Surgeon G. Robinson (Scots Guards) were the Medical Officers.

The 1st Coldstream left Wellington Barracks shortly after 7 a.m. on the 19th of February, accompanied by a dense and enthusiastic crowd, and, marching to Westminster Stairs, proceeded in two river steamers to Gravesend, where they embarked on board the *Manorah*. Remaining a few hours at Malta, they were detained a day at Suez, and reached Suakin on the 8th of March. The Battalion then landed without delay, marched about two miles, and encamped in an advanced position to cover the assembly of the troops; they were joined by the 2nd Scots and 3rd Grenadier Guards, who arrived respectively the 9th and 10th. There had been some alarms of a disquieting nature when we reached the seat of war. The Arabs frequently sent forward a few armed men at a time, who, crawling at night past the outposts into the centre of the camp, attacked and stabbed our soldiers and horses in the dark, even in the head-quarter camp or to the rear of it, where at least every one had a right to believe himself to be in safety, and guarded against depredations of the sort. This disagreeable method of warfare was not easy to suppress, and when the enemy was successful in his raid, it produced a "scare," which was calculated to disturb the equanimity of the troops. The dervishes, in short, were hovering very near us at night, firing into us from the bush (fortunately without much effect), though they seldom made any demonstrations in the daylight. Detachments were sent out as soon as it was dark, to watch all approaches leading to Suakin; but the nuisance only came to an end, when we moved out to attack the enemy, and drove him back from our neighbourhood. Meanwhile the Brigade camp, though it had never been disturbed, was withdrawn somewhat closer to the town on the 16th.

The orders which Sir G. Graham received were dated the 20th of February; and they directed him, in the first place, to destroy the power of Osman Digna, and, secondly, to give assistance and protection to the construction of the railway. The military occupation of the Hadendowa country, lying near the Suakin-Berber route, was to be accomplished; and it was indicated that this would be best done by the Indian troops, while the British portion of the army were to be placed in the hilly region, which is to be found a little beyond Tambuk wells (25 miles from Suakin), to a distance of 60 or 70 miles further on towards Berber. It was also intimated that possibly Berber might not be attacked before the autumn,[*] and, if so,—

"the railway cannot be pushed much beyond Ariab; and there, all the railway plant and material necessary for the 100 miles between it and Berber should be collected as soon as possible, so that the advance, when the cool weather begins, and Berber is taken, may be made at once."[†]

These instructions clearly show the intention of the British Government at this critical moment in their fortunes, when public indignation was rising against them; viz. to overthrow the power of the Mahdi at Khartum in the autumn of 1885, now that it was not found possible to achieve that object in the spring of the same year. This was to be effected by the co-operation of two expeditions, under the supreme command of Lord Wolseley,—one under his immediate leadership, concentrating in the province of Dongola, to pass the summer there, and to emerge therefrom when the suitable season came round for field operations; the other, under Sir G. Graham, with the objects (1) to crush Osman Digna, and to clear the country of the enemy, in order that the railway might be made, and (2) to construct that railway at least as far as Ariab (some 145 miles from Suakin), and to place troops for its protection "where the summer heats could be best endured."[‡]

Sir G. Graham reached Suakin March 12th, and next day the

---

[*] The date upon which Lord Wolseley ordered the River column to retire, was the 20th of February. See *ante*, chap. xvi., p. 391.

[†] Colvile, *Official Account*, part ii. p. 181. The full text of this despatch from the Secretary of State to Sir G. Graham is given in that work.

[‡] *Ibid.*, ii. 195.

railway was begun.* A few days had to be spent in completing the assembly of the force, and in perfecting the arrangements necessary for their supply. The wells in the neighbourhood were sufficient to provide the camels and horses with water, but as its quality and quantity could not be depended upon for the troops of the expedition, ships fitted with condensing boilers were brought to Suakin, and condensed sea-water was issued in tins for their use, and was transported to the various camps by camels or by railway.

The country near Suakin is a flat sandy plain, intersected by khors, or water courses (quite dry at this season of the year), which, extending westward some ten or twelve miles, is terminated by a line of hills running almost parallel to the sea coast. Near the town, the plain is fairly open for about two or three miles, but afterwards, and especially in the khors and at the foot of the hills, it is covered by thick masses of mimosa thorny scrub, many of which look somewhat like large gooseberry bushes six to eight feet high, and wide in proportion; in many places they are tangled by the prickly pear, and by rank grass and other undergrowth. The enemy was reported to have concentrated his main force of some 7000 men at Tamai, a village about 16 miles away in a south-westerly direction from Suakin. Another thousand or more were at Hashin, eight miles due east of the town, where a valley penetrates into the hills. It was here that the Arabs were supposed to live who troubled our nights. To the north-west is the village of Handub, eleven miles off, also occupied by dervishes; and to this place the railway to Berber would have to run.

It was evidently desirable that our first movement should be directed against Hashin. On the 19th of March, a reconnaissance was undertaken against it, and next day an attack upon the position was made in force; the 2nd Brigade in front, supported on the flanks by the Guards and Indian troops, covered by the cavalry; the horse artillery and a Gardner battery (4 guns) being in rear: altogether a little more than 8000 men. Arrived at a detached group of hills about a mile and a half from Hashin, redoubts were constructed there by the East Surrey Regiment, while the remainder continued to push forward, until the entrance

* It is worthy of remark that this was *not* a light railway, as had been originally proposed; but a line of the ordinary gauge, such as is constructed in England, for general traffic. See Map No. 8, p. 360.

of the valley, previously mentioned, was reached. The 2nd Brigade, supported by the Indian battalions, ascended the southern heights above this valley, and soon drove the enemy therefrom. The Arabs, estimated at 3000 strong, however, were favoured by the dense bush; they seemed to swarm through it, and, hovering round, they dashed into our men with the greatest bravery, whenever an opportunity presented itself. In this way, two squadrons of Indian horse were somewhat severely handled by an almost invisible foe. Meanwhile the Guards were in reserve, formed in square, just under the heights which Sir J. McNeill had taken on our left front, and close to a small rise in the ground on our right front, which we called Bee-hive Hill. The redoubts in rear being complete soon after midday, and garrisoned by the East Surrey, the 2nd and Indian Brigades were ordered to retire, the Guards to cover the movement. The Arabs, owing to the thick cover that concealed them, remained closer to our position than they could otherwise have done, and perceiving our return towards our camp, they opened a hot fire from the bush upon us, principally from Bee-hive Hill, which was returned with steady volleys. This proceeding soon silenced them, though the Brigade lost some men during this short period of the day—1 Officer, Captain Dalison (Scots Guards), and 2 men being killed, and 16 wounded. Our total casualties amounted to 48 Officers and men killed and wounded, and of these the Coldstream numbered 1 man died of wounds, and 8 wounded. The result of the action was that we had no further trouble as far as Hashin was concerned, and thenceforward the enemy's night raids on our camp ceased.

An advance was now made towards Tamai, the centre of Osman Digna's resistance, and, on the 22nd of March, Sir J. McNeill was sent forward to establish a post on the road to that place, eight miles off, with one squadron of the 5th Lancers, the Berkshire Regiment, the Marines, a detachment of the Naval brigade (with 4 Gardner guns), three Indian battalions, and the Madras Sappers. On the same day, the Coldstream proceeded towards Hashin, to convoy supplies to the East Surrey Regiment, who were still in the redoubts constructed on the 20th, and met with no misfortune, except that several of our men were struck down by sun apoplexy. On returning home in the afternoon, we saw clouds of dust rising out of the bush in the place where we conceived Sir J. McNeill's column to be, and wondered whether something unusual had happened there. On returning to camp we heard, at first, exaggerated accounts of what occurred, but it was not long before the real truth was known. The column, finding the bush exceedingly thick and no natural clearings in it, could only advance slowly, and halted some six miles from Suakin. The men then began to construct a zeriba; and, while so employed, they were necessarily scattered, some were unarmed, and a large number of camels blocked the ground. The enemy, lurking unseen in the scrub close by, crept up, and suddenly made a fierce onslaught on the force. Unfortunately, one of the Indian battalions was somewhat unsteady, and, though the Officers worked hard to rally the men, they were rushed, and carried away to the rear. Then followed a battle of short duration which is not easy to describe. The Berkshire—who gained the title of "Royal" for their day's work—stood manfully up to the Arabs, though half the battalion were collecting brushwood and the other half were at their dinners, and, together with the Marines, the Sikhs, and the remaining Indian battalion, they maintained a hard fight for the space of twenty minutes. They soon, however, gained the mastery, and drove the enemy back with great slaughter. Isolated combats took place at some distance from the zeriba on the road to Suakin, entailing considerable loss, and towards evening the telegraph wire was cut. But news had, before this, been received at head-quarters, to assure Sir G. Graham that the danger was over, and that the attack had entirely failed. The Arabs were computed at 5000 strong, and their losses at 1500 men. Our own casualties were severe; and amounted to 10 Officers and 131 men killed and missing, and to 5 Officers and 150 men wounded: total 296. Added to this, there were 157 native camel drivers killed and missing, and 19 wounded. Total *personnel* lost, 472 men; besides 501 camels. Among the wounded was Lieutenant Charteris, Coldstream Guards. This action, known as the battle of Tofrek, occasioned more losses on one day than in any other engagement during the whole war in the Sudan.

The Guards Brigade were sent early the following morning to reinforce the zeriba and to bring up supplies and water. Forming a square, and guarding 1200 camels, the march was slow, and took nearly six hours to accomplish. Many of the loads were indifferently packed, and repeatedly fell off; the drivers seemed to have little control over the animals, which were bad movers and difficult to guide. The weather, also, was oppressively hot, and the men suffered a good deal from thirst. Arriving shortly before noon, the force halted for some hours; the Grenadier Guards and the Indian Brigade then returned to Suakin with the wounded and empty camels, leaving the Coldstream and Scots Guards and the rest of the troops behind. The immediate neighbourhood of Tofrek was still covered with hundreds of dead and numerous camels, many of which were hamstrung, and had to be shot. Burial parties were actively at work, but it was not easy to dispose quickly of the mass of dead bodies, both of men and animals, that lay about in large numbers; added to which there was little shade to be had from the broiling sun, and the water ration for every purpose had to be reduced to a minimum. For the next few days, the position in the zeriba was therefore anything but a pleasant one, as may be readily imagined.

On the 24th, the Coldstream and the Marines began cutting a path one hundred paces broad towards Suakin. After some hours' work, they marched, under Colonel Lambton, about halfway to the town, to escort a convoy to Tofrek, consisting of 425 camels and 818 carts, with 8000 gallons of water, which was brought up to that point by Indian troops. The Arabs were still hovering near, and they fired upon the two battalions as they proceeded on their journey, but without inflicting much loss. On their return, however, the fire became somewhat hotter, and was delivered at closer ranges than before, so that Colonel Lambton was obliged to halt several times to return it, and to allow the wounded to be attended to. The square, crowded with carts and camels that would not keep a straight course, offered an excellent mark to the sharpshooters concealed in the bush; but we were able to check this attack by small volleys fired by marksmen at the spots where we saw the enemy's puffs of smoke appear. This lasted for an hour or more, when at last, to our great satisfaction, some of the most daring of the dervishes made an attempt to charge. They came on in line, guided by flags at each flank, in the most gallant manner, and directed their attack mainly against the left face of the square. But, unable to stand our fire, they were very soon defeated, and most of them were killed, though one or two did actually succeed in getting as far as our bayonets before they fell. After this event they left us alone, and we got back to the zeriba without further trouble. The casualties of the day amounted to 24, of which the Coldstream lost 2 men killed or died of wounds, and 8 wounded; three Officers were wounded, two belonging to the Royal Marines, and Captain Hon. N. Dalrymple, Brigade Major of the Guards Brigade; in addition, 5 native camel-drivers were killed.* Some of the camels lagged behind, their drivers having abandoned them while the fight was going on; others were squeezed out of the square, which was from the beginning too full to hold them, and thus more than a hundred were cut off by the enemy.

Next day, another convoy was taken from Suakin to the zeriba in the same manner, the escorts meeting each other halfway between the two places. This time it was not molested, but the occasion deserves mention, since a captive balloon was then first employed; the latter, attached by a rope to a waggon that moved in the square, enabled a proper look-out to be kept upon the enemy in the bush. On the 26th, however, there was another skirmish, but it was easily repelled with very little loss; and on this day, the Grenadier Guards relieved the Scots Guards at Tofrek, while the Coldstream remained there till the 28th, when they also returned to head-quarters. After the 26th no further difficulty was experienced with the Arabs; they were apparently disheartened, and had retreated from the neighbourhood. A move, therefore, was made to Tamai.

Early on the morning of April 2nd, a force of 8000 men marched through Tofrek to Tesela Hill, near Tamai, where a halt was made for the night.† Next day, the advance was continued, and Osman Digna's head-quarters were occupied after a very slight resistance. Tamai, like other villages in the country, is a mere collection of straw huts, and it was speedily fired and destroyed, while the enemy made off into the hilly region that lies to the south, where it would have been difficult, and indeed unnecessary, to pursue him. The column therefore returned to Suakin, and the attention of the troops was now directed more particularly to the protection of the railway, which meantime had been progressing. The Battalion lost only two men wounded, on the 3rd of April.

At this time, also, ponies having arrived, the Guards Mounted infantry detachments were formed into two companies (April

---

* Captain Dalrymple was succeeded as Brigade-Major by Captain Stopford.

† The New South Wales Battalion formed part of this force, having reached Suakin on March 29th.

5th): the Grenadier and Scots Guards company, under Captain St. John Mildmay, Grenadier Guards; and the Coldstream company, under Captain Ross-of-Bladensburg, to which was attached a half-company, furnished by the Royal Engineers, under Lieutenant Sandbach, R.E. Ten days later, a Camel corps was formed under the command of Major James, Scots Greys, consisting of 400 British and 100 native soldiers, divided into five companies, of which one was composed of Guardsmen (31 men taken from each of the three Battalions), under Lieutenants Neil Menzies, Scots Guards, and G. Wyndham, Coldstream Guards.

The railway, leaving Suakin in a north-westerly direction as far as Handub (11 miles distant), bore round towards the west at this point, and, passing through Otao (20 miles from Suakin) and Tambuk (25 miles), was to continue across the hilly country to Ariab; from thence it was to run to Berber, over a stretch of 100 miles of desert country, which is watered only by the wells of O-Bak, lying nearly halfway between these two places. To cover the construction of the line, a zeriba was made (April 6th) by the Coldstream, the New South Wales Battalion, artillery, etc., between Suakin and Handub, called No. 1 Station. On the 8th, Handub was occupied, the Scots Guards being at No. 1 Station. On the 16th, the latter pushed on to Otao without meeting with any resistance; and when the Coldstream followed on the 18th, the Scots moved to Tambuk, finding no enemy there. On the 24th, a reconnaissance by a portion of the Camel corps was made towards Es-Sibil; and by the 30th the railway was completed as far as Otao. During this time the men were constantly employed in clearing broad roads through the bush; in digging watering-places, which had to be deepened daily as the supply became exhausted; and in protecting the scattered parties of navvies at work on the line. There were not many Arabs about, though few nights passed without some shots being fired into the camp.

About the same period, also, reconnaissances were pushed in various directions to prevent any advance from Tamai, and to clear the neighbouring valleys of the enemy. The most important was one undertaken in the early morning of the 7th of May, against a chief who had collected a force at a place called T'Hakul, lying nearly 20 miles west of Suakin and 10 south of Otao. The Brigade took no part in this operation; but the company belonging to the Camel corps and the two companies of Guards Mounted infantry were present, and forming part of the force at Suakin, they paraded there a little before midnight on the 6th. A small column co-operated from Otao, and in the morning both appeared before the camp of the Arabs and surprised it; the enemy fled at our approach, leaving behind 1100 sheep, goats, and some camels. The columns then returned to Otao and Suakin respectively; the latter, however, on their way home, met parties of the enemy occupying heights within range of which they had to pass; after a few volleys he quickly disappeared. One Officer (of the Camel corps) and two men were wounded, of whom one (a sergeant) belonged to the Coldstream (Mounted infantry).

This was the last operation conducted by Sir G. Graham's force in the neighbourhood of Suakin. The district had just been pacified and relieved of the presence of the enemy: at this very moment, orders came to evacuate it, and to withdraw the troops therefrom, except a small garrison, which was to be left behind to guard the town.* We must briefly explain how this came about.

The British Government never had much sympathy with the policy of opposing the Mahdi, whose usurpation of power, founded upon rapine, massacre, and slavery, had been dignified into the movement of a people struggling for freedom! This strange opinion upon the upheaval that swamped every vestige of civilization in the Sudan, was doubtless one reason, but perhaps not the only reason, for the vacillating proceedings pursued there, and for the consequent inability to effect, even at great expense, any useful object. Unwilling to face with a firm resolution the questions that required solution in that region, and prevented by public opinion from adopting a policy of non-intervention, the Government did nothing till popular clamour forced them to some action, and then the steps they took, costing many lives and much treasure, could produce no beneficial results. Thus, as we have seen, was the brave intention of taking Khartum, and of restoring order there,

---

* With the dispersal of the force collected at T'Hakul, the political question of the Eastern Sudan may be said to have been solved for the time being; large numbers of the natives placed themselves unconditionally at the disposal of Sir G. Graham, and a decided movement was set on foot against Osman Digna, even among those who were considered to be his closest adherents. It may be remarked that, though Osman Digna appears as our principal opponent, he was not a military leader likely to give much trouble once his followers had been defeated; the fact being, that he himself never appeared on or near the scene of conflict, but was content to urge on his men from some safe position or inaccessible fastness. (Colvile, *Official Account*, part ii., pp. 217, 323.)

published in February; and so also, as soon as possible and upon the very first pretext, was that intention abandoned. An opportunity very soon arose to facilitate this procedure.

There was a dispute in Asia over the frontier between the Russians and Afghans, and, on the 30th of March, news reached London that the former, having agreed to make no forward movement until pending questions had been discussed, advanced and took possession of Panjdeh by force of arms—a place held to be a portion of the territories of the Amir of Afghanistan. For reasons connected with the safety of India, we had espoused the cause of that Prince, and were bound to see that his legitimate claims received proper consideration. It is unnecessary to describe either the Panjdeh incident, or those that led up to this act of aggression. It is sufficient to say that they created much excitement in England, and soon drew public attention from the Sudan. The crisis did not last long, and the dispute was soon settled, but it enabled Government to wash their hands of the whole of the troublesome business connected with Khartum.

"The first step taken towards opening the country for the railway [in the neighbourhood of Suakin], was an attempt to form an alliance with the neutral tribes dwelling on or near the Berber road; but it was soon discovered that any such alliance must be dependent on a fixed policy on the part of Her Majesty's Government. The tribes appeared to be anxious to come in, and to be thoroughly tired of the terrorism established by Osman Digna, but they one and all said they could not join us unless they were assured of our future protection against Osman Digna, and unless we undertook that we would not go away, as we had done in the previous year. In a telegram to the Secretary of State for War, dated April 12, 1885, Sir G. Graham asked whether he might give this assurance. In reply, the following telegram was sent to Lord Wolseley, on the 15th of April, by the Secretary of State for War: 'Construction of railway for any considerable distance to be suspended pending further consideration. Suakin to be held for the present, and any position in neighbourhood necessary for protection from constant attack, as last year. You should report on point to which railway should now proceed, and instruct Graham, with reference to his message of the 12th, not to enter into engagements with tribes inconsistent with this policy.'" *

This was, therefore, the end of the expedition to the Eastern Sudan, and, as a matter of fact, orders soon arrived to break

---

* Colvile, *Official Account*, part ii. p. 212.

up the forces assembled there. The Guards Brigade and the New South Wales contingent were the first troops to take their departure. The Coldstream, having marched from the front on the 14th of May, embarked on the 16th in the *Deccan*, and started next day for Alexandria, where they arrived on the 23rd. The Battalion remained in the harbour, on board ship, until the 9th of June, when they marched to Ramleh, and camped on the beach. They stayed there until the 1st of July, and, together with the Grenadiers, embarked on H.M.S. *Orontes*, and proceeded on the 2nd to Cyprus. Landing at Limasol on the 5th, they marched to Mount Troödos, and reached that place on the 9th; the Scots Guards followed a few days later, and the whole Brigade remained at Troödos till after the middle of August. Major-General Fremantle stayed behind in Egypt, and Colonel Lambton, being the senior Officer, assumed the command of the Brigade, while that of the Battalion devolved upon Colonel Sterling, until the 27th, when Colonel Clive, Grenadier Guards, arrived from England as Brigadier-General.

We left the Nile force getting into summer quarters in the province of Dongola, in the spring of the year, and confidently expecting to resume the offensive against Khartum as soon as the great heat should pass away. But on the 13th of April a telegram reached Lord Wolseley, informing him that, in the then condition of Imperial affairs, it was probable the forward movement might have to be abandoned. The announcement that this decision had been taken was made known in England on the 21st, though on the 11th of May the troops were ordered to retire northwards, and to evacuate the Sudan.

"As it was certain that anarchy would immediately follow our withdrawal, and probable that a retreat on our part would allow the dormant hostility of the natives to find vent, it was necessary that the retreat, especially of the advanced portion of the force, should be conducted as rapidly and unexpectedly as possible. Jaudet Effendi [the then Governor of Dongola], was at once informed of the intended retreat. He begged for fifteen days' start, before our policy was made generally known, in order that he might take what steps he could, to mitigate the murder and rapine for which he believed our retirement would be the signal. This was granted him, and he at once started up the river, and the movement was arranged to commence on the 21st of May." *

* Colvile, *Official Account*, ii. 167.

Once begun, the evacuation did not take long to accomplish; the enemy offered no opposition, nor did he try to press our retreat. He was wise enough to follow at a respectful distance, occupying the country as we abandoned it. Indeed, ever since the return of the Desert and River columns we experienced no further trouble with the Mahdi, who, relieved of the danger with which he was threatened by the British advance, turned his attention to other matters. He sent a considerable force to the south of Khartum, to put down a rising which began to imperil his authority in Kordofan, and, as soon as he became aware that we were definitely about to withdraw from the province of Dongola and from the vicinity of Suakin, he despatched more of his men to hasten the reduction of Sennar and Kassala, both of which were besieged at that moment. These two places fell in the middle of August.

The operation of withdrawing from the Sudan was extremely distasteful to British Officers. The inhabitants of Dongola had trusted us, and had served us; we had necessarily interfered with their government, disturbed the means at their disposal for taking care of themselves, and prevented them from making terms with the enemy. They had been induced by us to resist the Arabs, to incur their vengeance, and to rely for protection upon the power of England,—a nation who never deserted a friend or turned away from a foe. We were pledged to defend this unfortunate people, or to make some reasonable provision for their future safety, but, in the face of the peremptory orders received from home, any such arrangement was entirely out of the question. Hence it was more than distressing to be forced to abandon these natives to the slavery that was in store for them; and we cannot be astonished that they reproached us bitterly for deserting them in this help-less condition, and for leaving them to the cruel tyranny of the Mahdi. Many appeared anxious to fly from their homes, but they were restrained by the knowledge that, in that case, they must forfeit the whole of their property; while others were unable to procure sufficient transport for their families and effects.*

Nearly 13,000 natives accompanied the retreat, and by the end of June these refugees, the supplies, and most of the troops were north of Dongola. At this moment the Government of Mr. Gladstone came to an end, and Lord Wolseley, who had from

* Colvile, *Official Account*, ii. 169.

the first protested against the precipitate withdrawal of the expedition, was empowered by the new Cabinet to arrest the movement temporarily, until the situation had been considered. It is sad to relate, that the evacuation had been too well executed, and that it was then too late to return or repair the evil that had already been done. By the 21st of July, that portion of the British army destined to remain as a frontier force, for the protection of Egypt, had taken up a position some ninety miles south of Wady Halfa, and there they covered the construction of the Sudan railway, which was completed to Akasheh on the 7th of August. Meanwhile the dervishes did not invade the northern part of Dongola at once, for the Mahdi fell a victim to his own debauchery, and, dying on the 22nd of June, left affairs in the Sudan in an unsettled state.* Until, therefore, his successor, the Khalifa Abdulla, had consolidated his position, no further conquests were possible, and the province was only seized by him in the middle of August. After this, the enemy advanced northwards with the intention of invading Egypt, and he even ventured to lay siege to a British fort on the frontier, in the month of November. In December, however, he was attacked, and forced to retire, by Lieut.-General Sir F. Stephenson, who defeated him at Ginnis on the 30th.

This event ends the war in the Sudan. Long before it took place the Guards Camel regiment had been sent home. Starting from Dongola, where they remained for nearly three months, they marched thence on the 1st of June, and, proceeding mostly by river, they reached Alexandria on the 1st of July, having halted for two hours at Cairo, where they were received by Lord Wolseley and Sir F. Stephenson. At Alexandria, they had the good fortune to meet the Guards Brigade, then on their way to Cyprus. They left Egypt on the 4th, and arrived in London on the 15th. After an inspection by H.R.H. the Duke of Cambridge, the various detachments composing the Camel corps returned to their respective Regiments. The following Brigade Order appeared in London on the 21st:—

"Lieut.-Colonel Hon. E. Boscawen, Coldstream Guards, recently in command of the Guards Camel regiment in the Sudan, having addressed to the Major-General Commanding the Brigade of Guards his complete

* See Major Wingate, R.A., *Ten Years' Captivity in the Madhi's Camp*, 1882-92, (from original manuscripts of Father J. Ohrwalder, late Priest of the Austrian Mission at Delen, in Kordofan), p. 160. (London, 1892.)

satisfaction with the conduct and soldierlike qualities displayed by all ranks under his command in the late Nile expedition, the Major-General wishes to place on record his great pleasure at receiving such a report, and his high appreciation of the manner in which the several detachments composing the Guards Camel regiment have so completely maintained the reputation of the Brigade. This order to be read at the head of each Battalion at the first full parade." *

The casualties of the Coldstream inflicted by the enemy in the field have already been noted in their proper place; but no mention has been made of those who died of disease during the two expeditions. It appears that sickness was less common in the interior than was the case among the troops stationed on the coast of the Red Sea; and six men only of the Coldstream died of illness during the many months they were employed on the Nile. The Regiment, however, had to deplore the death of Lieutenant G. Sutton and of 13 men of the 1st Battalion who succumbed to the climate of Suakin; while several Officers and 110 men had to be sent to England invalided. Lieutenant Sutton, a young Officer of great merit and of much promise, fell ill a short time before the end of the expedition, and was sent for a short cruise, in the hope that his health might be thereby re-established. He returned, as he thought, better, and resumed duty; but a very few days later he was again obliged to be placed upon the sick-list, and, becoming rapidly worse, he died at sea, May 18th, on his way home, before the steamer reached Suez, to the great sorrow of his brother Officers.

The Guards camp at Mount Troödos was broken up, and the 1st Coldstream marched from that place on the 24th of August, down to Limasol, where they embarked on board the *Orontes* (26th) in company with the Grenadiers, the Scots Guards being on the *Poonah*. The Battalion reached Spithead early on the

* Colonel Boscawen's report to the Officers Commanding 1st and 2nd Coldstream Guards, contained the following: "As the various detachments forming the Guards Camel regiment are shortly to return to their several Battalions, I have the honour to report on the general conduct of the Non-commissioned officers and men of the 1st and 2nd Battalions Coldstream Guards, during the period of service on the Nile expedition. The peculiar work which all ranks have been called upon to perform has been trying and arduous, and for the most part quite novel to the men. Nevertheless, it gives me the greatest satisfaction to testify to the cheerful and zealous manner with which these exceptional duties have been throughout accomplished. The behaviour of the men in the field needs no comment from me. The period of inaction, subsequent to the campaign, has been perhaps not the least tedious to soldiers, who lately had seen a good deal of hard work and excitement, but their behaviour has been uniformly unexceptionable."

10th of September, and proceeded next day to London, where they received a hearty welcome from their friends and the public at large.

The following extract of a letter, written by Colonel Lambton soon after his return from the Sudan, to the Officer Commanding the 2nd Battalion, refers to the men belonging to the latter, and temporarily posted to the service Battalion for duty during the war:—

"Now that the men belonging to the 2nd Battalion have left us, I should like to express to you how satisfied I have been with their conduct during the late campaign. I am glad to see there has been no distinction between the two Battalions; all have done their best to keep up the credit and reputation of the Regiment."

Medals for the Sudan campaign were issued to Officers, Non-commissioned officers, and men on the 7th of November; and by General Order, January 10, 1886, it was intimated that Her Majesty the Queen had been graciously pleased to approve of the three Regiments of Foot Guards being permitted to bear the words "Suakin, 1885" upon their Colours. Early in 1883, the record of Marlborough's battles, which had been somewhat strangely passed over in the past, were also added to the Colours, and the Coldstream then showed the following honourable distinctions, viz. "The Sphinx, superscribed 'Egypt.' Oudenarde. Malplaquet. Dettingen. Lincelles. Talavera. Barrosa. Peninsula. Waterloo. Alma. Inkerman. Sevastopol. Egypt, 1882. Tel el-Kebir. Suakin, 1885."

In December, 1885, the Regiment stood as follows:—

Colonel.—General Right Hon. Sir Thomas Steele, K.C.B.
Lieut.-Colonels.—Commanding Regiment.—Col. G. Wigram, C.B.
        ,,   Battalions.—Colonels A. Lambton, C.B.; and J. B. Sterling.
Majors—Mounted.—Lieut.-Colonels R. S. Hall; Hon. E. Acheson; Hon. E. Digby; and Hon. H. Corry.
    Dismounted.—Lieut.-Colonels R. Follett; Hon. E. Boscawen, C.B. (Regimental Adjutant); F. Graves-Sawle; A. Moreton; and R. Pole-Carew (Military Secretary to the Commander-in-chief in India).
Captains.—Lieut.-Colonels J. G. Montgomery; F. Manley; and L. D. MacKinnon; Captains H. Wetherall; V. Dawson; J. Ross-of-Bladensburg (A.D.C. to Lord Lieutenant, Ireland); and A. Codrington (Adjutant); Major Hon. H. Legge; Captains J. Gladstone; D. Dawson (A.D.C. to the Commander of the Forces, Ireland,

H.S.H. Prince Edward of Saxe-Weimer); and H. Stopford (lately A.D.C. to the Commander of Forces, Ireland, Sir T. Steele).

Lieutenants.—Hon. A. Henniker-Major (Adjutant); G. V. Boyle; Hon. H. Amherst; H. Surtees (employed with Egyptian Army); W. Corbet (A.D.C. to Major-General Hon. R. Monck); G. P. Bouverie (lately returned from Special Service in Bechuanaland, South Africa); Hon. A. Fortescue (lately returned from Special Service in Bechuanaland, South Africa); B. Gosselin-Lefebre; Hon. R. Winn; P. Lovell; Earl of Wiltshire; Sir C. Miller, Bart.; C. Kindersley; D. Hamilton; Hon. Alan Charteris; H. Shute; E. Wigram; Granville Smith; C. Frederick; G. Wyndham; G. Milligan; C. Holland; Hon. W. Lambton; J. Drummond-Hay; F. Maude; R. Grenfell; F. Ramsden; C. Monck; Hon. V. Spencer; J. Hall; J. Sterling; H. Hawkes; Hon. E. Charteris; G. Taylor; S. Earle; J. Wingfield; Hon. E. Pakenham; Hon. H. Baillie-Hamilton; J. McNeile; R. Skeffington Smyth.

Quartermasters.—W. Webster; and H. Folson.

Medical Officers.—Surgeons-Major C. Read; G. Perry; and J. Magill, M.D.
    „   Surgeons A. Alexander; and W. Carte, M.B.

Solicitor.—R. Broughton, Esq.

The 1st Battalion were on this date quartered at Chelsea barracks (head-quarters and 5 companies), and at St. George's (3 companies); the 2nd Battalion at the Tower. The writer of this portion of the History of the Coldstream Guards here takes leave of them, and wishing them many a glorious addition to their illustrious records, now bids them, with much regret, farewell.

APPENDIX I.

1.

Major-General Sir John Byng to the Duke of York.

"Nivelles, June 19, 1815."

"SIR,

"Your Royal Highness, I am sure, will wish to be informed of the Conduct of the Brigade of Guards, and, unfortunately, that duty has devolved upon me from my respected friend, General Cooke, being severely wounded, having lost His Left Arm. In the brilliant affair of yesterday, both Brigades have suffered severely, but I have the Authority of the Duke of Wellington to say, they highly distinguished themselves, that from the commencement to the end of the Action their conduct was most excellent. It happened that Both had important duties to perform, which they gallantly executed. At the commencement of the Action my Brigade, which was on the extreme Right, had to occupy a House and Wood which it was of the utmost consequence we should keep. Lieut.-Colonel Macdonell, of the Coldstream, with two Light Companies, occupied the House, and the Wood by the Light Companies of the 1st Brigade and some Battalion Companies of the Battalion of the Coldstream, the whole under Lieut.-Colonel Lord Saltoun's Command. Against this post the first Attack of the Enemy was made, and was successfully resisted, as were the numerous efforts made to the close of the Day by the Enemy to get possession. The Duke of Wellington Himself in the early part of the day gave his particular attention to that point, and, when called to the Left by a serious Attack on that point, He confided it to my care, with directions to keep the House to the last moment, relieving the Troops as they required it,—and the whole of the Brigade, except two Companies, were required before the Action ceased; Colonels Hepburn and Woodford, affording me every assistance, and giving a fine example to their Battalions.

"The conduct of Lieut.-Colonel Macdonell in defending the House, even when it was on fire, and maintaining it, as ordered, has, I have no doubt, been particularly noticed to you by The Commander of the Forces. It was admirable, as was that of Lieut.-Colonel Lord Saltoun. About four o'clock, the command of the Division devolved upon me, and, having rode over to see the 1st Brigade just at the time the attack was made by the Enemy's Cavalry, I had an opportunity of witnessing the steady manner in which they received the several charges made to their front. I had also to witness the gallantry with which they met the last Attack made by the Grenadiers of the Imperial Guard ordered on by Bonaparte himself, the destructive fire they poured in, and the subsequent Charge which together completely routed the Enemy; a second attempt met with a similar reception, and the loss they caused to the French, of the finest Troops I ever saw, was immense. I beg you, Sir, to understand that my presence or advice to General Maitland never was required, I merely staid with Him as an humble Individual, when the assistance of every one was required. His own judgment and gallantry directed everything that was necessary. I cannot say too much in His praise, or in that of the several Commanders his Battalions had. The conduct, Sir, of every Officer and Man of both Brigades was everything I could wish; the Officers on every occasion being conspicuous for their Gallantry. Sincerely do I regret the loss of so many valuable Officers, such excellent Men. I hope I have not trespassed too far on Your Royal Highness in my wish to do justice to my gallant Friends and Soldiers. I believe every one who witnessed their Conduct will confirm my statement. The Staff of the Division afforded me every assistance; Lieut.-Colonel Sir Henry Bradford, Assistant Quartermaster-General, was wounded. My Brigade Major, Captain Stothert, has lost an Arm, and my Aide-de-camp, Captain Dumaresq, was shot through the Body.

"I propose recommending to the Duke of Wellington, Lieut.-Colonel Stanhope, of the First Guards, to do duty for Sir H. Bradford, and Captain Walton, Adjutant of the Coldstream, to succeed Captain Stothert as Brigade Major. Should I obtain His Grace's assent, I hope the Appointments will meet with your approval.

"I have, etc.
"(Signed) JOHN BYNG,
"Major-General."

2.

GENERAL ORDERS, NIVELLES, JUNE 20, 1815.

"The Field Marshal takes this opportunity of returning to the army his thanks for their conduct in the glorious action fought on the 18th inst., and he will not fail to report his sense of their conduct in the terms which it deserves to their several Sovereigns. . . .

"As the army is about to enter the French territory, the Field Marshal desires it may be understood by the troops of the several nations composing the army which he has the honor to command, that their Sovereigns are in alliance with the King of France, and that France therefore must be considered as a friendly country. No article is to be taken from any individual by any officer or soldier, without payment for the same. The Commissaries of the army will supply the troops with all that they require in the usual manner, and no requisition is to be made direct on the country or its magistrates, by any officer or soldier. The Commissaries will receive directions, either from the Field Marshal or from the Generals commanding the troops of the several nations (if these troops should not be supplied with provisions by the British Commissariat) to make requisitions as may be necessary for the supply of the troops, for which they will give the usual voucher and receipt; and they will understand that they will be responsible to issue and account for what they will thus receive from the country in France, in the same manner as they would if they purchased supplies for the troops in their own country respectively. . . ." *

3.

PROCLAMATION OF THE DUKE OF WELLINGTON TO THE FRENCH PEOPLE, JUNE 22, 1815.

"Je fais savoir aux Français que j'entre dans leur pays à la tête d'une armée déjà victorieuse, non en ennemi (excepté de l'usurpateur, prononcé l'ennemi du genre humain, avec lequel on ne peut avoir ni paix ni trève), mais pour les aider à secouer le joug de fer sous lequel ils sont opprimés. En conséquence, j'ai donné les ordres ci-joints à mon armée, et je demande qu'on me fasse connaître tout infracteur. Les Français savent cependant que j'ai le droit d'exiger qu'ils se conduisent de manière que je puisse les protéger contre ceux qui voudraient leur faire du mal. Il faut donc qu'ils fournissent aux réquisitions qui leur seront faites de la part des personnes autorisées à les faire, en échange des reçus en forme et ordre ; et qu'ils se tiennent chez eux paisiblement, et qu'ils n'aient aucune correspondance ou communication avec l'usurpateur ennemi, ni avec ses adhérents. Tous ceux qui s'absenteront de leur domicile après l'entrée en France, et tous ceux qui se trouveront absens au service de l'usurpateur, seront considérés comme ses adhérents et comme ennemis ; et leurs propriétés seront affectées à la subsistance de l'armée.

"Donné au Quartier-Général, à Malplaquet, ce 22 Juin, 1815." †

---

* *The Despatches of Field Marshal the Duke of Wellington, during his Various Campaigns, etc.*, (compiled by Colonel Garwood), viii. 156. (London, 1847.)
† *Ibid.*, viii.

APPENDIX II.

1.

GENERAL ORDER, PARIS, OCTOBER 28, 1815.

"Before the troops go into barracks or cantonments, an officer of each troop or company is to visit the barracks or cantonments which the soldiers are to occupy, and to ascertain the state in which they are. The name of the owner of the house in which the troops will be cantoned, and the names of the soldiers cantoned in the house, must be kept. On marching days, the barracks and cantonments of each company are to be visited by an officer, once if possible after the troops will have arrived, and once before they will march; and upon halting days the barracks and cantonments of the soldiers must be visited twice every day by the officer of the company or troop to which they belong; these visiting officers will observe whether any article has been taken away, if the troops are in cantonments, and will inquire whether the owner of the house has any complaint to make of the men. Non-commissioned officers must be cantoned with the squads to which they belong, and the officers as near as possible to their companies; the Field-officers with their regiments; the Generals and Staff as near as possible to their brigades and divisions.

"WELLINGTON." *

2.

Lieut.-Colonel Sir C. Broke to Lieut.-General Lord Hill.

"Paris, October 29, 1815.

"MY LORD,
        "I am desired by His Grace the Duke of Wellington to inform you that the circumstances attending the present situation of the army render it expedient that His Grace should request you will call the attention of the officers under your command to the necessity of the strictest discipline and most exact regularity of the troops in the cantonments which they are about to occupy; and in order to ensure the uniform conduct of the service, His Grace desires that the following points may be attended to :—

"Billets are to be made by the mayors, or persons acting for them. They are to be applied for by officers of the Quartermaster-General's Department of Divisions; or if there are no officers of the Quartermaster-

---

* *Supplementary Despatches, etc.*, xi. 215.

General's Department, by Staff officers of divisions or brigades; or if there are no Staff officers, by Quartermasters. Where there are no mayors or persons having authority to issue billets, the billets are to be arranged and portioned by the officers of the Quartermaster-General's Department of the Divisions; or if there are no officers of the Quartermaster General's Department, by Staff officers of divisions or brigades; or if there are no Staff officers, by Quartermasters. All billets when granted are to be made use of. If the owner of a house refuse a billet, it is to be made good, if necessary by force; but this measure must be sanctioned by the officers of the Quartermaster-General's Department's of Division; or if there are no officers of the Quartermaster-General's Department, by the Staff officers of divisions or brigades; or if there is no Staff officer, by the Quartermaster authorised to arrange the billets. If the owner of a house takes away his furniture, or by other means endeavours to deter officers from entering the billet, the Commanding officer is to place soldiers in the house. No inhabitant is to be required to accommodate persons that are not entitled to billets; and it is particularly desired that officers will not give grounds for complaint by taking their wives or families into billets without having the consent of the owner of the house to do so.

"Officers are to be warned against shooting over the country without having permission of the proprietors. The General Orders of the army have already given sufficient caution upon this subject.

"The situation of the troops will require that military precautions should be attended to. Alarm posts are to be established, guards and pickets are to be posted, and sufficient measures taken for the security of the communications and for the safety and tranquillity of the cantonments. The most efficient steps are to be taken for the prompt and certain circulation of orders, so that the whole or any part of the troops may be collected at the shortest notice.

"Attention must be paid in the billets of soldiers to the ammunition, and to its security against accident or robbery; for this the frequent company inspection will be a precaution.

"The parks of artillery are to be formed where they can be protected; they are never to be without guards, and troops should be sufficiently near to afford them support.

"If an attroupement or riotous assembly of the inhabitants against the military takes place, the troops are to be under arms, and the attroupement is to be fired upon. Any act of violence against the soldiery is to be immediately noticed, and the offenders are to be secured. The service must be respected. The General Officers are to take care that the discipline and good conduct of the troops merit the respect demanded. The mayors are to be informed of the measures that will be taken, and are to be desired to warn the inhabitants against taking part in the disturbances that may subject them to military punishment."

3.

The Same to the Same.

"Paris, October 30, 1815.

"MY LORD,

"It is the Duke of Wellington's desire that a place of rendezvous should be fixed upon for each division of the army. The routes by which the troops may best move to the place of rendezvous should be reconnoitred, and such instructions given as may render the assembly easy and expeditious. The places of rendezvous or general alarm posts of the troops under your Lordship's command should be:—

"For the 2nd Division—Versailles, or about the cantonments of the division that are nearest to Paris.

"For the 4th Division—Longjumeau, or about the cantonments of the division that are nearest to Paris.

"Baron Estorff's Cavalry—Bièvres, or about the cantonments of the brigade nearest to Paris.

"The Nassau troops—Ecouen or Pierrefitte, or about the cantonments of the troops nearest to Paris.

"The ground fixed upon should be clear of the towns or villages, and towards Paris. The troops when assembled are to be in marching order, with their baggage. If any other point of assembly is desired, the instructions that may be given will express it. The brigades and battalions of the divisions are, however, at the same time, to have their alarm posts."*

APPENDIX III.

From the Duke of York to the Duke of Wellington.

"Horse Guards, November 9, 1815.

"MY LORD DUKE,

"Having received an intimation from His Majesty's Government that a contingent British force, consisting of 30,000 troops, shall be maintained in France for a certain period after the definitive treaty of peace, and the period having now arrived for carrying into effect the organization of this force, and for removing the remainder of the British army to this country, I have the Prince Regent's commands to acquaint your Grace that the following are the corps selected to remain in France, according to this arrangement, under the command of your Grace, viz.:—

* *Supplementary Despatches, etc.,* xi. 218, 219.

APPENDIX.

CAVALRY.

	Present strength.	Recruits from England.	Total.
1st Dragoon Guards	392	58	450
2nd ,, ,,	418	32	450
3rd Dragoons	365	40	405
7th Hussars	357	93	450
11th Light Dragoons	387	63	450
12th ,, ,,	341	109	450
13th ,, ,,	343	70	413
15th Hussars	347	103	450
18th ,,	386	64	450
Waggon Train Troops	600	..	600

INFANTRY.

	Present strength.	Recruits from England.	Total.
First Foot Guards, 3rd Battalion	..	..	1200
Coldstream Guards, 2nd Battalion	996	204	1200
1st Foot, 3rd Battalion	..	..	1000
3rd Foot, 1st ,,	827	173	1000
4th ,, ,, ,,	662	150	712
5th ,, ,, ,,	1116	..	1000
6th ,, ,, ,,	781	69	850
7th ,, ,, ,,	868	132	1000
9th ,, ,, ,,	1051	..	1000
21st ,, ,, ,,	804	196	1000
23rd ,,	671	29	700
27th ,, ,, ,,	..	..	1000
29th ,,	808	22	830
39th ,, ,, ,,	842	108	950
40th ,, ,, ,,	694	106	800
43rd ,, ,, ,,	1044	..	1000
52nd ,, ,, ,,	987	13	1000
57th ,, ,, ,,	601	149	750
71st ,, ,, ,,	803	130	933
79th ,, ,, ,,	692	80	772
81st ,, ,, ,,	..	..	1000
88th ,, ,, ,,	1130	..	1000
91st ,, ,, ,,	848	100	948
95th ,, 1st ,, (six companies)	577	..	600
,, ,, 2nd ,, ,, ,,	534	..	600
Staff Corps	302	..	200
Cavalry and Infantry	..	..	27,613
Artillery	..	..	2000
Officers and Non-commissioned officers	..	..	3300
Total	..	..	32,913

"With regard to the cavalry, the detachments of men from the depôts in this country will be forwarded without delay; and your Grace will be pleased to order a transfer of horses from the corps that are to return to England to complete the regiments remaining in France to 420 horses each, leaving five dismounted men in each troop.

"Your Grace will order the 3rd Battalion of the First Guards to be completed to 1,200 from the 2nd Battalion. The 2nd Battalion of the Coldstream will be completed from the 1st Battalion in this country to the same number.

"Your Grace will also be pleased to order the transfer of such effectives as may be required from the 4th Battalion of the Royals, 3rd Battalion of the 27th, and 2nd Battalion of the 81st, to complete the 3rd Battalion of the former and the 1st Battalions of the two latter corps to 1,000 rank and file. The remaining transfers from the 2nd Battalions and depôts necessary to complete the corps in the manner specified in the foregoing list will be forwarded from this country without delay, and will probably reach their destination before the final departure of the troops returning home; but until their arrival, your Grace will keep such corps from among those destined for England as may be necessary to keep the contingent complete in the first instance.

"Having made this selection of the corps to remain in France as the British contingent under your command, it remains for me to convey to your Grace, the Prince Regent's command that the following corps shall be marched for embarkation to   ,* under the charge of the Staff that is not destined to remain in France, as soon as your Grace shall have completed your arrangements.

	R. and F.		R. and F.
1st Life Guards	233	36th Foot	416
2nd ,, ,,	191	37th ,, 2nd Battalion	542
Royal Horse Guards	302	38th ,,	654
3rd Dragoon Guards	310	41st ,,	860
1st Dragoons	293	42nd ,,	472
2nd ,,	298	44th ,, 2nd Battalion	737
6th ,,	309	51st ,,	558
10th Hussars	448	54th ,,	547
16th Light Dragoons	390	58th ,, 1st Battalion	630
23rd ,, ,,	384	59th ,, 2nd ,,	458
Waggon Train	800	62nd ,, ,, ,,	538
First Foot Guards, 2nd Battalion	720	64th ,,	508
Third ,, ,, ,, ,,	1139	69th ,, 2nd Battalion	454
1st Foot, 4th Battalion	500	73rd ,, ,, ,,	490
12th ,, 2nd ,,	610	78th ,, ,, ,,	327
14th ,, 3rd ,,	593	81st ,, ,, ,,	390
16th ,,	617	82nd ,, 1st ,,	825
25th ,, 2nd Battalion	426	90th ,, 1st ,,	820
27th ,, 3rd ,,	585	92nd ,,	526
28th ,,	497	95th ,, 3rd Battalion	480
30th ,, 2nd Battalion	575	2nd Garrison Battalion	992
32nd ,,	555	7th Veteran ,,	670
33rd ,,	470	Total	24,714
35th ,, 2nd Battalion	575		

* Blank in manuscript.

"I am further to acquaint your Grace that the Prince Regent has been pleased to approve of Lieut.-General Lord Combermere to command the cavalry and Lieut.-General Lord Hill the corps of infantry, under your command; and upon the calculation that the corps of cavalry will consist of three brigades, and that your Grace will find it expedient to form the infantry, exclusive of the Guards, into three divisions and eight brigades, the following are the Officers who it is proposed to attach to these respective corps:—

    Lieut.-General Sir Lowry Cole, G.C.B.
        ,,   ,, Sir Henry Clinton, G.C.B.
        ,,   ,, Sir Charles Colville, G.C.B.
    Major-General Sir James Kempt, G.C.B.
        ,,   ,, Sir Thomas Brisbane, K.C.B.
        ,,   ,, Lord Edward Somerset, K.C.B. (Cavalry).
        ,,   ,, Sir Thomas Bradford, K.C.B.
        ,,   ,, Sir John Lambert, K.C.B.
        ,,   ,, Sir Manley Power, K.C.B.
        ,,   ,, Sir C. Grant, K.C.B. (Cavalry).
        ,,   ,, Sir P. Maitland (Guards).
        ,,   ,, Sir John Keane, K.C.B.
        ,,   ,, Sir Frederick Adam, K.C.B.
        ,,   ,, Sir H. Vivian, K.C.B. (Cavalry).
Adjutant-General, Major-General Sir E. Barnes, K.C.B.
Quartermaster-General, Lieut.-General Sir George Murray, G.C.B.

"Your Grace will be pleased to make a selection of the Staff for the Adjutant-General and Quartermaster-General's Departments, as well as the Medical, Commissariat, and Pay Departments, which you think adequate to the service; and when your Grace shall have made your selection of the members and the individuals, I request you will send a list for the Prince Regent's final approval.

    "I am, my Lord Duke,
        "Yours sincerely,
            "FREDERICK."[*]

APPENDIX IV.

DISTRIBUTION OF THE BRITISH CONTINGENT IN FRANCE, APRIL 10, 1816.

CAVALRY.

Head-quarters.		Stations.	No. of Officers.	No. of Men.	No. of Horses.
1st Brigade Cassel	1st Dragoon Gds.	Frevent and adjacents	30	458	438
	2nd ,, ,,	Avesnes and adjacents	22	437	420
	2nd Dragoons	Bailleul	26	431	579

[*] *Supplementary Despatches, etc., of the Duke of Wellington*, xi. 228.

APPENDIX.

CAVALRY (continued).

Head-quarters.			Stations.	No. of Officers.	No. of Men.	No. of Horses.
2nd Brigade Samer	7th Hussars	Etaples and 14 detachments		25	459	430
	12th Lt. Dragoons	Fruges and 9 detachments		30	499	433
	18th Hussars	Deserves and 9 detachments		24	468	426
	R. H. Artillery	Samer and 4 detachments		4	170	189
3rd ,, Cassel	11th Lt. Dragoons	Wormhout and 4 detachments		28	462	405
	15th Hussars	Bourbourg and vicinity		24	496	437
	13th Lt. Dragoons	Hazebrouck and 7 detachments		27	394	398
	R. H. Artillery	Samer		4	164	171

INFANTRY.

FIRST DIVISION (Head-quarters, Cambrai):—

							No. of Officers.	No. of Men.	No. of Horses.
1st Brigade Cambrai	Grenadier Gds.	Cambrai					27	1259	75
	Coldstream Gds.	Cambrai			11	257	29		
		Marcoing			5	231	9		
		Gouzeacourt			4	226	9		
		Gonnelieu			1	3	3		
		Villers Glishain			3	116	5		
		Honnecourt			2	117	5		
		Villers Ploich and Beaugaart			3	116	10		
		Banteau and Bantouzelle			2	113	3		
		Total Coldstream Guards					31	1179	73
7th ,, St. Leger	43rd Regiment	Bapaume and 10 detachments					43	1079	69
	7th ,,	Amblainsville and 13 detachments					37	933	54
	23rd ,,	Hamelincourt and 13 detachments					39	722	52
	Commissariat	Sapignies, Farreuil, Bapaume					3	90	126
8th ,, Beaumez	27th Regiment	Bugny and 14 detachments					44	988	67
	40th ,,	Havincourt and 8 detachments					26	653	48
	1st Battalion Rifle Brigade	Bourlon and 5 detachments					30	503	57
	Commissariat	Bugny					1	30	46
Divisional R. Artillery	..	Bapaume					8	216	90
,, Commissariat	..	,,					1	10	17

APPENDIX.

INFANTRY (continued).

Head-quarters.			Stations.	No. of Officers.	No. of Men.	No. of Horses.
SECOND DIVISION (Head-quarters, St. Pol):—						
3rd Brigade	St. Pol	3rd Regiment	Croix and 15 detachments	35	1013	50
		39th ,,	Bethincourt and 18 detachments	43	968	62
		91st ,,	St. Pol and 18 detachments	43	992	61
		Commissariat	Vallum, Bailleul, Maisnil	2	90	140
4th ,,	,,	4th Regiment	Fauquembourg and 15 detachments	29	814	52
		52nd ,,	Upen de Aval and 24 detachments	39	1003	70
		79th ,,	Wizernes and 16 detachments	37	671	42
		Commissariat	Clety, Dohen	2	52	80
6th ,,	Lillers	6th Regiment	Lillers and 6 detachments	35	843	38
		29th ,,	Chocques and 5 detachments	31	861	59
		71st ,,	Norrein Fonte and 18 detachments	35	864	62
		Commissariat	Bourcq, St. Hilaire	1	40	74
		Royal Sappers and Miners	Well, Pernes, Floringham	8	101	63
Divisional R. Artillery		..	Lillers, St. Pol, Lillers Barbent	15	258	285
,, Commissariat		..	Le Parcq	2	34	49
,, R. Waggon Train		..	Aubigny and 1 detachment	4	76	104
THIRD DIVISION (Head-quarters, Valenciennes):—						
2nd Brigade	Valenciennes	3rd Battn. Royals	Valenciennes	36	1132	49
		57th Regiment	,,	43	705	30
		2nd Battalion Rifle Brigade	Les Celles and 2 detachments	29	553	40
5th ,,	,,	5th Regiment	Valenciennes	37	1152	49
		9th ,,	St. Amand	40	1032	36
		21st ,,	Valenciennes	42	1004	43
9th ,,	,,	81st ,,	,,	37	1076	40
		88th ,,	,,	34	1113	56
Royal Artillery		..	,, and St. Amand	13	376	304
,, Waggon Train		..	Raillencourt and 3 detachments	15	166	255
,, Staff Corps		..	Proville and 1 detachment	11	168	..
Commissariat Waggon Train		..	St. Pol, Valenciennes, Sancourt, Oissy, and 10 detachments	48	1343	1810

Note.—Several of the detachments were commanded by Non-commissioned officers only.*

* *Supplementary Despatches, etc.*, xi. 355.

APPENDIX V.

SHORT ACCOUNT OF THE BAND OF THE COLDSTREAM GUARDS.

The Band of the Coldstream Guards dates from the 16th of May, 1785, when twelve German musicians were enlisted by the Duke of York, Colonel of the Regiment, and were sent to England to replace the eight civilian performers who were hired by the month, for the purpose only of playing the King's Guard to the Palace and back. They were brought over by Mr. Eley, who was appointed "Music Major." Mr. Eley was succeeded by Messrs. Weyrauch, Denman, and Willman. In 1825, Mr. Charles Godfrey—who, having joined the 1st Royal Surrey Militia as drummer at an early age, entered the Coldstream in 1813—was appointed Bandmaster in 1825, by the Colonel, the Duke of Cambridge; and he remained in that position until his death in 1863, though his military service ended in 1834. The following Regimental Order was issued on the 18th of December, 1863:—"The Commanding Officer is desired by General Sir William Gomm to express his sense of the loss the Regiment has experienced in the decease of Mr. Godfrey; the acknowledged efficiency of the band is in itself a proof of his talents as bandmaster, whilst the esteem and respect which he has earned from all ranks, during a period of upwards of fifty years' service, sufficiently attest his worth as a man and a soldier." He was succeeded by his son, Mr. F. Godfrey, who retained the bandmastership until 1880, when Mr. Thomas was appointed; the latter was replaced by Mr. Rogan in 1896. The band consisted, in 1888, of a Bandmaster, two Sergeants, two Corporals, and forty Musicians.

Three negroes were added; they carried two tambourines and a set of Turkish bells, and they continued part of the band until 1837, when they were abolished.*

The Drums date from 1650, when the Regiment contained one Drum-Major and twenty Drummers; the former was reduced in 1657, and replaced in 1670, and a second Drum-Major was appointed in 1810. In 1758, four fifers were added to the two Grenadier Companies, two to each. On the 6th of November, 1815, "it being desirable that the several duties of the drum and fife should be performed in the same manner throughout the service, and it being essential that one general principle or system of instruction should be laid down for the guidance of Regiments," three

---

* Taken from *Music for the People*, by Robert A. Marr.

books, viz. *A Treatise on Music for the Study of Boys in Her Majesty's Service; Instructions for the Fife;* and *Instructions for Beating the Drum by Note*, which had been prepared by Drum-Major Potter of the Coldstream Guards, were sent by the Adjutant-General to the Officer Commanding the Regiment, for the use of the Coldstream. "It is His Royal Highness's command that, after a reasonable period, you will be pleased to forward a report of the progress of the drummers and fifers, of a nature calculated to enable the Commander-in-Chief to determine as to the expediency of the mode of instruction, therein prescribed, being generally adopted in the service. The treatise which has been prepared for boys intended to be trained as drummers and fifers, it is recommended to use in the Regimental School, in order that as soon as the boys are able to read and write they may be required to copy parts thereof on their slates, and which may also from time to time be explained to them by the Drum and Fife-Majors."

In reply, the Commanding Officer stated, on the 6th of January, 1816, that, having inspected the boys, they appeared completely acquainted with the duties of the drum and fife, in the course of one month's teaching according to the system proposed in the books above-mentioned; also that the boys belonging to the Regimental school of the Regiment, were prepared, without difficulty, in the mode proposed for the further instruction from "the Drum and Fife-Majors."

Subsequently, the following General Order was issued by H.R.H. the Commander-in-Chief, dated December 28, 1816: "The mode of instruction for drum and fife, practised in the Coldstream Regiment of Foot Guards, having been referred to several Regiments in order to ascertain whether its adoption would be attended with advantage, and the reports which have been received appearing satisfactory, the Commander-in-Chief, with a view of assimilating the respective 'Calls and Beats' throughout the several Regiments of Infantry, is pleased to command that the system of instruction for the drum and fife, introduced by Drum-Major Potter, of the Coldstream Guards, shall be considered as the established system, and be adopted accordingly."

APPENDIX VI.

I.

GENERAL ORDER TO THE ALLIED ARMY OF OCCUPATION, NOVEMBER 10, 1818.

"Ordre du Jour.

"Il est impossible au Feld Maréchal Duc de Wellington de prendre congé des troupes qu'il a eu l'honneur d'avoir sous ses ordres, sans leur offrir ses remercîmens pour la bonne conduite, par laquelle elles se sont distinguées pendant tout le temps de son Commandement. Trois ans se sont presque écoulés depuis que les Souverains Alliés ont bien voulu confier au Feld Maréchal le Commandement de cette partie de leurs forces militaires que les circonstances du moment leur avaient rendu nécessaire de continuer en France. Si cette mesure adoptée par Leurs Majestés s'est effectuée d'une manière qui leur a paru satisfaisante, ce succès ne doit être attribué qu'à la conduite conciliante observée en toute occasion par leurs Excellences les Généraux Commandans en Chef; au bon exemple qui a été donné par elles à leur subordonnés, les Généraux et autres Officiers de l'Armée, et à l'assistance que ceux-ci leur ont rendue; comme aussi à l'exacte discipline qui a toujours regnée dans tous les Contingents. Ce ne peut être qu'avec des sentimens de regret que le Feld Maréchal voit le moment arrivé où la séparation de l'Armée doit terminer les relations de service, et les liaisons, qu'il a eues avec Leurs Excellences les Généraux Commandans, et avec les autres Officiers de leurs Corps. Le Feld Maréchal ne peut se dissimuler combien ces relations ont été avantageuses pour lui; et il prie les Généraux Commandans en Chef des différens Contingents, de vouloir bien agréer eux-mêmes, et communiquer aussi à ceux qui sont sous leurs ordres, les assurances du vif intérêt qu'il ne cessera de prendre à tout ce qui les regarde, et combien lui seront chers les souvenirs des trois années pendant lesquelles il a eu l'honneur d'être placé à leur tête.

"Le Lieutenant-Général,
"Chef de l'Etat Major Général de l'Armée Alliée."*

---

* *Supplementary Despatches, etc.*, xii. 795.

2.

GENERAL ORDER, CAMBRAI, NOVEMBER 10, 1818.

"Upon the return to England of the troops which have so long served under the command of the Field Marshal, he again returns them his thanks for their uniform good conduct during the period in which they have formed part of the Army of Occupation. The Field Marshal has, in another Order, addressed to the Army of Occupation at large, expressed his sentiments regarding the conduct of, and his obligations to, the General Officers and Officers of the Army. These are especially due to the General Officers and Officers of the British Contingent; and he begs them to accept his best acknowledgments for the example they have given to others by their own good conduct, and for the support and assistance they have invariably afforded him to maintain the discipline of the Army. After a service of ten years' duration, almost without interruption, with the same Officers and troops, the Field Marshal separates from them with regret; but he trusts that they will believe that he will never cease to feel a concern for their honour and interest.

" WELLINGTON." *

3.

GENERAL ORDER, PARIS, DECEMBER 1, 1818.

"The Field Marshal has great satisfaction in publishing to the troops which have lately served under his command the following letter from H.R.H. the Commander-in-Chief, conveying the Prince Regent's gracious approbation of their conduct while serving in France.

"'Horse Guards, November 27, 1818.

"'MY LORD DUKE,

"'The Army of Occupation having now finally returned from France, I have the Prince Regent's commands to convey to your Grace the thanks of His Royal Highness for the discipline and good order which has been so successfully maintained, to the honour of the British arms, during the period it has been stationed in that country. I have frequently had occasion to address your Grace, by command of the Sovereign, in the language of just commendation of the brilliant victories achieved under the guidance of your genius; but although the events of peace do not furnish the grounds for conveying the warmth of expression which a sense of the distinguished actions of warfare so strongly called forth, yet the conduct of the army, while stationed in the country of their former enemy, where the discipline and good order established by your Grace

---

* *Supplementary Despatches*, etc., xii. 826.

were calculated to conciliate the inhabitants, and to uphold the character of the British arms in the view of surrounding nations, cannot fail to draw forth the Prince Regent's cordial approbation and thanks, as well as the gratitude of the country to your Grace and to them. I am commanded to request that your Grace will be pleased to make these sentiments known to the General and other Officers who have been under your command, in any manner you may think proper.

"'FREDERICK,
"'Commander-in-Chief.'" *

APPENDIX VII.

COLDSTREAM GUARDS HOSPITAL.

A HOSPITAL for the Regiment was first established in 1814, previous to which date the sick were attended in their own quarters. Premises were secured in Rochester Row, and a lease of seven years obtained, Dec. 25, 1814, at a rental of £90 per annum, by Colonel Hon. Henry Brand, at that time the Lieut.-Colonel of the Regiment. In June, 1823, the lease was renewed for twenty-one years, at £145 a year, to Colonels Woodford, Sir Henry Bouverie, and Macdonell. The lease was then again renewed, June, 1844, for fourteen years, at the same rent, and on payment of a fine of £200. In 1855 an addition was made to the premises on the south side, and a lease for this addition was granted to Colonels Hon. G. Upton and Lord Frederick Paulet, for $3\frac{1}{4}$ years, at a yearly rent of £113 10s. The lease of the whole premises was further renewed in 1858, for a term of forty years, to Colonels Hon. George Upton, Lord Frederick Paulet, and W. Newton, on payment of a fine of £315, and at a yearly rent of £185. The sum of £3850 was then spent on rebuilding the greater part of the Hospital. Before this lease expired, Government took over the Hospital, and this transaction, begun in 1881, was finally completed in 1889.

---

* *Supplementary Despatches, etc.,* xii. 856.

APPENDIX VIII.

THE NULLI SECUNDUS CLUB.

APPENDIX No. 256 of Colonel MacKinnon's *Origin and Services of the Coldstream Guards* (ii. 373) contains an account of the formation and history of the Nulli Secundus Club up to the year 1832. Since then, the rules were altered (1869) so as to render Officers eligible for ballot who leave the Regiment after having served therein for three years, (reduced to two years in 1896). On account of the new arrangements introduced into the Medical Service of the Brigade (see *ante*, p. 340), Medical Officers transferred to the Coldstream from another regiment of the Brigade, are eligible for election, provided they are members of the First or Third Guards Clubs. And lastly, the service of Medical Officers when attached to the Regiment, counts towards election to the Nulli Secundus Club; but they are not eligible for election until permanently appointed to the Regiment.

The signal honour graciously conferred upon the members of the Nulli Secundus Club by His Majesty William IV., of receiving them annually at dinner, has already been adverted to in the text (see *ante*, p. 92).

In the year 1883, the club held its centenary celebration, when all Officers belonging to the Coldstream, who were not members at the time, were invited to dinner. Colonel G. R. FitzRoy, Lieut.-Colonel of the Regiment, presided. The meeting took place at the Albion Tavern, Aldersgate Street, on May the 30th.

The following is the roll of members of the Nulli Secundus Club.

ORIGINAL MEMBERS.
Fremantle, J. E.
Bosville, Thomas B.
Webb, Nathaniel.
Knight, Francis.
Calvert, George.
Gascoyne, Isaac.

1783.
Gould, Charles.
Vachell, Richard.
Bridgeman, John.
Hewgill, Edwin.
Fraser, John Henry.
Calcraft, John.
Boscawen, Nicholas.

1784.
Fane, Hon. Thomas.
Sutton, John.
Wyndham, Hon. William.
Cavan, Earl of.

1785.
Thoroton, Thomas.
Finch, Hon. Edward.
Morshead, William.
Stopford, Viscount (afterwards Earl of Courtown).
Boscawen, William A. S.
Morgan, Charles (afterwards Sir Charles, Bart.).

APPENDIX.

1786.
Madocks, Joseph.
Parker, Hon. Thomas.

1788.
Morrison, Edward.
York, H.R.H. Duke of.

1789.
Spencer, John.

1790.
Saye and Sele, Lord.
Gregory, Richard.
Hotham, Charles (afterwards Sir Charles, Bart.).

1791.
Strathavon, Lord (afterwards Marquis of Huntly).
De Visme, William.
Eld, George.
Wynyard, William.
Calvert, Harry (afterwards Sir Harry, Bart.).
Windsor, Hon. Henry (afterwards Earl of Plymouth).
Nugent, George (afterwards Sir George, Bart.).

1794.
FitzRoy, Hon. George (afterwards Lord Southampton).
Hulse, Richard.
FitzRoy, Hon. W.
Buller, William.
Morris, Roger.
Howard, Kenneth A. (afterwards Earl of Effingham).
Dyke, George Hart.
Pomeroy, Hon. G.

1795.
Forbes, Hon. James (afterwards Lord Forbes).
Fuller, Joseph (afterwards Sir J.).
Brand, Hon. Henry (afterwards Lord Dacre).

1796.
Stanwix, Thomas S.
Brownrigg, Robert.

1797.
Vane, William Walter.
Dungarven, Lord (afterwards Earl of Cork).
Brice, Arthur.
Hotham, B.
Chester, Harry.

1798.
Wingfield, Hon. John (afterwards Hon. J. Wingfield-Stratford).
Armstrong, Thomas.

1799.
Upton, Hon. Arthur Percy.

1800.
Peacocke, W. M. (afterwards Sir W.).
Boulton, Richard.
Stirling, Gilbert (afterwards Sir Gilbert, Bart.).
Wynyard, Montague.
Lloyd, John A.

1801.
MacKinnon, Henry.
Sheridan, William (afterwards Sir William, Bart.).
Plunkett, Hon. Edward (afterwards Lord Dunsany).
Smith, George.
Phillips, James.
Jackson, Richard D. (afterwards Sir Richard).
Onslow, Mathew.
Cadogan, Hon. Henry.

1802.
Ross, John.
Acland, William P. (afterwards Sir W.).

1805.
Conyers, H. J.
Braddyll, Thomas.
Adams, Lucius F.

1806.
Cambridge, H.R.H. Duke of.
Woodford, Alexander G. (afterwards Sir Alexander).

1807.
Pringle, William Henry (afterwards Sir William).
Dalling, Edward.

APPENDIX.

1808.
Hamilton, William.
Bouverie, Henry Frederick (afterwards Sir Henry).

1809.
Sutton, Francis Manners.

1810.
Collier, George.
Barrow, Thomas.
Buller.*
Aylmer, Lord.
Vachell, H. V.

1812.
Simpson, John (Surgeon-Major).
Sullivan, Sir Henry, Bart.
Taylor, Herbert (afterwards Sir Herbert).
Lascelles, Edward.

1813.
MacKinnon, Daniel.
Wynyard, W. C.

1814.
Milman, Francis M.
Raikes, William Henry.
Sandilands, P.
Bowles, George (afterwards Sir George).
Bayly, Henry.

1815.
Gore, Thomas.
Steele, Thomas.
Walpole, Hon. John.
Walton, William L.
Harvey, J. V.
Prince, John.
Dawkins, Henry.
Buller.*
Talbot, John.
Percival, G. H.

1818.
Fremantle, John.
Hotham, Lord.
Morgan, G.
Rose, Thomas (Surgeon).
Bligh, Thomas.

1819.
Clifton, Edward.
Wedderburn, Alexander.
Chaplin, Thomas.
Armytage, Henry.
Maynard, Thomas (Surgeon).

1820.
Kortwright, William.
Campbell, Sir Colin.
Loftus, Henry.
Cuyler, Augustus.

1821.
Rous, Hon. W.
Whymper, William (Surgeon).

1822.
Buller, Frederick Thomas.
Drummond, John.
St. John Mildmay, Humphrey.
Gooch, Henry.

1823.
Shawe, C.
Salwey, Henry.
Girardot, Chas. A.

1825.
Bentinck, C.
Powys, Thomas.
Bentinck, H. (afterwards Sir Henry).
Montagu, Hon. John.
Bowen, Robert.
Forbes, Hon. James.
Forbes, Hon. W. (afterwards Lord Forbes).
Macdonell, James (afterwards Sir James).
Arbuthnot, Sir R.
Gomm, Sir William.
O'Neill, Hon. J. (afterwards Viscount O'Neill).
Waters, John.

1828.
FitzClarence, George (afterwards Earl of Munster).
Cornwall, William Henry.
Graves, Hon. W. (afterwards Lord Graves).
Short, Charles.
Cowell, J. S. (afterwards Sir J. Stepney Cowell-Stepney, Bart.).
Hall, Jasper T.

---

* Either William Buller (1794) re-elected, or Frederick William Buller elected.

1828.

Dundas, Hon. H. (afterwards Viscount Melville).
Murray, Henry.

1829.

Russell, F.
Broadhead, B.
Bentinck, George.
Northey, W. B.
Rawdon, John Dawson.

1830.

Howden, Lord (formerly John F. Cradock).

1831.

Ashburnham, Hon. J.
Codrington, W. (afterwards Sir William).
Wigram, Ely D.
Hope, Hon. J.
FitzClarence, Lord Frederick.

1832.

Hobhouse, Edward T.
Shelley, Sir John, Bart.

1833.

Paulet, Lord Frederick.
Hunter, William (Surgeon).
Hay, Charles M.

1835.

Pringle, J. H.

1836.

Horton, Wilmot.
Drummond, Gordon.
Daniell, H.

1837.

Upton, Hon. Arthur.

1839.

Paget, Frederick.
Wilbraham, Hon. E. Bootle.

1841.

Villiers, Hon. F.
Knox, George.
Brand, Hon. H. (afterwards Speaker, and Viscount Hampden).

1841.

Forbes, John.
Clitherow, John C.
Windham, Charles G.

1843.

Elrington, J. L.
Vansittart, Robert.

1843 to 1863.*

Strafford, Earl of.
Stewart-Balfour, W.
Hulse, R. S.
Alexander, Viscount (afterwards Earl of Caledon).
Johnson, George J.
Newton, W. S.
Bathurst, P.
Milman, Egerton.
Boyle, Hon. R.
Perceval, Spencer.
Tierney, M. E.
Dawson, Hon. T. Vesey.
Steele, T. M.
Wigram, James R.
White, C. H.
Cocks, C. L.
Somerset, Poulett.
Whyte-Melville, G. J.
Cowell, J. C. M.
Robinson, W. F. C. (Surgeon).
Halkett, James.
Harington, Sir J., Bart.
Carleton, Dudley (afterwards Lord Dorchester).
Vernon, G. A.
FitzRoy, Lord Charles (afterwards Duke of Grafton).
Upton, Hon. G. (afterwards Viscount Templetown).
Burdett, C.
Newdigate, F. W.
MacKinnon, Lionel D.
Cumming, H. W.
Walker, Sir G., Bart.
Dawkins, W. G. (withdrew July 24, 1873).
Wood, W. Mark.
Jolliffe, Hylton.
Dunkellin, Lord.
Burton, F. A. P.

---

* There is no record of the dates of the election of members between the years 1843 and 1863.

APPENDIX.

Baring, William.
Feilding, Hon. P. (afterwards Sir Percy).
Dering, E. H.
Reeve, W. R.
Eliot, Hon. G. C. C.
Baring, Charles.
Bouverie, H. M.
Armytage, H.
Byng, Hon. H.
Thellusson, A. G. B.
Trevelyan, Walter.
Crawley, P.
Strong, C. W.
Dunlop, Sir James, Bart.
Hardinge, Hon. A. (afterwards Sir Arthur).
Goodlake, G.
Bingham, Lord (afterwards Earl of Lucan).
Tower, Harvey.
Wyatt, John (Surgeon).
Dangan, Viscount (formerly Hon. W. H. Wellesley; afterwards Earl Cowley).
Lyon Fremantle, A. J. (afterwards Sir A.).
Le Conteur, J. H.
Heneage, M. W.
Holmesdale, Viscount (formerly Hon. W. Amherst; afterwards Earl Amherst).
Herbert Stepney, A. St. G.
Airey, J. T. (afterwards Sir James).
Hall, Julian.
Wigram, G. J.
Lambton, Arthur.
Edwardes, Hon. W. (afterwards Lord Kensington).
Cecil, Lord Eustace.
Feilding, Hon. William.
Blackett, C. E.
FitzRoy, G. R.
Boyle, Hon. W.
Conolly, J. A.
Lane, H. J. Bagot.
Seymour, W. F. (afterwards Lord William).
Burghersh, Lord (afterwards Earl of Westmoreland).
Legge, Hon. E. H.
Burnell, E. S. P.
Monck, Hon. Richard.
Thursby, R. H.
Greenhill-Gardyne, Charles.
Clarke-Jervoise, H.
Burnand, Norman.
Campbell, Hon. H. W.
Wynne, William.
Clyde, Lord.

1864.

Reeve, Ellis.
Manningham-Buller, Frederick.
Bonham-Carter, H.
Fortescue, H. G.
Hathorn, J. F.

1865.

Trotter, J. W. (Surgeon).
Herbert, H. A.
Baring, Hon. Denzil.
Howard, Hon. F. C.
Brand, H. R. (afterwards Viscount Hampden).
Cathcart, R. A. E. (afterwards Sir Reginald, Bart.).
Lee Mainwaring, C. W.

1866.

Dawson, Hon. V. (afterwards Lord Cremorne).
Chaplin, E.
Windsor-Clive, Hon. G.
Hamilton, Sir E., Bart.
Smyth, G. F.
Fremantle, FitzRoy.

1866.

Farquharson, R. (Surgeon).
Wallscourt, Lord.

1867.

Eyre, H. R.
Sterling, J. B.

1868.

Macpherson, G. G.
Myers, Arthur (Surgeon).
Thomas, C. D.

1869.

Vesey, Hon. J. (afterwards Viscount de Vesci).
Wellesley, Hon. Frederick.
Legge, Hon. Heneage.
Wilbraham, Rev. Charles P.
Kirkland, Vesey.
Ellice, Charles (afterwards Sir Charles).
Verner, William (afterwards Sir W., Bart.).
Williamson, David (of Lawes).
Crombie, Thomas.
Chichester, Hon. A. C.

Caulfeild, J. A. (afterwards Viscount Charlemont).
Maxse, H. FitzHardinge (afterwards Sir H.).
Adair, A. W.
Seymour, J. H.
Forbes, Sir William, Bart., of Craigievar (afterwards Lord Sempill).
Grey-Egerton, P. Le B. (afterwards Sir Philip, Bart.).
Warrender, Sir George, Bart.

1870.
Hall, R. S.

1871.
Alexander, C. J.
Ramsden, W. J. F.

1871.
Farquhar, Arthur.
Acheson, Hon. E. A. B.

1872.
Aldenburg-Bentinck, H. C.

1873.
Dawnay, Hon. L. P.
Digby, Hon. Edward (afterwards Lord Digby).
Turquand, William, M. G.
Lowry-Corry, Hon. Henry.
Follett, Robert W.
Boscawen, Hon. E. (afterwards Viscount Falmouth).

1874.
Otway, W. P.
Bruce, Hervey J. L.
Wood, A. R. M. (afterwards Lockwood).
Campbell, Hon. Ronald G. E.
Bertie, Hon. George A. V.
Ailsa, Marquis of.
Boyle, Edmond.
Greville-Nugent, Hon. R.

1875.
Whipple, John (Surgeon).
Graves-Sawle, Francis A.

1876.
Stapleton, Hon. M. (afterwards Lord Beaumont).
Pole-Carew, Reginald.
Moreton, Augustus.

1877.
Montgomery, James G. H.
Fortescue, Cyril D.
Manley, F. C.
Goff, R. C.
Arkwright, F. W.
Cavendish, Hon. C. (afterwards Lord Chesham).
Clark-Kennedy, Alexander.

1878.
MacKinnon, L. D.
Gordon, Lord Douglas.
Dawson, Vesey, J.
Ossulston, Lord.
Stradbroke, Earl of (formerly Hon. J. Rous), [present at the meeting].

1879.
Dawnay, Hon. Eustace.
Legge, Hon. Henry.
Codrington, Alfred.
Monck, Hon. H. (afterwards Viscount Monck).
FitzRoy, Alfred (afterwards Lord Alfred).
Montrose, Duke of.

1880.
Gladstone, J. R. (afterwards Sir John, Bart.).
Dawson, Douglas F. R.
Boyle, George.
Ross-of-Bladensburg, John.
Brand, Hon. Charles.
Sandhurst, Lord.
Durham, Earl of.
Lambton, Hon. F. W.
Read, C. C. (Surgeon).

1881.
Ormsby-Gore, Hon. George.

1882.
Stopford, Horace.
Henniker-Major, Hon. Arthur.

APPENDIX.

Magill, James (Surgeon).
Clarke-Jervoise, A. (afterwards Sir Arthur, Bart.).
Dawson, Hon. Anthony.

1883.
Amherst, Hon. Hugh.
Perry, George (Surgeon).

1884.
Surtees, H. C.
Corbet, W. O. (afterwards Sir Walter, Bart.).
Vincent, Edgar (afterwards Sir E.).
Levett, Theophilus.

1885.
Pleydell-Bouverie, George.
Fortescue, Hon. Arthur.
Gosselin-Lefebre, Bertram M. O.
Winn, Hon. Rowland (afterwards Lord St. Oswald).
Sebright, Guy.

1886.
Lovell, Peter Audley.
Wetherall, H. A. (withdrew 1895).
Wiltshire, Earl of (afterwards Marquis of Winchester).

1887.
Miller, Sir C. Hubert, Bart.
Kindersley, Charles P.
Charteris, Hon. Alan.
Shute, Henry D.
Frederick, Charles A.
Hamilton, Douglas J.
Somers-Cocks, Herbert.
Wigram, Eustace.
Smith, Granville.

1889.
Alexander, A. C. (Surgeon-Major).
Fenn, E. H. (Surgeon-Major).
Wyndham, George.

1890.
Milligan, G. D.
Holland, Hon. C. T.

Lambton, Hon. William.
Drummond-Hay, James A.
Maude, Frederick S.
Grenfell, Riversdale F.
Ramsden, Frederick W.

1891.
Monck, Cecil S. O.
Hall, John H.
Sterling, John T.
Hawkes, Henry B.
Earle, Sydney.
Churchill, Lord.
Taylor, George W.

1892.
Wingfield, John M.
Pakenham, Hon. Edward M.
Baillie-Hamilton, Hon. Henry R.
Carte, W. A. (Surgeon).
McNeile, John.
Smyth, R. Skeffington.
Cox, R. H. (Surgeon).
Stephenson, Sir Frederick.

1893.
Athlumney, Lord.
Drumlanrig, Viscount.
Sutton, Hugh C.

1894.
Campbell, Hon. John B.

1895.
Marker, Raymond J.
Feilding, Geoffrey P. F.

1896.
Lambton, William H.
Romilly, Lord.
Ponsonby, John.
Newtown-Butler, Lord.
Portland, Duke of.
Charteris, Hon. Evan.
Newdigate, Francis A.

APPENDIX IX.

GENERAL ORDER, No. 1, CONSTANTINOPLE, APRIL 30, 1854.

"The Queen having been graciously pleased to appoint General Lord Raglan, G.C.B., to be Commander of the Forces to be employed in Turkey in support of Her Ally, His Imperial Majesty the Sultan, and His Lordship having arrived, all reports, etc., are to be made to him through the channels prescribed by Her Majesty's Regulations.

"The Commander of the Forces avails himself of the earliest opportunity to impress upon the Army the necessity of maintaining the strictest discipline, of respecting persons and property and the laws and usages of the country they have been sent to aid and defend, and particularly of avoiding to enter Mosques, Churches, and private dwellings of a people whose habits are peculiar and unlike those of the other nations of Europe.

"Lord Raglan fully relies upon the General and other Officers of the Army to afford him their support in the repression of disorder, and he confidently hopes that the troops themselves, anxious to maintain the character they have acquired elsewhere, will endeavour to become the example of obedience to orders and of attention to discipline, without which success is impossible, and their presence would be an evil instead of an advantage to those whose cause their Sovereign has deemed it proper to espouse.

"The Army will for the first time be associated with an Ally to whom it has been the lot of the British nation to be opposed in the field for many centuries.

"The gallantry and high military qualities of the French Army are matters of history, and the alliance which has now been formed, will, the Commander of the Forces trusts, be of long duration, as well as productive of the most important and the happiest consequences.

"Lord Raglan is aware, from personal communication with the distinguished Officer who is appointed to command the French Army, Marshal St. Arnaud, and many of the Superior Officers, that every disposition exists throughout their ranks to cultivate the best understanding with the British Army, and to co-operate most warmly with it, and he entertains no doubt that Her Majesty's troops are animated by the same spirit, and that the first ambition of each Army will be, to acquire the confidence and good opinion of the other.

"By Command,
"(Signed)   J. BUCKNALL B. ESTCOURT,
"Brigadier-General and D. A. General."

APPENDIX X.

DEATH OF FIELD-MARSHAL LORD RAGLAN, G.C.B.

I.

GENERAL ORDER, HORSE GUARDS, JULY 4, 1855.*

"THE General Commanding-in-Chief has received Her Majesty's most gracious Commands to express to the Army the deep regret with which Her Majesty has to deplore the loss of a most devoted and able Officer by the death of Field-Marshal Lord Raglan, the Commander of the Forces in the Crimea.

"Her Majesty has been pleased to command that her sentiments shall be communicated to the Army, in order that the military career of so illustrious an Officer shall be recorded, not only as an honourable testimony of Her Majesty's sense of his eminent services, and the respect due to his memory, but as an example worthy of imitation by all ranks of her Army.

"Selected by the Duke of Wellington to be his Military Secretary and Aide-de-camp, he took part, nearly fifty years ago, in all the military achievements of our greatest Commander. From him Lord Raglan adopted, as the guiding principle of his life, a constant, undeviating obedience to the call of duty.

"During a long peace, his life was most usefully employed in those unwearied attentions to the interests and welfare of the Army, shown by the kindness, the impartiality, and justice, with which he transacted all his duties.

"When war broke out last year, he was selected by his Sovereign to take command of the Army proceeding to the East; he never hesitated— he obeyed the summons, although he had reached an age when an Officer may be disposed to retire from active duties in the field.

"At the head of the troops during the arduous operations of the campaign, he resumed the early habits of his life; by his calmness in the hottest moments of the battle, and by his quick perception in taking advantage of the ground, or the movements of the enemy, he won the confidence of his Army and performed great and brilliant services.

"In the midst of a winter's campaign, in a severe climate, and surrounded by difficulties, he never despaired.

* Kinglake, *Invasion of the Crimea*, viii. 283.

"The heroic Army, whose fortitude amidst the severest privations is recognised by Her Majesty as beyond all praise, have shown their attachment to their Commander by the deep regrets with which they now mourn his loss.

"Her Majesty is confident that the talents and virtues which distinguished Lord Raglan throughout the whole of his valuable life, will for ever endear his memory to the British Army.

"By Command of General the Right Hon. Viscount Hardinge,
"Commanding-in-Chief.
"(Signed)   G. A. WETHERALL,
"Adjutant-General."

2.

FRENCH ARMY OF THE EAST, No. 15 GENERAL ORDER.*

"Death has suddenly taken away, while in full exercise of his command, the Field-Marshal Lord Raglan, and has plunged the British in mourning.

"We all share the sorrow of our brave Allies. Those who knew Lord Raglan, who knew the history of his life—so noble, so pure, so replete with service rendered to his country—those who witnessed his fearless demeanour at Alma and Inkerman, who recall the calm and stoic greatness of his character throughout this rude and memorable campaign, every generous heart indeed, will deplore the loss of such a man. The sentiments here expressed by the General-in-chief, are those of the whole Army. He has himself been cruelly struck by this unlooked-for blow.

"The public grief only increases his sorrow at being for ever separated from a companion-in-arms, whose genial spirit he loved, whose virtues he admired, and from whom he has always received the most loyal and hearty co-operation.
"(Signed)   A. PÉLISSIER,
"Commander-in-chief."

"Head-Quarters before Sevastopol; June 29, 1855."

* Kinglake, *Invasion of the Crimea*, viii. 291.

APPENDIX XI.

1.

RETURN SHOWING THE AGES OF THE NON-COMMISSIONED OFFICERS AND MEN COMPOSING THE 1st BATTALION COLDSTREAM GUARDS WHICH PROCEEDED TO THE EAST IN FEBRUARY, 1854, AND OF THE DRAFTS SENT OUT DURING THE WAR WITH RUSSIA.

Battalion and Drafts.	Strength.	Date of Departure from England.	Under 20 years of age.	20 and under 25.	25 and under 30.	30 and under 35.	35 and under 40.	Over 40 years of age.	Age of the Oldest Soldier.
1st Battalion	919	23-2-54	42	300	286	165	110	16	43 years.
1st Draft	153	28-6-54	48	86	10	6	1	2	40 ,,
2nd ,,	58	27-10-54	26	26	2	3	1	—	36 ,,
3rd ,,	153	25-11-54	45	93	14	—	1	—	35 ,,
4th ,,	307	13-4-55	54	198	50	3	2	—	36 ,,
5th ,,	207	16-9-55	4	108	76	16	2	1	44 ,,
6th ,,	263	14-2-56	13	182	51	16	1	—	35 ,,
Total	2060		232	993	489	209	118	19	

2.

RETURN SHOWING THE PREVIOUS OCCUPATIONS OF THE NON-COMMISSIONED OFFICERS AND MEN COMPOSING THE 1st BATTALION, AND THE DRAFTS THAT WERE ENGAGED IN THE WAR WITH RUSSIA.

Battalion and Drafts.	Agricultural Labourers.	Manufacturing Mechanics, Cloth Weavers, etc.	Mechanics in occupations favourable to physical development, as Masons, etc.	Shopmen and Clerks.	Professional occupations.	No previous occupation, as boys, etc.	Total.
1st Battalion	694	103	83	13	1	25	919
1st Draft	128	10	14	—	—	1	153
2nd ,,	44	2	4	1	1	6	58
3rd ,,	121	14	15	1	1	1	153
4th ,,	240	23	43	1	—	—	307
5th ,,	122	40	42	3	—	—	207
6th ,,	174	46	39	1	—	3	263
Total	1523	238	240	20	3	36	2060

APPENDIX XII.

1.

RETURN OF THE TOTAL NUMBER OF OFFICERS AND MEN IN THE ARMY WHO HAVE BEEN KILLED IN THE CRIMEA, UP TO JUNE 1, 1856.*

	Officers.	Non-Com. Officers.	Men.	Total.
Cavalry	8	10	104	122
Artillery	10	10	111	131
Sappers and Miners	9	1	31	41
Infantry	119	140	2191	2450
Staff	11	—	—	11
Total	157	161	2437	2755

2.

RETURN OF TOTAL NUMBER OF OFFICERS AND MEN IN THE ARMY WHO HAVE BEEN WOUNDED IN THE CRIMEA; OF THE WOUNDED WHO HAVE SINCE DIED; OF THOSE WHO HAVE RECOVERED AND HAVE RETURNED TO THEIR DUTY; OF THOSE WHO HAVE DIED OF SICKNESS; AND OF THOSE INVALIDED, UP TO JUNE 1, 1856.*

	NUMBER WOUNDED.				NUMBER WOUNDED SINCE DIED.				NUMBER RECOVERED AND RETURNED TO DUTY.†		
	Officers.	N.-C. Offs.	Men.	Total.	Officers.	N.-C. Offs.	Men.	Total.	N.-C. Offs.	Men.	Total.
Cavalry	22	21	216	259	4	1	25	30	38	585	623
Artillery	30	37	595	662	1	4	48	53	98	1171	1269
Sappers and Miners	12	7	79	98	6	1	22	29	18	154	172
Infantry	422	514	9892	10828	73	79	1753	1905	528	8920	9448
Staff	29	—	—	29	2	—	—	2	—	—	—
Total	515	579	10782	11876	86	85	1848	2019	682	10830	11512

* *Annual Register*, 1856, "Public Documents," p. 347.
† The columns marked with † are published with the following remark: "There

	Number died from Sickness.†				Number Invalided End of War.†		
	Officers.	Non-Com. Officers.	Men.	Total.	Non-Com. Officers.	Men.	Total.
Cavalry	23	53	954	1030	70	850	920
Artillery	10	35	1263	1308	164	1953	2117
Sappers and Miners	5	7	168	180	41	176	217
Infantry	104	479	12935	13518	862	10602	11464
Staff	5	—	—	5	—	—	—
Total	147	574	15320	16041	1137	13581	14718

3.

RETURN SHOWING BY MONTHS THE NUMBER OF NON-COMMISSIONED OFFICERS AND MEN OF THE 1st BATTALION COLDSTREAM GUARDS WHO LOST THEIR LIVES DURING THE WAR WITH RUSSIA, BETWEEN FEBRUARY 23, 1854, AND JUNE 30, 1856, AND THE CAUSE OF DEATH.*

	Killed in Action or in the Trenches.	Died of Wounds.	Total Deaths by the Enemy.	Died of Disease.						Grand Total.
				Cholera.	Dysentery.	Fevers.	Diarrhœa.	Miscellaneous.	Total.	
1854.										
March	—	—	—	—	—	—	—	1	1	1
April	—	—	—	—	—	—	—	1	1	1
July	—	—	—	2	—	6	—	1	9	9
August	—	—	—	28	—	22	2	1	53	53
September	—	2	2	5	—	12	2	—	19	21
October	1	2	3	14	—	10	11	1	36	39
November	67	22	89	9	4	4	13	2	32	121
December	—	6	6	7	11	9	45	6	78	84
1855.										
January	2	3	5	2	12	14	61	13	102	107
February	—	4	4	—	11	16	42	14	83	87

are no documents in the Adjutant-General's Office which will afford the information specified in the above columns, and the same can only be obtained (and probably then only imperfectly) from the Officers Commanding in the Crimea."

* This table is not absolutely correct, as it accounts only for 691 instead of 699 Non-commissioned officers and men, who fell in the war, either killed, or wounded, or by disease. According to Dr. Wyatt, who does not classify the casualties by months, the total losses were 81 killed in action, 54 died of wounds, and 564 died by disease, or 699 men. But the above return has been given, as it indicates sufficiently the months during which the bulk of the men lost their lives.

	Killed in Action or in the Trenches.	Died of Wounds.	Total Deaths by the Enemy.	Died of Disease.						Grand Total.
				Cholera.	Dysentery.	Fevers.	Diarrhœa.	Miscellaneous.	Total.	
1855.										
March	—	2	2	—	4	8	15	2	29	31
April	—	—	—	—	3	8	6	1	18	18
May	—	—	—	3	2	5	2	1	13	13
June	—	—	—	25	—	10	4	2	41	41
July	—	1	1	—	—	9	1	1	11	12
August	4	5	9	2	—	6	1	—	9	18
September	—	—	—	1	—	2	1	—	4	4
October	—	2	2	1	—	4	1	1	7	9
November	—	2	2	1	—	5	2	2	10	12
December	—	—	—	—	—	1	—	2	3	3
1856.										
January	—	—	—	—	2	4	—	—	6	6
March	—	—	—	—	—	—	1	—	1	1
Total	74	51	125	100	49	155	210	52	566	691

APPENDIX XIII.

THE VICTORIA CROSS.

THIS, the most honourable and coveted Order that can distinguish a British soldier, was instituted by Her Majesty the Queen by Royal Warrant, dated January 29, 1856, for the purpose of rewarding Officers and men of the naval and military services, who, while serving their Sovereign in the presence of the enemy, perform "some signal act of valour or devotion to their country." The decoration, conferred upon those whose deeds of bravery, during naval operations or on the field, entitle them to belong to this highly prized Order, is called the Victoria Cross, and consists of a Maltese Cross of bronze, bearing the motto "For Valour," which is suspended—on the wearer's breast to the right of every other medal,—by a blue riband in the Navy, and by a red riband in the Army. The Order is open to every soldier and sailor, entirely irrespective of rank, of long service, or of wounds received in battle; it is bestowed only where "the merit of conspicuous bravery shall be held to establish a sufficient claim to the honour." Should a man obtain the Victoria Cross, and again be adjudged worthy of the same distinction, a bar is added (like a clasp) to the riband, and so on for every other act of bravery. Warrant and Petty officers and seamen of the Navy, and Non-commissioned officers and men

APPENDIX. 443

of the Army receive an annuity of £10 for the Victoria Cross, and £5 additional a year for every bar they may obtain.*

ROLL OF THE VICTORIA CROSS IN THE COLDSTREAM GUARDS.

No. 1. Brevet-Major Gerald Littlehales Goodlake.

For distinguished gallantry whilst in command of the sharpshooters furnished by the Coldstream Guards on October 26, 1854, on the occasion of the "powerful *sortie* on the Second Division," when he held the Windmill [Careenage] Ravine below the Piquet-house, against a much larger force of the enemy. The party of sharpshooters then under his command killed thirty-eight (one an Officer), and took three prisoners of the enemy (of the latter, one an Officer), Major Goodlake being the sole Officer in command. Also for distinguished gallantry on the occasion of the surprise of a piquet of the enemy, in November, 1854, at the bottom of the Windmill Ravine, by the sharpshooters, under his sole leading and command, when the knapsacks and rifles of the enemy's party fell into his hands.

No. 2. No. 3968 Private William Stanlock.

For having volunteered, when employed as one of the sharpshooters in October, 1854, for reconnoitering purposes, to crawl up within six yards of a Russian sentry, and so enabled the Officer in command to effect a surprise; Private Stanlock having been warned beforehand of the imminent risk which he would run in the adventure.

No. 3. No. 4787 Private George Strong.

For having, when on duty in the trenches, in the month of September, 1855, removed a live shell from the place where it had fallen.

No. 4. Brevet-Major John Augustus Conolly.

In the attack by the Russians against the position held by the Second Division, October 26, 1854, Major Conolly, then a Lieutenant in the 49th Regiment, while in command of a company of that regiment, on outlying piquet, made himself conspicuous by the gallantry of his behaviour. He came particularly under the observation of the late Field-Marshal Lord Raglan, while in personal encounter with several Russians, in defence of his post. He ultimately fell, dangerously wounded. Lieutenant Conolly

* *Annual Register*, 1856, "Public Documents," p. 344, where the whole Royal Warrant is published.

was highly praised in General Orders, and promoted into the Coldstream Guards as a reward for his exemplary behaviour on this occasion.

NOTE.—Captain Hon. R. Campbell would have been fifth on this list, had he survived his act of bravery. The following gives the circumstances under which Lieut. Lysons and Private Fowler (90th Regiment), who gallantly followed Captain Campbell, obtained the Victoria Cross: "On the 28th March, 1879, during the assault of the Inhlobane Mountain, Sir Evelyn Wood ordered the dislodgement of certain Zulus (who were causing the troops much loss) from strong natural caves commanding the position in which some of the wounded were lying. Some delay occurring in the execution of the orders issued, Captain Hon. Ronald Campbell, Coldstream Guards, followed by Lieut. Lysons, A.D.C., and Private Fowler, ran forward in the most determined manner, and advanced over a mass of fallen boulders, and between walls of rock, which led to a cave in which the enemy lay hidden. It being impossible for two men to walk abreast, the assailants were consequently obliged to keep in single file, and, as Captain Campbell was leading, he arrived first at the mouth of the cave, from which the Zulus were firing, and there met his death. Lieut. Lysons and Private Fowler, who were following close behind him, immediately dashed at the cave, from which led several subterranean passages, and firing into the chasm below, succeeded in forcing the occupants to forsake their stronghold. Lieut. Lysons remained at the cave's mouth for some minutes after the attack, during which time Captain Campbell's body was carried down the slopes." *

APPENDIX XIV.

I.

BRITISH FORCES EMPLOYED IN THE EGYPTIAN CAMPAIGN, 1882.†

General Sir Garnet Wolseley, G.C.B., K.C.M.G., Commander-in-chief.
General Sir John Adye, K.C.B., Chief of the Staff and Second in Command.

* *Hart's Army List*, 1896, p. 270 (a). Sir E. Wood states in the account, "One of the Bravest Deeds I ever saw" (*Pearson's Magazine*, February, 1896), already alluded to (*ante*, p. 337), that Captain Campbell fully recognised the risk to the leading man who should try to enter the Zulu stronghold, and when there was a delay in the execution of the order, he called out, "Then I will do it myself," and, jumping over a low wall, ran forward in the manner mentioned above.

† Maurice, *Official Account*, pp. 112, 121. This force amounted to 1,180 Officers, and 28,300 men. Reinforcements, 280 Officers and 10,800 men, were also held in readiness to proceed to Egypt. Total 40,560 of all ranks. (*Annual Register*, 1882, pt. i., 370.)

APPENDIX.

CAVALRY DIVISION. Major-General D. C. Drury Lowe, C.B.
  1st Brigade. Brigadier-General Sir Baker Russell, K.C.M.G., C.B.
    Three Squadrons of Household Cavalry (Lieut.-Colonel Ewart), one each from 1st and 2nd Life Guards, and from Royal Horse Guards; 4th Dragoon Guards; and 7th Dragoon Guards.
  2nd Brigade. Brigadier-General H. C. Wilkinson.
    13th Bengal Lancers; 2nd and 6th Bengal Cavalry.
  Divisional Troops. One Battery Royal Horse Artillery; Royal Engineers; Mounted Infantry; Commissariat and Transport; Medical Department.

FIRST DIVISION. Lieut.-General G. H. Willis, C.B.
  1st. Brigade. Major-General H.R.H. the Duke of Connaught, K.G. Brigade-Major, Captain Ivor Herbert, Grenadier Guards.
    2nd Grenadier Guards (Colonel P. Smith); 2nd Coldstream Guards (Colonel Wigram); 1st Scots Guards (Colonel Knox).
  2nd Brigade. Major-General G. Graham, V.C., C.B.
    2nd Royal Irish (18th); 1st West Kent (50th); 2nd York and Lancaster (84th); 1st Royal Irish Fusiliers (87th).
  Divisional Troops. Two Squadrons 19th Hussars; 2nd Duke of Cornwall Light Infantry (46th); two Batteries Royal Artillery; one Company Royal Engineers; Commissariat and Transport; Medical Department.

SECOND DIVISION. Lieut.-General Sir Edward Hamley, K.C.M.G., C.B.
  1st Brigade. Major-General Sir Archibald Alison, Bart., K.C.B.
    1st Royal Highlanders (42nd); 2nd Highland Light Infantry (74th), 1st Gordon Highlanders (75th); 1st Cameron Highlanders (79th).
  2nd Brigade. Major-General Sir Evelyn Wood, V.C., G.C.M.G., K.C.B.
    1st Sussex Regiment (35th); 1st Berkshire Regiment (49th); 1st Staffordshire Regiment (38th); 1st Shropshire Light Infantry (53rd).
  Divisional Troops. Two Squadrons 19th Hussars; 3rd Kings Royal Rifle Corps (60th); two Batteries Royal Artillery; one Company Royal Engineers; Commissariat and Transport; Medical Department.

CORPS TROOPS. One Battery Royal Horse Artillery; three Batteries Royal Artillery; Siege Train; Pontoon and Telegraph Troop; Field Park; three Companies Royal Engineers; Railway Section; two Companies Madras Sappers and Miners; Commissariat and Transport; Medical Department.

INDIAN CONTINGENT. Major-General Sir H. T. Macpherson, V.C., K.C.B.
  Infantry Brigade. Brigadier-General O. V. Tanner, C.B.
    1st Seaforth Highlanders; 7th and 20th Bengal Native Infantry; 29th Company Beluchi Native Infantry; one Mountain Battery.
  Additional Troops. 1st Manchester Regiment.
  Reserve at Aden. Two Native Regiments Infantry.

2.

EXTRACTS FROM GENERAL ORDERS ISSUED AFTER THE BATTLE OF TEL EL-KEBIR.

HEAD-QUARTERS, TEL EL-KEBIR, SEPTEMBER 14, 1882.

"The following telegram has been received from Her Majesty by the General Officer the Commander-in-chief:—

"'The Queen sends Her warmest congratulations, and thanks God for victory. Express to all my admiration, and sympathy and sorrow for heavy loss.'"

HEAD-QUARTERS, CAIRO, SEPTEMBER 16, 1882.

"1. Her Majesty desires to convey to Her Army hearty congratulations on the bloodless occupation of Cairo, on the capture of Arabi, and other rebels against the authority of the Khedive, and on the termination of a campaign in which Her brave troops have so greatly distinguished themselves.

"2. The General Commander-in-chief directs the following orders be read and explained to the men at three consecutive parades :—

"The Army-Corps in Egypt will shortly be assembled in Cairo. Its discipline will now be subjected to a scrutiny the more searching because fatigue and privation nobly borne and victory brilliantly achieved will naturally direct upon it the attention of the civilized world.

"The General Commander-in-chief therefore appeals to all ranks to show, by a strict attention to duty and discipline, that it is not only in the field that the British Army is distinguished.

"It must be remembered that the Army is here in Cairo as the friend of the people of Cairo, whom it has relieved from the despotism of rebellion.

"3. The police and gendarmerie are not to be disarmed, but, on the contrary, are in every way to be assisted and supported in their authority.

"The soldiery has already been disarmed so far as is considered necessary.

"4. No soldier will be allowed to leave barracks, except on duty, until 4 p.m. Sergeants must be posted at the gates to see that no one goes out improperly dressed. Belts must be pipeclayed. Tattoo will be sounded at 8 p.m., and patrols sent out until all men are brought to barracks. Passes are not to be given for any hour later than 10 p.m., and very sparingly. In the event of any drunkenness or outrage or breaking into houses being reported, the regiment complained of will be immediately marched two miles outside the town to Abrasia, and there quartered as long as the Army is at Cairo."

APPENDIX. 447

HEAD-QUARTERS, CAIRO, SEPTEMBER 17, 1882.

"The General Commanding-in-chief congratulates the Army serving in Egypt upon the brilliant success which has crowned its efforts in the campaign terminated on the 14th inst., by the surrender of the citadel of Cairo and of Arabi Pasha, the chief rebel in arms against the authority of His Highness the Khedive. In the space of twenty-five days the Army has effected its disembarkation at Ismailia, has traversed the desert to Zagazig, and has occupied the capital of Egypt. It has fought and defeated the enemy five times: on the 24th of August, at El-Magfar; on the 25th of August, at Tel el-Makhuta and at Mahsama; on the 28th of August and on the 9th of September, at Kassassin; and, finally, on the 13th of September, at Tel el-Kebir, where, after an arduous night march, it inflicted upon him an overwhelming defeat, storming his strongly entrenched position at the point of the bayonet, and capturing all his guns, about 60 in number. In recapitulating the events which have marked this short and decisive campaign, the General Commanding-in-chief feels proud to place upon record the fact that these brilliant achievements are to be ascribed to the high military courage and noble devotion to duty which have animated all ranks under his command. Called upon to show discipline under exceptional privations, to give proof of fortitude in extreme toil, and to show contempt of danger in battle, the General Officers, Officers, Non-commissioned officers, and soldiers of the Army have responded with zealous alacrity, adding another chapter to the long roll of British victories." *

3.

EXTRACT OF REPORT ON ARMY SIGNALLING IN EGYPT.

"To Lieutenant Lovell, Coldstream Guards, and Sergeant Dunster and men, my thanks are due for their willing and most efficient help rendered on more than one occasion. With the assistance of Lieutenant Lovell and a party of signallers, Coldstream Guards, to whom I am much indebted for most efficient help, communication was opened from Kassassin Lock to Ismailia. Sergeant Dunster, in charge of this party, rendered very good service, both on this station and later at Cairo."

---

* It is stated in the *Official Account*, p. 106, that, "on the 4th of October, the General had issued a congratulatory order, complimenting the troops alike upon their conduct in the campaign and upon their behaviour as conquerors in Cairo." This order is not given in the above work; and as it is not to be found in the Battalion Order-book, it has not been possible to reproduce it in this volume.

APPENDIX XV.*

STATIONS.

Date.	No. of Cos.	Stations.
March 1, 1833	8	1st Battalion from Knightsbridge Barracks to King's Mews Barracks.
Aug. 19, ,,	8	2nd Battalion from Dublin *via* Bristol to the Mews Barracks, in two wings—left wing on the 19th, and the right wing on the 22nd.
Aug. 30, ,,	8	1st Battalion from the Mews to Portman Street Barracks.
Feb. 28, 1834	8	1st Battalion from Portman Street to Windsor.
March 1, ,,	8	2nd Battalion from St. George's Barracks † to Knightsbridge, Kensington, and Magazine Barracks.
April 30, ,,	1	Of the 2nd Battalion from the Magazine Barracks to Chelsea, returning to the Magazine the next day.
,, ,,	1	Of the 1st Battalion from Windsor to London, returning next day.
May 16, ,,	4	Of the 1st Battalion from Windsor to Bagshot; this detachment was back in Windsor on the 21st.
Sept. 3, ,,	8	1st Battalion from Windsor to the Tower, on the 3rd and 4th.
,, ,,	8	2nd Battalion from Knightsbridge, Kensington, and Magazine Barracks to Wellington Barracks.†
March 3, 1835	8	1st Battalion from the Tower to St. George's Barracks.
,, ,,	8	2nd Battalion from Wellington Barracks to Portman Street Barracks.
Aug. 31, ,,	8	2nd Battalion from Portman Street to Windsor, *via* Hounslow.
Sept. 2, ,,	8	1st Battalion from St. George's to Wellington Barracks.
Oct. 26, ,,	4	Of the 2nd Battalion from Windsor to Brighton.
Feb. 29, 1836	4	Of the 2nd Battalion from Brighton to the Tower.
March 2, ,,	4	Of the 2nd Battalion from Windsor to the Tower.
March 3, ,,	8	1st Battalion from Wellington Barracks to Knightsbridge, Buckingham Palace, Kensington, and Magazine Barracks.
May 31, ,,	4	Of the 1st Battalion from Knightsbridge Barracks to St. John's Wood Barracks.
July 28, ,,	8	1st Battalion from London to Dublin, *via* Bristol, by two wings, on the 28th and 29th.
Aug. 30, ,,	8	2nd Battalion from the Tower to St. George's Barracks.
March 3, 1837	8	2nd Battalion from St. George's to Portman Street Barracks.
July 7, ,,	8	2nd Battalion to Windsor, to take part in the funeral of King William IV.; the Battalion returned to Portman Street about the 9th.

* Continued from Appendix 273 of MacKinnon's *Origin and Services of the Coldstream Guards* (ii. 450).

† By *Brigade Order*, Nov. 5, 1833, the King's Mews Barracks were called St. George's Barracks; and the new building erected near Bird-cage Walk, on the site of the Armoury and Recruit House, Westminster Barracks. The latter were immediately afterwards called Wellington Barracks.

APPENDIX.

Date.	No. of Cos.	Stations.
July 22, 1837	8	2nd Battalion from Portman Street to Hammersmith and adjacents during an election in the borough of Marylebone; Portman Street was re-occupied by the Battalion on the 28th.
Aug. 21, ,,	8	1st Battalion from Dublin to St. George's Barracks, in two wings on the 21st and 22nd.
Sept. 2, ,,	8	2nd Battalion from Portman Street to St. John's Wood, Magazine, Buckingham Palace, and St. George's Barracks and quarters adjacent.
Feb. 14, 1838	8	1st Battalion from St. George's *viâ* Hounslow to Windsor.
Feb. 15, ,,	8	2nd Battalion from St. John's Wood, Kensington, Magazine, Buckingham Palace to Wellington Barracks.
March 28, ,,	8	2nd Battalion from London, 28th and 29th, in four divisions to Winchester; two *viâ* Epsom, Guildford, and Alton, and two *viâ* Hounslow, Bagshot, and Basingstoke. From Winchester to Portsmouth, where the Battalion embarked, April 17th, for Canada, in H.M.S. *Edinburgh* and *Athol*, and landed at Quebec on May 11th.
June 26, ,,	8	1st Battalion from Windsor to London to take part in the Queen's Coronation, returning to Windsor on the 30th.
Aug. 31, ,,	8	1st Battalion from Windsor to Portman Street Barracks.
March 1, 1839	8	1st Battalion from Portman Street to Wellington Barracks.
Aug. 31, ,,	8	1st Battalion from Wellington Barracks to the Tower.
Feb. 29, 1840	8	1st Battalion from the Tower to St. John's Wood (4 companies), Buckingham Palace (1 company), Kensington (1 company), the Magazine (1 company), and Wellington Barracks (1 company).
Sept. 1, ,,	8	1st Battalion from St. John's Wood, etc., to Wellington Barracks.
March 1, 1841	8	1st Battalion from Wellington to Portman Street Barracks.
June 28, ,,	8	1st Battalion from Portman Street to Fulham, Parson's Green, and Walham Green, during an election in the borough of Marylebone; thence the right wing to Twickenham and the left wing to Hounslow (but not within two miles of Brentford, Bedfont, or Kingston), during the election in the county of Middlesex. The Battalion returned to Portman Street Barracks on July 9th.
Sept. 1, ,,	8	1st Battalion from Portman Street to St. George's Barracks.
March 9, 1842	8	1st Battalion from St. George's Barracks to the Tower.
Sept. 1, ,,	8	1st Battalion from the Tower, 7 companies to Portman Street, 1 company to the Magazine Barracks.
Oct. 22, ,,	8	1st Battalion from Portman Street and the Magazine to St. John's Wood, Kensington, Magazine, and Buckingham Palace Barracks.
Oct. 6, ,,	6	Of the 2nd Battalion left Quebec to return to England on board the H.M.S. *Calcutta*; landed at Spithead on the 31st, and proceeded by two trains to Winchester.
Oct. 19, ,,	2	Of the 2nd Battalion, from Quebec, on board H.M.S. *Pique*, to Spithead; arriving there November 12th; thence to Winchester.
Nov. 22, ,,	8	2nd Battalion from Winchester to St. George's Barracks.
March 1, 1843	8	1st Battalion from St. John's Wood to Windsor.
,, ,,	8	2nd Battalion from St. George's to Portman Street.

2 G

APPENDIX.

Date.	No. of Cos.	Stations.
Sept. 1, 1843	8	1st Battalion from Windsor to Wellington Barracks.
,, ,,	8	2nd Battalion from Portman Street to St. John's Wood (3 companies), St. George's Barracks (2 companies), Buckingham Palace, Magazine, and Kensington Barracks (1 company each).
March 1, 1844	8	1st Battalion from Wellington to Portman Street Barracks.
,, ,,	8	2nd Battalion from St. John's Wood, etc., to Wellington Barracks.
Aug. 30, ,,	8	1st Battalion from Portman Street to the Tower.
,, ,,	8	2nd Battalion from Wellington Barracks to St. George's Barracks.
Feb. 28, 1845	8	2nd Battalion from St. George's Barracks to Windsor.
March 8, ,,	8	1st Battalion from the Tower to Winchester.
Sept. 1, ,,	8	1st Battalion from Winchester to Portman Street Barracks.
,, ,,	8	2nd Battalion from Windsor to the Tower.
Feb. 26, 1846	8	2nd Battalion from the Tower to Winchester.
Feb. 27, ,,	8	1st Battalion from Portman Street to St. John's Wood (3 companies), Wellington Barracks (2 companies), and to Kensington, Buckingham Palace, and the Magazine (1 company each).
Sept. 1, ,,	8	1st Battalion from St. John's Wood, etc., to St. George's Barracks.
,, ,,	8	2nd Battalion from Winchester to Portman Street Barracks.
March 2, 1847	8	1st Battalion from St. George's to Wellington Barracks.
,, ,,	8	2nd Battalion from Portman Street to St. John's Wood (3 companies), and Buckingham Palace, Wellington, the Magazine, Kensington, and St. George's Barracks (1 company each).
Sept. 1, ,,	8	1st Battalion from Wellington Barracks to Chichester.
,, ,,	8	2nd Battalion from St. John's Wood, etc., to Wellington Barracks.
March 1, 1848	8	1st Battalion from Chichester to the Tower.
,, ,,	8	2nd Battalion from Wellington Barracks to Windsor.
Sept. 1, ,,	8	1st Battalion from the Tower to Windsor.
,, ,,	8	2nd Battalion from Windsor to St. George's Barracks.
March 1, 1849	8	1st Battalion from Windsor to St. George's Barracks.
,, ,,	8	2nd Battalion from St. George's Barracks to the Tower.
Sept. 1, ,,	8	1st Battalion from St. George's Barracks to St. John's Wood (3 companies), Wellington (2 companies), and the Magazine, Kensington, and Buckingham Palace (1 company each).
,, ,,	8	2nd Battalion from the Tower to Chichester.
March 1, 1850	8	1st Battalion from St. John's Wood, etc., to Portman Street Barracks.
,, ,,	8	2nd Battalion from Chichester to St. George's Barracks.
Sept. 4, ,,	8	1st Battalion from Portman Street to Windsor.
,, ,,	8	2nd Battalion from St. George's Barracks to St. John's Wood (3 companies), and St. George's, Wellington, Kensington, Buckingham Palace, and the Magazine (1 company each).
March 7, 1851	8	1st Battalion from Windsor to the Tower.
,, ,,	8	2nd Battalion from St. John's Wood, etc., to Wellington Barracks.

APPENDIX.

Date.	No. of Cos.	Stations.
Oct. 23, 1851	8	1st Battalion from the Tower to Chichester.
,, ,,	8	2nd Battalion from Wellington to Portman Street Barracks.
March 2, 1852	8	1st Battalion from Chichester to Wellington Barracks.
,, ,,	8	2nd Battalion from Portman Street to Windsor.
Sept. 1, ,,	8	1st Battalion from Wellington to Portman Street.
,, ,,	8	2nd Battalion from Windsor to the Tower.
March 2, 1853	8	1st Battalion from Portman Street to St. John's Wood (3 companies), and to Kensington, Buckingham Palace, the Magazine, Wellington, and St. George's Barracks (1 company each).
,, ,,	8	2nd Battalion from the Tower to St. George's Barracks.
June 14, ,,	8	1st Battalion from St. John's Wood, etc., to Chobham Camp, viâ Windsor.
July 14, ,,	8	1st Battalion from Chobham Camp to St. George's Barracks.
,, ,,	8	2nd Battalion from St. George's Barracks to Chobham Camp, viâ Chertsey.
Aug. 19, ,,	8	2nd Battalion from Chobham Camp to Chichester, in two wings, left wing on the 19th and right wing on the 20th.
Feb. 14, 1854	8	1st Battalion from St. George's to Chichester; the men of the Battalion who were not to proceed on foreign service were sent to Windsor.
,, ,,	8	2nd Battalion from Chichester to Windsor, leaving behind at the former quarter men who were to complete the 1st Battalion to 850 rank and file.
Feb. 22, ,,	8	1st Battalion from Chichester to Southampton; thence in ss. *Orinoco* to Malta, reaching that place on March 4th.
Feb. 23, ,,	8	2nd Battalion from Windsor to St. George's Barracks, and thence on the 28th to Wellington Barracks.
April 21, ,,	8	1st Battalion left Malta in H.M.S. *Vulcan*, disembarking at Scutari on the 29th, and was encamped there.
June 13, ,,	8	1st Battalion from Scutari to Varna in the steam-transport *Andes*, and encamped about a mile outside the fortifications there on the 14th.
July 1, ,,	8	1st Battalion marched from Varna to Aladyn, and was encamped there.
July 27, ,,	8	1st Battalion marched from Aladyn to the village of Gevreklek, and was encamped there.
Aug. 16, ,,	8	1st Battalion marched from Gevreklek to the vicinity of the Adrianople Road, about two miles to the south of Varna, and reached their new camp on the 18th.
Sept. 1, ,,	12	2nd Battalion from Wellington Barracks to Portman Street.
Sept. 7, ,,	8	Of the 1st Battalion, the left wing and the head-quarters embarked on board the steam-transport *Tonning*, on August 29th, and 2 companies on H.M.S. *Simoon*; the remaining 2 companies on H.M.S. *Vengeance*, the next day, August 30th, whence they were transferred to H.M.S. *Bellerophon* on September 4th. On September 7th the fleet left the coast of Turkey, and sailed into the Black Sea, approaching the Crimea, off Eupatoria, on the 13th. Next day, the 14th, the Battalion landed in the Crimea.
Sept. 20, ,,	8	BATTLE OF THE ALMA. 1st Battalion present.
Oct. 2, ,,	8	1st Battalion marched from the neighbourhood of the Alma on September 23rd, and, taking part in the flank march round

APPENDIX.

Date.	No. of Cos.	Stations.
		Sevastopol, encamped outside Balaklava near the village of Kadikeui; on October 2nd, the Battalion took up a position before Sevastopol.
Nov. 5, 1854	8	BATTLE OF INKERMAN. 1st Battalion present.
Jan. 31, 1855	1	Of the 2nd Battalion from Portman Street to Kensington Barracks.
Feb. 24, ,,	8	1st Battalion from before Sevastopol to Balaklava.
March 1, ,,	12	2nd Battalion from Portman Street and Kensington to St. George's Barracks.
March 26, ,,	1	Of the 2nd Battalion from St. George's Barracks to Wellington Barracks. This company rejoined head-quarters on April 10th.
June 13, ,,	12	2nd Battalion from St. George's Barracks to the Camp at Aldershot.
June 16, ,,	8	1st Battalion from Balaklava to before Sevastopol.
Aug. 28, ,,	12	2nd Battalion from Aldershot to St. George's Barracks, the Tower, and the Magazine and Kensington Barracks.
Sept. 15, ,,	2	Of the 2nd Battalion from the Tower to Portman Street. Between this date and the end of January, 1856, several changes took place in the stations of individual companies, and the Battalion then had 3 companies in Portman Street, 1 company in Buckingham Palace, the Magazine, and in Kensington Barracks, each, and the remainder in St. George's Barracks.
Feb. 29, 1856	12	2nd Battalion from St. George's Barracks, etc., to the Tower and Portman Street.
June 4, ,,	8	1st Battalion embarked at Kamiesh Bay (Crimea), on board H.M.S. *Agamemnon*, for England, and disembarked at Gosport on the 28th; thence to Aldershot.
June 26, ,,	2	Of the 2nd Battalion from Portman Street to rejoin head-quarters at the Tower.
July 9, ,,	10	1st Battalion from Aldershot to the Tower and St. John's Wood.
,, ,,	10	2nd Battalion from the Tower to Windsor. From August 26th to the middle of October, 1 company was encamped at Ascot; (each company of the Battalion proceeded there in succession for a few days).
Dec. 4, ,,	2	Of the 1st Battalion from St. John's Wood to the Tower.
March 3, 1857	10	1st Battalion from the Tower to Aldershot.
,, ,,	10	2nd Battalion from Windsor to Wellington Barracks.
Sept. 1, ,,	10	1st Battalion from Aldershot to Wellington Barracks and Buckingham Palace (1 company).
,, ,,	10	2nd Battalion from Wellington Barracks to Dublin. Between October 17th and December 21st, 2 companies were at the Curragh; (detachments of 2 companies at a time relieved each other successively, until the whole 10 companies had received musketry instruction there). During the following spring and summer 1 company at a time proceeded to Curragh or to Ash Camp for musketry practice.
Nov. 20, ,,	1	Of the 1st Battalion from Buckingham Palace to Wellington Barracks.
April 15, 1858	10	1st Battalion from Wellington Barracks to Windsor. During

APPENDIX. 453

Date.	No. of Cos.	Stations.
		the summer months the companies proceeded one after another to Ash Camp or to Ascot for musketry practice.
Sept. 1, 1858	10	1st Battalion from Windsor to St. George's, Kensington, and Magazine Barracks.*
,, ,,	10	2nd Battalion from Dublin to Wellington Barracks.
April 1, 1859	10	1st Battalion from St. George's, Kensington, and Magazine Barracks to Wellington Barracks. During the summer the companies proceeded separately, one after another, to Ash Camp for musketry.
,, ,,	10	2nd Battalion from Wellington Barracks to Portman Street and St. John's Wood Barracks.
July 1st, ,,	10	2nd Battalion thence to Aldershot, returning to the same West-end Barracks, August 2nd.
Sept. 1st, ,,	10	2nd Battalion from Portman Street and St. John's Wood to the Tower.
Oct. 1st, ,,	10	1st Battalion from Wellington Barracks to Portman Street and St. John's Wood Barracks.
April 3, 1860	10	1st Battalion from Portman Street and St. John's Wood to Wellington Barracks and Buckingham Palace Barracks.
,, ,,	10	2nd Battalion from the Tower to Windsor. Musketry by companies at Ash Camp during the summer.
June 15, ,,	10	1st Battalion from Wellington Barracks to Aldershot, returning to same London quarters July 17th.
June 28, ,,	2	2nd Battalion from Windsor to Wellington Barracks, returning to Windsor August 13th.
Oct. 2, ,,	10	1st Battalion from Wellington and Buckingham Palace Barracks, to St. George's, Kensington, and Magazine Barracks.
,, ,,	10	2nd Battalion from Windsor to Portman Street and St. John's Wood Barracks.
April 2, 1861	10	1st Battalion from St. George's, Kensington, and Magazine Barracks to the Tower. Musketry by companies during the summer at Ash Camp.
,, ,,	10	2nd Battalion from Portman Street and St. John's Wood Barracks to Wellington and Buckingham Palace Barracks.
July 19, ,,	10	2nd Battalion from Wellington Barracks to Aldershot, returning to the former quarters August 23rd.
Oct. 4, ,,	10	1st Battalion from the Tower to Dublin by Liverpool.
Dec. 12, ,,	10	2nd Battalion from Wellington and Buckingham Palace Barracks to the Tower, returning to the same quarters in the West-end on December 19th.
April 1, 1862	10	2nd Battalion from Wellington and Buckingham Palace Barracks to Portman Street and St. John's Wood Barracks. Musketry by companies to Aldershot and at Eastbourne, during the summer.
April 16, ,,	10	1st Battalion from Dublin to Wellington Barracks.
Aug. 5, ,,	10	1st Battalion from Wellington Barracks to Aldershot.
Sept. 5, ,,	10	1st Battalion from Aldershot to Windsor.
,, ,,	10	2nd Battalion from Portman Street and St. John's Wood Barracks to St. George's, the Magazine, Wellington, and Buckingham Palace Barracks.

* The new Kensington Barracks replaced the old buildings in April, 1858.

APPENDIX.

Date.	No. of Cos.	Stations.
Jan. 10, 1863	1	Of the 2nd Battalion from St. George's Barracks to Wellington Barracks.
April 1, ,,	10	1st Battalion from Windsor to Portman Street and Kensington Barracks.
,, ,,	10	2nd Battalion from St. George's Magazine, Wellington, and Buckingham Palace Barracks to Windsor. Musketry for both battalions by companies at Aldershot, during the summer.
July 4, ,,	4	Of the 1st Battalion from Kensington to Wellington Barracks, returning to the former quarter September 1st.
Sept. 15, ,,	1	Of the 1st Battalion from Portman Street to Chelsea Barracks.*
Sept. 25, ,,	10	1st Battalion from Portman Street and Kensington to St. George's (7 companies), Magazine (1 company), and Chelsea Barracks (2 companies).
,, ,,	10	2nd Battalion from Windsor to Wellington Barracks.
Oct. 1, ,,	1	Of the 1st Battalion from St. George's to Chelsea Barracks.
Oct. 15, ,,	1	Of the 1st Battalion from the Magazine to Chelsea Barracks.
April 1, 1864	10	1st Battalion from St. George's and Chelsea to Wellington (8 companies), Buckingham Palace (1 company), Magazine (1 company). Musketry by companies during the summer at Eastbourne.
July 5, ,,	10	2nd Battalion from Wellington Barracks to Aldershot, returning to the former station August 2nd.
Sept. 15, ,,	10	2nd Battalion from Wellington Barracks to Windsor.
March 31, 1865	10	1st Battalion from Wellington, Buckingham Palace, and Magazine Barracks to Windsor.
,, ,,	10	2nd Battalion from Windsor to St. George's (6 companies), and Chelsea Barracks (4 companies). Musketry for both Battalions by companies at Aldershot.
Aug. 2, ,,	10	2nd Battalion from St. George's and Chelsea to the Tower (8 companies) and St. John's Wood Barracks (2 companies).
Sept. 1, ,,	10	1st Battalion from Windsor to Chelsea Barracks.
Feb. 20, 1866	10	1st Battalion from Chelsea to Dublin.
March 1, ,,	10	2nd Battalion from the Tower and St. John's Wood to Chelsea Barracks. Musketry during the summer by companies at Aldershot.
Aug. 31, ,,	10	2nd Battalion from Chelsea to Wellington, Kensington, Buckingham Palace, and Magazine Barracks.
Sept. 13, ,,	10	1st Battalion from Dublin to the Curragh, till October 25th.
Dec. 21, ,,	1	Of the 2nd Battalion from Magazine to Wellington Barracks.†
Feb. 28, 1867	10	2nd Battalion from Wellington, Kensington, and Buckingham Palace Barracks to Dublin.
March 1, ,,	10	1st Battalion from Dublin to St. George's (6 companies) and Chelsea Barracks (4 companies). Musketry by companies at Eastbourne during the summer.
March 9, ,,	1	Of the 1st Battalion from St. George's to Chelsea Barracks.
Sept. 3, ,,	10	1st Battalion from St. George's and Chelsea to the Tower (8 companies), and St. John's Wood (2 companies).

* The barracks built in Chelsea were ready for occupation at this time.

† The Magazine Barracks were given up on this date as a Guards quarter, and were handed over to the Police authorities.

APPENDIX.

Date.	No. of Cos.	Stations.
Oct. 21, 1867	2	Of the 1st Battalion from St. John's Wood to the Tower.
March 4, 1868	10	1st Battalion from the Tower to Windsor. Musketry by companies at Aldershot during the summer.
March 4, ,,	10	2nd Battalion from Dublin to Chelsea (7 companies) and St. George's Barracks (3 companies). Musketry by companies at Aldershot during the summer.
April 22, ,,	2	Of the 2nd Battalion from St. George's to Chelsea Barracks.
May 16, ,,	2	Of the 2nd Battalion from Chelsea to St. John's Wood Barracks.
May 29, ,,	2	Of the 2nd Battalion from St. John's Wood to St. George's Barracks.
Sept. 1, ,,	10	1st Battalion from Windsor to Chelsea Barracks.
,, ,,	10	2nd Battalion from Chelsea and St. George's Barracks to Windsor.
March 3, 1869	10	1st Battalion from Chelsea to Chelsea and St. George's.
,, ,,	10	2nd Battalion from Windsor to the Tower and St. John's Wood Barracks. Musketry by companies to Aldershot during the summer.
July 6, ,,	10	1st Battalion from Chelsea and St. George's Barracks to Aldershot, returning to former quarters August 3rd.
Sept. 1, ,,	10	1st Battalion from Chelsea and St. George's Barracks to Wellington Barracks.
,, ,,	10	2nd Battalion from the Tower and St. John's Wood to Wellington, Kensington, and Buckingham Palace Barracks.
March 2, 1870	10	1st Battalion from Wellington to Wellington, Kensington, and Buckingham Palace Barracks.
March 3, ,,	10	2nd Battalion from Wellington, Kensington, and Buckingham Palace Barracks to Wellington Barracks. Musketry for both Battalions by companies at Aldershot.
Sept. 1, ,,	10	1st Battalion from Wellington, Kensington, and Buckingham Palace Barracks to Windsor.
,, ,,	10	2nd Battalion from Wellington to Chelsea Barracks.
March 1, 1871	10	1st Battalion from Windsor to the Tower.
,, ,,	10	2nd Battalion from Chelsea to Chelsea and St. George's Barracks. Musketry by companies for both Battalions at Aldershot, during the summer.
June 19, ,,	1	Of the 1st Battalion from the Tower to Kensington Barracks.
July 5, ,,	1	Of the 1st Battalion from the Tower to Kensington Barracks.
Aug. 8, ,,	10	2nd Battalion from Chelsea and St. George's Barracks to Aldershot and neighbourhood for manœuvres.
Sept. 26, ,,	10	1st Battalion from the Tower and Kensington Barracks to Chelsea and St. George's Barracks.
,, ,,	10	2nd Battalion from Aldershot manœuvres to Windsor.
April 6, 1872	10	2nd Battalion from Windsor to Dublin.
		1st Battalion by companies to Aldershot during the summer for musketry.
Aug. 15, ,,	10	1st Battalion from Chelsea and St. George's Barracks to Blandford and neighbourhood, for Salisbury Plain manœuvres.
Aug. 19, ,,	10	2nd Battalion from Dublin to the Curragh, returning to Dublin after a few weeks.
Sept. 14, ,,	10	1st Battalion from Salisbury Plain manœuvres to Wellington Barracks.

Date.	No. of Cos.	Stations.
April 24, 1873	10	2nd Battalion from Dublin to the Tower and St. John's Wood Barracks. The companies in latter quarter were withdrawn from May to July. Musketry by companies during summer at Ash and Windsor. 1st Battalion by companies to Gravesend and Ash for musketry during the summer.
Aug. 18, ,,	10	2nd Battalion from Tower and St. John's Wood to Cannock Chase and neighbourhood for manœuvres.
Sept. 12, ,,	10	1st Battalion from Wellington to Chelsea Barracks.
,, ,,	10	2nd Battalion from Cannock Chase manœuvres to Chelsea and St. George's Barracks.
April 28, 1874	10	1st Battalion from Chelsea to Windsor. Musketry by companies at Windsor and Aldershot. 2nd Battalion by companies to Gravesend for musketry.
Oct. 1, ,,	10	1st Battalion from Windsor to the Tower and St. John's Wood.
,, ,,	10	2nd Battalion from Chelsea and St. George's to Wellington Barracks.
Jan. 5, 1875	1	Of the 1st Battalion from St. John's Wood to the Tower.
April 3, ,,	10	1st Battalion from the Tower to Wellington, Kensington, and Buckingham Palace Barracks. Musketry for both Battalions by companies at Gravesend and Ash.
Oct. 1, ,,	10	2nd Battalion from Wellington to Chelsea and St. George's Barracks.
March 29, 1876	10	1st Battalion from Wellington, Kensington, and Buckingham Palace Barracks to Shorncliffe.
March 30, ,,	10	2nd Battalion from Chelsea and St. George's to the Tower.
Aug. 2, ,,	10	2nd Battalion from the Tower to Aldershot.
Sept. 1, ,,	10	2nd Battalion from Aldershot to Windsor.
,, ,,	10	1st Battalion from Shorncliffe to Wellington Barracks.
March 1, 1877	10	1st Battalion from Wellington to Chelsea Barracks. Musketry by half-battalions at Gravesend and Ash.
,, ,,	10	2nd Battalion from Windsor to Wellington, Kensington, and Buckingham Palace. Musketry by half-battalions at Ash.
June 22, ,,	10	1st Battalion from Chelsea to Aldershot, returning to the former quarter July 20th.
Sept. 4, ,,	10	2nd Battalion from Wellington Barracks, etc., to Shorncliffe.
March 1, 1878	10	1st Battalion from Chelsea to the Tower. Musketry by companies at Eastbourne.
,, ,,	10	2nd Battalion from Shorncliffe to Chelsea and St. George's Barracks. Musketry by half-battalions at Gravesend.
July 2, ,,	10	2nd Battalion from Chelsea and St. George's Barracks to Aldershot, returning to former quarter, 24th.
,, ,,	10	1st Battalion from the Tower to Windsor.
March 4, 1879	10	1st Battalion from Windsor to Wellington and Kensington Barracks. Musketry by half-battalions at Aldershot.
,, ,,	10	2nd Battalion from Chelsea and St. George's to Windsor. Musketry by companies at Aldershot.
July 1, ,,	10	1st Battalion from Wellington Barracks, etc., to Aldershot.
July 26, ,,	10	1st Battalion from Aldershot to Shorncliffe.
Sept. 2, ,,	10	2nd Battalion from Windsor to the Tower.
March 3, 1880	10	1st Battalion from Shorncliffe to Chelsea and St. George's Barracks.

APPENDIX.

Date.	No. of Cos.	Stations.
March 3, 1880	10	2nd Battalion from the Tower to Wellington Barracks. Musketry by companies for both Battalions at Aldershot.
Dec. 6, ,,	10	1st Battalion from Chelsea and St. George's to Dublin.
Feb. 24, 1881	10	2nd Battalion from Wellington to Wellington, Kensington, and Buckingham Palace Barracks. Musketry by companies at Aldershot and Pirbright.
June 2, ,,	10	1st Battalion from Dublin to New Pallas, returning 4th.
March 4, 1882	8	1st Battalion Dublin to Chelsea Barracks.
,, 7, ,,	8	2nd Battalion from Wellington, Kensington, and Buckingham Palace Barracks to Dublin.
May 10, ,,	8	1st Battalion from Chelsea to Pirbright Camp, returning to former quarter, 26th.
Aug. 1, ,,	8	2nd Battalion from Dublin to Egypt, embarking at Kingstown on board s.s. *Iberia*, and landing at Alexandria, 13th. Moved to Ramleh that day.
Aug. 18 ,,	8	2nd Battalion from Ramleh to Alexandria, embarked on board *Iberia;* landed at Ismailia, 22nd; moved forward to the front, 24th.
Sept. 13, ,.	8	BATTLE OF TEL-EL-KEBIR. The 2nd Battalion to Cairo by train on the 15th.
Oct. 31, ,,	8	2nd Battalion from Cairo to Alexandria by train; embarked there on board the *Batavia*, and reached Portsmouth on November 16th; thence by train to London, Chelsea Barracks.
Nov. 13, ,,	8	1st Battalion from Chelsea Barracks to Windsor.
March 1, 1883	8	1st Battalion from Windsor to the Tower.
March 27, ,,	8	1st Battalion from the Tower to Wellington Barracks (4 companies), and St. George's Barracks (4 companies). Musketry and company training at Pirbright by companies, one or two at a time; one company trained at Wimbledon. 2nd Battalion by companies to Aldershot and Pirbright for musketry, during the season.
July 10, ,,	8	2nd Battalion from Chelsea to Pirbright Camp.
July 28, ,,	8	2nd Battalion from Pirbright to Windsor.
July 31, ,,	8	1st Battalion from Wellington and St. George's Barracks to Chelsea Barracks (south wing).
March 20, 1884	8	1st Battalion from Chelsea to Aldershot.
May 5, ,,	8	1st Battalion from Aldershot to Chelsea. 2nd Battalion by companies to Pirbright for musketry.
July 15, ,,	8	1st Battalion from Chelsea to Wellington Barracks.
Aug. 28, ,,	8	2nd Battalion from Windsor to Chelsea and St. George's.
Feb. 19, 1885	8	2nd Battalion from Chelsea and St. George's Barracks to Wellington Barracks. For musketry and company training, two companies at a time, to Pirbright during the season.
,, ,,	8	1st Battalion from Wellington to Westminster Stairs, where the Battalion embarked in two river steamers for Gravesend; thence on board s.s. *Manorah*, and started for Suakin; disembarking there on March 8th, and proceeded to camp near Suakin.
March 23, ,,	8	1st Battalion from Suakin to Tofrek (McNeill's) Zareba, returning to near Suakin, 28th.
April 2, ,.	8	1st Battalion from Suakin to Tamai, returning to near Suakin April 4th.

Date.		No. of Cos.	Stations.
April 6,	1885	8	1st Battalion from Suakin to No. 1 Station (on the road to Berber); thence to Handub, 8th; thence Head-quarters and Right-half Battalion to Otao, 18th, followed by Left-half Battalion, 20th.
May 13,	,,	8	1st Battalion from Otao to Suakin; embarked on board s.s. *Deccan*, 16th; and steamed to Alexandria; remained on board for some days in the harbour; landed June 9th and marched to Ramleh.
July 1,	,,	8	1st Battalion embarked on board H.M.S. *Orontes*, and landed in Cyprus, 5th; marched from Limasol to the top of Mount Troödos in that island, 9th.
Aug. 24,	,,	8	1st Battalion from the camp on Mount Troödos, to Limasol, embarked in H.M.S. *Orontes*, 26th, and reaching Spithead, September 10th, and London, 11th, were quartered in Chelsea (5 companies) and St. George's Barracks (3 companies).
Sept. 16,	,,	8	2nd Battalion from Wellington Barracks to the Tower.

APPENDIX XVI.

1.

COLDSTREAM ROLL.*

758 Francis Miles Milman, *Ens.* 3 Dec. 1800; *Lieut.* 28 April 1804; *Capt.* 25 Dec. 1813; *Major*, 22 July 1830; *Lieut.-Col.* 10 Jan. 1837. To half-pay 8 Aug. 1837.

Sir John Lowther Johnstone, Bart., *Ens.* 17 Dec. 1800; *Lieut.* 1 Dec. 1804. Promoted Lieutenant in York Hussars 23 July 1802. Exchanged to the Coldstream from Captain in 21st Foot 1 Dec. 1804. Retired 26 March 1806.

760 Charles Maitland Christie, *Ens.* 5 March 1801; *Lieut.* 16 Aug. 1804. Retired 20 June 1810.

Frederick Morshead, *Ens.* 13 May 1801. Retired 23 May 1804.

George Heneage Finch, *Ens.* 14 May 1801; *Lieut.* 29 Dec. 1804. To half-pay of the Royal York Rangers 28 Feb. 1805.

Thomas Gore, *Ens.* 3 Sept. 1801; *Lieut.* 4 July 1805; *Capt.* 25 Dec. 1813. Promoted to Captain in 88th Foot 27 June 1805. Exchanged to Coldstream 4 July 1805. Retired 19 Feb. 1823.

Henry W. Vachell, *Ens.* 15 Oct. 1801; *Lieut.* 28 Nov. 1805. Died at Penzance 29 Aug. 1813.

765 Thomas Wood, *Ens.* 28 April 1802; *Lieut.* 27 March 1806. Retired 16 Jan. 1811.

William Henry Pringle (afterwards Sir William, K.C.B.), *Capt.* 17 Sept. 1802. Exchanged from Lieut.-Colonel of 4th Foot. Exchanged to Lieut.-Colonel of 1st Foot 1 Dec. 1808.

Richard Oriel Singer, *Ens.* 24 Dec. 1802, 3 Sept. 1803. To half-pay from date

---

* Continued from the 757th Name in Appendix No. 255 of Colonel MacKinnon's *Origin and Services of the Coldstream Guards* (ii. 504).

APPENDIX.

of appointment. Re-appointed from half-pay 3 Sept. 1803. Retired 4 Dec. 1803.

William Wharton Rawlins, *Ens.* 24 Feb. 1803. Retired 19 Dec. 1804.

Hon. George Pelham, *Ens.* 5 May 1803; *Lieut.* 17 April 1806. Retired 26 June 1810.

770 Herbert Taylor (afterwards Sir Herbert, G.C.H.), *Capt.* 25 May 1803. Appointed from Lieut.-Colonel on half-pay of 9th West India Regiment. Major-General 4 June 1813. Removed from the Coldstream 25 July 1814, being a General Officer.

Edward Jenkinson, *Ens.* 26 May 1803; *Lieut.* 29 May 1806. Died of wounds 24 Aug. 1809.

Matthew, Lord Aylmer (afterwards K.C.B.), *Capt.* 9 June 1803. Exchanged from Lieut.-Colonel on half-pay of 85th Foot. Major-General 4 June 1813. Removed from the Coldstream 25 July 1814, being a General Officer.

Charles Doyle, *Ens.* 28 July 1803. Promoted to Captain in 1st Garrison Battalion 13 March 1806.

Thomas Thoroton, *Ens.* 28 July 1803; *Lieut.* 6 Nov. 1806. Retired 6 March 1811.

775 Thomas Barrow, *Ens.* 12 Aug. 1803; *Lieut.* 25 Dec. 1806; *Capt.* 2 June 1814. To half-pay of Regiment 15 June 1830.

George Thomas Baldwin, *Ens.* 1 Oct. 1803; *Lieut.* 14 May 1807. Retired 9 March 1808.

Henry Frederick Cooke, *Lieut.* 5 Nov. 1803; *Capt.* 7 Nov. 1811. Exchanged from Captain in 28th Foot. Exchanged to Staff in North America 23 July 1812.

Sir Henry Sullivan, Bart., *Lieut.* 2 Dec. 1803; *Capt.* 24 Sept. 1812. Appointed from Captain in 66th Foot. Killed before Bayonne 14 April 1814.

William Clinton Wynyard, *Ens.* 3 Dec. 1803; 23 July 1807. Died in Sloane Street 27 April 1814.

780 William Fairfield, *Ens.* 5 Dec. 1803. Promoted to Captain in 60th Foot 25 July 1806.

George Bryan, *Ens.* 6 Dec. 1803; *Lieut.* 24 July 1807. Died of wounds received at Talavera 30 Sept. 1809.

Hon. William George Crofton, *Ens.* 7 Dec. 1803; *Lieut.* 10 March 1808. From Lieutenant in Royal Fusiliers. Killed 14 April 1814, before Bayonne.

Daniel MacKinnon, *Ens.* 16 Jan. 1804; *Lieut.* 25 March 1808; *Capt.* 25 July 1814; Major, 22 June 1826; *Lieut.-Col.* 22 July 1830. Died in London 22 June 1836.

Newton Dickinson, *Ens.* 3 Feb. 1804; *Lieut.* 12 May 1808. Retired 31 Jan. 1810.

785 Hon. John Walpole, *Ens.* 18 Feb. 1804; *Lieut.* 23 June 1808; *Capt.* 25 July 1814. Retired 27 April 1825.

Matthew Fortescue, *Ens.* 3 March 1804; *Lieut.* 4 Aug. 1808. Retired 18 July 1810.

Henry Dawkins, *Ens.* 10 March 1804; *Lieut.* 25 Aug. 1808; *Capt.* 25 July 1814. Exchanged to half-pay, unattached, 31 Aug. 1826.

Thomas Steele, *Ens.* 17 March 1804; *Lieut.* 1 June 1809; *Capt.* 18 Jan. 1820. Exchanged to half-pay, unattached, 1 June 1829.

William Lord Alvanley, *Ens.* 31 March 1804; *Lieut.* 22 Dec. 1808. Exchanged to Captain in 50th Foot 16 Aug. 1810.

790 Hon. Charles Vere Ferrars Townshend (afterwards Lord Charles), *Ens.* 28 April 1804. Resigned 6 Sept. 1804.

Edward Harvey, *Ens.* 24 May 1804; *Lieut.* 17 Aug. 1809. Killed 18 October 1812, before Burgos.

William Burroughs, *Ens.* 26 July 1804; *Lieut.* 28 Sept. 1809. Died of his wounds 26 April 1814.

Francis James, *Ens.* 7 Sept. 1804. Promoted to Captain in 81st Foot 3 March 1808.

George Bowles (afterwards Sir George, G.C.B.), *Ens.* 20 Dec. 1804; *Lieut.* 1 Feb. 1810; *Capt.* 27 May 1825; *Major*, 31 Dec. 1839. Retired upon half-pay, unattached, 30 May 1843.

795 John Boswell, *Ens.* 21 Dec. 1804; *Lieut.* 8 March 1810. Retired 12 Dec. 1810.

Hon. Francis Hay Drummond, *Ens.* 22 Dec. 1804; *Lieut.* 21 June 1810. Drowned 28 Oct. 1810, in Scotland.

Lord Alexander Gordon, *Lieut.* 28 Feb. 1805. From Captain in 5th Foot. Appointed Captain in 59th Foot, 29 May 1806.

Thomas Sowerby, *Ens.* 28 Feb. 1805; *Lieut.* 27 June 1810; *Capt.* 14 May 1817. Retired 16 April 1823.

Harry Parker, *Ens.* 18 April 1805. Killed 28 July 1809, at Talavera.

800 Edward Lascelles, *Ens.* 25 April 1805; *Lieut.* 28 June 1810. Died 30 Sept. 1815, at Barrington Park, Gloucestershire.

Hon. Edward Boscawen (afterwards Earl of Falmouth), *Ens.* 1 May 1805. Resigned 16 Nov. 1808.

Patrick Sandilands, *Ens.* 2 May 1805; *Lieut.* 19 July 1810. Promoted to a company in Third Guards 30 Aug. 1821.

William Henley Raikes, *Lieut.* 13 June 1805; *Capt.* 3 June 1813; *Major*, 27 May 1825. Exchanged from Captain in 66th Foot. Retired 21 June 1826.

His Royal Highness Adolphus Frederick, Duke of Cambridge, K.G., *Col.* 5 Sept. 1805. Died 8 July 1850.

805 Richard Greville, *Ens.* 12 Sept. 1805. Retired 7 May 1806.

John Fremantle, C.B., *Ens.* 17 Oct. 1805; *Lieut.* 2 Aug. 1810; *Capt.* 1 Aug. 1822; *Major* 23 June 1836; *Lieut.-Col.* 8 Aug. 1837. Retired on half-pay 31 Dec. 1839.

John Prince, *Ens.* 31 Oct. 1805; *Lieut.* 29 Oct. 1810. Died 2 Jan. 1818 in Hanover Street, London.

George Frederick Augustus, Lord Kilcoursie, *Ens.* 6 Feb. 1806; *Lieut.* 13 Dec. 1810. Retired 24 March 1813.

James Vigors Harvey, *Ens.* 10 April 1806; *Lieut.* 17 Jan. 1811. From Lieutenant in 4th Foot. Exchanged to half-pay of the Regiment 6 May 1819.

810 Charles Gregory, *Ens.* 1 May 1806. Promoted to Captain in Second Ceylon Regiment 4 Aug. 1808.

Peter Gaussen, *Ens.* 2 May 1806. Died 8 Oct. 1808, at Dartford.

William Lovelace Walton, *Ens.* 8 May 1806; *Lieut.* 7 March 1811; *Capt.* 20 Feb. 1823; *Major*, 10 Jan. 1837; *Lieut.-Col.* 31 Dec. 1839. To half-pay 8 May 1846.

William Lockwood, *Ens.* 21 Aug. 1806; *Lieut.* 5 Sept. 1811. Retired 7 Oct. 1812.

Edward Noel Long, *Ens.* 4 Dec. 1806. Drowned 9 March 1809, on passage to Portugal.

815 Hon. John Ashburnham, *Ens.* 1 Jan. 1807. From Lieutenant in the Royal Fusiliers. Drowned at sea, Dec. 1809.

Hon. John Wingfield, *Ens.* 16 April 1807; Died at Coimbra 4 May 1811.

Paulet St. John Mildmay, *Ens.* 14 May 1807; *Lieut.* 3 Oct. 1811. Gentleman Cadet from R.M.C. Retired April 22, 1812.

Alexander Wedderburn, *Ens.* 17 Sept. 1807; *Lieut.* 7 Nov. 1811; *Capt.* 17 April 1823. Retired 27 July 1838.

Charles White, *Ens.* 7 April 1808; *Lieut.* 30 Jan. 1812. Retired 15 Aug. 1821.

820 Thomas Bligh, *Ens.* 21 April 1808; *Lieut.* 13 Feb. 1812. Retired 14 May 1823.

APPENDIX. 461

Charles Augustus Shawe, *Ens.* 26 May 1808; *Lieut.* 23 April 1812; *Capt.* 28 April 1825; *Major*, 8 Aug. 1837; *Lieut.-Col.* 8 May 1846. Removed 9 Nov. 1846 on promotion to Major-General.

Lord William Fitzgerald, *Ens.* 4 Aug. 1808. Resigned 7 Sept. 1808.

George Henry Macartney Greville, *Ens.* 8 Sept. 1808; *Lieut.* 24 Sept. 1812. From Ensign in 9th Foot. Exchanged to Captain in the Royal Fusiliers 23rd Sept. 1813.

Michael Watts, *Ens.* 20 Oct. 1808. Killed 5 March 1811, at Barrosa.

825 Charles Antonio Fredinand Bentinck, *Ens.* 16 Nov. 1808; *Lieut.* 24 Sept. 1812; *Capt.* 27 May 1825; *Major*, 30 May, 1843; *Lieut.-Col.* 9 Nov. 1846. Gentleman Cadet from R.M.C. Retired on half-pay 25th April 1848.

John Talbot, *Ens.* 17 Nov. 1808; *Lieut.* 26 Nov. 1812. Retired 24 Oct. 1821.

Frederick William Buller, *Capt.* 1 Dec. 1808. Exchanged from Lieut-Colonel of the 1st Foot. Major-General June 4, 1813. Removed from the Coldstream 25 July 1814, being a General Officer.

George Harvey Percival, *Ens.* 16 March 1809; *Lieut.* 25 March 1813. Gentleman Cadet from R.M.C. Died 11 Nov. 1815.

William Stothert, *Ens.* 23 March 1809; *Lieut.* 2 June 1813. Retired 13 Dec. 1815.

830 Walter George Baynes, *Ens.* 6 April 1809; *Lieut.* 1 June 1813. Retired 4 Oct. 1820.

John Stepney Cowell (afterwards Sir John Stepney Cowell-Stepney, Bart.), *Ens.* 18 May 1809; *Lieut.* 9 Sept. 1813; *Capt.* 15 June 1830. Retired 21 June 1832.

Wentworth Noel Burgess, *Ens.* 1 June 1809. From Ensign in 52nd Foot. Killed before Burgos 19 October 1812.

William Ainslie, *Ens.* 25 Aug. 1809. Died in Dover Street, London, 24 March 1810.

John Mills, *Ens.* 21 Dec. 1809; *Capt.* 10 Jan. 1814. Resigned 31 Aug. 1814.

835 James Bradshaw, *Ens.* 4 Jan. 1810. Resigned 16 Dec. 1812.

Francis Love Beckford, *Ens.* 25 Jan. 1810. Resigned 29 Dec. 1813.

Samuel Bates Ferris, *Ens.* 1 March 1810. Retired 12 June 1811.

John Charles Buckeridge, *Ens.* 29 March 1810. Killed before Burgos 7 Oct. 1812.

John Lucie Blackman, *Ens.* 5 April 1810; *Lieut.* 10 Jan. 1814. Killed at Waterloo. 18 June 1815.

840 William Grimstead, *Ens.* 21 June 1810; *Lieut.* 25 Dec. 1813. Gentleman Cadet from R.M.C. Exchanged to Captain in Royal York Rangers 28 May 1818.

Beaumont Hotham (afterwards Lord Hotham), *Ens.* 27 June 1810; *Lieut.* 25 Dec. 1813, 10 Nov. 1825. Gentleman Cadet from R.M.C. Exchanged to half-pay of the Regiment 14 Oct. 1819, and from ditto 10 Nov. 1825. Promoted to Lieut.-Colonel on half-pay, unattached, 24 December 1825.

Hon. John Rous (afterwards Earl of Stradbroke), *Ens.* 28 June 1810; *Lieut.* 4 May 1814. Exchanged to Captain in 93rd Foot. 6 Nov. 1817.

Windham Anstruther (afterwards Sir W. Carmichael-Anstruther, Bart.), *Ens.* 5 July 1810; *Lieut.* 17 March 1814. Retired 26 Feb. 1817.

Charles Shirley, *Ens.* 19 July 1810; *Lieut.* 5 May 1814. Exchanged to half-pay of the Regiment, 4 Nov. 1819.

845 Charles Mackenzie Fraser, *Lieut.* 16 Aug. 1810. Exchanged from 50th Foot. Retired 16 March 1814.

John Harcourt Powell, *Ens.* 20 Sept. 1810. Retired 4 March 1812.

John Drummond, *Ens.* 22 Nov. 1810; *Lieut.* 26 May 1814; *Capt.* 22 June 1826. Exchanged to half-pay, unattached, 13 April 1832.

Hon. Robert Moore, *Ens.* 21 March 1811 ; *Lieut.* 2 June 1814 ; *Capt.* 1 April 1824. To half-pay of the Regiment from date of promotion to Captain.

Charles Andrew Girardot, *Ens.* 4 April 1811 ; *Lieut.* 1 Sept. 1814 ; *Capt.* 27 July 1826. Promoted to Lieut.-Colonel half-pay, unattached, 11 July 1826. Exchanged from ditto 27 July following. Retired 21 Sept. 1830.

850 Thomas Chaplin, *Ens.* 18 April 1811 ; *Lieut.* 6 Oct. 1814 ; *Capt.* 31 Aug. 1826 ; *Major*, 8 May 1846 ; *Lieut.-Col.* 25 April 1848. Gentleman Cadet from R.M.C. Promoted to Lieut.-Colonel half-pay, unattached, 15 Aug. 1826. Exchanged from ditto 31 Aug. following. Retired 22 Aug. 1851.

Edward Clifton, *Ens.* 25 April 1811 ; *Lieut.* 6 July 1815. Retired 27 Oct. 1819.

Henry Salwey, *Ens.* 13 June 1811 ; *Lieut.* 20 July 1815 ; *Capt.* 15 Feb. 1827. Promoted to Lieut.-Colonel half-pay, unattached, 30 Dec. 1826. Exchanged from ditto 15 Feb. following. Exchanged to ditto 6 Aug. 1829.

George Gould Morgan, *Ens.* 4 July 1811 ; *Lieut.* 26 Oct. 1815. Exchanged to half-pay of the Regiment 25 Feb. 1819.

James Macdonell, C.B. (afterwards Sir James, K.C.B.), *Capt.* 8 Aug. 1811 ; *Major*, 25 July 1821 ; *Lieut.-Col.* 27 May 1825. Exchanged from Lieut.-Colonel of Second Garrison Battalion. Major-General 22 July 1830.

855 Frederick Vachell, *Ens.* 19 Sept. 1811. From Ensign in 52nd Foot. Died of his wounds 13 May 1814.

Thomas Slingsby Duncombe, *Ens.* 17 Oct. 1811 ; *Lieut.* 23 Nov. 1815. Resigned 17 Nov. 1819.

Francis Eyre, *Ens.* 26 Dec. 1811. Retired 31 May 1815.

Henry Shirley, *Ens.* 30 Jan. 1812. Gentleman Cadet from R.M.C. Retired 5 May 1813.

Hon. James Forbes, *Ens.* 13 Feb. 1812 ; *Lieut.* 14 Dec. 1815 ; *Capt.* 22 July 1830. Cadet from R.M.C. Died at Florence 25 Feb. 1835.

860 William Pitt, *Ens.* 5 March 1812. Died of his wounds 24 April 1814.

Thomas Powys, *Ens.* 30 April 1812 ; *Lieut.* 22 Jan. 1818, 4 Nov. 1819. To half-pay of the Regiment from 25 Dec. 1818. Exchanged from ditto 4 Nov. 1819. Exchanged to half-pay, unattached, 30 April 1829.

Henry Loftus, *Capt.* 23 July 1812. Exchanged from the "Staff in North America." Died 11 July 1823, at Stifkey, Norfolk.

Henry Gooch, *Ens.* 23 July 1812 ; *Lieut.* 28 Oct. 1819 ; *Capt.* 26 Nov. 1832. Gentleman Cadet from R.M.C. Retired 11 June 1841.

Augustus Cuyler, *Ens.* 15 Oct. 1812 ; *Lieut.* 27 Feb. 1817. From Ensign in 69th Foot. Promoted to Lieut.-Colonel half-pay, unattached, 10 June 1826.

865 Mark Beaufoy, *Ens.* 12 Nov. 1812 ; *Lieut.* 15 May 1817, 14 Oct. 1819. To half-pay of the Regiment from 25 Dec. 1818. Exchanged from ditto 14 Oct. 1819. Retired 9 Feb. 1825.

William Kortright, *Ens.* 26 Nov. 1812 ; *Lieut.* 6 Nov. 1817, 25 Feb. 1819. From Ensign in 68th Foot. Promoted to Captain in 93rd Foot 11 Sept. 1817, and exchanged from ditto 6 Nov. following. To half-pay of the Regiment from 25 Dec. 1818; exchanged from ditto 25 Feb. 1819. Exchanged to ditto 10 Nov. 1825.

Henry Armytage, *Ens.* 27 Nov. 1812 ; *Lieut.* 28 May 1818, 6 May 1819 ; *Capt.* 4 Dec. 1828. Promoted to Captain in the Royal York Rangers 5 March 1818, and exchanged from ditto 28 May following. To half-pay of the Regiment 25 Dec. 1818. Exchanged from ditto 6 May 1819. Promoted to Lieut.-Colonel half-pay, unattached, 21 Nov. 1828. Exchanged from ditto 4 Dec. following. Exchanged on half-pay of the 22nd Light Dragoons, 24 Jan. 1840.

Hon. William Rufus Rous, *Ens.* 17 Dec. 1812 ; *Lieut.* 18 Nov. 1819. Cadet from R.M.C. Exchanged to Captain in 55th Foot, 19 Feb. 1823.

APPENDIX.

Henry John William Bentinck (afterwards Sir Henry, K.C.B.), *Ens.* 25 March 1813; *Lieut.* 18 Jan. 1820; *Capt.* 16 May 1829; *Major*, 9 Nov. 1846; *Lieut.-Col.* 22 Aug. 1851. Major-General 20 June 1854.

870 Francis Manby Shawe, *Ens.* 6 May 1813; *Lieut.* 5 Oct. 1820. Exchanged to half-pay, unattached, 13 April 1826.

Humphrey St. John Mildmay, *Ens.* 9 Sept. 1813; *Lieut.* 16 Aug. 1821. Exchanged to Captain in 35th Foot, 25 Dec. 1823.

Edward Sumner, *Lieut.* 23 Sept. 1813. Exchanged from Captain in the Royal Fusiliers. Died of his wounds 26 June 1815.

Frederick Thomas Buller, *Ens.* 30 Dec. 1813; *Lieut.* 6 Sept. 1821; *Capt.* 4 June 1829. Exchanged to Lieut.-Colonel half-pay, unattached, 3 Feb. 1832.

Henry Frederick Griffiths, *Ens.* 25 Jan. 1814. From the Stafford Militia. Died in the Tower of London 19 Jan. 1821.

875 James Frederick Buller, *Ens.* 26 Jan. 1814. Died 4 Jan. 1816, in Paris.

Hon. John Montagu, *Ens.* 27 Jan. 1814; *Lieut.* 25 Oct. 1821; *Capt.* 13 Aug. 1829. Retired 26 Jan. 1832.

George Richard Buckley, *Ens.* 17 Feb. 1814. Died 15 Aug. 1815, in Paris.

James Hervey, *Ens.* 15 March 1814. Exchanged to half-pay of the Regiment 15 April 1819.

Henry Vane, *Ens.* 16 March 1814; *Lieut.* 1 Aug. 1822. Died at Sidmouth 9 Aug. 1829.

880 Francis James Douglas, *Ens.* 17 March 1814. Died 29 May 1821.

Robert Bowen, *Ens.* 24 March 1814; *Lieut.* 19 Feb. 1823; *Capt.* 27 Jan. 1832. Promoted to Captain in 55th Foot, 30 Jan. 1823. Exchanged from ditto 19 Feb. following. Retired 15 Nov. 1833.

Frederick FitzClarence (afterwards Lord Frederick), *Ens.* 12 May 1814. Promoted to Captain in the Cape Corps of Infantry, 23 Feb. 1820.

Alexander Gordon, *Ens.* 19 May 1814. Killed at Cambrai 1 April 1818, in a duel with a French Officer.

Hon. Walter Forbes (afterwards Lord Forbes), *Ens.* 2 June 1814; *Lieut.* 20 Feb. 1823. Retired 20 April 1825.

885 Hon. Alexander Abercromby, C.B., *Capt.* 25 July 1814. From Lieut.-Colonel of the 28th Foot. To half-pay of the Regiment 25 Oct. 1821.

Sir Colin Campbell, K.C.B., *Capt.* 25 July 1814. From Major of 63rd Foot. Major-General 27 May 1825.

Sir Robert Arbuthnot, K.C.B., *Capt.* 25 July 1814. From the Portuguese Service. Exchanged to Lieut.-Colonel half-pay, unattached, 27 July 1826.

Hon. Hercules Robert Pakenham, C.B. (afterwards Sir H., K.C.B.), *Capt.* 25 July 1814. From Lieut.-Colonel of 26th Foot. Exchanged to Lieut.-Colonel half-pay, unattached, 15 May 1817.

Sir William Maynard Gomm, K.C.B. (afterwards G.C.B.), *Capt.* 25 July 1814; *Major*, 16 May 1829; *Lieut.-Col.* 23 June 1836; *Colonel*, 15 Aug. 1863. From Major of the 9th Foot. Major-General 10 Jan. 1837. Died 15 March 1875.

890 Henry Wyndham, *Capt.* 25 July 1814. From Lieut.-Colonel of Dillon's Regiment. Exchanged to Lieut.-Colonel of the 19th Dragoons, 11 July 1816.

Charles Short, *Ens.* 13 Oct. 1814; *Lieut.* 17 April 1823; *Capt.* 21 Sept. 1830. Gentleman Cadet from R.M.C. Retired 24 Feb. 1837.

William Leedes Serjeantson, *Ens.* 17 Nov. 1814; *Lieut.* 15 May 1823. Exchanged to Captain half-pay, unattached, 9 Dec. 1824.

Richard Beamish, *Ens.* 22 Dec. 1814. Gentleman Cadet from R.M.C. Placed on half-pay of the Regiment from 25 Dec. 1818.

Joseph Henry, Lord Wallscourt, *Ens.* 5 Jan. 1815. Died 11 Oct. 1816.

APPENDIX.

895 Jasper Taylor Hall, *Ens.* 1 June 1815, 15 April 1819; *Lieut.* 25 Dec. 1823. To half-pay of the Regiment 25 Dec. 1818. Exchanged from ditto 15 April 1819. Promoted to Captain in 35th Foot 13 Nov. 1823, and exchanged from ditto 25 Dec. following. Promoted to Major half-pay, unattached, 1 Aug. 1826.

John Simon Jenkinson, *Ens.* 6 July 1815, 28 Oct. 1819. To half-pay of the Regiment 25 Dec. 1818. Re-appointed from ditto 28 Oct. 1819. Retired 16 Jan. 1822.

William Henry Cornwall, *Ens.* 10 Aug. 1815, 5 Oct. 1820; *Lieut.* 9 Dec. 1824; *Capt.* 10 Feb. 1832. To half-pay of the Regiment 25 Dec. 1818. Re-appointed from ditto 5 Oct. 1820. Promoted to Captain half-pay, unattached, 6 Nov. 1824, and exchanged from ditto 9 Dec. following. To half-pay 26 May 1848.

Henry Murray, *Ens.* 21 Sept. 1815, 31 May 1821; *Lieut.* 21 April 1825. From Page of Honour to the Prince Regent. To half-pay of the Regiment 25 Dec. 1818. Re-appointed from ditto 31 May 1821. Exchanged to Captain half-pay, unattached, 5 Oct. 1826.

Edward John Duke, *Ens.* 26 Oct. 1815. Exchanged to 46th Foot 20 Aug. 1818.

900 Joseph Sidney Tharp, *Ens.* 23 Nov. 1815. To half-pay of the Regiment 25 Dec. 1818.

Hon. Percy Ashburnham, *Ens.* 28 Dec. 1815. Cadet from R.M.C. On half-pay of the Regiment 25 Dec. 1818.

Charles Loftus, *Ens.* 25 Jan. 1816. To half-pay of the Regiment 25 Dec. 1818.

Hon. George Charles Grantley Berkeley, *Ens.* 7 Nov. 1816, 16 Aug. 1821. To half-pay of the Regiment 25 Dec. 1818. Re-appointed from ditto 16 Aug. 1821. Exchanged to 61st Foot 19 June 1823.

Hon. Arthur Charles Legge, 27 Feb. 1817. From Ensign in 28th Foot. To half-pay of the Regiment 25 Dec. 1818.

905 John Waters, C.B., *Capt.* 15 May 1817. From half-pay Portuguese Service. Exchanged to Lieut.-Colonel half-pay, unattached, 15 Feb. 1827.

Thomas Kingscote, *Ens.* 15 May 1817. To half-pay of the Regiment 25 Dec. 1818.

Brinckman Broadhead, *Ens.* 17 Sept. 1817, 13 Sept. 1821; *Lieut.* 28 April 1825; *Capt.* 20 April 1832. To half-pay of the Regiment 25 Dec. 1818. Re-appointed from ditto 13 Sept. 1821. Retired 11 June 1847.

John Blenkinsopp Coulson, *Ens.* 22 Jan. 1818. To half-pay of the Regiment 25 Dec. 1818.

Charles Ricketts, *Ens.* 5 March 1818. To half-pay of the Regiment 25 Dec. 1818.

910 John Arthur Douglas Bloomfield (afterwards Lord Bloomfield), *Ens.* 9 April 1818. From Page of Honour to the Prince Regent. To half-pay of the Regiment 25 Dec. 1818.

Thomas Butler, *Ens.* 20 Aug. 1818. Exchanged from Ensign in the 46th Foot. To half-pay of the Regiment 25 Dec. 1818.

Hon. Henry Dundas (afterwards Viscount Melville, G.C.B.), *Ens.* 18 Nov. 1819; *Lieut.* 1 April 1824. Promoted to Major, unattached, 11 July 1826.

Frederick William Culling Smith, *Ens.* 18 Jan. 1820. From Cornet in 2nd Dragoon Guards. Promoted to Captain in the Royal Horse Guards 2 Jan. 1823.

Hon. William Thomas Graves (afterwards Lord Graves), *Ens.* 8 June 1820; *Lieut.* 10 Feb. 1825. From Page of Honour to the King. Retired 15 March 1830.

915 Arthur Richard Wellesley, *Ens.* 25 Jan. 1821. From Page of Honour to the King. Appointed Cornet in the Royal Horse Guards, 20 Dec. 1821.

Charles Murray Hay, *Ens.* 1 Nov. 1821; *Lieut.* 24 Dec. 1825; *Capt.* 22 June 1832; *Major,* 25 April 1848. From Ensign in 43rd Foot. Major-General 20 June 1854.

APPENDIX.

William Harcourt, *Ens.* 20 Dec. 1821. From Cornet in the 5th Dragoon Guards. Promoted to Captain half-pay, unattached, 19 May 1825.

George Bentinck, *Ens.* 17 Jan. 1822; *Lieut.* 13 April 1826. Promoted to Captain half-pay, unattached, 8 April 1826. Exchanged from ditto 13 April following. Exchanged to ditto 31 Dec. 1830.

William Brook Northey, *Ens.* 1 Aug. 1822; *Lieut.* 20 April 1826. To half-pay of the Regiment as Lieutenant and Captain from 25 May 1828.

920 John Dawson Rawdon, *Ens.* 29 Jan. 1823; *Lieut.* 10 June 1826; *Capt.* 15 Nov. 1833. From Ensign in 79th Foot. To half-pay, unattached, 13 May, 1842.

Hon. Thomas Ashburnham, *Ens.* 30 Jan. 1823; *Lieut.* 22 June 1826; *Capt.* 27 March 1835. Exchanged to 62nd Foot 7 Jan. 1842.

Hon. Henry St. Clair Erskine, *Ens.* 20 Feb. 1823; *Lieut.* 11 July 1826. From Ensign in 85th Foot. Died 24 May 1829, in London.

William John Codrington (afterwards Sir William, G.C.B.), *Ens.* 24 April 1823; *Lieut.* 20 July 1826; *Capt.* 8 July 1836; *Colonel,* 16 March 1875. From Ensign in 43rd Foot. Major-General 20 June 1854. Died 6 Aug. 1884.

Ely Duodecimus Wigram, *Ens.* 29 May 1823; *Lieut.* 1 Aug. 1826; *Capt.* 13 Jan. 1837. To half-pay, unattached, 10 Dec. 1847.

925 St. John Dent, *Ens.* 19 June 1823; *Lieut.* 15 Aug. 1826. From Ensign in 61st Foot. Retired 2 Aug. 1830.

Hon. Henry Sutton Fane, *Ens.* 27 Nov. 1823. From Ensign in the 93rd Foot. Promoted to Captain, half-pay, unattached, 22 Oct. 1825.

Hon. James Hope (afterwards Hope-Wallace), *Ens.* 8 April 1824; *Lieut.* 30 Dec. 1826; *Capt.* 8 Aug. 1837. Retired 29 March 1844.

Willoughby Cotton, *Ens.* 6 Nov. 1824; *Lieut.* 21 Nov. 1828. From Ensign in 62nd Foot. To the 70th Foot 26 July 1833.

Hon. Arthur Upton, *Ens.* 10 Feb. 1825; *Lieut.* 16 May 1829; *Capt.* 31 Dec. 1839; *Major,* 22 Aug. 1851; *Lieut.-Col.* 20 June 1854. Major-General 20 Feb. 1855.

930 Frederick Paget, *Ens.* 24 Feb. 1825; *Lieut.* 4 June 1829; *Capt.* 24 Jan. 1840. From Ensign in the 36th Foot. (Late Page of Honour to the King.) Retired 13 Dec. 1853.

Boyd Pollen Manningham, *Ens.* 21 April 1825. Retired 20 Sept. 1826.

Hon. Edward Bootle Wilbraham, *Ens.* 28 April 1825; *Lieut.* 13 Aug. 1829; *Capt.* 11 June 1841. Retired on half-pay 7 Aug. 1846.

Lord Montagu William Graham, *Ens.* 19 May 1825; *Lieut.* 16 March 1830. Retired 1 May 1840.

George FitzClarence (afterwards Earl of Munster), *Capt.* 6 July 1825. From Lieut.-Colonel on half-pay, unattached. Exchanged to ditto 4 Dec. 1828.

935 Francis Russell, *Capt.* 7 July 1825. From Captain and Brevet Lieut.-Colonel on half-pay of the 12th Dragoons. Died 24 Nov. 1832, in London.

Hon. Charles Howard, *Ens.* 22 Oct. 1825. From Ensign in the 70th Foot. Retired 30 Sept. 1829.

John Henry Pringle, *Ens.* 24 Dec. 1825; *Lieut.* 15 June 1830; *Capt.* 13 May 1842. To half-pay 29 Dec. 1846.

John Christie Clitherow, *Ens.* 8 April 1826; *Lieut.* 22 July 1830; *Capt.* 30 May 1843. From 2nd Lieutenant in the Rifle Brigade. Retired 3 March 1854.

Gordon Drummond, *Ens.* 10 June 1826; *Lieut.* 3 Aug. 1830; *Capt.* 29 March 1844; *Major,* 20 June 1854. Died 17 November 1856.

940 Lord Frederick Paulet, C.B., *Ens.* 11 June 1826; *Lieut.* 21 Sept. 1830; *Capt.* 8 May 1846; *Major,* 20 Feb. 1855; *Lieut.-Col.* 26 Oct. 1858. From Page of Honour to the King. Major-General 13 Dec. 1860.

APPENDIX.

Christopher Wilmot Horton, *Ens.* 29 June 1826; *Lieut.* 27 Jan. 1832. Retired 15 Oct. 1841.

Hugh Forbes, *Ens.* 11 July 1826. Promoted to Captain half-pay, unattached, 24 May 1831.

John Forbes, *Ens.* 1 Aug. 1826; *Lieut.* 10 Feb. 1832; *Capt.* 7 Aug. 1846. From Ensign in 53rd Foot. Retired 27 April 1849.

Montagu George Burgoyne, *Ens.* 2 Aug. 1826; *Lieut.* 20 April 1832. Retired 31 May 1833.

945 Edward Isaac Hobhouse, *Ens.* 15 Aug. 1826; *Lieut.* 22 June 1832. Retired 1 June 1833.

Robert Vansittart, *Ens.* 21 Sept. 1826; *Lieut.* 26 Nov. 1832; *Capt.* 9 Nov. 1846. Retired 23 June 1848.

William Stewart (afterwards Stewart-Balfour), *Lieut.* 5 Oct. 1826; *Capt.* 24 Feb. 1837. Exchanged from half-pay, unattached. To half-pay 25 Feb. 1848.

Charles Ash Windham, *Ens.* 30 Dec. 1826; *Lieut.* 31 May 1833; *Capt.* 29 Dec. 1846. Gentleman Cadet from R.M.C. Retired on half-pay 22 June 1849.

Charles Philip Wilbraham (afterwards Rev. C.), *Ens.* 21 Nov. 1828; *Lieut.* 1 June 1833. Retired 11 Sept. 1840.

950 George Knox, *Lieut.* 30 April 1829; *Capt.* 27 July 1838. Exchanged from Captain on half-pay, unattached. Retired 29 Oct. 1847.

John Frederick Gore Langton, *Ens.* 16 May 1829; *Lieut.* 15 Nov. 1833. Died 27 Oct. 1834 at Newton Park, near Bath.

James Loftus Elrington, *Ens.* 4 June 1829; *Lieut.* 5 Dec. 1834; *Capt.* 11 June, 1847. Retired 7 April 1848.

Henry Daniell, *Ens.* 13 Aug. 1829; *Lieut.* 27 March 1835; *Capt.* 29 Oct. 1847. Retired 2 May 1856.

Charles Atticus Monck, *Ens.* 1 Oct. 1829. Retired 24 April 1835.

955 Frederick Halkett, *Ens.* 11 June 1830; *Lieut.* 8 July 1836. Died in Canada 25 Oct. 1840.

Hastings Dent, 15 June 1830; *Lieut.* 13 Jan. 1837. Retired 5 July 1839.

Charles Whitley Deans Dundas, *Ens.* 3 Aug. 1830; *Lieut.* 24 Feb. 1837. From Ensign in 42nd Foot. Retired 21 April 1837.

Richard Samuel Hulse, *Ens.* 21 Sept. 1830; *Lieut.* 21 April 1837. Retired 8 Aug. 1845.

Edward Harvey, *Lieut.* 31 Dec. 1830. Exchanged from Captain on half-pay unattached. To half-pay unattached 21 June 1833.

960 Duncan Macdonald Chisholm, *Ens.* 24 May 1831; *Lieut.* 7 Aug. 1837. Retired 25 Dec. 1838.

Stephen Rowley Conroy, *Ens.* 27 Jan. 1832; *Lieut.* 8 Aug. 1837. Retired 5 Feb. 1841.

Hon. Frederick William Child Villiers, *Ens.* 10 Feb. 1832; *Lieut.* 27 July 1838. Exchanged to 73rd Regiment Foot 24 May 1844.

Henry Brand (afterwards Viscount Hampden), *Ens.* 20 April 1832; *Lieut.* 25 Dec. 1838. Retired 6 Sept. 1844.

George Herbert, *Ens.* 22 June 1832. Died 1838.

965 James Du Pré Viscount Alexander (afterwards Earl of Caledon), *Ens.* 31 May 1833; *Lieut.* 5 July 1839. Retired 27 March 1846.

Hon. Richard William Lambart, *Ens.* 1 June 1833. Retired 20 July 1838.

Wilbraham Spencer Tollemache, *Lieut.* 21 June 1833. Retired 19 July 1839.

George B. Mathew, *Lieut.* 26 July 1833. Exchanged to 85th Regiment 17 June 1836.

George John Johnson, *Ens.* 15 Nov. 1833; *Lieut.* 19 July 1839. Exchanged to 11th Light Dragoons 7 July 1848.

APPENDIX.

970 William Samuel Newton, *Ens.* 5 Dec. 1834; *Lieut.* 31 Dec. 1839; *Capt.* 25 Feb. 1848; *Major*, 18 Nov. 1856; *Lieut.-Col.* 13 Dec. 1860. Retired on half-pay 2 July 1861.

Hon. Charles Grimston, *Ens.* 6 Dec. 1834; *Lieut.* 24 Jan. 1840. Retired 1847.

George V. Mundy, *Ens.* 27 Feb. 1835; *Lieut.* 1 May 1840. Exchanged to 33rd Regiment 10 Sept. 1841.

Peter James Bathurst, *Ens.* 27 March 1835; *Lieut.* 11 Sept. 1840. From 75th Foot. Exchanged to 11th Light Dragoons 13 April 1846.

Egerton Charles William Miles Milman, *Ens.* 24 April 1835; *Lieut.* 5 Feb. 1841; *Capt.* 7 April 1848. Exchanged to 37th Foot 30 Nov. 1849.

975 Hon. Robert Boyle, *Lieut.* 17 June 1836; *Capt.* 10 Dec. 1847. From 85th Regiment. Died on board ship, off Varna, 4 Sept. 1854.

Hon. Louis Hope, *Ens.* 8 July 1836; *Lieut.* 11 June 1841. Retired 27 Jan. 1843.

Spencer Perceval, *Ens.* 13 Jan. 1837; *Lieut.* 15 Oct. 1841; *Capt.* 23 June 1848; *Major*, 26 Oct. 1858; *Lieut.-Col.* 2 July 1861. To Major-General 9 Nov. 1862.

Hon. Adolphus Edward Paget Graves, *Ens.* 3 Feb. 1837; *Lieut.* 13 May 1842. Exchanged to 59th Regiment of Foot 11 Aug. 1843.

Matthew Edward Tierney (afterwards Sir M. Bart.), *Ens.* 10 March 1837; *Lieut.* 27 Jan. 1843; *Capt.* 27 April 1849. Retired 3 Nov. 1854.

980 William Capel Clayton, *Ens.* 21 April 1837. Retired 1 June 1841.

Hon. Thomas Vesey Dawson, *Ens.* 11 Aug. 1837; *Lieut.* 30 May 1843; *Capt.* 22 Aug. 1851. Killed in action 5 Nov. 1854, at Inkerman.

Thomas Montagu Steele (afterwards Right Hon. Sir Thomas, G.C.B.), *Ens.* 20 July 1838; *Lieut.* 29 March 1844; *Capt.* 31 Oct. 1851; *Major*, 13 Dec. 1860; *Lieut.-Col.* 9 Nov. 1862; *Colonel*, 7 Aug. 1884. From 64th Regiment. To half-pay 24 Nov. 1863. Died 25 Feb. 1890.

John Agmondisham Vesey Kirkland, *Ens.* 27 July 1838; *Lieut.* 6 Sept. 1844. From Rifle Brigade. Exchanged to 20th Foot 12 June 1846.

Adolphus Frederick Alexander Woodford, *Ens.* 25 Dec. 1838. Retired 23 April 1841.

985 Charles Henry Ellice (afterwards Sir Charles, K.C.B.), *Ens.* 10 May 1839; *Lieut.* 8 Aug. 1845. Exchanged to 82nd Regiment 20 March 1846.

James Richard Wigram, *Ens.* 5 July 1839; *Lieut.* 27 March 1846. Retired 30 July 1847.

John Wingfield S. Fraser, *Ens.* 19 July 1839. Exchanged to 60th Foot 21 Jan. 1842.

Charles Henry White, *Ens.* 31 Dec. 1839; *Lieut.* 8 May 1846. From 30th Foot. To 14th Regiment Foot 4 May 1849.

Charles Lygon Cocks, *Ens.* 24 Jan. 1840; *Lieut.* 7 Aug. 1846; *Capt.* 20 June 1854. From 54th Foot. Retired 17 April 1860.

990 Poulett George Henry Somerset, *Ens.* 1 May 1840; *Lieut.* 28 Dec. 1846; *Capt.* 3 March 1854. From 33rd Foot. Retired 21 Dec. 1855.

George John Whyte-Melville, *Ens.* 11 Sept. 1840; *Lieut.* 29 Dec. 1846. From 93rd Foot. Retired 28 Jan. 1848.

James Charles Murray Cowell, *Ens.* 25 Sept. 1840; *Lieut.* 11 June 1847; *Capt.* 20 June 1854. Killed in action 5 Nov. 1854, at Inkerman.

William Verner (afterwards Sir William, Bart.), *Ens.* 5 Feb. 1841. Retired 18 Sept. 1846.

James Halkett, *Ens.* 23 April 1841; *Lieut.* 1 July 1847; *Capt.* 20 June 1854. From 29th Foot. Retired 9 March 1860.

995 Sir John Edward Harington, Bart., *Ens.* 1 June 1841; *Lieut.* 2 July 1847. Exchanged to 48th Regiment 10 Nov. 1848.

Dudley Wilmot Carleton (afterwards Lord Dorchester), *Ens.* 11 June 1841; *Lieut.*

13 July 1847; *Capt.* 14 July 1854; *Major*, 9 Nov. 1862; *Lieut.-Col.* 22 May 1866. From 60th Foot. Retired on half-pay 2 Sept. 1868.

George Augustus Vernon, *Lieut.* 10 Sept. 1841; *Capt.* 25 April 1848. From 33rd Foot. Retired 27 May 1853.

Hon. Augustus Charles L. FitzRoy (afterwards Duke of Grafton, K.G., C.B.), *Ens.* 15 Oct. 1841; *Lieut.* 30 July 1847; *Capt.* 14 July 1854. From 60th Foot. To half-pay, unattached, 23 Nov. 1855.

Hon. George Frederick Upton (afterwards Viscount Templetown, G.C.B.), *Capt.* 7 Jan. 1842; *Major*, 20 June 1854; *Lieut.-Col.* 20 Feb. 1855. From 62nd Foot. To Major-General 26 Oct. 1858.

1000 Charles S. Burdett, *Ens.* 21 Jan. 1842; *Lieut.* 29 Oct. 1847; *Capt.* 22 Aug. 1854. From 60th Foot. Retired 20 Dec. 1859.

Francis William Newdigate, *Ens.* 13 May 1842; *Lieut.* 10 Dec. 1847; *Capt.* 4 Sept. 1854. From 66th Foot. Retired 29 Nov. 1859.

William Charles Lyon, *Ens.* 27 Jan. 1843; *Lieut.* 28 Jan. 1848. From 92nd Foot. Exchanged to 92nd Foot 14 April 1848.

Lionel Daniel MacKinnon, *Ens.* 30 May 1843; *Lieut.* 25 Feb. 1848. Killed in action 5 Nov. 1854, at Inkerman.

Henry Wedderburn Cumming, *Lieut.* 11 Aug. 1843; *Capt.* 27 May 1853. From 59th Foot. Retired 20 Oct. 1854.

1005 Sir George Ferdinand Radzivill Walker, Bart., *Ens.* 29 March 1844; *Lieut.* 7 April 1848. From 26th Foot. Retired 6 Oct. 1854.

Hon. Francis John Robert Villiers, *Lieut.* 24 May 1844. From 73rd Foot. Exchanged to 60th Foot 4 April 1845.

William Gregory Dawkins, *Ens.* 6 Sept. 1844; *Lieut.* 25 April 1848; *Capt.* 6 Nov. 1854. From 49th Foot. To half-pay 23 June 1865.

William Mark Wood, *Lieut.* 4 April 1845; *Capt.* 13 Dec. 1853; *Major*, 2 July 1861; *Lieut.-Col.* 24 Nov. 1863. From 60th Foot. To half-pay 22 May 1866.

Hylton Jolliffe, *Ens.* 8 Aug. 1845; *Lieut.* 23 June 1848. Died of cholera 4 Oct. in Camp before Sevastopol.

1010 William Eccles, *Lieut.* 20 March 1846. From 82nd Foot. Exchanged to 6th Foot 21 Aug. 1849.

Ulick Canning, Lord Dunkellin, *Ens.* 27 March 1846; *Lieut.* 27 April 1849; *Capt.* 3 Nov. 1854. Retired 21 Dec. 1860.

Charles John Colville, *Lieut.* 13 April 1846. To half-pay 13 July 1847.

Francis Augustus Plunkett Burton, *Ens.* 8 May 1846; *Lieut.* 27 June 1851; *Capt.* 25 May 1855. Retired 30 Nov. 1855.

William Baring, *Lieut.* 12 June 1846. From 20th Foot. Retired 29 April 1853.

1015 Hon. Percy Robert Basil Feilding (afterwards Sir Percy, K.C.B.), *Ens.* 7 Aug. 1846; *Lieut.* 21 Aug. 1851; *Capt.* 23 Nov. 1855; *Major*, 23 Oct. 1867; *Lieut.-Col.* 4 Jan. 1871. From 85th Foot. To half-pay 5 Sept. 1877.

Edward Heneage Dering, *Ens.* 18 Sept. 1846. Retired 11 July 1851.

William Henry Reeve, *Ens.* 29 Dec. 1846; *Lieut.* 22 Aug. 1851; *Capt.* 30 Nov. 1855. Retired 20 July 1866.

Hon. Granville Charles Cornwallis Eliot, *Ens.* 11 June 1847; *Lieut.* 31 Oct. 1851. Killed in action 5 Nov. 1854, at Inkerman.

Charles Baring, *Ens.* 2 July 1847; *Lieut.* 29 April 1853; *Capt.* 21 Dec. 1855; *Major*, 2 Sept. 1868. Retired 13 Aug. 1872.

1020 Henry Montolieu Bouverie, *Ens.* 13 July 1847; *Lieut.* 27 May 1853. From Rifle Brigade. Killed in action 5 Nov. 1854, at Inkerman.

Henry Armytage, *Ens.* 30 July 1847; *Lieut.* 13 Dec. 1854; *Capt.* 26 Oct. 1858. Retired 23 Nov. 1870.

APPENDIX.

Hon. Henry William John Byng, *Ens.* 27 Aug. 1847; *Lieut.* 3 March 1854; *Capt.* 2 May 1856. Retired 17 Nov. 1863.
Charles Rodney Morgan, *Ens.* 29 Oct. 1847. Retired 31 Dec. 1852.
Arthur George Bethel Thellusson, *Ens.* 10 Dec. 1847; *Lieut.* 20 June 1854. Retired 13 May 1859.

1025 Thomas Francis Rolt, *Ens.* 28 Jan. 1848. From 63rd Foot. Retired 18 Feb. 1853.
Robert Desmond Sulivan, *Ens.* 25 Feb. 1848. Exchanged to 2nd Dragoon Guards 1 Aug. 1851.
Horace William Cust, *Ens.* 7 April 1848; *Lieut.* 14 July 1854. Killed in Action 20 Sept. 1854 at the Alma.
George Warrender (afterwards Sir G., Bart.), *Lieut.* 14 April 1848. From 92nd Foot. Retired 27 June 1851.
David Robertson Williamson, *Ens.* 25 April 1848. Retired 23 July 1852.

1030 Walter Trevelyan, *Capt.* 26 May 1848. From half-pay 83rd Foot. Died at Varna 21 Aug. 1854.
Philip Sanbrook Crawley, *Ens.* 23 June 1848; *Lieut.* 14 July 1854; *Capt.* 13 Dec. 1860. From 74th Foot. Retired 30 March 1867.
George Thomas Duncombe, *Lieut.* 7 July 1848. From 11th Light Dragoons. To 16th Foot 22 June 1849.
Clement William Strong, *Lieut.* 10 Nov. 1848; *Capt.* 6 Nov. 1854; *Major* 14 Aug. 1866. From 48th Foot. To half-pay 15 March 1867.
Sir James Dunlop, Bart., *Ens.* 27 April, 1849; *Lieut.* 14 July 1854. Died 10 Feb. 1858 at Hyères, France.

1035 Charles Townsend Wilson, *Lieut.* 4 May 1849; *Capt.* 8 Dec. 1854. From 59th Foot. Retired 25 May 1855.
Thomas Crombie, *Capt.* 22 June 1849. From half-pay, unattached. To ditto 9 Feb. 1855.
Hon. Arthur Edward Hardinge (afterwards Sir A., K.C.B.), *Lieut.* 22 June 1849; *Capt.* 20 Feb. 1855; *Major*, 15 March 1867; *Lieut.-Col.* 2 Sept. 1868; *Col.* 26 Feb. 1890. From 16th Foot. To half-pay 3 Jan. 1871. Died 15 July 1892.
Hon. Augustus Charles Chichester, *Lieut.* 21 Aug. 1849. From 6th Foot. Exchanged to 87th Regiment 6 May 1853.
Hon. George Augustus Spencer, *Capt.* 30 Nov. 1849. From 37th Foot. Retired 31 Oct. 1851.

1040 John Earl of Strafford, G.C.B., *Col.* 15 Aug. 1850. Originally in the Scots Guards. Died 3 June 1860.
Gerald Littlehales Goodlake, V.C., *Ens.* 27 June 1851; *Lieut.* 14 July 1854; *Capt.* 29 Nov. 1859; *Major*, 14 Aug. 1872. From Rifle Brigade. To half-pay 7 Aug. 1875.
Frederick Henry Ramsden, *Ens.* 11 July 1851, *Lieut.* 28 July 1854. From Rifle Brigade. Killed in action 5 Nov. 1854, at Inkerman.
William Hull, *Ens.* 1 Aug. 1851. From 2nd Dragoon Guards. Retired 17 Aug. 1852.
George Lord Bingham (afterwards Earl of Lucan), *Ens.* 14 Oct. 1851; *Lieut.* 22 Aug. 1854; *Capt.* 20 Dec. 1859. From Rifle Brigade. Retired 15 June 1860.

1045 Harvey Tower, *Ens.* 21 Nov. 1851; *Lieut.* 4 Sept. 1854; *Capt.* 9 March 1860. From 48th Regiment Foot. Died 17 Nov. 1870.
Hon. William Henry Wellesley, Viscount Dangan (afterwards Earl Cowley), *Ens.* 23 July 1852; *Lieut.* 21 Sept. 1854; *Capt.* 17 April 1860. Retired 11 Aug. 1863.
Hon. Robert Drummond Hay, *Ens.* 17 Aug. 1852; *Lieut.* 5 Oct. 1854. Died of wounds on voyage home from the Crimea 2 Oct. 1855.
Percy Scawen Wyndham, *Ens.* 31 Dec. 1852. Retired 24 Nov. 1854.

Edward Amelius Disbrowe, *Ens.* 18 Feb. 1853. From 85th Regiment. Killed in action 5 Nov. 1854, at Inkerman.

1050 Arthur James Lyon Fremantle (afterwards Sir Arthur, K.C.M.G.), *Ens.* 29 April 1853; *Lieut.* 6 Nov. 1854; *Capt.* 20 April 1860; *Major*, 28 April 1875; *Lieut.-Col.* 5 Sept. 1877. From 62nd Foot. To half-pay 10 Nov. 1880.

John Halkett Le Couteur, *Lieut.* 6 May 1853; *Capt.* 18 Nov. 1856. Retired 13 March 1868.

Cavendish Hubert Greville, *Ens.* 10 June 1853. Killed in action 5 Nov. 1854, at Inkerman.

Michael Walker Heneage, *Ens.* 13 Dec. 1853; *Lieut.* 23 Dec. 1854; *Capt.* 21 Dec. 1860. Retired 11 Dec. 1866.

Hon. William Arthur Amherst, Viscount Holmesdale (afterwards Earl Amherst), *Ens.* 3 March 1854; *Lieut.* 4 March 1855. Retired 18 July 1862.

1055 Arthur St. George Herbert Stepney, C.B., *Capt.* 15 July 1854; *Major*, 24 Nov. 1862. From 54th Foot. Retired on half-pay 14 Aug. 1866.

James Talbot Airey, C.B. (afterwards Sir J., K.C.B.), *Capt.* 15 July 1854; *Major*, 22 May 1866. From 22nd Foot. To half-pay 23 Oct. 1867.

[James Armar Butler, *Lieut.* 15 July 1854. From half-pay Ceylon Rifles. Died of his wounds, 22 June 1854, received during the siege of Silistria. Therefore never belonged to Regiment, though the gazette of appointment was not cancelled.]

St. Vincent Bentinck Hawkins Whitshed (afterwards Sir St. V. Bart.), *Ens.* 1 Aug. 1854; *Lieut.* 2 Oct. 1855. Retired 6 May 1859.

Julian Hamilton Hall, *Ens.* 2 Aug. 1854; *Lieut.* 13 Feb. 1856; *Capt.* 30 Oct. 1866; *Major*, 29 Sept. 1877; *Lieut.-Col. com. Battn.* 1 July 1881.* To half-pay 29 Sept. 1882.

Godfrey James Wigram, C.B., *Ens.* 3 Aug. 1854; *Lieut.* 14 Feb. 1856; *Capt.* 11 Dec. 1866; *Major*, 10 Nov. 1880; *Lieut.-Col. com. Battn.* 1 July 1881;* *Lieut.-Col. com. Regt.* 16 Dec. 1885. To half-pay 10 Nov. 1885. From ditto 16 Dec. 1885. Major-General 25 Dec. 1889.

1060 Arthur Lambton, C.B., *Ens.* 4 Aug. 1854; *Lieut.* 15 Feb. 1856; *Capt.* 18 Jan. 1867; *Major*, 1 July 1881;* *Lieut.-Col. com. Battn.* 29 Sept. 1882. To half-pay 29 Sept. 1886.

George Ernest Rose, *Ens.* 24 Aug. 1854; *Lieut.* 2 May 1856. Exchanged to Rifle Brigade 25 Aug. 1857.

Gordon Manyard Ives, *Ens.* 25 Aug. 1854. Retired 30 Nov. 1855.

Charles Pierrepont Lane Fox, *Ens.* 21 Sept. 1854. Retired 3 June 1856.

Lord Frederick George S. Leveson Gower, *Ens.* 6 Oct. 1854. From Rifle Brigade. Died 6 Oct. 1854, at sea.

1065 Charles John Bouchier, *Lieut.* 6 Oct. 1854. Retired 12 Jan. 1855.

John Baillie Baillie, *Ens.* 20 Oct. 1854. From 6th Dragoons. Retired 26 Oct. 1855.

Sir William Forbes, Bart. (afterwards Lord Sempill), *Ens.* 3 Nov. 1854. Retired 30 Jan. 1857.

Hon. William Edwards (afterwards Lord Kensington), *Ens.* 24 Nov. 1854; *Lieut.* 5 Feb. 1858; *Capt.* 15 March 1867. Retired 30 March 1870.

Hedworth H. Jolliffe (afterwards Lord Hylton), *Lieut.* 15 Dec. 1854. From 4th Light Dragoons. Retired 1 May 1855.

1070 Hon. William H. A. Feilding, *Lieut.* 15 Dec. 1854; *Capt.* 15 June 1860; *Major*, 7 Aug. 1875. From 62nd Foot. To half-pay 29 Sept. 1877.

John Augustus Conolly, V.C., *Lieut.* 22 Dec. 1854; *Capt.* 11 Aug. 1863. From 49th Foot. Retired 15 March 1870.

---

* By an order, 1 July 1881, the Majors were appointed Lieut.-Colonels commanding Battalions, and eight Captains were promoted Major (*ante*, p. 342).

APPENDIX. 471

William T. Markham, *Lieut.* 23 Dec. 1854. Retired 28 Dec. 1855.

Lord Eustace H. G. B. Cecil, *Lieut.* 26 Dec. 1854; *Capt.* 2 July 1861. From 88th Foot. Retired 28 July 1863.

Christopher E. Blackett, *Lieut.* 29 Dec. 1854; *Capt.* 9 Nov. 1862. To half-pay 18 Dec. 1875.

1075 George R. FitzRoy, *Lieut.* 29 Dec. 1854; *Capt.* 28 July 1863; *Major*, 5 Sept. 1877; *Lieut.-Col.* 10 Nov. 1880. From 41st Foot. To half-pay 10 Nov. 1885.

Henry F. B. Maxse (afterwards Sir H., K.C.M.G.), *Lieut.* 29 Dec. 1854. From 21st Foot. To half-pay 16 March 1858.

James A. Caulfeild (afterwards Viscount Charlemont, C.B.), *Lieut.* 12 Jan. 1855. From 17th Foot. Retired 5 Feb. 1858.

Henry J. Bagot Lane, *Ens.* 16 Jan. 1855; *Lieut.* 26 Oct. 1858; *Capt.* 30 March 1867. Retired 25 Dec. 1867.

Alexander W. Adair, *Ens.* 17 Jan. 1855; *Lieut.* 6 May 1859. Exchanged to 52nd Foot 16 March 1860.

1080 William Frederick E. Seymour (afterwards Lord William), *Ens.* 18 Jan. 1855; *Lieut.* 13 May 1859; *Capt.* 23 Oct. 1867; *Major*, 1 July 1881.* To half-pay 5 Sept. 1884.

Hon. William G. Boyle, *Lieut.* 19 Jan. 1855; *Capt.* 24 Nov. 1863. From 21st Foot. Retired 18 Jan. 1867.

Stapleton T. Mainwaring (afterwards Sir S. Bart.), *Ens.* 19 Jan. 1855. Retired 10 Dec. 1858.

Francis W. H., Lord Burghersh, C.B. (afterwards Earl of Westmoreland), *Capt.* 9 Feb. 1855. From half-pay, unattached. Retired 20 April 1860.

Hon. Edward Henry Legge, *Ens.* 12 Feb. 1855; *Lieut.* 29 Nov. 1859; *Capt.* 25 Dec. 1867. Retired 1 Sept. 1875.

1085 Edward Strelley Pegge Burnell, *Ens.* 13 Feb. 1855; *Lieut.* 20 Dec. 1859; *Capt.* 22 Jan. 1868; *Major*, 1 July 1881.* Retired to half-pay 26 March 1884.

Rowland Hill Gordon, *Lieut.* 23 Feb. 1855. From 38th Regiment. Exchanged to 42nd Regiment 7 Sept. 1855.

Walter Stirling, *Ens.* 23 Feb. 1855. Resigned 1 May 1857.

Frederick Horace Seymour, *Ens.* 24 April 1855; *Lieut.* 9 March 1860. Exchanged to Rifle Brigade 17 July 1860.

Hon. Richard Monck, *Lieut.* 1 May 1855; *Capt.* 17 Nov. 1863. From Rifle Brigade. To half-pay 29 Sept. 1877.

1090 Richard Hassell Thursby, *Ens.* 4 May 1855; *Lieut.* 17 April 1860; *Capt.* 2 Sept. 1868. Retired 21 March 1871.

Charles Greenhill Gardyne, *Lieut.* 6 July 1855; *Capt.* 22 May 1866. From 92nd Foot. Retired 22 Jan. 1868.

Henry Clarke-Jervoise, *Lieut.* 7 Sept. 1855; *Capt.* 20 July 1866. From 42nd Foot. Retired 4 July 1873.

Norman Burnand, *Ens.* 26 Oct. 1855; *Lieut.* 20 April 1860; *Capt.* 17 Feb. 1869. From 50th Foot. Retired 14 April 1874.

Sir George A. F. Houstoun Boswall, Bart., *Capt.* 23 Nov. 1855. From half-pay, unattached. Retired 23 Nov. 1855.

1095 Frederick Charles Manningham-Buller, *Ens.* 30 Nov. 1855; *Lieut.* 13 Dec. 1860; *Capt.* 30 March 1870; *Major*, 1 July 1881.* Died 10 Jan. 1884.

Hon. Henry Walter Campbell, *Lieut.* 28 Dec. 1855; *Capt.* 14 Aug. 1866. From Rifle Brigade. Retired 17 Feb. 1869.

William Wynne, *Ens.* 13 Feb. 1856; *Lieut.* 15 June 1860. Died 22 May 1863.

---

* See footnote to No. 1060, p. 470.

APPENDIX.

Ellis Philip Fox Reeve, *Ens.* 14 Feb. 1856; *Lieut.* 21 Dec. 1860; *Capt.* 30 March 1870. Retired 24 March 1871.

Hugh Bonham Carter, *Ens.* 15 Feb. 1856; *Lieut.* 2 July 1861. Retired 18 Nov. 1873.

1100 Hugh Granville Fortescue, *Ens.* 1 April 1856; *Lieut.* 31 Dec. 1861. Retired 8 Sept. 1865.

Hon. William Henry Bruce Ogilvy, *Ens.* 16 May 1856. Retired 19 Dec. 1856.

George Gervis Cameron, *Ens.* 16 June 1856. Died 26 Sept. 1859, in London.

John Fletcher Hathorn, *Ens.* 19 Dec. 1856; *Lieut.* 18 July 1862; *Capt.* 23 Nov. 1870. Retired 2 Aug. 1872.

Henry Arthur Herbert, *Ens.* 30 Jan. 1857; *Lieut.* 9 Nov. 1862. Retired 23 March 1866.

1105 Philip Le Belward Egerton (afterwards Sir P. Grey-Egerton, Bart.), *Lieut.* 25 Aug. 1857. From Rifle Brigade. Retired 31 Dec. 1861.

Henry Robert Brand (afterwards Viscount Hampden), *Ens.* 10 Dec. 1858; *Lieut.* 23 May 1863. Retired 10 Oct. 1865.

Hon. Denzil Hugh Baring, *Ens.* 6 May 1859; *Lieut.* 28 July 1863. Retired 16 May 1865.

Hon. Frederick Charles Howard, *Ens.* 13 May 1859; *Lieut.* 11 Aug. 1863. Retired 20 July 1866.

Reginald Archibald Edward Cathcart (afterwards Sir Reginald, Bart.), *Ens.* 21 Oct. 1859; *Lieut.* 17 Nov. 1863. From 68th Foot. Retired 3 Aug. 1866.

1110 Charles Walter Lee Mainwaring, *Ens.* 29 Nov. 1859; *Lieut.* 24 Nov. 1863. From 5th Dragoon Guards. Died 20 June 1866.

Hon. Vesey Dawson (afterwards Lord Cremorne), *Ens.* 20 Dec. 1859; *Lieut.* 16 May 1865; *Capt.* 4 Jan. 1871. Retired 19 Jan. 1876.

Edward Chaplin, *Ens.* 9 March 1860; *Lieut.* 8 Sept. 1865; *Capt.* 22 March 1871. Retired 27 Sept. 1876.

Hon. George H. W. Windsor Clive, *Lieut.* 16 March 1860; *Capt.* 13 March 1868. From 52nd Regiment. Retired 30 March 1870.

Sir Edward Archibald Hamilton, Bart., *Ens.* 17 April 1860; *Lieut.* 10 Oct. 1865. Retired 7 May 1867.

1115 George John FitzRoy Smyth, *Ens.* 20 April 1860; *Lieut.* 23 March 1866; *Capt.* 25 March 1871; *Major*, 1 July 1881.* Retired 10 Dec. 1881.

Colin, Lord Clyde, G.C.B., *Col.* 4 June 1860. Died 14 Aug. 1863.

Arthur Wilbraham, *Ens.* 15 June 1860. Retired 28 Oct. 1864.

FitzRoy William Fremantle, *Lieut.* 17 July 1860; *Capt.* 16 March 1870; *Major*, 1 July 1881.* From Rifle Brigade. To half-pay 8 Dec. 1884.

Henry Robert Eyre, *Ens.* 13 Dec. 1860; *Lieut.* 21 June 1866; *Capt.* 14 Aug. 1872. *Major*, 1 July 1881.* From 73rd Regiment. To half-pay 18 April 1885.

1120 Joseph, Lord Wallscourt, *Ens.* 21 Dec. 1860; *Lieut.* 22 May 1866. Retired 25 Dec. 1867.

William Chafyn Grove, *Ens.* 16 Aug. 1861. Retired 11 Sept. 1863.

John Barton Sterling, *Ens.* 31 Dec. 1861; *Lieut.* 20 July 1866; *Capt.* 5 July 1873; *Major*, 1 July 1881;* *Lieut.-Col. com. Battn.* 10 Nov. 1885; *Lieut.-Col. com. Regt.* 5 Feb. 1890. From 8th Regiment. To half-pay 10 Nov. 1889. From ditto 5 Feb. 1890. To ditto 5 Feb. 1895.

George Gordon Macpherson, *Ens.* 18 March 1862; *Lieut.* 20 July 1866. Retired 5 March 1870.

Charles Dashwood Thomas, *Ens.* 19 Dec. 1862; *Lieut.* 3 Aug. 1866; *Capt.* 19 Nov. 1873; *Major*, 1 July 1881.* Died 27 April 1882.

---

* See footnote to No. 1060, p. 470.

APPENDIX.

1125 Hon. John Robert William Vesey (afterwards Viscount de Vesci), *Ens.* 12 June 1863; *Lieut.* 14 Aug. 1866; *Capt.* 15 April 1874; *Major*, 10 Dec. 1881. To half-pay 15 Aug. 1883.

Charles Napier McMurdo, *Ens.* 28 July 1863. Retired 23 Aug. 1864.

Hon. Frederick Arthur Wellesley, *Ens.* 11 Aug. 1863; *Lieut.* 30 Oct. 1866; *Capt.* 28 April 1875. From Rifle Brigade. Retired 11 Jan. 1881.

Hon. Heneage Legge, *Ens.* 11 Sept. 1863; *Lieut.* 11 Dec. 1866. Exchanged 9th Lancers, 9 Nov. 1873.

Richard Spencer Hall, *Ens.* 24 Nov. 1863; *Lieut.* 18 Jan. 1867; *Capt.* 7 Aug. 1875; *Major*, 28 April 1882; *Lieut.-Col. com. Battn.* 29 Sept. 1886. From 7th Foot. To half-pay 29 Sept. 1890.

1130 Arthur Farquhar, *Ens.* 4 Dec. 1863; *Lieut.* 15 March 1867. From 62nd Foot. Exchanged to 15th Foot 29 March 1870. Killed in the Sudan 7 Oct. 1883.

Caledon James Alexander, *Ens.* 23 Aug. 1864; *Lieut.* 30 March 1867. Retired 24 June 1873

William John Freschville Ramsden, *Ens.* 28 Oct. 1864; *Lieut.* 8 May 1867; *Capt.* 1 Sept. 1875; *Major*, 12 Aug. 1882. Retired 2 May 1883.

Hon. Edward Archibald Brabazon Acheson, *Ens.* 16 May 1865; *Lieut.* 23 Oct. 1867; *Capt.* 18 Dec. 1875; *Major*, 29 Sept. 1882. To half-pay 9 March 1887.

James Steadman Hawker Farrer, *Capt.* 23 June 1865. From half-pay, late 84th Foot. Retired 30 Oct. 1866.

1135 Henry Charles Adolphus Frederic William Aldenburg Bentinck, *Ens.* 8 Sept. 1865; *Lieut.* 25 Dec. 1867; *Capt.* 19 Jan. 1876. Retired 16 February 1878.

Hon. Lewis Payn Dawnay, *Ens.* 10 Oct. 1865; *Lieut.* 25 Dec. 1867; *Capt.* 27 Sept. 1876. Retired 17 Dec. 1879.

Hon. Edward Henry Trafalgar Digby (afterwards Lord Digby), *Ens.* 23 March 1866; *Lieut.* 23 March 1868; *Capt.* 5 Sept. 1877; *Major*, 15 Aug. 1883. Retired 4 Dec. 1889.

William Michael Glynn Turquand, *Ens.* 22 May 1866; *Lieut.* 13 June 1868. Retired 6 Jan. 1875.

Hon. Henry William Lowry-Corry, *Ens.* 20 July 1866; *Lieut.* 2 Sept. 1868; *Capt.* 29 Sept. 1877; *Major*, 10 Jan. 1884; *Lieut.-Col. com. Battn.* 10 Nov. 1889. To half-pay 10 Nov. 1893.

1140 Robert William Webb Follett, *Ens.* 20 July 1866; *Lieut.* 17 Feb. 1869; *Capt.* 29 Sept. 1877; *Major*, 26 March 1884; *Lieut.-Col. com. Battn.* 29 Sept. 1890. To half-pay 29 Sept. 1894.

Hon. Evelyn Edward Thomas Boscawen, C.B. (afterwards Viscount Falmouth), *Ens.* 20 July 1866; *Lieut.* 5 March 1870; *Capt.* 16 Feb. 1878; *Major*, 8 Dec. 1884; *Lieut.-Col. com. Battn.* 10 Nov. 1893; *Lieut.-Col. com. Regt.* 5 Feb. 1895. Effective 1896.

Archibald Earl of Cassilis (afterwards Marquis of Ailsa), *Ens.* 3 Aug. 1866; *Lieut.* 16 March 1870. Retired 18 May 1870.

Waller Philip Hughes (afterwards Otway), *Ens.* 14 Aug. 1866; *Lieut.* 30 March 1870; *Capt.* 4 June 1878. Retired 20 Oct. 1883.

Hervey Juckes Lloyd Bruce, *Ens.* 30 Oct. 1866; *Lieut.* 30 March 1870; *Capt.* 24 Aug. 1878. From 52nd Foot. Retired on half-pay 4 July 1883.

1145 Amelius Richard Mark Wood (afterwards Lockwood), *Ens.* 11 Dec. 1866; *Lieut.* 18 May 1870; *Capt.* 5 Oct. 1878. Retired 7 Nov. 1883.

Henry James Wigram, *Ens.* 18 Jan. 1867. Retired 13 May 1869.

Frederick Assheton Des Vœux (afterwards Sir Frederick, Bart.), *Ens.* 15 March 1867; *Lieut.* 23 Nov. 1870. Retired 2 May 1871.

Francis Henry Lovell, *Ens.* 3 April 1867. Retired 24 November 1868.

Walter Bulkeley Barrington, *Ens.* 8 May 1867. Retired 12 May 1869.

1150 Edmund Robarts Boyle, *Ens.* 15 May 1867 ; *Lieut.* 4 Jan. 1871. Retired 31 Oct. 1871.

Hon. Ronald George Elidor Campbell, *Ens.* 25 Dec. 1867 ; *Lieut.* 22 March 1871. Killed in action at Kambula Hill, Zululand, 28 March 1879.

Henry Charles Duncombe, *Ens.* 26 Dec. 1867. Exchanged 71st Foot 27 Aug. 1870.

Lord George Francis Hamilton, *Ens.* 22 Jan. 1868. From Rifle Brigade. Retired 5 May 1869.

Hon. Reginald James Macartney Greville-Nugent, *Ens.* 13 June 1868 ; *Lieut.* 25 March 1871. Retired 7 Oct. 1871.

1155 Hon. George Aubrey Vere Bertie, *Ens.* 14 Oct. 1868 ; *Lieut.* 3 May 1871 ; *Capt.* 12 Jan. 1881 ; *Major*, 31 Jan. 1885. Retired 11 April 1885.

Francis Aylmer Graves-Sawle, *Ens.* 25 Nov. 1868 ; *Lieut.* 7 Oct. 1871 ; *Capt.* 10 Dec. 1881 ; *Major*, 18 April 1885 ; *Lieut.-Col. com. Battn.* 29 Sept. 1894. From 71st Regiment. Effective 1896.

Augustus Henry Macdonald Moreton, *Ens.* 17 Feb. 1869; *Lieut.* 31 Oct. 1871 ; *Capt.* 12 Aug. 1882 ; *Major*, 3 Aug. 1885. Retired 18 April 1888.

Hon. Miles Stapleton (afterwards Lord Beaumont), *Ens.* 5 May 1869 ; *Lieut.* 3 Aug. 1872. Exchanged to 20th Hussars 20 Aug. 1879.

Reginald Pole-Carew, C.B., *Ens.* 12 May 1869 ; *Lieut.* 14 Aug. 1872 ; *Capt.* 4 July 1883 ; *Major*, 10 Nov. 1885 ; *Lieut.-Col. com. Battn.* 5 Feb. 1895. Effective 1896.

1160 James Gordon Henry Graham Montgomery, *Ens.* 13 May 1869 ; *Lieut.* 25 June 1873 ; *Capt.* 19 Sept. 1883 ; *Major*, 10 Nov. 1885. To half-pay 10 July 1889.

Cyril Dudley Fortescue, *Ens.* 5 March 1870 ; *Lieut.* 5 July 1873 ; *Capt.* 20 Oct. 1883. Retired 8 Sept. 1885.

Francis Capel Manley, *Ens.* 16 March 1870 ; *Lieut.* 19 Nov. 1873 ; *Capt.* 7 Nov. 1883 ; *Major*, 29 Sept. 1886. To half-pay 29 July 1891.

Robert Charles Goff, *Lieut.* 29 March 1870 ; *Capt.* 2 March 1878. From 15th Foot. Retired 5 Oct. 1878.

Hon. Charles Compton William Cavendish (afterwards Lord Chesham), *Ens.* 30 March 1870. Transferred to 10th Hussars 1 Jan. 1873.

1165 Alexander William Maxwell Clark-Kennedy, *Ens.* 30 March 1870 ; *Lieut.* 15 April 1874. Retired 12 June 1874.

Frank Wigsell Arkwright, *Ens.* 18 May 1870 ; *Lieut.* 13 June 1874. Retired 15 Jan. 1879.

Hon. Alfred W. Charteris, *Ens.* 27 Aug. 1870. From 71st Regiment. Died on board *Simoon*, Gold Coast, 23 Nov. 1873.

Charles, Lord Ossulston, *Ens.* 23 Nov. 1870. Transferred to Rifle Brigade 28 Oct. 1873.

Lionel Dudley MacKinnon, *Ens.* 4 Jan. 1871 ; *Lieut.* 6 Jan. 1875 ; *Capt.* 10 Jan. 1884. Retired 7 May 1887.

1170 Lord Douglas William Cope Gordon, *Ens.* 28 Oct. 1871 ; *Lieut.* 28 Oct. 1871.* Retired 8 May 1880.

Vesey John Dawson, *Ens.* 28 Oct. 1871 ; *Lieut.* 28 Oct. 1871 ;* *Capt.* 25 Oct. 1884 ; *Major*, 10 July 1889. Effective 1896.

Hon. Eustace Henry Dawnay, *Ens.* 28 Oct. 1871 ; *Lieut.* 28 Oct. 1871.* Retired 5 Dec. 1883.

Hon. Henry Power Charles Stanley Monck (afterwards Viscount Monck), *Ens.* 28 Oct. 1871, *Lieut.* 28 Oct. 1871 ;* *Capt.* 31 Jan. 1885. Retired 19 Sept. 1885.

Alfred William Maitland FitzRoy (afterwards Lord Alfred), *Lieut.* 17 July 1872. From 52nd Foot. Retired 29 Oct. 1881.

---

* Gazetted Ensign and Lieutenant ; afterwards appointed Lieutenant, same date.

APPENDIX. 475

1175 Douglas Beresford Malise Ronald, Marquis of Buchanan (afterwards Duke of Montrose), *Sub.-Lieut.* 14 Aug. 1872. Transferred to 5th Lancers 27 Feb. 1875.

Hon. Henry Charles Legge, *Sub.-Lieut.* 31 Aug. 1872; *Lieut.* 31 Aug. 1873;* *Capt.* 18 April 1885; *Major*, 29 Sept. 1890. Effective 1896.

Alfred Edward Codrington, *Sub.-Lieut.* 1 Feb. 1873; *Lieut.* 1 Feb. 1873;* *Capt.* 18 April 1885; *Major*, 4 Dec. 1889. Effective 1896.

Hon. Charles Brand, *Sub.-Lieut.* 9 Aug. 1873; *Lieut.* 9 Aug. 1874.* Resigned 9 June 1880.

John Foster George Ross-of-Bladensburg, C.B., *Lieut.* 9 Aug. 1873; *Capt.* 18 March 1885; *Major*, 10 Nov. 1889. From Royal Artillery. Promoted Lieut.-Colonel half-pay 27 July 1896.

1180 Robert Johnston Barton, *Lieut.* 10 Nov. 1873. Exchanged from Capt. 9th Lancers. Killed in action at Inhlobane, Zululand, 28 March 1879.

John Robert Gladstone (afterwards Sir John, Bart.), *Sub-Lieut.* 6 Dec. 1873; *Lieut.* 6 Dec. 1873;* *Capt.* 9 Sept. 1885. Retired 16 July 1890.

Hon. William Mansfield (afterwards Lord Sandhurst), *Sub.-Lieut.* 24 Dec. 1873; *Lieut.* 24 Dec. 1875. Retired 19 Feb. 1879.

Douglas Frederick Rawdon Dawson, *Sub.-Lieut.* 21 Jan. 1874; *Lieut.* 21 Jan. 1874;* *Capt.* 19 Sept. 1885; *Major*, 29 July 1891. Effective 1896.

George Vere Boyle, *Sub.-Lieut.* 18 March 1874; *Lieut.* 18 March 1876. From 60th Foot. Retired 24 Nov. 1886.

1185 John George, Viscount Lambton (afterwards Earl of Durham), *Sub.-Lieut.* 29 April 1874; *Lieut.* 29 April 1876. Retired 6 Aug. 1879.

Hon. Frederick William Lambton, *Sub.-Lieut.* 11 July 1874; *Lieut.* 11 July 1875.* Retired 11 Feb. 1880.

Hon. George Ralph Charles Ormsby-Gore, *Sub.-Lieut.* 28 Aug. 1875; *Lieut.* 28 Aug. 1875.* From 16th Foot. Retired 5 Sept. 1883.

Horace Robert Stopford, *Sub.-Lieut.* 28 Aug. 1875; *Lieut.* 28 Aug. 1875;* *Capt.* 19 Oct. 1885; *Major*, 10 Nov. 1893. From 46th Foot. Effective 1896.

Hon. Hugh Rudolph Arbuthnot Gough, *Lieut.* 6 Oct. 1875. From 21st Foot. Retired 14 Sept. 1878.

1190 Hon. Arthur Henry Henniker-Major, *Lieut.* 20 Nov. 1875; *Capt.* 10 Nov. 1885, *Major*, 29 Sept. 1894. From West Suffolk Militia. Effective 1896.

Arthur Henry Clarke-Jervoise (afterwards Sir A. Bart.), *Lieut.* 5 Jan. 1876. Retired 6 Aug. 1879.

Hon. Anthony Lucius Dawson, *Sub.-Lieut.* 9 Feb. 1876; *Lieut.* 11 Feb. 1877. From 98th Regiment. Retired 23 March 1881.

Hon. Hugh Amherst, *Lieut.* 5 Sept. 1877; *Capt.* 16 March 1887. From 7th Royal Fusiliers. Retired 23 July 1890.

Herbert Conyers Surtees, *Sub.-Lieut.* 31 Oct. 1877; *Lieut.* 31 Oct. 1877;* *Capt.* 7 May 1887; *Major*, 5 Feb. 1895. From 49th Foot. Effective 1896.

1195 Edgar Vincent (afterwards Sir Edgar K.C.M.G.), *2nd Lieut.* 31 Oct. 1877; *Lieut.* 1 July 1881. From Berks Militia. Retired 25 Oct. 1883.

Walter Orlando Corbet (afterwards Sir W., Bart.), *2nd Lieut.* 31 Oct. 1877; *Lieut.* 1 July 1881; *Capt.* 25 Jan. 1888. Retired 25 April 1888.

Theophilus Basil Percy Levett, *2nd Lieut.* 13 March 1878; *Lieut.* 1 July 1881. From 74th Foot. Retired 19 Nov. 1881.

Edward Carolus Milner, *2nd Lieut.* 13 March 1878. Died 23 April 1878.

William John Arthur Charles James Cavendish-Bentinck (afterwards Duke of Portland), *2nd Lieut.* 25 May 1878. From 84th Foot. Retired 26 May 1880.

1200 Guy Thomas Saunders Sebright, *2nd Lieut.* 7 Aug. 1878; *Lieut.* 1 July 1881. From 106th Foot. Retired 19 Sept. 1885.

---

* Promoted to Lieutenant, ante-dated.

George Pleydell Bouverie, *2nd Lieut.* 19 Oct. 1878 ; *Lieut.* 1 July 1881 ; *Capt.* 25 April 1888 ; *Major*, 3 April 1895. Effective 1896.

George Francis Sutton, *2nd Lieut.* 19 Oct. 1878 ; *Lieut.* 1 July 1881. Died in Red Sea 18 May 1885.

Hon. Arthur Grenville Fortescue, *2nd Lieut.* 13 Nov. 1878 ; *Lieut.* 1 July 1881 ; *Capt.* 18 July 1888. Retired 10 April 1895.

Bertram Mont Orgueil Hadsley Gosselin-Lefebvre, *2nd Lieut.* 30 Nov. 1878 ; *Lieut.* 1 July 1881. From 24th Foot. Retired 10 Sept. 1887.

1205 Philip Gurdon, *2nd Lieut.* 22 Jan. 1879. Retired 29 Sept. 1880.

Hon. Rowland Winn (afterwards Lord St. Oswald), *2nd Lieut.* 19 Feb. 1879 ; *Lieut.* 1 July 1881 ; *Capt.* 10 July 1889. Retired 6 Dec. 1893.

Peter Audley David Arthur Lovell, *2nd Lieut.* 22 Feb. 1879 ; *Lieut.* 1 July 1881 ; *Capt.* 4 Dec. 1889. Retired 28 Aug. 1895.

Lawrence George Drummond, *2nd Lieut.* 13 Aug. 1879. To Scots Guards 27 Sept. 1879.

Henry Augustus Wetherall, *Lieut.* 20 Aug. 1879 ; *Capt.* 26 March 1884. Exchanged from Capt. 20th Hussars. Retired 25 Jan. 1888.

1210 Hon. Edward Knatchbull-Hugessen (afterwards Lord Brabourne), *2nd Lieut.* 27 Aug. 1879. Retired 23 March 1881.

Augustus John Henry Beaumont, Earl of Wiltshire (afterwards Marquis of Winchester), *2nd Lieut.* 27 Sept. 1879 ; *Lieut.* 1 July 1881 ; *Capt.* 16 July 1890. Effective 1896.

Sir Charles John Hubert Miller, Bart., *2nd Lieut.* 17 April 1880 ; *Lieut.* 1 July 1881 ; *Capt.* 23 July 1890. Retired 18 May 1892.

Charles Porcher Wilson Kindersley, *2nd Lieut.* 28 April 1880 ; *Lieut.* 1 July 1881 ; *Capt.* 29 Sept. 1890. From half-pay 52nd Regiment. Effective 1896.

Douglas James Hamilton, *2nd Lieut.* 28 April 1880 ; *Lieut.* 1 July 1881 ; *Capt.* 1 Jan. 1891. From 109th Regiment. Exchanged to Royal Fusiliers 23 May 1891.

1215 Hon. Alan Dudley Charteris, *2nd Lieut.* 29 Sept. 1880 ; *Lieut.* 1 July 1881. Retired 9 July 1890.

Henry Gwynn Deane Shute, *2nd Lieut.* 30 Sept. 1880 ; *Lieut.* 1 July 1881 ; *Capt.* 27 Jan. 1891. Effective 1896.

Herbert Haldane Somers-Cocks, *2nd Lieut.* 16 Oct. 1880 ; *Lieut.* 1 July 1881. Retired 4 Feb. 1885.

Eustace Rochester Wigram, *2nd Lieut.* 2 Feb. 1881 ; *Lieut.* 1 July 1881. Retired 30 April 1887.

Granville Roland Francis Smith, *2nd Lieut.* 30 March 1881 ; *Lieut.* 1 July 1881 ; *Capt.* 29 June 1891. From 20th Hussars. Effective 1896.

1220 Charles Arthur Andrew Frederick, *2nd Lieut.* 30 March 1881 ; *Lieut.* 1 July 1881 ; *Capt.* 29 July 1891. Effective 1896.

Francis Alexander Newdigate, *Lieut.* 10 March 1883. Retired 7 Oct. 1885.

George Wyndham, *Lieut.* 10 March 1883. Retired 3 June 1887.

Charles Henry Copeley Du Cane, *Lieut.* 25 Aug. 1883. Transferred to Royal Fusiliers 24 Dec. 1884.

George Dunbar Milligan, *Lieut.* 5 Dec. 1883 ; *Capt.* 29 July 1891. Retired 1 July 1896.

1225 Hon. Cecil Trevelyan Holland, *Lieut.* 30 Jan. 1884 ; *Capt.* 18 May 1892. Exchanged into Kings Royal Rifle Corps 20 July 1892.

Hon. William Lambton, *Lieut.* 6 Feb. 1884 ; *Capt.* 18 May 1892. Effective 1896.

James Adare Drummond Hay, *Lieut.* 6 Feb. 1884 ; *Capt.* 13 July 1895. Effective 1896.

Frederick Stanley Maude, *Lieut.* 6 Feb. 1884 ; *Capt.* 28 Aug. 1895. Effective 1896.

Riversdale Francis John Grenfell, *Lieut.* 6 Feb. 1884. Retired 29 Jan. 1890.

APPENDIX.

1230 Frederick William Ramsden, *Lieut.* 21 May 1884. Retired 8 May 1889.
Cecil Stanley Owen Monck, *Lieut.* 23 Aug. 1884; *Capt.* 28 Aug. 1895. Effective 1896.
Hon. Victor Albert Francis Charles Spencer (afterwards Lord Churchill), *Lieut.* 23 Aug. 1884. Retired 18 Sept. 1889.
John Richard Hall, *Lieut.* 31 Dec. 1884; *Capt.* 19 Nov. 1895. Effective 1896.
John Trelawney Sterling, *Lieut.* 31 Jan. 1885. *Capt.* 1 July 1896. Effective 1896.
1235 Henry Blundell Hawkes, *Lieut.* 4 Feb. 1885. *Capt.* 1 July 1896. From East Surrey Regiment. Effective 1896.
Hon. Evan Edward Charteris, *Lieut.* 7 Feb. 1885. Retired 15 March 1887.
George William Taylor, *Lieut.* 15 May 1885. From South Wales Borderers. Retired 8 Aug. 1888.
Sydney Earle, *Lieut.* 20 May 1885. *Capt.* 27 July 1896. From Liverpool Regiment. Effective 1896.
John Maurice Wingfield, *Lieut.* 10 June 1885. Effective 1896.
1240 Hon. Edward Michael Pakenham, *Lieut.* 7 Oct. 1885. Effective 1896.
Hon. Henry Robert Baillie-Hamilton, *Lieut.* 28 Oct. 1885. Effective 1896.
John McNeile, *Lieut.* 14 Nov. 1885. Effective 1896.
Randal Charles Edward Skeffington Smyth, *Lieut.* 25 Nov. 1885. Effective 1896.
James Herbert Gustavus Meredyth, Lord Athlumney, *Lieut.* 4 Dec. 1886. Effective 1896.
1245 Hon. John Beresford Campbell, *2nd Lieut.* 23 March 1887; *Lieut.* 9 July 1890. Effective 1896.
Maurice Abel Fremantle, *2nd Lieut.* 21 May 1887; *Lieut.* 16 July 1890. From Bedfordshire Regiment. Died at Hong-Kong 16 Jan. 1892.
Francis Archibald, Viscount Drumlanrig (afterwards Lord Kelhead), *2nd Lieut.* 18 June 1887; *Lieut.* 23 July 1890. Retired 8 July 1893.
Hugh Clement Sutton, *2nd Lieut.* 14 Sept. 1887; *Lieut.* 4 Sept 1890. Effective 1896.
Raymond John Marker, *2nd Lieut.* 15 Feb. 1888; *Lieut.* 29 Sept. 1890. Effective 1896.
1250 Geoffrey Percy Thynne Feilding, *2nd Lieut.* 25 April 1888; *Lieut.* 27 Nov. 1890. Effective 1896.
William Henry Lambton, *2nd Lieut.* 2 May 1888; *Lieut.* 1 Jan. 1891. Effective 1896.
Hon. John Gaspard Le Marchant Romilly (afterwards Lord Romilly), *2nd Lieut.* 5 May 1888; *Lieut.* 27 Jan. 1891. Effective 1896.
John Ponsonby, *2nd Lieut.* 15 Aug. 1888; *Lieut.* 29 June 1891. From Royal Irish Rifles. Effective 1896.
Charles John Brinsley, Lord Newtown-Butler, *2nd Lieut.* 22 Aug. 1888; *Lieut.* 15 Oct. 1891. Effective 1896.
1255 Guy Fremantle, *2nd Lieut.* 6 Feb. 1889; *Lieut.* 17 April 1892. From Worcestershire Regiment. Effective 1896.
Claude Julian Hawker, *2nd Lieut.* 22 May 1889; *Lieut.* 10 Aug. 1892. Effective 1896.
Reginald Longueville, *2nd Lieut.* 21 Sept. 1889; *Lieut.* 23 Feb. 1893. Effective 1896.
Cecil Edward Pereira, *2nd Lieut.* 29 Jan. 1890; *Lieut.* 6 July 1893. Effective 1896.
Thomas Elphinstone Case, *2nd Lieut.* 3 May 1890; *Lieut.* 8 July 1893. Effective 1896.
1260 Richard Arthur Starling Benson, *2nd Lieut.* 2 July 1890; *Lieut.* 1 Jan. 1894. Effective 1896.
Julian McCarty Steele, *2nd Lieut.* 29 Oct. 1890; *Lieut.* 24 June 1896. Effective 1896.

Nevile Rodwell Wilkinson, *2nd Lieut.* 29 Oct. 1890; *Lieut.* 1 July 1896. Effective 1896.
Thomas Henry Eyre Lloyd, *2nd Lieut.* 29 Oct. 1890; *Lieut.* 27 July 1896. Effective 1896.
Ronald Anthony Markham, *2nd Lieut.* 3 Dec. 1890; *Lieut.* 24 Aug. 1896. Effective 1896.

1265 Lawrence Challoner Garratt, *2nd Lieut.* 3 Dec. 1890. Effective 1896.
Edward Gardiner Alston, *2nd Lieut.* 4 March 1891. Retired 28 Nov. 1894.
Frederick Ivor Maxse, *Capt.* 23 May 1891. Exchanged from Royal Fusiliers. Effective 1896.
Henry Tracy Peel, *2nd Lieut.* 15 July 1891. From Kings Royal Rifle Corps. Died of Typhoid Fever, at Holyhead, 16 Oct. 1893.
Herbert William Studd, *2nd Lieut.* 25 July 1891. Effective 1896.

1270 Hon. Claude Heathcote-Drummond Willoughby, *2nd Lieut.* 5 Dec. 1891. Effective 1896.
Harry William Ludovic Heathcoat-Heathcoat-Amory, *2nd Lieut.* 5 Dec. 1891. Effective 1896.
Eric Thomas Henry Hanbury-Tracy, *2nd Lieut.* 25 May 1892. Effective 1892.
Sir Frederick Charles Arthur Stephenson, G.C.B., *Col.* 16 July 1892. Originally in the Scots Guards. Effective 1896.
Henry Seymour Rawlinson (afterwards Sir H., Bart.), *Capt.* 20 July 1892. Exchanged from Kings Royal Rifle Corps. Effective 1896.

1275 Reginald Champion, *2nd Lieut.* 31 Aug. 1892. From West Riding Regiment. Retired 25 Jan. 1893.
Charles Edward Wyld, *2nd Lieut.* 8 Feb. 1893. Effective 1896.
Hon. Leslie d'Henin Hamilton, *2nd Lieut.* 22 March 1893. Effective 1896.
Hon. Guy Victor Baring, *2nd Lieut.* 8 July 1893. Effective 1896.
Francis Charles Philips, *2nd Lieut.* 21 Oct. 1893. Transferred to 4th Dragoon Guards 6 March 1895.

1280 Harry Anthony Chandos Pole-Gell, *2nd Lieut.* 23 Dec. 1893. Effective 1896.
Torquhil George Matheson, *2nd Lieut.* 2 June 1894. Effective 1896.
Hon. George Arthur Charles Crichton, *2nd Lieut.* 28 Nov. 1894. Effective 1896.
Jocelyn Henry Clive Graham, *2nd Lieut.* 6 March 1895. Effective 1896.
Francis Douglas Farquhar, *2nd Lieut.* 29 April 1896. Effective 1896.

1285 Giles Stephen Holland, Lord Stavordale, *2nd Lieut.* 5 Aug. 1896. Effective 1896.
Ralph Henry S. Wilmot, *2nd Lieut.* 12 Aug. 1896. Effective 1896.
John Vaughan Campbell, *2nd Lieut.* 7 Sept. 1896. Effective 1896.
Francis Jenkins, *2nd Lieut.* 23 Sept. 1896. Effective 1896.

2.

COMMANDING OFFICERS OF THE COLDSTREAM GUARDS.

A.—COLONELS.

1 George Monck, Duke of Albemarle, K.G., Capt.-General, July 1650.
2 William, Earl of Craven, Lieut.-General, 6 Jan. 1688/9.
3 Thomas Talmash (or Tolemache), Lieut.-General, 1 May 1689.
4 John, Lord Cutts, Lieut.-General, 3 Oct. 1694.
5 Charles Churchill, General, 25 Feb. 1707/8.
6 William, Earl of Cadogan, K.T., Lieut.-General, 11 Oct. 1714.

APPENDIX.

COLONELS (*continued*).

7 Richard, Earl of Scarborough, K.G., 18 June 1722.
8 H.R.H. William, Duke of Cumberland, K.G., Field-Marshal, 30 April 1740.
9 Charles, Duke of Marlborough, K.G., 18 Feb. 1744½.
10 William, Earl of Albemarle, 5 Oct. 1744.
11 James, Lord Tyrawley, Lieut.-General, 8 April 1755.
12 John, Earl of Waldegrave, K.G., General, 15 July 1773.
13 H.R.H. Frederick, Duke of York, K.G., Field-Marshal, 27 Oct. 1784.
14 H.R.H. Adolphus, Duke of Cambridge, K.G., Field-Marshal, 5 Oct. 1805.
15 John, Earl of Strafford, G.C.B., Field-Marshal, 15 Aug. 1850.
16 Colin, Lord Clyde, G.C.B., General, 22 June 1860.
17 Sir William Maynard Gomm, G.C.B., Field-Marshal 15 Aug. 1863.
18 Sir William Codrington, G.C.B., General, 16 March 1875.
19 Rt. Hon. Sir Thomas Steele, G.C.B., General, 7 Aug. 1884.
20 Hon. Sir Arthur Hardinge, K.C.B., General, 26 Feb. 1890.
21 Sir Frederick Stephenson, G.C.B., General, 16 July 1892. Effective 1896.

B.—LIEUT.-COLONELS.

1 William Gough, July 1650.
2 Ethelbert Morgan, Oct. 1659.
3 Sir James Smith, Kt., M.P., 21 July 1665.
4 Edward Sackville, Major-General, Jan. 168½ till 1688.
5 James Bridgeman, 1691.
6 Sir William Seymour, 10 Aug. 1692.
7 William Matthew, 26 Feb. 169¾.
8 William Mathew, 1 Oct. 1702.
9 Edward Braddock, Major-General, 10 Jan. 170¾.
10 Richard Holmes, Major-General, 28 Sept. 1715.
11 Sir Adolphus Oughton, Bart., M.P., 12 Aug. 1717.
12 John Robinson, 3 Aug. 1733.
13 John Folliot, 30 Oct. 1734.
14 George Churchill, 1 April 1743.
15 Edward Braddock, 21 Nov. 1745.
16 Hedworth Lambton, 12 May 1753.
17 Hon. Bennet Noel, Lieut.-Major-General, 22 Dec. 1755.
18 Julius Cæsar, Major-General, 12 April 1762.
19 William A'Court, 20 Aug. 1762.
20 John Thomas, 23 Dec. 1763.
21 Henry Lister, 21 Nov. 1777.
22 Harry Trelawney, 23 Nov. 1785.
23 Anthony George Martin, Major-General, 26 May 1789.
24 Thomas Slaughter Stanwix, Lieut.-General, 2 Dec. 1795.
25 Edward Morrison, Major-General, 9 May 1800.
26 Andrew Cowell, Major-General, 19 Nov. 1800.
27 Hon. Henry Brand, C.B., (afterwards Lord Dacre), 25 July 1814.
28 Alexander Woodford, C.B., 25 July 1821.
29 James Macdonell, C.B., 27 May 1825.
30 Daniel MacKinnon, 22 July 1830.
31 Sir William Maynard Gomm, K.C.B., 23 June 1836.
32 Francis Miles Milman, 10 Jan. 1837.
33 John Fremantle, C.B., 8 Aug. 1837.
34 William Lovelace Walton, 31 Dec. 1839.
35 Charles Shawe, 8 May 1846.
36 Charles Antonio Ferdinand Bentinck, 9 Nov. 1846.
37 Thomas Chaplin, 25 April 1848.
38 Henry John William Bentinck, 22 Aug. 1851.
39 Hon. Arthur Upton, 20 June 1854.
40 Hon. George Upton, C.B. (afterwards Viscount Templeton), 20 Feb. 1855.
41 Lord Frederick Paulet, C.B., 26 Oct 1858.
42 William Samuel Newton, 13 Dec. 1860.
43 Spencer Perceval, 2 July 1861.
44 Thomas Steele, C.B., 9 Nov. 1862.
45 Mark Wood, 24 Nov. 1863.
46 Dudley Wilmot Carleton (afterwards Lord Dorchester), 22 May 1866.

LIEUT.-COLONELS (*continued*).

47 Hon. Arthur Hardinge, C.B., 2 Sept. 1868.
48 Hon. Percy Feilding, C.B., 4 Jan. 1871.
49 Arthur Lyon Fremantle, 5 Sept. 1877.
50 George Robert FitzRoy, 10 Nov. 1880.
51 Godfrey Wigram, C.B., 16 Dec. 1885.
52 John Barton Sterling, 5 Feb. 1890.
53 Evelyn, Viscount Falmouth, C.B., 5 Feb. 1895. Effective 1896.

C.—MAJORS COMMANDING BATTALIONS.

NOTE.—Up to 1711, the Regiment contained only one Major; another was then appointed, the senior having the rank of First Major, the junior, Second Major. This distinction was abolished by authority, dated September 11, 1821 (*ante*, p. 86), and the new rule applied retrospectively to the promotion that took place in July of that year. The Senior Major, however, still commanded the 1st Battalion, and the junior the 2nd Battalion. In 1864, this system was discontinued, and Majors were definitely posted to the Battalions they were appointed to command (*ante*, p. 307).

In the following list, First and Second Majors are indicated by *F* and *S* respectively; Senior and Junior Majors by *sen* and *jun*; Officers posted definitely to Battalions have the number *1st* or *2nd* entered against their names, to show which Battalion they commanded.

1 Abraham Holmes, July 1650.
2 Francis Nicols, Oct. 1659.
3 Sir James Smith, Kt., M.P., 11 March 166¼.
4 John Miller (formerly Adjutant-General), 21 July 1665.
5 Robert Winter, 1673.
6 Thomas Mansfield, 1676. (No Major for a year).
7 John Huitson, 1682.
8 James Bridgeman, 1688.
9 Sir William Seymour, 1691.
10 Henry Withers, 10 Aug. 1692.
11 William Mathew, 26 Feb. 169½.
12 Edward Braddock, 1 Oct. 1702.
13 Richard Holmes, Major-General, 10 Jan. 170¾. *F* 25 April 1711.
14 Henry Morryson, Brigadier-General, *S* 25 April 1711.
15 Sir Adolphus Oughton, Bart., M.P., *F* 28 Sept. 1715.
16 John Robinson, *S* 28 Sept. 1715; *F* 12 Aug. 1717.
17 Sir Tristram Dillington, Bart., M.P., *S* 12 Aug. 1717.
18 John Folliott, *S* 8 July 1721; *F* 3 Aug. 1733.
19 Henry Pulteney, *S* 3 Aug. 1733; *F* 30 Oct. 1734.
20 John Huske, *S* 30 Oct. 1734; *F* 5 July 1739.
21 George Churchill, *S* 5 July 1739; *F* 25 Dec. 1740.
22 William Douglas, *S* 29 Dec. 1740; *F* 2 April 1743.
23 Edward Braddock, *S* 2 April 1743; *F* 27 May 1745.
24 Maurice Buckland, M.P., *S* 27 May 1745; *F* 21 Nov. 1745.
25 Charles Russell, *S* 21 Nov. 1745; *F* 1 Dec. 1747.
26 Hedworth Lambton, *S* 1 Dec. 1747; *F* 17 Dec. 1751.
27 Hon. Bennet Noel, *S* 17 Dec. 1751; *F* 12 May 1753.
28 Julius Cæsar, Major-General, *S* 12 May 1753; *F* 25 Dec. 1755.
29 William A'Court, *S* 29 Dec. 1755; *F* 12 April 1762.
30 John Thomas, *S* 12 April 1762; *F* 20 Aug. 1762.
31 William Evelyn, *S* 20 Aug. 1762; *F* 23 Dec. 1763.
32 Hon. Martyn Sandys, *S* 23 Dec. 1763.
33 William Alexander Sorell, Major-General, *S* 11 Jan. 1769; *F* 3 Nov. 1769.
34 Francis Craig, *S* 3 Nov. 1769; *F* 15 Dec. 1773.
35 Henry Lister, *S* 15 Dec. 1773; *F* 8 Sept. 1775.
36 Thomas Clarke, *S* 8 Sept. 1775; *F* 21 Nov. 1777.
37 Charles Rainsford, *S* 21 Nov. 1777.
38 Harry Trelawney, *F* 5 May 1780.

Majors Commanding Battalions (continued).

39. Anthony George Martin, Major-General, *S* 7 June 1780; *F* 23 Nov. 1785.
40. Richard Grenville, Major-General, *S* 23 Nov. 1785.
41. Hon. Chapel Norton, Major-General, *S* 21 April 1786; *F* 26 May 1789.
42. George Morgan, Major-General, *S* 26 May 1789.
43. Lowther Pennington, Major-General, *S* 1 Feb. 1793; *F* 1 April 1795.
44. Thomas Slaughter Stanwix, Major-General, *S* 1 April 1795; *F* 23 June 1795.
45. William Morshead, Major-General, *S* 23 June 1795; *F* 2 Dec. 1795.
46. Edward Morrison, Major-General, *S* 2 Dec. 1795; *F* 30 Dec. 1797.
47. Andrew Cowell, Major-General, *S* 30 Dec. 1797; *F* 9 May 1800.
48. Richard Earl of Caven, Major-General, *S* 9 May 1800; *F* 19 Nov. 1800.
49. Hon. Edward Finch, Lieut.-General, *S* 19 Nov. 1800; *F* 18 June 1801.
50. John Calcraft, Lieut.-General, *S* 18 June 1801; *F* 4 Aug. 1808.
51. Kenneth Alexander Howard, Major-General (afterwards Earl of Effingham), *S* 4 Aug. 1808.
52. Sir Richard Downes Jackson, K.C.B., *F* 25 July 1814.
53. Alexander Woodford, C.B., *S* 25 July 1825; *F* 18 Jan. 1820.
54. Sir Henry Bouverie, K.C.B., *S* 18 Jan. 1820; *sen.* 25 July 1821.
55. James Macdonell, C.B., *jun.* 25 July 1821.
56. John Hamilton, *sen.* 27 May 1825.
57. William Henley Raikes, *jun.* 27 May 1825.
58. Daniel MacKinnon, *jun.* 22 June 1826; *sen.* 16 May 1829.
59. Sir William Maynard Gomm, K.C.B., *jun.* 16 May 1829; *sen.* 22 July 1830.
60. Francis Miles Milman, *jun.* 22 July 1830; *sen.* 23 June 1836.
61. John Fremantle, C.B., *jun.* 23 June 1836; *sen.* 10 Jan. 1837.
62. William Lovelace Walton, *jun.* 10 Jan. 1837; *sen.* 8 Aug. 1837.
63. Charles Shawe, *jun.* 8 Aug. 1837; *sen.* 31 Dec. 1839.
64. George Bowles, *jun.* 31 Dec. 1839.
65. Charles Antonio Ferdinand Bentinck, *jun.* 30 May 1843; *sen.* 8 May 1846.
66. Thomas Chaplin, *jun.* 8 May 1846; *sen.* 9 Nov. 1846.
67. Henry John William Bentinck, *jun.* 9 Nov. 1846; *sen.* 25 April 1848.
68. Charles Murray Hay, *jun.* 25 April 1848; *sen.* 22 Aug. 1851.
69. Hon. Arthur Upton, *jun.* 22 Aug. 1851.
70. Hon. George Upton (afterwards Viscount Templetown), *sen.* 20 June 1854.
71. Gordon Drummond, *jun.* 20 June 1854; *sen.* 20 Feb. 1855.
72. Lord Frederick Paulet, C.B., *jun.* 20 Feb. 1855; *sen.* 18 Nov. 1856.
73. William Samuel Newton, *jun.* 18 Nov. 1856; *sen.* 26 Oct. 1858.
74. Spencer Perceval, *jun.* 26 Oct. 1858; *sen.* 13 Dec. 1860.
75. Thomas Montagu Steele, C.B., *jun.* 13 Dec. 1860; *sen.* 2 July 1861.
76. William Mark Wood, *jun.* 2 July 1861; *sen.* 9 Nov. 1862.
77. Dudley Wilmot Carleton (afterwards Lord Dorchester), *jun.* 9 Nov. 1862; *sen.* 24 Nov. 1863.
78. Arthur St. George Herbert Stepney, C.B., *jun.* 24 Nov. 1863.
79. James Talbot Airey, C.B., 1*st* 22 May 1866.
80. Clement William Strong, 2*nd* 14 Aug. 1866.
81. Hon. Arthur Edward Hardinge, C.B., 2*nd* 15 March 1867.
82. Hon. Percy Robert Basil Feilding, C.B., 1*st* 23 Oct. 1867.*
83. Charles Baring, 2*nd* 2 Sept. 1868.
84. Gerald Littlehales Goodlake, V.C., 2*nd* 14 Aug. 1872; transferred to 1*st*, 20 July 1875.
85. Arthur James Lyon Fremantle, 1*st* 28 April 1875; transferred to 2*nd*, 20 July 1875.
86. Hon. William Henry Adelbert Feilding, 1*st* 7 Aug. 1875.
87. George Robert FitzRoy, 2*nd* 5 Sept. 1877.
88. Julian Hamilton Hall, 1*st* 29 Sept. 1877.
89. Godfrey James Wigram, C.B., 2*nd* 10 Nov. 1880.

* From Jan. 4, 1871, to April 28, 1875, Colonel Feilding, while Lieut.-Colonel of the Regiment, continued to command the 1st Battalion (*ante*, 315, 334).

APPENDIX.

LIEUT.-COLONELS COMMANDING.*

90 Arthur Lambton, C.B., 1*st* 29 Sept. 1882.
91 John Barton Sterling, 2*nd* 10 Nov. 1885.
92 Richard Spencer Hall, 1*st* 29 Sept. 1886.
93 Hon. Henry Lowry Corry, 2*nd* 10 Nov. 1889.
94 Robert William Webb Follett, 1*st* 29 Sept. 1890.
95 Evelyn Viscount Falmouth, C.B., 2*nd* 10 Nov. 1893.
96 Francis Aylmer Graves-Sawle, 1*st* 29 Sept. 1894. Effective 1896.
97 Reginald Pole-Carew, C.B., 2*nd* 5 Feb. 1895. Effective 1896.

3.
REGIMENTAL STAFF OFFICERS.†

A.—ADJUTANTS.

Hon. J. Hope, *jun.* 16 May 1829 ; *sen.* 10 Feb. 1832. Resigned 7 July 1837.
60 C. W. Horton, *jun.* 10 Feb. 1832 ; *sen.* 6 July 1837. Resigned 4 Sept. 1840.
D. M. Chisholm, *jun.* 8 July 1837. Retired 25 Dec. 1838.
Lord F. Paulet, *jun.* 25 Dec. 1838. Promoted 2 May 1846.
Hon. F. W. Child Villiers, 1*st Battn.* 4 Sept. 1840.‡ Resigned 27 May 1842.
W. S. Newton, 1*st* 27 May 1842. Resigned 30 Dec. 1845.
65 J. L. Elrington, 1*st* 30 Dec. 1845. Promoted 11 June 1847.
P. G. H. Somerset, 2*nd Battn.* 8 May 1846. Resigned 2 March 1849.
J. Halkett, 1*st* 11 June 1847. Resigned 8 Oct. 1850.
F. W. Newdigate, 2*nd* 2 March 1849. Promoted 4 Sept. 1854.
Hon. P. Feilding, 1*st* 8 Oct. 1850. Promoted 23 Nov. 1855.
70 Hon. H. W. J. Byng, 2*nd* 4 Sept. 1854. Resigned 2 Oct. 1855.
A. J. Fremantle, 2*nd* 2 Oct. 1855. Promoted 20 April 1860.
George Lord Bingham, 1*st* 21 Dec. 1855. Resigned 7 Aug. 1856.
Hon. R. Monck, 1*st* 8 Aug. 1856. Promoted 17 Nov. 1863.
W. F. E. Seymour, 2*nd* 20 April 1860. Resigned 1 Sept. 1863.
75 H. G. Fortescue, 2*nd* 1 Sept. 1863. Retired 8 Sept. 1865.
Hon. E. H. Legge, 1*st* 17 Nov. 1863. Resigned 24 Dec. 1867.
G. J. Wigram, 2*nd* 8 Sept. 1865. Resigned 14 Sept. 1866.
G. J. Fitzroy Smith, 2*nd* 14 Sept. 1866. Promoted 25 March 1871.
Hon. F. A. Wellesley, 1*st* 25 Dec. 1867. Resigned 19 Aug. 1871.
80 Hon. J. R. W. Vesey, 2*nd* 25 March 1871. Resigned 28 April 1874.
Hon. R. G. E. Campbell, 1*st* 19 Aug. 1871. Resigned 28 Oct. 1878.
Hon. E. H. Digby, 1*st* 29 April 1874. Resigned 1 April 1876.
Hon. E. E. T. Boscawen, 2*nd* 1 April 1876. Resigned 16 Feb. 1878.
Hon. A. H. Henniker-Major, 2*nd* 16 Feb. 1878. Resigned 2 Feb. 1886.
85 Hon. H. C. Legge, 1*st* 29 Oct. 1878. Resigned 29 Oct. 1885.
Hon. E. H. Digby, *regimental* 1 July 1881. Resigned 19 Sept. 1883.
Hon. E. E. T. Boscawen, *regt.* 19 Sept. 1883. Resigned 18 March 1887.
A. E. Codrington, 1*st* 29 Oct. 1885. Resigned 7 March 1888.

---

* By Royal Warrant, 1 July 1881, the Majors Commanding Battalions were called Lieut.-Colonels Commanding Battalions.

† Continued from Appendix No. 285 of MacKinnon's *Origin and Services of the Coldstream Guards*, vol. ii., p. 521.

‡ Adjutants ceased to change Battalions, about this time, when they became senior, and were definitely posted to Battalions (*ante*, 22, 308).

E. R. Wigram, *2nd* 3 Feb. 1886. Resigned 26 Oct. 1886.
90 C. A. A. Frederick, *2nd* 27 Oct. 1886. Resigned 28 Dec. 1888.
Hon. H. Amherst, *regt.* 16 March 1887. Resigned 25 March 1890.
F. S. Maude, *1st* 7 March 1888. Time expired 6 March 1892.
Hon. W. Lambton, *2nd* 29 Dec. 1888. Time expired 28 Dec. 1892.
Hon. A. H. Henniker-Major, *regt.* 26 March 1890. Resigned 26 Jan. 1891.
95 V. J. Dawson, *regt.* 27 Jan. 1891. Resigned 28 July 1891.
H. G. D. Shute, *regt.* 29 July 1891. Appointed Brigade-Major Brigade of Guards 1 Jan. 1894.
R. J. Marker, *1st* 7 March 1892. Time expired 6 March 1896.
C. S. O. Monck, *2nd* 29 Dec. 1892. Effective 1896.
H. C. Sutton, *regt.* 1 Jan. 1894. Effective 1896.
100 H. W. Heathcote Amory, *1st* 7 March 1896. Effective 1896.

B.—QUARTERMASTERS.

(Previous Rank—Appointment, etc.)

28 Thomas Dwelly, *Q.-M.-Serg.*; *2nd Battn.* 15 Oct. 1812. To half-pay 25 July 1837.
Benjamin Selway, *Ens.* and *Adj.* Surrey Local Militia; *1st Battn.* 26 Nov. 1812. Died 2 June 1836.
30 William Morse, *Sergt.-Major;* *1st* 28 June 1836. Died 21 June 1853.
Thomas Lea, *Sergt.-Major;* *2nd* 25 July 1837. Died 12 Feb. 1852.
Arthur Hurle, *Sergt.-Major;* *2nd* 13 Feb. 1852. Retired 27 Feb. 1867.
Alexander Falconer, *Sergt.-Major;* *1st* 1 July 1853. Retired 26 Feb. 1876.
Joseph Birch, *Q.-M.-Sergt.*; *2nd* 27 Feb. 1867. Retired 15 Oct. 1881.
35 William E. Reynolds, *Sergt.-Major;* *1st* 8 March 1876. Transferred to Guards Depôt 1 April 1885.
William Webster, *Ord. Room Sergt.*; *2nd* 15 Oct. 1881. Retired 24 July 1894.
Henry Folson, *Sergt.-Major;* *1st* 1 April 1885. Retired 14 May 1895.
Robert Grindel, *Superintend. Clerk Reg. Ord. Room*; *2nd* 25 July 1894. Effective 1896.
William W. Girling, *Q.-M.-Sergt.*; *1st* 15 May 1895. Effective 1896.

C.—MEDICAL OFFICERS.

31 William Whymper (Sir William), *Assist.-Surg.* 14 Nov. 1805; *Battn.-Surg.* 25 Dec. 1813; *Surg.-Major*, 24 Feb. 1825. To half-pay 29 April 1836.
Charles Herbert, *Assist.-Surg.* 3 March 1808. Resigned 24 Oct. 1810.
Thomas Clarke, *Assist.-Surg.* 20 April 1809. Resigned 3 Oct. 1810.
James Owen, *Assist.-Surg.* 4 Oct. 1810. Superseded 20 Feb. 1811.
35 Edward Nixon, *Assist.-Surg.* 25 Oct. 1810. Resigned 28 April 1813.
Thomas Maynard, *Assist.-Surg.* 21 Feb. 1811; *Battn.-Surg.* 28 May 1818. Died 1836.
George Smith, *Assist.-Surg.* 17 Dec. 1812; *Battn.-Surg.* 24 Feb. 1825. Retired 1836.
Septimus Worrell, *Assist.-Surg.* 29 April 1813. Exchanged to half-pay of the Regiment 23 Aug. 1821.
William Hunter, M.D., *Assist.-Surg.* 10 Feb. 1814, 24 Feb. 1825; *Battn.-Surg.* 4 Sept. 1836; *Surg.-Major*, 16 March 1838. Half-pay 25 Dec. 1818. Re-appointed 24 Feb. 1825. To half-pay 2 Sept. 1845.
40 Sherrington Gilder, *Assist.-Surg.* 28 May 1818, 23 Aug. 1821. On half-pay 25 Dec. 1818. Exchanged from ditto 23 Aug. 1821. Exchanged to half-pay First Foot Guards 20 June 1822.

APPENDIX.

Frederick Gilder, *Assist.-Surg.* 20 June 1822; *Battn.-Surg.* 16 March 1838. Exchanged from half-pay First Foot Guards 20 June 1822. To half-pay 14 April 1843.

George Chenevix, *Surg.-Major*, 4 Sept. 1836. To half-pay 16 March 1838.

James Wedderburn, *Assist.-Surg.* 21 Oct. 1836. Exchanged 2nd Dragoons 27 Aug. 1841.

Edward Greatrex, *Assist.-Surg.* 15 March 1838; *Battn.-Surg.* 14 April 1843; *Surg.-Major*, 2 Sept. 1845. To half-pay 3 April 1851.

45 William Thomas Christopher Robinson, *Assist.-Surg.* 23 March 1838; *Battn.-Surg.* 2 Sept. 1845; *Surg.-Major*, 4 April 1851. Died 20 Feb. 1853.

James Munro, M.D., *Assist.-Surg.* 27 Aug. 1841; *Battn.-Surg.* 4 April 1851; *Surg.-Major*, 20 Feb. 1853. From 2nd Dragoons. To half-pay 9 Jan. 1863.

Joseph Skelton, M.D., *Assist.-Surg.* 2 Sept. 1845; *Battn.-Surg.* 20 Feb. 1853. Died 8 April 1857.

Frederick Wildbore, *Assist.-Surg.* 4 April 1851. Resigned 1854.

John Wyatt, C.B., *Assist.-Surg.* 1 April 1853; *Battn.-Surg.* 9 April 1857; *Surg.-Major*, 9 Jan. 1863. From 5th Dragoon Guards. Died 3 April 1874.

50 Charles Vidler Cay, *Assist.-Surg.* 24 Feb. 1854; *Battn.-Surg.* 9 Jan. 1863 (Surg.-Major, 12 June 1866); *Surg.-Major*, 3 April 1874. From 97th Foot. To half-pay 30 Nov. 1878.

John William Trotter, *Assist.-Surg.* 26 May 1854 (Surg.-Major, 3 April 1874). To Scots Fusilier Guards on promotion, 3 May 1876.

Thomas Lawes Rogers, *Assist.-Surg.* 8 Dec. 1854. Resigned 16 April 1858.

Francis Bowen, M.D., *Assist.-Surg.* 11 May 1855. From Medical Staff. Appointed to Royal Hibernian School 31 May 1859.

W. H. Phipps, *Assist.-Surg.* 16 April 1858. Died 14 June 1858.

55 Andrew Spittal, M.D., *Assist.-Surg.* 28 Sept. 1858. From Medical Staff. Resigned 29 July 1859.

Robert Farquharson, M.D., *Assist.-Surg.* 29 July 1859. From Royal Artillery. Retired 14 Oct. 1868.

Arthur Bowen Richards Myers, *Assist.-Surg.* 26 Sept. 1859 (Surgeon in 1873). To Scots Guards on promotion 14 March 1883.

John Henry Connel Whipple, M.D., *Assist.-Surg.* 14 Oct. 1868 (Surgeon in 1873). From 21st Foot. To Grenadier Guards on promotion, 21 June 1885.

Constantine Caridi Read, *Battn.-Surg.* 3 April 1874; *Surg.-Major*, 30 Nov. 1878. From Grenadier Guards. To half-pay 8 Dec. 1885.

60 James Magill, M.D., *Surg.* 3 May 1876; *Surg.-Major*, 9 Dec. 1885. Promoted Surgeon Lieut.-Colonel 3 May 1896. Effective 1896.

George Perry, *Battn.-Surg.* 30 Nov. 1878 (Surgeon-Major 1876); *Surg.-Major*, 9 Dec. 1885. From Scots Guards. To Brigade-Surgeon Brigade of Guards 31 Dec. 1887. To retired pay 13 May 1888.

Alexander Charles Archibald Alexander, *Surg.* 21 April 1883; *Surg.-Major*, 8 Nov. 1888. From Army Medical Department. Effective 1896.

William Alexander Carte, M.B., *Surg.* 22 July 1885. From Medical Staff Corps. To Grenadier Guards on promotion 23 May 1891.

Robert Hippesley Cox, *Surg.* 7 April 1886. Resigned 11 March 1891.

65 Ernest Harrold Fenn, C.I.E., *Surg.-Major*, 13 May 1888. From Grenadier Guards. Seconded 8 Nov. 1888. To Scots Guards 26 Sept. 1894.

D.—SOLICITORS.

13 W. G. Carter, 29 Jan. 1824. Died 11 Nov. 1861.

R. J. P. Broughton, 7 Jan. 1862. Effective 1896.

APPENDIX.

4.
WARRANT-OFFICERS.*
A.—SERGEANTS-MAJOR.
FIRST BATTALION.

Appointed.		Retired.
Sgt.-M. in 1821.	Thomas Baker	Discharged June 3, 1823.
June 4, 1823.	Samuel Rook	Discharged Dec. 26, 1828.
Dec. 27, 1828.	William Morse (from 2nd Battn.)	Quarter-M. June 28, 1836.
June 20, 1836.	William Lundie	Discharged March 24, 1846
March 25, 1846.	Arthur Hurle	Quarter-M. Feb. 13, 1852.
Feb. 13, 1852.	Alexander Falconer	Quarter-M. July 1, 1853.
July 1, 1853.	Anthony Talbot	Dischd. Inval. Sept. 15, 1855.
Sept. 26, 1855.	Shepherd Carter	Discharged Feb. 24, 1865.
Feb. 25, 1865.	Thomas Samson	Discharged Jan. 24, 1871.
Jan. 25, 1871.	William E. Reynolds	Quarter-M. March 8, 1876.
March 8, 1876.	Henry Risebrook	Reverted Col. Sergt. Oct. 29, 1876.
Oct. 30, 1876.	Edward Dutton	Discharged Jan. 20, 1880.
Jan. 21, 1880.	Henry Folson	Quarter-M. April 1, 1885.
April 1, 1885.	Frederick Dickenson (from Depôt)	Garrison Sergt.-Major, Home District, Sept. 1, 1894.
Sept. 1, 1894.	Alfred Best	Effective 1896.

SECOND BATTALION.

Sgt.-M. in 1821.	David Newton	Discharged Sept. 29, 1823.
Sept. 30, 1823.	William White	Discharged Oct. 16, 1826.
Oct. 17, 1826.	William Morse	To 1st Battn. Dec. 27, 1828.
Dec. 27, 1828.	Thomas Lea	Quarter-M. July 25, 1837.
July 25, 1837.	Edward Geer	Died March 16, 1840.
April 25, 1840.	William Smeaton	Died Oct. 1, 1845
Oct. 2, 1845.	William Loomes	Discharged Sept. 11, 1849.
Sept. 12, 1849.	Richard Port	Dischd. Inval. May 25, 1853.
May 26, 1853.	George Pennymore	Discharged Jan. 31, 1860.
Feb. 1, 1860.	John K. Creagh	Discharged Feb. 26, 1867.
Feb. 27, 1867.	William Ewings	Discharged Jan. 22, 1878.
Jan. 23, 1878.	Alfred Spackman	Discharged June 28, 1881.
June 29, 1881.	Alfred Bustard	Discharged Oct. 6, 1885.
Oct. 7, 1885.	Joseph Brace	Garrison Sergt.-Major, Portsmouth, Jan. 31, 1893.
Feb. 1, 1893.	James Sparkes (from Depôt)	Garrison Sergt.-Major, Home District, April 2, 1895.
April 3, 1895.	Stephen Wright	Effective 1896.

B.—REGIMENTAL CLERKS.

Warrant-Officer.		Retired.
July 1, 1881.	Frederick J. Wray	Retired April 30, 1892.
May 1, 1892.	Robert Grindel	Quarter-M. July 24, 1894.
July 25, 1894.	William Johnson	Effective 1896.

* By Royal Warrant, 1 July 1881, the Sergeant-Major, Bandmaster, and Superintending Clerk at Regimental Orderly Room were appointed Warrant-officers

C.—BANDMASTERS.*

Warrant-Officer.		Retired.
July 1, 1881.	Cadwallader Thomas	Invalided April 8, 1896.
April 9, 1896.	John Rogan	From 2nd Queen's Royal West Surrey Regiment. Effective 1896.

D.—COLDSTREAM SERGEANTS-MAJOR OF THE GUARDS DEPÔT.

(Found in turn by the three Regiments.)

July 1, 1881.	Herbert Barrell	Discharged Aug. 30, 1881.
July 1, 1883.	Frederick Dickenson	To 1st Coldstream Guards April 1, 1885.
Jan. 23, 1888.	Herbert Martin	Retired at own request March 17, 1891.
May 13, 1891.	James Sparkes	To 2nd Coldstream Guards Jan. 31, 1893.

* See Appendix V. p. 424.

INDEX.

Abu Hamed, 383
Abu Klea, battle of, 384, 385
Abu Kru, battle of, 386
Airey, Col: [Gen: Sir J.], 141, 314
Aix-la-Chapelle, congress of, 67
Aladyn, 145
Aldershot, 268, 283, 296, etc. (see App. xv.)
Alexander I. of Russia, 32
Alexander II. of Russia, 252, 331
Alexandria, 354; forts of, bombarded, 355
Alison, Sir Archibald, Gen:, 355, 357, 358, 370
Alma, 167; battle of the, 168 ff
Amherst, Hon: W. [Viscount Holmesdale; Earl Amherst], 227
Angelo, Mr., 117
Arabi Pasha, 352, 353, 357, 363
Armament of the British infantry, 126, 259, 271, 317
Army Purchase abolished, 324
Army Reform, 124, 319-349
Austria; and Russia, 133, 148, 149
Azof, Sea of, 161, 245, 253, 274

Baker Pasha, Gen:, 374
Balaklava, 197; charge of, 198
Baltic Sea, 158
Baring, Capt: C. [Col:], 174, 314
Barracks (see App. xv.)
—— Buckingham House [Palace], 97, etc.
—— Chelsea, 270, 305, etc.
—— Kensington, 97, 300, etc.
—— King's Mews, 76; changed to St. George's, 97; etc.
—— Knightsbridge, 76; given up, 97; etc.
—— Magazine, 97; given up, 305; etc.
—— Portman Street, 76, 120; given up, 305; etc.
—— St. George's, 97, etc.
—— St. John's Wood; first used, 97; given up by Foot Guards, 305; etc.
—— Wellington, 97, 300, 305, etc.
—— Westminster, 97
—— Windsor. See Windsor.
Barrell, Sergt:-Major, 310
Barton, Capt: Robert, 336, 337
Bath, Order of, ceremony of investiture, 102; investitures in Crimea, 265
Bathurst, Lord, 19, 67, 71

Bayonet exercise, 117
Bentinck, Col: C., 118
—— Col: [Sir H.], 128, 140, 171, 216, 233, 266
Berber, 379, 380, 403, etc.
Beresford, Lord C., 382
Berlin Treaty, 338
Bertie, Capt: Hon: G., 336
Bicentenary of Coldstream, 120
Billeting system, 35
Bingham, Maj: Lord [Earl of Lucan], 141
Black Sea neutralized, 278
Blücher, Marshal, 8, 9, 11, 12, 14, 15, 17, 30, 35
Boat-race, 85
Bombardments of Sevastopol (see Sevastopol), 193, 252, 255, 256, 261
Bonaparte. See Napoleon I.
Bonham, Lt:-Col:, 339, 377
Boscawen, Col: Hon. E. [Viscount Falmouth], 377, 386, 408
Bosphorus, 137
Bosquet, Gen:, 155, 165, 200, 223, 244, 262
Bouverie, Sir H., 79, 83, 85, 86, 88
Bouverie, Capt: H., 227
Bouverie [Pleydell-Bouverie], Lt: G. [Maj:], 411
Bowles, Col: [Sir G.], 114, 117
Brand, Col: [Gen:] Hon. H. [Lord Dacre], 82, 83
Brigade of Guards, 13, 20, 57, 69, 77, 94, 138, 141, 150, 164, 170, 172, 188, 191, 200, 201, 213, 214-217, 220, 245, 246, 248, 251, 257, 267-269, 279, 284, 285, 300, 302, 304, 306, 313, 329, 330, 336, 344, 346, 347, 359, 360, 384, 399, 401, 406, etc.
——, General Officer appointed to command the, 290
Brighton, 97, etc.
Brown, Gen: Sir G., 141, 170
Buckingham House [Palace] Barracks. See Barracks.
Buller, Maj:-Gen:, 170, 210, 212
Buller, Gen: Sir Redvers, 337, 390
Bülow, Gen:, 14, 15
Burghersh, Lt:-Col: Lord [Earl of Westmoreland], 141
Burnaby, Col: F., 385

INDEX.

Butler, Maj : J. A., 146, 147
Byng, Gen : Sir John [F.-M. Earl of Strafford], 8, 13, 21, 88, 122, 284, 285, 303
Byng, Capt : Hon : H., 141

Cambridge, F.-M. H.R.H. Adolphus Duke of, 57, 120, 121
Cambridge, Gen : H.R.H. Prince George [F.-M. Duke] of, 118, 165, 216, 232, 235, 285, 290, 296, 297
Camel Corps, 377, 381, 383, 391, 408
Campbell, Gen : Sir Colin [Lord Clyde], 173, 189, 251, 266, 303, 307
Campbell, Lt :-Col : Hon : H., 141, 172
Campbell, Capt : Hon : R., 336, 337
Canada, 103; discontent in, 107; suppression of outbreak, 108; second outbreak, 110, 111; legislative union, 112
Canrobert, Gen :, 145, 155, 165, 183, 184, 225, 252, 253
Canteen system, improvements in, 299, 340
Carleton, Col : Dudley [Lord Dorchester], 247, 306, 307, 314
Carnot (1815), 43
Caroline, Queen, 80
Caspian Sea, 159
Castlereagh, Lord, 31
Casualties ; Waterloo campaign, 21 ; Alma, 171; Inkerman, 226; in Crimea, 290; Tel el-Kebir, 368; Abu Klea, 385; Hashin, 399 ; 24th March, 1885, 401, 402
Cathcart, Gen : Hon : Sir J., 183, 184, 215, 222
Cato Street Conspiracy, 79
Caucasus, 160
Chapel Royal, Whitehall, 77
Chapel, Royal Military, at Wellington Barracks, 104, 300, 349
Chaplin, Col : T., 116, 118, 120
Charteris, Lt : Hon : Alan, 395
Charteris, Lt : Hon : Alfred, 336
Chartists, 119
Chatham, 76, etc. (*see* App. xv.)
Chelsea Barracks. *See* Barracks.
Chichester, 117, etc. (*see* App. xv.)
Chobham Camp, 128, 296
Cholera, 95, 152, 183, 189, etc.
Cialdini, Gen :, 262
Circassia, 160, 255, 294
Citate, 135
Clarendon, Earl of, 255
Clinton, Gen : Sir H., 48, 88
Clive, Col :, 406
Clyde, Lord. *See* Campbell, Sir C.
Codrington, Lt : Alfred [Maj :], 357
Codrington, Gen : Sir W., 108, 151, 170, 210, 262, 266, 276, 333, 344

Colborne, Gen : Sir J. [F.-M. Lord Seaton], 107, 111, 112, 128
Coldstream Guards, 8, 12, 13, 32, 48, 55, 69, 76, 84, 87, 100, 105, 107, 112, 117, 128, 154, 208, 213, 224, 245, 299, etc. (*see* Brigade of Guards)
—— Colours. *See* Colours.
—— Establishment, (1814 and 1821) 75 ; (1854) 195 ; (1856) 293 ; changes in '81, 342, 343
—— Name of, 90
—— Officers, lists of, (1815) 23 ; in France, (1816) 49 ; (1825) 87 ; (1837) 99 ; in Canada, 108 ; ('48) 118 ; (1854) 287 ; to Crimea, 139 ; in Bulgaria, 151 ; Inkerman, 213 ; (1855) May, 250 ; Oct., 266 ; and Dec., 274 ; (1856) March, 278 ; and July, 286 ; (1865) 308 ; (1871) 316 ; (1877) 334 ; Egyptian Campaign, 356 ; Nile Expedition, 377, 378 ; Suakin Campaign, 395 ; Dec. '85, 410
Cole, Gen : Sir L., 48
Colonial troops, 394
Colours, 272, 300, 371, 410
Colville, Gen : Sir Charles, 11, 60
Combermere, Gen : Lord, 48, 84
Connaught, Gen : H.R.H. Duke of, 356, 358
Conolly, Lt : [Col :] 201, 287
Consort, Prince. *See* Prince Consort.
Convoy, attack on, near Gubat, 391
Convoy, attack on, near Suakin, 24th March, 1885, 401
Cookery, School of, 298
Corporal punishment in the Army, 101
Corry [Lowry-Corry], Hon : H. (*see* App. xvi.)
Council of Military Education, 296
Cowell, Lt :-Col : 217, 227
Craufurd, Gen :, 281, 285, 304, 307
Crawley, Capt : P. [Col :], 227
Crimea, position of, 161 ; invasion of, 154. *See* Crimean War.
Crimean War ; origin, 134 ; commenced, 135 ; formally declared, 138 ; women in camp, 144 ; Danube Campaign, 146 ; Austrian intervention, 148, 149 ; invasion of Crimea, 154 ; allied forces, 154 ; the Alma, 170 ; siege of Sevastopol, 184 ff; first bombardment, 193 ; Balaklava, 197 ; Inkerman, 204-230 ; the winter 1854-55, 234 ; commissariat, 235 ; sickness, 241 ; fall of Sevastopol, 265 ; later operations, 273, 274 ; conclusion of, 278 ; summarized, 288 ; (*see* Sevastopol, etc.)
Croydon, 97, 309, etc.
Cust, Capt :, 174
Cyprus, 355, 406

Dacre, Lord. *See* Brand.

INDEX.

Dalrymple, Hon: N. 402
Daniell, Col: 247, 250
Dannenberg, Gen:, 210, 212
Davoût, Marshal, 14, 16, 17, 25, 38, 42, 43
Dawson, Lt:-Col: Hon: T. Vesey, 209, 218, 227, 228
Dawson, Capt: [Maj:] Vesey, 390
D'Erlon, Gen:, 12
Deptford, 77, etc.
Devna, Lake of, 152
Digby, Col: Hon: E. [Lord Digby], 334
Disbrowe, Lt:, 227
Dobrudsha, 146, 148, 150
Dongola, 372, 377; advance to, 380 ff; evacuated, 407
Dorchester, Lord. *See* Carleton.
Double Rank, 20, 325, 342
Drummond, Col: Gordon, 150, 247, 250, 300
Drummond, Capt: Hon: R., 260
Dublin, 76, 335, 345, etc. (*see* App. xv.)
Durham, Earl of, 107, 108, 109, 112

Earle, Maj:-Gen:, 382, 390, 391
Education, Military, Council of, 296
Edward of Saxe-Weimar, Prince. *See* Saxe-Weimar.
Egypt, 350, 372; dual control, 352; British Protectorate, 371
Egyptian Army, 364
Egyptian War, Tel el-Kebir Campaign, 358–367; Nile Campaign, 372–392; Suakin Campaign, 393–408
Eliot, Capt: Hon: G., 151, 209, 217, 227
Eupatoria, 163, 244, 274
Evans, Gen: Sir De Lacy, 170, 210

Falconer, A., Quartermaster, 213, 335
Falmouth, Viscount. *See* Boscawen.
Feilding, Col: Hon: P. [Gen: Sir P.] 151, 213, 227, 314, 315, 334
Feilding, Col: Hon: W. [Gen:], 334
Fenians, 311, 313
Field-Officer in Brigade Waiting, 92, 290, 291
Finsbury, 76, etc.
Fire-service, 106
First Guards. *See* Grenadier Guards.
FitzClarence, Lt: [Gen: Lord Frederick], 80, 321
FitzRoy, Col: G. [Gen:], 334, 343, 344, 345
FitzRoy, Lt:-Col: Lord Charles [Duke of Grafton], 334, 340
Flank-march round Sevastopol, 181
Fleet in Crimean War, 138, 149, 178, 193, 273; in Egyptian War, 355, 359
Flogging in the Army, 101
Follett, Col: R. (*see* App. xvi.)

Forey, Gen:, 155, 165, 187
Forster, Rt: Hon: W. E., 347
Fortescue, Capt: [Lt:-Col:] Cyril, 339, 346
Fortescue, Lt: Hon: A. [Capt:], 411
Fouché, Duc d'Otranto, 7, 16, 17, 29, 42
Franco-Prussian War, 320
Fremantle, Col: [Gen: Sir A. Lyon], 334, 343, 376, 394, 406
Fremantle, Col: J., 90, 104, 105

Gemai, 380
George III., 73, 79
George IV., 69, 79, 81; coronation, 82; death, 96
Gevreklek, village of, 152
Ginnis, battle of, 408
Gipps, Gen: [Sir R.], 344, 345
Gladstone, Lt: [Capt: Sir J., Bart:], 395
Godfrey, Mr. [Bandmaster], 307
Gomm, Col: Sir W. [Field-Marshal], 49, 90, 98, 99, 307, 332
Goodlake, Capt: [Col:], 192, 200, 287, 334
Goodram, Private, 276
Gordon, Gen: C. G., 373; sent to Khartum, 375; message from, 382; death, 389
Gordon, Col:, [R.E.], 192
Gortchakoff, Gen: Prince Michael, 134, 146, 148, 212, 226, 260, 261, 272
Graham, Gen: Sir G., 359, 363, 375, 394, 397, 404
Graham, Lance-Sergt:, 20
Graves-Sawle, Col: F., 369, 378
Grenadier Guards, 8, 48, 76, 110, 128, 212, 213, 245, etc. (*see* Brigade of Guards)
Greville, Lt:, 217, 227
Grouchy, Marshal, 2, 9, 10, 12
Guards, Brigade of. *See* Brigade of Guards.
——— Camel Corps. *See* Camel Corps.
——— Club, 106
———, Coldstream. *See* Coldstream Guards.
——— Depôt, 310
———, First. *See* Grenadier Guards.
———, Grenadier. *See* Grenadier Guards.
——— Medical Service. *See* Medical Service.
———, Scots. *See* Scots Guards.
———, Scots Fusilier. *See* Scots Guards.
———, Third. *See* Scots Guards.
Gubat, 387, 388, 390
Gymnastic training, 297

Halkett, Capt: F., 111
Halkett, Col: J., 213
Hall, Col: Julian [Gen:], 334, 343
Hall, Col: R. S. (*see* App. xvi.)
Hamilton, Gen: F. [Sir F.], 315
Hamley, Sir E., 214, 358, 361
Handub, 398, 403

Hardinge, Capt: Hon: A. [Gen: Sir A.], 141, 265, 314
Hardinge, Sir H. [Lord Hardinge], 115, 126, 140, 290, 296
Hashin, battle of, 398
Hay, Col: [Gen:], 139, 151
Herbert, Col: I., 356, 378
Hicks Pasha, Gen:, 373
Higginson, Gen: Sir G., 335, 344, 345
Hill, Gen: Lord, 89, 106
Hope, Lt:-Col: Hon. James, 111
Hospital, regimental, 85
Hythe Musketry School, 127, 296

Indian troops, 358, 370, 397, 399, 400
Indigènes, 219, 223
Inkerman, 188; opposing forces, 205; the ground, 207; battle of, 210 ff; Russian retreat, 225; losses, 229; effects, 231
Ireland, 83, 97, 311, 345-348
Ismail Pasha (Khedive), 351
Ismailia, 357, 359

Jackson, Gen: Sir R., 79, 112
Jakdul, 382, 383

Kars, siege and fall of, 274
Kassassin, 361, 363
Kensington Barracks. See Barracks.
Kertch, 161, 253, 255
Khartum, 373, 378; Gordon sent, 375; two plans of relief, 379; fall of, 389
Khedive. See Ismail, and Tewfik.
King's Mews Barracks. See Barracks.
Kirbekan, battle of, 391
Knightsbridge Barracks. See Barracks.
Korti, 379, 381

Labedoyère, Gen:, 43
Lafayette, 4
La Marmora, Gen:, 254
Lambert, Gen: Sir J., 60, 70
Lambton, Col: A. [Gen:], 343, 401, 406
Lavalette, Gen:, 45
Leaning, Lance-Sergt:, 391
Legge, Capt: Hon: E. [Col:], 312
Lindsay, Gen: Hon: J. [Sir J.], 315
Lindsay, Lt: R. [Lord Wantage], 172, 217
Liprandi, Gen:, 197
Liverpool, Lord, 46
Lloyd, Lt: F. [Maj:], 339, 396
Louis XVIII., 7, 11, 18, 26; restoration of, 27, 29, 30; 45, 61
Louis Napoleon. See Napoleon III.
Louis-Philippe, 94, 119
Louvre, the, 41
Lovell, Capt: P., 339

Lucan, Gen: Earl of, 188
Lucan, Earl of. See Bingham.
Luders, Gen:, 146, 281
Lyons, Admiral Sir E. [Lord], 178, 184

Macdonald, Marshal, 39
Macdonell, Gen: Sir James, 20, 49, 83, 86, 107, 110, 114
Mackenzie Heights, 181, 196, 261, 272, 281
MacKinnon, Col: D., 49, 55, 59, 98
MacKinnon, Capt: L. D., 189, 209, 227
M'Neill, Gen: Sir J., 395, 399, 400
Magazine barracks. See Barracks
Magill, Surgn: [Surgn: Lt:-Col:], 377, 385
Mahdi, the (Muhammad Ahmad), 373, 374, 375, 408
Maitland, Gen: Sir P., 21, 49, 60
Malakoff, the, 185, 193, 255, 257, 262
Malta, 140
Manœuvres, 329
Medical service of the Brigade, changes in, 340
Menshikoff, Gen: Prince, 167, 168, 175, 181, 185, 196, 205, 231, 245
Metemmeh, 379, 387
Metropolitan police, 94
Military Chapel. See Chapel, R.M.
—— Education, Council of, 296
—— Establishment reduced, 74, 293
—— reforms, (1837-54) 124; (1871-85) 319-349
—— service, terms of, 322
Militia, 126, 268, 302
Milman, Col: F., 93, 99
Monck, Col: Hon: R., 303
Müffling, Baron, 30, 33
Muhammed Ahmad. See Mahdi
Musketry, 127, 140, 296, 339
Mussa Pasha, 147

Napoleon I., after Waterloo, 1-4; abdication, 5; surrender, 2
Napoleon II., 5
Napoleon III., 132, 252, 253, 274, 280, 295, 302
Napoleon, Gen: Prince, 155, 165
Newton, Lt:-Col: W. S., [Gen:], 247, 250, 300, 302, 304
Ney, Marshal, 43
Nicholas I. of Russia, 117, 132, 133, 138, 252
Nightingale, Florence, 240
Nile Expedition, 372-392
Nulli SecundusiClub, 92. (see App: viii.)

Omar Pasha, 135, 138, 145, 147, 274
Osman Digna, 374, 380, 397
Otao, 403
Otway, Lt:-Col:, 339

INDEX.

Paris; (1815) provisional government, 7, 13, 16; convention of St. Cloud, 18; occupied by allies, 28; review at, 31; allies in, 39-41; Treaty of, 48; supplementary convention, 52; (1856) Treaty of, 278
Paulet, Col: [Gen:] Lord F., 114, 233, 246, 250, 302, 304, 307
Paulet, Lord W., 241
Pavloff, Gen :, 211, 212
Pélissier, Marshal, 254, 256, 257, 261, 273
Perceval, Col: Spencer, 247, 250, 302, 304, 306
Perekop, isthmus of, 161, 245
Peronne, Highlanders at, 35
Pirch I., Gen :, 10, 11
Pirbright Camp, 338
Platform-money, 83, 95
Pole-Carew, Capt: [Col :] R., 357, 410
Police, 94
Portman Street Barracks. See Barracks.
Portsmouth, 300
Prince Consort, 122, 126, 128, 285, 296; death of, 304
Prince Imperial, 280
Prince of Wales; marriage of, 306; illness, 330
Promotion, 327, 341
Public duties in London, 76, 124, 267, 310, 311
Purchase, abolition of, 324

Queen Caroline. See Caroline.
Queen Victoria. See Victoria.

Raglan, F.-M. Lord, 141, 168, 174, 175, 184, 205, 225, 253, 256, 257
Raikes, Col: W. H., 86
Ramsden, Capt :, 227
Redan, the, 185, 193, 255, 257, 262, 263; evacuation of, 264
Reform agitation, 93
Reforms of Army, 124, 319-349
Regent, Prince. See George IV.
Regimental hospital, 85
— transport. See Transport.
Rewards; for Waterloo, 19, 20; in 1829, and 1836, 100; in 1845, 125
Richelieu, Duc de, 53, 59
Rokeby, Gen : Lord, 246, 247, 282, 285, 300, 301, 304
Ross-of-Bladensburg, Capt : [Lt :-Col :], 396, 403
Rowley, Lt :-Col: C., 378, 384
Royal Military Chapel. See Chapel, R.M.
Russian Empire, 130; policy of, 131

St. Arnaud, Marshal, 145, 161, 165, 168, 174, 175, 183

St. Cloud, Convention of, 18
St. George's Barracks. See Barracks.
St. John's Wood Barracks. See Barracks.
Sandbag battery, 188, 213-224
Saxe-Weimar, Col : [Gen :] H.S.H. Prince Edward of, 212, 315, 335
Scots Fusiliers. See Scots Guards.
Scots Guards, 8, 76, 87, 95, 128, 213, 245, 375, etc. (see Brigade of Guards)
Scutari, 141, 142; hospitals at, 240
Seaton, Lord. See Colborne.
Sevastopol, 157; plan of attack, 163; disembarkation for, 164; arrival before, 176; harbour of, 177; flank march round, 181; commencement of siege, 184; garrison and defences, 185, 186; distribution of allies, 189; first bombardment, 193; Balaklava, 197; Inkerman, 204-230; second bombardment, 252; third, 255; fourth, 256; fifth, 261; sixth, 261; fall of, 264, 265
Seymour, Lt :-Col : [Gen :] Lord William, 357
Shawe, Col : [Gen :], 104, 108, 118, 123
Shendi, 375, 379
Shorncliffe, 300, 311, 335 (see App. xv.)
Short service system, 322
Silistria, siege of, 146, 147
Simpson, Gen : Sir James, 257, 262, 263, 276
Sinope, battle of, 135
Smoking, customs concerning, 309
Soimonoff, Gen :, 210, 212
Somerset, Col : P., 141
Soult, Marshal, 10, 12, 105
Stanlock, Private, 287
Steele, Gen : Sir T., 141, 170, 304, 306, 307, 344
Stephenson, Gen : Sir F., 128, 141, 151, 246, 335, 376, 377, 408
Stepney [Herbert-Stepney], Col :, 307, 314
Sterling, Col : J. B., 344, 368, 406
Stewart, Lt :-Col : Donald, 375
Stewart, Sir Herbert, Gen :, 368, 381, 382, 383, 386, 388, 389
Stopford, Capt : Hon: F. [Col :], 402
Strafford, Earl of. See Byng.
Stratford de Redcliffe, Lord, 137, 265
Strong, Col :, 314
Strong, Private, 287
Suakin, 373, 374, 379, 397, 398
Suakin Campaign, 393-408
Sub-Lieutenant, rank of, 328, 340
Sudan, 372; rising in, 373; war in, 375, etc.; evacuation of, 407
Suez Canal, 351
Suleiman Pasha, 155
Sultan of Turkey, 132, 134, 137, 314
Sutton, Lt : G., 396, 409
Sydenham, Lord, 112, 114

Tactics, changes in, 320, 329
Talbot, Lt :-Col. Hon : R., 389
Talleyrand, Prince, 27, 29, 41
Tamai, 398, 399, 402
Tambuk Wells, 397
Tchernaya, battle of, 261
Tel el-Kebir, 357 ; Arabi's position at, 365 ; British march on, 366 ; battle of, 367
Tel el-Makhuta, 360, 361
Templetown, Viscount. *See* Upton, G.
Tewfik Pasha (Khedive), 352, 369
T'Hakul, 403
Thieleman, Gen : 9, 10, 11, 15
Third Guards. *See* Scots Guards.
Thompson, Mr. Paulet. *See* Sydenham, Lord.
Timofeyeff, Gen :, 226
Todleben, Gen :, 178, 186, 252, 257
Tofrek, battle of, 400, 401
Torrens, Capt : [Gen : Sir Arthur], 107, 222, 321
Tower, Capt : [Col :], 191, 195, 198, 209, 216, 259, 303
Tower of London, 76, 106, etc. (*see* App. xv.)
Transport, in Crimea, 143, 166, 237, 238, 273
——, Regimental, 329, 338
Troödos, Mt., 406, 409

Uniform, changes in, 91, 270, 315, 340
United States, 114, 294, 304
Upton, Col : Hon : A., 151, 246
Upton, Col : [Gen :] Hon : G., [Viscount Templetown], 151, 171, 213, 222, 233, 246, 302

Vandamme, Gen :, 15
Varna, 143, 145, 153
Victor Emanuel, 295
Victoria, Queen ; accession, 100 ; coronation, 104 ; sympathy with army, 271 ; address to Crimean troops, 284
Victoria Cross, 172, 192, 201, 218, 287 (*see* App. xiii.)
Vienna Note, the, 134
Volunteers, 302, 303
Von Sohr, Lt :-Col :, 15

Walton, Capt : [Col :], 22, 105, 116, 118
Wantage, Lord. *See* Lindsay.
Warley, 96, 101
Warrant officers introduced, 342
Washington, Treaty of, 114
Waterloo, battle of, 1 ; Napoleon after, 2-6 ; operations after, 9-15 ; political result, 24-27
"Waterloo men," 19, 20
Wellington, Duke of, 8, 10, 14, 15, 17, 30, 35, 49, 62, 63, 71, 106, 119, 122 ; funeral of, 123
Wellington Barracks. *See* Barracks ; and Chapel, R.M.
Wellington Pension, 20
Westmoreland, Earl of. *See* Burghersh.
Wigram, Col : [Gen :] Godfrey, 343, 344, 356
William IV., 79, 92 ; coronation, 95 ; death, 100
Willis, Gen : [Sir G.], 356, 360, 368
Willson, Col : M., 378
Wilson, Col : [Gen :] Sir Charles (R.E.), 382, 386, 388
Wilson, Capt : C. T. [Col :], 191, 219, 223, 224
Wilson, Gen : Sir Robert, 45
Wiltshire, Earl of, 395
Wimbledon Camp, 303
Winchester, 116, etc. (*see* App. xv.)
Winchester, Marquis of. *See* Wiltshire.
Windsor, 76, 91, etc. ; drag-hounds at, 299 (*see* App. xv.)
Wolseley, Gen : Lord [F.-M.], 356, 377, 397, 408, etc.
Women in the Crimea, 144
Wood, Gen : Sir Evelyn, 337
Wood, Col : Mark, 306, 307, 314
Woodford, Gen : Sir A., 60, 66, 77, 79, 83, 84, 86, 120
Woolwich, 77, etc.
Wyatt, Dr : J., 276, 279, 332

York, F.-M. H.R.H. Frederick, Duke of, 19, 49, 85 ; death of, 88

Zeriba, McNeill's, 400
Ziethen, Gen :, 15, 16, 64

THE END.

www.ingramcontent.com/pod-product-compliance
Lightning Source LLC
Chambersburg PA
CBHW060415300426
44111CB00018B/2861